Oxford Studies in European Law

General Editors: Paul Craig and Gráinne de Búrca

CIVIL PROCEDURE AND EU LAW

Civil Procedure and EU Law

A Policy Area Uncovered

EVA STORSKRUBB

OXFORD
UNIVERSITY PRESS

OXFORD
UNIVERSITY PRESS

Great Clarendon Street, Oxford OX2 6DP

Oxford University Press is a department of the University of Oxford.
It furthers the University's objective of excellence in research, scholarship,
and education by publishing worldwide in

Oxford New York

Auckland Cape Town Dar es Salaam Hong Kong Karachi
Kuala Lumpur Madrid Melbourne Mexico City Nairobi
New Delhi Shanghai Taipei Toronto

With offices in

Argentina Austria Brazil Chile Czech Republic France Greece
Guatemala Hungary Italy Japan Poland Portugal Singapore
South Korea Switzerland Thailand Turkey Ukraine Vietnam

Oxford is a registered trade mark of Oxford University Press
in the UK and in certain other countries

Published in the United States
by Oxford University Press Inc., New York

First published 2008

British Library Cataloguing in Publication Data
Data available

Library of Congress Cataloging in Publication Data
Storskrubb, Eva.
Civil procedure and EU law : a policy area uncovered / Eva Storskrubb.
p. cm. — (Oxford studies in European law)
Includes bibliographical references and index.
ISBN-13: 978-0-19-953317-6
1. Civil procedure—European Union countries. I. Title.
KJE3802.S76 2008
347.24'05—dc22 2008000170

Typeset by Newgen Imaging Systems (P) Ltd., Chennai, India
Printed in Great Britain
on acid-free paper by
Biddles Ltd., King's Lynn

ISBN 978-0-19-953317-6

1 3 5 7 9 10 8 6 4 2

For my family and fellow proceduralists

GENERAL EDITORS' PREFACE

It is axiomatic that the rules and precepts of civil procedure in any national legal system embody important values and principles. It is equally apparent that the nature of these values and principles vary as between legal systems. The degree of variance will of course depend upon the nature of the particular procedural precept, but it is also the case that there may in fact be a plethora of approaches, which differ in varying degrees, to the same procedural issue. It is therefore unsurprising that EU law should be concerned with rules of civil procedure, since the variance in the applicable national rules may hinder cross-border trade and lead to differential treatment of otherwise identical civil disputes. What is more surprising, given the practical significance of the topic and its intellectual interest, is that there has been relatively little systematic treatment of the topic.

This book is therefore especially welcome within the series. The author provides a well-organized analysis of the interaction between civil procedure and EU law. A glance at the particular topics covered reveals the importance of the subject matter: service of documents, establishing jurisdiction and enforcing judgments, enforcement of uncontested claims, legal aid, alternative dispute resolution, payment orders, small claims, and judicial network. The discussion of these topics is set within the broader framework of the regulatory debate within the EU, as to how and why particular topics should be regulated.

The book facilitates our understanding of judicial cooperation in civil matters through its analysis of the relevant EU legislation and enhances our comprehension of the way in which this policy area is affecting the interaction between civil procedure and EU law. The focus is both 'internal', considering the relevant material from an EU perspective, and 'external', placing the EU regulatory initiatives into a broader perspective. Comparison between topics is aided by using common structural features in each of the chapters dealing with particular topics. Thus each chapter proceeds through ordered discussion of legislative history, substantive content and normative implications.

The book will be of interest to all those concerned with civil procedure and more generally to those who study the regulatory interaction between the EU and Member States.

Paul Craig
Gráinne de Búrca

PREFACE

The European University Institute in Florence was a genuine oasis for me as a researcher, naturally in its beauty and physical environment, but more importantly in its unique academic and institutional make-up. I am thankful to the Academy of Finland for funding my research and to all the staff at the EUI who facilitated the practicalities of my research. Intellectually and collegially I am indebted to the faculty, researchers, and fellows of the Law Department. The open and creative atmosphere of the Department formed a fascinating and rewarding professional environment.

During the course of my thesis project, several Finnish officials helped me forward in my research through interviews, for which I am thankful. Kirsti Rissanen, Asko Välimaa, and Outi Kemppainen, all from the Ministry of Justice, as well as Mari Aalto of Finland's Permanent Representation to the EU, kindly gave time to discuss the development of a new policy area from the perspective of a particular Member State. Judge Allan Rosas and Heidi Kaila at the European Court of Justice also kindly gave time to discuss my area of research and helped me in locating references to relevant case law.

My traineeship from autumn 2005 to early spring 2006 in Unit C1 of Directorate General Justice, Freedom and Security at the EU Commission provided invaluable insights into the development of the policy area in real time. I am very grateful for the stimulating discussions that I had with my colleagues and for their warm support. Particular thanks go to Olivier Tell, in addition to Karen Vandekerckhove and Katja Lenzing.

There are a few people who have been very significant at various stages during my pursuit of and completion of a doctoral programme as well as in the publication phase of this work. I am abundantly grateful and privileged to express heartfelt thanks to them.

I would probably not have had the courage to embark upon a PhD project were it not for dedicated encouragement from Professor Dan Frände during my time as deputy Assistant in Procedural Law at the University of Helsinki and ever since. In his positive spirit and regimented work schedule I found a role model for my life as a researcher.

My former colleagues at Ross & Co in London provided another source of encouragement for my leap into the project and a very concrete source of inspiration for the topic. During our many walks in Temple gardens debating procedural tactics I had the good fortune to find a legal soulmate and motivating mentor in Ian Ross.

My supervisor at the EUI, Professor Jacques Ziller, gave me prompt, practical, and well-tailored advice as well as most kind support from the very beginning of my thesis project. His experienced reassurances of 'continue on your way' in addition to his enthusiasm for comparative access to justice paved the way for our French-Finnish *amitié*.

The members of my thesis jury, Professor emeritus Per-Henrik Lindblom of Uppsala University, Professor Burkhard Hess of Ruprecht-Karls-Universität Heidelberg, Professor Bruno De Witte of the EUI, and my supervisor gave their kind and enthusiastic encouragement for publication and sound suggestions for further improvement.

My editor Alex Flach and the team at Oxford University Press have guided me through the publication process with experience and professional ease whilst my current colleagues at Dittmar & Indrenius in Helsinki have generously and with full support given me time to dedicate to the publication process.

The PhD thesis and the completion of a doctoral programme which led to the publication of this work can admittedly at times be considered a solitary pursuit. In my most optimistic cheery moments and equally in my dark moments of exasperation I nonetheless never walked alone.

Shoulders and brains to rely on when my own barely managed to carry the daily weight of the thesis project were provided by two fellow proceduralists who are very dear to me. Whilst working on their own theses in Helsinki and Florence respectively, Gisela Knuts and Johanna Engström were invaluable troupers. They helped with sources, proof reading, and concrete ideas, but above all gave indefatigable inspirational and moral support.

I have been blessed with wonderful close friends who light up my life and form my extended family be they in Helsinki, London, Florence, or elsewhere. My heartfelt thanks go to them all unnamed. I do though particularly want to thank the 'GLBs' for always – always – being there to share and care. I also cannot but especially thank the 'Troikas', my flatmates, and other EUI *amici* for so much fun and joy during our Florentine adventure.

Finally, it is impossible to thank adequately my beloved parents and my beloved sister with family enough for their unwavering love and for countless happy moments together, from which I draw comfort, strength, inspiration, and much needed patience. 'Family Storskrubb' – you are my safe haven as well as the wind beneath my wings.

The cut-off date of this work is 31 August 2007. The responsibility for all submissions and for inevitable errors is that of the author alone.

Eva Storskrubb

Helsinki, September 2007

CONTENTS

TABLE OF CASES

EUROPEAN COURT OF JUSTICE

EUROPEAN COURT OF HUMAN RIGHTS

ENGLISH CASES

TABLE OF LEGISLATION

EUROPEAN COMMUNITY AND UNION LEGISLATION

EUROPEAN COUNCIL DOCUMENTS

COUNCIL OF THE EUROPEAN UNION DOCUMENTS

EUROPEAN COMMISSION DOCUMENTS (COM) AND COMMISSION STAFF WORKING PAPERS (SEC)

EUROPEAN PARLIAMENT DOCUMENTS

EUROPEAN ECONOMIC AND SOCIAL COMMITTEE DOCUMENTS

OTHER DOCUMENTS

1

Introduction

Intersections between Procedural and European Law

For the purpose of defining the subject matter of this work and its aims it is useful to step back, and consider the big picture. In the broadest sense, the backdrop is formed by the emergence of a truly global economy. The recent decades of technological advancement and relative freedom of international trade entail ramifications for transnational litigation. A larger volume of disputes together with the advent of labour and asset mobility constitute a plethora of acute challenges.[1] In the European Union context civil and commercial dispute resolution has also become a key issue. Therefore it is pertinent to identify actual cases, situations or scenarios in which civil procedural law and European law intersect and to have a grasp of the legal and political issues at the intersections.

First, the creation of the Internal Market and the four basic freedoms within the EU entail that entities can engage in cross-border trade with as little regulation and restriction as possible. If restrictions are necessary these are regulated in a similar manner for all, either through harmonization or approximation, i.e. creation of supranational rules, or through mutual recognition. When a cross-border commercial or civil dispute arises, e.g. litigation between two companies from different Member States under a sale of goods contract, or litigation between a consumer and a company from different Member States under a consumer sales contract, the smooth functioning of the Internal Market and cross-border trade can be disrupted. Such disruption of the Internal Market arises if there is a lack of or inadequate

[1] Bell (2003) pp. 1–5.

transnational procedural regulation, i.e. if the national procedural rules on jurisdiction, choice of law, service of documents, obtaining evidence abroad, and enforcement of foreign judgments are parochial and complex, regulated differently in each Member State. In addition, if litigants have to resolve their dispute in a foreign civil procedural system they will often have to engage foreign lawyers to protect their interests and will encounter problems due to the differences from their own procedural rules. In other words, even if jurisdiction and enforcement are mutually regulated there is still an additional complexity and financial burden of litigating abroad, which can be seen as a further disincentive to cross-border trade and a hindrance to the Internal Market.

Secondly, in certain instances Community law creates rights and obligations for private parties, which have direct effect either between one party and a Member State or even between two private parties. The realization of these rights between parties arises in national courts during civil and commercial litigation. Examples of specific areas of law in which this might arise are: competition law, employment law, consumer contract law, product liability law, and agency law. These are areas which EC law specifically regulates through Treaty articles and directives. It is for the national procedural system to provide the rules and remedies for the realization of the rights. However, the national procedural systems might not always provide for such procedural and remedial rules, or the existing national rules might have a limiting effect on the realization of EC rights flowing from such substantive EU norms. In addition, litigants are in effect treated unequally in different national jurisdictions, e.g. on questions of standing, time limits, or burden of proof. This causes a potential conflict with the fundamental EC law principle of uniform application and equality because the domestic procedural systems form a de facto obstacle to the uniform application of substantive EU norms.

Thirdly, the creation of a European Union at Maastricht in 1993, including the Third Pillar provisions on Justice and Home Affairs, and the political impetus for the Area of Freedom, Security and Justice introduced at Amsterdam in 1999, give rise and legitimacy to free-standing citizen requirements. These include fundamental notions such as the right to a fair trial and access to justice. In addition, once the Union sets itself social goals, the position of consumers, small and medium-sized companies, and other perceived economically weaker parties might influence the demands on the procedural systems; for example issues such as legal aid and special procedures for small claims arise. Furthermore, the EU Charter of Fundamental Rights provides the right to an effective remedy and the right to a fair trial[2] and the current draft Reform Treaty specifically includes effective access to justice as one of the aims for measures in the field of judicial cooperation.[3] Thus, from a concrete perspective litigants within the Union are taking part in civil proceedings that are under such modern civil procedural demands as efficiency, accuracy, and openness in addition to the pressure of keeping costs to the minimum.

These intersections were admittedly and deliberately presented in a simplistic factual manner and without analysis.[4] Nevertheless, in their plain exposition they demonstrate that the intersections between procedural law and European law are complex and arise in different instances and on different levels. Regarding the complexities of procedural law one commentator has eloquently noted: 'Procedure is not pure form. It is the meeting point of conflicts, of policies, of ideas. It is the "Cape Wrath" where Rapidity and Efficiency have to be combined with Justice; it is also the "Cape of Good Hope" where Individual Liberty has to be combined with Equality of Opportunities. Procedure is, in fact, the faithful mirror of all of the major exigencies, problems, and trials of our epoch – of the immense challenge of our time. Here, my fellow proceduralists, is our challenge. Here is our work.'[5]

The elaborated intersections form the backdrop against which the legal analysis and evaluation are conducted in subsequent chapters. The merit of each of these intersections as a positive or negative occurrence and the merit of the argument for or against a regulatory strategy vis-à-vis each of these intersections is the fundamental theme of this work. The challenge of this work is to mirror the exigencies and developments of transnational procedural cooperation on the European Union level and analyse its features of 'Cape Wrath' and 'Cape of Good Hope'.

[2] Art. 47.

[3] Art. 69d of European Council document CIG 1/07.

[4] Each of the intersections, even as presented baldly here, can be contested; e.g. the premise that transnational procedural complexities hinder cross-border trade can be contested by economic theory that argues for jurisdictional competition as a mechanism for innovation and choice. The merits of such arguments are at the heart of the functional debate discussed in this work.

[5] Cappelletti (1970–1) p. 886.

Uncovering the Policy Area Judicial Cooperation in Civil Matters

Approach to the Task

The latest and most overt response of the European Union to the pressures of the intersections between civil procedure and European law has been the creation of a novel policy area named 'judicial cooperation in civil matters'. Since the Treaty of Amsterdam entered into force in 1999 judicial cooperation in civil matters has become a specific EU policy area in its First Pillar, under the legal basis elaborated in Articles 61 and 65 of the EC Treaty. Since its advent, significant progress has been made in this policy area that has, in its legislative breadth (i.e. number of measures) and legislative reach (i.e. also affecting domestic litigation), arguably advanced very rapidly.

As a completely novel form of supranational procedural regulation judicial cooperation in civil matters, now that it has reached a certain level of development and implementation, is starkly topical and still under-researched. Hence the need to 'uncover' the policy area. In particular, as procedural law, because of its detailed nature, often warrants research into only one piece of legislation, or even one procedural aspect, there is a need for holistic analysis. The general aim of this work may be summarized as attempting to depict, as completely as possible, the policy area of judicial cooperation in civil matters, including all its generic procedural instruments, and attempting a critical assessment the success of these instruments.

However, the work also has a more ambitious aim because the analysis will hopefully go 'under' and 'over' the policy area, in the sense that the legal instruments should not simply be evaluated narrowly on their own technical premises. European law should not be seen as merely a technical set of rules since it represents an intricate web of politics, economics, and law, and should be evaluated from a contextual or critical perspective.[6] Similar considerations are arguably applicable to procedural law, for which a contextual approach with a strong historical perspective, analysing and comparing trends in procedural laws, helps commentators understand questions of harmonization and access to justice.[7] Therefore, to 'uncover' the policy

[6] Snyder (1990) p. 9f.

[7] Cappelletti (1989) outlines this methodology.

area the present analysis is also pitched at a meta level, asking 'why' and 'how' supranational procedure should be regulated.

Further, the investigation will adopt an 'outside' perspective in addition to the 'insider' Eurocentric perspective an analysis of an EU policy area inherently entails. It is believed that a contextual and meta-level analysis with both an inside and outside perspective would be valuable and warranted at a time when a systematic and cohesive analysis, which is essential for both academic doctrine and practising legal professionals including judges, is about to emerge among the experts in the European Member States vis-à-vis this new policy area. This work is an attempt to participate in the debate and in the forming of the emerging doctrine.

Aims and Outline

The aims of this work may briefly be summarized as: (i) to gain an understanding of the policy area judicial cooperation in civil matters through an analysis of specific legislative measures and proposals; (ii) to review how this policy area is affecting and changing the intersections between civil procedure and European law; (iii) to extrapolate some of the characteristics of this 'Brave New World' and analyse the implications from both an internal and an external perspective; and (iv) to outline some future projections.

The first and central aim of the work, to gain an understanding of the legislative breadth and content of the legislative instruments of the policy area judicial cooperation in civil matters, will be dealt with in Chapters 6–15. However, in order to be able to understand and analyse the specific legislative measures, the relevant context for the legislative initiatives will be dealt with in Chapters 2–5. This context entails presenting the important background legal and political developments within the European Union. This includes depicting in Chapter 2 prior and embryonic forms of procedural harmonization formed by the doctrine of the European Court of Justice and the ad hoc substantive law development within consumer law as a specific field of Community law.

These further include the constitutional development of a legal basis in the EC Treaty, described in Chapter 3, which sets the scene for the evolution of a new policy area. In addition, amendments to and development of the EC Treaty produced specific and particular institutional and structural characteristics for the new policy area that will be depicted in Chapter 4. The prior forms of harmonization as well as the evolution of a legal basis with its institutional particularities foreshadow the functional analysis of whether the policy area and its legislative measures are appropriate and legitimate.

Finally, the background context discussed in Chapter 5 includes situating the regulation in relation to broader themes of the European integration process: market building, citizenship, fundamental rights, subsidiarity, and governance. The emergence of a political impetus for the policy area and the broader themes and developments of European integration which were and are current and affect several policy areas must be recounted if a holistic understanding of the policy area is to be achieved. The broader themes to be dealt with aptly raise and give focus and depth to the questions of how and why the EU should regulate judicial cooperation in civil matters. The themes of subsidiarity and governance foreshadow the difficult choices to be made in relation to how to regulate, whereas the themes of market integration, fundamental rights, and citizenship highlight and illuminate some of the justifications and considerations which foreshadow the debate on why to regulate.

The second aim, to review how the policy area affects the intersections between procedural law and European law, together with the third aim, to extrapolate some of the characteristics of this 'Brave New World', will be achieved in Chapter 16. Based upon the findings in Chapters 6–15, in particular upon the analysis of each legislative measure and specifically upon the sections dealing with the normative implications of each measure, and based on the background context elaborated in Chapters 2–5, the analysis will focus on the legitimacy of the policy area and move to the meta level in order to carry out a holistic analysis. This analysis will be carried out at an introspective level, asking such questions as what regulations are missing from the policy area and how the constitutional conundrum of the policy area can be solved. However, in the final section of the chapter an external perspective is taken, which will attempt to situate the policy area in the broader streams of general and international procedural development. Thus the legitimacy of the policy area is opened up to renewed scrutiny. Finally, in Chapter 17 the fourth aim of providing projections for the future is fulfilled by elaborating proposals that the policy area should now address: internal coherence and consolidation, scrutiny and debate as to the precepts of mutual recognition and procedural rights, as well as tuning in to broader horizons.

A Novel Legal Concept of European Civil Procedure

Judicial Cooperation in Civil Matters: Practical Scope

This work focuses on the generic international civil procedure measures within the policy area. A number of measures that are regarded as not within the scope of this work are excluded from our discussion. The discrete regulation of insolvency proceedings[8] is excluded due to its particular nature and the fact that it does not have general relevance for every civil litigation case. Insolvency is increasingly also being considered as a separate topic in the domestic conception of civil procedure. Furthermore, measures within the policy area that are not generic, i.e. that concern only one discrete area of private law, are not included. In particular, family law measures do not fall within the scope of this work.[9] Finally, because the work deals with procedural regulation, substantive law[10] and conflict of law regulation[11] do not fall within its scope.

[8] The EU has enacted Regulation (EC) No. 1346/2000 in Insolvency Proceedings.

[9] Note that the general measures included in this work might be relevant for and apply to certain family law disputes, depending on the specific scope of each measure. In the EU the legal basis is the same for family law matters, Art. 65 of the EC Treaty, but there are also special institutional and structural rules (Art. 67(5)). The EU has enacted two Regulations in the field of family law: Regulation (EC) No. 1347/2000 on jurisdiction and the recognition and enforcement in matrimonial matters and in matters of parental responsibility ('Brussels II') and Regulation (EC) No. 2201/2003 on jurisdiction and the recognition and enforcement in matrimonial matters and in matters of parental responsibility, repealing Regulation (EC) No. 1347/2000 ('Brussels II bis'). In addition the following legislative initiatives and consultations are pending: COM (2005) 649 Proposal for a Council Regulation on jurisdiction, applicable law, recognition and enforcement of decisions and cooperation in matters relating to maintenance obligations; COM (2006) 399 Proposal for a Council Regulation amending Regulation (EC) No. 2201/2003 as regards jurisdiction and introducing rules regarding applicable law in matrimonial matters; COM (2005) 65 Green Paper on wills and succession; COM (2006) 400 Green Paper on conflict of laws in matrimonial property regimes including questions of jurisdiction and mutual recognition.

[10] A substantive law project is pending regarding contract law, COM (2007) 447 Second Progress Report on The Common Frame of Reference, and a specific substantive Directive has been enacted, Council Directive (EC) No. 80/2004 of 29 April 2004 relating to compensation to crime victims.

[11] (EC) No. 864/2007 Regulation of the European Parliament and of the Council of 11 July 2007 on the law applicable to non-contractual obligations ('Rome II'); and COM (2005) 650 Proposal for a Regulation of the European Parliament and the Council on the law applicable to

Chapters 6–15 discuss in turn the generic international civil procedure measures within the policy area of judicial cooperation in civil matters that this work deals with:

- the 'Service Regulation' (6)[12]
- the 'Evidence Regulation' (7)[13]
- the 'Brussels I Regulation' (8)[14]
- the 'Enforcement Order Regulation' (9)[15]
- the 'Legal Aid Directive' (10)[16]
- the 'Code of Conduct' for mediators and the proposed 'ADR Directive' (11)[17]
- the 'Payment Order Regulation' (12)[18]
- the 'Small Claims Regulation' (13)[19]
- the European Judicial Network (EJN) (14)[20]
- the European judicial training initiative[21] and other measures (15)[22]

contractual obligations ('Rome I'). These measures are linked to procedural ones in that they naturally form part of the mutual recognition programme, since harmonized conflict of laws is considered to lessen forum shopping and facilitate recognition and enforcement of judgments.

[12] Council Regulation (EC) No. 1348/2000 of 29 May 2000 on the service in the Member States of judicial and extrajudicial documents in civil or commercial matters OJ L160, 30 June 2000, p. 37.

[13] Council Regulation (EC) No. 1206/2001 of 28 May 2001 on cooperation between the courts of the Member States in the taking of evidence in civil or commercial matters OJ L174, 27 June 2001, p. 1.

[14] Council Regulation (EC) No. 44/2001 of 22 December 2000 on jurisdiction and the recognition and enforcement of judgments in civil and commercial matters OJ L12, 16 January 2001, p. 1.

[15] Council and Parliament Regulation (EC) No. 805/2004 creating a European Enforcement Order for uncontested claims OJ L143, 30 April 2004, p. 15.

[16] Council Directive (EC) No. 8/2003 of 27 January 2003 to improve access to justice in cross-border disputes by establishing minimum common rules relating to legal aid for such disputes OJ L26, 31 January 2003, p. 41.

[17] The European Code of Conduct for Mediators, 2 July 2004, see the website of the European Judicial Network: www.europa.eu.int/comm/justice_home/ejn/adr/adr_ec_en.htm (visited 16.8.2007). Proposal for a Directive of the European Parliament and the Council on certain aspects of mediation in civil and commercial matters, COM (2004) 718, OJ C49, 28 February 2006, p. 38.

[18] Council and Parliament Regulation (EC) No. 1896/2006 of 12 December 2006 creating a European order for payment procedure OJ L399, 30.12.2006, p. 1.

[19] Council and Parliament Regulation (EC) No. 861/2007 of 11 July 2007 establishing a European Small Claims Procedure, OJ L199, 31.7.2007, p. 1.

[20] Council Decision 470/2001 of 28 May 2001 establishing a European Judicial Network in civil and commercial matters, OJ L174, 27 June 2001, p. 25.

[21] Initiative of the French Republic with a view to adopting a Council Decision setting up a European judicial training network OJ C18, 19 January 2001, p. 9. The initiative has not been pursued and there is as yet no specific forecast of a legislative measure.

[22] The other measures include inter alia Council Regulation 743/2002 establishing a general framework for Community activities to facilitate the implementation of judicial cooperation in

These instruments and measures are dealt with in an order which broadly follows both the historic timeline of development and a progression from relatively traditional forms to more innovative and far-reaching forms of international judicial cooperation. In addition, the specific measures that regulate one aspect of judicial cooperation are dealt with first (Chapters 6–13) and the general overarching measures are dealt with in Chapters 14 and 15.

In order to provide structure and coherence to the analysis of the development and impact of these measures they can be divided into three broad groups. The first group (discussed in Chapters 6–9) deals with traditional aspects of private international law or civil procedural cooperation. The second group (see Chapters 10–13) is more disparate and includes measures that are innovative and go beyond the traditional forms of cross-border procedural cooperation. The third group (discussed in Chapters 14 and 15) brings together measures that are also innovative, but in addition are general and overarching, affecting the structures of the judicial cooperation systems. Commentators and the EU institutions have also regarded the judicial cooperation measures as having developed in stages, phases, or generations. Any broad categorization such as that employed in this work runs the risk of arbitrariness and generalization, and the present categorization of the measures into three groups is not intended to hamper the evaluation of each individual measure and the links between them.

Judicial Cooperation in Civil Matters: Legal Definition

As a legal concept judicial cooperation in civil matters is a novel one and it is not defined in the Treaty. The only way in which to try to characterize it is to consider the enacted instruments of the policy field and the list of measures in Article 65 of the EC Treaty and consider where they might fit into traditional legal definitions.[23] It is notable that 'private international law' as a term is not used in the EC Treaty and commentators use this concept in different ways. In some Member States private international law is

civil matters, OJ L115, 1 May 2002, p. 1. Note that the Framework Regulation will be replaced by new financial support measures for 2007–13 by the legislative measure pending. The specific proposal for Civil Justice is COM (2005) 122–5, which is still in the legislative process. According to the Parliament legislative tracking website http://www.europarl.europa.eu/oeil/ (visited 25.8.2007) the Parliament has held its second reading and a common position is scheduled in the Council for the end of 2007.

[23] Pataut (2004) p. 31.

predominantly considered to include only conflict of law questions.[24] Some of the commentators within the European law arena include all the measures of judicial cooperation in the concept of private international law. Others use the concept in the more narrow sense, including only questions of jurisdiction, enforcement, and conflict of laws.[25] Because of these contradictory practices, the term 'private international law' is used as little as possible in this work and the term 'judicial cooperation in civil matters' is used to denote the policy area. Private international law is hence not a helpful tool for describing in legal terms the policy area of judicial cooperation in civil matters.

European civil procedure is perhaps a more appropriate term for describing the policy area. The concepts of 'civil litigation', 'civil procedure', or 'civil proceedings' are part of the common and everyday language of lawyers, but we do not all necessarily easily manage to define the concepts, and the definitions vary between jurisdictions.[26] In most jurisdictions the proceedings in a civil matter can be delimited from proceedings in a criminal matter. In some jurisdictions there is also a differentiation between civil proceedings and administrative proceedings. In the EU context judicial cooperation in civil matters is demarcated in scope from criminal and administrative matters. Each measure might have particular delimitations but as a general rule their scope is that of 'civil and commercial' matters.[27] The Commission suggests that the same interpretation of 'civil and commercial' should apply to all these instruments in order to maintain consistency and that the essential impact of the scope is that criminal and tax matters are excluded.[28] Despite the delimitation from criminal and administrative matters, it is noteworthy that administrative procedure was the first arena in which the intersection with European and procedural law emerged,[29] whereas European criminal procedure has in its very recent mutual recognition and harmonization politics come close to its civil counterpart.[30]

[24] Inter alia the Finnish doctrine.

[25] Partsch (2003) and Von Hoffman (ed) (1998) include all the measures of judicial cooperation in the concept of 'private international law'. In contrast, Jessurun D'Oliveira (2002) includes only questions of jurisdiction, enforcement, and conflict of laws.

[26] Jolowicz (2000) p. 11f.

[27] Inter alia Art. 1 of the Service Regulation.

[28] COM (1999) 219 final, 4.5.1999, p. 10.

[29] Consider for example, from this arena, public procurement procedures, Directive 89/665 EEC, OJ L395, 30.12.1989, and subsequent amendments. See also Chapter 2.

[30] From the criminal arena the Proposal for a Framework Decision on certain procedural rights in criminal proceedings COM (2004) 328, 28.4.2004 can be noted. The analogies and

Quite apart from the issue of demarcation and separation from criminal and administrative proceedings, 'civil procedural law' or 'civil procedural regulation' as derived from the policy area of judicial cooperation in civil matters has a broad remit, including questions of enforcement and regulating the organization of the civil justice system, e.g. in the provision of legal aid and judicial training. Also, even though the main emphasis is on procedural rules for proceedings within the court system, so-called alternative dispute resolution rules for proceedings outside the official court system have also been developed. In sum, it is not surprising that in order to situate the concept within traditional categorizations of legal scholarship commentators have rightly suggested that the study of judicial cooperation in civil matters is situated at the crossroads of procedural law, private international law, and European Community law and as such is an interdisciplinary endeavour.[31]

One commentator has criticized the term judicial cooperation in civil matters for being inadequate and giving too narrow a title to a policy area that potentially will include measures beyond mere 'cooperation' and also affects citizens' rights beyond the mere 'judicial' or courtroom sphere.[32] This criticism is in part warranted; for example in English the concept judicial cooperation in civil matters includes the word 'judicial', which intimates and even literally indicates that courts are the relevant actors. Thus, the English wording clearly suggests that the policy area involves cooperation between courts in civil matters. Furthermore, as regards the English-language version, the use of the word 'matters' can be taken as a synonym for cases or claims, which then makes sense: that is, the policy area concerns courts cooperating in cross-border civil claims which have been brought before them. Hence, the English wording, albeit describing a significant part of the policy area well, perhaps implicitly excludes some of the scope of the term and gives the impression of a narrower policy area than exists in reality.

In contrast, the terms used in Finland and Sweden are very broad and general, in that they do not include any particular reference to courts as the relevant actors; instead the more generic terms '*rättsligt samarbete*' and '*oikeudellinen yhteistyö*' are used, which may be translated into English as

interesting comparisons between criminal and administrative procedure and civil judicial cooperation are unfortunately for reasons of space largely outside the scope of this work. However, the author does acknowledge that such comparisons could be very fruitful and interesting. See e.g. Gröning (2005), who raises the legitimacy of legislative competence for the criminal field and Lööf (2006), who raises critical issues with regard to procedural rights harmonization.

[31] Lebeau and Niboyet (2003) p. 221.

[32] Partsch (2003) p. 295.

'legal cooperation'. But the very generality of this concept means that its substantive meaning might not immediately be obvious, even to practitioners in the field, and one only becomes aware of the meaning by carefully examining all the measures encompassed therein. The general Swedish and Finnish wordings may also be considered misleading since they only hint at substantive law cooperation and include no term that refers to courts or procedures, i.e. the actual core of the policy area. Thus, one may conclude that the concept as a legal one, with its novel Community nature and general wording, is potentially amorphous, amoebic, and not very helpful. In contrast and notwithstanding that conclusion, the concept may be held to be helpful and to have merit in the sense that it is a new concept, which is distinct from developments in other national and international arenas. Furthermore, the concept will – with further dissemination of knowledge and with further consolidation of the legislative initiatives – become a distinct one within both the Community and national legal orders.

2

Background Developments: Forms of Procedural Harmonization

The Doctrine of the ECJ: National Procedural Autonomy versus Harmonization

This chapter will focus on internal EU background developments and attempt to give a historic context consisting of the relatively random legal developments which took place before the emergence of the policy area judicial cooperation in civil matters. The case law or doctrine of the ECJ as well as sundry or ad hoc private international law rules in EC secondary law show the nascent regulation before and alongside the development of a competence and legal basis in the field.[1] As one commentator has noted, these separate courses of development have together with the ideas, motives and justifications for them fused and thus take part in forming the new policy area of judicial cooperation in civil matters.[2] These two strands foreshadow the questions which will be raised in Chapter 5, namely how and why one should regulate judicial cooperation in civil matters on the European Community or Union level. The questions raise the debate on procedural harmonization and highlight whether the following quotation is apt in the European judicial arena: 'Procedural idiosyncrasy is not (like national costume or regional cuisine) to be nurtured for its own sake.'[3]

[1] Two other potential sources of background strands which have been identified by one commentator as having had a harmonizing influence on procedural law before the emergence of judicial cooperation in civil matters are Treaty Art. 12, which prohibits discrimination on grounds of nationality, and the Brussels Convention of 1968, see Kennett (2000) pp. 28–34.

[2] Ibid. p. 21.

[3] Bingham LJ (as he then was) in *Dresser UK Ltd v. Falcongate Ltd* [1992] 1 QB 502, 522 H, CA.

The Evolving Case Law

The direct effect of Community rights entails that these rights can be invoked before national courts. However, traditionally neither the EC Treaty (the Treaty of Rome, as amended) nor Community legislation laid down a general scheme of procedure or remedies for the enforcement of these rights. Therefore, it was for the national legal systems to determine the rules of procedure and enforcement.[4] Subsequently, the ECJ has clarified the conditions for this apparent 'national procedural autonomy' by imposing two Community requirements on national procedural rules: (i) the principle of non-discrimination or equivalence which provides that the forms of action available must be the same as for national law rights; and (ii) the principle of practical possibility or efficiency which provides that the procedural rules must not make the exercise of the EC right impossible.[5] This 'minimalist' approach by the Court was applied in the early 1980s.

However, it was soon clear that where both principles were satisfied the full or even reasonable enforcement of Community law was not necessarily guaranteed.[6] Consequently, there followed a group of cases, mostly in relation to national remedies, in which the adequacy and effectiveness of national rules in securing Community rights became of central importance,[7] e.g. the landmark case *Factortame I*.[8] There followed a group of cases in which the Court confronted the tension caused by the additional demand of effectiveness. These cases can be seen as the most interventionist of the Court's case law vis-à-vis national procedural and remedial rules.[9] After this period, which lasted until the early 1990s, some commentators consider that further cases have evened out the doctrine and returned to the core requirements. Thus, the emphasis has shifted to whether the application of national procedural rules renders the exercise of a Community right excessively

[4] Craig and De Búrca (1998) p. 213f., referring to cases C-6/60 *Humblet v. Belgium* [1960] ECR 559 and C-13/68 *Salgoil v. Italian Ministry for Foreign Trade* [1973] ECR 453.

[5] Case 33/76 *Rewe-Zentralfinanz eG and Rewe-Zentral AG v. Landswirtschaftskammer für das Saarland* [1976] ECR 1989.

[6] Craig and De Búrca (1998) p. 216f.

[7] Cases 14/83 *Von Colson and Kamann v. Land Nordrhein-Westfalen* [1984] ECR 1891, 222/84 *Johnston v. the Chief Constable of the Royal Ulster Constabulary* [1986] ECR 1651, and 222/86 *UNECTEF v. Heylens* [1987] ECR 4097. See also Craufurd Smith (1999) pp. 300f. and 307–10.

[8] Case C-213/89 *R. v. Secretary of State for Transport, ex parte Factortame Ltd and Others* [1990] ECR I-2433.

[9] Craig and De Búrca (1998) p. 228f., referring to cases C-271/91 *Marshall v. Southampton and South West Area Health Authority II* [1993] ECR I-4367 and C-208/90 *Emmott v. Minister for Social Welfare* [1991] ECR I-4269.

difficult.[10] In particular, the evening out of the doctrine was perceived in the balancing approach or proportionality test introduced by the Court, which entails weighing the restrictive impact of the national procedural or remedial rule against the legitimate aim that the rules uphold, e.g. the basic principle of legal certainty and judicial passivity which was at stake in the two central cases.[11]

Some commentators thus describe the evolution of the case law as having occurred in three distinct phases.[12] The three phases as described above have also been seen as a pendulum between the historical underlying policy aim of uniformity through legal integration and the current vision of regulatory diversity with only sectoral uniformity.[13] The doctrine of the ECJ has also, though, been interpreted as either a linear evolution, consistently applying the fundamental principles, or as somewhat more confused and contradictory.[14] For example a recent case again demonstrates that the intrusion into domestic procedures is incidental and the requirements of full effect are sometimes emphasized.[15]

Aside from the evolution of the general tenets and the principles of equivalence and effectiveness, it is important to observe that the ECJ has managed to deal with several specific procedural or remedial issues in some detail. The span of cases has raised the question of procedural effectiveness with reference to such diverging procedural rules as, inter alia, time limits, the admissibility of certain forms of evidence, the neutrality of expert witnesses, and the method for apportioning the costs of proceedings.[16] The doctrine is also still developing as, case by case, further questions arise concerning particular national procedural rules and specific further clarifications of the scope of application.[17]

[10] Craig and De Búrca (1998) pp. 229 and 233 referring to, among others, the case C-338/91 *Steenhorst-Neerings v. Bestuur van de Bedrijfsvereniging voor Detailhandel* [1993] ECR I-5475.

[11] Craig and De Búrca (1998) p. 233ff. referring to cases C-312/93 *Peterbroeck, Van Campenhout & Cie v. Belgian State* [1995] ECR I-4599 and C-430–431/93 *Van Schijndel & Van Veen v. Stichting Pensioenfods voor Fysiotherapeuten* [1995] ECR I-4705. See also Craufurd Smith (1999) p. 314ff.

[12] Inter alia Dougan (2004) pp. 28–33, and Prechal (2001) pp. 39–42.

[13] Dougan (2002) pp. 167–78.

[14] Craufurd Smith (1999) pp. 293–316 identifies the following periods: (a) the initial preference, (b) early tension in the case law, (c) tightening the screw I, (d) tightening the screw II, and (e) tightening the screw III.

[15] Case C-405/03 *Class International BV v. Colgate-Palmolive Company and others* [2005] ECR I-8735.

[16] Dougan (2004) p. 32f.

[17] Ibid. pp. 55–65, and Prechal (2001) p. 42ff

The Draft Constitution for Europe,[18] and the subsequent Constitutional Treaty[19] attempted to define and codify the role of the Member States in the judicial system of the Union, and in particular their obligation to ensure effective legal protection as elaborated by the doctrine of the ECJ. Hence, Article I-29 of the Constitutional Treaty included the obligation on Member States to 'provide remedies sufficient to ensure legal protection'. The negative referenda in France and the Netherlands in the spring of 2005 in relation to ratification of the Constitutional Treaty have been followed by a period of reflection and an agreement in June 2007 to convene an intergovernmental conference (IGC) and draw up a more limited 'Reform Treaty' instead of the Constitutional Treaty.[20] A draft of the Reform Treaty amending the EU Treaty and the EC Treaty has been published as a working document for the IGC.[21] Changes to this document are still possible but currently included is the obligation for Member States to 'provide remedies sufficient to ensure effective legal protection'.[22]

The body of ECJ case law, which mostly has developed through cases dealing with administrative rather than civil proceedings, is still very relevant and fulfils an essential role in upholding the effectiveness and uniform application of Community law rights before national courts. The role of the case law vis-à-vis national courts dealing with civil rather than administrative proceedings is also becoming more and more apparent.[23] In addition, it

[18] OJ C-169, 18.7.2003, p. 1.

[19] OJ C-310, 16.12.2004, p. 1.

[20] The projected timetable is that the Reform Treaty should be agreed by the end of 2007 and be ratified before June 2009. Information taken from the IGC homepage that can be found on the Council website http://www.consilium.europa.eu/ (visited 22.8.2007), further confirmed in Presidency Conclusions 11177/1/07 para. 11.

[21] CIG 1/07 of 23.7.2007.

[22] Ibid. proposed Art. 9f of the TEU.

[23] Andersson (1998–9) p. 816 refers to case C-126/97 *Eco Swiss China Time Ltd v. Benetton International NV* [1999] ECR I-3055, and Komninos analyses case C-453/99 *Courage Ltd v. Bernard Crehan* [2001] ECR I-6297 and the new prospects for private enforcement in light of the modernization debate on EC competition law. Further Prechal and Shelkoplyas (2004) p. 593f. mention specifically labour law and cases concerning equal treatment of men and women as a limited group in which private law and the procedural doctrine of the ECJ has arisen. However, they also note that any particular directive in the private law sphere or general questions of discrimination or free movement arising in a private law dispute might trigger the connection between the procedural doctrine of the ECJ and civil proceedings. Dougan (2004) pp. 34–8, deals with the scenario of individual rights being enforced against private parties, e.g. the principle of effectiveness in horizontal situations, mentioning product liability and equal treatment as examples. The author notes that for the most part the case law of the Court has not distinguished between vertical and horizontal cases but that one can envisage situations in

is most interesting to note that in a few cases with a national civil procedure rather than administrative procedure context, the case law here elaborated is in part sidelined and the ECJ has instead been prepared to use a more direct free movement and non-discrimination argument to analyse the national procedural rules.[24]

The overall theme and debate generated by the case law is an evaluation of its effectiveness in achieving uniformity and protection of the parties' rights. Regarding the effectiveness in achieving uniformity commentators observe that it is partly a 'chimera' since there is an inevitable diversity which counters the homogenizing effect.[25] Therefore, one major strand of debate within Community law, which the ECJ procedural case law also highlights, and which is tangential to judicial cooperation in civil matters, is the choice between centralized (directly before the Community Courts) and decentralized (indirectly before the national courts) enforcement of Community law.[26] Because the uniform application of Community law is the ultimate general aim of the Treaties and has been called a fundamental requirement of the Community legal order, the ECJ has had to reconcile this with the fact that in the absence of uniform rules of procedure and remedies there is a reliance on Member State national

which the principle of effectiveness is less easily translated into a suitable remedy in the private law sphere.

[24] Cases C-20/92 *Hubbard v. Hamburger* [1993] ECR I-3777, where a national procedural rule that required a legal professional from another Member State to give security for costs solely on the grounds of nationality amounted to unlawful discrimination under the Treaty, and C-389/92 *Mund & Fester v. Hatrex* [1994] ECR I-467, where a domestic procedural rule providing that seizure of property for enforcement purposes solely based on the grounds that the judgment emanated from another Member State also amounted to discrimination under the Treaty. In contrast is the case C-412/97 *ED Srl v. Italo Fenocchio* [1999] ECR I-3055 where a national summary procedure for obtaining a payment order, which could only be sought against domestic defendants, did not interfere with free movement of goods or capital.

[25] Harding (1997) discusses the general question of effectiveness of enforcement of Community law and the potential harmonization of enforcement measures.

[26] The interaction between these two paths of enforcement has been analysed by several authors, inter alia Craufurd Smith (1999) p. 290f. for a succinct comparison with the USA. For a synopsis of the debate see Dougan (2004) pp. 1–4. The discussion is not completely analogous because in judicial cooperation in civil matters one could not envisage an intrinsic role for the ECJ in the practical day-to-day handling of matters. However, some of the same general themes do echo in relation to the regulation of the policy area judicial cooperation in civil matters, e.g. the quest for efficiency through the means of decentralization and its limits. Furthermore, there is overlap, in that the strengthening of cooperation between national courts in the field of judicial cooperation in civil matters might impact in the long run and strengthen their role in the general context of the enforcement of Community law.

systems.[27] Hence the question is always one of the limits of the principle of uniform application in the context of the judicial protection of rights.[28]

From a practical perspective, among the positive features of the ECJ body of case law in question is the cooperation between the Court and the national courts, which removes an enforcement burden from the Community institutions and has positive influences in the Member State, as citizens and national courts can identify with, understand, and appreciate the harmony and consistency with their own system.[29] Thus, public acceptance of the Community and its law can be fostered and the principles of subsidiarity and proportionality are upheld.[30] Furthermore, a positive feature is the balance which the Court of Justice has been able to strike between the autonomy of the national systems and the need to ensure effective protection.[31] In addition, the inevitably incremental approach, by which the Court provides solutions to individual situations, has been considered beneficial as this method in a detailed manner and more easily identifies both acceptable and unacceptable procedural differences.[32] However, in contrast, the point has been made in relation to the aim of achieving effectiveness of Community law, that the judiciary, litigation, and Article 10 (former Article 5) of the EC Treaty all have their inherent limits. Further, the test of minimum effectiveness has been questioned as a substantive standard against which to pitch national rules and obtain protection for litigants.[33] Furthermore, the negative features include that the doctrine is ad hoc and clearly less normatively coherent and less comprehensive than a legislative scheme which would be systematic and politically legitimate.[34] In addition,

[27] Van Gerven (2000) p. 504f. in particular referring to cases C-143/88 and C-92/89 *Zuckerfabrik Suderdithmarschen and Zuckerfabrik Soest v. Hauptzollamt Itzehoe and Hauptzollamt Paderborn* [1991] ECR I-415, para. 26, and C-46/93 *Brasserie du Pêcheur S.A. v. Germany* [1996] ECR I-1029, para. 33.

[28] Van Gerven (2000) p. 504f. Girerd (2002) pp. 97–102 specifically notes the difficult balance between the national courts (together with their national procedural rules) and the ECJ and the principle of effectiveness in matters where the financial repercussions are significant for the Member States.

[29] Bridge (1984) p. 31.

[30] Ibid. p. 31, De Búrca (1997) p. 45f., and Curtin (1994) p. 649f.

[31] Jacobs (1997) p. 35f. and Curtin (1994) p. 649f.

[32] Himsworth (1997) p. 307.

[33] Van Gerven (2000) p. 532ff. proposes and argues for the positive test of 'adequate protection' as a more apt measure.

[34] Neville Brown (1997) p. 70f. The case law of the ECJ in relation to procedural law has also overlapped with or highlighted the general Community law debate regarding judicial

the doctrine introduces a lack of legal certainty which complicates the role of the national courts.[35]

The Regulatory Debate

From these practical evaluations of the features of the system stems a further theoretical and regulatory debate. First, the question can be put whether the Member States actually possess judicial procedural autonomy.[36] If such autonomy exists, it is clear from the development of the case law that it is curtailed and subject to considerable requirements and restrictions.[37] Also it is noteworthy that no such autonomy exists in the Community context if procedural rules are in themselves incompatible with the free movement of goods or discrimination on the grounds of nationality, e.g. that the procedural rules themselves imply a breach of a Treaty article or substantive EC law.[38] However, more often the question is less clear and the context is rather the enforcement of Community rights through the medium of national procedural law.

In this context, one commentator claims that the impression that national procedural law is applied as a matter of basic principle, which is derived from a residual competence of the Member States and which constitutes a manifestation of their sovereignty, is wrong.[39] National courts and Member States do not possess national procedural autonomy; rather national procedural law is merely an ancillary body of law which is used to ensure the effective application of substantive Community law.[40] In contrast, another

activism and judge-made law; Weatherill (2003) p. 93 provides a general discussion on 'judicial activism'.

[35] De Búrca (1997) p. 45f., Hoskins (1996) p. 376, Engström (2003) p. 177f., and Girerd (2002) p. 102.

[36] Interestingly, the debate regarding the limits or existence of national procedural autonomy has largely not tapped into the general supremacy of the EC law debate and the reception of EC by national courts: Slaughter, Stone Sweet, and Weiler (eds) (1998), and the articles therein. However, it is clear that the question of ***kompetenz-kompetenz*** and procedural law can collide and that since the national courts in general apply their own procedural law, *lex fori*, there is clearly a particular barrier to the reception of 'foreign' influence. Very interesting empirical research could be done in lower courts, even linked to different substantive fields, as noted by Mattli and Slaughter (1998) p. 276.

[37] Inter alia Szyszczak and Delicostopoulos (1997), in relation to the impact of *Van Schijndel* and *Peterbroeck* on the French rules of procedure.

[38] Dougan (2004) pp. 20–3.

[39] Kakouris (1997) p. 1389f.

[40] Ibid. p. 1390.

commentator prefers to define the question as one of procedural competence, which he contends resides with the Member States.[41] Another more recent commentator argues that the European legal order has moved from national procedural autonomy to a more subtle combination of national procedural competence and European procedural primacy.[42] A further commentator, as well as referring to the case law of the ECJ, importantly also refers to several other limitations in EC law to national procedural autonomy, inter alia the obligation to make a referral to the ECJ for a preliminary ruling in certain circumstances and the obligation to refrain from conflicting rulings in pending competition matters.[43] He thus contends that, notwithstanding national competence, in the sphere of procedural law there is a refined emanation of the general loyalty principle.[44] Finally an additional commentator dispels the myth and comments that the concept of procedural autonomy is not helpful, in particular, he notes, in relation to the strong case law of the ECJ regarding access to court, which can be seen as an independent right situated above national procedural autonomy.[45]

The second theoretical question, which follows from the negative answer to the first, i.e. that Member States do not possess national procedural autonomy, is what the regulatory approach is accomplishing in the broader perspective and whether its inherent diversity should be replaced by a harmonized set of procedural and remedial rules. It is clear that the approach of the ECJ is broadly achieving some form of approximation of procedural rules across the EU, albeit that it is very difficult to assess the level of this approximation.[46] Therefore, after a certain period of time, the focus of the regulatory debate shifted towards a unified set of rules even though it was of course recognized that as a general project it would be very difficult to raise questions of public and private law involving national procedural codes as well as rules on both state liability and private tort liability.[47] Also the difficulty of the project was perceived as stemming from political sensitivities.[48] Specifically, in relation to harmonizing civil procedural rules and

[41] Van Gerven (2000) p. 501f.

[42] Delicostopoulos (2003b) p. 599ff.

[43] Sevón (2003) p. 5f.

[44] Ibid. p. 3.

[45] Rosas (2004) p. 372. Further, Dougan (2004) pp. 4–14 categorizes part of the doctrine of the ECJ as creating a more general right to access to court.

[46] Andersson (2003) pp. 56–9.

[47] Craig and De Búrca (1998) p. 252; and Lindblom (1997a) pp. 15 and 46, in relation to the difficulty of the project of procedural harmonization.

[48] Crauford Smith (1999) p. 298.

national procedural codes, the Commission in 1990 requested a group of experts under the chairmanship of Professor Storme to study the approximation of the laws of procedure. The group published its report in 1994.[49] This launched an academic and theoretical debate on the consequences and potential desirability of civil procedural harmonization within the European Union.[50]

First, arguments from the more general debate on private law harmonization within the EU can be used in relation to civil procedural law. One commentator argues that a common private law represents a logical extension in order to facilitate the Internal Market.[51] However, in contrast, it is arguable that the private law systems of the Member States represent an intrinsic part of their culture and traditions so that proposals for uniformity would represent an excess of centralization contrary to the principle of subsidiarity.[52] Private law can play a significant role both as a symbolic expression of moral values and as an effective underpinning for basic social institutions. Therefore, the risk presented by the EU and potential harmonization is the risk of jeopardizing personal identity and the destruction of the social basis.[53] Where private law has been harmonized in the Single Market, there are clear instances of resistance to harmonization both in the legislature and in the courts. The reasons for this resistance can be explained by the link between private law and national cultural identity and the pressure to make new choices in relation to the underlying goals, social impact, and wealth distribution of private law.[54]

Similarly, civil procedural regulation embodies social distributive functions in society in that it embodies a social agenda of how we wish to resolve our disputes. Thus, despite their ostensibly technical nature, civil procedural rules too enforce a political choice, which does not necessarily converge across the Union and which should not necessarily be harmonized. The difficult balance which the Court of Justice has trodden, and which the case law application in the Member States already shows, is that there is a policy choice between protecting the individual's rights and the general legality of

[49] Storme (ed.) (1994).

[50] The substance of the Report has also raised debate, inter alia by Lindblom (1997a) p. 15, Himsworth (1997) p. 303 and Juenger (1997) p. 932.

[51] Collins (1995) p. 353. Further, Schwarze (2000) pp. 138–41 analyses the costs of market integration under diverging procedural rules.

[52] Collins (1995) p. 353.

[53] Ibid. p. 363. Further Wilhelmsson (2001) pp. 14–18.

[54] Caruso (1997) p. 28f.

government action.[55] In addition, harmonization could encounter resistance within the legal community. Furthermore, linking to the discussion on legal culture, it has been argued that within the EU, which recognizes legal pluralism, culture actually shows the limits of law. Understanding diversity is an important value in itself and should be pursued, rather than trying to reduce diversity by creating uniformity.[56]

Secondly, more particular and technical arguments also arise in relation to the harmonization of civil procedure. There are inherent limits to procedural harmonization, e.g. judicial organization and the existence and scope of methods of appeal are seen as too closely linked to the state and to constitutional law for harmonization to be attempted.[57] In addition, to create a complete codification suddenly could lead to increased complexity and fragmentation with issues of disintegration at the national level and divergences in implementation at the supranational level as a result.[58] There is an additional concern that the harmonization process would entail a 'lowest common denominator' result.[59] Furthermore, harmonization through codification could also lead to a disincentive for development since reform would be a very time-consuming process and create a sense of closure, with the new code monopolizing legal discourse and excluding alternative views of justice.[60]

Adopting a market-oriented perspective would see the Internal Market gain an increase in stability due to a decrease in forum shopping. However, forum shopping also has a positive impact for the consumers of the systems since it provides an incentive for development and improvement.[61]

[55] Prechal (2001) p. 52.

[56] Legrand (1997) p. 61ff., Prechal (2001) pp. 55–8. With regard to the general private law debate see Weatherill (2004a) p. 12f, who is not insensitive to cultural concerns but says that they can only be persuasive if they are pursued in a specific sectoral context. Hence, he argues against a general preference for local culture: 'Local culture can be exclusionary; local culture can be downright nasty. Part of the very point of EC law is that it puts to test the validity of local "cultural" preferences in the context of the benefits of integration (which are admittedly not unqualified).'

[57] Kerameus (1990) p. 62f. and (1998a) p. 123.

[58] Lindblom (1997a) p. 26.

[59] Andersson (2003) p. 64 and Walter (2003) p. 77.

[60] Lindblom (1997a) p. 23ff., Legrand (1997) p. 55, and Zuckerman (2002) p. 325. Kötz (1992) p. 31f. makes the same point in relation to unification through codification for private law in general. See further Weatherill (2004a) p. 13f., who notes that economic objections to harmonization, including proponents of regulatory competition, form one strand of anti-harmonization criticism.

[61] Lindblom (1997a) p. 23 and Legrand (2002) p. 68.

In addition, there is a danger of creating two separate procedural strands, the national one and the Community one, which might be counterproductive to integration.[62] The commentators therefore favour a more decentralized and flexible development of common procedural rules or standards, and emphasize the importance of simultaneously developing a common legal culture and education as well as fostering a discussion on the fundamental principles of procedure.[63] In particular, the specificity of procedural law raises the question whether market unification is the appropriate starting point for procedural reform. In terms of procedure, the value of efficiency is important but not paramount; more vital is the capacity of the system to produce just and fair outcomes.[64]

Interestingly, a parallel and analogous debate has arisen, with regard to a project of model transnational civil procedure principles elaborated by the American Law Institute (ALI) and UNIDROIT.[65] It is clear that the same issues concerning procedural rules and their embeddedness in the local legal culture or mentality and concerning the different societal goals behind diverging procedural systems arise as for the Storme project.[66] Furthermore, the question of how best to deal with problems arising out of transnational litigation is raised and the particular problems that cross-border litigants face are highlighted. Some criticize the system of creating uniform rules, noting that the real problem lies in application and that it would be harmful to the efficiency of global litigation to use this method; as an alternative, more in-depth comparison and reinforced cooperation models should pave the way for dealing with particular problems such as taking evidence and provisional measures.[67] The project has also raised a debate about how a multinational special system of procedure or procedural rules for only transnational disputes could be reconciled with and fitted into a system where we already have national rules and supranational cooperation. Many commentators note several problems with the method adopted, e.g. creating

[62] Prechal (2001) p. 57f.

[63] Lindblom (1997a) pp. 26f and 45f., Niemi-Kiesiläinen (1999) p. 254ff., Kerameus (1995) p. 405, Kötz (1992) p. 34ff., and Biavati (2001) p. 100f.

[64] Niemi-Kiesiläinen (1999) p. 251.

[65] The principles are available inter alia at: http://www.unidroit.org/english/principles/civilprocedure/main.htm (visited 23.8.2007).

[66] Debates in Fouchard (ed.) (2001). In particular, Mayer (2001) p. 24 and Muir Watt (2001b) p. 40. Further Zuckerman (2002) p. 325. Note, however, that the debate was based on a draft version of the ALI and UNIDROIT rules, and that changes were made to this draft before the final version of the rules was published.

[67] Muir Watt (2001b) p. 43ff.

potential discrimination and potential interpretation problems about scope and applicability, and are more inclined to favour other forms of cooperation which can be part of the current systems.[68]

Following upon the above points a further clarification has to be made in relation to the debate regarding harmonization of civil procedural law, namely that one has to distinguish carefully between the arguments against codification and complete unification and the arguments against harmonization or Europeanization.[69] 'Harmonization' is here used not as an umbrella concept but to denote a lesser degree of legal approximation or legislation, as distinct from unification.[70] 'Europeanization' is here used to denote the variety of forms of cooperation and legislation within the EU which might be less stringent than wholesale codification. Both technical and legal cultural arguments can be used against both 'unification' and 'harmonization'. Nevertheless, particularly in the procedural field the critical commentators seem to have a more balanced and nuanced view, which does not entirely exclude harmonization or Europeanization.[71] In addition, it is important to note that other commentators have for a long time been calling for European projects in the field.[72] Also, more recently, perhaps in parallel with the constitutional developments of the Community (on which see Chapter 3), and with the evolution of the broader themes of European integration (see Chapter 5), the focus has shifted from the 'utopian' debate on feasibility of a common civil procedural code to more concrete discussions on minimal measures necessary in order to realize such objectives as bringing the Union closer to its citizens.[73] Thus, the unattainable unification ideal has

[68] Inter alia, Niboyet (2001) p. 52ff. and Gaudemet-Tallon (2001) p. 70.

[69] Osman (2001) p. 89f. emphasizes that it is important to note and be aware of the small but clear nuances of difference between these concepts.

[70] The commentators use the terms 'harmonization', 'unification', and 'approximation' in a variety of ways, some including clear definitions, others giving no explicit definition. Sometimes translation of these terms is also difficult, e.g. Partsch (2003) p. 30f. chooses to use the French term '*rapprochement*' – partly to denote some kind of medium between harmonization and unification and partly to use a broad term which can encompass all kinds of coordination including harmonization and not excluding unification. Another example is Andersson (2003), who uses the term 'approximation' to denote a broader concept, similar to 'Europeanization'. The generic terms 'approximation' or 'Europeanization' do not allude only to legislative developments, whereas in the EC law context 'harmonization' as a term does have that connotation. In contrast, these terms can encompass a broad variety of measures and mechanisms.

[71] For a more recent view from the immediate post-Storme debate see Andersson (2003) p. 64f.

[72] Inter alia Partsch (2003) p. 25.

[73] Labayle (1997) p. 856.

progressively been replaced by the older idea of Europeanization.[74] Conceptually also the idea of integration through law or ideology has been challenged by regulatory differentiation.[75] Nonetheless, the tide might again be turning and these issues will resurface in Chapters 16 and 17.

Notwithstanding, the doctrine of the ECJ comprises one of the important strands for providing the necessary background context to the current civil procedural initiatives. The case law reveals the procedural divergences in the European Union and the early calls from the Court for legislation in the field. Furthermore, the cases reveal individual situations from which it becomes clear that European law rights are not enforced. Thus, it is discernible, on the practical and factual level, that there is heterogeneity in the Internal Market, when disputes arise. This heterogeneity in dealing with disputes is the core of the problem, which the current legislative initiatives also seek to address. The debate and the questions raised in relation to the doctrine of the ECJ are indeed also relevant to an analysis of the current legislative measures. They show that harmonization of the Internal Market is deemed necessary but that the pressure for centralized solutions is softened by respect for local diversity.[76] They also show that there is an inherent tension between decentralization and effectiveness. In sum, they confirm that the desirability and feasibility of procedural regulation is linked amongst others to issues of market integration, social cohesion and legal cultural diversity as well as particular concerns in relation to the functions of procedure and the functionality of procedure.

Substantive Regulation: Ad hoc Creation of European Procedural Rules

Sector-specific Regulation

Parallel to the case law of the EJC described above a different strand of development has taken place in the context of sector-specific substantive

[74] Boularbah (2003) p. 171.

[75] Dougan (2002) pp. 157–61.

[76] Weatherill (2003) p. 653 makes the general observation of the perceived need for uniformity in relation to internal market rules, but also observes that these are nevertheless subject increasingly to the forces of subsidiarity, flexibility, and new forms of governance. See further Chapter 5.

Community law regulation. However, the impetus for this strand of procedural development had the same source as the above case law, i.e. the realization that substantive Community law must be backed up by some form of procedural security in order that rights which have been created not be watered down or given different treatment in the various Member States. This development has been ad hoc and does not display the same kind of tracked evolution as the case law of the ECJ. Without going through the whole *aquis communautaire*, or the specific part of it which can be classified as civil and commercial substantive law, it is also difficult to ascertain every instance of such regulation. However, we can make certain general assumptions.

The first of these assumptions is that there has de facto been relatively little such regulation, partly perhaps because of a sensitivity on the part of the Community institutions vis-à-vis the question of competence.[77] The second of these assumptions is that the encroachment of these measures into the field of traditional judicial cooperation or private international law has mainly been of a conflict of laws nature.

Commentators on conflict or choice of law have realized that the substantive legislative instruments which include a choice of law article have often been made to deal with a specific or single issue or have predominantly taken into account substantive policy arguments and the particular interests involved in the relevant policy field. The question, not only of an academic nature, has then arisen whether or not these choice of law stipulations conflict with the mutual international rules laid down in the Rome Convention of 1980. An interesting debate has also arisen in relation to how such secondary Community law choice of law rules should be ranked and interpreted in relation to the four fundamental freedoms of the EC and the country of origin doctrine.[78] These choice of law rules cannot be used as examples of a nascent procedural regulation within the EU. Nevertheless, they can serve as a guide to the instances and areas of law in which the institutions have deemed it necessary to include any kind of rules adjacent to the purely substantive ones in order to make rights efficient. Thus, commentators note the following areas of Community legislation amongst those in which this has occurred: insurance law and provision of insurance services, labour law both in terms of discrimination rules and the posting of workers,

[77] Jayme and Kohler (1995) p. 4, and ECLG (1998) para. 6.

[78] Duintjer Tebbens (2004) inter alia pp. 112–15, and Jayme and Kohler (1995) inter alia pp. 36–9.

cultural heritage law and restitution for objects unlawfully removed, intellectual property law and Community trademark law, corporate law and the formation of European companies, as well as telecommunications law and e-commerce.[79]

One clear area of focus, very much linked to the feasibility of cross-border trade for small and medium-sized companies, is the reduction of payment periods and non-payment in commercial transactions. In particular the Late Payment Directive obliges the Member States to have certain procedural rules in place.[80] In addition the area of consumer law has seen several instances of choice of law and procedural law rules being inserted into the substantive legislative instruments.[81]

Case Study: Consumer Law

The area of consumer law is the sectoral field in which commentators have identified the greatest volume of regulatory focus on procedural issues and access to justice embedded in and interlinked with the substantive regulatory activity.[82] This is perhaps because the consumer *aquis* is an extensive and developed field of substantive EC law where the protective element, e.g. protecting the weaker party, is strong. Even at the domestic level the protection of consumers' rights, and specifically litigation rights, has increased the focus on procedural rules. Therefore, it is perhaps not surprising that such political efforts have also been made at the EC level. Hence, it is useful to use consumer law as a case study to briefly demonstrate the substantive ad hoc strand of procedural development.

In the field of consumer law a number of substantive directives were enacted before 1993 giving consumers specific protection in such diverse areas as misleading advertising, contracts negotiated away from business premises, consumer credit, package travel, the advertising of medicinal products, unfair

[79] Duintjer Tebbens (2004) pp. 102–11 and Jayme and Kohler (1995) pp. 5–10 provide different listings of substantive measures and their choice of law or jurisdiction rules. Andersson (2003) p. 56ff. notes instances of overlap between procedural law and secondary substantive EC regulation.

[80] Directive (EC) No. 35/2000, OJ L-200, 8.8.2000, p. 35. Kennett (2000) p. 42ff.

[81] Duintjer Tebbens (2004) pp. 102–11, and Jayme and Kohler (1995) pp. 5–10, provide different listings of substantive measures and their choice of law or jurisdiction rules, including consumer law measures.

[82] Kennett (2000) p. 40 also notes that consumer policy, based on Art. 153 (former Art. 129a) of the EC Treaty as a legal basis, is the most notable instance of a sectoral policy which has had a procedural law element.

contract terms, time-share development, and distance contracts.[83] These measures served two goals, first to establish a legal framework enabling all economic players to exploit the common market with fewer barriers, and secondly to facilitate public access to cross-border justice in the European Union.[84] These substantive directives notwithstanding, redress for consumers whose rights were aggrieved was, as in the past, left to the Member States' procedural laws.

Reliance on national procedural laws was not considered sufficient and was seen as creating undesired diversity in the Internal Market. Therefore the Commission launched a Green Paper consultation process in 1993 on 'Access of consumers to justice and the settlement of consumer disputes in the Single Market'.[85] Then in 1995 the Commission launched an in-depth study, 'The Cost of Legal Barriers to Consumers in the Internal Market', the main finding of which was that for consumers, cross-border disputes valued at less than 2000 ECU were not worth pursuing, even at the level of first instance proceedings.[86] As a result of these findings, which indicated a macroeconomic incentive to improve the situation, the Commission published a legislative proposal in 1996.[87] This proposal resulted in the Consumer Injunction Directive, which regulates collective consumer interests or grievances.[88] The Commission further adopted an Action Plan for the regulation of individual consumer disputes,[89] which resulted in a Communication regarding dispute prevention and in a Recommendation on principles for the out-of-court resolution of disputes.[90]

The Consumer Injunction Directive has been considered to be groundbreaking in that it clearly represents a very rare instance of secondary legislation intended to create or achieve a partial harmonization of national procedural rules. However, first it is noteworthy that the degree of harmonization is in reality quite modest. This is because the system created is one in which certain national organizations or agencies, 'qualified entities', which have been notified to the Commission and whose names are published, can

[83] Directives 89/450/EEC, 85/577/EEC, 87/102/EEC, 90/314/EEC, 92/28/EEC, 93/13/EEC, 94/47/EEC, and 97/97/EEC.

[84] ESC 742/2003, p. 4.

[85] COM (1993) 576, 16.11.1993.

[86] Freyhold et al. (1998) p. 276f.

[87] Ibid., Gasparinetti (1996) p. 227. See also COM (1995) 712, 24.1.1996.

[88] (EC) No. 27/1998, OJ L-166, 11.6.1998, p. 51.

[89] COM (1996) 13, 14.2.1996.

[90] COM (1998) 198–1 and 198–2; Tenreiro (2001) p. 111f.

bring an action for injunctive relief in all the Member States.[91] Thus, harmonization is rather a question of the mutual recognition of the legal capacity of certain collective interests. The *lex fori* and the local court can still examine whether the qualified entity has a right of action in the specific case and can decide which law is to be applied to the alleged infringement.[92] Furthermore, the directive does not deal at all with the actual procedural rules governing such an application for injunctive relief, e.g. rules on time limits, the form of pleadings, the service of documents, the taking of evidence, the hearing of submissions and evidence, and appeals of the decision. Thus, one can envisage that even organizations that are nationally adroit at defending collective consumer interests might still, because of the lack of information and experience, find it complex and time-consuming to bring actions in other Member States. Thus, one can also envisage that the proceedings would vary significantly between Member States in terms of time and cost, depending on the procedural rules but also on the resources of national courts to deal efficiently with caseloads.[93]

In addition, the directive stipulates that the remedy it is intended to create or support is an order that prohibits or requires the cessation of an infringement of a relevant consumer protection provision, as well as an order that failure to comply with will result in a costs consequence.[94] However, the wording is relatively vague and does not harmonize procedural practice in Member States with regard to injunctive relief, including the established jurisprudence in relation to, for example, the conditions and burden of proof to be granted an injunction. Therefore, it is still very likely that there will be

[91] Arts 3 and 4 of the directive. Note that the scope of the directive is limited to a list of substantive Community directives. Action can only be brought if there is an intra-Community infringement of any of the listed directives.

[92] Arts 2 and 4 of the directive. Osman (2001) pp. 110–15 notes that this choice of system is quite extraordinary because the goal of private international law has traditionally not been to treat international actors/parties equally with national ones, but rather to assure them legal certainty through a functioning system of reciprocity. However the author also notes that the directive treads a fine line between the national law of the actors and the *lex fori*.

[93] Viitanen (1999) pp. 553f and 560–4, for other lines of critique against the directive. These include that the directive does not resolve the problems of differences in substantive law, nor – on a more practical note – does it deal with how such intra-Community collective interest action should be funded. Furthermore, the author notes that a group action for compensation (rather than only injunctive relief) would be another important weapon in achieving access to justice for consumers.

[94] Art 2 of the directive. Note that the monetary sanction for non-compliance is not mandatory or harmonized, because this will only apply 'in so far as the legal system of the Member State concerned so permits'. Thus, fragmentation is added to the system.

fragmentation in the practice of the courts and in the procedural framework in the Community.[95] Finally, it is noteworthy that, because of the nature of representation by organizations, such a measure will only help a fraction of cross-border consumers who have a grievance. For this reason procedural measures which help individual consumers are also necessary.[96]

There is information that in the service sector in matters of banking, insurance, and real estate, there are increasing numbers of cross-border disputes involving consumers and concerning relatively high-value claims.[97] For individual consumer disputes it was recognized that the Brussels Convention gave little practical relief even in the context of enforcement.[98] Therefore in 1998 a number of practical measures were put in place, including a Communication which launched the publication of a European claim form for consumers and a Recommendation which outlined such principles as independence, transparency, and effectiveness for alternative dispute mechanisms where a third party is actively mediating between the parties.[99] These measures have subsequently been followed by a Recommendation for conciliation procedures where a third party is not actively mediating and the establishment of two networks.[100] The first network, 'EEJ-Net', consists of the national bodies that are involved in the extrajudicial settlement of disputes, and the second network, 'FIN-Net', is concerned specifically with financial services and their consumer complaint bodies.[101]

These measures have been considered relatively modest because they deal only with out-of-court dispute resolution mechanisms and are predominantly 'soft law', i.e. non-binding measures. The practical consequences of the obligation to cooperate amongst national entities entrusted with consumer dispute resolution will depend greatly on national resources and

[95] Nevertheless, the directive has contributed to procedural developments in the Member States and – depending on the prior national systems – in some instances led to major change: Osman (2001) pp. 107–10.

[96] Freyhold et al. (1998) p. 3.

[97] Ibid. pp. 1f. and 277.

[98] ECLG (1998) inter alia paras 7, 18.

[99] Tenreiro (2001) pp. 113–17, for a description and analysis of these measures. See also the Commission publication, *Consumer Disputes – Labyrinthian Thread* (1999), which aimed to inform citizens about the possibilities of recourse open to them.

[100] OJ L-109, 19.4.2001, p. 56.

[101] COM (2002) 196, 19.4.2002, Green Paper on alternative dispute resolution in civil and commercial matters, pp. 16–18, gives a good exposition of all the ADR measures in the field of consumer law.

intercultural understanding. The reason for the modest nature of these measures has been the difficulty and inability on the practical as well as political level of encroaching upon national procedural rules and embarking upon a harmonization of these, even in the limited area of consumer disputes.[102] Not surprisingly, these measures have not been considered sufficient. The specific vision of a European Area of Justice, and the renewed focus on citizens of the Union as part of the process of building that area, have rekindled the need for access to justice measures, both procedural and substantive, specifically for consumers.[103]

Hence it is evident that consumer law as a sector-specific example evidences the practical issues which are at stake and the complexities of cross-border dispute resolution. Because the value of the claims and the resources of the litigants are both often small in monetary terms the need for efficiency, and particularly for simplified and affordable procedures, becomes acutely visible. Therefore, the Community attempts to create access to cross-border justice for consumers can appropriately serve as an embryonic form of the policy area judicial cooperation in civil matters and as a case study for the more generic initiatives. However, one problem in this context is that because the value of the claims at stake is often low there are few references to the ECJ. Hence, no guiding or harmonizing case law has been developed in relation to procedural rules in the policy sector which would serve as a unifying factor and raise awareness and debate about questions of procedural harmonization.[104] Nevertheless, it is also evident that the same questions and issues arise for sectoral regulation as for the general harmonization debate discussed in the preceding section. Therefore, in relation to the second abstract question raised in the discourse, i.e. whether or not harmonization is desirable, the example of consumer dispute resolution substantiates some of the perceived drawbacks. Harmonization of procedural rules for consumer disputes would thus, like the general argument, be logical in an Internal Market perspective; but centralization of such structures has necessarily had to take into account local legal culture

[102] Tenreiro (2001) p. 113f. For consumer disputes such harmonization could conceivably be grounded legally in the competence basis established in Art. 153 (former Art. 129a).

[103] Wilhelmsson (2004). For a procedural law specialist 'substantive' access to justice measures might sound like an anomaly. Wilhelmsson is here referring to creating such legal obligations as a network liability between manufacturer and seller or a network liability in a selective distribution system, both of which would give consumers more parties from whom to seek redress.

[104] Kennett (2000) p. 35.

and distribution goals, as well as potential resistance from the legislature or the courts. Furthermore, there are perceived inherent limits to such harmonization, which have entailed the creation of a degree of fragmentation and the ensuing complexity in the measures. Therefore, a more decentralized approach has been adopted, but only partially, and this mutatis mutandis has created a tension with the goal of efficiency.

3

Setting the Scene: The Evolution of a Legal Basis

Pre-Amsterdam

The fundamental principle of legality of Community action or the doctrine of attributed competence is outlined in Article 5(1) of the EC Treaty (Treaty of Rome, as amended). This entails that the Community does not have general competence since it must act within the limits of its powers. Hence, the Community must have a legal basis within the Treaty for every legal act it adopts.[1] In particular the judgment of the ECJ in the *Tobacco Advertising*[2] case has highlighted the question of constitutional control over the limits of Community competence and led to a certain 'competence anxiety' for certain sectors of EC law. One commentator notes that the harmonization of private law for the purpose of reinforcing the Internal Market has had to be rethought and rejustified, raising the question of how far into private law the EC might legitimately reach.[3] The question of Community competence in the field of civil procedural law is therefore of paramount importance.

The issue of Community competence in the field of procedural law was raised in Chapter 2 in the elaboration of the case law of the ECJ with regard to the limits of civil procedural autonomy. One commentator notes that one could consider the competence as arising from either an interpretation of substantive Community competence such as in the case of consumer law depicted in Chapter 2 or the loyalty principle in Article 10 (former 5) of

[1] Craig and De Búrca (2002) p. 111.
[2] C-376/98 *Germany v. Parliament and Council* [2000] ECR I-8419.
[3] Weatherill (2004b) p. 643ff.

the EC Treaty.[4] Another commentator sees the case law as an adjunct to the twin doctrines of primacy of EC law and direct effect, being indispensable to the uniform application of Community law that is imperative for the Internal Market.[5] One can also construe the competence as arising from general principles of Community law, among these the right to access to a court, particularly as supported by Article 13 of the ECHR and Article 47 of the EU Charter of Fundamental Rights.[6]

However, these premises, for imposing conditions upon national procedural law on a case-by-case basis, are of a rather vague nature and as such did not entail that there was a fully fledged competence to regulate civil procedural law or judicial cooperation in civil matters at the Community level. Thus, the need for a more concrete competence or legal basis can be seen as emerging in parallel with the two strands of development outlined in Chapter 2. As one commentator put it in 1997, envisaging that there might be a role for what was then the Third Pillar, 'what will be "the next step"... in securing a coherent and effective system of enforcement of Community rights in the national courts?'[7] One should nonetheless not jump so far ahead because chronologically the EC Treaty had already in 1957 partly foreseen that judicial cooperation in civil matters could become necessary or relevant, which can be seen in Article 220 (now 293): 'Member States shall, so far as is necessary, enter into negotiations with each other with a view to securing for the benefit of their nationals:... 2. the simplification of formalities governing the reciprocal recognition and enforcement of judgments of courts or tribunals and of arbitration awards.'

This Article was the first vehicle for or seed of Community developments in the field, albeit clearly only at an intergovernmental level rather than through Community legislation.[8] Consequently, the Brussels Convention on Jurisdiction and the Recognition and Enforcement of Judgments was

[4] Prechal (1997) p. 6.

[5] Arnull (1997) p. 16. Thus, the procedural law case law from the ECJ has lent its weight to another academic debate or given rise to another offshoot of debate, namely the question of the reception of Community law and its principle of supremacy in national courts. This can also be characterized as the debate over judicial activism and ***komptetenz-kompetenz***, see inter alia Alter (2001) and Slaughter, Stone Sweet, and Weiler (1998).

[6] Dougan (2004) p. 52ff.

[7] Neville Brown (1997) p. 70f.

[8] Pipkorn (1981) p. 40ff. notes that the conventions did not form part of the Community legal order ***strictu sensu*** because their legal nature and legal effects derived from the national constitutional law of each of the signatory Member States. And as part of national law they were subordinated to the primacy of EC law.

agreed upon in 1968 between the Member States under this provision. In addition, during this period, the Member States also entered into the Rome Convention of 1980.[9] These Conventions together with their Protocols, which conferred jurisdiction on the ECJ to interpret the Conventions, have played a significant role in paving the way for a discussion on the need for unified procedural rules or cross-border procedural cooperation in the EU. The case law of the ECJ in relation to the Brussels Convention, showing tendencies both to unify interpretation and to refer to the national systems, can be seen as displaying the tension referred to above in the debate on procedural harmonization between effectiveness and decentralization.[10] However, it is also clear that these Conventions evidenced the technical limits of the intergovernmental route and thereby highlighted the potential for Treaty modification and attribution of competence.[11] Another potential legal basis provided in the Treaty of Rome was Article 100 (now 94) which allows for the approximation of laws which directly affect the functioning of the Common Market: 'The Council shall, acting unanimously on a proposal from the Commission and after consulting the European Parliament and the Economic and Social Committee, issue directives for the approximation of such laws, regulations or administrative provisions of the Member States as directly affect the establishment or functioning of the common market.'

In addition the Treaty of Rome provided for a further potential subsidiary legal basis, namely Article 235 (now 308), which allows for the promulgation of appropriate measures for the achievement of the objectives of the Community where the EC Treaty has not provided the necessary powers elsewhere.[12] This legal basis also requires unanimity in the Council but the available legislative measures are not limited to approximating directives. Furthermore, the initiatives can go beyond the purely economic sphere as there is no requirement of 'directly affecting the functioning of the common market'. However, in the very early developments of the Community and even later on during the birth of the Brussels and Rome Conventions, it is clear that the Commission did not consider using either of these legal bases

[9] Barrett (2001) p. 8 notes that there was no legal basis for the Rome Convention since conflict of laws is not mentioned in Art. 220 (now 293). However, the Treaty did not hinder a separate intergovernmental Convention between the Member States, which still clearly became part of the Community *aquis*.

[10] Kennett (2000) p. 29.

[11] Pipkorn (1981) p. 41f.

[12] Craig and De Búrca (1998) pp. 110–15 discuss the legality of Community action and in particular the debate surrounding Art. 308 (ex 235).

for the domain of judicial cooperation. In particular, due to the considerable potential competence accorded to the Community in Article 235 (now 308), the Member States in the Council were not, for reasons of political sensitivity willing or able to agree unanimously to use it as legal basis.[13]

The Single European Act in 1985 introduced amendments to the EC Treaty in order to make progress in the implementation of the Internal Market. Article 100a (now 95) was introduced as a derogation to Article 100 (now 94), and allowed for the approximation of laws by qualified majority voting to speed up the process of establishing the Internal Market. The Storme working group found in its Report that both articles, 100 and 100a, opened the way for legislative action approximating procedural laws. However, others have been more sceptical, pointing out that the legislative competence under these articles can only come into play if both the benefits and the disadvantages of approximation of procedural rules are weighed against each other.[14] In addition, some commentators did not consider that Article 100a (now 95) provided a basis for harmonization because the basic freedoms were thought not to be curtailed by differences in private international law.[15] Other authors, in contrast, consider that Article 100a (now 95) would provide a formidable legal basis for harmonization in that judicial cooperation measures support the functioning of the market by creating legal certainty and supporting the enforcement of civil and commercial rights in the market.[16] In addition, the divergences in judicial cooperation can lead to competition distortions and therefore Article 100a (now 95) would be the correct basis for harmonizing measures.[17]

Another point of view is that the scope of Article 95 (former 100a) and potential areas of harmonization are based on the functionality of the rules vis-à-vis the Internal Market, and private law regulations typically do not affect market access *per se* but the *inter se* relationship between market actors. Therefore the market obstacles come into play at a later stage in integration.[18] It is also possible to argue that the Storme project came during a historic period in which the political climate among the EC institutions was such that competence creep was not a concern and it was habitual to 'borrow'

[13] Partsch (2003) p. 242f.
[14] Lindblom (1997) pp. 22 and 27.
[15] Basedow et al. (2000) p. 699.
[16] Partsch (2003) p. 254f.
[17] Ibid. p. 258, further p. 240 in relation to Art. 100 (now 94).
[18] Israël (2000) p. 90f.

the Internal Market legal bases for varied tangential legislative projects.[19] Notwithstanding the scope of Articles 94 and 95 (ex 100 and 100a), the reality is that no legislative action was or has been taken by the Community in the field of judicial cooperation or procedural regulation on the basis of these articles.[20] However, towards the end of the 1980s there were attempts to create further means of judicial cooperation using the intergovernmental route and one commentator notes that these attempts, which ultimately failed, raised awareness of the lack of legal basis but also gave a hint of the move away from purely economic arguments for cooperation towards a more citizen-oriented focus.[21]

The next Treaty development was the Treaty of Maastricht which came into force on 1 November 1993. Before reviewing the obvious new potential legal basis of Article K, it is worth noting that some commentators also raise the Articles on citizenship of the Union, introduced at Maastricht, as a potential basis for harmonizing judicial cooperation in civil matters and private law within the European Union.[22] In particular they refer to the legal basis provided for in Articles 8A and 8E of the EC Treaty (now Articles 18 and 22) as well as the goals of Union citizenship as elaborated by Article B of the EU Treaty (now Article 2), which include the object of protecting the rights and interests of citizens.[23] This has been seen by commentators as clearly encompassing a goal of improving access to justice within the Union.[24] Many judicial cooperation projects could be considered as partly affecting the free movement of persons, i.e. affecting the economic working of the market, but also affecting the more personal sphere of persons, i.e. affecting Union citizens' access to justice. Thus, a combination of Articles 100a (now 95) and 8 (now 18) could have provided a suitable legal basis.[25]

[19] Weatherill (2004, 2) p. 634ff.

[20] However, this statement has to be qualified by the point that several of the secondary substantive legislative measures based on Art. 100a (now 95) have included provisions which can be characterized as procedural and/or pertaining to judicial cooperation in civil matters. Partsch (2003) p. 258ff. makes this point. Normand (1998b) p. 131f., noted that in 1998 the EC institutions could only make 'modest' inroads in the field due to the competence issue and the principle of subsidiarity.

[21] Rouchaud (2001) p. 20f.

[22] Partsch (2003) pp. 271–5 and Moccia (2004) p. 315f.

[23] Partsch (2003) pp. 269 and 275 mainly refers to Art. 8A (now 18) of the EC Treaty as a potential legal basis, whereas Moccia (2004) p. 315 refers to the goals in Art. 2 (formerly B) of the EU Treaty as the starting point for using citizenship itself as a legal basis, perhaps in the more figurative sense.

[24] Partsch (2003) p. 270.

[25] Ibid. p. 274f.

Nevertheless, again the reality is that the articles on citizenship have yet to be used as a legal basis for measures in the field of judicial cooperation in civil matters.

The Treaty of Maastricht did however introduce another new route for potential measures vis-à-vis judicial cooperation in civil matters in the Third Pillar, 'Justice and Home Affairs'. In particular, Article K.1 of the EU Treaty provided that: 'For the purposes of achieving the objectives of the Union, in particular the free movement of persons, and without prejudice to the powers of the Community, Member States shall regard the following areas as matters of common interest: . . . (6) judicial cooperation in civil matters.'

The Third Pillar had a different institutional structure and legislative process from the Community, remaining predominantly intergovernmental with conventions as the most likely instrument to be used in the field of judicial cooperation in civil matters. Two such conventions were subsequently signed, the Convention on Service of Judicial and Extrajudicial Documents and the Convention on Jurisdiction and the Recognition and Enforcement of Judgments in Matrimonial Matters. However, there were inherent disadvantages in the intergovernmental mechanism, and particularly in the new structure created within the Council for Article K matters.[26] Structural and political factors entailed that the development of measures was slow, being hampered by, for example, lack of objectives, targets, and deadlines, as well as by the requirement of unanimity.[27] Another critique of the Third Pillar, as it was regulated at the time, was the question of legitimacy and the absence of the usual checks and balances due to the lack of judicial review and parliamentary control.[28] Finally, the lack of appropriate legislative instruments and the fact that the convention system was cumbersome, requiring transposition through signature and ratification in each Member State, has been criticized.[29] As an example, slow transposition delayed the two conventions in the field of judicial cooperation in civil matters from entering into force before the Treaty of Amsterdam entered into force.[30]

[26] Kennett (2000) pp. 6–9.

[27] Barrett (1997) pp. 17–23.

[28] Ibid. p. 26–38.

[29] Ibid. 24f. on the general point of lack of suitable legal instruments. See also Barrett (2001) p. 9f.

[30] Rouchaud (2001) p. 22f. suggests that the fact that there were only two conventions under discussion during this period was perhaps caused by the lack of a mobilizing umbrella project, due either to the complexity of the questions or to Member States' protectiveness of their national sovereignty.

Post-Amsterdam

As a response to these structural deficiencies, the Treaty of Amsterdam, which came into force on 1 May 1999, removed the policy area of judicial cooperation in civil matters from the Third Pillar and placed it in the First Pillar, i.e. the Community sphere. Thus, Articles 61 and 65 were introduced in the EC Treaty. According to Article 61 the Council shall in order to establish progressively an Area of Freedom, Security, and Justice adopt measures in the field of, inter alia, judicial cooperation in civil matters. Article 65(1) elaborates these measures:

1. Measures in the field of judicial cooperation in civil matters having cross-border implications, to be taken in accordance with Article 67, and insofar as necessary for the proper functioning of the internal market, shall include:
   a) improving and simplifying:
      - the system for cross-border service of judicial and extrajudicial documents,
      - cooperation in the taking of evidence,
      - the recognition and enforcement of decisions in civil and commercial cases, including decisions in extrajudicial cases;
   b) promoting the compatibility of the rules applicable in the Member States concerning the conflict of laws and of jurisdiction;
   c) eliminating obstacles to the good functioning of civil proceedings, if necessary by promoting compatibility of the rules on civil procedure applicable in the Member States.

For the first time the EC Treaty contained a specific legal basis for judicial cooperation in civil matters and a specific enumerated list of potential measures to be adopted. Hence, one can say that the policy area was 'Communitarized' or 'Europeanized'. Nevertheless, it is somewhat anomalous that the policy area was included in the new Title IV of the Treaty, 'Visas, Asylum and Policies Related to Free Movement of Persons', together with immigration policy.[31] This location has been criticized from a conceptual, systematization point of view. Since substantively immigration policy relates to external parties who want entry into the Community and the external sphere of the Community in general, the issues are discrete and independent and do not

[31] Girerd (1999) p. 252 notes that Title IV was a late addition in the intergovernmental negotiations and that this evidences and is characteristic of the difficulties that the negotiators experienced in constituting the relevant policy domains.

overlap with judicial cooperation in civil matters. By contrast, commentators have seen the latter policy area as relating more to the internal sphere of the Community, to the Internal Market.[32] However, even though some commentators criticize the linking of private international law to the Area of Freedom, Security and Justice, other commentators find the association relevant and central to an understanding of the policy area.[33] The political explanation for the inclusion of judicial cooperation in civil matters in Title IV seems to have been that throughout the negotiations there was uncertainty as to whether the policy area belonged in the First or the Third Pillar. Finally, the Member States in favour of further developing this area within the Community framework were successful in including it in the First Pillar, their main aim thus being to avoid the unanimity requirement in the Third Pillar. However, as a concession to the Member States who opposed Community developments, it was finally included in Title IV.[34]

Notwithstanding the political explanation there are noteworthy legal consequences arising from the placement of judicial cooperation in civil matters in Title IV of the EC Treaty. First, Title IV contains some anomalous and particular institutional and structural characteristics.[35] It is important therefore to distinguish whether measures fall under Article 65 of the EC Treaty or any of the other potential legal bases, e.g. Articles 95 or 293 of the EC Treaty. One commentator argues that Article 65 should only be used when there is a clear link to the free movement of persons, the ensuring of which is the overriding purpose of Title IV. In other instances, also involving the free movement of goods and services, Article 95 would be the more appropriate legal basis.[36] Other commentators do not agree[37] and one author also suggests that it would have been beneficial to use Article 293 (former 220) of the EC Treaty in order to avoid the structural problems.[38]

[32] Partsch (2003) pp. 296ff. and 300ff. and Leible and Staudinger (2000–1) p. 226.

[33] Meeusen (2004) p. 49 takes this approach, whereas Rissanen (1999) p. 236ff. takes the opposite approach.

[34] Partsch (2003) p. 299f., Kohler (1999) pp. 10–14, and Labayle (1997) pp. 815–19 and 856–64, regarding the birth of Title IV of the EC Treaty and Art. 65, going through the different IGC phases and drafts leading up to the Treaty of Amsterdam. Further, Israël (2000) p. 83f. points out that judicial cooperation in civil matters did not receive the same attention as the core issues of immigration and asylum; he thus seems to imply that there is a certain ad hoc character to Art. 65 and its placement in Title IV.

[35] Chapter 4 provides a detailed analysis of the structural particularities of Title IV of the EC Treaty.

[36] Basedow (2000) p. 697ff.

[37] Inter alia Remien (2001) p. 72f.

[38] Beaumont (2002) p. 13f.

The opposing view is that Article 65, as *lex specialis*, prevails.[39] In practice none of the alternative older legal bases has been used, rather the approach adopted by the Community institutions[40] is that all measures have been based on Article 65.

The discussion on the appropriate legal basis already gives us an inkling of the second, related point. This is the issue of whether Article 65 of the EC Treaty, due to its placement in Title IV, is limited in its scope to measures pertaining to the free movement of persons, i.e. is limited in its horizontal scope. One of the early commentators presented this interpretation and it has been followed by many others, with slightly different justifications.[41] This interpretation sees the Community competence created in Articles 61 and 65 of the EC Treaty as quite narrow. This narrow scope, in conjunction with institutional constraints, would lead to the conclusion that the legal basis is not a practical means on which to base the evolution of judicial cooperation.[42] In retrospect it is clear that in practice this view has not been verified or empirically substantiated. On the contrary, several legislative initiatives having a horizontal rather than sector-specific scope have been passed in the Community based on Article 65. A later commentator therefore proposes that the systematic interpretation of the role of Article 65 as a legal basis in the Treaty is a fallacy since neither its genesis nor its actual wording suggests a sectoral approach, but rather a horizontal one.[43]

Despite not being sectorally limited Article 65 has two explicit limitations of scope in the legal basis itself, i.e. the limitations of 'matters having cross-border implications' and 'insofar as necessary for the proper functioning of the internal market'. In addition, there has been some debate as to whether the unusual wording 'improving and simplifying' and 'promoting the compatibility' also can be considered an attempt to limit the extent of

[39] Inter alia Meeusen, Pertegás, and Straetmans (2004) p. 3.

[40] Ibid. 11f., for a particular critique of the Santer Commission, which took the first initiatives in the field of judicial cooperation in civil matters in 1999; the authors implying that impatience to make progress with new legislative proposals entailed that a thorough analysis of the legal basis implications was dispensed with.

[41] Kohler (1999) p. 15ff. introduced this interpretation, based on a systematic interpretation of the EC Treaty, and was followed by Basedow (2000) and Israël (2000). Lindblom (1997b) pp. 312–16 notes that one can interpret the scope of Art. 65 in two ways and criticizes the lack of clarity. However, since he is sceptical about procedural harmonization he tends to support the narrow interpretation.

[42] Kohler (1999) p. 29.

[43] Partsch (2003) pp. 305–9. Note also that the commentator considers that even if the systematic interpretation can be made, one should admit that it was not the intention of the authors of the Treaty to make Art. 65 so narrow in its scope.

action.[44] In light of the debate on desirability and feasibility as well as the scope of any potential harmonization, at least the two explicit limitations seem significant. Several commentators have emphasized the importance of these limitations, some even suggesting that as a result of these, and as a result of a general restrictive or careful interpretation of Article 65, soft law rather than hard law mechanisms would be the most suitable form of regulation.[45] Even though such a restrictive approach has not been taken in practice, these limitations do necessitate that the Community legislative proposals, and thus the institutions, take them into account. This necessity can be seen in the reasons given for the legislative proposals and often later on in the preamble, confirming that the measure does indeed concern matters having a cross-border effect and that it is necessary for the proper functioning of the Internal Market.[46]

Initially these limitations do not seem to have played a major role in limiting the action of the Community institutions, partly due to the fact that most of the measures initially adopted are specifically mentioned in the list of measures and therefore their cross-border effect and necessity for the Internal Market is taken for granted.[47] In contrast, however, for the Legal Aid Directive the limitations clearly played a role in narrowing the scope of the Directive itself.[48] Similarly, the limitations affected the agreement between Member States in relation to the scope of the Payment Order Regulation and the Small Claims Regulation as well as the directive on certain aspects of mediation.[49] These contentious matters regarding the interpretation of the specific limitation go to the heart of whether the vision for the policy area is more restrictive or expansive. As one commentator notes, in the negotiations of the EC Treaty these words were revised several times but ultimately

[44] Meeusen (2004) p. 48.

[45] Kohler (1999) pp. 18–21.

[46] Inter alia the Service Regulation, Commission proposal COM (1999) 219, p. 5f., and Regulation (EC) No. 1348/2000 recitals (2)–(94) of the preamble and Art. 1(1).

[47] De Búrca (1999) p. 19 notes that a cross-border element should not be used as pretext where there is little effect on market integration, as mentioned below in relation to the principle of subsidiarity.

[48] Leroy (2003), cf. the original Commission legislative proposal COM (2002) 13 and the enacted Directive (EC) No. 8/2003.

[49] Jastrow (2004) p. 5. See inter alia COM (2002) 746, p. 6f. and COM (2004) 173, p. 7f., where the Commission argues for an expansive interpretation of the definition of 'matters having cross-border limitations'. In addition, see below, Chapters 12 and 13 respectively regarding the Order for Payment and Small Claims Regulations.

one could not know exactly what difference they would make.[50] Thus, the debate that was in a sense left open at Amsterdam has now resurfaced.

It has been argued, in the expansive vein, that the limitations should not hinder a proper horizontal approach to the policy area of judicial cooperation. Hence political support for a common market, for free movement, and for European citizenship should receive its legal concrete form notwithstanding the limitations.[51] Another expansive reading of the Internal Market condition is provided by commentators who note that its wording is more programmatic than that in Articles 94 and 95 of the EC Treaty. Hence, the condition actually goes beyond or expands the necessity requirement; the Internal Market should not merely function but should function 'properly'. This interpretation would allow the measures taken under Article 65 of the EC Treaty to not necessarily be constitutive of the Internal Market but rather to allow measures which give indirect support to the market, e.g. even measures which have fundamental human rights as their primary aim.[52]

In contrast, in the restrictive vein, these limitations have also been regarded as an emanation of the principle of subsidiarity and proportionality in the legal basis itself.[53] However, this observation should not result in the subsidiarity of the policy area being taken for granted. On the contrary the result should be a strict burden of justification in terms of the measures taken and their compatibility with the principle of subsidiarity. Thus, the strength of the limitations should also be compounded by and their remit analysed in the light of the principle of subsidiarity when the appropriate level of action for each measure is examined.[54] Nevertheless, in the end it is perhaps not surprising, as one commentator notes, that the 'technical merits or demerits' of Article 65 of the EC Treaty sometimes play a side role. As other policy areas have shown, the explicit terms of the Treaties have often been unable to constrain the dynamism in the legislative and political processes, and if legal bases have proved inadequate they have been amended in Treaty renegotiations.[55] Thus, it is not surprising that such amendments have in fact been proposed.

[50] Labayle (1997) p. 856.
[51] Van den Bossche (2003) p. 15.
[52] Leible and Staudinger (2000–1) p. 228f.
[53] Partsch (2003) p. 310ff.
[54] Chapter 5 provides a further analysis of the principle of subsidiarity.
[55] Kennett (2000) p. 12.

Future Treaty Reform

The Draft Treaty establishing a Constitution for Europe submitted by the Convention on the Future of Europe to the European Council in July 2003 proposed reform to the legal basis of Article 65.[56] Subsequently the Treaty establishing a Constitution for Europe also included reform proposals to the legal basis of Article 65.[57] Following the negative referenda in France and the Netherlands in the spring of 2005 a period and process of reflection took place.[58] Thereafter political agreement was reached in June 2007 among the Member States to convene an IGC in order to draw up a 'Reform Treaty'. The projected timetable is that the Reform Treaty should be agreed by the end of 2007 and the aim is for ratification by the Member States before June 2009.[59] A draft of the Treaty amending the EU Treaty and the EC Treaty has been published as a working document for the IGC.[60] Changes are therefore still possible at the IGC and one cannot be sure that Member States will ratify the Treaty. Nevertheless, in anticipation of final agreement in the IGC and ratification of the draft Treaty on the Functioning of the Union (the proposed new name for the EC Treaty), it is worth reviewing the draft legal basis in Title IV which regulates the Area of Freedom, Security and Justice. Section 3 of Title IV concerns judicial cooperation in civil matters and Article 69d (1)–(2) is the current draft proposal to replace Article 65(1) of the EC Treaty:

1. The Union shall develop judicial cooperation in civil matters having cross-border implications, based on the principle of mutual recognition of judgments and decisions in extrajudicial cases. Such cooperation may include the adoption of measures for the approximation of the laws and regulations of the Member States.
2. For the purposes of paragraph 1, the European Parliament and the Council, acting in accordance with the ordinary legislative procedure, shall adopt measures,

[56] OJ C169/2003, 18.7.2003, p. 1.

[57] OJ C310, 16.12.2004, p. 1.

[58] De Witte (2005) analyses the legal options if not all Member States ratify the Constitutional Treaty.

[59] Information taken from the IGC homepage that can be found on the Council website http://www.consilium.europa.eu/ (visited 22.8.2007), further confirmed in Presidency Conclusions 11177/1/07 para. 11.

[60] CIG 1/07 of 23.7.2007.

particularly when necessary for the proper functioning of the internal market, aimed at ensuring:

(a) the mutual recognition and enforcement between Member States of judgments and decisions in extrajudicial cases;
(b) the cross-border service of judicial and extrajudicial documents;
(c) the compatibility of the rules applicable in the Member States concerning conflict of laws and of jurisdiction;
(d) cooperation in the taking of evidence;
(e) effective access to justice;
(f) the elimination of obstacles to the proper functioning of civil proceedings, if necessary by promoting the compatibility of the rules on civil procedure applicable in the Member States;
(g) the development of alternative methods of dispute settlement;
(h) support for the training of the judiciary and judicial staff.

Some tentative conclusions can be drawn by comparing the proposed changes with Article 65 of the current EC Treaty. First, the changes in part reflect the current legal reality, by including alternative dispute resolution and judicial training, because such measures have been proposed and agreed at the legislative stage whereas they are not enumerated in Article 65. Therefore, the new wording reflects in a more complete and transparent manner the scope of Community action in the field. However, it is not fully clear and accepted that, for example, regulating alternative dispute settlement mechanisms actually falls within the competence of the area of judicial cooperation in civil matters under the present Article 65 or the EC Treaty wording. Nor is it clear, even if it is within its competence, that such action is desirable from the point of view of subsidiarity. Therefore the new enumeration can be seen as not just adding transparency but actually increasing the scope of competence of the EU.

This leads on to the second conclusion in relation to the changes, which is that there is a broadening of the competence. The addition of paragraph 2(e), 'effective access to justice', to a list of areas of action, which in essence have been and still are very practical, e.g. service of documents or obtaining evidence, is interesting. The addition may be intended only as programmatic support for the fundamental right of access to justice but it can also be seen as further potential broadening of the competence, under which therefore more proactive measures in relation to the effectiveness of procedures could be introduced. Another change that may appear slight but nonetheless may introduce potent change to one of the limiting conditions of the legal basis is the change in the Internal Market condition from 'in so far as necessary' to 'particularly when necessary'. This condition might hence no longer be considered and interpreted as a condition at all but solely as an added emphasis to the Internal Market necessity.[61]

Finally, to conclude this examination of the series of Treaty amendments which have given us a specific legal basis for the policy area of judicial cooperation in civil matters and as an introduction to the broader context discussed in Chapter 5, it is pertinent to observe that the Treaty goals of the EC and EU as outlined here have developed progressively. From there being no mention or vision of the goal of procedural approximation in the Treaty of Rome and from the vague notion of 'developing a close cooperation in the field of justice and home affairs' in the Treaty of Maastricht the Amsterdam era has given us a clearer vision in the Treaty itself by creating the goal of an Area of Freedom, Security and Justice.[62] This objective is specifically added to the general overarching objectives of the Union in Article 2 of the Treaty of the European Union. It is furthermore repeated in Article 61 of the EC Treaty in relation to civil cooperation and in Article 29 of the EU Treaty for criminal cooperation. The fact that there was a distinct idea of progression and development in the Treaty wording itself with regard to the Area of Freedom, Security and Justice, e.g. 'progressively establish', together with the specification of a five-year period, is very important when evaluating the political message, its weight, and the practical implications deriving from the Treaty.[63] Thus, there is an apparent attempt to provide coherence, vision, and pace to the legal basis reforms introduced, and to position them as part of a broader but distinct political project.[64]

[61] Rossi (2004) p. 65.
[62] Rouchaud (2003) p. 450ff. refers to this 'qualitative leap'.
[63] Labayle (1997) pp. 825ff. and 844f.
[64] Ibid. p. 823f., and Kennett (2000) p. 11.

4

Institutional and Structural Characteristics

The Hybrid Nature of Institutional Participation

The Legislative Process

Title IV of the EC Treaty (the Treaty of Rome, as amended), introduced at the Amsterdam IGC and including the new legal basis for judicial cooperation in civil matters, was not completely 'Communitarized'. Even though the new legal basis was hailed as providing more transparency, democratic legitimacy, and efficiency,[1] doubts arose because the Community method, including the legislative and judicial mechanisms of the First Pillar, were not fully implemented for the policy area.[2] The institutional features of Title IV of the EC Treaty have also been described as a hybrid, encapsulating the hesitant and incomplete transfer from the Third to the First Pillar, and raising questions about the substantive scope of competence.[3]

In relation to legislative mechanisms a specific and idiosyncratic legislative procedure was introduced in Article 67 of the EC Treaty. This procedure contrasted with the co-decision procedure under Article 251 of the EC Treaty in three respects, first in that the Commission did not have the sole right of initiative, but shared this right with the Member States.[4] The emergence of a right of initiative for the Commission, albeit shared

[1] Rouchaud (2001) p. 24.

[2] Monar (1998a) p. 329.

[3] Kohler (1999) p. 8.

[4] This derogation can be seen as a remnant of the intergovernmental cooperation era and perhaps also as a recognition of the many previous bilateral and multilateral mechanisms of judicial cooperation among the Member States that could be models for pan-Community projects, see inter alia Jongbloet (2003) p. 255.

with the Member States, from being very much on the sidelines during the Maastricht era has nevertheless been considered to have enormous importance for the policy area of judicial cooperation in civil matters. This follows from the fact that in areas in which it has the initiative the Commission traditionally shapes the legislative agenda. In addition, because the Commission is represented at all stages of institutional negotiations it becomes a broker trying to achieve agreement between the Member States in the Council.[5]

Secondly, in contrast to the normal Community legislative method under Article 251 of the EC Treaty, the European Parliament was, as in the prior intergovernmental period, not fully involved in the new idiosyncratic legislative procedure under Article 67 of the EC Treaty. The Parliament only had the right to be consulted rather than taking part in the decision-making process. Thirdly, the Council could not vote and agree by qualified majority voting, as is the practice under the normal Community method, but had to adopt legislation by unanimity. Thus, some of the criticisms of the Maastricht era could still be targeted at this quasi- or 'phasing-in' legislative procedure. In particular, the lack of one body with responsibility for taking initiatives, the lack of parliamentary control, and the requirement of unanimity could cause concern vis-à-vis both the efficiency and democracy of the procedure.[6]

The special arrangements or modified legislative method introduced in Title IV of the EC Treaty were only intended to be transitional and in force for a period of five years, up until 1 May 2004. According to Article 67 of the EC Treaty, during or after that five-year period, the Council acting unanimously could take a decision for all or parts of Title IV to be governed by the co-decision procedure of Article 251. In the Treaty of Nice, signed on 26 February 2001 (entered into force 1 February 2003), the Member States had already addressed the issue of the legislative procedure, introducing an amendment to Article 67 of the EC Treaty. Thus, specifically for judicial cooperation in civil matters, the co-decision procedure of Article 251 has, since February 2003, been the procedure to be adopted.[7] Thus, it is particularly noteworthy that the role of the European Parliament and

[5] Kennett (2000) p. 15ff.

[6] Barrett (ed) (1997) provides a detailed critique of the efficiency and democracy of the Third Pillar cooperation in the Treaty of Maastricht.

[7] The working draft for the potential future Reform Treaty follows this in that the 'ordinary legislative procedure', like the co-decision procedure, is applicable to judicial cooperation in civil matters. However, like the current EC Treaty, the potential future Reform Treaty excludes aspects relating to family law, for which unanimity in the Council is still required

its powers of negotiation in the policy area dramatically increased at this stage.[8]

The Role of the ECJ

The role and jurisdiction of the ECJ is significantly also specifically regulated for matters falling under Title IV, including those of judicial cooperation in civil matters, by Article 68 of the EC Treaty:

1. Article 234 shall apply to this title under the following circumstances and conditions: where a question on the interpretation of this title or on the validity or interpretation of acts of the institutions of the Community based on this title is raised in a case pending before a court or a tribunal of a Member State against whose decisions there is no judicial remedy under national law, that court of tribunal shall, if it considers that a decision on the question is necessary to enable it to give judgment, request the Court of Justice to give a ruling thereon.

...

3. The Council, Commission or Member State may request the Court of Justice to give a ruling on a question of interpretation of this title or of the acts of the institutions of the Community based on this title. The ruling given by the Court of Justice in response to such a request shall not apply to judgments of courts or tribunals of the Member States which have become 'res judicata'.

The jurisdiction differs from that for all other matters of the First Pillar, for which the Court's jurisdiction is regulated in Article 234 of the EC Treaty. Most significantly, the jurisdiction to give preliminary rulings is curtailed in that references can only emanate from national courts of last resort, from whose decisions there is no appeal. One commentator has suggested that the provision might not be so stringent and that it could perhaps be interpreted as only obliging courts of last resort while not preventing lower courts from making referrals, i.e. the provision would not change the general breadth of Article 234.[9] However, that interpretation cannot be held

unless unanimous agreement is reached that certain measures may be adopted following the ordinary procedure.

[8] Kennett (2000) p. 19, predicting this change.

[9] Ibid. p. 293. In contrast, regarding the other interpretation – that Article 68 derogates even more from the general framework for preliminary referrals, in that courts of final resort are not obliged to make referrals even when the question is unclear – see Partsch (2003) p. 285ff., and Girerd (1999) p. 243. Neither author supports this interpretation, declaring that such an obligation is clear from the intent and wording of the article. Labayle (2002) p. 95f. nevertheless states that it is for the Court itself to rule at some stage on the question, using either dynamic or textual interpretation to reach a conclusion.

to be valid since the more stringent interpretation has been confirmed by the ECJ. In the case *Warbecq v. Ryanair*[10] the Court refused jurisdiction to hear a preliminary referral concerning the interpretation of certain provisions in the Brussels I Regulation referring specifically to Article 68 and the fact that it was not disputed that the decisions of the Tribunal making the preliminary referral were amenable to appeal.[11]

Particularly in relation to judicial cooperation in civil matters, the entry into force of the Treaty of Amsterdam and Article 68 has thus significantly curtailed the existing and prior legal position. Both the Protocol to the Brussels Convention and the Protocol to the Service Convention conferring competence on the ECJ to interpret the Conventions were less stringent. Under these only courts of first instance were prevented from making preliminary referrals to the ECJ, whereas appellate courts of the second instance could make preliminary referrals.[12]

A further complexity, which arises as a consequence of the inability of lower courts to make preliminary referrals in judicial cooperation in civil matters cases, is the applicability of the *Foto-Frost* principle.[13] For the sake of uniformity, this long-standing principle prevents national courts from declaring a Community act invalid, e.g. for lack of attributed competence, without referring the question to the ECJ. Together with Article 68 of the EC Treaty the principle would result in national parties not being able to challenge the validity of Community legislation in the field of judicial cooperation in civil matters without taking their case to the highest court. One commentator suggests that the way to resolve this *fait accompli*, which is not alleviated by the strict standing rules in Article 230 of the Treaty for direct actions, is for lower courts not to apply or to disregard *Foto-Frost* where

[10] Case C-555/03 *Magali Warbecq v. Ryanair Ltd*, Order of the Court 10.6.2004. The decision of inadmissibility was foreshadowed in case C-24/02, *Marseille Fret SA v. Seatrano Shipping Company Ltd*, Order of the Court 22.3.2002. In para. 14 of the latter Order of the Court, the ECJ noted that if the new Brussels I Regulation had been applicable to the case at hand Article 68 of the Treaty would limit the right of preliminary referral to national courts from which their internal legal system permits no appeal.

[11] Nevertheless, there are conceivably ways in which judicial cooperation in civil matters and other matters falling under Title IV of the EC Treaty will still be affected by rulings from the Court answering questions emanating from courts of lower instance. As Partsch (2003) p. 285 points out, general questions such as compatibility with other parts of the Treaty or competence issues might still be admissible as preliminary referrals.

[12] Kennett (2000) p. 293 and Partsch (2003) p. 57f.

[13] Case 314/85 *Foto-Frost v. Hauptzollamt Lübeck-Ost* [1987] ECR 4199.

necessary.[14] However, it is as yet unclear what view the ECJ itself would take of such a liberty.

Another issue with regard to Article 68 of the EC Treaty is whether, as a result of the discrepancy between the respective wordings 'shall refer' and 'is obliged to call upon the court', its requirement for courts of last instance to refer to the ECJ is narrower than the general obligation to refer in Article 234 of the EC Treaty.[15] Commentators adduce the argument that since there is a regrettable prohibition of referrals from lower courts a less stringent obligation upon higher courts might be beneficial to the length of proceedings. Admittedly there is a risk of potentially denying justice in cross-border cases through lengthening the dispute by a referral to the ECJ, thereby giving the other party more time to dissipate assets or giving one party the opportunity to use a protracted jurisdiction issue as a procedural tactic.[16] Nevertheless, it is highly unlikely that despite the difference in wording the ECJ would interpret the obligation upon higher courts in any other manner than in accordance with the *CILFIT* doctrine developed for Article 234.[17]

The second derogation and change from the normal Community judicial framework introduced in Article 68 of the EC Treaty is a new procedural route for the Commission, Council, or Member States to request a ruling on the interpretation of provisions of Title IV of the EC Treaty and any secondary legislation. Such rulings will not apply to national court judgments which have become res judicata. This creates a somewhat similar procedure to that introduced in the 1971 Protocol to the Brussels Convention, a procedure which was inspired by French law and is called *pourvoi dans l'intérêt de la loi*.[18] However, the procedure is more flexible under Article 68 of the EC Treaty than under the Protocol, since not only the Member States but also Community institutions, albeit not the European Parliament, can request a ruling and since the question does not have to pertain to inconsistent national judgments, but can relate to a much wider spectrum.[19] One commentator observes that this new procedural route is abstract and general, and has the characteristics of traditional consultative and collaborative procedures, but in a sense lacks their

[14] Arnull (1999) p. 116f.

[15] Labayle (1997) p. 863.

[16] Leible and Staudinger (2000–1) p. 227f.

[17] Nascimbene (2005) p. 491.

[18] Basedow (2000) p. 695.

[19] Partsch (2003) p. 287f.

precision and finality.[20] The similar procedure available under the Protocol to the Brussels Convention was never used, i.e. the provision was obsolete in practice.[21] Whether that will be so under Article 68 of the EC Treaty remains to be seen. However, as the new provision has been criticized as artificial and not fitting into the logic of the Community judicial system, it is perhaps not surprising that so far there appears to have been no request under this provision for a ruling from the Court.[22]

The reason for these derogations from the normal Community judicial mechanism, in particular preventing national lower courts from seeking preliminary rulings, seems – according to several commentators – to have been a fear of overloading the Court with excessive litigation which was expected in relation to immigration and asylum matters, also belonging to Title IV of the EC Treaty.[23] If the jurisdiction of the ECJ had not been restricted there would have been concerns about how the already overburdened Court would accommodate such claims and guarantee legal certainty and rapidity of response, as is urgently needed in such cases.[24]

However, this point of view can be seen as a lateral or Court-centred one. From the perspective of the Member States there was also a political concern that the ECJ would gain jurisdiction in such sensitive matters as asylum and immigration. Thus, to appease those who were most opposed to Europeanization, the negotiators were focused on how to restrict the impact of the ECJ, since a complete exclusion of the Court's jurisdiction was not an option.[25] Notwithstanding the practical or political arguments, the commentators subsequently agree that these derogations raise a concern because they set a dangerous precedent in destroying the unity of the Treaty provisions on the jurisdiction of the ECJ. As one commentator notes, the logic of 'agreement at all cost' seems to have taken an unprecedented dominance in the Treaties at the expense of progressive congruence.[26] The restriction on preliminary rulings also importantly undermines the guarantee of uniform and consistent interpretation of the measures, which would add legitimacy to the process of integration.

[20] Labayle (2002) p. 97.
[21] Partsch (2003) pp. 58 and 288.
[22] Labayle (2002) p. 97.
[23] Albors-Llorens (1998) p. 1287, Labayle (2002) p. 77, and Girerd (1999) p. 242.
[24] Labayle (2002) pp. 75f. and 77.
[25] Ibid. p. 93. See also Alter (2001) p. 205, regarding the Treaty of Amsterdam, judicial activism in the EU, and political attempts to curtail the ECJ.
[26] Girerd (1999) p. 260.

Furthermore, the continuing dialogue between the ECJ and the national courts and the development of EC law will be weakened.[27] The clear risk is that there will be a 'cacophony' of legal interpretation between the Member States and even internally within Member States.[28] Furthermore, as has already been noted, the restriction seriously undermines the judicial protection available to private parties and practically guarantees considerable time and costs if litigants have to appeal up to the highest tier in order to obtain clarity.[29] Since the legal basis in Article 65 of the EC Treaty has been used instead of other potentially alternative legal bases for all legislation enacted so far in the field of judicial cooperation in civil matters, these concerns have grounds to be realized.[30]

An additional cause for concern is the fact that the restrictions to ECJ jurisdiction were introduced simultaneously with the Treaties' specific affirmation that fundamental human rights are an integral part of the Community legal order. This is ironic since the very areas in which ECJ jurisdiction is limited by Article 68 of the EC Treaty are ones in which fundamental human rights questions are inherent.[31] In particular, in relation to judicial cooperation in civil matters, the historic example of the ECJ case law on the Brussels Convention shows the valuable and important role the Court has played in ensuring coherence of interpretation and simultaneously protecting the interests of citizens and parties, e.g. in the right to a defence. This essential role would clearly also be useful in relation to the other new judicial cooperation measures being implemented.[32] Thus, it is most unfortunate that due to the sensitive nature of the visa and immigration questions also

[27] Albors-Llorens (1998) p. 1288 and Monar (1998a) p. 330ff. Further, Barrett (1997) p. 26ff., who writes in relation to the Maastricht era but whose points are still largely relevant; and Louis (2003) p. 257, who identifies the pillar structure as a challenge to the integrity of the European judicial structure and as one of the problems to be dealt with either at Nice or in the Draft Constitution.

[28] Girerd (1999) p. 243.

[29] Girerd (1999) p. 245f. Twomey (1999) p. 371 makes this point in relation to asylum and immigration matters.

[30] See Chapter 3. Girerd (1999) p. 254f. makes the same point with regard to the traditional free movement articles of the Treaty and the specific legal basis for immigration, etc. in Title IV.

[31] Ibid. p. 244f. The Treaty of Amsterdam amended Article F (now renumbered Article 6): 'The Union is founded on the principles of liberty, democracy, respect for human rights and fundamental freedoms, and the rule of law, principles which are common to the Member States.'

[32] Labayle (2002) p. 80.

dealt with in Title IV, the jurisdiction of the Court is curtailed for judicial cooperation in civil matters.

The regrettable curtailment of the right to refer matters for a preliminary ruling might in some instances not have such dramatic and unwanted consequences. In case C-175/06 *Alessandro Tedesco v. Tomasoni Fittings SrL and RWO Marine Equipment Ltd*[33] which is pending, Advocate General Kokott considers that even though the referring court, the *Tribunale Civile Di Genua*, is a court of first instance its specific procedural decision to make a request for evidence under the Evidence Regulation might be the object of a referral for a preliminary ruling because there is no appeal from the procedural decision and it constitutes a decision in a procedure separate from the main proceedings.[34]

Under Article 67 of the EC Treaty the Council is, as with the legislative process derogation, empowered during or after a five-year period to act unanimously and to decide to adapt the provisions relating to the ECJ. However, in stark contrast to the position in relation to the legislative process, and notwithstanding the elapse of the period in 2004, the Council has not taken any decision relating to the jurisdiction of the ECJ, which therefore is unchanged and remains limited.[35] This demonstrates that no automatic progression was built into the EC Treaty and that progress depends on the unanimous will of the Member States.[36] This delay might be attributable to the planned introduction by the Treaty Establishing a Constitution for Europe (then under discussion)[37] of an amendment whereby lower national courts would also have been able to lodge such requests.[38]

However, since the ratification of the Constitutional Treaty by all the Member States was thwarted by the negative referenda in two Member States in 2005, the Constitutional Treaty will not alleviate the position of

[33] OJ C-154, 1.7.2006, p. 8.

[34] Opinion dated 18.7.2007, available on the ECJ website http://curia.europa.eu/, paras 20–28.

[35] Labayle (2002) p. 74f., affirming that even though the ECJ opposed a general acceptance of the system of exceptions or derogations introduced at Amsterdam, the Treaty of Nice did not reopen the matter. Also confirmed by the Commission in COM (2005) 184, p. 4, 'Hague Action Plan', where the Commission states its belief in the essential right of individuals to access the ECJ.

[36] Den Boer (1999) p. 312.

[37] OJ C-310, 16.12.2004, Article III-369 of the Constitutional Treaty.

[38] Dougan (2003) p. 792 and Louis (2003) p. 262 confirm that the Convention on the Future of Europe agreed to remove the restrictions on jurisdiction for Title IV and emphasize that, as a consequence of the 'suppression of the pillars', this was one of the successes of judicial reform introduced in the Draft Constitution.

the ECJ. Nevertheless, political agreement was reached in June 2007 among the Member States to convene an IGC in order to draw up a 'Reform Treaty', which is projected to be agreed by the end of 2007 and ratified before June 2009.[39] A draft of the Treaty amending the EU Treaty and the EC Treaty has been published as a working document for the IGC.[40] Changes are still possible, but in anticipation of the final agreement in the IGC it is worth noting that Title IV of the draft Treaty on the Functioning of the Union (the new proposed name for the EC Treaty) would not appear to limit the right of referring matters for preliminary ruling to the ECJ.

During the period of reflection, and perhaps because of the failure of the ratification of the Constitutional Treaty, the Commission lodged a Communication proposing that the Council take a decision to adapt the provision of Title IV of the EC Treaty relating to the ECJ.[41] In order to ensure effective judicial protection the Commission proposes that the general mechanism under Article 234 of the EC Treaty regarding preliminary referrals be applicable to inter alia judicial cooperation in civil matters.[42]

Therefore, the period in which preliminary rulings can only emanate from national courts of last resort has already been extended far beyond the five-year period set out in Article 67 of the EC Treaty.[43] It appears that 'if and when' the Reform Treaty enters into force or 'if and when' the Council makes a separate decision based on the Commission proposal, only then could the ECJ play a truly significant role in the field of judicial cooperation in civil matters, because not only would it have 'normal' jurisdiction over preliminary referrals but this would also arguably entail an increased role vis-à-vis fundamental rights and subsidiarity, questions which shape the legality for Community action in the field.[44]

[39] Information taken from the IGC homepage that can be found on the Council website http://www.consilium.europa.eu/ (visited 22.8.2007), further confirmed in Presidency Conclusions 11177/1/07 para. 1.

[40] CIG 1/07 of 23.7.2007.

[41] COM (2006) 346.

[42] Ibid. inter alia pp. 7f. and 11. The Commission presents its arguments under the headings 'Ensure the uniform application and interpretation of Community law', 'Strengthen judicial protection', and 'Remedy a gap in judicial protection in civil matters'. The Commission's proposal is supported by the Parliament, A6 82/2007 and T6 140/2007.

[43] Hence, the Council could hypothetically be exposed to an action under Article 232 of the Treaty compelling it to act: Partsch (2003) p. 289.

[44] Tridimas (2004) p. 140.

The Flexible Nature of Member State Participation

Apart from the idiosyncrasies of Title IV of the EC Treaty in relation to the legislative process and the scope of jurisdiction of the ECJ, a further complexity is added by the Protocols of the UK, Ireland, and Denmark to the Treaty of Amsterdam (Protocols Nos 4 and 5 to the Treaty). In these Protocols the relevant Member States 'opted out' of the policy areas covered by Title IV of the EC Treaty, apparently wishing to retain national control over immigration and asylum matters.[45] Thus, since judicial cooperation in civil matters also falls within Title IV of the EC Treaty, all matters in this policy area are affected by the introduction of such 'flexibility' or 'variable geometry', as it has been termed.[46] The exclusion of these Member States means that they will not be bound by Community legislation enacted within Title IV of the EC Treaty. In relation to judicial cooperation in civil matters, the measures of which are often enforced or conducted between Member States, there is clearly an added complexity. Because measures adopted under Title IV will not apply between all Member States, in any case involving one of the excluded Member States, parties and authorities will have to look to other binding international conventions which might apply instead. The application of the relevant international convention might lead to very different results from those that might obtain with the application of the relevant European measure, thus introducing procedural advantages and disadvantages, i.e. inequalities, into the system.[47]

Furthermore, on a general level the exclusion of some Member States also threatens the unity of the Community law system and might limit possible further developments since not all Member States have an equal stake in and reciprocal approach to the policy area.[48] However, fortunately the fragmentation that is introduced by the Protocols is counterbalanced by 'opt-in' clauses. For the UK and Ireland Article 3 of Protocol No. 4 allows them to give notice, within three months of the submission of a legislative proposal, that they wish to adopt that measure. In practice, both the UK and Ireland have opted in to all the measures adopted so far in the field of judicial cooperation in civil matters.

[45] Basedow (2000) p. 695.

[46] Monar (1998a) pp. 321f. and 332ff., who explains the diverging Member States' interests that led to the flexibility but is critical of the fragmentation thus introduced.

[47] Boele-Woelki (2000) p. 68.

[48] Partsch (2003) p. 293.

Denmark, on the other hand, is in a different situation. According to Article 7 of Protocol No. 5, Denmark may inform the Member States that it no longer wishes to avail itself of all or part of the Protocol. However, this change must be made in conformity with national constitutional law, according to which a referendum would have to be held in Denmark.[49] The above-mentioned complexities thus arise in practice in judicial cooperation matters and civil proceedings where one party or a court is Danish. However, an amendment to the Danish Protocol was envisaged in the Constitutional Treaty, which, had it entered into force, would have enabled Denmark to apply a similar system of opt-in as the UK and Ireland.[50] The present working document for the IGC projected to draw up a Reform Treaty in 2007 also currently appears to introduce such a change.[51] Additionally, in advance of any potential Treaty reform entering into force, a project has been completed for international conventions to be signed between the EU and Denmark, specifically including Denmark within the framework of two of the Regulations in judicial cooperation in civil matters, the Service Regulation and the Brussels I Regulation.[52] Hence from July 2007 the provisions of these two Regulations will apply to Denmark.

In the explanatory memorandum to the proposed conventions, the Commission states that the objective is to amend the current situation, which jeopardizes uniformity and legal certainty. The project is, however, seen as exceptional and transitional, and this presumably means that there will not be similar projects for all the measures of judicial cooperation in civil matters, and that it is hoped that the entire situation will be remedied in a future Treaty revision.[53] Furthermore, it is noteworthy that the requirements imposed by these conventions on Denmark will be identical to those of the Member States vis-à-vis the substantive realm of the Regulations

[49] Paulino Pereira (2001a) p. 44.

[50] This is envisaged in CIG 60/03, p. 56, Art. 3 of the new Annex. See similarly the final version in CIG 87/04 ADD2 of 6.8.2004.

[51] CIG 2/07 of 23.7.2007, p. 59.

[52] Ekelmans (2001) p. 484, regarding the Service Regulation. Wilderspin and Rouchaud-Joët (2004) p. 24f. discuss the specific problems and questions of external competence that might arise during negotiations between Denmark and the EU. The Convention project between Denmark and the EU was confirmed in COM (2005) 184, p. 39, the 'Hague Action Plan', and the specific legislative proposals are in COM (2005) 145 and COM (2005) 146. The Agreements were signed between the EU and Denmark on 19 October 2005. Council approval was obtained in Council Decision (EC) No. 790/2005. Final approval was achieved in the Parliament, T6-105/2006 and T6-106/2006, and in the Council, Decisions (EC) No 325–326/2006. Denmark ratified the agreements on 18 January 2007.

[53] COM (2005) 146, p. 2.

concerned and that the ECJ will have the same jurisdiction for requests for preliminary rulings.[54]

The Complex Nature of External Relations

Finally, a further structural question arising from of the Communitarization of judicial cooperation in civil matters is the extent to which the Community and the Member States have external competence in this policy area.[55] The question is particularly important because the transnational aspect of this policy area entails that there has for the past century been a wealth of international, multinational, and bilateral treaties, both ad hoc and in the context of such international organizations as the Hague Conference on Private International Law, the UN, and the Council of Europe. Furthermore, simultaneously with the EU's development of the policy area of judicial cooperation in civil matters, several other international organizations have been redefining their roles in the field of international procedural law and have been taking new initiatives.[56]

On the very general level it is undoubtedly clear that because of the increase of Community measures in the field, the Member States are losing their external competence to the Community, and this change will have a considerable influence on practice within certain international organizations.[57] The loss of sovereignty in the field of judicial cooperation, specifically in jurisdiction litigation, also naturally affects the outcome of individual cases and restricts the application of domestic law by national courts. This is a consequence of the primacy of EC law, but when there are cases involving both third state courts and Member State courts the scope of inter alia the Brussels I Regulation has been subject to extensive debate before and after significant ECJ case law.[58]

[54] Ibid. pp. 2f. and 13f.

[55] Wilderspin and Rouchaud-Joët (2004) pp. 4–15 provide an overview of the general theory of external competences.

[56] Hess (2004) p. 82f.

[57] Inter alia, Wilderspin and Rouchaud-Jöet (2004) p. 3f. and Borrás (2004) p. 123ff.

[58] As a prominent example case C-281/02 *Andrew Owusu v. N.B Jackson et al.* [2004] ECR I-1383, has shed light on the question of the mandatory nature of the Brussels Convention vis-à-vis a dispute between a claimant and one defendant domiciled in a Member State, but where other defendants were domiciled in a third State to which the matter at hand also had close connections. The ECJ held that the principle of legal certainty as one of the aims of the Brussels

Furthermore, at a more structural level, both as between the Member States and also in relation to other international conventions already in force at the time of conclusion of a Community measure, each measure taken will have its own singular effect, depending on the circumstances. First, each Community regulatory measure will need to clarify its relationship with pre-existing treaties or conventions (and this can also include a clarification as to whether the Member States in the future can amongst themselves agree bilateral or multilateral arrangements).[59]

Secondly, however, at a purely future and external level, the adoption of internal measures will confer power, so-called external competence, on the Community to negotiate and adopt international instruments in the subject area in question. Since there is no explicit external competence in the EC Treaty, the *AETR* doctrine based on the case law of the ECJ is applicable to the measures enacted in the area of judicial cooperation in civil matters.[60] However, due to the principle of affectation the Community measure must be affected by an international measure in order for the Community to have external competence to negotiate it. Further, mixed agreements are those where the content of the international measure includes areas within the competence of both the Member States and the Community, so-called shared competence. The precise degree of Community and Member State external competence in the field is a complex question.[61] When the

Convention and the mandatory nature of its provisions on the Member States precludes the national court from declining jurisdiction based on a discretionary *forum non conveniens* reasoning under English law. Inter alia Fentiman (2006) pp. 713–18 provides a critique of *Owusu*. Further debate and cases regarding the reach of the jurisdiction rules when there is a third-country connection to the dispute will certainly arise: Harris (2005) pp. 942–50, Fentiman (2006) pp. 718–32. Further, Nuyts (2003b) pp. 73–89 analyses a theory of reflexive effect regarding the interaction of jurisdiction between Member States and third countries, and Gottwald (1997) p. 143f. notes that when the Brussels jurisdictional regime was designed there was more focus on the internal coherence of the system than on the external consequences, widely acknowledged as resulting in unfairness to third-country litigants. Further, note Pataut (2003) inter alia pp. 367–71 and 384f., regarding the territorial delimitation of the Brussels I Regulation.

[59] Thoma (2002) pp. 408–13 analyses the Brussels I and II Regulations in this respect.

[60] COM (2002) 654, p. 20, where the issue is mentioned in relation to conflict of laws regulation. The conferral of competence on the Community once internal regulation is adopted is a general principle of Community law emanating from case 22/70 *Commission v. Council (AETR or ERTA)* [1971] ECR 263 and subsequent case law. Lavranos (2006) p. 1088 summarizes the doctrine of the ECJ.

[61] Wilderspin and Rouchaud-Joët (2004) inter alia pp. 7–10 in general and 28 dealing specifically with the Brussels I Regulation. Paulino Pereira (2001a) p. 45 does not take a stance on the question, but just gives the different opinions. Beaumont (2002) p. 26 points out that at the time of the negotiations for the global jurisdiction convention in the Hague Conference, the

competence is shared, with the Community having competence for the issues which directly affect the Community instruments, and the Member States having competence for the rest, the Community and the Member States are under an obligation to cooperate and find a uniform position on overlapping grey areas. The competence evaluation must be casuistic, i.e. made separately for each international project that arises.[62] Therefore, for judicial cooperation in civil matters as a policy area the nature of external competence will be heterogeneous, depending on which measure is at issue.[63]

Even if overlapping and mixed competence entails practical difficulties for the negotiation, conclusion, and implementation of the international project, these difficulties cannot influence the allocation of competence and it is incumbent upon the Member States and the Community institutions to find a *modus vivendi* for their cooperation.[64] This question was relevant to the global jurisdiction convention project in the Hague Conference on Private International Law, which ultimately succeeded, though in more limited form.[65] For the global jurisdiction convention the Commission and the Council did adopt a formal agreement on their mutual working method, but without agreeing on the nature of the competence, i.e. whether it was exclusive or mixed.[66] This question also arose when the Brussels I Regulation was to be extended to Denmark, where the Council and Commission recognized that competence most likely fell exclusively to the Community.[67]

The ambit of Community external competence has also been the object of an Opinion procedure before the ECJ under Article 300(6) of the EC

Commission and Council agreed not to determine the question but to use an ad hoc pragmatic solution.

[62] Wilderspin and Rouchaud-Joët (2004) pp.16 and 27–48, and Thoma (2002).

[63] Hess (2004) p. 99.

[64] Wilderspin and Rouchaud-Joët (2004) p. 8.

[65] O'Brien (2003) p. 491ff. Further, Beaumont (2002) p. 25 states that one of the reasons for the Commission's haste in proposing the Brussels I Regulation was to enable it to gain competence in the Hague Conference negotiations. Wilderspin and Rouchaud-Joët (2004) p. 34 confirm that for the more limited project in the Hague Conference the Commission considered that the Community had exclusive competence. That project was restricted to a convention on exclusive choice of court agreements in international business-to-business cases in civil or commercial matters; the convention was signed on 30 June 2005, see the Hague Conference on Private International Law website, http://www.hcch.net. Hess (2004a) p. 93, agrees that the Community does have exclusive external competence to negotiate this limited convention because under the Brussels I Regulation prorogation of jurisdiction is applicable to both internal and external matters and thus the competence has been conferred on the Community.

[66] Hess (2004a) p. 84f.

[67] Ibid. pp. 98–9.

Treaty. Here the Council asked the ECJ to give an Opinion on the external competence of the Community in relation to the negotiation of the revision of the Lugano Convention on jurisdiction and enforcement of judgments in civil and commercial matters.[68] The ECJ Opinion gave the Community exclusive competence to negotiate and conclude the Lugano Convention, based on a detailed analysis of the relationship between the relevant Community legislation and the envisaged external measure.[69] In conducting this analysis the Court found that the jurisdictional and enforcement rules of the Brussels I Regulation formed a global system which had implications for external parties, notwithstanding the disconnection clause.[70] Further, the Court identified several instances where the envisaged Lugano Convention could affect the application of the Brussels I regime and its coherence.[71] Consequently, because this would affect the uniform application of Community law and the functioning of its regime, the Community must have exclusive competence to negotiate and conclude the measure.[72]

The decision of the ECJ is significant. The fact that the Community for the first time has been awarded exclusive competence in the policy area will affect the Member States because it is now apparent that in specific cases they will have to concede the negotiating role in a field which still has strong links to sovereignty and territoriality. From the structural and administrative point of view, the decision also necessitates change. In particular, a number of bilateral jurisdiction and enforcement treaties between even one Member State and a third country might have to be seen as a matter of Community competence. In these instances a practical working model will have to be found between the Commission and the Member States with regard to human resources and other administrative matters.

For the other generic procedural measures of judicial cooperation in civil matters, e.g. the Service or Evidence Regulation, the question of external competence has yet to be brought to the fore in practice but has been

[68] Request for Opinion 1/03, decision handed down 7.2.2006, available on http://www.curia.eu.int/, case comment, Lavranos (2006).

[69] Opinion, paras 124 and 133.

[70] Ibid. paras 130, 143–4. Lavranos (2006) pp.1096–9 analyses the disconnection clauses.

[71] Opinion, paras 145–6 and 153.

[72] Ibid. paras 161, 172–3. Lavranos (2006) p. 1095f. notes that the ECJ shifted its approach from previous doctrine by taking into account the Community legislation and the level of harmonization, but also the nature of the envisaged agreement and future developments in Community law. In addition, the ECJ focused on assessing whether the envisaged agreement would affect the uniform application of Community law. He therefore characterizes this as a broader analysis, i.e. including policy considerations.

addressed by one commentator who suggests that the external competence is shared rather than exclusive.[73] However, it is not only these projects of a procedural law nature that might raise the competence question. Any international substantive law measure, which only as a secondary matter regulates civil law jurisdiction, can potentially affect judicial cooperation in civil matters and therefore also comes within the competence of the Community, e.g. the 2002 Protocol to the 1974 Athens Convention on the carriage by sea of passengers and their baggage.[74] The multitude of such measures will add to the organizational tasks of cooperation between the Commission and the Member States and amply show how broad the reach of the policy area may be.

On a less technical level, concern has been raised about procedural cooperation and the consequences of Community competence, e.g. the effects on the diversity and quality of the comparative debate and ensuing work within international fora such as the Hague Conference and the different branches of the UN.[75] Concern has also been raised at the favouring of the regional or European approach, which thus becomes entrenched at the expense of the more universal or global needs for judicial cooperation.[76] There is a risk that there will be competition between the international institutions.[77] Finally, there is a risk that the phrase 'fortress Europe' might in future also be applicable to private international law and international, procedural law, since the Community can be a source of paralysis in international negotiations because of the inflexible requirement of internal agreement between all Member States and the Commission before a measure can be ratified.[78] 'Fortress Europe' would also suggest that the Community is more interested in removing barriers within its own free-trade area than in ensuring fair jurisdiction rules for parties from outside the area.[79]

[73] Hess (2004a) pp. 90–5 and 98–9.

[74] Wilderspin and Rouchaud-Joët (2004) pp. 25–48. Further, Borrás (2004) pp. 107–17, dealing separately with (i) conventions coinciding totally with the Community measure, (ii) conventions with partial coincidence, and (iii) bilateral conventions.

[75] Boele-Woelki (2000) p. 75, Gillies (2003) pp. 364 and 373f., specifically in relation to jurisdiction over consumer contracts, as well as Beaumont (2002) p. 14, who makes the comment that exclusive or mixed competence would result in the common law countries being 'swallowed up in a civil law oriented EU voice'.

[76] Boele-Woelki (2000) p. 76, Gillies (2003) p. 380ff., and Aalto (2000) p. 333f.

[77] Remien (2001) p. 73.

[78] Beaumont (2002) pp. 14, 26–9 advocates and favours a less centralized federal model.

[79] Ibid. p. 27.

As a consequence of the Europeanization of the policy area of judicial cooperation in civil matters, the external competence of the Community in this field has perhaps come as a surprise to actors in the field and has been rather reluctantly acknowledged.[80] The doctrine of external competence has developed within the realm of substantive law and hence is not easily transposed to the procedural and private international law domain.[81] Nevertheless, commentators argue that the Member States and the Community institutions should try to resolve these concerns and find a working method which would ensure that the Community could act with diplomatic strength in the area.[82] Such an outcome will also be important when the Community becomes a member of international organizations in the field. An example of this development is the Community membership as of April 2007 in the Hague Conference on Private International Law.[83]

In sum, even though the centre of gravity has now changed towards the Community, Europeanization of the policy area is not a one-way process. The Member States have subjected the policy area to strict requirements relating to the conferral of powers, subsidiarity, and institutional constraints.[84] Nevertheless, commentators identified its potency, and it is today possible to say that for judicial cooperation in civil matters the new legal basis of Article 65 of the EC Treaty has entailed progress and not been a mere 'cosmetic exercise'. Furthermore, despite the restrictive and unsatisfactory institutional features of Title IV of the EC Treaty the Title has entailed a giant leap forward towards expansion of Community law in the sovereignty-sensitive policy domain.[85]

[80] Boele-Woelki (2000) p. 76.

[81] Borrás (2004) pp.100 and 106.

[82] Wilderspin and Rouchaud-Joët (2004) p. 48.

[83] Hess (2004a) p. 100. See COM (2005) 639 Proposal for the accession of the European Community to the Hague Conference on Private International Law and (EC) No. 719/2006 Council Decision of 5 October 2006 on the accession of the Community to the Hague Conference on Private International Law. The proceedings were lodged in anticipation of amendments to the Statute of the Hague Conference and the membership follows the entry into force on 1 January 2007 of the amendments to the Statute of the Hague Conference, which made it possible for certain Regional Economic Integration Organisations, in particular the EC, to become a Member of the Hague Conference. Gaudemet-Tallon (2004) p. 80f. notes that membership will not solve all the problems of coordination between the Member States and the EU.

[84] Meeusen (2004) p. 47.

[85] Den Boer (1999) p. 303.

5

The Emergence of a Policy Area and the Broader Context

Political Impetus

The Area of Freedom, Security, and Justice

The creation of the Area of Freedom, Security, and Justice, and concurring legal bases for judicial cooperation in civil matters (amongst other matters) has been considered one of the major innovations of the Treaty of Amsterdam, albeit that the Treaty was mainly consolidating in nature and aimed to improve processes and enhance efficiency rather than extend Community powers.[1] The new general policy vision of an Area of Freedom, Security, and Justice, specifically enunciated in Article 2 of the EU Treaty, is the stepping stone for the policy area and the most tangible emanation of its original political impetus. Several factors contributed to this impetus becoming the focus of the IGC leading up to the Treaty of Amsterdam. Amongst these have been suggested disillusionment with the old Third Pillar, the fragility of the democratic order in some candidate Member States, the perceived threat of organized crime and migration but also the failure of the negotiators to advance in other areas.[2]

The vision of an Area of Freedom, Security, and Justice offered a new paradigm for discourse and a new representation of Europe focusing on the individual citizens and on the concept of security. This vision counteracts the darker spin created by the concept of 'Fortress Europe'. However, security can also be an anomaly when grouped with justice, and from the justice

[1] Craig and De Búrca (1998) p. 32.
[2] Twomey (1999) p. 351.

perspective security can actualize the perennial difficulty of balancing overall efficiency of procedure with fairness of results.[3] Therefore commentators analysing the glossy promise of Freedom, Security, and Justice raise questions about protection of participation and the social legitimacy of the project.[4] Such legitimacy questions might also surface for judicial cooperation in civil matters when one reviews the development in detail.[5]

Aside from the general visionary projection of the Area of Freedom, Security, and Justice the political will and high priority given to judicial cooperation in the Union in both civil and criminal matters is evidenced by the enlargement process to include the 10 'new' Member States in May 2004.[6] An important part of the accession process was the three Copenhagen criteria, formulated by the European Council in 1993. The first so-called political criterion is relevant to procedural law since it presupposes functioning structures to uphold the rule of law, human rights, and democracy.[7] More pragmatically, the intent was to make membership conditional upon the existence of a functioning court system and a guarantee of upholding the right to a fair trial in the broad sense. Broken down this might also be considered as including the practical structures, knowledge, and capability of participating in judicial cooperation in civil matters.

Another fundamental condition for accession of the candidate countries was the third Copenhagen criterion entailing the ability to take on the aims of the Union. In practice this is also relevant for procedural law since it entailed an obligation on the Enlargement States to transpose into their national legal systems the *aquis communautaire* including all the new measures of judicial cooperation in civil matters which were not

[3] Ibid. pp. 352, 357, 360, and 370 makes this point in the context of immigration and asylum policy. The same general logic applies by analogy to judicial cooperation in civil matters albeit that this is a politically less sensitive policy area which relates more tangentially to security.

[4] Ibid. p. 372f. These concerns, by analogy applied to judicial cooperation in civil matters, might have a less dramatic tone in this context but serve as an important reminder of and pointer to the legitimacy issue.

[5] Chapter 16 analyses the legitimacy of the policy area.

[6] Rissanen (2004) p. 349f. Poland, Czech Republic, Slovak Republic, Estonia, Latvia, Lithuania, Hungary, Slovenia, Cyprus, and Malta acceded on 1 May 2004. This round of EU enlargement had been precipitated by the fall of the Berlin wall and the changed geopolitical climate in Europe after the cold war. In 1991 the EC entered into Europe Agreements to link the countries more closely and establish a forum for dialogue. In 1997 the EU opened membership negotiations and concluded association agreements (so-called Europe Agreements) to structure the pre-accession process.

[7] Heiss and Supron-Heidel p. 156f.

exempted.[8] According to commentators, as the accession process progressed, more attention was focused on judicial reform and a reconstruction of the legal institutions.[9] However, the most visible political emphasis on functioning judicial cooperation structures and the commitment of the EU to create these is the third 'safety clause' of the Accession Agreements.[10] Under the safety clause the Commission can undertake protective measures if within three years of membership, serious discrepancies are evident in the implementation of judicial cooperation in civil matters.[11]

Progression of the Project

A clear demonstration of political impetus and the progression of the project is evidenced by the institutional support, from the Commission and the Member States in the Council, in a stream of policy documents instigating and monitoring the creation of the Area of Freedom, Security, and Justice. The documents focus on outlining and steering the actual implementation of the new vision by the European institutions. They follow as a consequence of the change in responsibilities and the new opportunities available since the ending of the preceding intergovernmental era of cooperation in Justice and Home Affairs.[12] They also demonstrate institutional effort to comply with the five-year deadline in the Treaty of Amsterdam for the creation of Area of Freedom Security and Justice.[13]

The first important document is the joint Action Plan of the Commission and of the Council, which was submitted to the Vienna European Council in December 1998.[14] It aims to reflect the priorities and timetable but also

[8] Ibid.

[9] Ibid. pp. 157 and 161. The authors also note, pp. 147–54, that as a consequence of increased trade the market need for international procedural rules on jurisdiction and enforcement, etc. was evident in the Central and Eastern European countries. They had been eager to sign and enforce conventions amongst themselves but also within the auspices of the Hague Conference on Private International Law and the Council of Europe. Some of them had also sought to become signatories to the Lugano Convention prior to their EU membership.

[10] Rissanen (2004) p. 349f.

[11] Art. 38, Act concerning conditions of accession and adjustments to the Treaties on which the European Union is founded, OJ L236, 23.9.2003.

[12] Council and Commission Action Plan OJ C-19, 23.1.1999, p. 1, paras 1–3.

[13] Art. 61 of the Treaty.

[14] OJ C-19, 23.1.1999, p. 1. Note, however, that from 1997, prior to the entry into force of the Treaty of Amsterdam, the institutions were already preparing for the new framework within the existing justice and home affairs cooperative framework. See priorities identified by the European Parliament, OJ C-371, 8.12.1997, p. 207.

to set out a general philosophy.[15] In relation to justice the Action Plan confirms that the aim is to give citizens a common sense of justice and improve the day-to-day life of people in society through improving access to justice and judicial cooperation between Member States. Judicial cooperation in civil matters is said to represent a fundamental stage in creating a European judicial area and one which many believed had developed too slowly.[16] Thus, it could already be seen both that the policy area was given greater synergy than was present in the very slow intergovernmental method and that pressure towards change would be more difficult to resist.[17]

A year after the Action Plan, the European Council met at Tampere in Finland for a special meeting on the Area of Freedom, Security, and Justice. In the Conclusions of the Tampere European Council, the particular aims and objectives of separate policy fields are further fleshed out.[18] First, however, the Conclusions proclaim that European integration has accomplished an Internal Market and a common currency and is now challenged to achieve free movement of citizens within the Union under safe and fair parameters. This entails creating a genuine judicial space, which generates legal certainty as citizens can approach any court as easily as in their own Member State and as judgments are mutually recognized.[19] The three overall objectives for the envisaged European area of justice are: better access to justice, mutual recognition, and greater convergence in civil law. Under each of these headings, several specific measures to be implemented are mentioned. On the basis of the Tampere Conclusions, the Commission published biannual updates, so-called scoreboards.[20] The scoreboards became increasingly detailed as new legislative proposals were added under the existing chapter headings. The scoreboards clearly added to the transparency of the work being undertaken by the institutions and give a very thorough overview of the development of the Area of Freedom, Security, and Justice. Pursuant to the May 2004 deadline set by the Treaty of Amsterdam, the Commission published a final

[15] OJ C-19, 23.1.1999, p. 1, in particular paras 4–5.

[16] Ibid. paras 15–16.

[17] Kennett (2000) p. 6.

[18] Presidency Conclusions No. 200/1/99, 16.10.1999. Aalto (2000) p. 327 makes the point that the Tampere Conclusions have no legal binding effect. However, in their listing of measures and timetables they do provide an incentive for the other institutions to act.

[19] Presidency Conclusions No. 200/1/99, paras 1, 2, and 5.

[20] COM (2000) 167, 24.3.2000 was the first scoreboard and COM (2003) 812, 30.12.2003 the penultimate one.

scoreboard or Communication providing an assessment of the achievements and failures in implementing the Tampere agenda.[21]

The Commission Communication of June 2004 provides the first suggestion of a continued or second phase of political impetus and institutional support for developing the Area of Freedom, Security, and Justice. With regard to judicial cooperation in civil matters the main proposals and future orientations include: to continue and increase the work on the mutual recognition programme; to foster greater mutual trust; and to monitor the implementation of the Community legislative measures adopted to date. Interestingly the Commission also sees it as necessary to avoid having two separate legal regimes, one relating to disputes with a cross-border element and the other relating to purely internal disputes.[22] The Commission refers to the Constitutional Treaty, perhaps envisaging a broadening of the legal basis in Article 65 of the EC Treaty, e.g. by deleting the reference to 'cross-border'.[23] Notwithstanding the fact that the limits to the competence still remain, the Commission statement shows a new, bolder, or unification-oriented political vision for the judicial space. The Commission explains that the creation of a dual system would be inconsistent with the aim of a single area of justice and could raise questions of discrimination as well as complicate legislation at the expense of transparency.[24]

An additional clear political impetus and mandate for continuing to create genuine judicial space was given in the European Council's Hague Programme of 2004, which outlines a new multi-annual agenda.[25] The Programme states that it is 'grounded in the general principles of subsidiarity, proportionality, solidarity and respect for the different legal systems and traditions of the Member States'. The approach taken to judicial cooperation in civil matters is moderate and pragmatic, recognizing the need for 'an explicit effort to improve mutual understanding among judicial authorities and different legal systems'. There is an emphasis on measures improving mutual understanding, including an effective European training network for judicial authorities, exchange programmes for judicial authorities, and

[21] COM (2004) 401, 2.6.2004.

[22] Ibid. p. 11.

[23] Just such a deletion was made in the Draft Constitution but during the intergovernmental conference the same condition was again inserted. Thus, in the Constitutional Treaty the legal basis was not broadened in this way and neither has such a broadening been envisaged in the future Reform Treaty, see Chapter 3.

[24] COM (2004) 401, p. 11, n. 11.

[25] Presidency Conclusions 1492/04, Annex I, p. 11f.

workshops to promote cooperation between the legal professions.[26] It is also noteworthy that the Programme mentions that the institutions of the EU should ensure coherence with the international legal order and continue to have close cooperation with the Hague Conference and the Council of Europe so as to 'coordinate initiatives and maximise synergies'.

Following the Hague Programme the Commission launched its five-year Action Plan.[27] Confirming the orientations of the Hague Programme, the Action Plan outlines twin strategies for civil justice: namely, first to strive towards effective access to justice by focusing on the enforcement of judgments and the completion of the mutual recognition programme; and secondly to build confidence, mutual trust, and a European judicial culture through training and networking.[28] A part of these strategies is a move towards consolidation and overall coherence, i.e. towards a more holistic view of the system being created. Among the projected measures the Commission intends to draw up are a Specific Programme on judicial cooperation in civil and commercial matters and a Strategy on the external aspects of Union policy.[29]

Finally, aside from the interaction and dynamics between the Community institutions, the individual Member States themselves – through the means of the rotating Presidency of the Union – contribute to the political impetus behind the policy area. Without reviewing all the past Presidencies, it is noteworthy that at a time when the Amsterdam five-year implementation period had passed and at a time when there was some doubt as to the general legitimacy of the European project,[30] the UK Presidency in the second half of 2005 placed strong emphasis on civil justice, causing one commentator to note that 'the case is made that civil law had a significant impact, more, perhaps, than in any previous Presidency'.[31] The policy area is thus shown to have a strong and continuing political impetus, and seems to be growing progressively stronger.[32]

[26] Ibid. pp. 36f. and 40f.

[27] COM (2005) 184, 10.5.2005.

[28] Ibid. p. 11.

[29] Ibid. p. 29f.

[30] The generally perceived crisis of confidence in the direction of the European Union resulted from the negative referenda in the spring of 2005 in France and the Netherlands over the acceptance of the Constitutional Treaty.

[31] Baroness Ashton of Upholland writing in ***Brussels Agenda***, Jan. 2006, the monthly publication of the UK Law Societies joint office in Brussels.

[32] The Austrian and Finnish Presidencies of 2006 were committed to implementing the Hague Programme, and during the Finnish Presidency a mid-term review of the Hague

Thus, it is evident from the development of both the legal basis, outlined in Chapter 3, and the political impetus, as outlined here, that there has been a significant qualitative leap vis-à-vis the aims, forms, and framework for judicial cooperation in civil matters in the EU.[33] However, it is also evident that ever-deepening integration gives birth to and fosters many complex issues. The European Parliament's recommendation to the Council and European Council, in anticipation of the Hague Programme, foreshadows these by raising, both generally and in detail, the need to enhance the legitimacy and credibility of the Area of Freedom, Security, and Justice. The Parliament also emphasizes that the Area of Freedom, Security, and Justice has to be aligned to the promotion of fundamental rights in the Union and to the strengthening of the concept of European citizenship.[34] This statement raises issues of the broader context in which the policy area is developed to which we turn below.

The Broader Context

General

It is important to understand that the generation of broader issues within the EU can help explain some characteristics or trends of the current civil procedural regulation and that this regulation does not exist in a vacuum. In particular, in the context of the EU the main political and historical phases have coloured the regulatory and legislative activity.[35] Furthermore, commentators have found, when analysing the developments of national procedural systems, that procedural regulation is very closely linked to general trends in society. One commentator has professed that 'Procedure is not pure form. It is the meeting point of conflicts, of policies and ideas' and procedural

Programme was conducted, see Council Document 16065/05. The German, Portuguese, and Slovenian Presidencies for 2007 and the first six months of 2008 have issued a Trio Programme. In relation to the Area of Freedom, Security, and Justice the emphasis and priority are not on the generic civil procedure measures, but these are mentioned, as are general goals of enhancing cooperation between courts, developing E-justice, and judicial training, Council Document 17079/06 DQPG.

[33] Rouchaud (2001) p. 23.

[34] T-22/2004.

[35] See inter alia Craig and De Búrca (1998) pp. 3–48. Further, Raitio (2003) p. 10 advocates a historical and teleological approach to EC law interpretation in conducting research.

scholars are studying 'the great waves of history: the socioeconomic as well as the intellectual changes, revolutions and stagnations of history'.[36] In relation to the question of how to regulate within judicial cooperation in civil matters as a new policy area of the EU one can arguably not adopt the traditional view of 'integration through law', seeing Community law as basically moving forward in a process of ever-deeper convergence.[37] This view, based on a historical observation of the expansion of Community law, is today arguably an orthodox approach. The opposite approach, seeking to limit expansion and regulatory differentiation as a pragmatic attempt to resolve tensions, must also be taken into account.[38] Therefore, two holistic themes of European integration and regulatory strategy have been chosen as important, even though their link with the current regulation on civil procedure might at first glance seem more tenuous. These are the principle of subsidiarity and its impact on the scrutiny of the need for supranational regulation, and the new governance programme launched by the EU institutions and its impact on the forms of regulation.

How Regulate?

Subsidiarity and Proportionality

Closely related to the question of the existence of Community competence and the adequacy of a particular legal basis for action (see Chapter 3), with its institutional particularities (see Chapter 4), is the question of when such competence is properly exercised.[39] The competence question is the prior question, and is of course the main area in which to check the adventurous use of competence.[40] However, if the competence question is resolved positively a further constitutional enquiry arises governed by the principles of subsidiarity and proportionality, which are set out in Article 5(2)–(3) of the EC Treaty and in a Protocol to the Treaties.[41] The principles entail that

[36] Cappelletti (1970–1) p. 885f.

[37] Dougan (2002) pp. 154–7.

[38] Ibid. pp. 158–61.

[39] Weatherill (2004a) pp. 21–32 notes that the existence of competence and the choice of exercising competence are fundamentally different in principle but that in practice they are closely associated.

[40] Weatherill (2004b) p. 658.

[41] The principle of subsidiarity was introduced at Maastricht in Art. 3(b) of the Treaty. It was renumbered as Art. 5(2) by Amsterdam and remains unchanged by the Treaty of Nice. In order to attempt to give the principle more practical or operational value a Protocol on its application was attached to the Treaty of Amsterdam. See Weatherill (2003) pp. 654–61 for an overview of

Community action is appropriate if a proposed action cannot be achieved by the Member States, but can by reason of scale or effect be better achieved by the Community. However, any action by the Community must not go beyond what is necessary to achieve the objectives of the Treaty. In the Protocol there is a further enumeration of material criteria, namely the requirement of a transnational dimension and the requirement of market distortion. The Protocol also contains several procedural checks and balances for how the institutions should take the principles into account in the legislative process. Amongst the latter is the obligation of the institutions and Member States to justify using either qualitative or quantitative indicators to show compliance with the principles of any legislative proposal.

Subsidiarity and proportionality can be seen as the political answer chosen for reconciling the increasing European integration with the Member States' national interests; they also counter the federal deficit or legitimacy crisis of the European Union.[42] After it has first been determined that the Community has the competence to act, the principles can be seen as a second filter which aims to determine whether Community intervention or regulation is appropriate or not. One commentator claims that the ethos behind the principles is that of restricting intervention by the Community.[43] However, the more moderate view is that there is no entrenched preconception in favour of State action at the expense of the Community but that the appropriate level is determined *in casu*.[44]

The application of the principles of subsidiary and proportionality as justiciable questions has been affirmed by the ECJ. Nevertheless, their reach and strength are less than clear and they have been held to be weak judicial swords.[45] Because the most intense level of judicial scrutiny would bring into play issues of separation of powers, the ECJ has often shown deference to discretion in policy making and applied the principle of proportionality in such a manner that only manifestly unreasonable measures would be

the principle of subsidiarity and in particular the varying and developing political and legal perceptions of the principle in the EU. Further, Bermann (2002) pp. 75–9 notes that the principle of proportionality had previously been a part of Community law, often as a means of testing the compatibility of national law with Community requirements.

[42] Estella (2002) pp. 82–5, and De Búrca (1999) p. 8f.

[43] Estella (2002) pp. 80 and 91.

[44] Weatherill (2003) p. 654.

[45] Bermann (2002) p. 80f. notes that the principle of proportionality introduces several levels of legal analysis, from the weakest kind of reasonability requirement to a costs versus benefits test, and further even to an enquiry into whether a measure is excessive because the objective could satisfactorily have been achieved by imposing fewer costs.

overruled.[46] The Court has avoided elaborating a substantive merits test for the principle of subsidiarity, and has instead 'proceduralized' it. The case law to date thus tells us that the focus is on the obligation of the institutions to justify and make reasoned findings vis-à-vis subsidiarity.[47]

This weakness of the principles as a judicial tool should also be borne in mind for the policy area under analysis, albeit that the most effective use of the principles and their clearest impact actually fall outside the sphere of judicial review. The principles still have significant impact in the political sphere of the legislative process. This is reconfirmed in the draft of the potential future Reform Treaty where the principle of subsidiarity is reinforced by the involvement of national parliaments, which can require the Commission to review a legislative proposal if one-third of them object to it on grounds of subsidiarity. Furthermore, the ECJ can hear actions on the grounds of infringement of the principle of subsidiarity brought by Member States on behalf of their national parliaments.[48] Even though the Reform Treaty has not yet entered into force, the proposed reforms display a vision whereby subsidiarity is an important and integral part of the question of levels of regulation in the EU and also, fundamentally, questions of competence.

On a general level, in relation to judicial cooperation in civil matters, subsidiarity highlights the question of what action is best done at the Community as opposed to national, regional, or even global, levels. This question is theoretically and constitutionally important, as well as intensely practical. However, difficulties arise when it is not possible to decide on the appropriateness of Community action, because the criteria can offer arguments both for and against and furthermore have an ideological underpinning.[49] Therefore it is a question of values, interests, and political choice.[50] Furthermore, because the Commission is the primary actor making legislative proposals

[46] Ibid. p. 82f. in relation to the principle of proportionality.

[47] Ibid. p. 85ff.

[48] For the reforms to the working of the principle of subsidiarity in the Constitutional Treaty see inter alia Tridimas (2004) pp. 132–5. The reforms proposed in the Constitutional Treaty have been carried through in the draft Reform Treaty, confirmed by Council Document 11218/07, p. 4. The Reform Treaty is currently set to be agreed in the 2007 IGC and the aim is ratification by the Member States before 2009; the IGC homepage that can be found on the Council website http://www.consilium.europa.eu/ (visited 22.8.2007).

[49] Weatherill (2003) p. 660.

[50] Estella (2002) p. 112f. and De Búrca (1999) p. 19f. In contrast, Rouchaud-Joët (2003) p. 452 mentions the principle of subsidiarity as playing a role in the EU institutions' decision on whether or not to adopt a measure in the area of judicial cooperation in civil matters, namely the Enforcement Order Regulation.

and offering a qualitative or quantitative justification in its explanatory reports, it is possible that it uses the justifications to advance its policy preferences and uphold Community intervention.[51] In judicial cooperation in civil matters most of the regulatory activity relates to cross-border or transnational matters; therefore, the principle of subsidiarity can be used to reinforce the political argument for regulation without a proper weighing of the different values at stake.[52] This potential preference for Community action is reinforced by the fact that there will be many policy areas in which the comparative efficiency calculation favours Community action, as the *raison d'être* of the Community will require centralized action and uniform application. But the very question of whether the Community should act has increasingly become a subject of debate and this very principle is receiving renewed attention.[53] And the principle can, as one commentator suggests, have a more subtle influence on the form that Community action takes, which ties in with the theme of governance.[54]

Governance

The emergence of the principle of subsidiarity in the EU can be explained both by general trends in domestic administrative laws, which recognize the limits of a top-down approach to regulatory mechanisms and create more participatory and decentralized models, and also by the perceived democratic deficit in the EU, which stimulated increased delegation to lower levels and more dialogue with civil actors. The doctrine of subsidiarity, together with the background forces mentioned, has also contributed to the growth of pressure towards new approaches to governance in the EU.[55] Governance has been defined by the Commission as 'rules, processes and behaviour that affect the way in which powers are exercised at the European level'.[56] New or modern governance is a term of political science. It has emerged to describe the shift in Western Europe away from the interventionist hierarchical welfare state to cooperation of the state and private actors in public policy making.[57]

[51] Estella (2002) p. 126f.
[52] Biavati (2001) p. 90. Weatherill (2004) makes the same point in the general private law context.
[53] Bermann (2002) p. 87.
[54] Craig and De Búrca (2002) p. 136.
[55] Scott and Trubek (2002) p. 6ff.
[56] COM (2001) 428, 25.7.2001, p. 8.
[57] Mayntz (2002) p. 1f.

According to one definition of new governance its important characteristics are: that it is broader than government as it encompasses non-state actors; that networks are created and interact as an alternative to markets and hierarchies; that the networks function on trust and autonomy; and that the state can only steer the networks imperfectly.[58] Furthermore, the post-regulatory state characteristically employs a variety of norms, including 'soft' law, the role of which can be seen as putting procedures in place, steering the actors involved in policy making, rather than as substantively regulating.[59] Prominent features of governance are the participatory element and the involvement of private actors, including civil society. In the legal literature new governance in the EU has been defined as mechanisms which depart from the classic 'Community method'[60] and which thus might include other institutional players in the legislative process or might not necessarily give rise to legislative binding acts for the purposes of creating uniform rules.[61] New governance has been seen to emerge pragmatically within the EC in policy areas which are politically sensitive or have previously been completely within the national sphere of competence. New governance in these areas can respect national parameters and answer the political concern for legitimacy.[62]

From the legal point of view, the new governance mechanisms that have developed in the EU have several shared characteristics, including broader participation in policy making by private actors, dialogue and coordination between actors from different levels, acceptance of legislative diversity rather than uniformity, more reliance on soft law and mutual surveillance through benchmarking performance as well as sharing best practices.[63] In the EU earlier policy initiatives have retrospectively been seen as phenomena of new approaches to governance.[64] One commentator notes that a clear transformation of the regulatory system has occurred in the EU throughout the 1990s, resulting in the new governance rhetoric, based on more openness in decision making. This transformation entails that ancillary procedures,

[58] Rhodes (1997) p. 52f.

[59] Scott (2003) p. 20.

[60] 'The Community method' is a term that refers to the regular legislative procedure within the European Community, at present the co-decision procedure in Article 251 of the EC Treaty.

[61] Scott and Trubek (2002) p. 1f.

[62] Weatherill (2003) p. 679.

[63] Ibid. p. 5f.

[64] E.g. the new approach to harmonization and the principle of subsidiarity. See Lebessis and Paterson (1997) p. 10f and De Búrca (1999) p. 1f.

e.g. consultation with experts, participation by interested parties, and comitology, are associated with decision making and form a complex web, the coordination of which can also be seen as a multifaceted network.[65]

The political conceptualization and formal introduction of a new governance project in the EU commenced with an academic survey commissioned by the Commission and published in 1997.[66] Thereafter the Commission conducted a broad consultation which led to the White Paper on European Governance in 2001.[67] The White Paper makes a number of proposals for change in order to achieve the five guiding principles of openness, participation, accountability, effectiveness, and coherence. The new governance project has of course its critics and it is clear that new forms of governance can be questioned from the perspective of legal legitimacy and they must be followed by a novel institutional balance.[68] Nevertheless, these general transformations have the capacity to influence and transform individual substantive policy areas within the EU.

The new governance approach to regulation was debated and introduced within the institutions during the same period in which the Area of Freedom, Security, and Justice was introduced and its implementation commenced after the Treaty of Amsterdam entered into force. Therefore, it is plausible that the institutions, when envisaging proposed new measures in the area of judicial cooperation in civil matters, have been influenced by the highly topical new governance mechanisms and regulatory techniques. In addition, the opposite is true, i.e. that civil justice can, through the dynamic relationship between citizen actors with the governing courts, form a logical and vital dimension of local but simultaneously integrated governance which could reinforce the new governance theme.[69] There are several ways in which these new governance mechanisms can impact on the policy field of judicial cooperation in civil matters. Early commentators in the field argued that softer forms of regulation could be the appropriate form of action.[70] It is also interesting that softer forms of governance can be seen as having links

[65] Azoulay (2002) pp. 120–6 and 126–9.

[66] Lebessis and Paterson (1997).

[67] COM (2001) 428, 25.7.2001.

[68] Azoulay (2002) p. 129–37. Further, Weatherill (2003) p. 680 notes that new governance systems can themselves become complex and less transparent, which leads to the circular problem of creating the same issues as it was intended to combat and therefore again being questioned from the point of view of legitimacy.

[69] Hartnell (2002) pp. 118–38.

[70] Kohler (1999) p. 18f.

to strong concerns about procedural harmonization, which led commentators to advocate diverse forms of cooperation rather than full-scale codification. A commentator makes the point generally for private law that today harmonization, as conventionally understood, increasingly co-exists with 'softer' forms of governance showing a general willingness to extol flexibility and diversity.[71]

The earlier measures enacted to date in judicial cooperation in civil matters fall within the more classic mould of harmonizing techniques, but in the later measures, and those to be implemented in the future, soft law would allow for a more nuanced relationship between Community regulation and projects on the national and global levels. The measures enacted so far also have a markedly decentralized approach, which in itself is characteristic of a new approach to governance.[72] In addition, the measures affect and involve private interests, civil society, and certain professions, in addition to local judicial authorities. Consequently, multilevel interaction involving actors from the private and local sectors is almost inevitable and highly beneficial, as evidenced by the consultation processes launched by the Commission in relation to proposals and measures in this field.[73] Finally, as the implementation of judicial cooperation in civil matters in practice depends on cooperation between the private and local parties involved, follow-up, in the form of benchmarking or exchange of best practices, can be seen as very constructive, and is to some extent already taking place through the European Judicial Network in civil matters.[74]

Why Regulate?

Interlinked with but also separate from the questions of whether there is Community competence in a certain field, and which regulatory levels and governance forms the exercise of such competence takes, there is also the

[71] Weatherill (2004a) p. 15ff.

[72] An example is the Regulation on obtaining evidence, (EC) No. 1206/2001, where new 'direct channels' replace the previously favoured centralized systems.

[73] Inter alia the consultation processes on ADR and on conflicts of law and small claims launched by: COM (2002) 196, 19.4.2002, Green Paper on alternative dispute resolution in civil and commercial matters; and COM (2002) 746, 20.12.2002, Green Paper on a European order for payment procedure and on measures to simplify and speed up small claims litigation.

[74] Articles 9–12 of the Decision to establish the EJN, (EC) No. 470/2001, provide for national contact points and other national actors involved in judicial cooperation in civil matters to meet biannually to exchange experiences and data, identify best practices, and discuss problems that they have encountered.

question of the substantive political support and justification for development. In this respect we can see several general themes within the European integration maze which support and reinforce the development of judicial cooperation in civil matters. These are also themes which might serve and have served as justification or motivation for Community action in the field. The first is the market integration or economic analysis justification. This is perhaps classic in the EU law sense, but currently when the EU has been transformed from a common market project to a diverse constitutional entity it is important to remember and highlight this theme. Two other themes, which are relevant and which can be said to have foreshadowed civil procedural regulation at the Community level, are European citizenship and fundamental human rights. These have developed more recently than the idea of the common market but are now staples of EU political jargon and because of their general nature have the potential of 'spillover' and overlap with many policy areas. As the European Parliament has recently noted, and as we shall see below, it is 'impossible to dissociate the implementation of the Area of Freedom, Security and Justice from a policy of protection and promotion of fundamental rights and citizenship within the Union'.[75]

Market Integration

From the suitable metaphor that procedural law has a service function vis-à-vis substantive law,[76] it is perhaps evident but nonetheless necessary to reiterate that the harmonization of procedural rules has been considered a sine qua non for market creation. This is so because of the recurring point that the bases of the EC free trade area, the cornerstones of the Internal Market, namely the four fundamental freedoms, the free movement of goods, services, workers, and capital, are less likely to be realized in practice notwithstanding the liberalization of import and export (emigration and immigration) rules if there are significant procedural disincentives within the Community. However, interestingly and perhaps surprisingly from a proceduralist's perspective, this was not initially realized or considered a priority. Or as one commentator notes, only when the Internal Market was substantively complete was the true significance of procedural obstacles revealed.[77] Thus, the Strategic Programme for the Internal Market of 1993 and the

[75] T-22/2004, para. I.
[76] Andersson (2003) p. 64.
[77] Kennett (2000) p. 39.

Green Paper on Access to Justice for Consumers are two Commission documents which highlight this issue.[78]

From a general macro-level perspective one can state that procedural complexity creates barriers to trade, and also often discrimination, which entails that conditions are not equal for all participants in the supranational market. From a general micro-level perspective, companies and citizens will be faced with increased, even insurmountable, complexity, delay, and costs, as soon as there is a cross-border element to a transaction they undertake and they will therefore be less inclined to engage in transnational business.[79] To alleviate these discrepancies is the basic incentive for all international procedural cooperation between states. However, in the EC context one can see it as fundamental too, in the sense of providing the means for executing otherwise illusory economic freedoms. Conversely, the same discrepancies and remedies can be seen as correcting unwanted effects of the Internal Market.[80] Thus companies and businesses that enter into transactions across borders can in a dispute find that they have fewer procedural rights or less procedural protection than in their 'home state', from such diverse procedural institutions as legal aid, provisional relief, the availability of ADR, or small claims procedures. Thus the Member States of the European Union, having created an Internal Market, are obliged to correct such unwanted effects which stem from procedural differences set up for the benefit of companies and citizens.

From the perspective of companies, the opening of frontiers and the change from predominantly national markets to international ones has evidently led to greater complexities; above all the managing of risk has assumed a novel character, particularly since during the same time period companies have also faced a general trend of increased litigiousness or assertiveness in disputes.[81] Companies have therefore turned to the mechanism of arbitration for better risk and litigation management, and have also favoured ADR. However, particularly in the Community context the mosaic of different procedural systems is an anomaly that businesses, which expect simplicity, efficiency, and competitiveness in the system, wish to see rectified. From

[78] COM (1993) 256–1 and 256–2 as well as COM (1993) 576.

[79] Consumer perspective: ECLG (1998) Annex II, where it is noted that since the Internal Market does not have trustworthy and accessible legal structures for consumers they face macro-economic direct and indirect costs. However, aside from these static costs there are also dynamic cost effects on the economy as a whole and on economic growth.

[80] Rouchaud (2001) p. 21.

[81] Vincke (2003) p. 17.

the point of view of this interest group Member State parochialism and arguments of sovereignty or subsidiarity in the context of procedural law do not make sense.[82] Nonetheless the corporate justifications for procedural regulation are unfortunately not surveyed or substantiated by statistics.[83]

In contrast, the EU has analysed the macroeconomic effects from a consumer perspective and found that the absence of legal certainty leads to economic slow down. The lack of legal certainty is a much heavier burden and the litigation risk is more difficult to calculate for occasional litigants such as consumers and small and medium-sized companies than for larger enterprises which are often multiple players. Therefore, the former parties will avoid the risk and refrain from taking advantage of the Internal Market. Furthermore, the cost and duration of procedures, if lengthy, may deter parties from taking legal action. Hence, it is contended that there is an additional risk that because of lax procedural systems sellers or producers will take advantage of weaker parties. These combined effects lead to macroeconomically detrimental results.[84]

The Community development of and the debate regarding procedural harmonization has, from the first tentative steps of intergovernmental cooperation in jurisdiction and enforcement matters, been influenced by the common market and market integration. The European jurisdictional scheme that is today taken for granted is actually highly original because apart from being structured to take into account certain procedural aims it also takes into account and is moulded by what one author has identified as Community aims, e.g. legal certainty and the division of competence.[85] Most notably, a new paradigm has emerged beside and perhaps above the traditional international procedural aims of sovereignty and good administration, namely free economic movement in which the interests of private market actors are protected.[86]

In this context case C-412/97 *Italo Fenocchio*[87] is notable. The ECJ found that a national summary procedure for a payment order did not hinder free movement even if it was limited and could not be brought against a foreign defendant. Despite the argument that the limitation in scope of the national procedural rule could cause Italian undertakings to prefer business relations

[82] Ibid. pp. 19–23.
[83] Ibid. pp. 16 and 18.
[84] Kennett (2000) p. 39, Freyhold et al. (1998) pp. 276–9.
[85] Fallon (2003) pp. 25f. and 57ff.
[86] Ibid. pp. 54–7 and 61f.
[87] C-412/97 [1999] ECR I-3845.

with customers in the same Member State and could therefore interfere with free movement, the Court held that procedural law had a too indirect effect to be considered an obstacle. The case was first interesting in that it drew attention to the link between procedural rules and market action. Secondly, the case also again demonstrates that subsidiarity and national procedural autonomy are pitched finely against the need for the development of particular cross-border or international procedural rules. The ruling in the case regarding the indirect effect between the particular national procedural rule and the Internal Market can perhaps today be seen as superseded by the very rapid developments that have taken place thereafter. The ECJ might today itself have more support for a teleological and practical interpretation emphasizing the economic efficiency aspect and might perhaps reach a different conclusion. In this sense *Italo Fenocchio* arguably came just before a new era in which the development of procedural rules and a new procedural ethos of efficiency were linked to the better functioning of the market.

The link between market integration and procedural law can also be seen in parallel with or as an analogy to the substantive field of private law and the debate regarding *lex mercatoria*, globalization, and European private law. In this debate a turning point at the transnational level called 'new pragmatism' has been evidenced, arguably due to the economic rationale on both a macro and a micro level. First, the transaction costs of divergences in national laws are seen as an obstacle or a 'globalization trap' which must be removed; secondly, the drive to enhance productivity and a rationalization of processes in economic terms impact on the evolution of transnational law and tend to take precedence over state sovereignty.[88] Hence modern global social economic processes have a more direct link to the evolution of law. Furthermore, linking in with the question discussed earlier of how to regulate, the economic processes have led to a trend towards an informal and more pluralist style of law making and legal norms in the private law sphere where full-scale codification demonstrates in its formalism a paradox with the new pragmatism. Hence, governance techniques, legal culture, and the judiciary are important tools and mechanisms in the development of a mutual private law.[89] Therefore, it is also relevant to recognize the influence of market integration on regulation of procedural law and judicial cooperation, pressing towards harmonization but also towards more pluralist modes of common rules.

[88] Berger (2004) p. 43f.
[89] Ibid. pp. 45 and 53ff.

Citizenship

The Treaty of Maastricht formally introduced the concept of European Union citizenship in the Treaties and constitutional framework of the EC and EU.[90] The main normative expression of this concept, Article 8 of the EC Treaty, deals only with a limited number of rights, which can be characterized as electoral rights and the right to reside freely.[91] Thus, there is no mention of the other two facets which in the social science literature have been ascribed to citizenship, the social element and the civil element.[92] The latter element is relevant for procedural law and encompasses the right to justice and the due process of law.[93] More specifically the civil element of citizenship can be seen as encompassing a right to knowledge of the law, of procedure, and of the range of legal help available, as well as participation in legal processes in available and accessible institutions.[94] Notwithstanding the narrow scope of Article 8 of the EC Treaty, one of the objectives of the EU, set out in Article 2 of the EU Treaty, is to 'strengthen the protection of the rights and interests of the nationals of its Member States through the introduction of a citizenship of the Union'. Furthermore, the three objectives ascribed to citizenship at Maastricht were broad: to encourage free movement, to enhance democratic legitimacy, and to form the basis for the creation of a European identity.[95]

Therefore, based on these broader normative premises, commentators have argued that even pre-Maastricht there was a move towards focusing on citizens and their needs in day-to-day life in developing judicial cooperation

[90] This formal introduction of a concept of citizenship and corollary rights in the Treaties of the EC and EU does not of course mean that prior dimensions of cooperation and integration in Europe, e.g. the Council of Europe and the ECHR, as well as direct elections to the European Parliament from 1979 onwards, could not also be seen as a 'thin form' of evolving European citizenship, see Heater (2004) p. 103ff. The formal introduction was also preceded by several prior attempts to introduce such a concept, dating back to 1975, see Rissanen (2004) p. 350.

[91] On the introduction of the different rights, e.g. residence rights and electoral rights, and their limitations and for a critique see inter alia O'Leary (1998), pp. 91–103 and Jessurun D'Oliveira (1995) pp. 77–82.

[92] One of the early twentieth-century political science theories on citizenship was developed by T. H. Marshall in 1949. He developed a perception of citizenship as a bundle of rights – civil, political and social – and theorized that these evolved historically one after the other. In the civil element he includes: the liberty of the person, freedom of speech, thought and faith, and the right to own property and to conclude valid contracts, as well as the right to justice: inter alia Heater (2004) p. 113ff.

[93] White (1993) p. 236.

[94] Ibid. 236ff.

[95] O'Leary (1998) p. 84ff.

in civil matters.[96] Furthermore, it has been argued that Maastricht refocused the discussion on the relationship or partnership between the Member States, the Community institutions, and most importantly the individuals in ensuring the effectiveness of the Community legal order. The constitutional imperative, through the concept of citizenship, was that Community rights are respected. In addition, the goal of making Europe more relevant to its citizens was coupled with the ambition of the effective enforcement of Community law and the creation of a consistent and coherent system.[97] Therefore, the historical coincidence between the genesis of Union citizenship and judicial cooperation in civil matters is noteworthy. Furthermore, later on the political documents introducing the Area of Freedom, Security, and Justice indicate at least a rhetorical link between citizenship and judicial cooperation in civil matters.[98] The Commission displayed rhetoric supporting such a link in a communication to the Constitutional Convention: 'Since the Amsterdam Treaty, the establishment of a coherent and balanced area of freedom, security and justice has formed part of the objectives of the Union and is one of the European Union's essential missions now and looking ahead to enlargement. This objective, a corollary to the establishment of an integrated, frontier-free economic area, helps to give the idea of European citizenship its full meaning.'[99]

Citizenship thus led to a more practical expectation of an efficient system for the enforcement of rights and can be seen to have initiated calls for a European judicial space. On the theoretical level the creation of a European judicial space has been argued to be a logical extension of the ideals which motivated the foundation of the European Communities and perhaps a way of giving effect to the idea of citizenship.[100] In the eloquent and ideological wording of one commentator: 'Procedural law lies at the heart of society. If a European society is to be created in the Union, a common system of procedural law must be developed.'[101] Furthermore, again in the theoretical vein, in relation to private law harmonization in general it has been argued that if the current projects are rooted in the market function only they become superficial. Therefore in the EU context citizenship as a symbolic concept

[96] Rouchaud (2001) p. 21.
[97] Szyszczak (1996) pp. 351–2.
[98] Action Plan, paras 2, 15, and 16. European Council Conclusions 1999, para. 2.
[99] COM (2002) 247.
[100] Barrett (1997) p. 6.
[101] Storme (1999) p. 238.

can actually have the practical function of supporting private law, and arguably also civil procedural law developments.[102]

Another view emphasizes law as a potential source of both collective and individual empowerment, which makes universal access to the law fundamental to social participation. Furthermore, because of the social embeddedness of law our perceptual framework is structured by ideas of justice and rights, making equality of access to justice fundamental to people's sense of themselves as citizens.[103] More pragmatically, one commentator argues that the principle of legitimate expectations is inherent in citizenship and that the right to a fair trial is such an expectation. Further, this expectation creates an obligation, not only at the national level but at the supranational level, to ensure judicial cooperation or procedural structures that work. In particular in the EU context citizens should be able to realize their four freedoms of free movement, and should be provided with efficient procedural guarantees to this end.[104]

Hence, there are several strands of doctrinal argument which support the hypothesis that there is a link and an interaction between citizenship and the emergence of an EU civil justice system. Furthermore, this interaction can be seen as operating in both ways, citizenship fostering a judicial space but also judicial cooperation in civil matters developing and giving substantive meaning to citizenship.[105] The interaction has also been seen as a practical development, with the current European regulation of cross-border procedural issues taking citizens as a starting point, rather than emphasizing state interests.[106] Furthermore, citizenship of the Union has had a considerable impact on the case law of the ECJ, particularly in the context of the free movement of persons, and as a dynamic concept it may come to influence the emerging case law regarding judicial cooperation in civil matters.[107] However, the rhetoric can be misleading, as demonstrated by the non-inclusion critique after the introduction of EU citizenship and the apparent paradox between non-inclusion and the freedom element of the Area of Freedom, Security, and Justice.[108] Thus, it cannot be assumed that EU citizenship

[102] Moccia (2004) pp. 315 and 326f.

[103] Sommerlad (2004) p. 350.

[104] Rissanen (1999) p. 239.

[105] Hartnell (2002) p. 66ff.

[106] Hess (2003) p. 221f.

[107] Rissanen (2004) p. 356f, Weatherill (2003) p. 488ff., and Rossi (2004) pp. 72–5.

[108] Inter alia O'Leary (1998) p. 90f, specifically with regard to citizenship. Walker (2004) pp. 12ff. and 24f. gives a broader view of the competing values and justifications as well as the

positively reinforces European integration or policy area developments; it should not just be a tool of discourse or legitimation but provide a concept of rights and a basis for the exercise of such rights.

The civil element or bundle of rights ascribed by political scientists to citizenship, which includes access to justice, poses two distinct problems from a legal perspective because these are actually at the confluence of citizenship rights and fundamental human rights.[109] First, citizenship in its narrow sense equals nationality, and in the modern understanding nationality is not considered a condition for the exercise of access to justice rights and due process rights.[110] Therefore, the Tampere conclusions at several instances refer to all people rather than to citizens, and when the EU institutions refer to citizens they are employing a wider meaning than nationality. This is of course positive, but can also be seen as unfortunate because of the confusion thereby created.[111] As has been noted, in political science one should make a distinction between formal citizenship, i.e. membership of a nation-state, and substantive citizenship, the array of civil, political, and social rights.[112] However, in using citizenship as a broad concept the institutions regrettably seem to indicate a kind of watered-down sense of substantive citizenship which is more discourse than rights. This is evidenced by the fact that even though we can perhaps identify a clear spirit of legal certainty and efficiency for 'citizens' behind the new procedural regime these are often not enforceable rights *per se* but just broad policy objectives.[113]

Secondly, however, because civil citizen rights coincide with fundamental human rights, e.g. the right to fair trial elaborated in national procedural laws and constitutions, in Article 6 of the ECHR, and in Article 47 of the Charter of Fundamental Rights of the European Union, these already include detailed and sophisticated case law, albeit in part outside the EU framework, which do affect the rights of citizens of the Member States. In particular as we shall see, the new procedural regime raises the difficult question of the

multi-layered explanations for the development of a 'Genuine European Area of Justice' as a political priority.

[109] Twomey (1994) p. 119 notes that there is no jurisprudential consensus on the distinction between citizens' civic rights and human rights.

[110] Gardner (1994) p. 41f.

[111] Sankari (2006) p. 78f., in relation to the Hague Programme.

[112] Bottomore (1992) p. 66.

[113] Monar (1998b) pp. 177 and 181 notes that EU citizenship rights are incomplete because they are guaranteed and implemented at the national level and he suggests that substantial progress could be achieved by expanding access to the ECJ.

balance between the fair trial right to enforcement and the fair trial rights of the defence.[114] Therefore these complex questions might in fact provide the true core for creating the justice facet of the civil part of citizenship in Europe rather than the more bland policy statements. As one commentator notes, the concept of European citizenship is 'law and policy in flux', but together with the developing role of fundamental human rights in the EU it promises to be increasingly significant.[115] Such a development would also mirror domestic experience in which both the citizenship perspective and fundamental rights have been considered as catalysts for procedural development and as current forces strongly influencing quality demands on procedural rules.[116]

Fundamental Human Rights

Like the concept of European citizenship, fundamental human rights hint at a step beyond the largely economic focus of market integration and could be used or necessitated by a European identity formation built around shared constitutional values and attempting to legitimize and support the ever-deepening inclusiveness of the Union.[117] Fundamental human rights are very much an emerging theme within the EU context. In parallel to EC market integration the Council of Europe, another European organization, has since the 1950s achieved unprecedented success in concluding the European Convention on Human Rights (ECHR) and in establishing an independent European Court of Human Rights before which individuals can seek redress against Member States for human rights violations.[118]

According to some commentators the ECHR, notably Article 6 on the right to fair trial and the doctrine on Article 6 in judgments of the Court of Human Rights, provides one parameter in Europe that concurs to procedural unification.[119] Notably, during the 1980s and 1990s, Article 6 became one of the most frequently used articles in bringing claims to the Strasbourg Court and hence precipitated an abundant human rights case law regarding procedural issues, amongst which can be singled out the doctrine on reasonable

[114] Inter alia Niboyet (2001a) pp. 945, 947, and 949 specifically in relation to the Brussels I Regulation and the enforcement of judgments, and Yessiou Faltsi (2002) pp. 202–10, for an analysis of the ECHR case law.

[115] Weatherill (2003) p. 475.

[116] Virolainen (2003) p. 190ff, for a Finnish perspective.

[117] Weatherill (2003) p. 485.

[118] De Vel (2001) p. 27f.

[119] Kerameus (1998a) p. 130f., and for a further developed view Kerameus (2003) p. 259.

length of proceedings, the parameters of a full and appropriate hearing, and safeguards of judicial impartiality.[120] This success of another international organization, parallel to the emergence of the citizenship concept in the EU, has put fundamental human rights on the table of the EU. The rise of fundamental human rights in the EU legal order can, as at the national level, be explained by a concrete social need to present the essence of law for citizens in a transparent manner. There is a perception that the Union can no longer look backward to history to create an identity but has to look to the concrete values of today to forge legitimacy.[121] A key to understanding the evolution of the EU legal order and the recent emergence of judicial cooperation in civil matters is arguably the twin purposes, market integration and the protection of the individual, which will continue to affect the Union and its ongoing 'constitutionalization' process.[122]

More practically, the ECJ has historically increasingly had to deal with fundamental human rights adjudication.[123] This has been accompanied by revisions in primary Union law, first by a tentative affirmation in the preamble to the Single European Act in 1987 and secondly at Maastricht by an explicit recognition in the Treaties of the respect for fundamental human rights: Article 6 of the EU Treaty. As one commentator notes the policy areas developed within the Area of Freedom, Security, and Justice at Amsterdam have to be considered in the context of this new fundamental human rights provision.[124] Furthermore, the Council has passed a recent regulation to establish an EU Agency for Fundamental Rights, which seemingly demonstrates how committed the EU is to creating a fundamental human rights umbrella.[125]

From Article 6 of the EU Treaty and its recognition of the principles of 'liberty, democracy, respect for human rights and fundamental freedoms, and the rule of law' commentators have derived a commitment to access to justice and the right to a fair trial.[126] More specifically, in relation to human

[120] Kerameus (2004) p. 154f.

[121] Rissanen (2004) p. 351.

[122] Weatherill (2003) p. 96.

[123] For an introduction to the topic see Craig and De Búrca (1998) pp. 299–31 and Craig (2002) 197f.

[124] Labayle (1997) p. 822f.

[125] (EC) Regulation 168/2007. According to information from the Commission the Agency will become fully operational during 2007: http://ec.europa.eu/justice_home/fsj/rights/fsj_rights_agency_en.htm (visited 24.8.2007).

[126] Rissanen (1999) p. 229. Even though these rights are more specifically elaborated in Art. 6 of the ECHR, the author notes that they are inherent in the concepts of democracy and the rule of law.

rights and procedural law at the EU level, one commentator notes that access to court is one of the central tenets of the rule of law ideal, which the case law of the ECJ has emphasized and guaranteed by developing a clear EC principle of access to court.[127] In these cases the ECJ elaborated and introduced in the EC context the requirements of the right to an independent and impartial tribunal, with flanking protection such as the disclosure of reasons for a decision.[128] Further, also specifically, the ECJ has in the context of prior private international law cooperation had to take into account and deal with the right to be defended, and has stated that the observance of the right to a fair hearing is a fundamental principle of Community law derived from the mutual constitutional traditions common to the Member States. Therefore, a negative condition can be inferred from the case law that the procedural simplification judicial cooperation aims to achieve is not permissible if it undermines the right to a fair hearing.[129] However, the recognition of the right to a fair trial within Community law can also be seen as making a positive contribution to the development of judicial cooperation. This can be evidenced in some of the early case law of the ECJ which raised procedural issues such as legal aid.[130]

The importance of fundamental human rights was significantly enhanced in the EU context with the advent of the EU Charter of Fundamental Rights proclaimed at Nice in December 2000,[131] which includes in Article 47 the right to an effective remedy and to a fair trial:[132]

Everyone whose rights and freedoms guaranteed by the law of the Union are violated has the right to an effective remedy before a tribunal in compliance with the conditions laid down in this Article.

Everyone is entitled to a fair and public hearing within a reasonable time by an independent and impartial tribunal previously established by law. Everyone shall have the possibility of being advised, defended and represented.

Legal aid shall be made available to those who lack sufficient resources in so far as such aid is necessary to ensure effective access to justice.

[127] Rosas (2004) pp. 364–9. Note that the commentator distinguishes this strand of case law from other cases with regard to national procedural rules, see Chapter 2 above.

[128] Dougan (2004) pp. 4–14.

[129] Case C-7/98 *Dieter Krombach v. Andre Bamberski* [2000] ECR I-1935, inter alia paras 38 and 43.

[130] Case C-122/96 *Saldanha* [1997] ECR I-5325.

[131] OJ C-364, 18.12.2000, p. 1.

[132] The articles in Taruffo and Varano (2002) discuss Art. 47 and its impact in the European judicial space.

The protection and fundamental access to court in this Article is even broader in scope of application than the fair trial guarantees of the ECHR, on which it is partly modelled, because it extends to all rights and obligations arising from the Treaty, i.e. including civil, criminal, and administrative matters.[133] The Charter did not have legally binding force though the Constitutional Treaty intended to give the Charter legal force but also included so-called horizontal clauses delimiting the scope of application of the Charter.[134] The Constitutional Treaty will not enter into force and the current draft Reform Treaty before the IGC suggests that a reference be made in the EU Treaty to the Charter and that a separate Declaration shall deal with its binding force.[135]

Notwithstanding potential limitations of applicability and of non-legally binding force, Article 47 reinforces the case law and doctrine of the ECJ discussed above in Chapter 2. Secondly, being based on both Articles 6(1) and 13 of the ECHR it explicitly provides the right to a remedy before a court, entailing that a non-judicial remedy would be inadequate.[136] Therefore, it might be held to create an enforceable individual right to an effective remedy before both national courts and Community courts.[137] Commentators have focused on how this will affect the standing of private litigants before the ECJ and similar questions.[138] However, it might also more subtly provide inspiration or a standard for judges to refer to and respect.[139] In the context of judicial cooperation in civil matters it might influence the balance

[133] Dougan (2004) p. 5.

[134] Arnull (2004) p. 99f., who notes that the horizontal clauses confirm that the Charter was not designed to convert the Union into a general human rights organization and that the effect of the Charter on the Member States is more limited than that of the general principle of fundamental rights recognized by the ECJ.

[135] Council Document 11218/07, p. 12f. The proposed draft Declaration gives the Charter legal binding force, but like the horizontal clauses notes that the Charter does not extend the field of application of EU law. Note also that a special Protocol to the Treaties is also envisaged to clarify the application of the Charter specifically for the United Kingdom.

[136] Arnull (2004) p. 109. See also CONV828/03, 9.7.2003, for the Explanations to the Charter updated by the Convention on the Future of Europe, p. 41f., at http://european-convention.eu.int/.

[137] Craig (2002) p. 209ff. on the enforceability of the provisions of the Charter as individual rights, which is left open in the Charter itself and will have to be clarified in future practice and case law. Rosas (2004) p. 371, notes that the case law of the ECJ already gives a directly enforceable individual right to access to court and that the incorporated Article in the Constitutional Treaty was probably intended to be directly applicable.

[138] Inter alia Arnull (2004) pp. 109–12.

[139] Both national judges and the ECJ, see inter alia Diez-Picazo (2002) p. 51, and Biavati (2002) pp. 213–15.

between due process rights and the claims of efficiency, which was evident in the *Krombach* judgment.[140] In this judgment the ECJ took an unprecedented step from a private international law perspective and transformed the public policy concept of inward-looking national values to a positive outward-looking common European value of procedural fairness.[141] Thereby the Court also took a substantive methodological step, a 'merger of values', in merging the economic interests of the Community with the human rights values of the Council of Europe.[142]

This emphasis on procedural rights can also be seen as part of the emerging 'judicial globalization' trend, i.e. that in order to form a global cooperative system judges are reluctant to question foreign substantive law but are rather moving towards a procedural threshold of due process.[143] The *Krombach* judgment and Article 47 not only are significant in terms of the ambit of the public policy exception in enforcement matters, but show that judicial cooperation measures and national practices will not be acceptable if certain fundamental rights are not upheld. This might also influence for example how the sanctions in the various judicial cooperation in civil matters regulations are analysed, e.g. the obligation to serve documents in a particular manner or within a particular time and the sanctions for not having done so.[144] These kinds of predictions as to the potential role fundamental human rights will play in the future in litigation between private parties with respect to cross-border civil litigation can be reinforced by the predictions in the field of substantive private law.[145] As has been observed in recent case law, derogations from the economic free movement freedoms of the Treaty, fundamental to the Community legal order, have been permitted and justified in the light of fundamental human rights.[146] Thus it is clear that

[140] Case C-7/98 *Dieter Krombach v. André Bamberski* [2000] ECR I-1935.

[141] Muir Watt (2001a) p. 539f.

[142] Ibid. pp. 544 and 549ff.

[143] Buxbaum (2004) pp. 82–4 elaborates upon this trend in the US context. Azoulay (2002) p. 117ff. provides a similar scenario from the sphere of Community administrative law. Particularly notable is the idea of balance between protection of procedural rights and efficiency.

[144] Mignolet (2003) p. 329ff. raises the issue that sanctions or reparations in questions of procedural irregularity under the regulations have to a large extent been left unregulated.

[145] Cherednychenko (2006) pp. 45–53 and 53–6.

[146] Cases C-112/00 *Eugen Schmidberger Internationale Transporte und Planzüge v. Republic of Austria* [2003] ECR I-5659 and C-36/02 *Omega Spielhallen- und Automatenaufstellungs GmbH v. Oberbürgermeisterin der Bundesstadt Bonn* [2004] ECR I-9609. See Morijn (2006) for an analysis of the cases and for an evaluation of what the Constitutional Treaty might have brought to this new and evolving case law, which balances Common Market freedoms with fundamental rights.

there is a potential for an alignment of EU private law with fundamental human rights requirements.[147]

Furthermore, the crucial issue is whether the right to an effective remedy and to a fair trial also influences the development of civil procedural regulation as a policy area. The draft declaration to the Reform Treaty clarifies that the Charter does not establish any new power or tasks for the EU or modify powers or tasks defined by the Treaties. Nevertheless, it is inevitable that the inclusion of the Charter in the potential future Treaty might influence the interpretation and nature of policy developments of the Union, albeit in a subtler way than establishing or modifying powers.[148] For example, in relation to judicial cooperation in civil matters, Member States or Community institutions that propose procedural reform could invoke the fundamental human rights clause as a legitimizing argument or as a higher standard which needs to be achieved. Particularly if the right to an effective remedy is linked to the proposed 'effective access to justice' in the legal basis, the fundamental right might become a powerful policy-legitimizing tool in the sphere of judicial cooperation. In addition, if the ECJ elaborates upon both of these and the Court develops the substantive criteria in a proactive direction this could lead to a qualitative and higher standard being developed for the policy area.[149] In contrast, in the interplay between fundamental rights and procedural regulation one can also identify an inverse influence, i.e. judicial cooperation in civil matters might despite its technical character itself contribute to bringing in fundamental notions of justice in the arena of cross-border litigation.[150]

[147] Cherednychenko (2006) p. 51ff.

[148] De Búrca (2003) p. 21. See also Rissanen (2004) p. 353.

[149] Craig (2002) p. 20 mentions without endorsing or refuting the argument that the ECJ should not adopt minimum but maximum standards for fundamental rights. In addition, at p. 213ff. he mentions that the relationship between Art. 41 of the Charter, the right to good administration, and Art. 230 of the Treaty, even in light of the limitation in Art. 52(2) of the Charter, could result in the ECJ using the fundamental right as a reason for broadening the scope of judicial review under Art. 230.

[150] Hartnell (2002) p. 92.

6

Service of Documents

Legislative History

On 26 May 1997 the Council adopted a Convention on the service in the Member States of the European Union of judicial and extrajudicial documents in civil or commercial matters. This Convention had been in progress since 1993 when the Council of Ministers for Justice set up a Working Party on Simplification of Document Transmission. After several drafts, questionnaires, and negotiations the final draft was adopted by the Council in 1997.[1] The legal basis for the Convention was Article K.2(3) of the Treaty on the European Union. However, the Convention was not yet ratified when the Treaty of Amsterdam entered into force. On 4 May 1999, three days after the Treaty of Amsterdam entered into force, the Commission proposed a Directive on the service in the Member States of judicial and extrajudicial documents in civil or commercial matters.

The proposal marked the first initiative of the Commission in the area of judicial cooperation in civil matters, brought within the Community framework by the Treaty of Amsterdam.[2] The specific legal basis for the new proposal was Article 61(c). The proposal clearly fell within the scope of judicial cooperation in civil matters since Article 65(a) specifically includes improving and simplifying the system for cross-border service of judicial and extrajudicial documents in the list of measures. The proposal was in substance based on the unratified Convention. The justification for the proposal was therefore more formalistic. Since the Convention had not yet been ratified, transposing it into a Community instrument would have the effect

[1] For a more detailed account of the steps leading up to the Convention, see COM (1999) 219, pp. 3–4.

[2] Ibid. pp. 4–5.

of ensuring its entry into force in the whole Community at the same date. Due to the obvious legal differences in the two types of instruments some technical legal changes were also made in the proposal which departed from the Convention.[3] The European Parliament suggested in its Report that the type of instrument should be changed to a regulation as these instruments allow for rapid and homogenous implementation of Community law and had already been chosen for the Communitarization of other conventions.[4] This recommendation was accepted and adopted by the Commission in its amended proposal.[5] After the amended proposal had been transmitted to the Council in March 2000, the 'Service Regulation' was adopted on 29 May 2000 and entered into force on 31 May 2001.[6]

The aim of the Service Convention was, according to the Commission, to create a mechanism that would better serve the needs of justice and reduce delays than previous ones had. In particular the Hague Convention of 1965 was no longer considered suitable for providing the speed required in a European judicial space that was becoming ever more consolidated.[7] The Convention aimed to balance two different procedural values. The first was to create a new system for transmission which would be flexible and prompt, utilizing modern techniques of communication, and the second was to continue to protect the interests of the addressee.[8] The aims of the Regulation are very similar to those of the Convention. However, with the inclusion of the Community dimension the political justifications and reasons broadened beyond procedural efficacy. The expedited transmission of documents is seen as a part of establishing the Area of Freedom, Security, and Justice. This is an area in which, according to the Commission, litigants should be able in practice to assert their rights, enjoying facilities equivalent to those available in the courts of their own country. This vision stems, according to

[3] Ibid. pp. 4, 6–7.

[4] A5 60/1999, p. 5.

[5] COM (2000) 75, p. 3. The term regulation is hereafter used in this section to denote the new proposed instrument, even though some of the references are to documents which were adopted prior to COM (2000) 75 and therefore in practice still use the term directive for the proposed instrument.

[6] Council Regulation (EC) No. 1348/2000 of 29 May 2000 on the service in the Member States of judicial and extrajudicial documents in civil or commercial matters, OJ L-160, 30.6.2000, p. 37.

[7] Paulino Pereira (2001b) p. 75. Note, however, that commentators who have a more global outlook on trans-frontier litigation consider that the Hague Convention of 1965 has been a success, see inter alia McClean (2002a) p. 55.

[8] Paulino Pereira (2001b) p. 75f.

the Commission, from the free movement of persons and is needed for the sound operation of the Internal Market.[9] The Economic and Social Committee adds that access to justice is a human right and that notwithstanding the marked differences in legal systems, the Member States must face up to civil society's growing demand for equity and justice and for comparable conditions of legal certainty and protection.[10] The European Parliament considers the proposed instrument to be a highly desirable advance since Community legislation is often criticized on grounds of legal certainty for resembling international conventions. However, the Parliament considers that transposing the Convention into a Community instrument must be seen as only a first step.[11]

Finally, as regards the aims of the Regulation, it is pertinent to note the specific vital procedural position of service. This explains why the Regulation serves an important need and why its aims, both the micro-level aim of ameliorating service between Member States and the macro-level aim of being the first Regulation in the establishment of a European judicial space, have broader implications. In any cross-border dispute issues of initially establishing jurisdiction and finally enforcing a judgment are difficult, sensitive, and important to the resolution of a dispute and the realization of the rights of the individual parties. This is underlined by the fact that due service on a cross-border defendant in sufficient time is often a requisite for a court to establish jurisdiction or to recognize a judgment for enforcement.[12] However, service, including transmission and notification, can be considered to form a technically complex procedure, both in practice and as a matter of law.[13] Additionally one should bear in mind the significant structural and legal differences between Member States' procedural rules regarding service, in particular the divide between highly formal and more liberal approaches.[14] Furthermore, one should bear in mind that this complexity

[9] COM (1999) 219, p. 5.

[10] ESC 947/1999, pp. 1–2, 4.

[11] A5 60/1999, p. 19.

[12] For example Art. 27 of the Brussels Convention requires refusal of recognition and enforcement of a judgment if a defendant in default of appearance had not been duly served, and the current Brussels I Regulation (EC 44/2000), Art. 43(2), includes the same requirement. See inter alia Kaye (1998) p. 159ff., who elaborates on why international transmission matters, in particular explaining the importance of the requirement of due service for jurisdiction and enforcement. See also Kennett (2000) pp. 184–90.

[13] Bambust (2003) p. 241.

[14] Kennett (2000) pp. 174–84 (for an exposé of the different approaches in national law of the Member States) and p. 196.

can not only easily lead to technical errors but also be exploited by parties to frustrate litigation.[15] Hence, there is a real need for help and cooperation between Member States in relation to the transmission of documents.

The indispensable nature of cooperation in cross-border service is underlined by the fact that it is the oldest form of international judicial cooperation and by the fact that in statistical terms this form of cooperation is voluminous.[16] However any envisaged system of cross-border cooperation in relation to the service of documents has to find a balance between the principle of national sovereignty, the need for speed, and the rights of the defence.[17] Thus, there are several possibilities, and the one which is traditionally seen as most efficient is also the one which encroaches most upon national sovereignty, i.e. a method of direct channels of transmission.[18] Notwithstanding efficiency, the challenge in a European context is to fulfil the positive obligations of a fair trial which influence inter alia the methods of service adopted, the language issues, the cost of service, and the time between service and hearing.[19] As we shall see below and also with regard to the Evidence Regulation and the Enforcement Order Regulation, even within the EU the principle of national sovereignty can still play a role, e.g. in the minimum standards approach to mutual regulation of procedural matters. However, at the forefront of the debate on these measures is very clearly the difficult balance between the virtue of efficiency and the fundamental rights of the defence.

Substantive Content

In the practical transmission of documents the Regulation introduces several innovations. First, the aim is to establish more direct, decentralized,

[15] Ibid. p. 173f.

[16] Schlosser (2000), p. 89. McClean (2002a) pp. 15–23 provides an overview of the different forms of international procedures of service and a historic overview of international cooperation in the first half of the 20th century.

[17] Bambust (2003) p. 241 notes that the sovereignty of states creates two separate issues vis-à-vis cross-border service: on the one hand a conflict between laws and on the other hand a conflict between authorities. Respect for each other's sovereignty has in practice traditionally caused the process to become very protracted.

[18] Ekelmans (2001) p. 482.

[19] Fricero (2002) elaborates upon the human rights aspects, in particular those stemming from Art. 6 of the European Convention on Human Rights, with regard to service of documents.

channels for transmission. Thus, Article 2 establishes the principle of direct transmission between authorities, so-called 'transmitting' and 'receiving' agencies, which the Member States have designated. This innovation differs from the Hague Convention of 1965 and several bilateral conventions, which often add centralized bodies and further stages to the procedure.[20] However, the Regulation also envisages that the Member States will nominate a central authority to facilitate the process by helping to solve any transmission difficulties and in exceptional circumstances forwarding documents for transmission.[21] Secondly, the transmission of acts between the agencies is allowed by appropriate means. There is no list of means by which transmission can take place, and it is hoped that leaving the decision on this to the agencies will facilitate speed as they can make their choice taking into account the procedures under domestic law, the circumstances of the case, and the type of link-up that can be established with the foreign counterpart agency.[22] Naturally it is expected that all modern forms of transmission, including e-mail, will be utilized in the future.[23]

Furthermore, the Commission publishes and updates information on such matters as the transmitting agencies, the central authorities, and the languages and methods of transmission that are accepted by each Member State for use between the agencies.[24] The Commission also publishes and

[20] COM (1999) 219, p. 10. In practice the Service Regulation has not in all instances established completely decentralized models in the Member States. Most notably Sweden, England, and Wales have adopted a half-way house between centralization and decentralization. Kennett (2000) p. 203 notes that England and Wales have disputed the assumption that decentralization will necessarily be more efficient. The diversity in different types of agencies established for receiving and transmitting has also been criticized for not bringing the system closer to the citizens, see Spinelli (2002) p. 87ff.

[21] Art. 3. Kaye (1998) p. 168 gives examples of such exceptional circumstances: (1) where, despite repeated requests and after a reasonable time, the decentralized agency has not responded, (2) where there are force majeure situations such as strikes and natural catastrophes. Bambust (2003) pp. 247–57 provides a general overview of the new role of the central bodies and pp. 258–69 offer some observations about the initial work of these entities.

[22] COM (1999) 219, p. 13.

[23] Paulino Pereira (2001b) p. 77.

[24] This information also includes how the provisions on the date of service, diplomatic service, postal service, direct service, and judgment in default are applied in each Member State. The first Communication of this information took place in OJ C-151, 22.5.2001, p. 4 (corrigenda in OJ C-65, 19.3.2003). The subsequent updates have been published in: (1) OJ C-202, 18.7.2001, p. 10; (2) OJ C-282, 6.10.2001, p. 2; (3) OJ C-13, 17.1.2002, p. 2; (4) OJ C-136, 11.6.2003, p. 11; and (5) OJ C-37, 11.2.1004, p. 12. This information has now been consolidated into a Communication, which is updated regularly on the Commission website: http://www.europa.eu.int/comm/justice_home/judicialatlascivil/html/docservdocs_en.htm.

updates a separate manual containing information about the receiving agencies and a glossary of documents that may be served under the Regulation.[25] This information is a practical means which is intended to ease the task of both the practitioners and the relevant officials involved.[26] In addition the transmission of documents is assisted in a practical manner by a number of standard forms which must be used in effecting service between the agencies. These include inter alia a form for the Request for Service, a form for Acknowledgement of Receipt, and a form for Certificate of Service or Non-service of Documents.[27]

The forms are available in all official languages on 'European Judicial Atlas in Civil Matters', an Internet database and help site created and updated by the Commission.[28] The language of the forms used in a particular factual scenario is not specifically regulated. However, the language in which the forms are to be completed is in part regulated.[29] Thus, the Request form should be completed in the language of the requested state, either its official language(s) or any other language that it has additionally notified as acceptable. Thus, if the form is filled in by the transmitting agency itself it might have to arrange for a translation of a few brief points in the form. Similarly, when the receiving agency is sending back to the transmitting agency a Certificate of Service it should complete the form in the language of the transmitting agency. Again, the authority might thus have to have some points translated.[30]

Thirdly, the requirements regarding the form of the documents to be served are less stringent than according to several of the multilateral and bilateral conventions. There is no requirement that the documents be legalized in any manner.[31] In addition the documents do not have to be translated

[25] The first manual and glossary was published as Commission Decision 2001/781, OJ L-298, 15.11.2001, p.1 and updated by Commission Decision 2002/350, OJ L-125, 13.5.2002, p.1. The manual and glossary are now regularly updated on the Commission website: http://www.europa.eu.int/comm/justice_home/judicialatlascivil/html/docservdocs_en.htm.

[26] COM (1999) 219, pp. 6 and 13.

[27] The Forms are annexed to the Regulation, OJ L-160, 30.6.2000, pp. 44–52 and are also available on the Commission website: http://www.europa.eu.int/comm/justice_home/judicialatlascivil/html/.

[28] http://www.europa.eu.int/comm/justice_home/judicialatlascivil/html/.

[29] Kerameus (2002) p. 113f. makes the point that the Regulation marks a departure from the Hague Service Convention in that it is more flexible and open to the multilingual reality in the EU, i.e. introducing a more diverse principle and procedure for the language issue.

[30] Ekelmans (2001) p. 485.

[31] COM (1999) 219, p. 14.

if the addressee understands the language of the document.[32] However, if the documents are not translated, the applicant is to be advised by the transmitting agency that the addressee may refuse if he or she does not understand the language or the language is not one of the official languages of his Member State.[33] Similarly, to protect the interests of the addressee, when service is effected upon him or her, the receiving agency is obliged to provide information of the possibility to refuse to accept service on grounds of the language of the document.[34]

Fourthly, in order for the transmission and subsequent service to be prompt, the Regulation includes certain 'deadlines' or suggested time periods which the authorities should try to follow. The first of these is that the receiving agency should send the transmitting agency an acknowledgement of receipt form as soon as they have received documents, if possible within seven days. If the receipt fails to arrive within a reasonable time after the expiry of the seven days, the transmitting agency should resend the documents in order to not waste any time if the documents have gone astray.[35] The second time period is that the receiving agency should try to effect service within one month in accordance with the rules laid down in that Member State. After service has been effected, the receiving agency should send a certificate of service to the transmitting agency.[36] The manner in which service is effected is notably not dealt with in the Regulation. Article 7 only mentions that the receiving agency shall serve the document or have it served, either in accordance with the law of its own Member State, or in a particular manner requested by the transmitting Member State unless that method is incompatible with its own law. Thus, there is basic subjection to the national law of the Member State carrying out service as to the method and execution of service.[37]

[32] The Regulation thus does not oblige the applicant to translate the document into one of the official languages of the receiving Member State. Conversely, however, the Regulation gives the addressee the right to refuse the document if it has not been translated into a language he does understand. If a dispute arises as to whether or not the addressee understands the language the question can be raised in the court seized of the procedure in connection with which the document was transmitted. See Arts 5 and 8 of the Regulation and COM (1999) 219, pp. 14, 15, and 17.

[33] Art. 5.

[34] Art. 8.

[35] Art. 6 and COM (1999) 219, p. 15.

[36] Arts 7 and 10.

[37] Kaye (1998) p. 170f.

Fifthly, the Regulation introduces several subsidiary methods of service in certain prescribed circumstances. The first of these is the traditional method of transmission not through the agencies but through consular or diplomatic channels. This method has been considered extremely time consuming, therefore the Regulation limits its use to 'exceptional circumstances'.[38] In contrast, the Regulation also provides for a more speedy subsidiary method using diplomatic or consular agents, namely service of documents directly though these channels. However, the Member States are allowed to derogate from this Article and oppose such service unless it concerns a national of the Member State in which the documents originated.[39] Further subsidiary means of service which are intended to simplify the system of service abroad are service by post and direct service. Service by post entails that each Member State shall be free to effect service by post to persons residing in another Member State.[40] It is notable that the Member States cannot derogate from this Article completely, in contrast to the Hague Service Convention.[41] However, the Member States may specify the conditions under which such service is effective in their systems.[42] This introduction of a slight amount of formalism into the liberal form of service is due to the fact that legal certainty and protection of the addressee are values which entail that some supervision of the process is needed.[43]

The Member States may also authorize direct service, i.e. the parties are allowed to make direct contact with the relevant authorities in the receiving state and request service, without the transmitting agency as a go-between.[44] The main discrepancies for the parties and perhaps even for lay litigants vis-à-vis using these latter two subsidiary means of service are the language

[38] Art. 12. Kaye (1998) p. 173, and Kennett (1998) p. 290, note that 'exceptional circumstances' are considered to be the same sort of force majeure scenarios envisaged also in Art. 3(c).

[39] Art. 13.

[40] Art. 14(1).

[41] Kennett (1998) p. 290.

[42] Art. 14(2).

[43] Schlosser (2000) p. 91, and dealing in particular with the EU Service Convention (forerunner to the Regulation) at p. 112f. He criticizes the vagueness of the formal requirements of service by post and suggests both a uniform requirement of using registered mail and certain requirements regarding the envelope and the documents themselves.

[44] Art. 15. This is the way that I read the Article and the way that it has been explained by the commentators, Kaye (1998) p. 173, Kennett (1998) p. 291, and Johansson (2002) p. 162. However, note also that the Mainstrat 'Study on the Application of Council Regulation (EC) No. 1348/2000 on the Service of Judicial and Extra Judicial Documents in Civil and Commercial Matters' (2000) has a different interpretation of the Article and the concept of direct service, pp. 65–8.

question, i.e. in which language to approach the agency, and whether there are any derogations. Thus there are some lacunae and complexities in these methods despite their ostensible simplification.[45]

A clarificatory ruling has been rendered by the ECJ concerning these alternative means of transmission (which are grouped in Chapter II of the Regulation under the heading 'Other means of transmission and service of documents') and their relationship with the principal method of service elaborated by the Regulation. In the case C-473/04 *Plumex v. Young Sports N.V.*[46] the *Hof van Cassatie van België* made a preliminary referral to the ECJ asking (a) whether the principal method of service takes precedence over a secondary method of service, being postal service in the relevant case, when both are legally effected and (b) how this affects the calculation of the commencement of a procedural time limit.

The opinion of Advocate General Tizzano was that a literal and teleological interpretation of the Regulation provided no hierarchy between the different methods of service, which also follows from the objectives of the Regulation to simplify and accelerate service.[47] With regard to which date of service is relevant where there are multiple attempts to serve, the Advocate General refers to Case C-443/2003 *Götz Leffler v. Berlin Chemie AG*,[48] regarding the need for uniform application and autonomous interpretation of the Regulation. Therefore, to ensure the clear and homogenous application and in light of the objectives of speed and simplification the date of service should be that of the first service effected.[49] The Court's judgment is helpfully straightforward and confirms the verdict of the Advocate General that there is no hierarchy between the various methods of service elaborated in Chapter II of the Regulation.[50] Consequently, all legal effects which follow from service must be calculated from the first validly effected service.[51] The Court relies on a literal interpretation of the Regulation and on its purpose and spirit, which is the intention to expedite service while respecting the legitimate interests of the parties.[52]

[45] Vanheukelen (2003) pp. 220f. and 223f.
[46] ECR [2006] I-1417.
[47] Ibid. Opinion paras 22–25.
[48] [2005] ECR I-9611.
[49] ECR [2006] I-141, Opinion paras 32–40.
[50] Ibid. judgment para. 22.
[51] Ibid. para. 29.
[52] Ibid. paras 20–1, 30–2.

Finally, an important feature is the rules on date of service, which was one of the questions debated between the Member States during the negotiations for the Convention.[53] The Commission also notes that the question is one in which there are differences between the Member States' systems.[54] Therefore the result is a compromise between two elements. In principle, the date of service is the date on which the document is served in accordance with the law of the Member State in which service is effected. However, if there is a national time limitation running in the Member State of origin, the applicant's right to legal certainty is protected and a cumulative date of service is that when the document is deemed served according to the Member State of origin.[55] The provisions for judgment in default are not innovative, but follow the system of other conventions. The proceedings should be stayed until the judge is sure that the document has been served and the defendant has had enough time to prepare a defence. Even when judgment in default has been entered, relief can be applied under certain conditions. In relation to judgment in default, the provisions allow the Member States some room to derogate or set conditions.[56]

Normative Implications

The Regulation specifically replaces the existing mechanisms for transmission of documents between Member States, i.e. the Protocol to the Brussels Convention of 27 September 1968 on Jurisdiction and the Enforcement of Judgments in Civil and Commercial matters and the Hague Convention of 15 November 1965 on the Service Abroad of Judicial and Extrajudicial Documents.[57] However, the Member States are empowered individually or acting in concert to expedite the transmission of documents. Also the Member States are allowed to maintain or adopt provisions which expedite transmission

[53] Paulino Pereira (2001, 2) p. 78.
[54] COM (1999) 219, p. 18f.
[55] Art. 9.
[56] Art. 19.
[57] Douchy (2002) pp. 55–66 analyses the conflict between conventions or legal orders (international and Community ones) that was introduced by the Service Regulation. However, the author does not dispute the primacy of EU law and notes that this political choice of legal order was made when the Treaty of Amsterdam was signed and Title IV EC and Art. 65 were introduced.

provided they are compatible with the Regulation. Such provisions must be notified to the Commission.[58]

Initial Conclusions on the Impact and Effect of the Regulation

Regarding the impact and effect of the Regulation, the European Parliament stressed in its opinion prior to the adoption of the Regulation that it is a first step in simplifying and harmonizing document service across the Community. Nonetheless, there is a clear shift from prior methods of inter-state cooperation between the EU Member States to methods which are closer to the national procedural systems and to more direct forms of cooperation, which underlines that the limits of national sovereignty do not 'menace' judicial cooperation in civil matters.[59] Thus, the initial evaluation of the Regulation must be that even as a first step it offers a substantial simplification in the procedure. Particularly for the applicant party who is attempting to serve documents in another Member State, the fact that there is no legalization requirement and the fact that the documents do not necessarily have to be translated are major developments. Furthermore, the fact that there are specific forms to use, which are translated into all official languages, greatly eases the burden and workload of both the practitioners and the transmitting authorities. Also the fact that a more individualistic approach is taken to the language question, supporting the reality of linguistic plurality in the EU, can be considered as developing 'justice with a human face'.[60]

Notwithstanding these improvements, it is questionable whether all potential users of the system have yet reaped its benefits. One practical, albeit legal technical, question that is of immediate concern is the sphere of application of the Regulation, since it states in Article 1 only that it shall apply in civil and commercial matters. Even though the parameters of this concept have been established in the case law of the ECJ in relation to the Brussels Convention, since that Convention and the Brussels I Regulation have specific additional exclusions, the question arises for example whether the Service Regulation can be resorted to in arbitration matters.[61] And even this initial but crucial question of scope can *in casu* give rise to difficult subsidiary questions regarding which entity has the interpretative discretion and competence over the question, the transmitting or receiving agency.

[58] Art. 20.

[59] Hess (2003) pp. 217 and 220f.

[60] Kerameus (2002) p. 118.

[61] Vanheukelen (2003) p. 198ff.

Furthermore, what are the sanctions or remedies if there has been a fault in interpretation, and how does such a discrepancy affect prescription and other time limits of the claim at issue? Thus, the fairly vague nature of the scope of the Regulation can challenge and in practice mitigate its attempts to achieve procedural economy and legal certainty.[62]

Even in cases where the question of scope is straightforward, there are questions in relation to practical expediency. It is not always clear that the procedures have been easily accessible to the parties and practitioners. They might not have had enough information about the system, and the authorities with whom they have dealt might not have been fully informed or organized. Furthermore, it is not clear that procedures have been rapid. There is no mechanism in the Regulation which guarantees that the authorities adhere to the seven-day deadline to acknowledge receipt or the one-month time limit for effecting service. In addition, there is no control over how long it takes for the transmitting agency to initially deal with the request and transmit it to the receiving authority. Similarly, there is no control over how soon after effected service the receiving authority shall inform the transmitting authority and the transmitting authority convey that same information to the applicant party or the court which has stayed its proceedings pending effected service. Therefore, in reality the procedure still has several stages in which delay can arise.

The efficiency of the system in any given case is also very much dependent on the efficacy of both of the designated national authorities involved.[63] The efficiency of each designated national authority is in turn dependent on resources, which for the courts and legal services vary greatly across the Member States.[64] Furthermore, the efficiency of the designated agencies in dealing with international litigation matters in each Member State will depend on their prior arrangements and level of experience. Naturally systems which have previously already been decentralized will adapt more easily, whereas systems which have been centralized will not necessarily adapt

[62] Ibid. p. 199. This is so even though most commentators consider that the specific exclusions of the Brussels I Regulation do not apply to the Service Regulation: inter alia Lebois (2003) p. 280 and Ekelmans (2001) p. 483 as well as Lebeau and Niboyet (2003) p. 223.

[63] Castellain (2002) pp. 78–81 notes that there is a difference between transmission, e.g. the contact between the designated agencies, and service, e.g. the actual serving of the document on the party in question. The author apparently questions whether speed and efficiency will be achieved between agencies by the Regulation rule of 'any appropriate means'. The author thus is one of the commentators to support a system of professional agents and suggests that a secure system of electronic document transmission be established between these.

[64] Girard-Thuilier (2001) p. 62.

as quickly. Additionally, some legal systems and agencies will have more experience in dealing with the problems of international procedural assistance than others.[65] Additionally, the simplifications achieved might still be hampered by linguistic problems between the Member States.[66]

Apart from the efficiency of the system, there are also some lacunae in the Regulation. One such discrepancy in the Regulation, which can be held to introduce an unnecessary element of legal uncertainty, is the vague terms of the requirements for when postal service is accepted.[67] However, the most glaring lacuna which ties in several issues crucial to cross-border litigation is the issue of translation of documents and the possibility for the addressee to refuse service on grounds of the language of the documents.[68] The Regulation provides an option to not translate the documents where the addressee understands the language of the Member State of transmission. The most obvious scenario is that he/she is a national of that Member State but residing in another Member State. However, another scenario is that of a commercial transaction conducted in a language mutual to the parties but not necessarily an official language in the Member State of the addressee.[69]

The first problem which arises is that of proof of whether the addressee understands the language or not.[70] The Regulation does not deal with this, but the Commission suggests that it therefore is for the court seized of the procedure in connection with which the documents were served to decide according to its national procedural rules.[71] However, even if the court seized finds that the language was correct, the court of enforcement, perhaps in the Member State of the addressee, might take a different view at the enforcement stage and is not bound by the seized court's finding when

[65] Kennett (1998) p. 295f.

[66] Hess (2003) p. 224f.

[67] Schlosser (2000) p. 112f.

[68] Hess (2003) p. 230, who calls not for clarifying case law from the ECJ but for legislative reform. Vanheukelen (2003) p. 208f. notes that, in comparison to the Hague Service Convention of 1965, the translation provisions of the Service Regulation better provide for the rights of the defence. Nevertheless, the question arises whether not just formal documentary requirements such as translation are necessary but also practical substantive advice to the defendant of the implications of service.

[69] Kennett (1998) p. 302.

[70] Vanheukelen (2003) p. 209f. naturally notes that for the parties this entails a factual burden of proof, which can itself be complex since the comprehension of a foreign language is a relative notion and can be difficult to prove in practice.

[71] COM (1999) 219, p. 17. See also Kennett (1998) p. 303.

checking whether due service has taken place for enforcement purposes.[72] Other problems which arise are whether the addressee should have a certain time, e.g. a couple of days, to decide if he accepts service or not, whether it is possible to cure the defect of non-translation and what the consequences of unjustified refusal are.[73] Interestingly and as predicted by the commentators, cases do arise in relation to the issue of translation.[74] In a pending referral to the ECJ from the *Bundesgerichtshof* for a preliminary ruling, C-14/07 *Michael Weiss v. Industrie und Handelskammer Berlin, intervener Nicholas Grimshaw & Partners*, the questions relate amongst other matters to the right to refuse if the annexes to a document are not translated and whether a party can be deemed to 'understand' the language if the language has been agreed upon in the contract as the language of communication.[75]

Judgment has also been rendered in the first case lodged with the Court regarding the Regulation, a preliminary referral, C-443/2003 *Götz Leffler v. Berlin Chemie AG* made by the *Hoge Raad der Nederlanden*.[76] This case does not concern all the aforementioned questions but does clearly highlight a couple of these. In essence the *Hoge Raad* asks whether it is possible to rectify non-translation when the defendant has refused to accept service under Article 8 of the Regulation, and whether the national procedural law applies to such rectification. Furthermore, the *Hoge Raad* is concerned with the effects of the 'faulty' service, whether it renders service inoperative in its entirety. Advocate General Stix-Hackl found first, with regard to the consequences and legal effect of 'faulty' service, e.g. with regard to the language of documents, that it would not be efficient to refer to the national procedural rules because the Regulation is intended to form an independent tool in order to achieve effective mutual treatment of litigants in the Area of Freedom, Security, and Justice.[77] Therefore, the consequences must derive from the Regulation. Conducting an evaluation and balancing the interests of both

[72] Kennett (1998) p. 304 and Kaye (1998) p. 163 referring to Case 228/81 [1982] ECR, p. 2723. See also Schlosser (2000) p. 104ff., who accounts for the same problem in a more international context and relates cases from the USA and Japan.

[73] Vanheukelen (2003) p. 214ff. notes that Austria is the only Member State to have promulgated national rules for these questions. Thus, the principle of legal certainty necessitates mutual deadlines and sanctions for non-translation and rectification.

[74] Schlosser (2000) p. 102 and Kennett (2000) p. 208ff.

[75] *Ingenieurbüro Michael Weiss und Partner GbR v. Industrie und Handelskammer Berlin, intervener Nicholas Grimshaw & Partners Limited*, pending referral reported OJ C-56, 10.3.2007, p. 22.

[76] [2005] ECR I-9611.

[77] Opinion paras 61–5.

litigants do not permit the conclusion that service has been entirely ineffectual as a result of faulty service. Rather the Advocate General suggests that the best solution would be for faulty service to entail a stay of proceedings until proper service has been effected.[78] The procedure by which to rectify faulty service, Advocate General Stix-Hackl argues, does not require a referral to the national rules of *lex fori*. Instead, and logically, in order to ensure legal certainty and equal treatment of litigants, the normal course of service in accordance with Articles 7–9 of the Regulation should once more come into play, in a sense simply leading to procedure under the Regulation being recommenced.[79]

The Opinion of the Advocate General was well argued, but the expectation was that the Court would perhaps be more careful, i.e. defer to national procedural rules. Indeed the Court has in its judgment in Grand Chamber to tread a very delicate line with regard to national procedural autonomy. On the first question, the potential nullity and rectification of faulty service due to non-translation, the Court notes that even though this is not specifically elaborated in the Regulation its provisions clearly envisage or justify precluding nullity and accepting the possibility of remedying lack of translation.[80] The Court also notes that the objective of creating an Area of Freedom, Security, and Justice, giving the Community a new dimension and legal competence for judicial cooperation in civil matters, testifies to the intention of the Member States to place these measures within the Community legal order. Therefore, the measures are to be interpreted autonomously and national law cannot prevail since it would prevent uniform application.[81] Hence, Article 8(1) must be constructed as giving an opportunity to rectify service by sending a requested translation.

To the more detailed question regarding procedure to rectify and date of service the Court answers that even though the Regulation is silent, general principles of Community law and other provisions of the Regulation can provide some guidance. Therefore, for purposes of legal certainty non-translation must be remedied in accordance with the normal procedure under the Regulation.[82] Furthermore, as regards the consequences, the dual date system established in Article 9 of the Regulation ensures that both

[78] Ibid. paras 67–86 and 103(1).

[79] Ibid. paras 98–102 and 103(2).

[80] Ibid. judgment paras 37–41. The Court specifically refers to recitals 2, 6, and 9 as well as to Arts 5 and 8.

[81] Ibid. paras 44–5.

[82] Ibid. paras 62–4.

parties are given equal protection. Thus, the applicant can benefit from the initial date of service whereas the defendant can be deemed served only when the translated version has been served.[83]

Thus far the Court can be seen as supporting the Advocate General's solution and not providing space for national procedures to apply. However, the Court is more nuanced and realizes that, other than the guidance and uniform interpretation it has given with regard to remedying non-translation, national courts and national procedure will also play a role in these situations.[84] Therefore, the Court repeats its well-established principles of non-discrimination and effectiveness vis-à-vis national procedural rules, specifically noting that the national court must safeguard both parties' rights. The Court goes on to elaborate that within the context of domestic procedure and the national court's discretion, the party who has been served must be given adequate time to prepare his defence but that the party effecting service must be protected against refusals to accept documents which constitute an abuse of process, e.g. where it is apparent that the addressee understand the language in which the documents are served.[85] In addition, the Court specifically elaborates that a time limit for remedying service and providing translation of the documents might be imposed by a national court and that the suggestion of a one-month time limit by some governments might be appropriate but this must be determined by the national court in light of the specific circumstances in the case.[86] In sum, the case has highlighted explicit lacunae in the Regulation but the Court managed to give several substantive clarifications and successfully clarified the relationship with national procedural discretion. The content of this first judgment of the Court with regard to the Service Regulation, and indeed the first regarding any of the measures of judicial cooperation in civil matters, can be applauded.

In conclusion, the evaluation of the legal framework provides evidence, despite the unifying judgment C-443/2003 *Götz Leffler v. Berlin Chemie AG*, of differences in the efficacy of the Member States' legal services that will entail that the harmonizing effects of the Regulation remain patchy. Therefore, there is a clear risk that the goal of the Commission, that litigants should be able to assert their rights, enjoying facilities equivalent to

[83] Ibid. paras 65–7.
[84] Ibid. paras 49–51 and 69.
[85] Ibid. para. 52
[86] Ibid. para. 64.

those enjoyed in the courts of their own country, is far from achieved. Similarly, the system therefore falls short of fulfilling the aim propounded by the Economic and Social Committee, the aim of confronting civil society's growing demand for equity and justice and for comparable conditions of legal certainty and protection.

The differences in efficacy are not the only features of the system which act against harmonization. In addition, the fact that service itself is still effected according to the national systems adds an element of diversity and complexity to the system. The fact that each national procedure in essence remains unharmonized is also shown by the dualism in Article 9 on date of service. One commentator even states that the multiplicity and derogations in particular in relation to date of service significantly reduce the whole point of the Regulation.[87] Thus, the Regulation still contains evidence of the different choices made by Member States in protecting parties and also of their wariness in accepting unified rules.[88]

Another issue is the latent complexity in the system, which still allows for alternative channels of service, e.g. consular and diplomatic channels, albeit that these are supposed to be the exception.[89] The number of potential derogations and transitional periods, as well as the minimum characteristics of the rules on service, bear the hallmarks of and are a legacy of the Convention as originally envisaged, and this as an intergovernmental measure was much more cautious. Thus, the Regulation has been criticized for similarly maintaining these characteristics and maintaining diversity.[90] Finally, the lacuna in the Regulation regarding open questions in relation to the provisions on translation of documents also shows a potential in the Regulation for complexity and divergent national application, at least until clarifying case law from the ECJ develops.

[87] Douchy (2002) pp. 68–72, who notes that it is unfortunate that the dual date system does not attach certain consequences, such as time limits, to either of the dates, thereby leaving the parties to the mercies of different systems.

[88] Ibid. p. 71f. Spinelli (2002) p. 85ff. notes that we are still continuing to debate how best to serve documents across borders because no convention or regulation has yet put in place a complete operational model for the matter.

[89] A5 60/1999, p. 17. Hess (2003) p. 229 also makes the point that the subsidiary methods of service, including the opportunities for the Member States to derogate or make reservations to these, raise questions about the uniformity of the regime put into place.

[90] Ekelmans (2001) p. 488.

The Study on the Application of the Service Regulation and the Commission Report

These initial conclusions regarding an evaluation of the impact of the Regulation are to a large extent echoed in the 'Study on the Application of Council Regulation (EC) No. 1348/2000 on the Service of Judicial and Extra Judicial Documents in Civil and Commercial Matters' (hereinafter the 'Study').[91] This Study was commissioned by the Commission from an outside entity, the company MainStrat, in order to obtain an empirical analysis of the application of the Regulation. The Study only covers the 14 States (excluding Denmark) that were Member States of the EU prior to 1 May 2004. The Study is primarily an empirical analysis of the functioning of some of the elements of the Regulation. However, the authors also draw conclusions from the data obtained, give opinions, and present proposals for reform. It is naturally however most relevant in the present context to see what conclusions the Commission will draw from the empirical data and what reform proposals it may present.

The Study states that the Regulation is an important tool in achieving a European judicial space and that it has had a positive impact. However, the Study acknowledges that the results also show that there is room for improvement in the technical and practical application among Member State agencies and other parties involved in applying the Regulation.[92] The Study also states that the task in itself, to reflect the opinion of the professionals involved in the system of transmission, turned out to be quite complex because the members of the diverse professions involved, e.g. judges, legal practitioners, bailiffs, and public administrators, had widely varying functions and interests.[93]

The Study first deals with speed of transmission and concludes that there has generally been an improvement, even though most respondents thought that the level of improvement varied between Member States.[94] Furthermore, as regards speed, the Study points out that notwithstanding the 'deadlines' for the receiving agency to report back to the transmitting agency, i.e. regarding receipt of documents, the inability to effect service within one

[91] The Study can be found on the Commission website: http://www.europa.eu.int/comm./justice_home/doc_centre/civil/studies/doc/study_ec1348_2000_en.pdf.

[92] The Study, p. 6f.

[93] Ibid. p. 12.

[94] Ibid. pp. 23 and 78.

month, and a certificate of service, these are often sent back with considerable delay. Thus, the transmitting agencies are at the mercy of the efficiency of the receiving agencies.[95] In addition, even if publication of the names and details about the agencies involved has contributed to the increased speed, the fact that there is a diversity among the Member States agencies vis-à-vis the type of body involved and the number of bodies comprises an element of complication and difficulty in practical application.[96]

In practice it is still, for example, difficult for the agencies involved to find the correct contact information, and also they may not yet have precise knowledge about and familiarity with the mechanisms of the Regulation; furthermore there are real language barriers which can slow down communication between agencies.[97] In practice, the standard forms may not have reached their full potential to simplify proceedings, since the Study shows that sometimes the forms are not used at all or are incompletely utilized, or the language requirements are not followed – with ensuing difficulties in communication and cooperation between agencies.[98]

The Study further deals with areas of the Regulation which are potentially complex in application. The first concerns the obligation to inform the addressee of his or her right to refuse to accept service of a document due to non-translation. The Study illuminates many of the legal uncertainties surrounding this issue, as highlighted above.[99] Interestingly, the Study also reveals that more than half of the respondents had made use of the possibility to serve in a language other than the official language of the receiving Member State,[100] and the narrative comments also show that the respondents are well aware that refusal to accept can be a procedural tactic and that this has the potential to paralyse the transmission and service procedure.[101] Another issue which has perhaps unexpectedly been identified as a complexity is that of cost of service.[102] The Regulation clearly states that services rendered by the authorities in the receiving Member State shall be free of charge, and that payment by the applicant shall only be asked for if private entities are

[95] Ibid. pp. 23f. and 79–83.
[96] Ibid. p. 23.
[97] Ibid. pp. 25–30 and 84–9.
[98] Ibid. pp. 39 and 93–8.
[99] Ibid. p. 41ff.
[100] Ibid. p. 100.
[101] Ibid. pp. 101–8.
[102] Kennett (2000) pp. 200 and 210 did however note that the issue of costs had already arisen under the Hague Convention and was likely to arise again under the Service Regulation.

entrusted with service in the receiving Member State, as is traditional in some Member States.[103] However, the system has been described as 'neither transparent nor equal', there is no clarity as to what the costs comprise and what the costs are in different Member States. In contrast, the private entities that charge for service experience problems in extracting payment.[104]

Finally, as regards methods of service, the Study deals with two of the subsidiary methods, postal service and direct service. Both methods are, according to the empirical data, employed by the agencies and professionals involved. However, it seems that postal service is much more common than direct service.[105] The main criticism in the Study of these methods is the lack of legal certainty they introduce. As regards service by post the Study identifies uncertainty as to whether or not delivery has been effected as the main problem in practice, e.g. due to the fact that no acknowledgement of receipt is returned or that it is not filled in completely.[106] As regards direct service the main problems in practice are uncertainty as to the exact meaning of the provision and unfamiliarity with the practical means for operating the provision.[107]

The Study and in particular its empirical analysis were contracted out by the Commission in order to serve as one source of information for the Commission Report, which the Commission was obliged to make under Article 24 of the Regulation following up on the application of the Regulation.[108] Apart from the Study, the Commission gained information from a meeting of the European Judicial Network, a public hearing, and a meeting of the Advisory Committee on Service of Documents. The Commission Report was published in October 2004 and is succinct, but does not yet make any clear suggestions for reform.

One of the conclusions to be drawn from the Commission Report is that on a few crucial problematic questions, e.g. costs of service and date of service, the Member States have very divergent and strong views based on their particular, and different, national systems. The Commission is not at this stage

[103] Art. 11.

[104] The Study, pp. 53–8 and 112–18, the words quoted can be found on p. 117.

[105] Ibid. pp. 118f. and 124f.

[106] Ibid. pp. 63f. and 120–4.

[107] Ibid. pp. 66ff. and 126ff.

[108] Strictly the Article obliges the Commission to present its Report no later than June 2004 and every five years thereafter to present a report on the application of the Regulation. The Commission did not quite reach the first deadline. Its Report, COM (2004) 603, was published on 1 October 2004.

prepared to support any one national method, as is evident from the following quotation: 'In the view of the Commission, the Regulation is intended to function with different systems of serving documents, and it should neither encourage nor discourage the one or the other system.' Nonetheless, at this stage the Commission does not suggest any harmonized new procedure, but just hints at a compromise solution.[109] This feature of the Report underscores one of the inherent weaknesses of the Regulation in that it upholds national diversity rather than brings procedures closer to each other. Therefore there is complexity in its application as well as in its potential reform.

Another view taken by the Commission in the Report is that there is need for further training because the professionals and authorities involved in the application of the Regulation are still in an adaptation phase. However, the Commission does not in the Report give any indication of how, e.g. at the national or supranational level, such training would be organized and whether there would be any obligation on Member States or parties involved to organize or participate in such training.[110] Finally, one practical recommendation that the Commission does suggest is that the multitude of information on relevant decentralized district courts as well as other information included in the manual prescribed by the Regulation should no longer be published in the Official Journal but only be posted on the 'European Judicial Atlas in Civil Matters', which is the Commission's database and Internet help site.[111]

Further indications regarding the future reform of the Service Regulation were given in the discussion paper published for the hearing organized by the Commission in February 2005.[112] The suggestions mentioned in the document are inter alia the following: that receiving agencies be under an obligation to serve documents within 30 days; that addressees be informed in writing of their right to refuse the document under certain circumstances due to the language of the document; that there be a seven-day procedural time limit for such a refusal; that costs of service in countries where there

[109] COM (2004) 603, p. 6.

[110] Ibid. See in particular pp. 3 and 8.

[111] Ibid. p. 7. The link for the Judicial Atlas is: http://www.europa.eu.int/comm/justice_home/judicialatlascivil/html/. The Atlas is a superb Internet site and no doubt offers valuable support to practitioners and officials working in the field. However, since the Internet might not be accessible to all parties who need this highly relevant information, some other means of public dissemination of the information should also be arranged.

[112] The discussion paper was available on the Commission website on the specific news site: http://www.europa.eu.int/comm/justice_home/news/events/news_events_en.htm (visited 20.4.2005). The Paper is not an official document of the Commission and has no SEC or COM number and is not published in the Official Journal.

is a separate profession for such services be fixed and the sum be communicated to the Commission; and that Member States cannot prescribe their own criteria for service by post but all Member States must accept service by registered mail with acknowledgement of receipt.

Thus, the suggested amendments reflect some of the significant concerns raised about the practical functioning of the Regulation. These suggestions have been adopted in the Commission proposal to amend the Regulation.[113] In addition, the proposal includes a further amendment to Article 8 concerning translation, which is no doubt occasioned by Case C-443/2003 *Götz Leffler v. Berlin Chemie AG*. Thus, Article 8(3) would in its amended form stipulate that service of non-translated documents can be rectified in the event of refusal through service in accordance with the Regulation of the same documents in translated form. The date of service is the date on which the document accompanied by translation is served in accordance with the law of the Member State where the addressee lives, but if necessary to protect any rights of the applicant the date of service of the initial document shall also be valid. The proposal also includes a suggested amendment to clarify the provision on direct service, from which it would no longer be possible to derogate. Hence, according to the proposed Article 15 direct service, which all interested parties should be free to pursue, entails that they contact directly the relevant officials in the Member State of service rather than going through their own transmitting agency.

The proposal for amending the Service Regulation is progressing towards the last stages of the legislative process.[114] Both the Economic and Social Committee and the Parliament rapporteur support the aims of the proposed amendments to the Service Regulation and acknowledge the need for clarification of the Regulation. The Parliament has also advocated further clarifications to be introduced that have been taken into account in the Commission's modified legislative proposal.[115] The amendment process for the Service Regulation has underscored how vital the Regulation is to the judicial cooperation system but also that there are challenges to meet in creating legal certainty and protecting the litigating parties.

[113] COM (2005) 305 initial legislative document and COM (2006) 751 modified legislative proposal.

[114] The Council has published a Common Position, 08703/5/2007, and the Commission has published its communication thereto, COM (2007) 400. According to the Parliament's legislative tracking website, http://www.europarl.eu.int/oeil/ (visited August 2007), a second reading is preliminarily scheduled for the autumn of 2007.

[115] ESC 231/2006 para. 1.1 and A5 24/2006 p. 9.

7

Obtaining Evidence

Legislative History

The Proposal for a Regulation on cooperation between the courts of the Member States in the taking of evidence in civil and commercial matters was made, not by the Commission, but by a Member State, Germany, and published in November 2000.[1] The right of initiative of Member States under Article 67 of the EC Treaty was introduced by the Treaty of Amsterdam and derogated from the standard 'Community method'. This right of initiative ceased to exist after the Treaty of Nice entered into force. Germany has been particularly active in making proposals during the period available for Member State initiatives.[2] Because the proposal was made by a Member State there was no official or published opinion of the Commission. Instead in accordance with pre-Nice Article 67 procedures the European Parliament was consulted[3] and the European Economic and Social Committee gave an opinion of its own initiative[4] before the final unanimous decision of the Council. The 'Evidence Regulation'[5] entered into force on 1 July 2001 but the system of cooperation in taking evidence between Member States has only been operational from 1 January 2004.[6] The specific legal basis for the proposal was EC Treaty Article 61(c) and the proposal clearly fell within

[1] OJ C-314, 3.11.2000, p. 1.

[2] The other proposal was for a Regulation on Insolvency, made together with Finland. The only other Member States to have used their right of initiative are Finland (together with Germany) and France (judicial training).

[3] A5 73/2001.

[4] ESC 228/2001.

[5] Council Regulation (EC) No. 1206/2001 of 28.5.2001 on cooperation between the courts of the Member States in the taking of evidence in civil or commercial matters, OJ L-174, 27.6.2001, p. 1.

[6] Art. 24.

the scope of judicial cooperation in civil matters since Article 65(a) specifically includes in the list of measures improving and simplifying cooperation in the taking of evidence.

Political support for legislation can be found in the Tampere European Council conclusions, which recalled that legislation in the area of procedural law should be prepared, in particular the cooperation of courts in taking evidence.[7] However, because the proposal was made by a Member State there is no published explanatory memorandum, as there always would be for legislative initiatives taken by the Commission. Therefore, the first institutional source of the underlying legal and political aims as well as the principles of the proposal is the preamble to the Regulation. According to the preamble, it is often essential in a civil or commercial matter to take evidence in a Member State other than the one in which the matter is pending. The preamble points out that there is no binding instrument in force between the Member States concerning the taking of evidence because the Hague Convention of 1970 is only applicable between 11 of the 15[8] Member States. Also, the Service Regulation on transmission of documents is not enough. Hence, it is necessary to continue to improve cooperation between the courts of Member States in the taking of evidence.[9]

However, more broadly, beyond mere transnational procedural efficiency, the preamble mentions that it is to ensure the proper functioning of the Internal Market that it is necessary to improve cooperation between courts and to accelerate and simplify procedures. In addition the overriding reason for the improved judicial cooperation in civil and commercial matters is the broader objective of implementing the Area of Freedom, Security, and Justice.[10]

The second source of the underlying political and legal aims and principles can be found in the reports of the Economic and Social Committee (ESC) and the European Parliament. The Economic and Social Committee mentions one important additional legal perspective, which is that the purpose of international legal assistance in general is to offset the difficulties which arise as a result of the inability of the courts to exercise powers outside their territorial jurisdiction, and that the interests of the principle of legal certainty require that all Member States should be governed by one legal

[7] Presidency Conclusions No. 200/1/99, 16.10.1999, para. 38.

[8] ESC 228/2001, para. 2.4. The Hague Convention of 1970 has not been ratified by Austria, Belgium, Greece, or Ireland.

[9] Preamble, recitals 6–7.

[10] Preamble, recitals 1–2.

instrument in this respect.[11] The explanatory report to the Opinion of the European Parliament mentions first that the establishment of an Area of Freedom, Security, and Justice confers an essential role on the members of the judiciary in the process of European integration. However, because the activities of the judiciary are confined within national frontiers the effectiveness of judicial action is easily diminished. Thereafter it is stated that it is impossible to create an area of freedom unless a judicial dimension is established.[12]

Furthermore, the report notes that the differences between the legal and judicial cultures of the Member States may create obstacles in the lives of ordinary people and prevent them from exercising their rights. One such example is, according to the report, cooperation between courts in taking evidence. The report also mentions that civil courts have to deal with an increasing number of cross-border cases and need to learn to work together. For all the aforementioned reasons the report welcomes the German initiative and states that the proposal fills a legal void, which has discriminated against the free movement of ordinary people who have run the risk of being denied prompt access to justice.[13]

Finally, taking a more proceduralist view of the aims of the Regulation, one sees that the reasoning underlines and supports the aims of the Regulation and the points made above by the institutions. First, one may note that the examination of a witness in a court of one jurisdiction for the purpose of being used in proceedings in another jurisdiction, i.e. taking evidence abroad, is another classical form of judicial cooperation, aside from service of documents, which has been regulated in the modern international arena since the 1905 Hague Convention on Civil Procedure.[14] Furthermore, commentators note that even though this form of cooperation is not nearly as frequent as cooperation in the service of documents the need for cooperation in the taking of evidence, and the number of cases in which the need arises, is increasing.[15] Commentators also state that this is and is likely to remain one of the pre-eminent issues to resolve in transnational litigation.[16]

However, to the proceduralist commentators it is clear that for a number of reasons this form of judicial cooperation is different from others. First,

[11] ESC 228/2001, paras 1 and 2.5.
[12] A5 73/2001, p. 9.
[13] Ibid. p. 9f.
[14] Schlosser (2000) p. 118.
[15] Inter alia Bruneau (2001) p. 1768.
[16] De Vos and Rechberger (1998) p. 687.

providing evidence requires more active collaboration than the more passive form of assistance present in the service of documents.[17] Secondly, more difficulties can arise because evidence is an area of procedural law in which the legal systems are very divergent, as the case law over the years has confirmed. These divergences exist, for example, in the modes and forms of collecting evidence for the proceedings and presenting evidence in the proceedings. One of the crucial differences is the different perspectives, including those with strong ideological and historical roots, as regards the role of the judge and of the parties in collecting evidence. These differences were perhaps underestimated until case law provided evidence of the divide.[18] The difference is at its most stark in the collecting of evidence against the will of a party.[19] The discovery process in the USA and to a lesser extent the disclosure procedure in the UK are generally perceived as differing from the modes and forms of collecting documentary evidence in civil law countries. These divergences have caused an accumulation of procedures, with the ensuing complications to and errors in cross-border cooperation.[20]

One must also note that taking evidence or obtaining information abroad include several elements: specific information needed from the opponent, specific information needed from a third party, and general information needed.[21] These elements also introduce an inherent complexity into judicial cooperation because legally they have different implications and will be dealt with in a different manner in both the national and transnational procedural context. Naturally, the complexities outlined above have given rise to delay and costs. Additionally, parties taking advantage of the procedural complexities or conducting 'forum shopping' have also become issues. Due to the expertise and experience needed to deal with these complexities, the introduction by the Hague Convention of 1970 on Taking Evidence Abroad of central authorities to whom requests must be directed, was considered great progress, notwithstanding that this step also introduced some delay.[22]

Further complications are caused by the fact that the taking of evidence has in some instances been considered a matter of sovereignty or executive rather than judicial control.[23] In the context of the European Union

[17] Mougenot (2002) p. 18.
[18] De Vos and Rechberger (1998) pp. 688f. and 691f.
[19] Ibid. p. 696f.
[20] Schlosser (2000) p. 114ff.
[21] Ibid. p. 166f.
[22] Ibid. pp. 120 and 403f., McClean (2002a) p. 106ff.
[23] Hess (2003) pp. 216f. and 219f., Mougenot (2002) p. 17.

and its Area of Freedom, Security, and Justice such sovereignty arguments can be considered to have been replaced by Article 10 of the Treaty and the obligation upon Member States to act with loyal cooperation and reciprocity in the cross-border judicial field.[24] Thus, the Evidence Regulation is an attempt both to regulate this form of judicial cooperation, taking into account the practical problems that have arisen, and to introduce efficiency into the system.[25]

Substantive Content

In the practical taking of evidence, the aim of the Regulation is to introduce efficiency and speed.[26] First, the aim is to be achieved, as in the Service Regulation, by establishing more direct, decentralized, channels for transmission. Thus, Article 2 establishes the principle of direct transmission, between competent courts, called the 'requesting' and 'requested' court. Each Member State must draw up a list of competent courts and include details of the territorial and special jurisdiction of the courts. This innovation aims to eliminate any intermediate stages which could complicate and delay the forwarding of a request.[27] In contrast to the Service Regulation and the proposal made by Germany (see above), the final version of the Evidence Regulation makes no provision for a Member State to designate a single centralized requesting and a single centralized requested agency. Therefore the system for taking evidence is clearly a decentralized court system.[28]

The Evidence Regulation thus clearly departs and distinguishes itself in method from the Hague Convention and several bilateral conventions, which often add centralized bodies and further stages to the normal request procedure. However, the Evidence Regulation does include the requirement that each Member State designate a central body the tasks of which are to supply information and solve any difficulties arising in respect of a request. The central authority should only in exceptional cases be involved in the forwarding of a request to the competent court.[29] However, in contrast to the

[24] Hess (2003) p. 221.
[25] Ibid. p. 220f.
[26] Preamble, recital 8.
[27] A5 73/2001, p. 11.
[28] Compare Arts 2 and 3 of the Regulation with those of the German proposal.
[29] Art. 3(1).

central bodies designated under the Service Regulation and notwithstanding decentralization, the central bodies are under the Evidence Regulation most likely to play a significant role since they will deal with requests for taking evidence under the second mode envisaged in Article 17.[30]

Secondly, speed and efficiency are to be achieved by Article 6, which obliges the courts to use the swiftest possible means and allows for any appropriate means of communication and transmission of requests.[31] The Member States are obliged to list the technical means of receipt that are available and acceptable to their courts.[32] Thirdly, the requirements regarding the form of the request and all accompanying documents are less stringent than those in several of the multilateral and bilateral conventions. There is no requirement that the documents be legalized in any manner.[33] However, in contrast to what is often the case under the Service Regulation, the documents have to be in or be translated into the official language of the requested Member State or any other language which that Member State has indicated it can accept.[34] A manual containing information about the competent courts, the means of transmission, and the languages that they accept is published and regularly updated by the Commission. The manual or directory eases the task of both the practitioners and the relevant officials involved.[35]

Fourthly, to speed up the transmission of requests and subsequent taking of evidence, the Evidence Regulation introduces both a specific system of forms and clear deadlines. The forms which are intended to facilitate and speed up the work of the court officials are annexed to the Evidence Regulation and include forms A to K. There are specific forms for, amongst other matters: request for taking evidence, acknowledgement of receipt of a request, request for information missing in the original request, notification of the parties or the court of the time and place for taking evidence and under which conditions they may participate, and notification of refusal to

[30] Art. 3(3).

[31] Art. 6.

[32] Art. 22.

[33] Article 4(2).

[34] Arts 4(3) and 4(5). Bruneau (2001) p. 1769 notes, interestingly, that the Regulation does not in this respect go as far as the Hague Convention, which stipulates that all signatory states should accept letters rogatory in either English or French if they do not specifically make a reservation at the time of accession to the Convention.

[35] Art. 19(1) and A5 73/2001, p. 14. The manual itself can be found on the website of the European Judicial Network in Civil and Commercial Matters: http://ec.europa.eu/civiljustice/. All information is also available on the Judicial Atlas in Civil and Commercial Matters: http://ec.europa.eu/justice_home/judicialatlascivil/html/te_information_en.htm.

execute a request. The forms are very detailed and sometimes can form a means of interpreting the intent and practical consequences of the Evidence Regulation.[36]

The deadlines include: (1) that the requested court shall within seven days of receipt send an acknowledgement of receipt to the requesting court;[37] (2) the requested court must within 30 days notify the requesting court if information is missing or a deposit is necessary;[38] (3) most importantly, a requested court which has received a complete request is obliged to execute it within 90 days;[39] if it is not possible to execute within 90 days the requested court is under an obligation to inform the requesting court of the grounds for the delay and give an estimate of the time it will take for execution.[40]

The Evidence Regulation envisages two modes of taking evidence: either the requested court takes the evidence or the requesting court takes evidence directly in the other Member State. Interestingly, the possibility of a third or subsidiary mode of taking evidence, i.e. using diplomatic or consular agents, was envisaged by the German proposal but not included in the final version of the Evidence Regulation.[41] It is also significant that the two methods of evidence can be seen as representing and potentially reconciling very different prior views among the Member States as regards providing international cooperation in evidentiary matters. Generally, the first mode is a more formal approach and resembles the one in use in the civil law jurisdictions and the second is more informal and resembles the one in use in England and Wales and other common law jurisdictions.[42]

It is important to note that the Evidence Regulation tries to specify in some detail the information to be presented in the request. Were this not the case it would be difficult, under both modes of taking evidence, for the authorities in the requested Member State, either the court or the central body, to deal with or process the request. The information required in the request includes inter alia the questions to be put to witnesses, any potential rights of witnesses to refuse to testify under the requesting Member State's

[36] Lebeau and Niboyet (2003) p. 232.

[37] Art. 7.

[38] Art. 8.

[39] Art. 10.

[40] Art. 15.

[41] Compare Art. 19(2) of the German proposal (OJ C-314, 3.11.2000, p. 1) and Art. 21 of the Regulation.

[42] De Vos and Rechberger (1998) pp. 719–26. Note however that the second mode is not quite so open and liberal as the customary practice in common law jurisdictions.

law, and any special form required. Also, if the request relates to documents or objects to be inspected these must be enumerated and described. Any special technical methods or special procedures requested should where appropriate be explained.[43]

Despite these specifications, intimating that evidence includes witnesses, documents, and objects, the concept of evidence and the relevant forms of evidence possible are not defined and are left open to each national system to interpret according to its rules on evidence. The only limit on the concept of taking evidence is that it must be intended for judicial proceedings which are commenced or contemplated.[44] Commentators from civil law countries often see this limitation as a safeguard against excessive 'fishing expedition' requests for evidence from common law jurisdictions, but of course it applies equally to all requests which lack specificity and connection.[45] In relation to Article 1(1) the Council declared at the adoption of the Evidence Regulation that pre-trial discovery, the so-called 'fishing expedition', is excluded from the scope of the Regulation.[46]

The concept of taking evidence, the requirement of commenced or contemplated judicial proceedings, and the requirement of specificity all arose in the case C-175/06 *Alessandro Tedesco v. Tomasoni Fittings SrL and RWO Marine Equipment Ltd* which constitutes a pending reference for preliminary ruling from the *Tribunale Civile Di Genova*.[47] The first question referred asks whether a request for a description of goods under Italian law and in the terms of the order made by the Italian court is a form of evidence under the Evidence Regulation. The request for a description of goods in a patent dispute such as this entails the location and documentation of the object that potentially breaches the patent and/or the seizure of business records or samples relating to the object.

In anticipation of the ECJ findings the Opinion of Advocate General Juliane Kokott is very interesting. She notes with regard to the first question referred that the concept of taking evidence, which is of crucial importance

[43] Art. 4 and forms A and I annexed to the Regulation.

[44] Art. 1(1).

[45] Lebeau and Niboyet (2003) p. 224f. Note also that the commentators make the point that the English disclosure procedure under the Civil Procedure Rules of England and Wales is much more restrictive than the US discovery procedure, which meant that Art. 1(2) of the Regulation sufficed and no such reservations as are included in Art. 23 of the Hague Convention were needed in the Regulation.

[46] Council Document No. 10571/01.

[47] OJ C-154, 1.7.2006, p. 8.

to the scope of the Evidence Regulation, must be interpreted autonomously in light of its wording, history, and aims, and further must not be interpreted narrowly since that would hamper the stated aim of the Regulation, i.e. to support the smooth functioning of the Internal Market.[48] With reference to Articles 1(1) and 4(1) as well as to the Commission handbook giving practical guidance on the Evidence Regulation, the Advocate General notes that the concept of taking evidence is not a narrow one, but includes inter alia inspection of objects and expert evidence, wherefore the description of goods in this case should in principle fall within the scope of the Regulation.[49] Furthermore since the Member States have enacted Directive EC 2004/48 regarding amongst other measures the preservation of evidence in intellectual property disputes, and since such interim measures are inseparably linked to the taking of evidence, such measures should fall within the ambit of the Evidence Regulation.[50]

Furthermore, the Advocate General also deals with the requirement that evidence be taken for proceedings that are commenced or contemplated and argues that no kind of procedure that strives to establish facts before the main proceedings have been commenced should be excluded from the scope of the Evidence Regulation. Referring to the Council declaration on the Regulation, she states that the taking of evidence must be sufficiently specific and precise that a link to a contemplated procedure can be established. Measures to trace evidence cannot be allowed but the measures must constitute direct evidence themselves.[51]

Finally, regarding the scope of the Evidence Regulation and its relationship to the Brussels I Regulation the Advocate General notes that in the case C-104/03 *St. Paul Dairy Industries*[52] the ECJ specifically held that pre-trial interim measures to preserve evidence do not fall within the ambit of Article 31 of the Brussels I Regulation and that if they did it would be a circumvention of the Evidence Regulation. Therefore the ECJ has implicitly held that such interim measures to preserve evidence constitute the taking of evidence within the meaning of the Evidence Regulation.[53]

[48] Opinion dated 18.7.2007, available on the ECJ website http://curia.europa.eu/, paras 42–3.

[49] Ibid. para. 44.

[50] Ibid. paras 46–52, 56–62.

[51] Ibid. paras 67–74.

[52] [2005] ECR I-3481.

[53] Opinion dated 18.7.2007, available on the ECJ website http://curia.europa.eu/, paras 80–94.

For the first mode of taking evidence the requested court shall execute the request in accordance with the laws of its Member State.[54] However, the Regulation also stipulates that if any special procedure provided for by the law of the requesting Member State or any specific type of technology is requested, these requests should be complied with unless they are incompatible with the law of the forum or unless to do so would entail major practical difficulties.[55] If it is provided for by the law of the requesting court, the parties shall have the right to be present at the taking of evidence. In relation to their participation the requested court is obliged to inform them of the time and place as well as any conditions under which they may participate, as prescribed by the law of the forum.[56] The same provisions apply to representatives of the requesting court. These representatives naturally include any judicial personnel designated by the requesting court, but may also include any other person such as an expert appointed by the requesting court.[57]

The possibility for the parties and the representatives of the requesting court to participate constitutes an important facet of the system and represents major progress.[58] In particular if the evidence is taken by modern methods of communication, e.g. telephone or videoconferencing, their participation is also very practical because they do not need to travel. However, their participation ensures immediacy in the presentation of evidence.[59]

Under this first mode of taking evidence the requested court shall where necessary use any coercive measures available under the law of its Member State in the execution of the request.[60] The Regulation specifies the instances in which the requested court can refuse to execute the request. These include that a person can claim the right to refuse to give evidence under the law both of the requested court and of the requesting court. In addition the requested court can only refuse if the request falls outside the scope of the Regulation or the functions of the judiciary, is incomplete, or is not supported by a necessary deposit. If execution is refused, the requesting

[54] Art. 10(2).

[55] Art. 10(3) and 10(4).

[56] Art. 11.

[57] Art. 12.

[58] Lebeau and Niboyet (2003) p. 227f.

[59] Välimaa (2001) p. 860f. mentions as a typical example that a witness would be required to give evidence before a Finnish district court, and a telephone or video conference would be organized from the courthouse to the requesting courthouse. The author also indicates that Finnish courts should in principle be open to allow the requesting court also to ask questions of the witness.

[60] Art. 13.

court shall notify the requested court within 60 days of the receipt of the request.[61] In contrast, where execution is successful, the requested court should also without delay send the evidence to the requesting court with a confirmation of execution certificate.[62]

For the second mode of taking evidence the request is not sent to a court in the requested Member State but to the central body which decides whether or not direct taking of evidence by the foreign court officials is accepted. The central body shall inform the requesting court of its decision within 30 days of receipt. The taking of evidence directly can only take place if it can be performed on a voluntary basis, e.g. the witnesses agree to be heard, and must be executed by a member of the judiciary or by any person such as an expert designated by the requesting court.[63] Furthermore, the central body can lay down conditions according the law of its Member State under which the taking of evidence should be carried out. The central body can also assign a court of its Member State to take part in the taking of evidence to ensure that the conditions are applied properly. Without prejudice to the conditions laid down, the requesting court shall execute the taking of evidence in accordance with the law of its Member State.

There are only limited grounds on which the central body can refuse to allow the direct taking of evidence. These include that the request falls outside the scope of the Regulation, that the request does not contain all the necessary information, and that the taking of evidence is contrary to the fundamental principles of the law of the requested Member State.[64] Finally, under both modes of taking evidence, the Regulation stipulates that the execution of a request shall not give rise to a claim for reimbursement of any taxes or costs. However, if the use of interpreters, experts, any special procedure or technology is required, the requesting court shall ensure reimbursement if the requested court so requires. The duty for the parties to bear these costs is governed by the law of the Member State of the requesting court.[65]

Normative Implications

The Regulation specifically prevails over the existing mechanisms between the Member States for cooperation between courts in taking evidence, most

[61] Art. 14.
[62] Art. 15.
[63] Art. 17(1)-(4).
[64] Art. 17(4)–17(6).
[65] Art. 18(2).

notably the Hague Convention 1970 on the Taking of Evidence Abroad and the Hague Convention 1954 on Civil Procedure. However, the Member States are allowed to maintain or conclude agreements or arrangements which further facilitate the taking of evidence provided they are compatible with the Regulation. Such provisions must be notified to the Commission.[66] It is difficult to know how much practical impact the Regulation will have. So far the Regulation has been operational since January 2004 and the first review report of the Commission is due in 2007.[67] However, first it is clear that as the Regulation applies to all Member States, unlike the Hague Convention of 1970, it has simplified and unified procedures. Furthermore, by simplifying and speeding up procedures, it is argued that the Regulation's more decentralized approach has introduced a very welcome reform.[68]

The Hague Convention of 1970 created a more cumbersome administrative system between the authorities rather than the courts of the states involved. In contrast, under the Regulation the Member States' agencies play a less central role and the contact between the courts is more direct.[69] Nevertheless, because central bodies are involved in the second mode of taking evidence introduced by the Regulation, the decentralization introduced is not complete. Future empirical data should show which of the modes has been applied more frequently, which in turn will indicate how big a role the central bodies play.

Another issue vis-à-vis the Regulation's aim of introducing simplification and speed is that, as with the Service Regulation, despite the simplified system, with the different forms to be used and the deadlines, there is no guarantee that either the courts or the central bodies will deal promptly with requests. Future empirical data will, it is hoped, indicate whether the Regulation has achieved the desired simplification and speed. However, if an analogy can be drawn from the Study on the application of the Service Regulation, it will take time in practice before these aims are achieved due both to national differences in experience and resources and to language differences leading to communication problems.[70]

[66] Art. 21.

[67] Arts 23 and 24.

[68] Hess (2003) p. 220ff. Note also Schlosser (2000) pp. 120 and 403f. Even though Schlosser hails the establishment of central bodies as significant progress, he also realizes that in the context of the EU the involvement of these bodies has given rise to unnecessary delays.

[69] Mourre (2003) p. 423f.

[70] See Chapter 6 above regarding the empirical data from the Study on the application of the Service Regulation.

On the very practical level, one must note that collecting evidence is more complex than simply transmitting a document. The Regulation emphasizes and encourages the use of modern methods of communication and modern methods of taking evidence, e.g. teleconferencing and videoconferencing.[71] The explicit mention of these methods at several places in the Regulation is hailed by commentators as one of its central features and as a very important practical development which helps both the parties and the courts in requesting evidence from abroad because technology mitigates distance.[72] However, it will no doubt take time before these opportunities are available to all the courts of the Member States. Additionally these methods at present often entail considerable costs, which might still have to be borne by the parties.[73]

One striking feature of the Regulation is the wholly unprecedented possibility that the requesting court may (with permission from the central body) take evidence directly in the requested Member State. This should speed up the obtaining of evidence. Interestingly, however, inexperience with this method and the lack of national procedural rules or practices to support it might at least initially lead national courts to opt for the first method rather than the second, direct one.[74]

The Regulation also differs from the conventional interstate systems of cooperation in its limited approach to the right to refuse execution. There is no general public policy ground on which a court can refuse to execute a request, such as Article 12(b) of the Hague Convention of 1970. There are nonetheless more restrictive grounds which can lead to a refusal to execute. This restrictive approach can first be seen in relation to the first method by which the requested court executes the taking of evidence. For this method the limited grounds for refusal are set out in Articles 10 and 14 of the Regulation. Under Article 10 the requested court has the right to refuse to take evidence according to a particular requested procedure if this procedure is incompatible with its own law or by reason of major practical difficulties. This arguably does not constitute a traditional *ordre public* clause since according to a literal interpretation there is no right to completely refuse to take evidence; it is only the requested form of taking evidence or procedure itself that can be refused. Thus, if witness evidence is requested in

[71] Arts 10(4) and 17(4).

[72] Välimaa (2001) p. 860.

[73] Hess (2003) on the provision on videoconferencing in Art. 17 of the Regulation.

[74] Mougenot (2002) p. 21.

a manner incompatible with the law of a requested Member State, it should comply with the request but execute the hearing of the witness according to its own procedural law.[75] Some commentators contend that this right of refusal should be interpreted in a spirit of comity, and that only a mode of evidence which is explicitly forbidden under the law of the requested state can be refused. Thus, the simple fact that a similar form of evidence does not exist in the national system is not enough.[76] In addition, however, the other ground for refusal in Article 10 is more novel, modern, and tenable. It is foreseeable in practice that the 'major practical difficulties' test might be used more frequently than traditionally *ordre public* grounds have been, as it is conceivable that courts can refer to their heavy caseloads and lack of resources, at least to delay complying with a request.

Furthermore, under Article 14, the requested court is specifically denied the right to refuse execution on the ground that one of its Member State courts has exclusive jurisdiction over the dispute in question; on the other hand it is granted the right to refuse execution if the request is not within the ambit of the Regulation or the function of the judiciary. The latter of these specifications is uncontroversial and is clearly intended to make it clear that matters of an administrative rather than a civil or commercial nature are excluded.[77] The former of these specifications, however, also emphasizes procedural comity and is aligned to the thinking behind the Brussels I Regulation that only the one court first seized should deal with the question of jurisdiction. Thus, one can in these more limited rights of refusal to execute see a shift away from an emphasis on state prerogatives and procedural protectionism to an emerging common system for cross-border disputes based on a duty of cooperation.[78]

[75] Lebeau and Niboyet (2003) p. 225f. give as an example a religious oath, which would not be taken by witnesses in France due to the principle of *laïcite*. The commentators further suggest that French courts might consider refusing extensive discovery requests on the grounds either that the forms of evidence are incompatible with French law or that major practical difficulties are entailed.

[76] Välimaa (2001) p. 861.

[77] Mourre (2003) pp. 435 and 438f. Admittedly the central body can under Art. 17 refuse the direct taking of evidence if the request is contrary to a fundamental principle of law in the Member State but Mourre (p. 441) states that there has to be '*une grave contrariete à l'ordre public de l'Etat requis*'.

[78] Ibid. p. 428 points out that the lack of a public policy exception shows a vote of confidence in the legal systems of the Member State. Hess (2002a) p. 11f. notes that to include the possibility of direct taking of evidence is a departure from previous underlying legal theory, according to which such an act would have been impermissible as a sovereign act within a foreign country.

The ambit of the right to refuse execution under Articles 10 and 14 will no doubt be subject to interpretation and it is hoped that clarifying case law from the ECJ will develop. The right of refusal under these Articles arises in the pending case C-175/06 *Alessandro Tedesco v. Tomasoni Fittings SrL and RWO Marine Equipment Ltd.* Advocate General Kokott has in her Opinion noted that as a general principle the right of refusal should be limited to exceptional cases but that it is a question for the national court to establish whether the exceptional circumstances are present.[79] However, the Advocate General also refers to established case law holding that when EC law refers to national law the Member States cannot take measures which hinder the effect of the EC law, and that the ECJ may interpret the Regulation in order to establish the boundaries which national law has to respect.[80] Regarding the right to refuse, the Advocate General also notes that the national court cannot refuse on grounds of lacking jurisdiction if it is not the court itself taking the evidence but an officer appointed by the court. Furthermore, the fact that under common law it is mainly the parties who are responsible for procuring evidence in civil matters cannot form a ground of refusal since it is too general and would obviate the practical meaning of Article 10(3) of the Evidence Regulation.[81] Therefore, it is for the requested court to enforce the request of the requesting court as far as possible, within the limits of its own legal system. In practice, when the requested method cannot be followed to the letter due to constraints in national law, the request should not immediately be completely refused. According to the Advocate General the requested court is first under a duty to consider whether the requested measure can be tailored to conform with the national requirements or whether an analogous national method might be used to enable the request to be executed rather than refused.[82]

The very practical guidance of the Advocate General correlates with the opinion of commentators who contend that the basic ideology of judicial cooperation in the EU rests on mutual recognition and that the minimum rights of refusal constitute an emanation of this ideology. Furthermore, the grounds and instances of refusal are intended to focus more on protecting

He sees Art. 10 of the Treaty as integral in replacing the old notion of sovereignty with a duty to cooperate.

[79] Opinion, paras 97 and 99.

[80] Ibid. para. 98.

[81] Ibid. paras 105–7.

[82] Ibid. para. 111.

the human rights of the parties than on the interests of the relevant State.[83] However, in order to complete the picture it should be noted that some vestiges of sovereign interest are still guarded by the Member States. For the second mode of taking evidence, direct execution by the requesting court on the territory of the requested Member State, the central body can under Article 17 refuse the direct taking of evidence if the request is contrary to a fundamental principle of law in the Member State. This is a more traditional *ordre public* clause, and interestingly does not follow the wording of the Brussels I Regulation of 'manifestly contrary', even though one commentator points out that due to comity and the otherwise restrictive limitations there has to be a serious incompatibility with public policy for the Article to come into play.[84]

Notwithstanding the innovations of the Regulation vis-à-vis efficiency and comity, the Economic and Social Committee points out that differences in national systems in relation to a number of issues constitute a significant underlying problem in cross-border matters. These differences concern: evidentiary rules[85] such as inter alia rules on the role of the judge in evidential matters; the pre-procedural or procedural character of providing evidence; the degree to which parties themselves are obliged to give documentary and witness evidence; the scope of documentary, witness, and expert evidence; and the rules on the burden of proof.[86] As long as these rules remain different, there is an inherent risk of conflict of laws between the different systems in the course of cooperation between courts in cross-border matters.[87] Articles 1(1) and 10(2) of the Regulation provide that the request is made in accordance with the law of the requesting Member State and that the request is executed in accordance with the law of the requested Member State. Thus, there is a clear system providing for which set of laws is applicable, with the

[83] Välimaa (2001) p. 683.

[84] Mourre (2003) p. 441.

[85] ESC 228/2001, para. 1.4. This discrepancy or clear lack of harmonization through referral back to the national systems is also mentioned by Lebois (2003) p. 292f., who states that this shows the limits of a step-by-step political approach.

[86] Jolowicz (1993) pp. 135–44 demonstrates that there are great differences in the conceptual, theoretical, and legal cultural underpinnings as well as in the practical functioning of the procedural rules governing the fact-finding process. His particular examples include the parties as a source of information or fact and the use of experts. In addition, despite a recent trend towards convergence, there are diverse interpretations of the broader question of the role of the parties and the judge.

[87] ESC 228/2001, para.4.5.

requested court's law being in a stronger position, but there is also a risk of incomplete results due to the differences.

For example, the rules of the requesting court's Member State may allow for a certain witness to give evidence, but the rules of the requested court's Member State may provide for such a witness to be privileged. In such a situation Article 14(1) of the Regulation results in the witness evidence not being provided to the requesting Member State. In another scenario the rules of the requesting court's Member State may provide for disclosure by the parties of all documents in their possession that are relevant to the dispute, but the rules of the requested court's Member State may oblige the parties only to disclose documents that are relevant to their own submissions and may have further provisions for specific disclosure at the request of the other party. Because the Regulation does not provide any definition of evidence, there is still room for very different views about taking evidence against the will of a party. In certain jurisdictions such an obligation is fully accepted, in others there is a strong principle against it, even though there is a trend towards a more open approach if the evidence is considered relevant.[88] This might result under Article 10 of the Regulation in a limited execution of the request, in accordance with the more stringent rules on disclosure of Member State B, and therefore 'incomplete' evidence being provided for the proceedings in Member State A.

The Economic and Social Committee further points out that the Regulation must not result in an erosion of protective safeguards for citizens,[89] but in the examples above protective rules in the Member State of the requested court are favoured above the procedural rules in the requesting Member State. As one commentator points out, the differences in the evidence rules entail that the Regulation is logically only a first step which, he argues, will be followed by harmonization of the procedural rules on evidence in order to reduce the burden that legal fragmentation imposes on the parties.[90] An illustration of this burden is that litigating parties and citizens not only are having to use but perhaps also are subject to 25 different evidentiary systems in the territory of their own Member State, a situation which clearly raises issues of legal certainty and complexity. This can be seen as one reason for the balance in the Regulation between the method of direct taking of

[88] De Vos and Rechberger (1998) p. 696f.
[89] ESC 228/2001, para. 5.3.
[90] Hess (2002a) p. 12.

evidence and the control and supervision exercised by the central body. It can also be considered an argument for Europeanizing evidentiary rules.[91]

Pending the ultimate decision of the ECJ the Advocate General's Opinion in the case C-175/06 *Alessandro Tedesco v. Tomasoni Fittings SrL and RWO Marine Equipment Ltd* shows that there can be a clarifying and therefore harmonizing interpretation of the scope of the Evidence Regulation, in the particular case the definition of 'taking of evidence', that might resolve some diverging national differences, align practice of cooperation, and alleviate the risks elaborated above. The case therefore demonstrates the vital role that the ECJ can come to play in both facilitating the practice of cooperation and harmonizing the interpretation of the evidentiary procedural rules in the decentralized system.

Another problem which arises from the differences in the evidentiary systems and which reinforces the point that there is still room for 'forum shopping' among procedural laws on evidence is that the Regulation itself does not contain any coercive methods for obtaining evidence. Any mechanisms to, for example, force a witness to give evidence follow from the law of the requested Member State only. Thus there is an added inefficiency arising from diversity or non-harmonization.[92] However, even if there is no harmonization of evidentiary rules *per se* at this stage of development, commentators contend that the gradual and perhaps even difficult development of cooperation between courts under the Regulation might pave the way for an 'impregnation', or progressive infiltration of the legal systems at least as regards the judicial culture and practice in taking evidence.[93] Finally, the last critique of the Regulation, which does not detract from its potential achievements, is the regrettable non-inclusion of official trans-border information on legal issues such as evidentiary or factual matters. Even though there is a Council of Europe Convention on the Information on Foreign Law,[94] apparently this has not been widely successful and expert evidence on legal questions will arguably often be needed in civil or commercial cross-border disputes.[95]

[91] Hess (2003) pp. 222f. and 226.

[92] Ibid. pp. 226f. and 232

[93] Lebeau and Niboyet (2003) p. 221f.

[94] Of 7 July 1968, published in Council of Europe series ETS No. 62. Also available at: http://conventions.coe.int/.

[95] Schlosser (2000) p. 395f.

8

Establishing Jurisdiction and Enforcing Judgments

Legislative History

Regulation 44/2001[1] is also called the 'Brussels Regulation', or more specifically the 'Brussels I Regulation'.[2] The Regulation is the product of a revision of the Brussels Convention of 1968. It is clear that the 1968 Convention together with the interpretive case law of the ECJ in relation to it has had a dramatic effect on international procedural cooperation and could in itself be considered to form one of the separate strands of background development which foreshadowed the genesis of the policy area judicial cooperation in civil matters.[3] The revision process and the related work and negotiations were already under way in December 1997 when the Council instructed an ad hoc working party composed of representatives of all the Member States to work on the parallel revision of the Brussels and Lugano Conventions.[4] Simultaneously the Commission submitted a proposal for a Convention to replace the Brussels Convention on the basis of Article K.3(2) of the Treaty on European Union (TEU).[5]

[1] Council Regulation (EC) No. 44/2001 of 22 December 2000 on jurisdiction and the recognition and enforcement of judgments in civil and commercial matters, OJ L-12, 16.1.2001, p.1.

[2] The Brussels I Regulation concerns jurisdiction and the recognition and enforcement of judgments in civil and commercial matters generally with specific substantive exclusions including family matters. The Brussels II Regulation concerns specifically divorce, legal separation, and marriage annulment matters, as well as parental responsibility matters relating to these.

[3] Kennett (2000) pp. 29–34.

[4] The Lugano Convention, nearly identical to the Brussels Convention, was entered into in 1988 between the Member States of the EU and the States belonging to EFTA (the European Free Trade Association).

[5] COM (1997) 609, p. 20.

This proposal was superseded by the entry into force of the Treaty of Amsterdam and the continued negotiations in the Council working group. In July 1999 a new Commission proposal, this time for a Regulation to replace the Convention, was published.[6] The specific legal basis for the new proposal was Article 61(c). The proposal clearly fell within the scope of judicial cooperation in civil matters since Article 65(a) specifically lists improving and simplifying recognition and enforcement and since Article 65(b) specifically includes promoting the compatibility of rules on jurisdiction. However, the legislative procedure and negotiations for the revision of the Regulation suddenly at this stage became protracted since technological and global commercial developments had precipitated the need for a concurrent strategy on e-commerce which can be hugely affected by jurisdictional rules.[7]

The Economic and Social Committee gave its opinion on the proposal in March 2000[8] and the European Parliament published its report in September 2000.[9] Thereafter, taking into account the proposed amendments of the Parliament and accepting some of them, the Commission published an amended proposal[10] in October 2000, which was passed by the Council in December 2000 and entered into force on 1 March 2002.[11]

Apart from the explanatory memorandum to the Commission proposal, two other background sources are relevant for analysing the aim and purposes behind the Regulation and the general changes it introduces. The first of these is the Commission Communication 'Towards greater efficiency in obtaining and enforcing judgments in the European Union',[12] which was adopted in December 1997. The aim of the Commission was to present practical proposals to further facilitate recognition and enforcement and to generate debate.[13] In this Communication the Commission recognizes that recognition and enforcement procedures take too long and cost too much, and can consequently create obstacles and disincentives to the

[6] COM (1999) 348, p. 1.

[7] Kennett (2000) p. 55f. gives an account of this facet of the negotiations and the legislative process.

[8] ESC 233/2000, p. 6.

[9] A5 253/2000, p. 4.

[10] COM (2000) 689, p. 243.

[11] There have been subsequent amendments to the Regulation of a technical nature mainly affecting the Annexes. See Corrigenda OJ L-307, 24.11.2001, p. 28, Regulation (EC) No. 1937/2004, Regulation (EC) No. 2245/2004, and Corrigendum OJ L-50, 23.2.2005, p. 20.

[12] COM (1997) 609, p. 3.

[13] Ibid. p. 4f.

free movement of judgments. This is particularly the case in the context of private law relations.

The most radical solution would be to completely abolish the recognition procedure, exequatur, but to do this would be inconceivable to the Member States because of the wide procedural differences between them as regards enforcement. Therefore, the object is to simplify as much as possible without complete abolition.[14] Another way of simplifying enforcement or of offsetting delay in enforcement would be to deal with the provisions for provisional and protective measures. However, these are substantively different in the Member States.[15] Other issues raised by the Commission in its Communication include the potential creation of a European procedure for payment orders, instead of the fragmented summary procedures available in some but not all Member States.[16] Furthermore, the Commission highlights the issue of enforcement proper, i.e. that after recognition the actual execution of a judgment varies greatly in the Member States.[17]

The second general background document to bear in mind in relation to the Brussels I Regulation is the Council 'Draft programme of measures to implement the principle of mutual recognition of decisions in civil and commercial matters'.[18] The motivation for the programme came explicitly from the Tampere European Council which stated that the principle of mutual recognition should become the 'cornerstone' of judicial cooperation. Two problems are highlighted, first that mutual recognition is limited because many areas of private law do not fall within the ambit of existing measures. Secondly, the Brussels regime does not remove all obstacles to free movement of judgments.[19] In the areas of private law covered by the Brussels Convention the programme specifically raises concerns in relation to the small consumer and commercial as well as uncontested claims.[20]

The programme proposes to streamline the existing measures and strengthen their effects in the Member States by limiting the reasons for non-recognition, removing the public policy test, and establishing provisional enforceability and protective measures at the European level. This is the first series of measures. The second series of measures involves complete

[14] Ibid. pp. 6 and 8ff.
[15] Ibid. p. 10f.
[16] Ibid. p. 12ff.
[17] Ibid. p. 14f.
[18] OJ C-12, 15.1.2001, p.1.
[19] Ibid. p. 2; Haibach (2005) p. 296.
[20] OJ C-12, 15.1.2001, p. 3f.

abolition of the recognition requirement.[21] The programme also proposes measures that are ancillary to mutual recognition. Amongst these are the setting up of minimum standards for certain aspects of civil procedure, or if these are insufficient a certain degree of harmonization of procedures, this being a potential necessary precondition for the abolition of the exequatur. Many of the same ideas, proposals, and reasons are propounded in the Commission Communication of 1997 and the Council Programme of 2000.

From the point of view of the Brussels I Regulation, it is interesting to note that the mutual recognition concept of the Single Market has been and is being used in the context of judicial cooperation of civil matters and that efficient enforcement of judgments is seen as a crucial issue for the Internal Market. The concept of mutual recognition and enforcement is also seen as a key, from which stem the ancillary needs of general procedural harmonization and harmonization of provisional measures.[22] In addition to these background Community documents, it is pertinent to note that the effectiveness of enforcement has been raised in both the Storme Report[23] and the more recent ALI/UNIDROIT Principles of Transnational Procedure adopted in 2004.[24] The recourse to proper enforcement procedures has also been recognized by the European Court of Human Rights.[25] These sensibilities and the understanding of the central importance of enforcement have no doubt influenced the Community institutions. Apart from the reform of the recognition and enforcement procedures proposed and achieved in the Brussels I Regulation the European Enforcement Order Regulation (which will be dealt with in Chapter 9) is part of the Community attempts to deal with this issue.[26]

[21] Ibid. p. 5.

[22] Note however that, if one adopts a strict interpretation, the political concept of 'mutual recognition' is not to be confused with the legal concept of recognition of judgments, notwithstanding that the latter forms part of the former in its technical emanation: Tubeuf and Lebois (2003) p. 374f.

[23] Storme (1994) p. 108ff., where an order for payment, i.e. a simplified form of enforcement, 'as an expedient, cost-advantageous and uncomplicated dispute settlement is a fundamental demand of modern procedural law'.

[24] The Principles are available inter alia at: http://www.unidroit.org/english/principles/civilprocedure/main.htm (visited 23.8.2007). See in particular Principle 29 regarding effective enforcement.

[25] Case *Hornsby v. Greece*, 19.3.1997, Reports (1997-II).

[26] The Commission also sees the reform of the Rome Convention regime (including both the Rome I and Rome II projects) as supporting the mutual recognition programme. Harmonized choice of law rules would obviate part of the forum shopping that is perceived to take place, thereby supporting the common jurisdictional scheme. Harmonized choice of law rules would in addition obviate *ordre public* defences based on the application of the wrong law, thereby supporting the common enforcement scheme.

Furthermore, the explanatory report accompanying the proposal for the Brussels I Regulation commences in a similar fashion by pointing out that the reinforcement of judicial cooperation in civil matters is fundamental to the creation of a European judicial area with benefits for its citizens. Secondly, the report mentions that the Internal Market creates a need for clear rules on jurisdiction and a need to improve and speed up the recognition and enforcement of judgments.[27] The aims and purposes in relation to jurisdiction and to recognition and enforcement in the proposal for a Regulation to replace the Brussels Convention differ from one another. In relation to jurisdiction the aim is to update the Brussels Convention and take into account new forms of commerce, most notably electronic commerce, and in so doing to strike a balance between the parties. The aim is also to introduce uniform modern standards for jurisdiction. In relation to recognition and enforcement the aim is to simplify the formalities in order to create an automatic and rapid procedure.[28]

In general there is also an aim of continuity, which means that the Regulation corresponds to the Convention it replaces to the extent that no change is deemed necessary and some of the changes, particularly to the jurisdiction rules, correspond to the established case law of the ECJ.[29] A further aim of the Regulation is to create, through the choice of instrument (i.e. using a regulation and not a directive), direct and uniform application in the Member States and to create legal certainty.[30] Finally, these internal political goals at the European level underscore the proceduralist perspective that regulating jurisdiction and thus avoiding concurrent jurisdiction is crucial to saving the parties expense and inconvenience but also support the rule of law and respect for the efficacy of courts in a modern society. In addition, by curbing a race to court it is intended to avoid procedural confusion and injustice.[31]

Substantive Content

The scope of the Regulation is the same as for the prior Convention. Thus, according to Article 1 the Regulation applies to civil and commercial matters, excluding revenue, customs, or administrative matters. Furthermore, the

[27] COM (1999) 348, para. 1.1.
[28] Ibid. paras 2.1 and 4.1.
[29] Ibid. para. 4.2 and A5 235/2000, p. 29.
[30] ESC 233/2000, paras 2.2.2 and 3.2.1.
[31] Bell (2003) p. 12.

following categories are also excluded: the status or legal capacity of natural persons; rights in property arising out of matrimonial relationships, wills, and succession; bankruptcy; social security disputes and arbitration proceedings. According to the transitional provisions regulating its temporal scope the Regulation will only apply to proceedings instituted after its entry into force. As an exception, even if proceedings were instituted before the entry into force, judgment rendered after that date shall be enforced in accordance with the new regime.[32]

In territorial scope, however, the Regulation initially differed from the Convention in that Denmark, due to its particular Protocol to the Treaty of Amsterdam, is not participating in the area of judicial cooperation in civil matters and was therefore initially excluded from the Regulation. In practice this entailed that the former Brussels Convention applied to situations in which a Danish party was the defendant in the action (and the claimant party was from another EU Member State). However, when the defendant was from another EU Member State and the claimant was Danish the Regulation would apply.[33] In July 2007 an international agreement between the EU and Denmark entered into force, which entails that the Brussels I Regulation provisions are extended to Denmark.[34]

Chapter II of the Regulation on Jurisdiction is in its main characteristics the same as for the prior Convention. Under Article 2, persons domiciled in a Member State shall be sued in the courts of that Member State, i.e. the principle of defendant's domicile as the general basis for jurisdiction is retained. Thereafter, sections 2–7 of Chapter II deal with: special jurisdiction; jurisdiction in the specific areas of insurance and consumer and employment contracts; exclusive jurisdiction; and prorogation of jurisdiction.[35] Finally sections 8–10 of Chapter II deal with examination as to jurisdiction, lis pendens, and related actions and provisional measures. The aims of jurisdictional reforms are to update the system and achieve a high level of

[32] Art. 66.

[33] Mourre (2003) p. 24f.

[34] See above, Chapter 4.

[35] Thus, the system of several alternative jurisdictions for many disputes does not change in its fundamentals and still leaves considerable freedom for litigants, in particular claimants, to choose a jurisdiction. This very 'liberal' system does however inherently cause some degree of forum shopping. Forum shopping is not necessarily considered to be illicit or wrong even though the merits and delimitation of such a liberal system have been debated in the literature. See Nuyts (2003a) pp. 5–9. The ECJ has also in its case law recognized some limits to forum shopping, which might be categorized as jurisdictional fraud and abuse of process, ibid. pp. 10–17 and 18–30.

predictability and clarity as well as to avoid conflicting judgments.[36] However, the Communitarization of the Convention into a regulation does not represent a grand reform of the rules of jurisdiction, rather some housekeeping is done to gaps and uncertainties which have been identified in the previous convention system.[37]

Both the previous convention system and the current Regulation with its innovations are addressing a major issue, which is that venue is an important matter for litigants and both parties will always therefore wherever possible forum shop and seek the most beneficial forum.[38] Neither the Convention nor even the Regulation completely eliminates forum shopping but they do attempt to provide more certainty for litigants and this should allow them to calculate their risks.[39]

The main innovations in the jurisdiction part of the Regulation are, first, that there is a separate definition of domicile for legal persons, whereas the definition of domicile for natural persons remains to be determined in accordance with the national choice of law rules of the relevant Member State court which is seized.[40] The second main innovation is that the alternative jurisdiction in Article 5(1) for contracts also now contains a separate definition of the place of performance, particularly for the sale of goods and provision of services.[41] The change attempts to remedy the diversity resulting from the previous clause which the Court, in a much criticized line of doctrine, had held to refer back to the *lex casusae*.[42]

[36] Preamble, recitals 11–12. See also Droz and Gaudemet-Tallon (2001) pp. 609–11.

[37] Generally ibid. pp. 630–43, for an exposé of all the changes introduced to the jurisdictional regime.

[38] Bell (2003) pp. 14–18 and 23–48. This commentator identifies a host of procedural and substantive differences in domestic laws which might influence the choice of venue and cause the parties to forum shop.

[39] Ibid. pp. 34f., 53f.

[40] COM (1999) 348, p. 6.

[41] Ibid. p. 14. See also Beaumont (2002) pp. 15–24, who gives a detailed account of the negotiations which resulted in this change and highlights some of the consequences. He states that the negotiations on this particular point were the most protracted of all the jurisdiction issues. See also Kennett (1993) for an interesting historic analysis of the jurisdictional rules in the Brussels Convention (as apply now to the Regulation) for contract cases. She takes the view, p. 103f., that the approaches chosen in the Convention can be traced back to historic influences in the Member States and that sometimes the ECJ's technical interpretation lacks transparency and can be manipulated by national courts which are seeking a certain result. Her critique, p. 107, that the historic rules of jurisdiction might not be suited to the modern commercial climate has to some extent been answered by the reform of the contract rule in the Regulation. Nevertheless, the fact remains that national courts will apply these taking into account their own particular historic traditions.

[42] Gottwald (1997) p. 146ff.

The third main innovation concerns the special jurisdiction for consumer contracts. Under Article 16(2), proceedings brought against a consumer must exclusively be brought in the consumer's domicile. However, consumers' entitlement to sue in their domicile under certain circumstances is extended by new Article 15(c).[43] The criteria in the Convention have been reframed to take into account developments in marketing techniques, in particular the reality of consumer contracts concluded over the Internet.[44] Now a consumer can sue in his own domicile, as an exception to the rule of the defendant's domicile, if the contract has been concluded 'with a person who pursues commercial or professional activities in the Member State of the consumer's domicile or, by any means, directs such activities to that Member State'.

The fourth main innovation regarding jurisdiction rules entails that the lis pendens rules become more effective by the provision of an autonomous definition of the date on which a case is 'pending'. This fills a gap in the Convention that permitted potential abuse and unfairness, and which had been revealed by ECJ case law.[45]

Chapter III of the Regulation, Recognition and Enforcement, is to a large extent a modification of the prior Convention. In particular, Article 33 introduces the principle of automatic recognition. This is said to be founded on the mutual trust between the Member States' judicial authorities and entails that proceedings cannot be recommenced in another Member State.[46] In practice, Annex V of the Regulation contains a standard-form certificate which should be issued by the court or competent authority in the Member State where judgment was given. This certificate and a copy of the judgment are the only documents to be provided in order to apply in another Member State for formal recognition or a declaration of enforceability. Upon completion of these formalities the ex parte application has to be granted without any ex officio review of the limited possibilities of non-recognition.

Only if the decision granting enforceability is appealed in accordance with Article 43 of the Regulation can a party raise any of the grounds for non-recognition in Articles 34 and 35. These have been narrowed down, and include the following: (1) manifestly contrary to public policy, (2) judgment

[43] Stadler (2005) p. 1639ff.

[44] COM (1999) 348, p. 16.

[45] Ibid. p. 20. See also Schütze (2002) p. 58f., for a brief outline of the problems that had arisen due to the wording of Art. 21 of the Convention and the relevant ECJ case law. See also Möller (1996) p. 219 for a Nordic view of the problem. The central case of the ECJ is C-129/83 *Zelger v. Salinitri* [1984] ECR 2396.

[46] COM (1999) 348, p. 21.

was given in default when the defendant had not been given adequate time to prepare his defence provided that he used any means of appeal available to him, and (3) irreconcilable judgment has already been given in a Member State. Further to these limited grounds for non-recognition, the Regulation specifically mentions that the foreign judgment may under no circumstances be reviewed as to its substance and neither may the jurisdiction of the court of origin be controlled by the court of enforcement.[47] Further, in line with the case law of the ECJ, the public policy clause has been further restricted by the addition of the additional criterion 'manifestly', and the assessment of public policy has to focus on the effects in the Member State rather than the decision as such.[48]

The novel enforcement regime hence entails an inversion of the burden of proof regarding the regularity of the original proceedings and an inversion of the dispute itself from being claimant initiated to putting the burden of initiative on the defendant.[49] It is thus intended that simplified procedures will speed up enforcement and that reframing the restrictive grounds will improve the free movement of judgments.[50] Furthermore, Article 47 provides that when a judgment must be recognized in accordance with the Regulation, the applicant is entitled to avail himself of any available provisional or protective measures that are available in the Member State of enforcement.[51] The declaration of enforceability shall also carry with it the same power.

[47] Arts 34 and 35. As an exception the enforcement court is allowed to ensure that certain heads of jurisdiction which protect the weaker party are complied with, e.g. consumer protective jurisdiction in Art. 15. These restrictions are not novel but already existed in the context of the Brussels Convention. Lopez-Tarruella (2000–1) p. 125f. further notes that a substantive or jurisdictional error cannot be used as grounds for *ordre public*, which gives further evidence of the emphasis on mutual recognition and mutual trust under both the Convention and the Regulation.

[48] Ibid. pp. 124 and 126–9. Interestingly, the author notes that the ECJ had not accepted any situation as constituting public policy under the Convention before the *Krombach* judgment.

[49] Tubeuf and Lebois (2003) p. 385.

[50] COM (1999) 348, p. 21f. Note that since the judge cannot make a substantive review of the foreign judgment the examination of public policy must in essence focus on very clear and 'manifest' issues and cannot lead to any 'veiled' substantive review of the case. However, since there is no restriction on reviewing the procedural regularities (except the prohibition to review jurisdiction), and since public policy after the *Krombach* judgment of the ECJ does include procedural due process guarantees, the extent to which the enforcing court should deal with this matter is unclear. See Tubeuf and Lebois (2003) p. 383f.

[51] Art. 31 of the Regulation deals with the provision of pre-judgment provisional relief and is the same as the previous Art. 24 of the Brussels Convention. There has been some case law concerning the scope of the provision, one criticism of which concerns the lack of an agreed

Normative Implications

Jurisdiction

The Regulation did not abrogate the Brussels Convention, which was still in force between the Member States of the EU and Denmark until July 2007[52] or the closely related Lugano Convention, which is still in force between the Member States of the EU and Norway and Switzerland.[53] However, between the Member States themselves the Regulation supersedes the Convention and other bilateral or multilateral treaties.[54] The latter will nevertheless continue to have effect in matters falling outside the scope of the Regulation.[55] It is also relevant to remember that the Regulation does not prejudice any specific jurisdictional rules that are contained in other Community instruments or in national legislation pursuant to such instruments.[56]

It is difficult to know what practical impact the revision of the Convention into a Regulation will have. The Regulation has been in operation since 2002 and the first review report of the Commission is due in 2007. Nevertheless, in relation to jurisdiction, it is clear that the Regulation has introduced very welcome innovations, which will create uniform modern standards and which will most likely achieve more uniform application and legal certainty since they remove references to national rules. In relation to the new lis pendens rule and the new definition of seizure, there has been significant progress in relation to what has been described as the paradigm of resistance by the

definition of 'provisional measures' and the case law of the ECJ which does not allow the mutual recognition of such measures when they have been granted ex parte, see inter alia Andrews (2003) pp. 278–81. Furthermore, the new Art. 47 specifically also deals with post-judgment (but pre-enforcement and exequatur) provisional relief, which commentators have hailed as positive. However, neither Article deals with another facet of provisional relief which some commentators argue should be dealt with within the auspices of judicial cooperation in civil matters, namely domestic litigation which needs to provide protective relief on a worldwide basis and the mutual recognition of such an order: ibid. pp. 269–77, for proposed rules to that effect.

[52] An international agreement entered into force on 1 July 2007, which entails that the Brussels I Regulation provisions are extended to Denmark. See also Chapter 4 above.

[53] Poland was a contracting party of the Lugano Convention of 1988 until May 2004 when Poland became a Member State of the EU. Note that in March 2007 a diplomatic conference was held in Brussels to conclude the negotiations on a new Lugano Convention to replace the old one and to align the Lugano regime with the Brussels I Regulation.

[54] Arts 68 and 69.

[55] Art. 70.

[56] Art. 67.

Member States to common procedural regulation.[57] Hence it can be said that the reform solves the previous problems and has met with the approval of the commentators.[58]

However, notwithstanding the clarification further new questions of interpretation are possible.[59] In addition, it has also been noted that the 'first step taken to commence proceedings' test that has been introduced still creates imbalances between jurisdictions in that some jurisdictions can be seized upon lodging without service and this allows them a tactical advantage over jurisdictions in which the first step is service.[60] Also the parties, and in particular citizens or small businesses, notwithstanding the added transparency and the abolition of some of the possibilities for forum shopping, are still obliged to obtain specific national comparative legal information concerning the 'first step taken' test in order to be fully aware of their rights.[61] It must also be noted that some recent cases have shown the limits and *in casu* weaknesses of the lis pendens rule to protect the parties from abuse of process and have also arguably shown a risk in the formalistic systematic interpretation of the ECJ. The debate will no doubt continue – however unlikely it is that there will be a complete change.[62]

In relation to the new definition of place of performance for sale of goods and service contracts, it is also clear that the reform entails more foreseeability and simplicity.[63] However, one commentator points out that the definition in practice only creates a second jurisdiction for sales contracts and is more or less redundant for many service contracts since it results in the place being the defendant's domicile which in any event is the general rule.[64] Another commentator gives such examples as cases in which the claimant is trying to recover a money debt or is pleading failure of design or manufacture as cases

[57] Boularbah (2003) p. 192.

[58] Schütze (2002) p. 62 and Geimer (2002) p. 25.

[59] Gaudemet-Tallon (2002) p. 268f. mentions some examples: (1) Within what time frame must a claimant who has seized through service lodge the claim with the court? (2) In the era of electronic communication how does one establish the exact time of seizure?

[60] Kennett (2001) p. 732.

[61] Nuyts (2003a) pp. 9f. and 31ff. argues that the lis pendens rule can still be used for forum shopping purposes and should in exceptional cases be considered illicit as an abuse of process.

[62] Bell (2003) p. 62ff.; Hartley (2000) pp. 166–70, specifically regarding the case C-159/02 *Turner v. Grovit*; and Hartley (2005) pp. 815–23, regarding the same case as well as case C-116/02 *Gasser v. MISRAT.*

[63] Gottwald (1997) p. 146ff. describes the history of the contract jurisdiction clause and its inherent limits.

[64] Stoffel (2002) p. 192f.

in which the new definition will make a difference.[65] However this Article, apart from perhaps being redundant in some cases, still has several inherent uncertainties; more precisely, it is envisaged that it will give rise to the interpretive litigation necessary to clarify the concepts themselves.[66]

This is because the question of place of performance arises in practice for particular goods and services, which is the main obligation, and where they are delivered or provided.[67] Furthermore, it is unclear which law is to be applied to the question of what constitutes a service or to the analysis of the 'under the contract' test for sale of goods.[68] These uncertainties appeared in a first preliminary referral to the ECJ regarding the new Article 5 of the Brussels I Regulation: C-386/05 *Colour Drack GmbH v. LEXX International Vertriebs GmbH.*[69] In that case the goods were delivered to purchasers in several different locations within one Member State, and they in practice constituted the sub-buyers or clients of the main buyer under the relevant contract. One would expect that the Court might adopt reasoning in stages, stating that if possible on the facts a principal place of delivery must be established.[70] However, if it is not possible to distinguish between principal and secondary deliveries, several solutions seem possible.

The alternative solutions are, first, that none of these multiple places of performance of the same obligation are accepted as 'the place of performance' under Article 5(1)(b); secondly, that all of the places are accepted for the purposes of establishing jurisdiction but that each dispute must be brought separately in the particular place of delivery and hopefully joined with others under national procedural law;[71] and thirdly, that any of the places is considered competent to establish jurisdiction over all the deliveries.

Arguably, the ambit and practical consequences of the simplification of procedures would be significantly lessened if the Court chose the first

[65] Beaumont (2002) p. 23f.

[66] Gaudement-Tallon (2002) p. 163f.; Stadler (2005) p. 1648.

[67] Niboyet (2001a) p. 945f. mentions inter alia distribution and franchising contracts as examples.

[68] Droz and Gaudemet-Tallon (2001) pp. 634–6.

[69] C-386/05, referral reported in OJ C-10, 14.1.2006, p. 11. Judgment dated 3.5.2007 not yet reported but available on the ECJ website: http://curia.europa.eu/en/index.htm.

[70] In line with its case law under the Brussels Convention in *Shenavai*, case 266/85, [1987] ECR 239, where several contractual obligations were at stake the Court held that jurisdiction must be concentrated before the courts of the principal obligation.

[71] This alternative would follow the ruling of the Court under the Brussels Convention in case C-420/97 *Leathertex* [1999] ECR I-6747, in which the Court held that each dispute concerning each separate obligation must establish jurisdiction independently under Art. 5(1).

alternative; if that were so, most cases would fall under the default position and the old, more complex *Tessili v. Dunlop* test,[72] or even fall completely out of the scope of Article 5 if the *Besix*[73] ruling is followed. The second option, by the referral to national law would also introduce significant disadvantages in terms of multiplication of fora, delay, and uncertainty. The third option seems most in line with an '*effect utile*' interpretation of the simplification introduced by the reform of Article 5. However, this solution is admittedly liberal, particularly if the facts are different from those of *Colour Drack v. LEXX* and multiple deliveries are effected in several Member States.[74] In conclusion, there is still a latent complexity and a necessity for citizens or small enterprises, as either claimants or defendants, to have access to intricate legal analysis if they are to be fully aware of their rights and the potential business risks and transaction costs.

The ECJ has in its judgment chosen a step-by-step approach, stating that where there are multiple places of delivery of goods a place of principal delivery must if possible be determined on the basis of economic criteria, which would then form the relevant place of jurisdiction under Article 5(1)(b). However, if a principal place of delivery cannot be established each of the places of delivery has a sufficiently close link to the dispute and the claimant can choose any of these for establishing jurisdiction over all the claims relating to the contract.[75] Notably, the ECJ specifically limited its ruling to matters where there are several places of delivery within one Member State. Therefore, there is still uncertainty what the applicability and interpretation of Article 5(1) would be where there are deliveries in several Member States.[76]

It is however clear that the ECJ here departed markedly from its previous case law under the Brussels Convention, predecessor to the Regulation, specifically stating that the place of performance for each obligation in question must not be established but that the place of delivery forms the sole jurisdiction for all claims arising out of the contract.[77] It is also clear that the ECJ case law under the Regulation is novel, in the sense that the

[72] Gaudemet-Tallon (2002) pp. 149f. and 155f.; C-12/76 *Tessili v. Dunlop* [1976] ECR 1473.

[73] C-256/00 *Besix* [2002] ECR I-1699, in which the Court held that when it is impossible to locate the place of performance of the obligation at stake Art. 5(1) cannot apply and the general rule of Art. 2 will be applied in default.

[74] Gaudemet-Tallon (2002) p. 159f.

[75] C-386/05, referral reported in OJ C-10, 14.1.2006, p. 11. Judgment 3.5.2007, reported in OJ C-140, 23.6.2007, p. 4, available in full on the website http://www.curia.eu.int/, paras 40–2.

[76] Ibid. para. 15.

[77] Ibid. para. 39.

origins, objectives, and scheme of the Regulation must be taken into account in interpretation.[78] The recitals, in this case those relating to the aims of unification and predictability, play an important role in finding and determining the objectives of the reformed system.[79]

In relation to jurisdictional reform, the most controversial of the innovations when the Commission proposal was published was clearly the extension of consumers' right to sue in their own domicile for contracts entered into over the Internet.[80] This extension specifically allowed a consumer to sue in the courts of the place where he is domiciled, i.e. not just in his own Member State of domicile but in a local place within that State.[81] First, concerns had been raised by the industry that companies engaged in electronic commerce would have to deal with potential litigation in every Member State. Secondly, the notion of 'directing activities' was not considered to provide legal certainty.[82] Thirdly, both parties, business and consumer organizations, argued that either the 'country of destination' or the 'country of origin' principle would deter their interest groups and therefore would not contribute to the availability of cross-border e-commerce.

In relation to the first point, it is clear that the extension of consumers' rights to sue in their own domicile is a political choice and confirms the intention supported in the Council to protect the weaker party to a contract.[83] Because the consumer is the weaker party, who often pays in advance for the transaction to take place and cannot influence the unilateral terms of contract that are offered, the balance in relation to jurisdiction leans towards the consumer.[84] Notwithstanding this, the business community should be offered some degree of legal certainty and ability to anticipate in which states they could be sued.

In relation to the second point, there has been considerable uncertainty as to what the 'directing activities' test entails. Even though the Commission did not in its explanatory report specifically state that passive websites could establish jurisdiction it is clear to one commentator that the interpretation

[78] Ibid. para. 18.

[79] Ibid. paras 19, 24, and 32.

[80] Kennett (2000) p. 55f. notes that the negotiations for a Regulation were abruptly halted due to lobbying from e-commerce interests and to the previously unforeseen need to take into account and create an e-commerce strategy.

[81] Art. 16(1). See also Droz and Gaudemet-Tallon (2001) p. 639.

[82] COM (1999) 348, p. 17.

[83] Ibid. p. 15.

[84] Øren (2003) p. 672.

was intended to be broad.[85] However, another commentator points out that a legal interpretation would also have to take into account vendors' so-called ring-fencing activities, by which they try, using technical means, to specify the Member States whose consumers they are willing to enter into contracts with.[86] The Commission and Council have subsequently issued a joint declaration[87] on the interpretation of Article 15(1)(c) which makes it clear that the mere accessibility of a website is not enough, the site has to include an invitation to enter into a contract over the Internet. The declaration thus introduces a distinction between passive and active websites similar to that first developed in the US doctrine.[88] However, there is still practical uncertainty, depending on the circumstances of each case, and only case law from the ECJ and national courts will be able to ascertain the specific interpretation of 'directing activities'.[89]

Unfortunately, the first preliminary referral to concern Article 15(1)(c), albeit not relating to electronic communication, has not been answered substantively by the ECJ.[90] A new pending preliminary referral might however provide the ECJ with an opportunity to give some guidance.[91] Finally, the 'directing activities' issue also highlights the point that the updating of the Brussels regime has, aside from this important Article, not been able to deal with all issues which might arise vis-à-vis jurisdiction in a virtual business relationship.[92]

[85] Berliri (2003) p. 50, referring to the distinction elaborated by US courts between passive, interactive, and active websites in relation to the question of establishing jurisdiction. See also Øren (2003) pp. 683–6, for a discussion of the potential helpfulness of the US distinction in interpreting the Brussels I Regulation.

[86] Øren (2003) pp. 690–4.

[87] Council Document 13742/00. Not published in OJ but available at: http://ec.europa.eu/civiljustice/homepage/homepage_ec_en_declaration.pdf.

[88] Mourre (2003) p. 178f.

[89] Gaudement-Tallon (2002) p. 230f., who refers to a theory of 'focalization', which relies on the intent of the operators, as one possible way of distinguishing and interpreting the ambit of the provision.

[90] C-234/04 *Kapferer v. Schlank & Schick GmbH* [2006] ECR I-2585. Based on its reply to the preceding questions the Court was not obliged to answer the substantive questions regarding Art. 15(1)(c) of the Regulation.

[91] C-180/06 *Renate Ilsinger v. Martin Drescher (administrator in the insolvency of Schlank & Schick GmbH)* (pending, referral reported OJ C-165, 15.7.2006, p. 12). It is not clear from the referring questions whether the sending of prize notifications to consumers, the activity relevant in the case, was done by electronic or regular postal means (referral reported OJ C-165, 15.7.2006, p. 12).

[92] Inter alia Girsberger (2002) provides an overview of several interpretation issues which arise when establishing jurisdiction in an e-business context. One other change in the new

Enforcement of Judgments

Regarding the reforms in the area of recognition and enforcement, the revised Regulation moves in the direction envisaged by the early policy documents, the Commission Communication of 1997 and the Council Programme of 2001. The exequatur procedure is not yet completely removed but the new combined recognition and declaration of enforceability procedure should become quicker, more standardized, and thus also less expensive. In addition, the applicant can, with the support of Article 47, avail himself of potential provisional measures immediately. Thus, enforcement and protection of judgment creditors should be improved.[93]

However, first it is noteworthy that the reforms can also be questioned from the perspective of procedural equity. As the defences to recognition are no longer applied in the first stage ex officio but have to be raised in the second appellate procedure by the defendant, the fairness of the procedure becomes an issue. Hence, the legal protection of the judgment debtor is lessened, even though some commentators consider that the court could raise such defences and conduct an ex officio examination at the first appellate stage.[94] Furthermore, the protection is lessened as the public policy exception becomes more restricted (and it should be noted that in the future it could even be removed), whilst the national procedural rules and constitutional standards still remain different.[95]

The extent to which the national systems will accept this or converge as to the interpretation of 'manifestly against public policy' is unclear, in particular since the procedural rights of the defence can be held to fall under public policy.[96] In the wake of the ECJ judgment in *Krombach* there are clear

Brussels I regime takes heed of the electronic environment, namely Art. 23(2), which authorizes the conclusion of a prorogation agreement by electronic means. However, this naturally raises further questions of factual interpretation.

[93] Coulon (2002) p. 148, as to the importance of provisional measures in comparison with the previous system. Niboyet (2001a) p. 948 notes that this provision provides efficiency but since the possibility is dependent on the national law of the Member State in question, fragmentation and uncertainty are foreseeable. Droz and Gaudemet-Tallon (2001) p. 650 assess this reform positively and note that it shows the spirit of mutual recognition.

[94] Tubeuf and Lebois (2003) p. 383f. note that diverging opinions have been mooted in the doctrine.

[95] Stoppenbrink (2002) p. 641. Hess (2002a) p. 9f. confirms the view that the elimination of the exequatur procedure must be accompanied by a prior reconciliation of procedural law.

[96] Coulon (2002) p. 144ff. refers to French case law under the Brussels Convention period to show that the rights of the defence have been held to be part of *ordre public* and have been grounds for refusal of recognition. Droz and Gaudemet-Tallon (2001) pp. 646–7 and Niboyet

indications of a progressive bottom-up integration in which the national courts are internalizing a common public policy concept that emphasizes procedural fair trial standards.[97] This emphasis on procedural rights can be perceived as part of the emerging trend towards judicial globalization, i.e. that in order to form a global cooperative system judges are reluctant to question foreign substantive law and find a substantive reason to support public policy arguments but are rather moving towards a procedural threshold of due process.[98] The emphasis on common procedural values to be protected under *ordre public* can also be perceived as a narrowing of the scope of public policy and a new approach which protects fundamental Community principles.[99] On the other hand, the emphasis on procedural public policy might entail a broadening of the concept and might link the free circulation of judgments in the EU to the dynamically developing Strasbourg case law of Article 6 of the European Convention on Human Rights (ECHR) and create a dialogue between courts; only further practice will tell.[100]

In addition, the protection of the judgment debtor is lessened by the narrower grounds upon which he can resist enforcement of a default judgment.[101] The new regime specifically places a burden of activity on the debtor. If he has been able to appeal the default judgment in the original Member State but has remained inactive he cannot use a mere irregularity regarding service as an argument against enforcement. This change specifically negates previous case law of the ECJ under the Brussels Convention system.[102] Therefore, a first ruling from the ECJ with regard to this specific

(2001a) p. 948 analyse the restricted *ordre public* clause and the inclusion of procedural *ordre public* within the remit of the clause. Further, Tubeuf and Lebois (2003) pp. 378–81 argue that the *Krombach* judgment of the ECJ and the inclusion of procedural public policy in the *ordre public* concept have not been changed by the transformation from Convention to Regulation, even though this groundbreaking case has not occasioned an explicit change of wording in the new Regulation.

[97] Muir Watt (2001a) pp. 549–54.

[98] Buxbaum (2004) pp. 82–4 elaborates upon this trend in the US context. Prechal and Shelkoplyas (2004) pp. 600–10 analyse the many faces of public policy and the complexity of construing and interlinking national and international standards. In particular, with regard to the ECJ itself, the authors note that the question of procedural public policy often arises.

[99] Lopez-Tarruella (2000–1) p. 128f. also refers to the case C-126/97 *Eco Swiss China v. Benetton* [1999] ECR I-3055.

[100] Gaudemet-Tallon (2002) pp. 323–8. Further, Boytha (2006) pp. 640–7.

[101] Art. 27 of the Brussels Convention was amended and narrowed. The current Art. 34(2) of the Regulation stipulates that ‘unless the defendant failed to commence proceedings to challenge the [default] judgment when it was possible for him to do so’ he can resist enforcement.

[102] Gaudemet-Tallon (2002) p. 340.

changed paragraph of the Regulation is very interesting. In *ASML v. SEMIS* the *Oberster Gerichtshof* referred questions for a preliminary ruling essentially dealing with the extent of the burden of activity upon the defendant and the conditions under which he is deemed to have been able to take action in the original Member State.[103]

In this respect, before reviewing the *ASML v. SEMIS* judgment, it is worthwhile looking at the earlier Court of Justice judgment in *Verdoliva*.[104] The case concerns the rule in the Brussels Convention, which has not changed in the Brussels Regulation, that an appeal against a declaration of enforceability shall be lodged within one or under certain circumstances two months of service thereof.[105] The Court ruled that in case of non-service or irregular service the time limit does not start running even if the defendant against whom enforcement is being sought has knowledge of the declaration.[106] Thus, one can see a tension within the Regulation itself, and perhaps in ensuing case law, between strict service rules to protect the defence and more practical service considerations to facilitate free movement of judgments.

In the *ASML v. SEMIS* ruling the ECJ clarifies that the question to be answered is whether Article 34(2) of the Regulation requires that the default judgment be duly served or whether it is sufficient that the defendant should become aware of its existence at the stage of enforcement proceedings in the State where enforcement is sought.[107] The ECJ further notes that Article 34(2) is silent as to the requirement dealing only with the service of the document that instituted proceedings. The ECJ also specifically notes the change introduced in the Regulation, that Article 34(2) does not necessarily require due service of the document instituting proceedings but does require that the rights of the defence are effectively respected.[108] The objective of the provision is that a mere formal irregularity which does not adversely affect the rights of the defence is not sufficient for applying the

[103] C-283/05 *ASML Netherlands BV v. SEMIS Semiconductor Industry Services GmbH* [2006] ECR I-12041.

[104] C-3/05 *Gaetano Verdoliva v. J. M. Van der Hoeven et al.* [2006] ECR I-1579, para. 15.

[105] Art. 43 of the Regulation (Art. 36 of the Convention).

[106] Inter alia paras 26–37 of the *Verdoliva* judgment. The Court reasoned that in light of the objectives of the Convention, the rule is specifically intended to protect the rights of the defence and provide an exact date from which the computation of the strict time limit is made. This double function would not be achieved if simple knowledge were enough to trigger the running of the time limit.

[107] C-283/05 *ASML Netherlands BV v. SEMIS Semiconductor Industry Services GmbH* [2006] ECR I-12041.

[108] Ibid. paras 17 and 20.

exception to recognition and enforcement.[109] Among the objectives of the Regulation are to ensure free movement of judgments and simplify formalities. However the Court states that this cannot be attained by undermining in any way the right to a fair hearing and refers amongst other to the *Verdoliva* case.[110] Respect for the rights of the defence is also a part of the Regulation scheme, in addition to which fundamental rights including procedural rights form an integral part of the general principles the observance of which the Court ensures.[111]

The ECJ finds that only knowledge of the content of a judgment ensures that it is possible for the defendant within the meaning of Article 34(2) to commence proceedings to challenge. Due service of the default judgment does not need to have taken place in all respects, the conditions laid down in Article 34(2) apply; but the defendant must at least be acquainted with the contents of the judgment by having been served with it in sufficient time for him to arrange his defence before the court in the Member State where the judgment was given, and the defendant is not required to take steps beyond normal diligence.[112] The judgment of the ECJ therefore demonstrates and emphasizes that the rights of the defence are part of the scheme of the Regulation despite the new reforms introduced, which place a larger burden of activity upon defendants. The judgment demonstrates that some of the concern raised regarding the reforms might be resolved by clarifying case law that protects the rights of the defence.

A separate criticism of reform of the recognition and enforcement regime is that there is no guarantee that the novel system will be more efficient and improve the rate of enforcement. This criticism hinges upon the fact that the systems of the Member States still remain procedurally unharmonized in relation to the procedural rules for recognition and enforcement applications themselves, and there are significantly different procedural systems as regards execution. In some Member States, execution requires no court at all, only public or even private bailiffs or enforcement agents, whereas in other Member States courts are involved in the process. Also the actual methods of execution vary.

[109] Ibid. para. 47.

[110] Ibid. paras 23–4.

[111] Ibid. paras 25–8. The ECJ refers to the European Court of Human Rights regarding the rights of the defence and refers inter alia to the case *Hadjianastassiou v. Greece*, 1992 A. No. 252, in which the defendant's lack of awareness of the grounds for a judgment within the period allowed for appeal against the judgment constituted an infringement of Arts 6(1) and (3) of the ECHR.

[112] Ibid. paras 39–49.

A judgment debtor may thus prevaricate in the hope that the creditor will be deterred by having to deal with a foreign system of execution, he may intend to avoid compliance and actively hide assets, or he might have genuine difficulties in making payment.[113] In none of these situations are there any mechanisms in place which specifically would assist the cross-border creditor.[114] In addition, as long as Member States have different rules for protective measures post-judgment in anticipation of execution and for access to information regarding the debtor's assets, enforcement will be fragmented and diverse.[115]

Furthermore, some of the greatest problems in the cross-border recognition and enforcement process, which comprises such issues as appeals, stays of execution, and provisional enforcement, are created by an unclear delimitation of powers between the court of origin and the court of enforcement. Neither of these difficult questions has been addressed by the Regulation.[116] Therefore, it is questionable how much the Regulation contributes to creating a European judicial area. From a review of the early policy documents, it may be seen that the Regulation has only implemented one of the first steps envisaged in the Council programme for mutual recognition.[117] However, it must be added that for the limited group of uncontested claims part of this critique no longer holds true since the European Enforcement Order Regulation has become operational.[118]

Furthermore, it is noteworthy that revision of the Convention and the Regulation have not introduced additional access to the ECJ. Under the 1970 Protocol to the Convention, only national courts that were the final instance or appellate courts could make a request for a preliminary ruling to the Court on the interpretation of the Convention.[119] This referral mechanism has been seen as one of the most successful features of the Convention as compared with other international procedural treaties.[120] Similarly, under Article 68 of the Treaty preliminary referral can only be made to the Court by national courts over whom there is no appeal. In particular in relation to

[113] Kennett (1997) pp. 421–4.

[114] This was highlighted in Commission Communication COM (1997) 69.

[115] Geimer (2002) p. 21; and Kennett (1997) pp. 421–4.

[116] Kennett (2000) pp. 231–41.

[117] Haibach (2003) p. 299f., who compares the development in the EU through secondary legislation to the US Supreme Court case law on the Full Faith and Credit clause of the US Constitution.

[118] See below Chapter 9 for a presentation and analysis of the Enforcement Order Regulation.

[119] Inter alia Dashwood et al. (1987) pp. 53–60.

[120] Geimer (2002) p. 33.

the Brussels I Regulation this is a regrettable. Because the rules on jurisdiction and enforcement are highly technical and contain many new autonomous definitions, e.g. 'directing activities', legal certainty and uniform application would benefit from a body of case law built up relatively promptly. Such a development is hampered by the fact that the jurisdictional issues have to be argued on appeal in the national courts before a referral can take place.

Finally, it can be noted that the European model for organizing international jurisdiction remains highly original. The Brussels Convention and its Jenard Report introduced a double or direct system that solves both jurisdiction and recognition issues, thus allowing for more harmonization and legal certainty and avoiding discrimination.[121] It is a system with a clear preference for preventing jurisdictional disputes rather than favouring a posteriori resolutions. It is also a system characterized by alternative jurisdictions, although these are exhaustive, thus neither including forum non conveniens argumentation nor allowing review of jurisdictional decisions by other courts.[122]

However, the emergence of a coherent European jurisdictional law still derives from a variety of sources. As a consequence of this diversified background, and because of the multiplicity of objectives, both procedural and Community related, there are tensions in the system which might hamper its transparency or sense of direction.[123] One commentator has identified as the main procedural aims the protection of the rights of the defence and good administration of justice; the latter includes the proximity of the court to the conflict, efficiency, and cost awareness.[124] However, in the new Communitarized context these aims have to be adapted to and mixed with the Internal Market aims which, as a new paradigm, wish to support the interests of cross-border actors. Thus, predictability and certainty as well as mutual recognition are important aims. But in some instances the protection of a party, even in the economic context, overrides other aims and thus represents a common or general interest protected by the Community.[125] In sum, jurisdictional regulation in the Community is today a multifaceted whole and is still finding its aims and boundaries.

[121] Kennett (1993) p. 87f. and Fallon (2003) p. 36f. See Juenger (1994) and Opeskin (1994) for an interesting dialogue on the aims behind different private international law systems and the merits or otherwise of forum shopping.

[122] Fallon (2003) pp. 40–4. Note, however, that several commentators are critical of this system, which they consider too rigid: Kohler (1985) p. 581ff.; and Hartley (2005) pp. 813ff. and 826ff.

[123] Kennett (1993) p. 106f.

[124] Fallon (2003) pp. 46–51.

[125] Ibid. pp. 54–60.

9

Enforcement of Uncontested Claims

Legislative History

On 18 April 2002 the Commission proposed a Council Regulation creating a European enforcement order for uncontested claims.[1] The further work in the institutions was slower than for the previous measures adopted in the field of judicial cooperation in civil matters. This was perhaps because the enforcement order, which entailed abolishing the exequatur procedure, is an original and thus, even if only by virtue of its very novel nature, a controversial instrument. Even though, as we shall see, the procedure is national, the enforcement order itself has become transnational and in that sense goes beyond the traditional territorial scope of a judgment.[2] Thus, it has been held that the measure goes to the heart of domestic procedural law and this is the source of its Europeanization.

In 1997, when the Commission first proposed an enforcement order, it recognized that the power of governance underlying the enforcement of a judgment is an expression of national sovereignty and that there were major barriers to creating a mutual enforcement order.[3] Nonetheless, the Commission proposal came five years later, in 2002, the Economic and Social Committee (ESC) gave its opinion in December 2002,[4] and the European

[1] COM (2002) 159.

[2] Baker (2003) paras 9–10, p. 986f.

[3] COM (1997) 609, p. 1, paras 17–18. Rouchaud-Joët (2003) p. 452 notes that the choice of method for creating measures to fulfil the objectives of the mutual recognition programme must be based on legal considerations of subsidiarity, proportionality, and complexity, as well as on political considerations regarding the level of confidence and trust achieved. The author considers that the Commission's approach is a gradual one, which reflects the current state of evolution of the regime.

[4] ESC 1348/2002.

Parliament published its first Report in March 2003.[5] As the Treaty of Nice had entered into force on 1 February 2003, introducing Article 67(5), the co-decision procedure of Article 251 was adopted for the first time, for a measure in the field of judicial cooperation in civil matters.[6] Therefore, after the first reading in the European Parliament and the Commission's Amended Proposal,[7] the Council adopted a common position.[8] Thereafter, the Commission made a declaration[9] in relation to the common position and the common position was transmitted to the European Parliament for its second reading and second Report.[10] Finally, after the second reading in the Parliament, the Council and the Parliament together signed and adopted the 'Enforcement Order Regulation'.[11]

The Regulation entered into force on 21 January 2005 but became applicable from 21 October 2005. The legal basis could, according to the Commission, be found in Articles 61(c) and 65.[12] Even though Article 65 does not specifically mention either abolishing the exequatur or creating an enforcement order, it is easy to see that such measures might fall under the general task mentioned in Article 65(b), 'improving and simplifying:... the recognition and enforcement of decisions in civil and commercial cases'. One commentator disagreed and contended that a measure which completely abolishes the exequatur procedure goes beyond merely improving and simplifying and thus cannot fall under this subparagraph.[13] Notwithstanding this, commentators have also inferred both that Article 65(c) was the correct specific legal basis as it referred to 'eliminating obstacles to the good functioning of civil proceedings' and that this entailed a new era for judicial cooperation in civil matters as the EU was hereby moving from traditional forms of cooperation to a deeper procedural unity.[14]

[5] A5 108/2003.

[6] The Draft Constitution, OJ C-169/2003, 18.7.2003, p. 1, also followed this in that the 'ordinary legislative procedure', like the co-decision procedure, is applicable to judicial cooperation in civil matters. However, both the Nice Treaty and the Draft Constitution excluded aspects relating to family law, for which unanimity in the Council is required.

[7] COM (2003) 341.

[8] OJ C-79E, 30.3.2003, p. 59.

[9] COM (2004) 90.

[10] A5 187/2004.

[11] (EC) No. 805/2004, Council and Parliament Regulation creating a European Enforcement Order for uncontested claims, OJ L-143, 30.4.2004, p. 15.

[12] COM (2002) 159, p. 2.

[13] Tagaras (2004) p. 4.

[14] Hess (2003) p. 223f.

However, the legal basis also provided that all measures have to be necessary for the proper functioning of the Internal Market. According to the Commission, this condition was fulfilled for the Enforcement Order Regulation since the Brussels I Regulation did not remove all obstacles to the unhindered movement of judgments. The streamlining of recognition and enforcement created by the Brussels I Regulation was still too restrictive, and therefore the aim of the Enforcement Order Regulation was to abolish the exequatur for uncontested claims. The purpose stated in Article 1 of the Regulation was to permit the free circulation of judgments without any intermediate proceedings. This was, according to the Commission, a necessity for businesses, addressed a concern of the economic sector, and was in the interest of the proper operation of the Internal Market.[15] This link between the idea of the four fundamental freedoms and the free circulation of judgments is not a new one, and has in the academic debate been called an enforcement 'passport'.[16] This link to the four fundamental freedoms of free movement in the EC and mutual recognition of judgments as the 'fifth freedom' has also been mentioned in the case law of the ECJ.[17]

This link between mutual recognition of judgments, including gradual abolition of the exequatur, and the Internal Market was also made in the Council Draft programme of measures to implement the principle of mutual recognition of decisions in civil and commercial matters.[18] The motivation for the programme came explicitly from the Tampere European Council, which stated that the principle of mutual recognition should become the 'cornerstone' of judicial cooperation. In the areas of private law covered by the Brussels Convention the programme specifically raised concerns in relation to inter alia uncontested claims.[19] The programme aimed in its second series of measures to achieve the complete abolition of the recognition requirement but recognized that ancillary measures such as setting up minimum standards for certain aspects of civil procedure might be a necessary precondition to this.[20]

[15] COM (2002) 159, p. 2.

[16] Normand (2003) p. 237. Note though, that the term 'passport' has also been used in the literature on judicial cooperation in civil matters to describe the standard form and system developed for serving of documents, see inter alia Spinelli (2002) p. 92.

[17] Lesauvage (2003) p. 48ff. The commentator notes that the notion of free movement of judgments can be found in the Jenard Report and that the expression has thereafter penetrated the doctrine of the Court, first, by appearing in Opinions of Advocates General Darmon and Tesauro and secondly, as used by the Court itself in case C-145/86 *Hoffmann v. Krieg.*

[18] OJ C-12, 15.1.2001, p. 1.

[19] Ibid. p. 3f.

[20] Ibid. p. 5.

The Commission stated that its proposal for the Enforcement Order Regulation was in accordance with the programme and that in order to strengthen the mutual trust between the Member States' legal systems some minimum procedural standards would be laid down in the Regulation.[21] The ESC emphasized the beneficial aim of the proposal, i.e. that through the avoidance of costs and delay the Regulation offered considerable advantages for creditors. The overall economic advantage was also considerable, since according to the ESC's statement an estimated 90 per cent of all judgments being enforced between Member States were based on uncontested claims.[22] Similarly, the European Parliament in its first Report welcomed the proposal as an appropriate complement to the free movement of services and trade in the Internal Market, assisting creditors to enforce their claims.[23]

Substantive Content

The scope of the Enforcement Order Regulation is limited, like that of the Brussels I Regulation, to civil and commercial matters, thus excluding revenue, customs, and administrative matters.[24] The Regulation also only applies to claims for payment of specific sums which are uncontested. Thus, only specific monetary claims which have fallen due or for which the

[21] COM (2002) 159, p. 3f.

[22] ESC 1348/2002, para. 3.1.

[23] A5 108/2003, p. 14.

[24] Art. 2. Also excluded are matters relating to the status or legal capacity of natural persons, property rights arising out of a matrimonial relationship, wills and succession, bankruptcy proceedings, social security, and arbitration. Tagaras (2004) p. 7f. notes that in contrast to the Brussels I Regulation the European Enforcement Order Regulation specifically excludes 'liability of the State for acts and omissions in the exercise of State authority, ("*acta iure imperii*"). This addition might appear slightly odd since such matters have normally been construed as falling outside the scope of 'civil matters' under the Brussels Convention. This question was raised in a case pending before the ECJ at the time of the EEO negotiations: C-292/05 *Lekhoritou and others v. Germany*, judgment 15.2.2007 reported OJ C-82, 14.4.2007, p. 5, available on the website http://curia.europa.eu/en/index.htm.

The ECJ has in its judgment re-confirmed its settled case law that actions between a private party and a public authority fall outside the scope of the Brussels Convention where the public authority is acting in the exercise of its public powers in the specific context of acts perpetrated by armed forces in the course of warfare. The potential explanation for the specific mention in the Enforcement Order Regulation is that since the Regulation abolishes *ordre public* defences, the Member States wanted a specific exclusion as protection in the event that such claims were ever considered 'civil and commercial'.

judgment indicates a due date are relevant. This naturally includes claims with interest which result from unequivocal legislative provisions and which can also be interpreted as including claims for periodic payments (e.g. rent) and index-linked orders.[25] The definition of uncontested is naturally very important for the scope of the Regulation and was subject to varying opinions and final compromise during the legislative phase.[26] The definition is in Article 3 and encompasses, first, claims to which the debtor has expressly agreed by admission or settlement; secondly, claims to which the debtor has never objected in compliance with the relevant procedural requirements; and thirdly, claims where the debtor has not appeared in court after initially having objected to the claim in the course of proceedings (such conduct amounting to tacit admission of the claim).[27] Both the second and third types of claim include a reference to national procedural law, since their practical application will depend on the relevant national procedural framework. One commentator points out that this is unfortunate since it would be more helpful to have an autonomous interpretation in order to achieve uniform application of Community law.[28] Other commentators note that the usefulness of the Regulation to creditors will depend on how the courts interpret these provisions.[29]

After a judgment has been handed down in an uncontested claim, which falls under the Regulation Article 3 definition of uncontested, the creditor can apply in the Member State of origin for the judgment to be certified as a European Enforcement Order. Such an application shall be granted if certain conditions are fulfilled. The first is that the judgment is enforceable in the Member State of origin. In order for the procedure to be less cumbersome, this condition does not entail that the judgment has to be final (as was originally envisaged), and thus it can also be provisionally enforceable. The second condition is that the proceedings themselves meet certain minimum requirements, which are elaborated in Chapter III of the Regulation.[30]

[25] Tagaras (2004) p. 9; and Shúlleabháin (2007) p. 3.

[26] Tagaras (2004) p. 9f.

[27] The fourth category within the definition of uncontested claims (see Art. 3(1)(d)) consists of claims to which the debtor has expressly agreed in an authentic instrument (which is defined in Art. 4 as inter alia an arrangement relating to maintenance obligations authenticated by the authorities). Zilinsky (2006) p. 477f. notes that Art. 3(1)(c) was especially drawn up for the purposes of German law and its *Mahnverfharen* procedure.

[28] Tagaras (2004) p. 10.

[29] Shúlleabháin (2007) p. 4.

[30] Art. 6.

Before returning to these minimum procedural requirements, which the Commission states are to ensure protection of the rights of defence, it is pertinent to note that the application is to be lodged with the court of origin but the application procedure itself is not regulated by the Regulation but left to the Member States' national procedural rules. Therefore, it is for these national rules to determine the complexity and cost of such application proceedings. However, it is apparent from the system that this is supposed to be an ex parte procedure and that the debtor may only be heard when exercising any of the remedies available to him. Notwithstanding the many different procedures which the Member States' national rules will lay down for dealing with such certificate applications, the Commission contends that this application procedure is one of the prime advantages of the Regulation in comparison to the exequatur procedure, since the certification is done by the court of origin, which will be familiar with the case at issue.[31] However, it is to be hoped that the composition of the court of origin is not the same when dealing with the certification as when handing down judgment, because if it were, it would be to confirm its own decision on jurisdiction and minimum requirements.[32]

The minimum procedural standards which have to be fulfilled in order for the judgment to be eligible for certification are intended to provide the debtor with the means to defend himself against the claim if he wishes to do so. First, the jurisdiction of the judgment court must fulfil certain of the exclusive and specific protective jurisdiction rules of the Brussels I Regulation.[33] Secondly, if there is no admission of the defendant there are detailed rules with regard to the proper service of the documents, outlining the relevant information and documents to be served and the accepted methods of service.[34] The information to be provided includes inter alia the amount of the claim including interest, the reason for the claim, the procedural requirements

[31] COM (2002) 159, p. 6.

[32] Tagaras (2004) p. 12. Zilinsky (2006) p. 479 considers that it is possible that at the same court another judge than the one who rendered judgment deals with certification but notes that this is determined by national law. Shúlleabháin (2007) p. 5, apparently agrees but also considers that a completely different court in the Member State of origin can issue the certificate.

[33] Art. 6(1)(b), ensuring that the special jurisdiction rules laid down in the Brussels I Regulation for insurance, consumer contracts, and exclusive jurisdiction have been complied with. For claims against consumer debtors Art. 6(1)(d) further lays down the specific requirement that the proceedings were brought and judgment was given in the debtor's domicile within the meaning of the Brussels I Regulation.

[34] COM (2002) 159, p. 10; see also Arts 13–17.

for contesting the claim, and the consequences of absence or default.[35] It is notable that this obligation for information is one of the cornerstones of the Regulation, because it is on the basis of the uncontested nature of the claim, as well as on the basis of sufficient information having been provided to the debtor, that the Member States have accepted mutual trust and direct enforcement.[36] The obligation to provide information is also the main mechanism by which the Regulation strives to protect the defendant debtor and to offer procedural fairness guarantees.

The accepted manners of service are grouped into two categories: service with proof of receipt by the debtor, e.g. personal service with a receipt signed by the debtor, and service without proof of receipt by the debtor, only allowed where the debtor's address is known with certainty.[37] During the course of negotiations the most controversial of the methods of service was postal service without proof of receipt, which according to some legal traditions is natural and according to others insufficiently guarantees the debtor's rights.[38] Therefore, in the Regulation this method of service is specifically limited to certain conditions.[39] With regard to the minimum standards, it is noteworthy that they do not include any specific time frame either for service or subsequent to service for the defendant to prepare a defence. This is particularly surprising, since both the Commission proposal and the amended proposal include an Article referring to 'sufficient time to arrange for defence'.[40] If the judgment and proceedings fulfil the above requirements and the debtor has been given an opportunity to challenge the judgment and has not availed himself of this option the European Enforcement Order (EEO) certificate shall be handed down.

In order to further protect the debtor but also to assist the creditor, there are rules regarding cure and review of the minimum standards. Thus, first, if service of proceedings has not fulfilled the minimum requirements, the judgment itself can be served with the acceptable means and if full challenge of the judgment is possible and the debtor fails to take this opportunity,

[35] Arts 16 and 17.

[36] Baker (2003) para. 15, p. 988.

[37] Arts 13 and 14. Zilinsky (2006) p. 483 notes that the notion of certainty is unclear and will have to be clarified by the ECJ in future case law.

[38] Tagaras (2004) p. 15f.; Normand (2003) p. 250ff.

[39] Arts 13(1)(c), 14(1)(c)–(e), and 14(3).

[40] Both COM (2002) 159, p. 11 and COM (2003) 341, p. 17 mention 14 days, calculated from the date of service, as the minimum time that is 'sufficient' to arrange a defence. Art. 19(1)(a)(ii) is the only Article in the final version of the Regulation to mention service in sufficient time, but does not include any parameters for what 'sufficient' time might be.

certification is also possible. Secondly, if service was made by any of the accepted means without proof of the debtor's receipt, if service was not effected in sufficient time, or if the debtor was prevented from objecting to the claim by reason of *force majeure*, certification can only take place if the debtor has been entitled to review of the judgment.[41]

The minimum standards, including the list of accepted methods of service and the list of matters of which the defendant is to be informed, are specifically minimum ones, which entails that it is at the discretion of each Member State whether or not to adapt its national rules on service; as long as the minimum is adhered to more stringent or stricter national rules on service are still accepted.[42] Despite their minimum character, it is also clear that these rules are the first in the new policy area of judicial cooperation in civil matters to have the potential to harmonize national civil procedural rules. They set a standard for service, and particularly the informative content of serving a claim or a summons, which must exist in the national proceedings for the judgment to fulfil the criteria for EEO certification.[43] However, it is also clear that these minimum standards, which were relaxed slightly in the legislative process, are at the heart of the question of whether mutual trust will be achieved through the Regulation.[44]

Under the crucial Article 5 of the Regulation, a judgment which has been certified as an EEO in the Member State of origin shall be recognized and enforced in the other Member States without a declaration of enforceability being needed or without any possibility of its recognition being opposed. However, the enforcement procedures themselves are governed by the law of the Member State of enforcement; the only requirement laid down in the Regulation is that the enforcement procedures are applicable under the same conditions as for judgments handed down in the Member State of enforcement.[45] The Member States are obliged to provide the public and professional circles, in particular via the European Judicial Network, with information about the methods, procedures, and competent authorities of enforcement.[46] The only possible grounds for refusal of enforcement in the

[41] Art. 19.

[42] COM (2002) 159, p. 10.

[43] Preamble, recital 19. See also Tagaras (2004) p. 17 and Hess (2003) p. 233f. Zilinsky (2006) p. 480f. emphasizes that the Member States are not required to adapt their national procedural laws to meet the requirements set out in the Regulation, but if they do not certification of judgments under the Regulation will not be possible.

[44] Andersson (2005b) p. 248ff.

[45] Art. 20.

[46] Art. 29.

Member State of enforcement are either an irreconcilable earlier judgment which involves that same cause of action, and which was not and could not have been raised as an objection in the proceedings in the Member State of origin, or an irreconcilable earlier international convention. Under no circumstances may either the judgment or its certification in the Member State of origin be reviewed as to their substance in the Member State of enforcement.[47] Hence, there is no customary *ordre public* exception, such as e.g. Article 34(1) of the Brussels I Regulation, in the EEO Regulation.

Furthermore, nor is there, in the Member State of origin, any ordinary appeal against the decision to issue a certificate. The Enforcement Order certificate may however be rectified in the Member State of origin if it contains a material error, or may be withdrawn if it was clearly granted in error.[48] These mechanisms are the result of a compromise between the views of the Commission and the Parliament, the former proposing no possibility of appeal and the latter objecting. Even though these mechanisms are worded relatively stringently, e.g. rectification is possible due to a 'material error' and withdrawal is possible if the certificate was 'clearly wrongly granted' and 'only in case of clear violation of Article 5', the remedies thus available to the debtor defendant come close to a genuine appeal.[49] If the debtor avails himself of either of these mechanisms he may also apply for a stay of enforcement in the Member State of enforcement and such a stay may be ordered in 'exceptional circumstances', which makes it clear that this is envisaged in a limited number of cases.[50]

Normative Implications

The (EEO) Regulation does not abrogate any previous conventions or such instruments since it creates in itself a new unprecedented type of legislation in the field of transnational enforcement.[51] However, there is of course the

[47] Art. 21. However, Art. 23 does stipulate that enforcement can be limited, made conditional, or under exceptional circumstances stayed where the debtor has challenged the judgment or certificate in accordance with Art. 10 or Art. 19 of the Regulation.

[48] Art. 10.

[49] Tagaras (2004) p. 12f.

[50] Art. 23.

[51] Art. 22 entails that agreements made by Member States with third countries prior to the entry into force of the Brussels I Convention are not affected by the Enforcement Order Regulation. However, on the contrary this also seems to entail that new such agreements cannot be

external competence limitation, which follows upon Community legislation and entails that the Member States cannot enter into subsequent international Conventions in the field.[52] The (EEO) Regulation neither abrogates nor conflicts with any Community legislation. On the contrary, this and the Brussels I Regulation are complementary, i.e. if a creditor cannot seek EEO certification of his judgment for an uncontested claim, e.g. because the minimum procedural requirements are not met, he can seek recognition and enforcement under the Brussels I recognition and enforcement procedure. The latter option is always open to him; there is no obligation on the creditor to use the EEO system.[53]

However, it is clear that in practice there might arise complex questions of overlap. For example, the creditor applies for both a declaration of enforcement in the Member State of enforcement and an (EEO) certificate in the Member State of origin, and these instances reach different conclusions as to the enforceability of the judgments. One opinion is that these decisions would not cause a lis pendens effect under Article 21 of the Brussels I Regulation. Thus, both instances come to their own decision, and the subsequent potential application for enforcement under an (EEO) certificate has to be evaluated anew in the Member State of enforcement.[54] Furthermore, the (EEO) Regulation and the Service Regulation are complementary, since the Service Regulation applies to cases in which transnational service is necessary. If such a matter is also uncontested and potentially eligible for an (EEO) certificate, service is to be effected in accordance with the Service Regulation, i.e. the two instruments apply together.[55] The (EEO) Regulation applies between all Member States, except Denmark.[56] Thus, presumably a Danish creditor cannot apply for such a certificate in Denmark, nor will creditors from other Member States be able to enforce with such a certificate against debtors in Denmark.

entered into after the entry into force of the Brussels I Regulation. See also Beaumont (2002) p. 14f. regarding the relationship between the former Art. 49 of the Brussels Convention and the Brussels I Regulation, as well as the problem of external specialist conventions.

[52] See Chapter 3 above regarding external competence in the field of judicial cooperation in civil matters.

[53] Beaumont (2002) p. 15, and Art. 27.

[54] Tagaras (2004) p. 21f.

[55] Art. 28; and Preamble, recital (21).

[56] According to recitals (24) and (25) of the Preamble the UK and Ireland have opted in to the Regulation, but Denmark will not take part. See also Art. 2 of the Regulation.

The (EEO) Regulation has been applicable from 21 October 2005 but it is difficult to know its consequences and effect; one can only make predictions. As to ascertaining its effectiveness, it is noteworthy that the Regulation does not provide for a follow-up report to be prepared, in contrast to the Service Regulation, the Evidence Regulation, and the Brussels I Regulation, which is an unfortunate discrepancy.[57] Particularly since the (EEO) Regulation is a completely new type of instrument, with potentially far-reaching consequences for debtors and creditors, an obligation to produce a follow-up report would have been appropriate. Another factor which makes the need for follow-up urgent is that the (EEO) Regulation for uncontested claims has been called a 'pilot project', i.e. a trial instrument, which if it is successful can perhaps be extended to other types of claim.[58]

The main aim of the Regulation is that, through the mutual trust shown in the abolition of the exequatur, creditors will save time and costs because they will not need to apply separately for enforcement in the Member State of enforcement; this is naturally particularly advantageous if the creditor wishes to enforce in several jurisdictions. As one commentator notes, the right to enforcement recognized by the European Court of Human Rights coupled with the principle of the free movement of judgments in the EU responds to the needs of big and small economic operators and reinforces the credibility of the law.[59] Thus, the (EEO) Regulation can also be considered to support economic actors and to reinforce the law. Notwithstanding the positive development that the Member States have moved towards greater mutual trust also by drastically reducing the grounds of refusal of enforcement in the respective legal systems, there are several weak points in the Regulation.

The aim to reduce the time and cost of enforcing uncontested claims, thereby assisting creditors and the working of the Internal Market, might for several reasons remain unattained. Even though the exequatur procedure has been abolished, an application procedure in the Member State of origin has been introduced. Since this procedure has not been harmonized there is a risk that time and costs will accumulate and vary greatly between the Member States, depending on the resources of each Member State's court system. Furthermore, as the court of origin itself is obliged to deal with this

[57] ESC 1348/2002, para. 4.11.

[58] See Council Document 10480/01, JUSTCIV 88 (29.6.2001); Baker (2003) para. 57, p. 991; and Boschiero (2003) p. 404.

[59] Fricero (2003a) p. 61f.

new application procedure, there is also the problem of inexperience since in the past international enforcement matters have often been dealt with by a centralized body within the national court systems rather than by each local district court. Therefore, one can expect, at the least, a certain period of adaptation by the national district courts.

Furthermore, in relation to speed and lower costs, the debtor can, simply by filing a perfunctory defence, always prevent the claim from becoming 'uncontested' within the meaning of the Regulation. And even if the claim is 'uncontested' and the EEO certificate is issued, there is also a possibility that the rectification procedure will be used more frequently than was envisaged and thus the parties, by raising an argument in the Member State of origin about whether or not the order was 'clearly wrongly granted', could introduce an element of appeal and delay enforcement. One commentator calls these inherent risks the fragile efficiency of the Regulation.[60]

It is furthermore noteworthy that the minimum procedural standards for service and provision of information to the defendant, which were the result of a compromise between systems, might be very difficult to apply in some jurisdictions.[61] For example, in countries which normally apply postal service, this form of non-personal service now has to be coupled with an explicit review procedure if claimants are to be able to apply for an EEO certification. If such a procedure does not exist at present it will entail either that there will be very few EEOs issued in such jurisdictions or that nationally a new tier of procedure will have to be introduced.[62] Thus litigants in general in all Member States, in particular non-repeat litigants who are citizens or small or medium-sized enterprises (SMEs), will be faced with a complex exercise to identify the internal procedures to follow so that their future judgment will be certifiable. And if they have to use more cumbersome procedures than normal to do so, the speed and cost benefits might be mitigated.

Linked to these concerns about speeding up procedures and reducing costs in the Member State of origin is the fact that the Regulation and its preparatory documents again highlight the still inherent discrepancy that execution mechanisms themselves are not harmonized. Therefore, creditors in possession of a certificate will still have to apply for enforcement via varying foreign procedural mechanisms in the Member State or States of enforcement, with

[60] Baker (2003) para. 40, p. 991.

[61] Crifò (2005) pp. 209–13 outlines the nature of the compromise between personal and non-personal service.

[62] Ibid. pp. 217–23 has analysed the Regulation vis-à-vis the Civil Procedure Rules in England and Wales and in this process identified precisely this problem.

documents translated into the relevant official language,[63] and to foreign enforcement authorities.[64] Depending on the Member State in question, these proceedings can still entail considerable time and expense. Also, notwithstanding that neither the judgment nor the certificate can be reviewed as to their substance in the Member State of enforcement, there might in the national enforcement procedures themselves be other mechanisms of objection or appeal which the debtor can raise, further increasing the time and cost of enforcement.[65]

The propounded aim of the Regulation of assisting creditors, but also providing minimum procedural guarantees for defendant debtors, is furthermore a difficult one to attain. Commentators have raised qualitative concerns regarding the system created. As one commentator notes, the Regulation does unquestionably illustrate a shift towards effective enforcement and a move away from the rights of the defence.[66] The first concern is that since the minimum procedural criteria for granting an enforcement order certificate are only minimum criteria, there is also a risk that there will be differences between Member States, introducing an element of complexity and uncertainty into the system.[67] With regard to the minimum criteria,

[63] Art. 20. Each Member State may indicate languages other than its own official one(s) which it can accept. The translation stage, which has partly been successfully excluded in the Service Regulation, always adds cost and expense for the enforcing party.

[64] See Chapter 8 above for exactly the same critique vis-à-vis the Brussels I Regulation. See also Kennett (1997) pp. 421–4. For a more recent source see the same author, Kennett (2002) p. 256, who identifies the enforcement agents as the main difference between Member States, particularly the divide between States which have specialized government agents and States which have more diffuse systems with a number of remedies/agents. Kennett (2002) pp. 258–62 also notes that if there is a political will to create better transnational enforcement mechanisms some preliminary issues need to be agreed upon, e.g. the social ethos to be achieved (the balance to be struck between the rehabilitation of the creditor and the legitimate interest of the creditors); the status of enforcement agents; the division of power between the agents, the creditors, and the courts; as well as the intrusion into the private sphere of the debtor.

[65] Kennett (2003) pp. 94–107 elaborates on the issues relating to harmonization of enforcement mechanisms. Furthermore, at p. 110f., the commentator notes that aside from the enforcement problem of mutual recognition there is the problem of effective enforcement mechanisms, which are transparent enough to encourage foreign creditors to attempt cross-border enforcement. Because enforcement laws are deeply embedded in national legal cultures the best way forward for harmonization is to focus on methods of enforcement rather than the structures of the enforcement system, setting common targets and reviewing progress together. Furthermore, at p. 108f., the commentator notes that improvements might be made in a crucial area, namely exchange of information between enforcement agents, and even advocates a separate enforcement data agency to coordinate the flow of information.

[66] Andersson (2005b) p. 248f.

[67] ESC 1348/2002, para. 5.3. The Committee sees this as a weakness in the Regulation.

specifically the fact that service through alternative modes other than verifiable personal service is allowed, this has been considered too loose a minimum standard that does not provide enough security for debtors.[68]

In addition, the fact that a court in the Member State of origin issues the certificate and ensures that the adequate minimum standards are observed can be problematic if national courts, for reasons of even unconscious parochialism, do not thoroughly scrutinize the judgments of their colleagues or the standards of their own system.[69] Also, in relation to the observance of minimum standards and their transposition into national law, there is no specific direct sanction which will apply to the Member States in such a situation.[70] In addition, concerns have been raised with regard to human rights, raising the question of whether the Regulation provides sufficient fairness and procedural guarantees to the debtors for their rights of defence to be protected.[71] The case law of the European Court of Human Rights explicitly includes enforcement within the realm of Article 6 of the European Convention on Human Rights (ECHR) and the right to a fair trial.[72]

[68] Tarzia (2003b) p. 457f.

[69] Hess (2002b) p. 125, in particular footnote 21, where support is given for the view that national judges are so much a part of their own legal order that they often do not perceive its procedural deficiencies. Tarzia (2003b) p. 456f. notes that the favouring of the court of origin is unusual and of concern.

[70] Baker (2003) para. 29, p. 990. However, the general EC law principles of State liability for breach of EC law would of course be applicable in a specific case if the party were to pursue such a claim.

[71] Tagaras (2004) p. 19.

[72] The leading case is *Hornsby v. Greece* (1997) 24 EHRR 250 in which the Court of Human Rights made a clear and general dictum confirming that Art. 6 of the ECHR applied to the enforcement of judgments. The case has subsequently been followed and further elaborated by other cases such as *Estima Jorge v. Portugal* [1998] HRCD 447. See Yessiou Faltsi (2002), in particular pp. 202–10, for an analysis of the consequences of the Court of Human Rights case law. Furthermore, the cases show the emanation of the principle of procedural effectiveness in the enforcement sector but also show that proportionate and balanced protection will be given to both the claimant/creditor and the defendant/debtor. See also Van Compernolle (2003b) pp. 475–8, for an overview of the case law development. The commentator notes that the first group of cases to emerge from the European Court of Human Rights specifically concerned the length of proceedings, and the cases acknowledged enforcement as the third stage of procedure for human rights purposes (i.e. after the stages of access to procedure and progress of procedure itself). Furthermore, the Court judged that enforcement was to be considered part of the procedure for calculating the length of proceedings. However, after these initial cases the Court in *Hornsby* took a further step and considered enforcement itself to be a fundamental right. See also Kodek (2005) pp. 310–33, who draws the conclusion that none of the procedural guarantees of Art. 6 concern enforcement proceedings, since these do not generally constitute a determination of a dispute relating to civil rights. The commentator rather vaguely further suggests that Art. 6 subjects enforcement proceedings to a general fairness requirement.

On the one hand, the human rights argument supports an efficient mode of enforcement, were there no means of enforcement, i.e. no means of realizing the rights created by a judgment or realization after a prolonged period of time, that in itself would be a potential violation of fair trial. Furthermore, because the ECHR applies to enforcement procedures, these themselves should perhaps fulfil the conditions required for fair trial, amongst which are independence, impartiality, and expediency. On the other hand, the enforcement procedure and its efficiency have to be balanced with the right of the defence to be fully heard, and execution itself can, in accordance with the principle of proportionality, take into account the social rights of the defendant.[73] One commentator forcefully states that efficiency concerns should not curtail the defendant's right to appeal in the Member State of enforcement and states that such a curtailment could be seen as breaching the principle of right to contradiction.

Thus the exclusivity of the Member State of origin can be seen as a flagrant inequality and denial of the right of the defence to be heard.[74] The rights of the defence should, according to one observer, not be overridden for the sake of achieving procedural efficiency, thus there should always be a possibility of reviewing the decision to grant the certificate.[75] However, apart from the rights of the defence to be fully heard, there are also other guarantees within the right to a fair trial, e.g. the independence of the court and the obligation to give reasons, which can either systematically or *in casu* be breached.[76] In addition, one commentator has argued that the national procedural systems provide different levels of protection and that mutual recognition rests on a 'fictive' equality between procedures.[77] Therefore, in order to guarantee

[73] Baker (2003) paras 16–29, p. 988f.; and Van Compernolle (2003b) pp. 478–82. Note, however, that Kodek (2005) pp. 310–18 is sceptical that the ECHR would apply fully to execution procedures because these might not fall within the definition of 'determination of civil rights and obligations' and in practice many execution procedures, e.g. ex parte ones, would have problems with the qualitative standards of Art. 6. The commentator thus considers that on the basis of the current case law we only know for certain that the reasonable time requirement applies to enforcement proceedings.

[74] Tarzia (2003a) p. 87f.

[75] Baker (2003), in particular paras 28 and 39, p. 990f.

[76] Fricero (2003a) pp. 71–7 and (2003b) pp. 180–3, who in relation to human rights obligations and enforcement procedures emphasizes the principles of legal certainty, reasonable time, and equality of arms as important and also gives examples of how these principles could influence and affect enforcement procedures and their development. She mentions inter alia the defendant's right to protection from poverty and social exclusion as well as the creditor's right to proportionate costs of the proceedings.

[77] Tagaras (2004) p. 19 links this critique to the 2004 EU enlargement and incorporation of ten new Member States into the matrix of the policy area judicial cooperation in civil matters,

in practice a fair trial in each case, it has been argued, the EEO Regulation should have itself been preceded by a directive harmonizing national procedures, or else the *ordre public* grounds for refusal of enforcement should not have been abolished.[78] Another vein of substantive critique linked to both the rights of the defence and its balance with efficiency contends that the sectoral and gradual approach taken in the Regulation is unwise and that a more vertical approach for simplifying exequatur would have been more coherent.[79]

Finally, the general aim of displaying, supporting, and creating mutual trust between the Member States through the abolition of the *ordre public* clause has raised concern. As mentioned, this revolutionary abolition means that the only grounds on which an EEO can refused enforcement are irreconcilability with an earlier judgment, and that no other grounds – including *ordre public* – may be invoked.[80] As a symbolic gesture and as an expression of political willingness to display mutual trust this is very important and gives an intimation of further and deeper integration. It has, however, been noted that as a practical change it might not be of significant consequence, as under the previous regimes in place, the Brussels Convention and the Brussels I Regulation, it has been rare for the *ordre public* argument even to be raised let alone be successful. Thus it is rare for enforcement to have been refused on this basis.[81] The new and uncharted territory for mutual trust is evidently that of procedural trust rather than substantive trust. There have as yet been no cases referred to the ECJ under the EEO Regulation but it is to be hoped that such cases will emerge in the future in order for clarification to be provided on the practical and technical issues as well as the matters of principle raised above.

arguing that the timing is too early for mutual trust to have developed between judicial systems and courts which have not been working together for very long and which have very different legal cultures. This argument may nevertheless be seen as no more than one of timing and the concerns raised might be proven wrong as they might lessen over time when all Member States, old and new, adapt to cooperation.

[78] Hess (2002b) p. 125f. The proposal for a harmonizing directive as regards procedural standards was suggested in the Anglo-German-Swedish proposal or declaration of intention of 12.1.2001, an internal Council document presented to the Civil Law Committee 5259/01 JUSTCIV5.

[79] De Leval (2002) pp. 132–6.

[80] Zilinsky (2006) p. 486 notes that the abolition of the public policy clause has been heavily criticized and that some commentators have suggested that public policy could be invoked in the execution proceedings since these are still regulated completely by national law. He disagrees with this proposal and refers to the legislative process and the specific amendment to the Commission's proposal.

[81] Tagaras (2004) p. 19; and Kohler (1985) p. 575f.

10

Legal Aid

Legislative History

As part of achieving an Area of Freedom, Security, and Justice, the Tampere European Council called on the institutions to establish minimum standards to ensure adequate legal aid in cross-border matters.[1] Therefore, the Commission first issued a Green Paper[2] on legal aid in civil matters and organized a hearing with national experts and professional bodies. Thereafter the Commission commenced preparation of a legislative proposal, also organizing a further meeting with national experts before publishing its proposal in January 2002.[3] The elaboration of the Directive was based on a recognition of the European trend towards proliferation of cross-border disputes, which increasingly could concern citizens who were unable to obtain access to justice due to lack of resources. In addition, there was a recognition both that differences between national legal aid systems could create obstacles for the citizens and that a cross-border element would inherently also generate additional expenditure for the citizens in question.[4]

The right to legal aid and the creation at a national level of different legal assistance schemes for litigants with limited means has in the procedural debate been recognized as the 'first wave' of the modern access to justice movement and has continued to occupy a central role in that movement.[5]

[1] Presidency Conclusions No. 200/1/99, 16.10.1999, para. 30.
[2] COM (2000) 51.
[3] COM (2002) 13.
[4] Ibid. p. 2.
[5] Cappelletti and Garth (1981) pp. 4–11.

The equality principle underlying the rule of law has been understood to place the state under an obligation to formalize the theoretical right of access to justice into a substantive citizen right to legal aid. Access to formal law thus has been understood to underpin modern citizenship and to be a precondition for achieving access to social justice.[6] The right has also been recognized as an inherent part of the right to a fair trial under Article 6 of the European Convention on Human Rights (ECHR) since the well-known judgments by the European Court of Human Rights in *Golder v. United Kingdom* and *Airey v. Ireland*.[7]

The Council of Europe has also made efforts to support and promote the development of legal aid schemes in its Member States.[8] Most recently, the Council of Europe Commission for the Efficiency of Justice, established in 2002, conducted a pilot study collecting data and conducting an empirical comparative survey on legal aid in its Member States.[9] Furthermore, the right has also been recognized in the EU Charter of Fundamental Rights and was as part of the Charter included in Chapter II of the Constitutional Treaty: 'II-47 Legal Aid shall be made available to those who lack sufficient resources insofar as such aid is necessary to ensure effective access to justice.'

However, as regards legal aid specifically in cross-border disputes the measures which were created prior to the Directive were of a limited nature,

[6] Sommerlad (2004) p. 350f.

[7] *Golder v. United Kingdom*, 21.2.1975 (1979–80) 1 EHRR 524 (unreported), and *Airey v. Ireland*, 9.10.1979 (1979–80) 2 EHRR 305. Leroy (2003) pp. 299–305 analyses the doctrine on legal aid developed in the extensive European Court of Human Rights case law. Mowbray (2004) pp. 98–103 also provides an exposition of the case law of the European Court of Human Rights specifically in relation to legal aid in civil proceedings. The main conclusion to be drawn is that the Member States are not under a positive obligation to establish general schemes of legal aid for civil proceedings, but legal aid may be required *in casu* under Art. 6(1), e.g. in practice the unavailability of legal aid has *in casu* been found to violate Art. 6(1).

[8] Resolution (76)5, Legal aid in civil, commercial and administrative matters, 18 February 1976, and Resolution (78)8, Legal aid and advice, 2 March 1978. See also Recommendation (81)7, Measures facilitating access to justice, 14 May 1981, pp. 7f. and 22–5.

[9] European Commission for the Efficiency of Justice (CEPEJ), *European Judicial Systems 2002 – Facts and figures on the basis of a survey in 40 Council of Europe Member States* (2005). The report is based on data for the year 2002 and in general the report shows that if public funding for courts and legal aid per inhabitant is measured as a percentage of the average gross salary there are not many differences between eastern and western European countries. In most countries public expenditure in these areas is between 0.1 and 0.3 per cent of the average gross salary. In relation to legal aid only, however, the study shows substantial differences in budget, in the allocation of funds, and in the income level of citizens covered, e.g. the amount granted per case varies between 34 and 2,433 Euro.

e.g. the Hague Convention of 1980 to facilitate access to justice only provided for cross-border service to be free of charge and for mutual recognition of the assessment of the right to legal aid in cross-border recognition and enforcement decisions. In addition, the same Convention only applied to some of the EU Member States.[10] Another limited form of cooperation in legal aid matters has, through the Strasbourg Agreement of 1977 and the Hague Convention of 1980, been the setting up of transmitting and receiving authorities for cross-border applications for legal aid.[11] However, in practice these mechanisms have been little used partly because they are not well publicized and because there are high information barriers about the scope of benefit schemes in the signatory states.[12] One commentator has even gone so far as to say that there are 'extreme problems' in the application of the convention.[13]

In addition the Brussels Convention and the current Brussels I Regulations provide that legal aid beneficiaries in one Member State are extended the most favourable legal aid or assistance mechanism in the Member State of enforcement as regards the procedure for obtaining recognition or an enforcement certificate. However, this mutual recognition is limited in that there will be a new examination of potential legal aid entitlement in the Member State of enforcement if the litigant wants to proceed with actual execution through the available public routes of enforcement.[14] Thus, one can say that at a European level, prior to the Directive the cross-border litigant was only provided with legal aid or support mechanisms linked thereto in a piecemeal fashion. In particular it has been noted that consumers, as potential low-income litigants, perhaps might not benefit from the non-discrimination protection in the Treaty vis-à-vis legal aid in another Member State.[15]

One may also contend that the criteria and mechanisms of national legal aid systems, e.g. whether legal aid also covers the other side's expenses if a case is lost, whether a contingent fee system is available, and whether legal expenses insurance exists and the extent of its cover, are factors which will

[10] Leroy (2003) p. 308f.

[11] Ibid. p. 306, referring to the European Agreement of 27 January 1977 on the Transmission of Applications for Legal Aid, within the auspices of the Council of Europe.

[12] Paterson (1993) p. 159.

[13] Freyhold et al. (1998), p. 72.

[14] Art. 44 of the Brussels Convention, now Art. 50 of the Brussels I Regulation. See also Leroy (2003) pp. 310–14.

[15] ECLG (1998) para. 26.

influence the choice of forum in cross-border claims and opportunities of bringing such claims.[16] This background can be seen in the propounded aims of the Directive, in that the general aim of the Directive is to improve access to justice in cross-border disputes by establishing minimum common rules relating to legal aid.[17]

In more explicit terms, the purpose is to avoid the situation that the poorest people are excluded from the European judicial area because they cannot exercise their rights effectively.[18] Effective exercise of rights is also intended to contribute to the smooth operation of the Internal Market.[19] The Commission states that its proposal is intended to follow from and support the Charter of Fundamental Rights, the ECHR, and the Hague Convention of 1980 on International Access to Justice.[20] The Economic and Social Committee (ESC) emphasizes that progressive integration raises the number of cross-border disputes for both small businesses and individual citizens. According to the Committee it is important that these litigants are treated in the same manner as national residents, and therefore this and the other overriding principles of the proposal are to be welcomed.[21] The European Parliament Report also mentions the Charter on Fundamental Rights, in particular its Article 47(3), and welcomes the proposed Directive as an opportunity within the Internal Market to put into practice the right to legal aid.[22]

The Commission presented its proposal for a Directive in January 2002. The ESC gave its opinion on 29 May 2002 and the European Parliament Report is dated 7 September 2002.[23] Thereafter the 'Legal Aid Directive' was adopted on 27 January 2003 and entered into force on the date of its publication in the Official Journal, 31 January 2003.[24] The Member States were given nearly two years, until 30 November 2004, to transpose the Directive into national law, i.e. bring into force laws necessary to comply with the

[16] Paterson (1993) pp. 157, 166f. and 169.
[17] Art. 1.
[18] COM (2002) 13, p. 3.
[19] Ibid. p. 4.
[20] Ibid. p. 3f.
[21] ESC 687/2002, paras 2 and 4.
[22] A5 312/2002, p. 29.
[23] ESC 687/2002 and A5 312/2002.
[24] (EC) No. 8/2003, Council Directive of 27 January 2003 to improve access to justice in cross-border disputes by establishing minimum common rules relating to legal aid for such disputes OJ L-26, 31.1.2003, p. 41. Note that the Directive was quite speedily adopted just before the Treaty of Nice entered into force, i.e. before the legislative procedure of co-decision was applicable to judicial cooperation in civil matters.

Directive.[25] The Commission's approach to regulating legal aid differed in two notable ways from that taken in relation to previous measures in the field of judicial cooperation in civil matters.

First, the Commission's proposal for the Directive was based on Article 65(c). This is a very general subparagraph (unlike subparagraphs (a) and (b) which mention quite specific tasks) and it refers to 'eliminating obstacles to the good functioning of civil proceedings if necessary by promoting compatibility of the rules on civil procedure applicable in the Member States'. The proposal for a directive on legal aid was the first Commission measure within the field of judicial cooperation in civil matters to be based on this more general legal basis. This might have occasioned the matter to be perceived as slightly more sensitive than previous proposals and thus might have caused the need for extensive external consultation prior to the publication of the proposal. Additionally, the use of the general legal basis might also have been the reason for some caution in the use of legislative instrument in that, instead of proposing a regulation the Commission proposed its first directive in the field. It is notable that both the ESC and the European Parliament addressed the legal basis question with regard to the proposed Directive and explicitly accepted that competence to adopt it generally fell within the scope of Article 65(c).[26]

Secondly, there was some debate as to whether all aspects of the Commission's initial proposal fell within the scope of Article 65. This followed from the fact that the proposal could have been interpreted as affecting disputes which were not of a cross-border nature and thus would have fallen foul of the limiting condition in Article 65 which specifically restricts legislative competence to cross-border matters.[27] Therefore, the Commission was not able to maintain its argument that it would be inconsistent and discriminatory for the Member States to provide a better support mechanism for cross-border disputes than for purely domestic matters, nor to maintain its corollary suggestion that a general minimum standard should be the object of the Directive. Notwithstanding the fact that the final Directive did not support this view, it is inevitable that the minimum standards for solely transnational disputes can and might cause spillover, i.e. affect and put pressure on the purely domestic systems to reform.[28]

[25] Art. 21, which also states that specifically for Art. 3(2)(a) of the Directive the Member States have more time for transposition, until 30 May 2006.

[26] ESC 687/2002, para. 2.9, and A5 312/2002, p. 25.

[27] Leroy (2003) p. 317; and Boularbah (2003) pp. 184 and 188f.

[28] Leroy (2003) p. 317. See also the Commission proposal for a regulation creating a European order for payment procedure, COM (2004) 173, p. 7f., in which the Commission adopted the same

Substantive Content

Chapter I of the Directive establishes its scope. First, it is limited to civil and commercial matters. These are not defined in the Directive, but the Commission mentions that they naturally include employment and consumer matters. The Commission also mentions that this approach vis-à-vis the Directive's scope is 'in the spirit of Council Regulation 44/2001', i.e. the Brussels I Regulation.[29] Secondly, the scope is limited to cross-border disputes. In the context of the Directive a cross-border dispute is defined as one in which the party applying for legal aid is domiciled or habitually resident in a Member State other than where the relevant court is sitting or where the decision is to be enforced.[30] The third limitation of the scope of the Directive is that the parties entitled to receive appropriate legal aid are solely natural persons, thus in practical terms excluding small businesses.[31]

Chapters II and III of the Directive specify the minimum standards of legal aid that must be offered to natural persons in cross-border civil or commercial disputes by the Member State in which the court is sitting. First, the legal aid must include costs in relation to pre-litigation advice, legal representation in court, and exemption from or assistance with the court fees. Moreover, legal aid might also cover, depending on the national system in force, the costs of the opposing party in the event that the legal aid recipient loses the case.[32] The Directive also specifically obliges the Member State in which the court is sitting to grant legal aid for the specific cross-border-related costs of language interpretation and translation as well as travel costs.[33] Furthermore, the Directive specifically mentions that legal

kind of justification again for a measure that is more general than specifically targeted at cross-border matters. The final resolution of the Payment Order Regulation shows the difficult practical legal definitional demarcation of cross-border and domestic matters and also evidences the latent political sensitivity of the policy area. This might have ramifications for regulating ADR and small claims as well as other future measures. See Chapter 16 below for further analysis.

[29] COM (2002) 13, p. 5. See Chapter 1 above for the point that all the measures in judicial cooperation in civil matters are intended to follow the general autonomous definition of 'civil and commercial' as was first stipulated and given meaning in ECJ case law specifically vis-à-vis the Brussels Convention and now to the Regulation regime. The scope of some of the measures is limited, including the Brussels I Regulation, but these limitations are specific to each measure.

[30] Art. 2(1). The Member State in which a party is domiciled is according to Art. 2(2) determined in accordance with Art. 59 of the Brussels I Regulation. However, Art. 59 of the Brussels I Regulation does not define the domicile of a person but refers to the national law of the judge seized of deciding the question to which domicile is relevant.

[31] Art. 3. [32] Art. 3. [33] Art. 7.

aid should be granted for ADR mechanisms if the parties are obliged by law to resort to these or if the parties have been ordered to do so by the court.[34]

At the end of proceedings, if the judgment is to be enforced in the Member State of the sitting court, legal aid shall continue to be granted for the enforcement expenses, including both the enforcement order procedure and different procedures for forced execution. Legal aid shall also continue in the event of an appeal.[35] In addition, the Member State where the legal aid recipient is domiciled is obliged to provide legal aid covering the assistance of a local lawyer before the legal aid application has been received by the Member State in which the court is sitting and also covering the costs of translation of the legal aid application.[36]

A fundamental and important point in relation to the provision of legal aid, whether the minimum provision outlined above or a more generous national scheme, is that Member States shall grant legal aid without discrimination to Union citizens and third-country nationals residing lawfully in a Member State.[37] However, these entitlements to legal aid can naturally be conditional upon an assessment of the economic status of the applicant, to be based on objective factors.[38] The Member States may also reject applications for actions which appear to be manifestly unfounded or take the nature of the action into account in defamation claims.[39] The Member States are not obliged to provide legal aid cover at all if the proceedings are designed for litigants in person[40] or if the applicant enjoys other alternative mechanisms that cover the cost of proceedings.[41] In addition the Member States may request that the recipients pay reasonable contributions towards the costs of proceedings or refund the sum in part or in whole if their financial situation has substantially improved.[42] One facet of the goal of transparency in the procedures is that the authorities dealing with applications must give reasons if they do not support a request and the applicant must have the right to appeal that decision.[43]

[34] Art. 10. [35] Art. 9.

[36] Art. 8. [37] Art. 4.

[38] Art. 5. Since there are marked differences in the living standards and cost of living in different Member States it was apparently not possible for the Directive to impose a common European financial threshold for eligibility for legal aid, as is done by statute in several Member States. Thus, the Directive instead focuses on the fact that any factors taken into account in the assessment of the applicant's financial situation must be objective. The Directive also specifically mentions that a national threshold must not impede the granting of legal aid to an applicant from another Member State where the cost of living is different if this fact can be supported by evidence.

[39] Art. 6. [40] Art. 3(3).

[41] Art. 5(5). [42] Art. 3(4)–3(5).

[43] Art. 15.

The procedure for applying for cross-border legal aid is also regulated in Chapter IV of the Directive. The legal aid application may be made either directly or to the competent authority in the Member State of domicile, the transmitting authority, which shall assist the applicant in ensuring that all the documents are compiled and translated into the official or accepted languages of the receiving Member State.[44] The application is made on a standard form and there is also a form for the transmission of an application.[45] Within 15 days of receipt of an application the authority in the Member State of origin shall transmit the application to the receiving authority in the Member State of litigation.[46] The Member States are obliged to inform the Commission by the transposition date which are the relevant authorities as well as which languages and means of transmission they accept.[47] Another facet of the above-mentioned goal of transparency is that the authorities are obliged to cooperate with one another in order to provide the public and professional bodies with information on the various legal aid systems.[48]

Normative Implications

As between the Member States and in relation to its subject matter the Directive takes precedence over other bilateral and multilateral agreements including the European Agreement on transmission of applications for legal aid (Strasbourg 1977) and its additional protocol (Moscow 2001) as well as the Hague Convention of 1980 on International Access to Justice.[49] The Directive applies between all the Member States except Denmark, which entails that cross-border applicants from other Member States will not be guaranteed legal aid under the Directive when Denmark is the Member State in

[44] Art. 13.

[45] Art. 16. At the time of publication of the Directive, the standard forms were not yet prepared. The deadlines for establishing the forms were 30 May 2003 (transmission form) and 30 November 2004 (application form). These are now available on the Judicial Atlas website operated by the Commission: http://ec.europa.eu/justice_home/judicialatlascivil/html/la_information_en.htm.

[46] Art. 13.

[47] Art. 14.

[48] Art. 18.

[49] Art. 20. Apart from taking precedence over international agreements between the Member States the Directive also entails external competence for the Community in further international negotiations.

which the relevant court is sitting.[50] However, it is less clear whether Danish citizens and third-country nationals resident in Denmark will be refused cover when applying cross-border for legal aid in the other Member States.[51] A further potential inherent discrimination in the Directive, as pointed out by the ESC, which emphasizes that access to justice is a fundamental right, is the exclusion of third-country nationals whose residence status is not yet regularized.[52] In addition, an unfortunate exclusion from the scope of the Directive is the limitation to natural persons only. Both the Parliament and the ESC advocated the inclusion of at least non-profit legal persons too.[53]

Despite these limitations the Directive, through the introduction of the non-discrimination principle, represents a considerable step forward and remedies the previous territorial scope of legal aid under which cross-border litigants fell between systems. On a practical and national level the Directive furthermore clearly raises awareness of the cross-border problem and obliges the Member States to take this into account and to organize structures to deal with it. On the European level, as commentators have pointed out, the traditional and prior national scope of legal aid rules could have been seen as a breach of the Treaty's free movement and non-discrimination rules.[54] Secondly the introduction of a specific obligation to cover cross-border legal costs also represents a considerable advance, since even if litigants previously qualified for legal aid cover the domestic context of the aid entailed that the litigant himself would have had to cover expenses for translation or travel.[55] Thirdly, the introduction of standard forms and a time limit for the transmitting authorities to send on applications for legal aid, with the aim of greater simplicity and efficiency, are welcome.[56] Thus, for cross-border

[50] Recital 33 of the Preamble to the Directive confirms that the United Kingdom and Ireland will participate in the adoption of the Directive. Recital 34 confirms that Denmark is not taking part in the adoption of the Directive and is not bound by it or subject to its application.

[51] Art. 1(3) and Art. 4 read together warrant the conclusion that these persons cannot apply under the Directive and thus there would be inherent discrimination. However, Denmark is party to the European Agreement on transmission of applications for legal aid (Strasbourg 1977) which entails that between Denmark and some of the Member States there is a channel for transmission of cross-border applications.

[52] ESC 687/2002, paras 3.3–3.5 and 4.2.

[53] ESC 687/2002, paras 2.3 and 3.10, A5 312/2002, p. 10.

[54] Wilderspin (2001) p. 66f., and Kamál Yuille (2004) p. 883f.

[55] Wilderspin (2001) p. 69.

[56] Ibid. p. 70f. The author states that the previous system introduced under the European Agreement (Strasbourg 1977) has been comparatively little used, reflecting insufficient knowledge. The author also states that delays in transmitting applications may seriously compromise the applicant's chances of being considered in due time.

disputes, the Directive does seem to have improved access to justice. The Directive has been operational since the transposition date of 30 November 2004 and the Commission has not yet lodged before the ECJ any proceedings for failure of transposition by the Member States. However, nor has the Commission published any follow-up report on the functioning of the Directive; it is difficult therefore to gauge its practical impact so far.

Nevertheless, the system which has been introduced provides only a bare minimum. It is noteworthy that the Directive does not deal with the organization or quality of legal aid. The Directive does of course outline the scope of legal aid, and in this context a positive factor is that pre-litigation advice which might previously have been excluded in some national systems is specifically mentioned. However, the Directive in this respect clearly missed an opportunity, in that the final version only included a watered-down version of the provision that was suggested in the initial proposal, which stated that if the court orders the losing party to pay the winner's costs and the losing party has been legally aided, that party would not be obliged to pay or the costs would also be covered by the State. As many commentators consider this so-called indemnity principle to be one of the obstacles to access to justice, to have included the original provision would have given further support to litigants with less means and would have lowered the cost threshold of going to court.[57] Furthermore, with regard to the scope of legal aid the Directive does not address the substantive content of measures covered, e.g. it leaves untouched typical national limitations on legal aid work, meaning that counsel may only work a certain number of hours or may be remunerated at significantly less than market value.[58]

Consequently the 'minimum' introduced does not address the heterogeneity among the Member States vis-à-vis the 'quality' of the legal aid provided. Similarly, the Member States are left to organize the conditions for legal aid, e.g. they are allowed to keep or introduce financial thresholds for eligibility.[59] One commentator points out that the heterogeneity of these conditions constitutes a deterrent for potential cross-border applicants.[60]

[57] Leroy (2003) p. 315f.; and Michalik (1999) p. 148 specifically from the English perspective.

[58] Kamál Yuille (2004) pp. 886–93 gives an overview of the legal aid mechanisms in some of the Member States and also, p. 917, touches upon 'quality' considerations.

[59] Art. 5 deals with conditions relating to financial resources. Specifically Art. 5(3) allows for thresholds, but importantly Art. 5(4) states that a threshold may not prevent legal aid applicants if they prove that they are unable to pay the cost of proceedings as a result of the differences in cost of living between Member States.

[60] Wilderspin (2001) p. 69.

In addition, another commentator points out that the documentary proof asked for by Member States to show financial eligibility can be a cumbersome hurdle even for national litigants but for the cross-border applicant the burden is of course greater and the Directive does not harmonize these hurdles.[61] Furthermore, the Directive only envisages a situation in which the authorities and courts of two Member States are involved and does not address a scenario in which enforcement has to take place in a third and even a fourth country. Any additional legal aid for such expenses is not specifically covered by the Directive. Finally, even though there is a 15-day deadline for national transmitting authorities to send on applications, there is no time limit within which the receiving authority must process the application. Thus, there is an inherent potential for delay and different treatment depending on the efficiency and resources of each national system.

For these above-noted reasons, it is doubtful whether the Directive goes far enough. The Directive might indeed 'improve' access to justice in cross-border disputes, but it will not significantly change the current national systems. Hence, one commentator views the Directive as only the first step to a more comprehensive and extensive positive duty for Member States.[62] However, any hope of a uniform or more harmonized level of regulation within the European Union or of more advanced legal aid schemes is perhaps illusory or at least optimistic. As the Commission also has intimated, the potential opposition, which is seldom explicitly acknowledged by Member States, is deeply political but also obviously financially dependent. In other words, the divergences between national legal aid systems reflect structural and cultural idiosyncrasies which it would be difficult to erode.[63] These idiosyncrasies, as well as the intricate relationship between the legal and political determination of citizenship, access to justice, and the development of legal aid schemes, would affect any attempts to introduce reform.[64]

Apart from these political or state-sponsored, European-level limits to legal aid, there is another limit to the Directive. This is that, outside the scope of the Directive but in some jurisdictions of great importance in the provision of access to courts and legal representation, there are additional private alternative schemes for litigants with low financial means. It is to be

[61] Kamál Yuille (2004) p. 887f. gives Italy as an example of a cumbersome application procedure.

[62] Kamál Yuille (2004) p. 884f.; and Leroy (2003) p. 327.

[63] COM (2000) 51, p. 6.

[64] Sommerlad (2004) finds that the current political climate is unsupportive of broad access to justice or legal aid schemes, explaining this by the predominant privatized citizenship model.

hoped that such schemes, e.g. pro bono and other private initiatives, would also receive attention and be developed within the EU.[65] Such alternative schemes should also be encouraged to develop an awareness and capacity not only to deal with national litigation scenarios but also to take into account the increasing number of cross-border disputes and the particular costs problems related to these.[66] Furthermore, apart from the 'charitable' and 'judicare' modes of legal aid there are a number of other options that several Member States use or have considered when the pressure on state funds has been perceived as too high and in the process of dismantling the welfare state model of the 1960s and 1970s.[67] Such alternatives as regulating legal expenses insurance or contingent fees for cross-border claims have yet to be debated or considered.

Finally, another facet of a broad definition of legal aid which is also excluded from the Directive is the so-called 'droit au droit', i.e. the right to legal information from professionals or specialized bodies.[68] In this context it is worth noting that even just lack of information regarding the particularities of Member States' legal aid systems and alternative modes of financial assistance can in practice lead to a reluctance to bring a cross-border claim.[69] This 'information deficit' is an interesting point which, though the Directive does not deal with it at all, has indeed been reflected in the creation of other Community instruments, most notably the European Judicial Network.[70]

[65] Kamál Yuille (2004) pp. 894–10, where she compares the development and importance of alternative schemes in the United States and Europe.

[66] Wilderspin (2001) p. 71f. describes the development of alternative schemes in the Member States.

[67] Paterson (1993) pp. 150–65, who defines four principal legal aid models: (1) charitable, (2) judicare, (3) salaried, and (4) mixed. In addition, pp. 165–72, he analyses alternatives to legal aid such as contingent fees, contingent legal aid funds, and legal expenses insurance.

[68] Leroy (2003) p. 269 lists the following in his broad definition of the substantive content of legal aid: exemption from court fees, exemption from paying court officials, free legal advice and representation by a lawyer, and access to information or the provision of information on rights and obligations by professionals or specialized bodies.

[69] Paterson (1993) p. 159 notes that barriers to information about the scope, limits, and coverage of legal aid in other legal systems create obstacles for litigants.

[70] The information deficit has also been noted by the Council of Europe, e.g. in its 'Recommendation on measures facilitating access to justice' (1981). For an analysis of the European Judicial Network see below, Chapter 14.

Alternative Dispute Resolution

Legislative History

The Green Paper on Alternative Dispute Resolution (the latter also referred to by the generally accepted acronym ADR) was adopted by the Commission and presented to the Council on 19 April 2002.[1] The purpose of the Green Paper was to initiate a broad-based consultation. This resulted in a wealth of answer and comments, which were followed by a public hearing on the Green Paper in February 2003.[2] In addition, the Economic and Social Committee (ESC) gave its opinion on 11 December 2002 and the European Parliament passed a resolution on 12 March 2003.[3] Subsequently, a Draft European Code of Conduct for Mediators, dated 6 April 2004 was published on the Commission's website, and thereafter officially launched at a conference in July 2004.[4]

Furthermore, in October 2004, the Commission published a proposal for a Directive on certain aspects of mediation.[5] Initially the Commission had timetabled the Directive for adoption in 2006.[6] In addition, the UK Council Presidency in 2005 specifically named ADR as one of its four priorities in the field and the 2006 Presidencies were also committed to finalizing the project.[7]

[1] COM (2002) 196.

[2] Ibid. p. 4, and COM (2003) 291, p. 41.

[3] ESC 1394/2002, and A 58/2003.

[4] The Code of Conduct can be found on the Commission's website at: http://ec.europa.eu/civiljustice/adr/adr_ec_code_conduct_en.htm.

[5] COM (2004) 718.

[6] COM (2005) 184, p. 29.

[7] The United Kingdom held the Presidency of the Council between July and December 2005. For a list of priorities in the field of justice see the Presidency website http://www.eu2005.gov.uk/ (visited 4.9.2005). See also Council Document 1605/05, p. 44, outlining the operational priorities of the Austrian and Finnish Presidencies during 2006.

However, the Directive proposal is subject to the co-decision procedure and the European Parliament was slow to progress the matter, and this is perhaps symptomatic of its more cautious general approach to supranational regulation in the field.[8] The Parliament eventually published its Report and presented its position after the first reading in March 2007.[9] In the meantime the Council has made some progress in its internal negotiations.[10] Therefore, it is projected that a common position will be reached at the end of 2007.[11] In the amended legislative proposal of the Parliament the Directive would have to be transposed by 1 September, with the exception of its Article for which the date of compliance by the Member States is proposed to be 1 September 2009.[12]

This first section of the chapter will endeavour to present all the measures themselves. However, it will also focus on analysing the Green Paper and the findings of the consultation process, in part because the extensive consultation process already foreshadows some of the key issues, in part because the consultation process gives evidence of the different and sometimes contrary stakeholder interests in regulating ADR at the EC level.

The political impetus for the Green Paper and subsequent legislative initiatives can be seen in a number of sources. First, the European Council, according to the Commission, repeatedly emphasized the importance of alternative means of cross-border dispute resolution for the creation of the Area of Freedom, Security, and Justice.[13] Secondly, the Lisbon European Council in March 2000 in particular invited the Commission and the Council to promote consumer confidence in electronic commerce through ADR systems.[14] In addition, the Brussels European Council in December 2001, which was concerned with employment relations, emphasized the

[8] The ESC published its Opinion in 2005: ESC 688/2005.

[9] A6–74/2007, 22.3.2007, and T6–88/2007, 29.3.2007.

[10] The Council adopted a common understanding under the UK Presidency in December 2005. This common understanding reflects the Council's negotiated position regarding the substantive aspects of the Directive. However, due to differences in opinion the issues of subsidiarity and cross-border definition were left untouched and not included in the compromise achieved so far.

[11] Information obtained from the European Parliament legislative tracking site: http://www.europarl.europa.eu/oeil/ (visited 6.8.2007).

[12] T6–88/2007, amendment 34.

[13] Action Plan OJ C-19, 23.1.1999, p. 1, para. 41(b) and Presidency Conclusions No. 200/1/99, 16.10.1999, para. 29.

[14] Presidency Conclusions No 100/1/00, para. 11. This objective was reaffirmed at the European Council at Santa Maria De Feira in June 2000, Presidency Conclusions No. 200/1/00, para. 22.

importance of preventing and resolving social conflicts by means of voluntary mediation mechanisms.[15] The additional impetus and inspiration for the Green Paper seems to have come from the increased awareness of ADR as a means of improving access to justice in many Member States, in many other international fora, and in many private dispute resolution organizations.[16]

The pragmatic aim of the Green Paper was first to consult and secondly to familiarize a broader public with the existing rules and regulations and to make the initiatives taken by Member States and the Community more visible.[17] However, the Green Paper can also be interpreted as having a more wide-ranging aim, which can be inferred from the text itself, in particular from the enthusiastic statement of the Commission that ADR offers a solution to the quest for access to justice.[18] The Commission identifies access to justice as a fundamental right, referring to Article 6 of the ECHR. However, the Commission also identifies that there is a problem of unachieved access to justice, which is created by the increasing volumes of disputes as well as the increasing length and cost of proceedings. This problem tends to affect cross-border disputes even more than others.[19] The Commission propounds that ADR can play an integral part in improving access to justice and complement the traditional judicial procedures, thereby helping the parties enter into a dialogue and constituting a means of achieving social harmony.[20]

The ESC supports this last point, and emphasizes that ADR is a 'functional subsidiarity', i.e. ADR is a complementary way of resolving disputes that involve civil society.[21] Similarly but more pragmatically the Parliament emphasizes the complexity and technical nature of issues facing the potential litigant which can be mitigated by recourse to a quicker and less stressful ADR route.[22] The need for quicker, simpler, and more cost-effective resolution of disputes, which in addition removes the pressure on court systems, thus permeates the political justification and impetus for the proposed measures on certain aspects of ADR.

[15] Presidency Conclusions No. 300/1/01, para. 25.
[16] COM (2002) 196, pp. 5 and 9–10.
[17] COM (2002) 196, p. 5.
[18] COM (2004) 718, p. 3.
[19] COM (2002) 196, p. 7.
[20] Ibid. p. 8.
[21] ESC 1394/2002, para. 2.1.1.
[22] A 58/2003, p. 6f.

However, the Commission also raises justifications which are Community linked and supranational, e.g. the discrepancies in national systems, which create legal uncertainty in the Internal Market and potential discrimination, the concerns for the free provision and receipt of mediation services, and the need to simplify the regulatory framework for economic actors.[23] The impetus and aims for the subsequent measures, the Code of Conduct, and the proposed Directive stem from the responses to the Green Paper and from an interaction between the institutional or public side and the private stakeholders or mediation service provider side. Furthermore, the interaction between these has to take into account the different regulatory choices, the legal basis.

Therefore, it is significant to note that Article 65 of the Treaty, in its list of defined measures to be taken within the field of judicial cooperation in civil matters, does not specifically mention alternative dispute resolution. It is also noteworthy that in its Green Paper the Commission does not mention which legal basis it would propose for any potential legislative measures for ADR. However, since the Green Paper is clearly part of the Commission's strategies in relation to judicial cooperation in civil matters and has been published in the context of Article 65 of the EC Treaty,[24] there is a presumption that any proposed measure would be based on that Article[25] and must by default fall within the more general subparagraph 65(c): 'eliminating obstacles to the good functioning of civil proceedings, if necessary by promoting the compatibility of the rules on civil procedure applicable in the Member States'. From this point of view Article III-269 in the Treaty establishing a Constitution for Europe was illuminating in that it specifically contained a new subparagraph 2(g), 'the development of alternative methods of dispute settlement', which it appears will still be included in the projected future Treaty reform.[26]

Therefore, the new wording can be held to depict in a more complete and transparent manner the scope of Community action actually taking place in the policy field. The new wording would also arguably extend Community competence. However, before any Treaty reform enters into force, Article 65(c) remains the relevant legal basis. It can be argued that particularly in relation to this more general subparagraph the limiting conditions of Article 65 are relevant and should be interpreted in a strict

[23] COM (2004) 718, pp. 3–5.

[24] The ESC also propounds this understanding, ESC 1349/2002, para. 1.1.

[25] However, there is nothing to prevent Art. 95 from forming the legal basis. See inter alia Basedow (2000) pp. 696–9, Partsch (2003) pp. 238–323.

[26] See above, Chapter 3.

manner. It thus follows that ADR legal acts should only be adopted in relation to 'matters having cross-border implications' and only 'in so far as necessary for the proper functioning of the internal market'. However, in contrast to this analysis, the Commission has proposed that the Directive on certain aspects of mediation apply to both cross-border and purely domestic disputes. The justification offered by the Commission for this stance is that it would be arbitrary and might be discriminatory to promote mediation in relation only to cross-border disputes.

Nevertheless, it is relatively clear that the proposal as it stands does not fall within the competence attributed to the EC in Article 65 and is therefore not covered by this legal basis. Therefore, one would expect that the proposal would have to be revised through a similar course of events as was necessary for the adoption of the Legal Aid Directive and of the Payment Order Regulation.[27] It is notable that even if a new legal basis enters into force, it seems likely to include the limitation of 'cross-border implications'.[28] The delimitation between 'cross-border' and 'domestic' matters is of great importance for the attribution of competence and for the legality of EU action.[29] It has also become a key political question for the whole policy area, and demonstrates the ambivalence of the legislators, i.e. the Member States and the Parliament, towards judicial cooperation in civil matters. However, in practice, of course, should measures in the field of ADR enter into force they are most likely to interact with purely domestic measures and influence these through a 'spillover effect'. Thus, it is clear that in any event the foray of the EU into the field of ADR will bring a new dimension to it.[30]

In this context it is notable that the Parliament proposal to amend the Commission's proposed Directive takes the legal basis issue into account. The Parliament suggests that the Directive will apply if at the date on which the parties agree to mediate at least one of the parties is domiciled or habitually resident in a different Member State from any other party.[31] However,

[27] See Chapters 10 and 12.

[28] Nonetheless, the Charter of Fundamental Rights, including its 'right to effective access to justice', might entail that discrimination claims, such as the ones propounded by the Commission, will be more relevant and perhaps even successful.

[29] See inter alia ESC 688/2005, para. 1.7 noting that the Member States have sole responsibility for their domestic judicial systems and therefore a constraint is placed upon the Directive, which can only assist or enable the Member States to maintain and ensure effective legal systems.

[30] Koulu (2005) p. 550f.

[31] A 74/2007, p. 12. Habitual residence of domicile is to be determined in accordance with the Brussels I Regulation or the Brussels II Regulation. Note that it is proposed that the Article in relation to confidentiality in mediation has a separate rule regarding scope in respect

the Parliament notes that it considers that the promotion of mediation should apply domestically too and therefore proposes a recital in which the Member States be encouraged to apply the provisions of the Directive internally. Specifically the Parliament notes that limits to the scope of the Directive should not limit rules of national law that provide for enforceability of mediation agreements, confidentiality, or the suspension of limitation periods.[32]

Substantive Content

The Green Paper

First, the Green Paper introduces a definition of ADR and outlines its substantive scope. ADR is defined as 'out-of-court dispute resolution processes conducted by a neutral third party'. This definition is specifically supposed to exclude arbitration. Furthermore, the definition is intended to focus on 'conventional ADR', i.e. ADR other than in the context of judicial proceedings.[33] The definition does not however seem to distinguish between ADR mechanisms where the third party makes a binding decision, and ADR mechanisms where the third party only makes a recommendation or does not adopt a formal position in the resolution of the dispute. For the purposes of the Green Paper ADR is considered to fall within the substantive scope of civil and commercial law matters, which is a broad and diverse scope including employment, family, and consumer law.[34] However, it is important to remember that ADR is traditionally a voluntary consensual process based on party autonomy. Hence, the dispute can only relate to those rights of the parties that are negotiable. Therefore, even though the scope of the Green Paper is broad, non-negotiable rights within civil and commercial law, e.g. in family, competition, and consumer law, are excluded from the Green Paper.[35]

of a situation in which, on the date that the parties agree to mediate, the court that would be seized in the event of subsequent judicial proceedings is in another Member State than that of the domicile or habitual residence of at least one of the parties.

[32] Ibid. p. 7.

[33] COM (2002) 196, p. 6, even though in the presentation of Member State ADR initiatives some schemes which are unconventional or set in the context of judicial proceeding are also included. This discrepancy introduces confusion, thus the scope of the Green Paper is not entirely clear.

[34] Ibid.

[35] Ibid., in particular footnote 4.

Secondly, the Green Paper goes on to survey the various developments of ADR, first in the Member States and then at the level of the European Community. At the EU level, the most far-reaching ADR initiatives have been taken in the field of consumer protection. These measures include Recommendations adopted by the Commission in 1998 and 2001 as well as two networks of national bodies. These networks are EEJ-Net, which is involved in consumer support and information, and FIN-Net, which comprises competent national ADR bodies in the area of financial services and consumers.[36]

Thirdly, the Green Paper introduces two sets of questions to consult on in relation to any future potential European regulation of ADR. The first set of questions is of a general nature and pertains to the overall approach to regulation of ADR and commences with the initial question, 'What approach should be followed?'[37] Should importance be given to setting in place Community-wide rules on ADR, the aim being as the Commission puts it to 'further reinforce convergence on national laws and practice on ADR'? Or should the Community pursue its policy aimed at research and cooperation with regard to comparative law, which could be geared towards defining common principles in areas relevant to ADR? Following on from this initial question are further issues, such as the most appropriate instrument to be used and the need for any measure adopted to respect the principles of subsidiarity and proportionality. An additional question which follows from and is linked to the discussion of the initial approach is whether initiatives should be taken field by field or should as far as possible govern all fields of civil and commercial law.[38]

The second set of questions moves on to examine the content and substance of any potential ADR regulation. The different questions which arise are grouped under three separate headings: ADR and Access to Justice, Minimum Quality Standards, and Status of Third Parties. First the Commission deals with the question of recourse, which revolves around the fact that even though recourse to ADR is consensual, contractual clauses on ADR do exist. The binding character of these clauses can easily become an issue between the parties and can limit or delay their seizing of the courts, and in different Member States these clauses have different legal consequences, which create

[36] Ibid. pp. 16–17. The Commission Recommendations on principles for ADR facilities and ADR procedures can be found at: OJ L-115, 17.4.1998, p. 31, and OJ L-109, 19.4.2001, p. 56.

[37] Ibid. p. 23.

[38] Ibid. p. 24.

legal uncertainty. In addition, recourse to ADR or alternatively to traditional court procedures is affected by limitation periods. The question here is whether commencing ADR could lead to a suspension of the time limit within which to bring proceedings.[39] Secondly, the Commission discusses minimum quality standards, including ethical rules, and the obligation of confidentiality on all parties involved in ADR. In particular the confidentiality of the third party is important and the third party should be obliged to divulge information only under specific instances of applicable law, e.g. in relation to suspicions of money-laundering.[40]

Furthermore, in relation to the settlement agreement, there is first the issue of how to ensure that the agreement is consensual and the consent of the parties is valid. The Commission mentions a period of reflection before signing, a period of retraction after signing, and a confirmation stage as possible guarantees of the mutual consent. In relation to the effectiveness of the settlement agreement there is the apparent problem of legal qualification or enforceability, and a clear heterogeneity amongst the solutions adopted in Member States, apart from the problem of international enforceability.[41] Finally, the Commission raises the status of the third parties. The Commission considers third party training and potential accreditation to be pivotal to the functioning and quality of ADR as well as to the free provision of ADR services. Therefore, the question is which kind of initiatives should be taken at the Community level to support training, to establish minimum accreditation criteria, or to regulate third party liability.

The responses to the Green Paper showed a great diversity in positions and opinions.[42] The respondents welcomed action at the European level in raising awareness of ADR, envisaging an educational and promotional role for the EU with regard to ADR. However, on the question of whether legislation should be drawn up, the opinions diverged, with some respondents firmly against legislation opposing others who favoured minimum rules to ensure some homogeneity. Several respondents raised the risk of undermining national developments and the risk of compromising the contractual freedom of parties by introducing legislation.[43] Issues of subsidiarity and governance are thus visible and highly relevant in the responses of commentators or interest groups on ADR. In relation to the question of field by field or generic measures, a majority of the respondents agreed that ADR measures

[39] Ibid. p. 24ff.
[40] Ibid. pp. 28–9
[41] Ibid. p. 31f.
[42] JAI/19/03, 31.1.2003, p. 1.
[43] Ibid. p. 2.

should not be generic, but should be adopted separately for different fields of civil and commercial law.[44] This is not surprising since one of the obvious criticisms of the Green Paper was that it did not take into account the idiosyncratic aspects and nature of such diverse areas as family and consumer law.[45] This also reflects a more diverse approach that supports the principles of subsidiarity and governance, since for each discrete area an assessment will have to be made of the appropriate forms of regulation and the specific interest groups and stakeholders should have an opportunity to be involved. With regard to the responses to the substantive questions,[46] and in particular to the question of possible harmonization of ethical standards for third parties, the responses show that the conduct of the third party, including his/her integrity, impartiality, and neutrality, form a very important aspect of mediation and ADR. Most of the interest groups would accept the need for a clear ethical framework and have developed their own guidelines.[47] Hence, the respondents considered that ethical conduct should be comparable in the Member States. However, some of the respondents considered it preferable that ethical rules be developed by professional associations and institutions, whereas others were in favour of a European code of ethics or a mediation charter.[48]

The Code of Conduct

The Code of Conduct is the first measure to be adopted as part of the follow-up to the Green Paper. The Commission has confirmed that as a result of consultation it considered that promotion of self-regulation was the most appropriate policy instrument to ensure the quality of mediation services.[49] The Code of Conduct is an initiative that has been developed by a group of stakeholders with the assistance of the Commission. The website of the European Judicial Network has a link to the Code and to an explanatory

[44] Ibid. p. 3.

[45] 'CEDR response to the Commission Green Paper on Alternative Dispute Resolution', pp. 5 and 9, can be found at http://www.cedr.co.uk.

[46] Only the question of ethical standards will be dealt with specifically here since it foreshadows the Code of Conduct.

[47] 'CEDR response to the Commission Green Paper on Alternative Dispute Resolution', p. 14.

[48] JAI/19/03, 31.1.2003, p. 5.

[49] SEC (2004) 1314, p. 5. It is interesting to note that this position, which reinforces governance and subsidiary aspects of the debate, might also be the result of very active lobbying from the mediation service providers and contrasts with the concerns about quality raised by consumer interest groups.

statement from the Commission regarding the Code.[50] According to this statement, the Code sets out a number of principles to which individual mediators can voluntarily commit. Organizations providing mediation services can also make such a commitment. Adherence to the Code is undertaken without prejudice to national legislation. The Code does not represent the official position of the Commission and it will not carry out any verification process as to whether the Code is being adhered to. Thus, the Commission has supported a self-regulatory approach and assisted the ADR professional community in developing ethical rules rather than proposing binding Community legislation. However, the Commission is very much involved in the process and it seems as if the supranational level might be appropriate for some stages and tasks such as publishing information, encouraging meetings, and exchanges of best practices.[51]

Substantively the Code of Conduct is applicable to all kinds of mediation in civil and commercial matters. The principles set out in the Code cover all areas of mediation, under four headings: (i) Competence and appointment, (ii) Independence and impartiality, (iii) The mediation agreement, process, settlement, and fees, and (iv) Confidentiality. Hence, the Code states inter alia that the mediator shall be competent and knowledgeable; shall disclose information concerning his/her background upon request by the parties; shall not act or continue to act if his/her independence is or may be seen to be affected; shall also be committed to serve the parties equally.[52] Furthermore, the mediator shall ensure that the parties have understood and expressly agreed to the terms of the mediation agreement and that all parties have an adequate opportunity to be involved in the process. The mediator is also obliged to conduct the proceedings taking into account the circumstances of the case (including possible power imbalances), the rule of law, any wishes of the parties, and the need for a prompt settlement.[53] In addition, the mediator shall ensure that any understanding is reached by all parties and that all parties understand the terms of the agreement; the mediator may also within the limits of his/her competence inform the parties how to formalize their agreement and the possibilities for enforcing it.[54] Finally, the mediator shall

[50] Available on the website of the European Judicial Network: http://ec.europa.eu/civiljustice/.

[51] This role of the Commission is mentioned on the CEDR website news pages (dated 21.7.2004) as the outcome of the discussions at the conference to launch the Code of Conduct: http://www.cedr.co.uk/news/archive/.

[52] Code of Conduct, paras 1–2.

[53] Ibid. para. 3.1–3.2.

[54] Ibid. para. 3.3.

keep confidential all information arising out of or in connection with the mediation.[55]

The Proposed Directive

The legislative process is at the time of writing at the stage where the Parliament has published its report proposing a number of changes to the Commission's initial proposal. Hence, the text will take both proposals into account, in the knowledge that the final statute might be further modified and might differ from both of these. As regards defining mediation and mediator the Commission proposes that mediation is 'any process... where two or more parties to a dispute are assisted by a third party to reach an agreement on the settlement of the dispute' and mediator is 'any third party conducting a mediation, regardless of the denomination or profession of that third party'. In particular mediation shall 'not include attempts made by the judge to settle the dispute within the course of judicial proceedings'.[56] The Parliament wishes to clarify and modify the definitions by noting that mediation is a structured process of a voluntary nature that shall be respected as such where suggested or ordered by a court. This may include mediation conducted by a judge who is not responsible for the judicial proceedings concerning the particular dispute. To the definition of mediator the Parliament, which in its Report stresses the need for ensuring quality of mediation, wants to add 'reasonable expectations that the mediation will be concluded in a professional, impartial and competent manner'.[57]

First, the proposed Directive on certain aspects of mediation is intended to ensure a sound relationship between mediation and judicial proceedings through common minimum rules and necessary tools to promote mediation without nevertheless making it compulsory. Therefore, without prejudice to national legislation, the Commission proposal prescribes that courts may when appropriate invite the parties to use mediation or require the parties to attend an information session on the use of mediation.[58] The Parliament suggests however that the information sessions should not be required of the parties but that the court may invite the parties to attend if such sessions are held and are easily available.[59]

[55] Ibid. para. 4.
[56] COM (2004) 718, Art. 2.
[57] A6–74/2007, pp. 12f. and 22.
[58] COM (2004) 718, proposed Art. 3.
[59] A6–74/2007, p. 14.

The Commission proposal suggests that the Commission and the Member States shall encourage the development of voluntary codes of conduct for mediators and the Member States shall promote the training of mediators.[60] The Parliament emphasizes the need for ensuring quality of mediation, and proposes to place the burden of this encouragement on the Member States and to add that both initial and further training, as well as a system of certification for national bodies offering training courses, should be encouraged.[61]

The Member States are also according to the Commission's proposal obliged to ensure that settlement agreements reached by the parties can be confirmed in an official form, which renders them enforceable in a similar way to a judgment under national law.[62] The Parliament suggests a crucial addition or clarification that this option of making an agreement enforceable should only be open to a party with the explicit consent of the other parties to the agreement.[63]

Article 6 of the Commission proposal deals with the confidentiality of mediation. In particular, the evidence of mediators with regard to specific aspects, e.g. the willingness of a party to accept a settlement proposal, shall not be admissible in judicial proceedings. The wording of the Parliament amendment does not outline a list of specific matters to hold confidential but rather proposes wording that neither the parties nor the mediator would be entitled or compelled to disclose 'information arising out of or in connection with the mediation'. Further, the Parliament proposes that the Member States shall not be precluded from enacting stricter confidentiality measures.[64]

The final substantive rule of the Commission proposal is Article 7, which prescribes that limitation periods for matters subject to mediation shall be suspended when the parties agree to mediation, are ordered to avail themselves of mediation by a court, or are subject to an obligation to mediate under national law. If the mediation has ended without settlement the period resumes, and according to the Commission proposal the period shall in any event extend for one month. The Parliament proposes different wording on the suspension of the time limit and does not include a one-month respite rule.[65]

[60] COM (2004) 718, proposed Art. 4.

[61] A6 74/2007, pp. 13, 22, and 25.

[62] COM (2004) 718, proposed Art. 5.

[63] A6 74/2007, p. 15. Certain prescribed circumstances are excluded from the confidentiality rule.

[64] Ibid. p. 16ff.

[65] Ibid. p. 18f.

Finally, it is notable that the Parliament has introduced a number of additions to the Commission's proposal. Amongst these are that the Member States shall be obliged to ensure that information is available to citizens, in particular via the Internet, on how to contact mediators and mediation providers; and that the Member States shall encourage legal practitioners to inform their clients about the possibility of mediation.[66] The Parliament also supports a certain consolidation of the measures regarding ADR by proposing that the Directive place an obligation on the Commission to publish the Code of Conduct for Mediators in the Official Journal. It is also proposed in the recitals to the Directive that the Member States should encourage and promote the Code of Conduct for Mediators as well as the Commission Recommendations for consumer mediation.[67] Further consolidation is proposed by stating in the recitals to the Directive that it also applies to consumer mediation and that the principles set out in the Commission Recommendation on principles for out-of-court bodies involved in the consensual resolution of consumer disputes should be incorporated and taken into account in such mediation.[68] Finally the Parliament proposes the inclusion of a review clause in the Directive that the Commission submit a report on the application of the Directive, accompanied if necessary by proposals to adapt the Directive. The report should consider the impact of the Directive on the development of mediation and whether further harmonization of the periods of limitation and prescription are necessary.[69]

Normative Implications

Regulatory Questions

The Community initiatives in relation to ADR, within the framework of judicial cooperation in civil matters including the initial Green Paper as well as the subsequent Code of Conduct and the proposal for a Directive on certain aspects of mediation, do not yet abrogate any other ADR regulations whether at the international or national level. As the Green Paper mentions, the Community initiatives will be at the confluence of a number of current ADR measures, e.g. at the international level within intergovernmental

[66] Ibid. p. 19. [67] Ibid. p. 10.
[68] Ibid. p. 6. [69] Ibid. p. 20.

as well as non-governmental organizations.[70] In addition the Community's own consumer law initiatives and several developments at national levels show that this is indeed an area of dispute resolution which is evolving and which is being developed to match modern needs.[71]

Therefore, a more global or holistic view of the Commission's initial question – what approach should be followed, or reframed, and which level of regulation is suitable for ADR – might suggest that these other levels of activity might, rather than necessitate Community action, entail that there is no need for it. The same conclusion might also follow from a subsidiarity and proportionality analysis. Hence, it is interesting to note that the Resolution of the European Parliament and the explanatory statement of its rapporteur both give a cautious response to the Green Paper's queries about the level of regulation.[72] Without completely negating Community initiatives on ADR, the Resolution very clearly expresses concern, implying that the Community might not be the appropriate level of actor, and that action might conversely be adequately achieved by the Member States. This view is supported inter alia by reference to the current innovations taking place in the field of ADR in the Member States, which might be stifled by supranational regulation. Further support for this view derives from the facts that the legal systems of the Member States differ greatly in the area of ADR and that the area is very much linked to the values and legal culture of each Member State.[73]

Similarly, the ESC is cautious about ADR legislation because of the principle of subsidiarity, mentioning local, regional, and national levels.[74] The emphasis placed on the different levels of appropriate regulation also echoes many of the governance arguments, which emphasize the flexibility of regulation over rigid structures. Thus, if measures are to be taken at the Community level the question of the form of regulation arises, taking into account the specific nature of ADR as a flexible mechanism based on party autonomy. These points are underlined by the European Parliament's statement

[70] COM (2002) 196, p. 11f.

[71] Alternative dispute resolution in the broad sense is of course not a new phenomenon, see inter alia De Roo (2001) p. 97; and Galanter (1981) pp. 161–9, who calls it access in the 'shadow of the law'. Van Rhee (2005) p. 185ff. also provides a brief historic outline of conciliation in procedural codes in Europe. However, ADR emerged in the 20th century as one of the 'waves' in the access to justice movement and as one of the responses to the perceived crisis in modern justice systems: Cappelletti and Garth (1981) p. 4.

[72] A5 58/2003.

[73] Ibid., in particular paras G, J, 2, and 4.

[74] ESC 1349/2002, para. 2.2.

that some degree of coordination and coherence is desirable but that self-regulation initiatives should be promoted. The Parliament further mentions other softer forms of regulation as an option, namely recommendations, codes of conduct, and exchanges of best practice.[75] The ESC also advocates softer regulation forms, which it calls a 'measured way', such as a reference framework, exchanging good practices, and creating networks.[76]

These suggestions entail that regulation would depart from the classic 'Community method', e.g. as regards the legislative instrument chosen and the binding and uniform effect of the measures chosen. In other words directives and regulations would be rejected in favour of soft law measures which support flexibility and diversity. Similar concerns were partly visible also in the summary responses to the Green Paper from stakeholders and are most likely one reason why the measures taken so far, i.e. the Code of Conduct and the proposed Directive, reflecting subsidiary and governance concerns, clearly represent a different regulatory choice from the other measures within judicial cooperation in civil matters.[77] Commentators also argue that Community initiatives should not stifle the wider international dimension of ADR regulation and should pay attention to providing consistency with these.[78]

Finally the view of the Parliament rapporteur on the Commission's proposed Directive is interesting in this context and underlines the debate. She notes that she initially questioned the need for the Directive and feared the stifling effect of a Directive but the online consultation carried out by the Parliament and a hearing of experts found overwhelming support for the Directive despite critique of the legal basis issue. Therefore, the Parliament has attempted to propose a 'light-touch' Directive that reflects existing guidelines and can serve to encourage the use of mediation in the Member States.[79] Hence, the Parliament wants the Directive to promote mediation and provide alternative access with a framework that protects parties' interests but is regulatorily light and allows solutions to emerge through the market.[80]

[75] A5 58/2003, pp. 7 and 11.

[76] ESC 1349/2002, para. 2.2.4.

[77] Koulu (2005) p. 549. Note also that within the EU, ADR measures can also be seen in an analytical context of 'regulation theories', e.g. self-regulation versus public action and soft versus hard law, and therefore there are connections with other mainly substantive law fields in EC law: ibid. pp. 553f. and 556.

[78] Meeusen, Pertegás, and Straetmans (2004) p. 9.

[79] A6 74/2007, p. 22.

[80] Ibid. p. 23.

The Code of Conduct

We cannot yet evaluate the full impact of the Code of Conduct, i.e. ascertain how many mediators and organizations sign up to it and assess how they manage to conduct meetings and exchange best practices. At the time of writing around 70 mediators or organizations of mediators have signed up.[81] The substantive normative content of the Code is not controversial and in certain elements it resembles the standard-model mediation rules or the model mediation procedures of mediation centres that exist in several Member States. However, because these procedures also cover matters other than just the mediators' conduct, the style and content of the European self-regulation measure does have a novel touch. The duties of the mediator under the headings 'Procedure' and 'Fairness of the Process' are particularly interesting in that the mediator is given quite heavy case-management-like duties, e.g. to ensure that all parties understand the process and the agreement, as well as to conduct the proceedings taking into account possible power imbalances.[82]

Future practice, including monitoring and enforcement, will reveal the impact on the quality of mediation services and any potential harmonizing and beneficial effects for litigants of the supranational , albeit self-regulatory, regulation. However, the Code of Conduct might not be tailored to deal with some of the specific problems which arise in cross-border mediation, and which can be contrasted with experiences and developments in the arbitration sector. For example, as is likely to happen more frequently than before in disputes between consumer and corporate interests or between small- and medium-sized business interests, the parties will speak different languages, will potentially be unaccustomed to mediation procedures, and will live in states with different national dispute resolution cultures. Such matters form real practical obstacles to the provision of cross-border mediation services and put pressure on the skills of the mediator.[83] These issues are not dealt with in the Code of Conduct and it is to be hoped that exchange of best practices between mediators will take place and that this might contribute to alleviating such difficulties.[84]

[81] According to a list published and regularly updated and available on the Commission website: http://www.europa.eu.int/comm/justice_home/ejn/adr/adr_ec_list_org_en.pdf (visited 16.8.2007).

[82] Code of Conduct, paras 3.1 and 3.2.

[83] Jagtenberg (2001) p. 91f.

[84] Nor are they dealt with in the proposed Directive on certain aspects of mediation. However it its Opinion the ESC, 668/2005, para. 3.3 also notes that in order to provide equal opportunities and access to mediation in the Member States, training of mediators is needed.

A further problem with mediation, as compared with arbitration, is that not all Member States have the highly specialized and institutionalized bodies needed to facilitate the use of the procedure, but also to monitor and enforce the upholding by officiating arbitrators (or in our case mediators) of agreed rules of conduct. Thus, parties to mediation should have some safety valve or recourse if the mediator does not in practice adhere to the code. The Code of Conduct as published does not deal with this aspect at all, and this is regrettable, in particular when single mediators sign up to it.[85] When participating in launching the Code of Conduct the Commission strongly emphasized the monitoring and enforcement of the self-regulatory measure as a key to establishing trust and ensuring a high quality of mediation services, and noted that subsequent evaluations of the self-regulation procedure will have to focus on these aspects to establish whether self-regulation is sufficient.[86]

The Proposed Directive

The Commission also stated when launching the Code of Conduct that it would in parallel prepare and propose a Directive. Thus the current proposal should be seen in this context, and the provisions of the Directive that encourage development and adherence to voluntary codes of conduct and other quality control mechanisms for mediation services show the complementary nature of the measures. However, in other respects the proposed Directive provides a more mixed and less structured picture. Also, because it is still at the stage of proposal, it is very premature to assess its potential impact. Nonetheless, certain points can be made about the proposed Commission draft and the Parliament's proposal for amendments.

First, although the choice of a Directive as the legislative instrument shows respect for the Member States' diverse national systems and some notion of governance, with such large differences between them transposition will potentially also entail the adoption nationally of highly divergent approaches and methods. Thus, there is a risk that there will be little transparency and that the Community norms will have little effect. Secondly, the proposed Directive is substantively very 'uneven' in that some provisions are highly

[85] If mediators or mediation bodies sign up to the Code of Conduct they will sometimes have monitoring and enforcement structures or may be subordinated to such structures as members of mediation organizations.

[86] Speech by Mr Faull, Director-General, DG Justice, Freedom and Security, European Commission, 18 April 2005. Available on EJN website: http://ec.europa.eu/civiljustice/adr/adr_ec_code_conduct_en.htm.

programmatic whereas others are detailed and specific.[87] An example of the programmatic provisions is the obligation to 'encourage training': the extent or scope of this positive obligation on Member States is unclear.[88] Similarly, the possibility for courts to invite the parties to use mediation, in Article 2 using the wording 'may, when appropriate', is normatively extremely vague and does not prescribe any obligation at all.[89] Therefore, pessimistically, one might expect the results to be 'patchy' within the Community and that the Member States in which mediation or ADR already exists or is encouraged will continue their practices and that in other Member States in which there is no legal culture to encourage mediation the influence of the Directive will be minimal.

In contrast, the national courts are obliged to refrain from ordering disclosure of evidence by the mediator and to treat such evidence as inadmissible. Similarly, the national courts are presumably obliged to enforce and adhere to a suspension of a time limit when a dispute has been the object of mediation and perhaps to resume judicial proceeding when no settlement is reached.[90] Thus, ostensibly there will be some very specific forms of harmonization of national procedural rules, with respect to evidence and suspension of time limits. However, again the question arises as to the extent to which these rules are implemented differently in the Member States. For example, when the time limit would have run out during the period of mediation and mediation is unsuccessful, does 'suspension' entail freezing for the time of mediation but obliging the parties to commence proceedings the following day or does it entail giving them additional time, calculated from when mediation was entered into, to lodge their claim at court?

Such varying possibilities of interpretation and implementation would inherently lead to differences in procedural treatment in different Member

[87] Koulu (2005) p. 546f.

[88] COM (2004) 718, proposed Art. 4, and A6 74/2007, p. 13.

[89] The Commission, SEC (2004) 1314, p. 5, clarifies that Member States are not under an obligation to make mediation compulsory. The proposed Directive does, however, oblige the Member States to give their courts the right to hold an information session on mediation with the parties to the dispute. The consumer interest group, ECLG (2004) p. 4, notes that if this is taken as a formal obligation the mediation itself would in small consumer cases aggravate delay, even introduce an element of formality and vexation into the procedure. Therefore, the group opposes any text which might force consumers to mediate in the course of proceedings. In the European Parliament's proposed amendments, A6 74/2007, p. 14, there is no obligation to hold a mediation information session; on the contrary, this is just an option.

[90] COM (2004) 718, proposed Arts 6 and 7. Furthermore the European Parliament proposed amendments, A6 74/2007, pp.16–19.

States. Such differences are of course inherently accepted for Directives but in the context of procedural rights, which might fall under the Charter of Fundamental Rights and the constitutional rights of access to justice, there is a possibility that the ECJ would and could impose a standard and see a need for a further harmonization because the minimum is not enough. Hence, in the long run, a minimum harmonization Directive could have a spillover and positive regulatory effect.

Thus, the proposed Directive can be seen as a very tentative step towards resolving and perhaps mitigating some of the cross-border hurdles and as a positive step in promoting mediation. But many of the cross-border hurdles remain, e.g. the proposal does not deal with the question of the law governing the settlement agreement and potential review of the agreement and the actual procedure for making it enforceable.[91] The speed and efficiency of potential enforcement of an agreement would be crucial in rendering the Directive effective.[92]

Furthermore, some of the choices made in the proposal are quite schematic from the point of view of the total procedural systems into which these have to fit and of legal cultural diversity. In particular, the emphasis on confidentiality is in itself important in encouraging parties to mediate. But one may ask whether this needs to extend to the negotiation or procedural tactics of the parties, as in Article 6(1)(a) which protects the confidentiality of the information that a party was willing to engage in mediation. Particularly when the court has under proposed Article 3(1) invited the parties to consider mediation, but also otherwise, the court is (e.g. in England and Wales) allowed to take into account an unreasonable refusal or an uncooperative tactic in ordering costs.[93] This approach takes a more holistic vision of the interaction between proceedings and ADR in the specific resolution of a dispute by forcing the parties to adopt clear positions and not abuse the procedures for tactical purposes, e.g. in order to create delay.[94]

[91] An obligation on the Member State of origin to have a procedure by which the agreement at the request of the parties is rendered enforceable (unless the agreement is contrary to the law of that Member State) was included in the Council version after its first reading of the Commission proposal. Such an enforceable title would for civil and commercial matters have to be enforced in the other Member States by means of the procedure available in the Brussels I Regulation.

[92] ECLG (2004) p. 6.

[93] Civil Procedure Rules of England and Wales, Part 44 Rules 3 and 5, in particular Rule 5(3)(a)(ii). Note, however, that the Council amendments to the Commission proposal include a more general confidentiality rule and would not prevent the parties from disclosing such facts in subsequent litigation.

[94] This view is supported by ECLG (2004) p. 7; this group also notes from the consumer perspective that the court should be able to take into account the good or bad faith of a party, and any unreasonable behaviour during the mediation.

This approach also takes a more holistic view of proceedings and ADR in the general creation of a functioning dispute resolution system.[95]

Finally, the Preamble of the proposed Directive on certain aspects of mediation states that the proposed Directive respects fundamental rights. This statement does not analyse the compatibility of ADR or cross-border mediation with the requirements of fair trial elaborated in Article 6 of the ECHR and Article 47 of the EU Charter of Fundamental Rights. The European Court of Human Rights has in its case law clarified that not every stage in the procedure needs to comply with all the requirements of fair trial, e.g. with independence, impartiality, *audiatur et altera pars*, and publicity. Derogations from these requirements are conditional upon there being an effective possibility of judicial review or upon the parties having entered into the procedure on a voluntary basis.[96] Furthermore, most mediation procedures have not been considered to fall within the ambit of Article 6 ECHR since it applies to the determination of civil rights rather than their voluntary negotiation and it only applies to courts or tribunals.[97]

Notwithstanding this case law, and depending on how each Member State implements the potential Directive, e.g. whether court-annexed mediation or not, there is a real tension with the very high procedural guarantees elaborated in the ECHR and EC realization of rights contexts and the freedom to derogate from these provided in ADR.[98] For example in some jurisdictions the question of whether courts can make compulsory an initial attempt to mediate and the matter of costs sanctions against parties who have resisted mediation have been considered to highlight tensions between mediation and Article 6 of the ECHR.[99] In the ADR critical literature one of the central issues is how to protect the weaker party and his rights, the argument being that ADR can dilute substantive and procedural law and create a situation where small and weak parties are forced to resort to ADR whereas arbitration

[95] Note that the Commission explains that 'a level playing field for mediators' is the primary and valid aim behind the proposed confidentiality rule. Notably it has been modelled on the UNCITRAL model law on commercial conciliation as a tool for promoting consistency between different rules on mediation. See SEC (2004) 1314, p. 6f.

[96] De Roo (2001) p. 103f. referring to case *De Weer*, 27.2.1980, (A 35).

[97] Knuts (2005) pp. 198–201, referring inter alia to cases *Le Compte, Van Leuven and De Meyre*, 23.6.1981 (A 34), regarding the concept of determination of rights and *Coëme et al. v. Belgium*, 22.6.2000 (2000–VII), regarding the concept of a court.

[98] Lindblom (2006), pp. 115 and 127f.

[99] CEDR, *Mediation Moot*, Second European Mediation Congress material available at http://www.cedr.co.uk/. The leading cases include *Dunnett v. Railtrack* [2002] 2 All ER 850 and *Halsey v. Milton Keynes NHS Trust* [2004] EWCA (Civ) 576.

and civil procedure proper are reserved for large and financially strong parties.[100] In this vein it is interesting that the Commission's proposal for a Directive does not include any form of control over mediators and schemes but that the Parliament has proposed a system of certification. Furthermore, it is noteworthy that the consumer interest lobby does not consider the Code of Conduct to be a sufficient quality guarantee.[101]

The Green Paper, the Code of Conduct, and the proposed Directive leave many questions unanswered. First is the issue of the level at which ADR should be regulated. Despite the enthusiasm of the European institutions for including ADR within the framework of judicial cooperation in civil matters there seems also to be consensus that national development and evolution should not be stifled and that any supranational regulation should fit ADR into the national legal cultures. Furthermore, as regards the form of supranational regulation there is a clear shift towards 'softer' measures like self-regulation. However, the institutions' current, more careful approach seems somewhat hesitant as they oscillate and balance different interests without clearly advocating either subsidiarity or governance but instead still trying to regulate incrementally. Therefore, the issue of how much Community intervention in the field of ADR is appropriate will be present in the future too, and the scope of this intervention, i.e. for cross-border disputes alone, or also for domestic disputes, is still very much alive.

The second fundamental question which remains unanswered and should be further addressed is whether ADR mechanisms can be regulated for all fields of civil and commercial matters generically or whether specific initiatives should be developed. This would entail bearing in mind in developing the systems the particularities of the common types of dispute in such diverse fields as consumer, family, and labour disputes as well as purely commercial business-to-business disputes. The conduct of the mediator and issues such as time limits, which are the object of the current two generic EU initiatives, are common to all fields and as such can be regulated generically. But if the EU is going to go further and develop more holistic ADR mechanisms, as we have seen in the field of consumer law,[102] these would perhaps have more impact if they were more targeted.[103]

[100] Lindblom (2006), p. 114.

[101] ECLG (2004) pp. 3–6 and 9.

[102] See Tenreiro (2001) pp. 113–17.

[103] ECLG (2004) p. 2 are in their response to the proposed Directive critical from a consumer law perspective and note that consumer disputes would require a specific sectoral approach.

These fundamental questions, however, do not address the basic underlying question, i.e. what is the purpose of the system? In the supranational context, as in the national one, the purpose of dispute resolution mechanisms is linked to the complementary nature of all the mechanisms available in a legal system. Rather than repeating the truisms about the benefits of ADR e.g. lower costs for the parties and governments, the possibility of reparative compromise, and efficiency and flexibility, we should know what the purpose is in order to be able to tailor the mechanisms.[104] Is the effectiveness of provision of mediation services across the Community the real goal, is efficiency in dispute resolution the paramount concern, or is social consensus the important added value? All of these possible purposes can also however be contested; e.g. as we see for most of the measures in judicial cooperation in civil matters efficiency is very important but not at any cost. This foray of the EU into ADR, the third wave of the access to justice movement, should occasion an in-depth debate about the difficult equation of factors including ever higher expectations of procedural guarantees, the perceived vices of length and costs for the parties, and the public costs for governments. When these are brought together with the other measures outlined in this section, one can perhaps even see a contradiction, as one critical commentator puts it in referring to the access to justice movement and the theory that it has developed in stages or 'waves': 'The third wave can potentially obliterate the achievements of the first and second ones.'[105]

[104] Lindblom (2006) pp. 114–20, regarding the pros and cons of ADR; the author himself is critical of ADR. Ibid. pp. 109–114 for a discussion of the functions in society of procedure; note that the author is sceptical about the possibility of ADR fulfilling these.

[105] Lindblom (2006) p. 126, free translation from Swedish.

12

Payment Order

Legislative History

The order for payment procedure proposal falls within a group of initiatives of the Commission and the EU institutions to remedy problems perceived in cross-border debt collection.[1] Other initiatives include the Directive combating late payment in commercial transactions and the European Enforcement Order.[2] According to Article 5(1) of the Directive on late payment, 'Member States shall ensure that an enforceable title can be obtained, irrespective of the amount in debt, normally within 90 calendar days . . . provided that the debt or aspects of the procedure are not disputed.' Notwithstanding some optimism on the part of the Commission, this provision has not occasioned significant modifications or specific transposition measures in the national procedural codes, as Member States have deemed their current procedures capable of providing redress within 90 days.[3] Therefore, the Commission states that the Directive can only be considered a careful first stage, not the final step in the process towards the establishment of an

[1] For a background to the problem and the history of the Directive combating late payment, see Milo (2003) pp. 379–83.

[2] (EC) No. 35/2000 of the European Parliament and of the Council of 29 June 2000 on combating late payment in commercial transactions OJ L-200, 8.8.2000, p. 35 and (EC) No. 805/2004, Council and Parliament Regulation creating a European Enforcement Order for uncontested claims OJ L-143, 30.4.2004, p. 15.

[3] Boularbah (2003) p. 186f. In contrast the author notes that Art. 3 of the Directive has had some impact on national procedural rules, i.e. brought about a change in the Member States which have not traditionally applied the indemnity principle. Freudenthal (2003) p. 363f. confirms that the Directive did not occasion any change in the Dutch procedural law other than a statement that whenever there is a general review of the procedural law the legislator will pay attention to the question of expedient debt recovery.

efficient European recovery procedure for uncontested claims.[4] Similarly, the European Enforcement Order Regulation can be seen as another step in this process as it eliminates the exequatur or recognition procedure, thereby combating delay in cross-border enforcement of judgments which have not been contested.

Both these measures are arguably necessary for businesses and economic actors and for ensuring the proper operation of the Internal Market.[5] As the Commission notes, from a market perspective, consequences of late payment, such as high, deterring interest rates, can be effective in dissuading only if they are accompanied by rapid and inexpensive redress procedures.[6] However, neither the Directive on combating late payment nor the European Enforcement Order manages to deal with the situation of a creditor who in a cross-border case has to bring a claim against a defendant in another Member State where an efficient procedure for the collection of debts does not exist, or where the procedure is more complex than that in his own Member State. More generally, apart from the specific needs of the cross-border litigant, the Storme group also in 1994 emphasized that order for payment procedures are cost advantageous and expeditious and should be used to reprieve the overburdened judicial systems of uncontested claims.[7] The Commission agrees and notes that where statistics are available the percentage of uncontested claims ranges between 50 and 80 per cent in national civil courts of first instance. When combined with the fact that swift recovery of debts is of paramount importance to economic operators, the situation implies a multifaceted problem for the Member States' judicial systems.

It becomes imperative to distinguish the truly contentious matters as soon as possible and deal with the other matters in a streamlined fashion so as to make efficient use of the limited resources allocated to adjudication.[8] One commentator offers further support for order for payment procedures by noting that amongst the over one million cases in which such a procedure is used in France, only 6 to 8 per cent of the matters are contested and transferred

[4] COM (2002) 746, p. 13.

[5] Ibid. p. 14.

[6] Ibid. p. 12.

[7] Storme (1994) p. 108.

[8] COM (2004) 173, p. 4f. Note that the Council of Europe has also in its 1981 'Recommendation on Measures Facilitating Access to Justice' and its 1984 'Recommendation on the Principles of Civil Procedure Designed to Improve the Functioning of Justice' supported simplified procedures which render final decisions quickly for undisputed or liquidated claims.

to ordinary proceedings.[9] Hence, it is not surprising that as part of the Area of Freedom, Security, and Justice, the Tampere conclusions mention orders for payment as an element instrumental to smooth judicial cooperation and enhanced access to the law.[10]

Therefore, the Commission initiated a debate and a proposal in relation to an order for payment procedure. First, on 20 December 2002, the Commission published a Green Paper.[11] The Economic and Social Committee (ESC) gave its opinion on the Green Paper in June 2003 and the European Parliament Report is dated 30 January 2004. Thereafter, in March 2004, based on the results of the consultation, the Commission transmitted its proposal for a Regulation creating a European Order for Payment Procedure to the Parliament and the Council for the first stage of the co-decision procedure.[12] In February 2005 the ESC published its Opinion,[13] but the European Parliament and Council took a longer time for their first readings. The Parliament resolution effectively represents amendments as agreed with the Council.[14] The amended proposal published by the Commission in February 2006,[15] followed by the common position of the Parliament and the Council[16] and the second Parliament reading,[17] resulted in a final legislative act at the end of 2006,[18] the 'Payment Order Regulation'. The substantive part of the Payment Order Regulation will be applicable from December 2008.

From the initial Commission proposal it is apparent, though not explicit, that the proposal was based on Articles 61(c) and 65, i.e. that the Commission considered that the measure falls within the scope of judicial cooperation in civil matters. However, since the Commission, both in the Green Paper and even more explicitly in the initial proposal itself, suggested a broad interpretation of the limitations in Article 65, the proposal and Green Paper left some space for adopting the measure on an alternative legal basis.[19]

[9] Perrot (2003) p. 388.

[10] European Council Conclusions, No. 200/1/99, para. 38.

[11] COM (2002) 746.

[12] COM (2004) 173.

[13] ESC 133/2005.

[14] T 499/2005. The Parliament Committee in charge of the matter had already published its Report in July 2005, see A5 240/2005.

[15] COM (2006) 57.

[16] 7535/3/2006.

[17] A6 316/2006 and T6 440/2006.

[18] (EC) No. 1896/2006 Regulation of 12 December 2006 creating a European order for payment procedure OJ L-399, 30.12.2006, p. 1.

[19] In the Green Paper, COM (2002) 746, p. 13, the Commission states that Arts 61(c) and 65 are not the only possible legal basis for a measure creating a European order for payment procedure.

In relation to the scope of the proposed Regulation, the Commission first specifically dealt with the traditional cross-border scenario, and observed that the contrast between a rapid recovery procedure available for purely domestic claims and the delays and expenses that ensue in a cross-border recovery claim, which has to go through normal civil proceedings, is intolerable in matters which are uncontested. Furthermore, this creates a disincentive for bona fide economic operators to extend their activities to the common market. Therefore, a uniform European order for payment procedure would considerably enhance access to justice.[20]

However, secondly, the Commission supported making the Regulation universally applicable, i.e. applicable to domestic claims too. There are several arguments in favour of this view beginning with the reverse discrimination logic that in Member States which do not have a debt-collection procedure for domestic claims a discrepancy between creditors in the different markets would be created and could cause distortions of competition. Also, every claim might potentially take on a cross-border nature at the stage of enforcement. But such distinctions and analysis of the details are not suitable for examination during the order for payment procedure itself which is by nature speedy, simple, and schematic. Finally, the Commission argued that a tool, which is of fundamental economic significance for the Internal Market and which is intended to provide an optional tool, should be able to apply to both types of claim and still fall within a flexible interpretation of the limitation 'matters with cross-border implications'.[21]

The ESC agreed, with regard to the scope of the proposed Regulation, that the situation facing creditors is the same whether the facts of the case are cross-border or not, and that an additional and separate European payment order procedure would not be advisable. However, this position was moderated by a suggestion that this could be achieved in steps, the first being to introduce the system for solely cross-border matters.[22] In its further response the ESC went even further and stated that there should be only one common order for payment procedure, and that when it enters into force all national

The most obvious alternative legal basis would be Art. 95. This legal basis is also mentioned as an option by the ESC: ESC 742/2003, p. 5, para.3.1.2. However, interestingly Freudenthal (2003) p. 364 notes during discussions on the Directive to combat late payment, the Member States resisted legislation which could impact on national procedural laws, and raised doubts as to whether the measures could be construed as falling within the legal basis of Art. 95.

[20] COM (2004) 173, p. 6, and COM (2002) 746, p. 8.

[21] COM (2004) 173, p. 7f. and COM (2002) 746, p. 10f.

[22] ESC 742/2003, p. 4f., para. 3.1.2.

procedures should cease to have effect or be abrogated.[23] The Regulation would apparently still be compatible with the principles of subsidiarity and proportionality even though the 'optional' nature of the procedure would only entail a choice between the order for payment procedure and more formal 'ordinary' civil proceedings.[24]

The European Parliament was more cautions, noting in its explanatory statement that it would be desirable for the parties to have the option of using the procedure in domestic matters as well, in order to avoid unequal treatment of creditors. However, in its resolution the Parliament stated that any proposal should apply to cross-border cases only, but give the Member States the right to introduce the procedure domestically also.[25] As far as the aims of a potential order for payment procedure go, the ESC fully supported the creation of an efficient order for payment procedure, mentioning in particular that for parties the economic risk or costs risk of collecting a debt or bringing a claim become more transparent and reasonable.[26] The European Parliament also supported the aims of the proposed measure, stating that the issue of uncontested claims for litigants be they citizens or firms, illustrates how vital it is to make progress towards judicial cooperation in civil matters.[27]

Subsequent negotiations in the Council and Parliament have evidenced the resurgence of the 'cross-border issue' and placed it at the centre of the debate regarding the future of this measure and other concurrently pending measures in the field of judicial cooperation in civil matters. As with the Directive on Legal Aid, the Member States were not prepared to follow the Commission's more liberal interpretation of the Treaty wording, 'cross-border implications'; rather there was a very strong majority in favour of restricting the scope of application. The crucial question here is how to limit the scope of the Regulation in a legally sensible and practicable manner which does not create anomalies and discrimination. The scope is hence worded as follows: 'For the purposes of this Regulation, a cross-border case is one in which at least one of the parties is domiciled or habitually resident in a Member State other than the Member State of the court seised.'[28]

[23] ESC 133/2005, p. 6, para. 4.9.1.

[24] ESC 133/2005, p. 2, paras 1.5 and 1.6.

[25] A5 41/2004, pp. 8 and 12.

[26] ESC 742/2003, p. 1, para. 1.1.

[27] A5 41/2004, p. 12.

[28] Art. 3(1). Domicile shall according to Art. 3(2) be determined in accordance with the Brussels I Regulation. The time when the cross-border nature of a claim should be evaluated is

There remain cases, e.g. where both parties are domiciled in one Member State but enforcement has to take place in another Member State, in which the simplified payment order mechanism will not be available, which could raise a discrimination argument. There might in practice also hence follow spillover effects at the domestic level from the Regulation which might negate or circumvent the strict scope of application. We have therefore potentially but glimpsed the reach of the policy area judicial cooperation in civil matters and its significance for domestic as well as transnational litigation.

Substantive Content

The substantive scope of the Regulation is generally the same as for the other measures in judicial cooperation in civil matters, i.e. it applies to all civil and commercial cases with the autonomous and coinciding definition based on paragraph 1 of the Brussels I Regulation and the case law of the Court.[29] Furthermore, the Regulation excludes insolvency, social security, and rights arising out of matrimonial relationships.[30] Also, significantly, the Regulation excludes claims arising from non-contractual obligations, e.g. tort claims, unless these have the subject of an agreement or admission of debt or relate to a liquidated debt arising from joint ownership of property.[31] However, the Payment Order Regulation is by its very nature more

according to Art. 3(3) the moment when the application for a payment order is lodged. Note that the Commission proposed and argued that the place of habitual residence of the parties should be referred to as a 'State' rather than 'Member State', because the narrower wording would prevent non-EU domiciled claimants from using the payment order procedure and could also not be used against non-EU domiciled defendants. Such a solution would according to the Commission be questionable from the point of view of existing international obligations of the EU such as GATT 1994, GATS, and TRIPS, as well as the Lugano Convention and potentially the Agreement on the European Economic Area, COM (2006) 57, p. 4.

[29] Art. 2(1) also specifically excludes liability of States for acts or omissions in the exercise of State authority '*acta iure imperii*': see Chapter 10 above regarding the Enforcement Order Regulation.

[30] Art. 2(2)(a)–(c) regulates the substantive exclusions, and it is noteworthy that in other substantive areas of law, e.g. employment law, the mere fact that such matters are dealt with by specialized tribunals does not exclude them from the scope of the proposed Regulation. Thus, they do still fall within the ambit of 'civil and commercial matters'.

[31] Art. 2(2)(d). Naturally, the exclusion of tort claims limits the scope of the Regulation significantly. However, considering the automated order for payment procedure its character is only suitable for very straightforward and liquidated claims, which tort claims seldom are. Therefore, the delimitation is warranted and justified.

restricted in its scope. The establishment and applicability of the procedure is limited to the recovery of liquidated pecuniary claims which are 'for a specific amount', are payable, and 'have fallen due'.[32]

On the basis of the Green Paper consultation process, the Commission proposed that there would be no other limitations to the applicability of the procedure, in particular that there would be no upper ceiling in monetary terms. Thus, a creditor can for any pecuniary claim, i.e. a claim for any sum of money, small or very large, apply for the payment order if he considers the matter to be uncontested and the sum is precise and liquidated. The Commission stated that it would not make any sense to put an upper ceiling on the sum potentially to be collected and that it was to be left to the creditor's judgement, presumably acknowledging that the likelihood of the matter being contentious increases with the value of a claim.[33] Commentators also note that creditors should have this possibility regardless of the amount claimed, because an upper limit would only make sense if ordinary proceedings offer greater protection to defendants. This is not the case specifically in judgment in default procedural rules, and generally if one agrees that the idea of *l'inversion du contentieux* as the basis for order for payment procedures does not in itself breach the defendant's right to be heard.[34]

The fundamental question in designing the functioning of the payment order procedure has been to choose between a 'minimum' and a 'maximum' system for rapid debt recovery.[35] In the descriptive terms of the Commission, the choice has been between the 'evidence' and the 'no-evidence' models.[36] The Commission chose in favour of the no-evidence model, and the logic of its proposal followed from this.[37] This has also been carried through in the Regulation. Thus, a creditor can make an application for a European order for payment by using a standard form indicating the names and addresses of the parties, the amount of the claim (including any interest), the cause of action, and a brief description of the facts, as well as a description of evidence supporting the claim.[38] The standard form, Annex I of the Regulation,

[32] Art. 4. These criteria have to be fulfilled at the time when the application for a European order for payment is submitted.

[33] COM (2004) 173, p. 9.

[34] Rechberger and Kodek (2001) pp. 17ff. and 71.

[35] Correa Delcasso (2003) p. 258.

[36] COM (2002) 746, p. 17f.

[37] COM (2004) 173, p. 10f.

[38] Art. 7(2)(e) and Recital 14 oblige the applicant to describe evidence which he relies on to prove the correctness of his claim.

is largely very helpful and straightforward: for the cause of action several alternatives are given and the creditor has only to choose one of the options given, i.e. the various types of sales and service agreements listed such as rental agreement, agreement for the supply of gas, water, or telephone, or insurance contract. Similarly, for describing the relevant evidence required the form gives the following alternatives: written, oral, expert, inspection, and other.

The Regulation specifically stipulates that representation by a lawyer or other legal professional shall not be mandatory for the application or for the statement of opposition.[39] A further stipulation, which is intended to enhance the simplicity and schematic nature of the application, is that the signature can be made in the form of an electronic signature. Even though the proposal does not yet mandate the creation of electronic application systems in the Member States, the acknowledgement of the electronic signature is a step in this direction and is intended to support national systems, some of which are already utilizing automatic data processing or electronic communication to speed up debt-recovery procedures.[40]

On the basis of the application, and upon verification that the formal requirements are fulfilled, and upon an examination that the claim and the jurisdiction appear to be founded and admissible, the court seized shall issue a European payment notification. The Court has an obligation to do so 'as soon as possible' and 'normally within 30 days of the application'.[41] If the requirements are not met or the claim is clearly unfounded or inadmissible the court shall reject the application.[42] If necessary a procedure is also elaborated for the completion, rectification, or modification of the application prior to the court issuing the order.[43] The local court is charged with ensuring that the order is served on the defendant and there are very specific rules regarding the information and advice to the defendant, which should be included in the order. The aim is to advise the defendant of his procedural

[39] Art. 24.

[40] Art. 7(6): an electronic signature should fulfil the requirements set out in Directive (EC) No. 93/1999 on the Community framework for electronic signatures. However, such electronic signatures shall not be required if and to the extent that an alternative electronic communications system exists in the courts of the Member State of origin, is available to a certain group of pre-registered authenticated users, and permits the identification of those users in a secure manner. Such communication systems shall be notified by the Member States to the Commission.

[41] Arts 8 and 12(1).

[42] Art. 11. The claimant cannot appeal the decision but can pursue a new application or avail himself of another available procedure.

[43] Arts 9–10.

options, the basis for the order, and the consequences thereof.[44] Articles 13 and 14 of the proposal also enumerate very specific and elaborate minimum standard methods of service. The intention is clearly that the methods should prove full legal certainty that service was effected or a very high degree of likelihood that the document has reached its addressee, and any methods based on a 'legal fiction' are not considered sufficient.[45]

The defendant has one month from the date of service to submit a statement of defence, otherwise the court of origin will declare its payment order enforceable.[46] The statement of defence can be made on a standard response form, which shall be supplied to the defendant with the notification. It must only contain a clear statement of contestation, no reasons or justifications are necessary, and legal representation is not mandatory. This statement can also be signed electronically.[47] If the defendant lodges a statement of defence the proceedings shall be transferred and continue in accordance with the rules of ordinary civil procedure.[48] The Commission's initial legislative proposal envisaged two chances for the defendant to respond. First, the application would be notified to the defendant, to which he could respond, and secondly, if a payment order were granted, the defendant could appeal.[49] In contrast, the Commission's amended proposal and the final Regulation are more streamlined and the defendant has only one chance to respond once the order is served upon him. If he does not respond it becomes enforceable.

However, it is still envisaged that the defendant can in exceptional circumstances apply for review of the order after the expiry of the time limit if it has been served on him without proof of receipt, and service was not effected in time for him to arrange a defence or he was prevented from objecting by reason of force majeure. Furthermore, review is possible if the order was clearly wrongly issued, e.g. based on false information, or there were other exceptional circumstances.[50] If such an application for review is lodged it is without prejudice to the enforceability of the order *per se*, but the court in the Member State of enforcement may upon application 'limit enforcement

[44] Art. 12(3)–(4).

[45] Recitals 19 and 20.

[46] Arts 16 and 18.

[47] Arts 16 and 24. The conditions for the electronic signature are the same as for the claimant's application, see above footnote 40.

[48] Art. 17. Note however that the claimant can explicitly choose to terminate the proceedings at this stage.

[49] COM (2004) 173, proposed Arts 7–9.

[50] Art. 20(1)–(2).

to protective measures, make enforcement conditional upon provision of security, or stay enforcement. If the review is found by the court to be justified the order for payment shall be null and void.'[51]

If a defendant does not oppose the order or apply for its review, a European payment order is declared enforceable by the court of origin 'without delay'. This does not, however, obviate the need to fulfil any national formal prerequisites for enforceability in the Member State of origin. Once the order has become enforceable it shall be recognized in the other Member States without any possibilities of opposition.[52] This abolition of exequatur is quite 'revolutionary' and was not envisaged in the Commission's initial proposal.[53] Thus, when applying for enforcement in another Member State the claimant shall only produce the copy of the order, with appropriate means of authentication, and if necessary a translation.[54] The Regulation specifically mentions that enforcement can only be opposed on grounds of an irreconcilable earlier decision. Under no circumstances can the order be reviewed as to its substance.[55]

To support the system created the Payment Order Regulation stipulates some additional rules. First, the costs of court fees for obtaining the order for payment are to be neutral in comparison to the court fees for ordinary civil proceedings. Hence, if the claim is contested and has to be transferred and continued in ordinary civil proceedings the total costs for court fees should not be higher than if only ordinary civil proceedings had been initiated.[56] How this principle of neutrality is to be complied with is left to the

[51] Arts 20(3) and 23.

[52] Arts 18 and 19.

[53] COM (2004) 173, p. 9f., where the Commission clarifies that the questions of recognition and enforcement are left exclusively to the Brussels I Regulation and the European Enforcement Order Regulation. See also Green Paper, COM (2002) 746, p. 47, where the Commission notes that if the payment order has to be enforced cross-border it will certainly fall within the scope of the enforcement order. Further, the payment order system could even completely abolish certification as an enforcement order. However, that would presuppose the adequate protection of the rights of the defence primarily concerning the service of documents, which so far the proposal does not do. It now appears that since the amended Commission proposal includes very detailed service rules, the abolition of exequatur has become possible.

[54] Art. 21. The Member States may indicate any of the official EU languages other than their own that they accept without translation.

[55] Art. 22. The irreconcilable earlier decision or order has to involve the same cause of action between the same parties and fulfil the conditions of enforcement. In addition, the irreconcilability must not have been raised as an objection in the proceedings in the Member State of origin.

[56] Art. 25.

Member States to organize, the aim naturally being that creditors should not be dissuaded by comparatively high court fees from using the procedure. Secondly, in order to assist creditors in lodging the application, the Member States are obliged to inform the Commission which courts in their system will have jurisdiction to issue a European order for payment, which courts will internally be competent to deal with review procedures, as well as the means of communication and languages accepted. The Commission is subsequently obliged to make the information public, through the Official Journal and other appropriate means.[57] The Member States are also obliged to provide information on costs of service and enforcement authorities in particular via the European Judicial Network.[58]

Normative Implications

As between the Member States the Payment Order Regulation is a completely new measure that will be applicable from 12 December 2008.[59] The Regulation is not intended to abrogate any prior arrangements. Furthermore, at the national level the procedure would not abrogate domestic order for payment procedures, but provide an optional tool for creditors to use.[60] The Regulation is thus sensitive to national procedural systems and also should be welcomed as hopefully providing creditors, both citizens and SMEs, with a rapid debt-recovery mechanism. However, the Regulation might not fulfil its aim and might raise some problematic issues. The limitation of competence in Article 65 of the Treaty to 'matters having cross-border implications', which remains in the projected future Treaty reform, has revealed a fundamental discrepancy in the Commission's original legislative proposal.[61] This discrepancy and any potential unwelcome 'competence creep' have been avoided by the introduction of the 'cross-border' definition.

[57] Art. 29.

[58] Art. 28.

[59] Art. 33. Arts 28, 29, 30, and 31 dealing with the information to be provided by the Member States, Annexes to the Regulation, and the Committee to assist the Commission will be applicable from 12 June 2008.

[60] Art. 1 and Recital 10. Compare the proposal to the ESC's Opinion, which does advocate abrogation of national order for payment procedures in favour of the common one: ESC 133/2005, p. 6, para. 4.9.1.

[61] Inter alia Correa Delcasso (2001) p. 72.

However, the Regulation in its Recitals takes a slightly different approach to the existing situation. It aims overtly to tackle the issue of recovering uncontested claims, the national procedures for which are said to vary substantially, resulting in impediments to justice and distortion of competition. Thus, Community legislation should ensure equal treatment for all, which is to be achieved not through harmonizing or replacing domestic procedures but by creating an additional procedure.[62] This final statement in the Recitals is highly significant but perhaps obscures the fact that a new and independent procedure is being created. With several parties wary of harmonization or of possible effects on national procedural laws, the current, apparently bland, proposal might turn out to be the progenitor of a completely new regime. It is after all a complete new generic civil procedure tool with its own rules governing all issues from commencement of proceeding to extraordinary review. It does not deal simply with one limited procedural step in transnational litigation, e.g. service of documents, but creates a parallel and virtually complete procedure for undisputed claims. Notwithstanding its substantive limits or the 'cross-border' definition, reform of the Member States' procedural systems is likely, most obviously in those that do not at present have a domestic order for payment procedure.

Secondly, with regard to the promise of creating a rapid, efficient, and transparent procedure at a lower cost the envisaged system certainly has positive features. For example, the emphasis on supporting electronic communications and perhaps creating an electronic highway together with simplified standard forms, which avoid the need for translation and legal counsel, will undoubtedly enable the simplification and speeding up of the procedure.[63] However, it is notable that no time limit has been imposed within which national court authorities are required to deliver the order for payment and the declaration of its enforceability. The phrases 'normally within 30 days' and 'without delay' are highly programmatic and could rarely be considered concrete obligations. Therefore, the speed of the procedure will depend, as noted for other measures, on the capacities of the national systems to cope and on their resources and efficiency. Thus, there is an inherent risk that creditors will be treated differently in different jurisdictions, the very problem that the procedure seeks to resolve.

In addition, even though the forms are clear and concise to a professional mind, there is no guarantee that laypersons will be able to complete the

[62] Recitals 7–10.

[63] Freudenthal (2003) p. 368.

forms, and since there are no rules for translation of the forms it is unclear whether there is such an obligation and upon whom its rests.[64] Also, since the claimant should indicate on his application jurisdictional grounds, based on the Brussels I Regulation, and grounds for his case falling within the 'cross-border' definition, there is a clear risk that laypersons will need professional guidance. Therefore, even though professional representation is specifically not mandatory, there are de facto a number of cases, for example those of a relatively high monetary value, where the use of counsel could be beneficial to the parties from the very beginning and thus the procedure will not necessarily create significant costs benefits for the parties.[65]

Inevitably also the Regulation raises the issue of complexity and transparency, as it is intended to provide an 'optional' tool in addition to national procedures. Thus a multitude of parallel procedures may coexist, with no provision in the proposal for any form of precedence between the procedures. An alternative to this optional parallel system has been proposed. In this the national procedures for order for payment proceedings remain the only such procedure, but these are applicable to cross-border debt-collection claims too; a certain harmonization of these procedures would pave the way for mutual recognition of the enforcement title thus obtained.[66]

In addition, a particular procedural problem arises in relation to which is the appropriate jurisdiction for cross-border disputes, a decision that should be derived from the Brussels I Regulation. This entails that in some cases there are alternative or exclusive jurisdictions. Furthermore the Brussels I Regulation has specific rules on lis pendens and concurrent proceedings to avoid the problem of double proceedings and conflicting judgments. In the Green Paper the Commission asks whether it would not provide more legal certainty and simplicity if the Payment Order Regulation contained a specific jurisdictional rule taking precedence over other such rules and entailing that the defendant's domicile would be the exclusive jurisdiction. This would also avoid problems of cross-border service during the order for payment procedure itself. This suggestion is supported by the commentators.[67] However, the European Parliament gave a contrary opinion that the

[64] ESC 133/2005, p. 11f.

[65] Ibid. p. 10f., para. 5.9 even suggests that it be mandatory in some cases to have legal representation.

[66] Correa Delcasso (2001) p. 73.

[67] Correa Delcasso (2003) p. 260. The ESC seems to support the Green Paper idea of regulating the jurisdiction but suggests that the jurisdiction rule should be incorporated into the Brussels I system, see ESC 742/2003, p. 7, para. 3.1.9.

Brussels I criteria should not be altered because that would weaken the coherence of the jurisdictional system established in the Union.[68] This latter position is now chosen in the Regulation, except when the defendant is a consumer. Thus, there are no specific rules for jurisdiction as the Commission notes that the Brussels I Regulation strikes such a fair balance between the interests of the parties that no justification could be made for departing from the system.[69]

The practical question which then arises is how the court seized with an application for a payment order can deal with the jurisdiction question. In some jurisdictions the courts are obliged to deal with this question ex officio at the first application or at the bringing of the action. In most jurisdictions the courts would deal with this as a preliminary issue and hear the parties' evidence as to jurisdiction in a preliminary hearing or first pre-trial conference, in other jurisdictions the courts would wait to hear arguments on the question as the first question at the full trial hearing. The Regulation makes no provision for such a hearing, unless the defendant opposes and the matter is transferred to ordinary proceedings. As commentators have noted, however, it should be envisaged that courts can reject applications on the basis of no international jurisdiction.[70] Under the Regulation it therefore seems as if the seized courts will have to deal with the issue of jurisdiction ex officio.[71]

One commentator notes that in the national context it is clear that the judge with an order for payment application before him will verify that certain conditions are fulfilled, including jurisdiction, and that the judge is explicitly expected to be vigilant because the defendant has at this stage no part or face in the procedure.[72] The scrutiny is carried out under the verification and examination of the formal requirements and grounds for the claim introduced in the proposed Regulation.[73] But the remits of this scrutiny are not dealt with and it seems as if a very schematic analysis is envisaged. This conclusion is based on the explicit statement in the Regulation that the scrutiny can be automated and the explicit statement in the Recital

[68] A5 41/2004, p. 12.

[69] COM (2004) 173, p. 9. See Art. 6 which includes a specific rule for the situation where a consumer is the defendant, in which instances the jurisdiction of the defendant's domicile shall be the only applicable one.

[70] Rechberger and Kodek (2001) p. 19 recognize the problem but apparently draw the opposite conclusion, i.e. that if the defendant does not raise any objection the court will have to grant the payment order regardless of whether it has international jurisdiction or not.

[71] Arts 6 and 8.

[72] Perrot (2003) p. 389f.

[73] Arts 6 and 11.

that the examination does not have to be carried out by a judge.[74] This could be problematic because there is no monetary detriment to the creditor if he makes an application. Thus, there is perhaps a certain risk of abuse by unscrupulous creditors, or concern as to the degree of prudence and the lack of experience of creditors.[75]

The quite schematic nature of the procedure can be contrasted with similar national procedures in which the threshold to be applied is slightly higher because the procedure entails a summary review of the merits and/or evidence in support by the court seized. Another concern is that the Regulation does not address the point made by the Commission in its Green Paper that when the court seized checks the admissibility of the application some guidelines on the thoroughness of this application and a certain safety valve for unfounded claims are important.[76] This aspect of the Regulation touches upon a central question, namely the difficult choice between the defendant's responsibility to prevent a decision being made against him and the principle of minimum protection of the defendant.[77] The principle of respect for the rights of the defence is linked to a more general tension in the modern procedural debate and current developments, namely the tension between the need for speed and efficiency and the protection of the rights of the parties.[78] However, most commentators seem to regard the rights of the defence in order for payment procedures as generally being protected, since they are not so much negated as simply deferred until the defendant intimates that the matter is contentious.[79]

However, this point has not yet been tested against the ever-evolving case law of human rights in Europe.[80] Another concern with regard to the rights

[74] Art. 8 and Recital 16.

[75] ESC 742/2003, p. 6, para. 3.1.7. See also ESC 133/2005, p. 5, para. 4.6, where it is noted that the procedure should take such factors into account or be so regulated that businesses cannot use it as cover for irregular practices, e.g. exerting pressure on consumer clients or using the mechanism for money laundering.

[76] COM (2002) 746, p. 30f.

[77] Ibid.

[78] Perrot (2000) p. 427.

[79] Ibid. Correa Delcasso (2001) p. 70f. agrees with Perrot. Further, Rechberger and Kodek (2001) p. 18.

[80] The European Court of Human Rights has for the purposes of Art. 6 of the ECHR held that it is sufficient that the defendant is given an opportunity to be heard, not that he or she actively exercises that right and takes part in proceedings. However, Rechberger and Kodek (2001) p. 18 make the point that Art. 6 might be interpreted differently in the different national order for payment procedures, depending upon when the enforceable decision is rendered, i.e. after the period for filing an objection has passed, or before such period has expired.

of the defence is the minimum standards for the service of documents, the methods including postal service without proof of receipt, delivery to the defendant's mailbox, or delivery to a post office with a written notification in the mailbox. Interestingly, both commentators and the European Parliament consider the preferred method of service to be a system of personal service through professional bodies or specialized personnel.[81] The commentators specifically link these very high standards of service and the recorded passing of information to the defendant to the deferral of rights of contradiction and to the acceptability of the so-called reversal of the dispute, *l'inversion du contentieux*, which occurs in an order for payment procedure. However, the question to be decided is whether the availability of these safeguards can be considered as providing 'effective' access to justice and protection of the imbued principle of the defendant's right to be heard.[82]

Finally, one of the perceived benefits of the envisaged European order for payment would be its immediate enforceability in the other Member States.[83] However, even though there can be no revision of the substance of the payment order, perhaps procedural *ordre public* can play a role.[84] The ECJ judgment in *Krombach*, that such direct mutual recognition could not be pursued without some safety valve to support the rights of the defence, is instructive here.[85] If many problematic cases emerge when the Regulation comes into force, it may be necessary to ask whether the problem of and the quest for efficiency should not be targeted in another way, e.g. against the methods of execution proper.[86] Fortunately, the Regulation includes

[81] A5 41/2004, pp. 8 and 13; Correa Delcasso (2001) p. 79; and Perrot (2000) p. 427.

[82] Perrot (2000) p. 425f. makes the point that the rights of the defence are an imbued principle in our modern adjudication but that the real challenge in practice becomes how to realize these rights and simultaneously achieve the goal of efficiency.

[83] The Parliament notes that there would be added value if the payment order obviated the need for resorting to exequatur and thus enabled the recoverability of uncontested claims – which creditors would otherwise be disinclined to pursue: A5 41/2004, p. 8. Correa Delcasso (2001) p. 80f. also notes that the suppression of exequatur would be one facet of an ideal European model.

[84] Since there is no public order exception in the Regulation such an argument would be very difficult to justify.

[85] C-7/98 *Dieter Krombach v. Andre Bamberski* [2000] ECR I-1935, in particular para. 44: 'recourse to the public policy clause must be regarded as being possible in exceptional cases where the guarantees laid down in the legislation of the State of origin and in the [Brussels] Convention itself have been insufficient to protect the defendant from a manifest breach of his right to defend himself before the court of origin, as recognised by the ECHR'.

[86] Correa Delcasso (2003) p. 262f. Kennett (2003) p. 110 notes that there are two cross-border 'enforcement problems', namely recognition and the mechanisms themselves, and outlines the

an obligation for the Commission to prepare, five years after its entry into force, a detailed report on its functioning.[87] For this purpose the Member States are explicitly obliged to provide the Commission with information on such issues as court fees, speed of procedure, efficiency, and ease of use.[88] The elaborate review or report clause shows that there is an awareness of the novel significance of the measure, perhaps of its potential weaknesses, as well as of the need for research in order to establish best practices and the best forms of regulation.[89]

very varied approaches amongst the Member States to the structures of enforcement mechanism systems and their methods: pp. 94–107.

[87] Art. 32. [88] Ibid. [89] Ibid.

Small Claims Procedure

Legislative History

The most recent of the generic procedural legislative proposals in the field of judicial cooperation in civil matters was published by the Commission 15 March 2005, regarding the establishment of a European small claims procedure. Both the European Parliament and the Economic and Social Committee (ESC) published some initial comments on a small claims regulation as a response to the Green Paper consultation which the Commission launched in 2002.[1] The Parliament published its legislative report and position on the Commission proposal at the end of 2006.[2] Agreement was reached in June 2007 and the Small Claims Regulation is set to be applicable in the Member States from 1 January 2009.[3]

The Commission based its proposal on Article 65(1)(c) of the EC Treaty 'eliminating obstacles to the good functioning of civil proceedings' since small claims procedures are not specifically mentioned in the list of measures under Article 65. In addition, the Commission's proposal is in line with its interpretation and analysis, that the legal basis does not limit the scope of the proposed rules to cross-border matters. The same issue arose at the proposal stages for a Legal Aid Directive, for a Regulation creating an Order for Payment Procedure, and for the Mediation Directive, and in all of these instances the Council rejected the Commission's proposed wider interpretation.

[1] COM 2002 (746).

[2] A6 387/2006 and T6 593/2006. The ESC had previously published its report: ESC 230/2006.

[3] (EC) No. 861/2007 Regulation of 11 July 2007 establishing a European Small Claims Procedure, OJ L-199, 31.7.2007, p. 1.

The justifications for the Commission's analysis of the legal basis in relation to small claims were further elaborated. Apart from the argument that it would be counterproductive and inappropriate to create a duality of regimes inconsistent with a single and coherent area of justice, the Commission further adduces that applying the same procedure to purely domestic small claims helps eliminate distortions of competition and thus does have cross-border implications and is necessary for the proper functioning of the Internal Market. The Commission thereafter states that the Internal Market limitation in Article 65 is a restriction of the cross-border requirement, which it claims can be confirmed by the negotiations leading to the adoption of Article 65 of the EC Treaty.[4] However, the Council and the Parliament still chose to limit the scope of application of the Regulation to cross-border matters and used the same definition for cross-border as for, inter alia, the Payment Order Regulation: 'For the purposes of this Regulation, a cross-border case is one in which at least one of the parties is domiciled or habitually resident in a Member State other than the Member State of the court or tribunal seised.'

In relation to the substantive objectives behind regulating small claims procedures at the European level, the Commission in its Green Paper had noted already that the complexity of legal systems, including the delay and costs of proceedings, is a particularly virulent problem in the case of small claims where because the values are relatively speaking small the individual parties might be discouraged from exercising their rights.[5] That this problem needs particular solutions is evidenced by the fact that many of the Member States have specific small claims procedures and many of those which do not, nevertheless provide simplified alternatives to the ordinary procedure.[6] The Council of Europe had also in 1981 highlighted the need for simplified procedures in small claims cases.[7] The added cross-border cost for litigants in the Internal Market is a further discouragement to potential small claims litigants, which is evidenced by a study in the field of consumer disputes.[8] In addition, the Commission contends that more generally than in consumer matters the expense of obtaining a cross-border judgment is often

[4] COM (2005) 87, p. 5f.

[5] COM (2002) 746, p. 49.

[6] Ibid. pp. 51–8 for an overview of these national measures. See also Serverin (2001), a study commissioned by the Commission, for an overview of the national procedures. For policy justifications see SEC (2005) 351, p. 2f.

[7] Council of Europe Recommendation R (81)7, pp. 8 and 25f.

[8] Freyhold et al. (1998) p. 276f.

disproportionate to the amount of money at stake, and especially so when the amount of the claim is low.[9] Simultaneously the number of cross-border claims is rising in line with the increase in the free movement of persons, goods, and services.

Consequently, the Commission suggests that there is a need for action at the supranational level.[10] The extended impact assessment carried out by the Commission admits that the size and nature of the problem are under-researched, data on cross-border shopping are relatively limited, and even scarcer is information on how many disputes arise and whether these go to litigation.[11] However, legal sociological research refers to the unprotected group who do not litigate because barriers are too high as 'no-shotters' and these economic actors must according to the Commission be given some idea of how the law will operate, as well as some simplified rules as a safeguard.[12] If the expected costs of the litigants can be reduced through a European procedure, the increase in access to justice will be coupled with an economic benefit through an increase in trade, thereby increasing the aggregate welfare for all consumers and businesses in the market.[13] If the time period within which judgment can be obtained is reduced to six months from the Member State level, which is between four and 24 months, this would also make a significant contribution to access to justice and to confidence in the legal systems, ultimately increasing trade.[14]

According to the Commission if the theoretical scope of the Regulation is estimated at five million cases per year, seven million citizens affected, and a turnover of eight billion euros (case value plus direct costs of proceedings), the projected benefits will indeed have a chance of making an impact.[15] Furthermore, the ESC has also emphasized that people should not be obstructed in exercising their rights in the European Area of Justice and the Parliament mentions that the prime object of the European judicial space is to simplify the legal context within the Union.[16] The Parliament also mentions that the

[9] COM (2002) 746, p. 59.

[10] COM (2005) 87, p. 3f. The European Council also called for measures in the field at Tampere, No. 200/1/99, paras 30–1. In addition the Programme for Mutual Recognition, OJ C-12, 15.1.2001, p. 1, also calls for simplifying and speeding up the settlement of cross-border small claims.

[11] SEC (2005) 351, p. 4f.

[12] Ibid. p. 8f.

[13] Ibid. p. 11.

[14] Ibid. p. 14f.

[15] Ibid. pp. 12ff. and 17f.

[16] ESC 724/2003, p. 11 and A 41/2004, p. 10.

small claims area illustrates the importance of progress in judicial cooperation and that the rapid recovery of small claims is an absolute necessity for trade and for the Internal Market.[17] The Hague Programme reconfirmed, in November 2004, that an instrument concerning small claims is a project which the Union will actively pursue.[18]

Substantive Content

The Regulation is intended to simplify and speed up litigation concerning small claims and to eliminate intermediate steps from the recognition and enforcement procedures for judgments rendered in such proceedings.[19] The procedure established by the Regulation shall be available to litigants as an alternative to the procedures existing under the laws of the Member States. Therefore, the procedure is not obligatory even in cross-border small claims matters but only serves as an 'optional tool'. The Regulation does not, however, deal with what happens if a claimant brings a claim under the European small claims procedure and the defendant objects and prefers a national small claims procedure to apply or even argues that 'normal'/'regular' rules of proceedings should apply. Or conversely, if the claimant issues his claim under a 'normal procedure' but the defendant would like the matter to be dealt with as a European small claim. Unless the defendant's views and interests are taken into account, the procedure is only an alternative tool for claimants. The ESC noted in its response to the Commission Green Paper that if an obligatory small claims procedure is introduced there must be a possibility of transfer to normal proceedings.[20] However, since the Regulation does not deal with this question the general default position under Article 17 of the Regulation applies, i.e. that the procedural law of the Member State in which the proceedings are conducted governs the question. This could have been drafted more clearly and regulated more explicitly, as the obligatory or optional nature of the measure and its consequences is one of the key matters raised by the Commission in its Green Paper.[21]

[17] A 41/2004, pp. 6 and 12.
[18] European Council Conclusions, No. 14292/04 Annex I, p. 40.
[19] Art. 1.
[20] ESC 742/2003, p. 12, para. 4.1.6.
[21] COM (2002) 746, p. 64f.

Furthermore, it is notable that the Regulation does not deal with the issue of international jurisdiction. However, Annex I, Form A, refers to the application of the Brussels I Regulation. Consequently, the European small claims procedure can be lodged cross-border by claimants following the jurisdictional rules of the Brussels regime. For small claims litigants this means that they will have to be aware of these rules and might have to issue a claim in another Member State.[22]

The scope of the Regulation applies in the same way as the other measures of judicial cooperation in civil matters, i.e. to civil and commercial matters generically, hence not to administrative matters. In addition there are some substantive exclusions in Article 2(2)(a)–(e) that are similar to those in the Brussels I Regulation; these include matters concerning: legal capacity, rights to property arising out of a matrimonial relationship, maintenance obligations, wills and succession, bankruptcy and analogous proceedings, social security, and arbitration. Interestingly, there are further subparagraphs of substantive exclusions which state that matters concerning (f) employment law, (g) tenancies of immovable property with the exception of actions on monetary claims, and (h) violation of privacy and of rights relating to personality, including defamation, are also excluded from the scope and thus cannot be the object of a small claims procedure. This does not follow the standard Brussels I Regulation exclusions and there is no particular explanation in the documentation to explain why these areas have been singled out to be excluded.

The Tampere European Council conclusions specifically mention the need for accelerated rules for 'small consumer and commercial claims, as well as maintenance claims'.[23] By contrast, the Commission notes in its Green Paper that certain types of claim might not be suited for an accelerated small claims procedure and specifically mentions personal injury litigation, which often entails extensive expert evidence, and family law claims. The ESC only noted in its response to the Green Paper that it considered that the procedure should only apply to disputes which fall within the remit of ordinary courts of first instance in the Member States. The policy arguments for excluding each of these very different types of civil dispute most likely differ and are probably justifiable. With regard to the whole

[22] Chapter 12 above regarding the order for payment procedure raises a jurisdiction issue similar to that for the small claims procedure.

[23] Tampere European Council Conclusions, No. 200/1/99, para. 34.

systematization of judicial cooperation in civil matters such exclusions create less legal certainty, transparency, and clarity.

Further, as regards the scope of the Regulation, there are important limitations in its application since according to Article 2 it applies only 'where the total value of a monetary or non-monetary claim excluding interests, expenses and outlays does not exceed EUR 2000 at the time the procedure is commenced'.[24] This is the regulatory choice made as a response to the Commission's Green Paper in which the threshold for small claims is a key question.[25] The Commission seems to have taken a view that a quantities threshold and criteria are the right way of limiting small claims procedures and even states that 'Since the notion of the term "Small Claims" is quantitative, it seems necessary to set a quantitative threshold.'[26] Therefore, the Regulation more or less sidestepped qualitative criteria. This is of concern for the obvious reason that even if it is true that in principle and in practice many 'small claims', e.g. under a threshold of 2,000 euros, warrant and justify a simplification of procedural rules in order to make the costs for the litigants more proportionate to the interest at stake, there are also consumer, agency, personal injury, business contract, or other matters which are of low monetary value but legally complex. Such cases have the potential, both at national and supranational level, of creating important precedents, and therefore a qualitative analysis of their suitability for small claims would benefit the legal system as a whole.

Furthermore, cases that are not of a precedent nature might still be complex and need extensive taking of evidence. A qualitative analysis of their suitability for small claims would therefore benefit the litigants in question. Hence, some national systems, which have a small claims procedure, allow some kind of 'safety valve' to enable the court to transfer the matter to 'normal' proceedings.[27] The schematic nature of the threshold of 2,000 euros in the Regulation, which includes no 'safety valve', might therefore raise concern. One potential consequence is that parties will attempt to use Article 19,

[24] Recital 10 clarifies that for the purpose of facilitating calculation of the value of the claim, all interest, expenses, and disbursements should be disregarded. This should affect neither the power of the court to award these in the judgment nor the national rules on calculation of interest.

[25] COM (2002) 746, p. 62f.

[26] Ibid. p. 62.

[27] According to Serverin (2001) pp. 14–17, Finland and Sweden are the only Member States to have no thresholds, just a qualitative approach (among the 15 'old' Member States, 12 provided material for the report). Interestingly, the value thresholds varied significantly between the domestic procedures.

which refers to national procedural rules. However, such an attempt would not seem to be possible since the application of Article 19 is subject to the provisions of the Regulation.[28] It would be clearer to have a 'safety valve' in the Regulation itself, which might subsequently result in case law from the ECJ to guide the national courts and to harmonize the standards of which matters might be considered complex and more suitable for resolution in 'normal' proceedings. Further, if qualitative criteria were applicable, the Regulation could apply in cases which are for monetary settlement but for which the value is not yet clearly assessable, or additionally in cases which are for non-monetary remedies.

Chapter II of the Regulation deals with the various steps of the small claims procedure itself. The procedure is commenced by the claimant lodging a completed claim form, which is a standardized form that should according to the Regulation be available at all courts and tribunals where the procedure can be commenced. Furthermore, the Regulation prescribes that Member States shall ensure that practical assistance is available to help the potential claimant complete the form.[29] Upon the lodging of a claim form the court may ask the claimant to rectify the application within a specified time and where the claimant fails to rectify the claim or where the claim is clearly unfounded or the application inadmissible the application shall be dismissed.[30]

Otherwise the court shall proceed and is responsible for serving the claim form together with an answer form on the defendant. Upon receiving a response from the defendant, in the format of a completed answer form, the court is responsible for serving the response on the claimant; the latter is apparently only allowed to lodge a written rebuttal if the defendant makes a counterclaim.[31] The main rule is that the streamlined and court-assisted small claims procedure is to be written only, and unless the court considers that further written details, the taking of expert witness or party evidence, or an oral hearing are necessary it shall deliver a judgment.[32]

[28] Another possible consequence is that in complex small claims the national courts in practice, under Arts 7–9 of the Regulation, organize their hearing and taking of evidence to match 'normal' proceedings. However, this kind of application is hardly transparent and could create discrimination between litigants in different Member States due to varied practice.

[29] Arts 4(5) and 11.

[30] Art. 4(4).

[31] Art. 5.

[32] Arts 5(1) and 7.

In order to provide for efficiency there are also deadlines in the Regulation. Hence, it stipulates that the court shall serve on the defendant the claim form within 14 days of receiving a completed claim form. The defendant is allowed 30 days to submit his response, which shall be served on the claimant within 14 days of receipt.[33] Furthermore, the court shall within 30 days of receipt of the defendant's response deliver judgment.[34] However, if the court considers that an oral hearing is necessary or that further details or evidence must be obtained the 30-day period commences from the time of the hearing or receipt of evidence.[35] The procedural time limits mentioned above may be extended in exceptional circumstances, when it is necessary in order to safeguard the rights of the parties. In addition, if in exceptional circumstances it is not possible for the court or tribunal to respect the time limits the court or tribunal shall take the required steps as soon as possible.[36] A future analysis of the practice of national courts and the cases in which such 'exceptional circumstances' are invoked will demonstrate the impact of this provision, and it is hoped that potential case law of the ECJ will create guidelines in relation thereto.

In addition to the time limits set out in the Regulation, there are a host of rules to ensure that the proceedings are as simple as possible and bear upon the parties and augment costs to the lowest degree. Therefore, the court may use different means of modern technology to hold the hearing itself or to take evidence.[37] Furthermore, the parties are not required to be represented, by a lawyer or other legal professional, and the court shall not require the parties to make a legal assessment of the claim and shall also support the parties in procedural questions.[38] The proposed Regulation also adds to the simplification of procedures by specifying that the courts shall serve documents, both out of and in their own jurisdiction, by registered letter with acknowledgement of receipt. Alternative methods of service, being the ones outlined in the Enforcement Order Regulation, should not be resorted to unless service cannot be effected in that manner.[39]

[33] Art. 5.

[34] Art. 7(1). Note that if the defendant lodges a counterclaim the 30-day deadline for the court commences when the claimant lodges his response.

[35] Art. 7(2).

[36] Art. 14.

[37] Arts 8 and 9.

[38] Arts 10 and 12.

[39] Art. 13.

As regards language of documents the Regulation stipulates that the claim form and other documents are to be submitted in the language of the court, and if the court receives documents in any other language it may require a translation if it appears necessary for the giving of the judgment.[40] Where a party has refused to accept a document because it is not in an official language of the Member State where the document is dispatched, or a language that the addressee understands, the court shall inform the other party with a view to providing a translation.[41]

The Regulation also deals with costs, with the possibilities for appeal and review, as well as with enforcement of the small claims judgment. The main rule is that the unsuccessful party shall bear the costs of the proceedings, albeit not where they were unnecessarily incurred or disproportionate to the claim.[42] As regards appeal, the Commission notes in its Green Paper that to restrict appeal would have the benefits of reducing costs and duration as well as producing faster legal certainty. However, to completely exclude appeal might be problematic from a fair trial point of view. The possibility of an appeal against the judgment rendered in small claims proceedings is hence specifically left open to the Member States to regulate in their national procedural law. However, they are obliged to inform the Commission whether appeal is possible or not.[43] As regards review of the judgment the defendant can apply for review if he acts promptly, and in the same fashion as under Article 19 of the Enforcement Order Regulation, if service was not effected with proof of receipt and was not effected in sufficient time for the defendant to prepare his defence or if *force majeure* prevented the defendant from entering a defence.[44]

A judgment delivered in small claims proceedings shall be immediately enforceable notwithstanding any appeal. Furthermore, as in the procedures laid down in the Enforcement Order Regulation, a certificate of enforceability shall be issued in the Member State of judgment.[45] It is noteworthy that for small claims, which can be contested and are not of an uncontested nature, the proposal follows the simplified enforcement route of the Enforcement Order Regulation rather than the streamlined enforcement route of

[40] Art. 6(1)–(2).

[41] Art. 6(3).

[42] Art. 16.

[43] Art. 17.

[44] Art. 18.

[45] Art. 20. Enforcement may be limited or stayed where a party has challenged the judgment or applied for a review of the judgment: Art. 23.

the Brussels I Regulation. This can be seen as a further step in abolishing exequatur. Enforcement proper in the Member State of enforcement, e.g. the execution mechanisms themselves, are not dealt with by the proposed Regulation and therefore fall under national procedural law. However, an additional simplification is introduced for execution by the specific mention of the fact that the party seeking enforcement shall not be required to have an authorized representative or a postal address in the Member States of enforcement.[46] Possible refusal of enforcement is limited, as in the Enforcement Order and Payment Order Regulations, to the grounds of an irreconcilable earlier judgment.[47]

Normative Implications

The Small Claims Regulation will not abrogate national procedural laws. On the contrary, the intention is that the new procedure shall be available to litigants in parallel with potential existing national small claims procedures. Consequently, the intention is that national Member State authorities shall cooperate and provide information to the general public and to professional circles, in particular through the European Judicial Network, about this new optional European small claims procedure.[48]

The optional aspect of the proposal raises several issues. First amongst these is the question of the compatibility of the proposal with the principle of subsidiarity. It is true that the Member State cannot guarantee equivalence of small claims rules and therefore the argument for compatibility with subsidiarity is that to achieve equivalence Community action is necessary. However, the envisaged parallel system might not achieve equivalence since there is limited harmonization. Furthermore, one may ask whether such a parallel system is necessary or proportionate to achieve the objective of simplifying procedures for litigants if as both the Commission Report and the Green Paper note many of the Member States have some form of small claims procedures already.[49] In addition, since no small claims litigants, even

[46] Art. 21(3). Cf. the Brussels I Regulation (EC) No. 44/2001, Art. 40(2).

[47] Art. 22.

[48] Art. 24.

[49] Stürner (2003) p. 185 finds that there is no real need for harmonization of small claims procedures. See also report by Serverin (2001) p. 21, and COM (2002) 746, pp. 51–8. If the information contained in these is correct there are no generic small claims (or simplified/alternative)

cross-border ones, are obliged to follow the Regulation procedure but can use national procedures, specific to small claims or otherwise, the proposal might not achieve the intended equal footing or address the problem of distortion of competition.[50]

As the Commission itself pointed out in its Green Paper, if the procedure is optional and not obligatory, the practical scope of its application could be significantly limited.[51] Also, there is a general point of concern about the added complexity for courts and litigants in Member States, in particular in those which have a domestic small claims procedure, to adapt to and choose between the two alternatives, a complexity which in consequence partly defeats the purpose of simplification in the sense of introducing transparency across all national systems.

The aims of the Regulation are simplification and to create mechanisms which can assist lay litigants to avail themselves of the system without recourse to legal counsel. Thus, commentators considered that standard forms and simple rules for initiating the procedure were vital for any small claims system to function.[52] Furthermore, the use of advanced electronic technology has been suggested and propounded as a means of creating cost efficiency.[53] Hence, naturally the requirement that the court assist the litigants when lodging a claim and during the proceedings, the requirement that the court serve all documents, the predominantly written procedure, as well as the deadlines in which the court should effect all its obligations, are beneficial features of the proposed procedure and should achieve simplification and efficiency. Furthermore, regardless of the fact that the Regulation does not introduce a procedure for lodging by e-mail or the use of electronic

procedures in Austria, Belgium, Denmark, Luxembourg, and Finland (there was no response from Greece, Italy, and the Netherlands). (The Commission is unclear as to whether or not there are such procedures in the Netherlands and Portugal.) The information in Serverin's report can be contrasted with Haibach (2005) p. 594, who states that there are specific small claims procedures in the UK, Ireland, Sweden, and Spain, whereas in Germany and France there is a simplified way of introducing the procedure, and in Austria, the Netherlands, and Finland there are other procedural simplification tools which achieve the same result. These sources do not record whether there are any small claims procedures in the new Member States which joined in May 2004. If the lack of small claims procedures in these Member States is the true concern of the Commission this is not explicit in its proposal, COM (2005) 87.

[50] Kodek (2003) p. 361 notes that the expected effect on the market of the harmonization of payment orders and/or small claims is debatable and that the merits of the proposed systems depend on the structure of the procedural system in each Member State.

[51] COM (2002) 746, p. 64.

[52] Laukkanen (2003) p. 191.

[53] Ibid. p. 191 and Stürner (2003) p. 185.

signatures the Green Paper recognizes these as future possibilities.[54] In addition, all forms of telecommunication, such as videoconferencing, are possible for the potential oral hearing and collecting of evidence.[55] The simplified and strict review and enforcement certificate procedure also allows for streamlining and quicker redress. Thus, in its impact assessment evaluation the Commission adduces that for the potentially seven million European citizens involved in small claims litigation each year, the reduction of the duration of the procedure to six months would be a significant improvement and the reduction in costs and time at the recognition and enforcement stage would also further reduce costs and duration by 20 per cent.[56]

However, it is interesting that all these simplifications increase the pressure, with regard to both resources and personnel, on the decentralized local first instance courts, which will be major 'protagonists' in such small claims procedures. It appears that the proposed Small Claims Regulation is a measure in the policy area of judicial cooperation in civil matters which might significantly encroach upon the court structure or affect structural concerns within the national court systems.[57] The implementation of the Regulation implicitly expects a certain level of resources within the national courts. In particular, since no national functions or prior supranational systems are being abrogated, personnel and their time will have to be allocated to carry out such new and additional tasks as assisting potential claimants to fill in the forms and to serving all the documents. This raises the concern of whether all Member States will be able to provide the same level of resources. If not, there is risk of fragmentation and discrimination. Secondly, it is unsatisfactory for resources to be allocated from elsewhere in the domestic judicial systems, possibly resulting in fewer resources and longer waiting periods for other categories of claims where there are no specified deadlines for court tasks and caseload management.

Another development related to the nature of the simplifications introduced in the proposed Regulation is the explicit stipulations which affect the role of the judge and the parties in litigation. Not only are the courts as administrative units given tasks and deadlines by the Regulation, but the

[54] COM (2002) 746, p. 67.

[55] Arts 8 and 9.

[56] Haibach (2005) p. 601.

[57] The Service and Evidence Regulations as well as the Legal Aid Directive also added tasks and pressures for domestic local courts. The order for payment procedure will also, like the small claims procedure, necessitate the introduction of additional structures in the local court systems.

judges themselves are obliged to assist the parties in procedural matters and cannot ask the parties to present argument on the legal analysis of the matter. This might oblige judges to fundamentally change their traditional role in civil proceedings, a role which is inextricably linked to the national legal culture. Even though there is a recognized trend in the modern western civil procedural reforms to move towards more case management in order to achieve efficiency the variations of this in different jurisdictions reflect differing legal cultures.[58] Furthermore, the goal of uniform procedures available across Europe will most likely not be achieved in the short term, since it is precisely the legal cultural differences that will influence how judges approach the wide discretion they are given to 'respect the right to a fair trial and the principle of an adversarial process' when deciding on the necessity for an oral hearing or in the means of proof and the extent to which evidence is taken. Thus again the spectre of fragmentation of practices between jurisdictions is raised.

Finally one can, as with the Enforcement Order Regulation in particular and the Order for Payment Procedure, question whether the difficult balance between efficiency and the rights of the parties will be struck in a fair manner by abolishing the intermediate measures and supporting immediate recognition and enforcement in Member States other than the Member State of origin.[59] Despite the low value of the claims in question, there might be strong matters of principle involved or complex analyses of jurisdictional issues or substantive law that might have significant ancillary impact, e.g. on the future business practices of either party or as a general precedent for a specific type of contractual clause. In particular, since again only the country of origin and the court of origin decide whether all the minimum guarantees have been fulfilled for enforcement, this might disadvantage the defendant party and implies a very high level of mutual trust between the Member States.

[58] Van Rhee (2005) pp. 189–93 and 314ff.

[59] See above Chapters 9 and 12 regarding the Enforcement Order and Payment Order Regulations.

14

Judicial Network

Legislative History

The initial political documents in the process of moving towards implementation of the Area of Freedom, Security, and Justice mooted the idea or concept of a judicial network. First among these was the Action Plan which stated that one of the aims was to examine the possibility of extending the concept of a European Judicial Network in criminal matters to embrace civil and commercial proceedings.[1] The Tampere European Council conclusions also included a recommendation that an easily accessible information system be established, maintained, and updated to provide information to the public on the European area of justice.[2] These policy documents raised for the first time the issue of an inherent access to justice, a matter which the Council of Europe had in 1981 placed first among the principles established in a recommendation for access to justice at the national level, namely that of the availability of information to the public.[3] The Commission subsequently acted upon these two political proposals.

Initially, the Commission included the proposed European Judicial Network ('the Network' or EJN) in its communication reviewing progress on the creation of the Area of Freedom, Security, and Justice.[4] Thereafter, the Commission presented the proposal for a Council Decision to establish the Network.[5] Subsequently, the Report of the European Parliament[6] and

[1] Action Plan, OJ C-19, 23.1.1999, p. 1, para. 40(d).
[2] Presidency Conclusions, No. 200/1/99, para. 29.
[3] Council of Europe, Recommendation No. R (81)7, pp. 6 and 12f.
[4] COM (2000) 167.
[5] COM (2000) 592.
[6] A5 91/2001.

the Opinion of the Economic and Social Committee (ESC)[7] were published, after which the Commission's amended proposal was adopted by Decision of the Council.[8]

The objective of the Network stems from the single market and the four freedoms, with the ensuing substantial expansion of cross-border civil and commercial exchanges. As the Commission argues in its explanatory memorandum, the expansion 'raises more and more acutely the question of how members of the general public and firms are to exercise their rights in a cross-border context'.[9] The objective of the Network is therefore to ensure the sound operation of judicial procedures in cross-border matters by improving judicial cooperation mechanisms between the Member States. According to the Commission the ultimate goal is to simplify the life of citizens facing cross-border litigation and improve access to justice.[10] In particular, the Commission wants to offer added value for litigants and promote access to justice by providing an information system, which is maintained by the Network.[11]

According to the Commission, the proposal is justified by the inherent 'cross-border' element which necessitates action at the Community level. Furthermore, the Commission considers that the existing bilateral, multilateral, and international arrangements for judicial cooperation mechanisms do not hinder Community action, which is taken without prejudice to these. On the contrary the Commission envisages a role for the Network in areas not covered by the existing arrangements and also a role of supporting the existing mechanisms, e.g. by identifying best practices and disseminating knowledge of these.[12] In addition, the Commission has high hopes for the Network, which it expects to develop into an essential instrument that permits an integrated approach and serves as a forum for discussion and monitoring, as well as fosters development of practical initiatives.[13]

[7] ESC 227/2001.

[8] Amended proposal, COM (2001) 234, and (EC) No. 470/2001 Council Decision of 28 May 2001 establishing a European Judicial Network in civil and commercial matters, OJ L-174, 27.6.2001, p. 25.

[9] COM (2000) 592, p. 3.

[10] Ibid. p. 3f. See also Recitals 2, 3, and 14.

[11] Ibid. pp. 4 and 7. See also Recital 14.

[12] Ibid. p. 4f.

[13] Ibid. p. 5f.

Substantive Content

The application of the Network does not cover the entire Union. In accordance with the protocols of Denmark, UK, and Ireland to the Treaty of Amsterdam, Denmark will not participate in the Network whereas the UK and Ireland are participating.[14] However, in substantive application the Network is very broad in that there is no definition of 'civil and commercial', and specifically the Commission states that the intention is to avoid 'compartmentalization'.[15] Therefore, it is possible to envisage the application of the Network's cooperation and information mechanisms in a broad range of legal matters, including family, employment, and consumer law matters, apart from the obvious contract law, and other commercial law matters.

The vision and intention is that the Network should have two distinct practical functions or tasks. The first function is to assist or be the facilitating go-between in judicial cooperation between the Member States in civil and commercial matters. The second function is to establish and maintain an information system for the public.[16] The Network must consist of members or participants in order to function at all and to fulfil its goals, and is hence formed by several categories of member. Most relevant of these members, considered to be the 'cornerstones' of the Network, are the central contact points, one designated by each Member State.[17] There is no precise definition of the professional make-up of the national contact points or of how they operate within that national system. Due to their obligations and tasks one would assume that the contact points will be civil servants within a relevant national ministry or other administrative body, in some cases within the court system. The Decision itself refers to the contact points also by using the terminology 'authorities'. Other members of the Network fall into the following categories: (1) authorities provided for in other instruments of judicial cooperation in civil and commercial matters; (2) liaison magistrates working in the criminal network when they have responsibilities in civil or commercial matters; and (3) any other appropriate judicial or administrative authority whose membership is considered useful by the Member

[14] Recitals 18 and 19.
[15] COM (2000) 592, p. 5.
[16] Ibid. p. 4.
[17] Ibid. p. 9.

State to which it belongs.[18] The Member States were obliged to notify the Commission by June 2002 of the names and contact details of the national contact points as well as their communication facilities and knowledge of languages.[19]

In order for the Network to achieve its first function, i.e. to facilitate judicial cooperation, the contact points are obliged to provide any necessary information, to facilitate the processing of requests, and to seek solutions to any difficulties that arise.[20] However, since information about the designated contact points is not made public it appears that they are therefore not to be directly approached by litigants. Rather, liaison in practice presumably takes place between contact points themselves once they have been alerted to concrete problems within their national systems. The exact role and operational format of contact points within each Member State are not regulated, but one might envisage them as having a kind of monitoring and support function. This may be deduced from the Decision, which states that the contact points shall be at the disposal of local judicial actors and other authorities, thus emphasizing the support function.[21] This presumed interchange between contact points and their monitoring of national systems is further supported by the Decision itself, which obliges the collegiate body of contact points to meet at least once every six months to exchange experiences and identify problems and best practices.[22] Furthermore, the additional Network members are also according to the Decision supposed to participate in meetings, which the Commission will convene when appropriate. The meetings are intended to provide a platform for discussion and the exchange of experiences, but can also be held on specific issues.[23] In addition, the Decision stipulates that a secure and limited-access electronic information exchange system should be established for dissemination of information between members of the Network.[24]

In order for the Network to achieve its second function, i.e. to establish and maintain an information system for the public, the contact points are obliged to assist with the preparation and updating of the system. The Decision specifies that this shall take place through the completion and

[18] Art. 2.
[19] Arts 2(5) and 20.
[20] Art. 5(2).
[21] Art. 5(1).
[22] Arts 9 and 10.
[23] Arts 11 and 12.
[24] Art. 13.

updating of practical and concise information sheets.[25] The contact points are obliged to draw up guidelines for progressively establishing these information sheets, but the Decision specifies that at least the following subjects should be covered: principles of the legal system, judicial organization, procedures for initiating court claims including small claims and appeals, legal aid, service of documents, enforcement of judgments, interim relief and seizure of assets, alternative dispute resolution possibilities, and operation of the legal profession.[26] With regard to the information system, the Decision further stipulates that the system should be Internet based and comprise the following categories: Community instruments, national measures, and international instruments in force. The website should also make links to other sites, in particular those where the original information is to be found.[27] The information is to be updated regularly, even though no definite updating deadlines are stipulated, and the contact points are responsible for the accuracy of the information provided.[28]

Notwithstanding the central role of the contact points in the Network, it is notable that the Commission also plays a major role. With regard to the first function of the Network the Commission shall in close cooperation with the Council organize the meetings of the Network. Specifically, the Commission is the convener of meetings, and is also obliged to chair meetings and provide secretarial services. The Commission is further given the task of preparing the agenda for meetings and preparing a report after each meeting.[29] With regard to the second function the Commission is responsible for managing the information system. The Decision envisages that this includes: constructing the website, providing Community law information, and progressively translating and installing information on the website.

The Commission sees the establishment and development of the Network as a gradual process and states that the Network is to be flexible and open to evolution.[30] The Decision contains a review clause, which obliges the Commission to produce evaluation reports every five years, commencing in 2005.[31] In particular the decision specifies that the report shall consider among other matters the question of public access to the contact points,

[25] Arts 5 and 15.
[26] Arts 5 and 15.
[27] Art. 14.
[28] Arts 16 and 18.
[29] Arts 11 and 12.
[30] COM (2000) 592, p. 7f.
[31] Art. 19.1.

access to and the involvement of the legal profession in Network activities, and synergies with the Network for the extrajudicial settlement of consumer disputes.[32] The first report was published in 2006 and the information provided therein and the Commission's further suggestions are analysed below.

Normative Implications

The Network is a completely novel structure, and does not as such abrogate the existing structures of any legal instruments. However, it is noteworthy that the Network is one of the measures of judicial cooperation in civil matters most visibly influenced by the thinking developed in the field of criminal judicial cooperation has.[33] It seems that the Judicial Network in criminal matters[34] in its setting up and its success was a forerunner to and served as a model for the Network.[35] It is also noteworthy that another potential influence on the Network was the White Paper on Governance, which was published shortly after the Commission's proposal for the Network. It is plausible that the Commission was influenced by the highly topical new governance mechanisms and regulatory techniques, including the concept of networks, when envisaging proposed new measures in the area of civil and commercial matters. The Decision to create the Network has been applicable since 1 December 2002, even though the contact points had been designated prior to the entry into force of the Network.[36]

Initial Conclusions on the Impact and Effect of the Network

The Network may be seen as an inherently natural, supporting structure with the potential to contribute to a change in legal thinking and to

[32] Art. 19.2.

[33] Kennett (2000) p. 53.

[34] Established by Joint Action 98/428JAI.

[35] A5 91/2001, p. 12. There has also been some influence from the criminal field in the judicial training, cooperation, and funding structures. Therefore, the overarching measures in particular are perhaps the first to remind us of such a link, which in many national systems is stronger and natural. Because these are general measures there is a possibility that these tentative and initial influences and links might grow stronger in the future and affect the whole policy area.

[36] Art. 21.

the acquisition of sufficient knowledge by the relevant actors.[37] And as an objective of the Network is the creation of a flexible and non-bureaucratic tool, it is clear that it is expected to support the mutual recognition programme.[38] However, before the publication of the Commission's follow-up report there was no verifiable measure of the practical efficacy of the Network, i.e. whether it had indeed solved practical problems between its members and thus contributed to smoother transnational cooperation.[39]

Apart from the practical effects of the Network it is relevant to analyse also some pervading theoretical issues arising from the existence and intended function of the Network, in particular to evaluate it as a holistic structure for the whole policy area. At the institutional level it is pertinent to consider the consequences of the Network's decentralized approach. One commentator notes that the idea that institutionalization is only associated with the development of supranational rules perhaps rests on its own self-reinforcing path dependency. He continues his argument by claiming that even new forms of governance, which do not conform to the classic Community method, have led to a Europeanization of policy and an institutional shift through new discourses and forums.[40] This is a particularly interesting observation when applied to the Network, because without much previous Community procedural regulation in civil and commercial matters, a new highly organized forum and discourse are created through the Network. Thus, notwithstanding decentralization, there is actually an institutional shift from the purely national to the supranational level.

In addition, policy coordination through the Network has potential as a tool for Europeanizing or converging policy rather than fostering diversity. Hence one can even say that the diversity of national systems offers an institutional explanation for the emergence of the Network and it also conditions domestic adaptation under the system.[41] However, even though there is ample room for national contextualization, there are several incentives for convergence in a process which creates trust and cooperative orientations

[37] Hess (2003) p. 227.

[38] Tenreiro and Seoane (2003) p. 468.

[39] Hess (2003) p. 228.

[40] Armstrong (2003) p. 172f. makes this argument in relation to the 'open method of coordination', a new mechanism of Community political and legal interaction in the fields of employment and social law. The same argument can be used by analogy in the context of judicial cooperation in civil matters.

[41] Ibid. p. 180.

among participants and encourages learning dynamics.[42] In addition to the supranational and converging elements, the Network includes a potential for centralization in the central role accorded to the Commission. This can be seen in the explanatory memorandum to the proposal, in which the Commission emphasizes its own role in the Network and even obliges the national contact points to cooperate and coordinate closely with the Commission.[43] Also, the limited membership of the Network, and the fact that most participants can be seen as civil servants with the requisite technical expertise, resemble the centralization features of the comitology system.[44] Thus, the tentative vision of the Network as new governance in procedural law has to be modified by what is in essence an alternative picture of the Network as 'old' governance, as a centralized bureaucracy with ensuing Europeanization.

In terms of practical administration, it is pertinent to consider whether the Network will manage its two functions efficiently. There is first a concern that it will not achieve coherence and transparency. It is a further cooperation structure separate from the existing structures, which are not supposed to be prejudiced by it.[45] Therefore, it is not clear what further facilitative assistance the Network contact points can offer, bearing in mind that the existing cooperation structures may have been in place for a considerable time and might have very specific procedures. If the Network contact points instead are to promote coordination of the existing mechanisms and uniformity, it is difficult to see how this can be done without affecting existing mechanisms and without undermining the Member States' own powers in the implementation of the existing mechanisms.[46] Such process of coordination would underline the point above that the Network is Europeanizing procedures from above instead of ostensibly fostering diversity.

Secondly, there is a concern that the Network's facilitative task will be difficult and not constructive. National procedures are closely linked to national legal cultures; they are also highly technical and form a system,

[42] Ferrera, Matsaganis, and Sacchi (2002) p. 227 make this argument in relation to the open method of coordination. Again an analogy can be drawn to the context under discussion.

[43] COM (2000) 592, p. 8.

[44] Craig and De Búrca (1998) p. 138ff., inter alia, provide an explanation of comitology or the committee system. See further Azoulay (2002) p. 125f. for a view on its role in the regulatory system of the EU.

[45] Structures in place to achieve these aims include initiatives within the Hague Conference on Private International Law, the Council of Europe, and the EU itself, as well as bilateral or multilateral treaties amongst and between the Member States.

[46] ESC 227/2001, p. 6f.

whereby each particular part of the procedure, even judicial co-operation mechanisms, fits and links into the procedural system as a whole. Therefore, identifying best practices, seeking solutions to problems that arise, and exchanging experiences at Network level demand an in-depth knowledge of the procedural systems and a genuine comparative understanding if the results are to be constructive. Notwithstanding the existence of a genuine comparative understanding, it might be difficult to find mutual solutions due to the particular linkages and technicalities of each unharmonized procedural system. An analogy can be made drawing on Scharpf's critique of the White Paper on Governance in relation to economic governance: successful market integration has led to a need for a mutual judicial space but perhaps also exposes the fundamental asymmetries between the legal systems with the resultant difficulty in finding effective European solutions.[47]

Thirdly, the fact that the cooperation is created at the civil service level, perhaps including some judges in the category of any other appropriate authority, does not necessarily foster a genuine area of justice in which national courts, judges, and professionals are the practical participants. Horizontal dialogue between the national courts is important for the reception of EU law and would be particularly important when the matter concerns assistance between Member States in civil and commercial matters, because the assistance itself is given by national courts and national judges.[48] Disappointingly, the Network does not create a direct link between national courts at any level of the court structure or judiciary, and does not therefore match the hopes of the commentators.[49] Similarly, if one considers some of the other probable stakeholders, i.e. the legal profession and the parties themselves, it is clear that potential groups in civil society, such as organizations representing consumers or small and medium-sized enterprises (SMEs) who could be interested in mitigating obstacles to cross-border civil litigation, are not provided with a role or consulted.[50] Thus, the actors involved are mostly on the same horizontal level and are a closed group.

Finally, the attempt to promote access to justice and provide information to citizens through the Network's website can be seen as a successful tool, but one which might however have only a limited effect. The ESC notes that not all potential litigants have access to the Internet, and the percentage of

[47] Scharpf (2001) p. 3f.

[48] See inter alia Slaughter, Stone Sweet, and Weiler (2001) p. xiif., and Edward (2004) p. 2f.

[49] Inter alia Paulino Pereira (2001a) p. 48. However, there is of course potential that this might take place in the framework of the judicial training initiative.

[50] ESC 27/2001, p. 8f.

the population with an Internet connection in the Member States differs.[51] Furthermore, the litigants will in any event have to obtain more information than is provided on the Internet, and specific advice in relation to their particular case. Hence, one cannot yet see the information service as a complete Community public legal service, which is accessible and free of charge for everybody.[52]

The Commission Report

The Report published by the Commission on the Network's first three years underscores some of the issues raised and encourages a debate about the future of the Network.[53] Of all the measures in the area of judicial cooperation in civil matters the Network stands out as a structure with the widest substantive span, possibly dealing with the full range of issues such as service, evidence, and legal aid. The Network also stands out because it has a broader reach, practically involving all the national actors in one project thereby creating a Community-wide interface for the actors involved. Therefore, despite the issues that have emerged the Network has the potential to be a valuable tool for the policy area. The Commission also sees the Network as a supporting structure with potential for the future consolidation of the judicial space in Europe. This view can be seen in its Communication on the future orientations of the policy area, in which emphasis is given to the important role of the Network in the crucial functioning and implementation of the Community legislation that has been adopted in the field.[54]

In relation to the first task the Network held its inaugural meeting on 4 December 2002.[55] From the Commission's Report it is also known that the Network held four annual meetings of its contact points in 2003 and 2004 and five meetings in 2005.[56] In addition the Network has organized

[51] Ibid. p. 9.

[52] Ibid. p. 8f.

[53] COM (2006) 203, p. 7ff.

[54] COM (2004) 401, p. 11.

[55] COM (2003) 291, p. 39.

[56] COM (2006) 203, p. 1f. The Report, under heading 2.1, confirms that in 2005 there were 93 contact points in total. Most Member States have designated between two and five contact points whereas the countries which have created subdivisions of the Network might have even more contact points. In its Report the Commission is concerned that some of the contact points are combining their tasks with other functions (e.g. being the central authority for matters of judicial cooperation) and wishes that each Member State would designate at least one full-time contact point.

an annual meeting each year for all of its four categories of members.[57] The focus of the Network during its first years has apparently been its information website as well as the development of the Network's future structure and functioning.[58] Thus, one can perhaps say that the Network, apart from the very concrete task of providing the information site, has been trying to find its role and create synergies. The initial meetings, tasks, and discussions within the Network have undoubtedly been important in creating personal contacts and mutual trust between its members, which together with their goodwill is the basis for the functioning of the Network.

There is no official information at present on whether the Network has been successful in facilitating cross-border judicial cooperation through the intranet specifically created for this purpose. However, the Commission's Report does tell us that a rudimentary initial reporting system logged 363 such requests for 2003 and 2004 involving seven Member States contacted by 15 Member States; it appears that these figures do not represent the total. Since then, with the objective of obtaining more exhaustive statistics, the Commission has created an online register. Notwithstanding the fact that not all cases were included in these numbers, and bearing in mind that the Network is only an additional tool where there are problems and cooperation mechanisms that need further support, the number of matters is relatively low. Therefore, it is suggested that the Network needs to be better known amongst and have clearer channels to its current primary users, the national judges and the designated national central authorities for specific judicial cooperation issues.[59] Ultimately this of course depends on the national systems and practices. The Report does nevertheless note that in the cases logged the Network was able to reduce delay in the handling of the matter and was able to assist in solving the cooperation exchange, thereby fulfilling its task of additional simplification and facilitation.[60]

In relation to the second task, the website providing the information system was launched in March 2003, offering a wealth of information about the legal systems of the Member States as well as about the relevant international

[57] Ibid. p. 1. According to the Commission there are in total 424 members of the Network. Since 93 of these are national contact points, the other 331 fall into the additional categories: (1) authorities provided for in other instruments of judicial cooperation (159); (2) liaison magistrates in the criminal network (13); and (3) any other appropriate judicial or administrative authority (159).

[58] COM (2006) 203, p. 3f.

[59] Ibid. pp. 5 and 9f.

[60] Ibid. p. 5.

institutions and bodies.[61] Today the Network has therefore over 10,000 web pages covering 19 main themes for each of the 27 Member States in 22 different languages.[62] Between July and September 2005 there were on average 100,000 monthly visits to the site, and in 2003 the European Information Association awarded a prize to the Network for its website. In addition to the website an information campaign has been launched to create awareness of the direct impact that judicial cooperation in civil matters has on citizens and enterprises and to create awareness of the Network.[63] Furthermore, the Commission has together with the Network and national experts produced practical brochures called Practice Guides for two legislative measures in the realm of judicial cooperation in civil matters.[64]

Thus, the Network has endeavoured to facilitate access to justice through the tool of access to information. It has been considered as giving high-quality information via an accessible and user-friendly site that would not otherwise be available to citizens without great effort through more cumbersome channels.[65] For the future, the Commission considers that the pedagogical role of the Network could be further developed, e.g. by creating online discussion groups around specific judicial cooperation topics and acting as a 'forum of debate' for practical application problems, thereby facilitating exchanges on best practices.[66]

The Report furthermore deals with future challenges to the Network and notes that one crucial question is opening access to the Network both to legal practitioners and to the public in general and citizens needing help and information. Thus, the Commission has addressed the Network's participatory deficiency and lack of openness, which were recognized in the review clause of the Decision itself, and which form one of the significant critiques of the Network. There are two potential ways of opening up the Network, corresponding to

[61] http://ec.europa.eu/civiljustice/index_en.htm (visited 25.8.2007).

[62] The Commission is responsible for the coherence and translation of the information together with the practical running of the website, which is a formidable task. In accordance with the Decision the contact points are responsible for the national information provided for the website.

[63] COM (2003) 291, p. 9. See also COM (2006) 203 p. 5.

[64] The Practice Guides currently published are for the Brussels II Regulation (which as a measure falls outside the scope of this work) and the Evidence Regulation. These Guides are also available on the Network's website.

[65] COM (2006) 203, p. 7. However, it should be noted that some Member States are slow to provide information to the website or to update it. Translation has become a major issue since the 2004 enlargement and not all web pages are yet available in all languages.

[66] COM (2006) 203, p. 10.

the parallel functions of facilitating cooperation and providing information. The first of these is to let other parties participate in the annual meetings and have access to knowledge about these meetings and about the accrued experience and functioning of judicial cooperation between the contact points. This approach would appear to be most suitable for fulfilling the need of the Network to engage and interact with the legal profession, including bailiffs, lawyers, and notaries. A specific mandate in the Hague Programme is to establish cooperation between legal professionals and organize Europe-wide conferences. Hence, the Commission proposes as a first step that the Network could create a 'privileged partnership' for the legal profession, where representatives could attend Network meetings and representatives of the legal profession would have access to the national contact points in particular cases.[67]

The second approach to opening up the Network is to provide public access to the contact points for anybody. This would suit the broader public and the increasing number of citizens who find themselves faced with cross-border legal problems. This option is perhaps more controversial in that the resources of the contact points, and their position within national administrations, might not allow them essentially to become free legal advice or information clinics. However, it has been argued that the Network must develop the information side of its function and move beyond the 'faceless' website. The Commission therefore proposes that an online communication system might be established, using the precedent and methods established through the alternative dispute resolution networks for consumers, SOLVIT and EEJNET.[68]

In conclusion, the first potential development of the Network is for the group of actors presently involved in it to expand it through learning and new initiatives into a general coordinating structure for civil procedural regulation. The second potential development is for it to encourage more participation by stakeholders. Were the Network to fulfil its potential in these two ways, it would become a real tool for building a genuine European area of justice. It would become the interface in which judges, professionals, and interest groups for litigators would learn about, develop, and facilitate cross-border and European procedures.

[67] COM (2006) 203, pp. 7f. and 10. It appears that there are different views in the Member States about this proposal, with some being concerned that the legal profession could abuse access to the contact points in matters which are within their own remit. However, some Member States already allow access to the contact points by legal professionals and encourage their participation.

[68] Ibid. p. 7.

15

Judicial Training and Other Measures

Legislative History

Since 1997, various separate projects have aimed at increasing the level of knowledge within the judiciary of EC and EU matters, e.g. within the auspices of the Robert Schumann Project and the Grotius criminal and civil projects. In 2004 it was calculated that through different funding programmes for civil and criminal matters 4.5 million euros were earmarked for judicial training projects.[1] In addition the European Institute for Public Administration (EIPA) in Maastricht and its European Centre for Judges and Lawyers in Luxemburg, founded in 1992, as well as the European Law Academy (ERA), founded in Trier in 1992, both supported by the EU, disseminate knowledge and training in European law.[2] Since the nature of these initiatives is piecemeal, and since most of them entail the holding of seminars and conferences with a limited audience attending, they can perhaps not be characterized as judicial training in the strict sense, i.e. practical and holistic education given to a corps of judges.

From this perspective, a further, EU-wide initiative emerged in 2000 when a number of national training agencies with responsibility for training members of the judiciary set up an informal network through the adoption of a charter, the so-called Bordeaux Charter. However, because that network did not have legal personality and could not obtain funding from the EU or the Member States, the Charter was expressly designed to be recognized subsequently at the EU level, hence forming the background to the Decision

[1] It is unclear how much of these funds go to the civil field. COM (2005) 34, p. 9 gives a strong indication that in the civil field projects providing for the exchange of judges have been very few from these avenues of funding.

[2] COM (2006) 356, p. 6.

to create a European Judicial Training Network which was proposed by the French Government.[3]

The French Government suggested Articles 31 and 34(2) of the EU Treaty (Treaty of Maastricht, as amended) as a legal basis for the proposal, which only envisaged a training network in the field of criminal law and criminal judicial cooperation. However, the European Parliament in its Report and Opinion proposed an amendment to broaden the scope of the network to both criminal and civil judicial cooperation, which would have altered the legal basis to Article 42 of the EU Treaty as well as Articles 65 and 67 of the EC Treaty (Treaty of Rome, as amended).[4] When the Council subsequently, in June 2003, dealt with the proposal it decided that 'at present it would not be appropriate to pursue the discussions on the initiative of France'; it noted also that matters had progressed vis-à-vis the Bordeaux Charter, which was being incorporated under Belgian law and thus the independent European Judicial Training Network (EJTN or Training Network) would have legal status.[5] Therefore, the Council stated that it welcomed the establishment of the EJTN for both civil and criminal matters, that it encouraged the Member States to strengthen the EJTN, that it urged the EJTN to establish close links to the European institutions, and that it invited the Commission to examine how it could assist the Training Network. Furthermore, it invited the Commission and the EJTN to report on the functioning of the Training Network so that the Council could in the future reconsider the French initiative.[6]

In March 2003 before the Council decided to not to proceed with the French initiative the European Parliament in a Resolution indicated that it intended to launch a pilot project to promote the training and exchange of judges in Europe on the basis of the Erasmus model. This parallel initiative was launched for 2004 and 2005 whereby proposals could be submitted for funding exchanges which comprised at least four partners from at least three Member States.[7] The programme continues and will according to the Commission boost resources for judicial training in the coming years.[8]

[3] Initiative of the French Republic with a view to adopting a Council Decision setting up a European judicial training network OJ C-18, 19.1.2001, p. 9.

[4] A5 276/2002, and T5 430/2002.

[5] See website of the EJTN: http://www.ejtn.eu/.

[6] Council document 9702/03, p. 3f.

[7] Reported on the Commission website at: http://www.europa.eu.int/comm/justice_home/funding/exchanges/ (visited 9.6.2004). Apparently this project was initially targeted at magistrates in the criminal field.

[8] COM (2006) 356, p. 5.

Following from these previous tentative attempts to create EU-wide judicial training measures a new wave of political impetus is evident. First, it is noteworthy that the draft Reform Treaty mentions judicial training for both civil and criminal judicial cooperation in the respective proposed legal bases for these policy areas.[9] Secondly, even within the framework of the current Treaty bases, following the European Council Hague Programme, the Commission's Action Plan projects several measures in relation to judicial training, including the creation of a judicial training network for both civil and criminal matters from the existing structures.[10] The Commission has also published a Communication on judicial training, noting that coordination of the training of judges is a challenge and an aim to be achieved in order to properly support the implementation of the corpus of legislation in the field and in order to foster the emergence of mutual trust.[11] There is also support from the Member State Presidencies for the creation of a 'European judicial culture' and for networking between judges and judicial authorities.[12]

The Commission notes that judicial training varies among the Member States as regards initial training, continuing training, duration of training, and access to training.[13] The EU cannot interfere with the organization of judicial training in the Member States, but can strengthen mutual trust, develop training, and ensure sufficient resources for judges, prosecutors, and lawyers to receive training of the equivalent level and quality.[14] Hence, it is foreseeable that there will be further developments and perhaps even more Community-led structures with regard to judicial training and exchange of the judiciary in the future. It must also be noted that apart from the political support, judges themselves have shown their willingness to cooperate and also openness towards the comparative law methodology.[15] On a more theoretical note, for judges coordination with other jurisdictions is slowly

[9] CIG 1/07 Arts 69d(2)(h) and 69e(1)(c). These were also included in the non-ratified Constitutional Treaty Arts III-269 and III-270.

[10] COM (2005) 184, p. 26.

[11] COM (2006) 365, p. 2.

[12] Council Document 1605/05, p. 43, elaborating the operational priorities of the Austrian and Finnish Presidencies of the EU during 2006. Furthermore, the German, Portuguese, and Slovenian Presidencies for 2007 and the first six months of 2008 have issued a Trio Programme which supports enhancing cooperation between courts and developing e-justice and judicial training: Council Document 17079/06 DQPG.

[13] COM (2006) 356, p. 3f.

[14] COM (2006) 356, p. 4.

[15] Berger (2001) p. 885f.

being put on an equal basis with the classical task of preserving and developing the domestic legal system, and a horizontal comparative law analysis is increasing in significance as a sub-institutional integrative process unfolds in the EU.[16] Therefore it is relevant to consider in the following section the content of the French proposal and the parameters of the existing independent EJTN.

Substantive Content

The aim behind the judicial training initiative proposed by France was to help foster a genuine European judicial culture which could be based on mutual understanding and trust. Therefore, national bodies responsible for training would cooperate in a network structure and ensure a degree of coherence and continuity between the systems.[17] The objectives of the Training Network would inter alia be to further mutual knowledge, deepen knowledge of the European aquis, analyse training needs, exchange experiences on training, and encourage coordination of training.[18] The proposal included an annual working programme of the Training Network focusing on three strands of action: enhancing knowledge of the European legal systems and languages; organizing courses and exchanges between the judiciary; and creating training tools and educating trainers.[19] It was suggested that the Training Network would be assisted by a scientific committee of knowledgeable experts with practical experience.[20] It was further suggested that the Training Network have a secure electronic exchange network and a public website.[21]

The current independent European Judicial Training Network has been functioning, first from 2000 on the basis of a mutual Charter, and since 2004 as a non-profit registered organization with a secretariat in Brussels. The members of the Training Network are the national bodies responsible

[16] Ibid. p. 887ff.

[17] Recitals (2)–(5) of the Proposal.

[18] Proposed Art. 3. Further objectives would be to develop training measures for third countries where the EU is called upon to restore the rule of law and to help structure training measures in States applying for membership of the Union.

[19] Proposed Art. 4.

[20] Proposed Art. 8.

[21] Proposed Art. 6.

for judicial training in the Member States and the ERA.[22] The General Assembly of the Training Network meets annually to determine the general policy and activities, the Secretary General represents the Training Network and manages the secretariat for a period of three years, and three working groups deal with the training programme, the website, and external relations. The main activity of the Training Network to date has been to hold training courses in each of its member bodies for the Europe-wide judiciary. So, each domestic training body is invited to offer places to judges from other Member States in relevant legal fields (i.e. criminal, civil, commercial, administrative, labour, and European law, as well as the general fields of societal issues and languages).

In 2006 it was expected that over one thousand judges or other officials would have participated in training courses offered via the Training Network, and for 2007 almost 160 training activities at 14 training institutions were offered.[23] The Training Network is also responsible for coordinating the European Parliament's exchange programme for judicial authorities; 230 judges, public prosecutors, or trainers benefited from short-term internships in 2006 and the aim for 2007 has been for 400 exchanges to take place.[24] These activities are a remarkable step forward in such a short period of time and the exponential growth of activity between 2004 and 2005 shows that there is a drive, a potential, and a need to be harnessed. The Training Network seems to be only at the start of its evolution, with new projects such as launching a newsletter in 2006 and a permanent discussion forum being considered. Furthermore, the Training Network intends that attention will also be turned to evaluation of the courses held, so that monitoring and also development can commence.[25]

Building upon the ideas of the French initiative and the practical existence of the Training Network, the Commission notes that the training of judges falls within the domestic competence of the Member States. Nevertheless, according to the Commission the Community should focus on providing added value and financial support to existing structures.[26] The Commission stresses that this does not prevent the Member States from exercising their

[22] It appears that Cyprus among the current Member States has not yet become a member. (EJTN website http://www.ejtn.eu/, visited 25.8.2007.)

[23] This is a huge increase from 2004 when 550 judges from 19 countries were able to benefit. Information obtained from the EJTN website: http://www.ejtn.eu/.

[24] Ibid.

[25] Ibid.

[26] COM (2006) 356, p. 8.

full responsibility for judicial training and also enumerates principles which it considers the domestic systems should take into account when organizing their training systems.[27] Naturally, the Commission has very little real power to influence these issues, which depend heavily on the level of national funding for training structures.

At the European level, the Commission however sees an opening for the Community to undertake concrete action and have a real impact, through financial support for the existing structures and through cooperation between the Training Network, ERA, EIPA, and the Judicial Networks in civil and criminal matters.[28] The EU funding will be channelled through the Framework Programme for Fundamental Rights and Justice for 2007–2013. After this period the Commission envisages that a further evaluation can be carried out of the need for other measures in the field of judicial training.[29]

Normative Implications

The current independent Training Network, funding for judicial training by the EU, and any future Community structure which would build upon this do not abrogate any previous structures but provide an innovative and new interface. As the European Parliament notes the Training Network is the first structured and holistic effort in the field. It should not be confused with other networks such as the European Judicial Network (EJN) in civil matters or with the Commission's funding programmes in the field of judicial cooperation in civil matters; rather, it should be seen as a valuable addition to these structures, all of which are intended to support and service the policy area as a whole.[30] However, any potential future structure does raise crucial issues which perhaps underlie the reluctance of the Council, or lack of political support amongst the Member States, to move forward on the French initiative. These issues also permeate the debate on the need for such structured cooperation and are interlinked.

[27] Ibid. p. 6f. The Commission notes that judicial training should incorporate an EU dimension which should include familiarizing judges with European legislative instruments, improving the language skills of judges, and developing familiarity with the legal systems of other Member States.

[28] Ibid. p. 9.

[29] Ibid. p. 9.

[30] A5 276/2002, p. 18f.

The first is the key issue of funding which relates to the potential structure itself, but also invariably to the national judiciaries, national court structures, and national training structures for the judiciary. The second is the issue of cultural difference and mutual understanding. As one commentator notes, the jurisprudence of the ECJ regarding the Brussels Convention has been significant in paving the way for necessary technical procedural harmonization in the Community, but has at the same time successfully avoided becoming a victim of either of two insurmountable obstacles, e.g. the diverse organization of justice in the Member States and the ideological antagonisms between procedural systems. However, these matters do need to be addressed in the near future. The commentator makes an analogy with technological hardware and software, i.e. the upgrading of the software can sometimes be prevented by the older hardware.[31] The case law of the ECJ has also in *Mund v. Fester* touched upon the underlying hardware where it held that the Member States could be seen as a single entity for the purpose of fulfilling the objective of free movement of judgments, i.e. that the enforcement systems and courts should be presumed to be the same in order to support the common market.[32] From this presumption follows the determination to achieve this single entity for the purpose of the common market.

Regarding the issue of funding, one commentator notes that judges have become a central element in our society and that the main guarantee for proper functioning of courts lies in the training, recruitment, and selection of judges.[33] Therefore, it follows that in a European context the cooperation and potential harmonization of recruitment and training of judges is also fundamental, if European courts are to trust one another. This comment is interesting because few commentators deal with the judiciary and some categorically exclude it from the scope of potential harmonization. That one of the early proponents of harmonization has turned towards the question of the judiciary is therefore relevant and indicative of the new emphasis on this aspect of the broader picture. Significantly he notes that concrete measures to harmonize judicial training are a key to mutual trust, also thereby a key to the potential successful abolition of exequatur in the enforcement of

[31] Kerameus (2003) p. 256f.

[32] Case C-398/92, [1994] ECR I- 467. See in particular paras 11, 19, and 20. The Court found a rule of the German civil procedure code, which held that the fact that a judgment was to be enforced abroad was considered sufficient grounds for a seizure order over property in Germany, to be discriminatory and not justified under the Treaty.

[33] Storme (2001) pp. 58f. and 63.

judgments.[34] Thus, the more holistic measures such as the EJN or judicial training are tied in with the specific single practical measures to show that they are not an adjunct to these or a further step on the road, but perhaps an important preceding step to make the policy field work effectively.

Nevertheless, reverting to the funding issue, the procedural rules themselves are important, in addition to the judiciary, the court structure, and financial resources. Both of the latter are also in constant need of review. In particular, the financial resources of courts are a recurring issue. One source states that the only country in the world that does not provide inadequate financial support for the operation of its courts is Costa Rica.[35] Hence, in practice if the local courts do not have sufficient resources for their work and are overburdened, the effects of training at the supranational level will not yield significant results. Also, exchanges between judges and training officials could reveal both how different the Member State systems are as well as differences in financial support. Therefore, the gains might be unevenly distributed and paradoxically courts and judges in Member States which have comparatively more resources and structures might gain from the initiative. Furthermore, the question that will have to be resolved is where the responsibility for funding the supranational training structure will ultimately lie.

A practical example raised in the literature is the specific problem of delay in civil procedure. Here too the role of the national judiciary is important because, following the academic and professional focus on this aspect of the mutual fair trial standard, it can be observed that the obstacle to Europeanizing procedural standards across Europe lies in part in the infrastructure and cultural framework of procedure rather than in the procedural rules *per se*. Thus the reasoning of local judges is an important factor, with one commentator suggesting that national courts should adopt an 'applied comparative law approach' and a more 'pro-European approach'. But structural issues are another important factor, and therefore measures concerning the organization and administration of the judiciary might also be necessary.[36]

The independent Training Network and the French judicial training initiative, as well as any future Community measures in the field, form in parallel with the EJN a first embryonic attempt to move in the direction of addressing such issues as infrastructure and the cultural framework of national courts. With regard to the cultural aspects, the measures address

[34] Ibid. p. 63.

[35] Ibid. p. 49.

[36] Oberhammer (2003) p. 441.

more directly than the EJN the issue of concrete dialogue between national judges, in the form of face-to-face meetings between them. At the global level such meetings are increasingly common, taking place in several institutionalized fora such as the Organisation of Supreme Courts of the Americas, the Common Law Judiciary Conference, and the Association of Judges of the Baltic States. There are also increasing numbers of bilateral 'summits' and less formal meetings sponsored by law schools and non-governmental organizations.[37] Such gatherings contribute to the growing judicial globalization in which judges are beginning to perceive each other as fellow professionals in a profession which transcends borders, a perception which forms the very core of the process and its end result.[38] In the EU context there are several examples of mutual learning between courts, mostly from reported supreme or higher court cases.[39] This is indeed significant but the aim is to involve judges at all levels. Ultimately mutual understanding has to be successful in order that the end result is not circular, i.e. the end result should not deepen an initial perception of difference or misunderstanding which is the actual crux of the matter.

For local national judges to rise to the challenge of positive reinforcement as cross-border actors despite their deeply entrenched cultural perceptions might be a complex and lengthy process. It is also one which is not at all predictable as researchers have found that judicial behaviour may be influenced by several divergent factors.[40] Fortunately, practical cases other than general meetings show that the emphasis is not on the cultural differences or similarities, but rather on negotiation and direct communication in order to find the best solution.[41] In any event, because there is a widespread realization that judicial systems are lagging behind in the globalization and European integration processes and because the benefits of mutual legal training will take some time, perhaps even a generation, to emerge it is desirable that such measures are pursued now.[42] The urgency can also be seen in the point of view of one interest organization, which noted in 1998 that legal certainty

[37] Slaughter (1999–2000) p. 1120f.

[38] Ibid. p. 1123f.

[39] Van Gerven (2006) pp. 69–72.

[40] See the collection of articles in Slaughter, Stone Sweet, and Weiler (eds) (1998).

[41] Westbrook (2003) p. 567ff. notes that there has been little academic attention paid to this type of judicial activity and gives international insolvency and *forum non conveniens* matters as two practical examples of such direct negotiation.

[42] Interestingly, judicial training was suggested as one measure to remedy the problems of access to justice for consumers in the Internal Market in a study prepared for the Commission in 1998: Freyhold et al. (1998) p. 92ff.

for litigants in cross-border Europe cannot be attained through legislation alone but through legal actors, such as consumers, having confidence in the judicial persons and institutions.[43] Therefore these relational aspects of justice might quickly become the true key to success. However, as with the EJN one can say that notwithstanding that most European litigators would agree that a structure to bridge differences and support mutual understanding among local judges is an important objective, difficult tensions with subsidiarity and fragmentation still exist.

Other Initiatives and Measures

Funding for Support Activities

Under the Maastricht Treaty's Third Pillar there were specific short-term funding projects in place for civil matters, the so-called 'Grotius' and 'Grotius civil' programmes for the exchange of legal practitioners, and the Robert Schumann action programme to increase awareness within the legal professions.[44] However, in the context of the new policy area of judicial cooperation in civil matters a broader and more permanent structure, which would also be flexible and effective, was considered necessary.[45] Hence, the General Framework Regulation[46] was enacted for the period 2002–2006, supported by the European Parliament and the ESC.[47] Thus, projects which promote judicial cooperation, improve mutual knowledge, ensure sound application of Community instruments, or improve information to the public have been selected by the Commission and given financial support.[48] Projects can be set up by the Commission itself, or be submitted by other institutions and public or private organizations and must consist of exchanges, work placements, studies and research, meetings and seminars, or the dissemination of information.[49]

[43] ECLG (1998) Annex II.

[44] OJ L-287, 8.11.1996, OJ L-43, 14.2.2001, and OJ L-196, 14.7.1998.

[45] Recital 8.

[46] (EC) No. 743/2002, Council Regulation establishing a general framework for Community activities to facilitate the implementation of judicial cooperation in civil matters, OJ L-115, 1.5.2002, p. 1.

[47] A5 339/2001, p. 9 and ESC 1324/2001, paras 2.1–2.4 and 4.

[48] Art. 2.

[49] Arts 3–6.

A number of projects have been funded during this period. An important project, to be realized within the auspices of the Commission itself, which was also the first project to be financed, was the development of the Civil Judicial Atlas.[50] The Atlas is a tool available on the Internet, with a link from the EJN website amongst others, for practitioners and officials working with any of the various measures of judicial cooperation in civil matters, e.g. the taking of evidence or the provision of legal aid.[51] In practice the Atlas provides an alternative to the cumbersome route of searching in the latest paper manual published in the Official Journal for the up-to-date forms and contact details of each local court or authority involved. Instead, by clicking on the map and other icons of the Atlas, a practitioner in Florence (Italy) can find details for the District Court of Seinäjoki (Finland) and the relevant forms in Finnish.

Another type of project is the publication *Enforcement of International Contracts in the European Union* (Antwerp: Intersentia, 2004) which is the result of a research project funded by the Commission under the framework programme, coordinated by four European universities, and bringing together 14 experts from 11 European universities. This is a joint analysis of the coherence between the Brussels I and Rome I Regulations in the period when the latter was still a proposal in the legislative process. The experts have managed to compile a general report which they hope will contribute to the coherent development of the policy area.[52]

Another issue, which perhaps also indicates a certain amount of fragmentation in the initial stages of creating the European judicial space, is the geographical spread of the projects and the breadth of their reach. In 2004, before the accession of the 'new' Member States, project leaders came from only five Member States. But in practice the polarization might not be very great because seven others were involved in projects, in addition to which three of the accession countries were also involved.[53] It is to be hoped that most Member States are involved in projects but some Member State governments, professional training institutions, and universities might be

[50] Tenreiro and Seoane (2003) p. 470. See also COM (2005) 34, p. 4f., which is the Commission interim report on the implementation of the framework programme. The other Commission-led projects include a database of case law and an information campaign to raise the awareness of legal practitioners.

[51] http://ec.europa.eu/justice_home/judicialatlascivil/html/index_en.htm (visited 25.8.2007).

[52] Meesuen , Pertegás, and Straetmans (eds) (2004), p. 1f.

[53] COM (2005), 34, p. 7.

more active in applying for funding and participating in projects.[54] However the Commission, countering fragmentation and attempting to foster widespread knowledge, emphasizes the condition that project results must be published and disseminated.[55]

Upon the expiry of the current framework programme and in line with the preparation of the next general financial projections for the Union, the Commission has taken the opportunity to establish a new umbrella Framework Programme for Fundamental Rights and Justice which in essence covers all the separate policy areas of the Area of Freedom, Security, and Justice. The programme for each of the policy areas will still be composed of different legislative instruments but the intention is to ensure political coherence and logistical simplification and flexibility in management.[56] For judicial cooperation in civil matters the new emphases are, first, that synergies are to be found and projects coordinated with the European Judicial Network and, secondly, that better grouping – together with criminal judicial cooperation – is intended to be complementary and helpful to judges and practitioners.[57] For the whole period 2007–2013 the projected expenditure on civil justice is 106.5 million euros.[58] Thus, it is clear that funding will continue and that it is seen as very important to increase effort in monitoring the application of the relatively new civil justice aquis and significant to the effort to achieve mutual recognition in a wider sense.[59]

Cooperation with the Council of Europe

Apart from using the ECHR and the well-known Article 6 fair trial standards, the Council of Europe has through its various Committees sought to influence and develop access to justice in its Member States, amongst which are all the EU Member States. Thus, for example, Recommendations published in 1981 and 1984, 'Measures facilitating access to justice' and 'Principles of civil procedure designed to improve the functioning of justice', albeit having no legally binding force, foreshadowed issues such as small claims,

[54] Ibid.

[55] COM (2005) 34, p. 8.

[56] COM (2005) 122, p. 3ff. The specific proposal for Civil Justice is COM (2005) 122–5, which is still in the legislative process. According to the European Parliament's legislative tracking website http://www.europarl.europa.eu/oeil/ (visited 25.8.2007) the Parliament has held its second reading and a common position is scheduled in the Council for the end of 2007.

[57] COM (2005) 122, p. 7f.

[58] Ibid. p. 9.

[59] Ibid. p. 6.

public access to information, the use of modern technology, and encouraging mediation in certain types of cases. In addition, more recently the current Commission for the Efficiency of Justice (CEPEJ) within the Council of Europe (COE) has created a framework programme, 'A new objective for judicial systems: the processing of each case within an optimum and foreseeable timeframe' and has set up a scheme for an ongoing evaluation of European judicial systems.[60] Thus, the COE, having different goals and instruments than the EU, strives in what can be termed a 'softer' way to influence public policies of justice, and thereby at the national level contributes to improving justice for citizens.

Notwithstanding the difference in outlook since the EU began to develop its policy area of judicial cooperation in civil matters, there are obvious synergies and mutual interests between the two institutions. Therefore forms of cooperation with the COE, which might prove significant and interesting as support structures for the EU policy area, have started to develop. A first concrete example is the co-organization of the annual European Day of Civil Justice on 25 October, which was first celebrated in 2003. The intention is that, together with the Member States, the EU and COE institutions will use the day to organize workshops and events which publicize civil justice and provide information. Another example is the competition for the Crystal Scales of Justice Award, which honours innovative practices that have contributed to the quality of civil justice.[61] The broader idea is to use the competition as a means for disseminating amongst policy-makers and the judicial community information about interesting and successful measures which have been created in one Member State but which might provide ideas and possibilities for improvement in other States.

[60] See the website of the Council of Europe: http://www.coe.int/T/E/Legal_Affairs/Legal_co_operation/Operation_of_justice/.

[61] The first prize was awarded in 2005 to the Court of Appeal of Rovaniemi Finland and courts in its jurisdiction for a successfully completed quality project. A description of the project can be found at the Finnish Ministry of Justice website at: http://www.oikeus.fi/uploads/wz1uke8tvs.pdf (visited 3.2006). The core idea is to influence the main factor in the quality of adjudication, i.e. the professional skill and competence of the judge. The main tool consists of systematic discussions among the judges and between the judges and stakeholders. In 2006 the prize was awarded to the Regional Court of Linz, Austria. The winning initiative is the Court's Service Centre, a central point where citizens can obtain all necessary information and can apply to use the Court's services.

16

The Legitimacy of the Policy Area: Rethinking the Procedural Landscape

Brave New World

Review of the Legislative Measures

One commentator has, in the face of the Europeanization of private law, written:

> We cannot return to a world of local law unsullied by transnational influences. History tells us that this is anyway not the normal state of affairs in Europe. And, looking into the future, the pressures of transnational trade make it all the more improbable that reliance on established domestic processes can meet the prevailing challenges.
>
> ...it is possible for jurists to collaborate in identifying the way forward for a sharing of responsibility in the evolution of a European private law which must be based in perceptions more sophisticated than a mere glorification of harmonization, just as it must not exaggerate the inviolability of national legal culture and thinking.[1]

In the face of the Europeanization of cross-border procedural law the purpose of this chapter is to gather all the threads of information, the seeds of understanding, from the background and substantive analyses of judicial cooperation in civil matters, and to conduct a holistic evaluation. The question, which begs an answer, is the character and role of the policy area, which might perhaps be called a 'Brave New World',[2] within the traditional procedural landscape. On the basis of the analyses of the procedural measures and

[1] Weatherill (2004b) p. 659f.

[2] Referring to the novel published in 1932 by Aldous Huxley. The title comes from Miranda's speech in Shakespeare's *The Tempest*, Act V, Scene I: 'O wonder! How many goodly creatures are there here! How beauteous mankind is! O brave new world, That has such people in't!'

their normative implications in Chapters 6 to 15 as well as the background themes and issues raised in Chapters 2–5 the purpose is to 'uncover' the policy area. Is it a dystopia or a benign utopia?[3] First, the practical functioning and procedural implications of our three categories of measures will be reviewed together and the main trends emerging from the separate measures will be identified. Secondly, the constitutional and regulatory implications, emerging separately and collectively for our three categories, will be debated. This analysis will have an insider perspective, from the point of view of the European Union and its supranational constitutional and regulatory parameters. Thirdly, a different perspective will be adopted, looking outward towards procedural trends, international procedure, and procedural functions, considering the impact of the policy area on these and vice versa. It is hoped that these stages of analysis will 'uncover' judicial cooperation in civil matters so we can address its legitimacy and project its future.

The Brave New World created by all the measures outlined above is undoubtedly a challenge for the national jurisdictions and is also a formidable challenge for researchers.[4] An evaluation of the first group or first phase of measures, Chapters 6 to 9, demonstrates several crucial features of the new system. First, all of the four measures clearly envisage decentralization and direct channels of cross-border cooperation to the very lowest level of local first instance courts. In addition, through practical and modern tools, such as standard forms and manuals, now available on the online site of the Judicial Atlas, the measures strive towards avoiding delay and practical complexity. Traditional mechanisms of international procedure, such as diplomatic channels, central authorities, and the double checks of the exequatur procedure, are all abolished or streamlined. Some measures set out procedural deadlines for the courts or other designated bodies to follow. Again, the aim is effective procedures and lower costs. Minimum standards and mutual recognition are propagated: e.g. the Service Regulation enumerates several possible methods of service that have to be accepted; under the Evidence Regulation requests can only be refused in limited circumstances and Member States have to accept other forms and methods of taking evidence if possible; for enforcement under the Brussels I Regulation the grounds of refusal are limited, and for enforcement under the Enforcement Order

[3] Huxley himself apparently referred to the Brave New World as a 'negative utopia' (see http://en.wikipedia.org/).

[4] The Brave New World that is being analysed is naturally not static and the policy area is still in evolution. However, the cut-off date for this work is the end of August 2007.

Regulation if minimum procedural standards are upheld direct enforcement is possible.

The second phase of measures, Chapters 10 to 13, also demonstrates several of these features in a significantly novel context and therefore provides further depth and force to them. Decentralization and direct channels are also predominant here, now giving local courts international procedural tasks in the fields of legal aid, small claims, and payment orders. A further element of decentralization is the bringing in to the realm of regulation of local private actors, albeit through a model of self-regulation, in the field of mediation and alternative dispute resolution. For these measures modern tools designed to introduce efficiency and keep costs low are available, i.e. standardized procedural forms and specific deadlines within which the courts are to act and progress proceedings, thus creating streamlined access to justice for litigants. A further feature, which is specifically underlined in the Legal Aid Directive and the Small Claims Regulation, is the obligation upon courts and Member States to cooperate and to provide information on procedures through the European Judicial Network (EJN), thereby emphasizing transparency and clarity through the provision of and access to proper information for litigants.

A central theme of this particular group is that of simplification of procedural rules, with the introduction of optional new, ostensibly simplified, procedural mechanisms and the facility for litigants to avail themselves of these tools without counsel. In addition, not only courts (under the Evidence Regulation), but also litigants (under the Payment Order Regulation and the proposed Small Claims Regulation), are encouraged to use new technology to lodge such procedures, thereby increasing speed and decreasing cost. Finally, mutual recognition and mutual trust as well as minimum standards are very much in evidence for this category of measures too. In particular the Payment Order Regulation, which concerns uncontested claims, but also the Small Claims Regulation, which is intended to apply to contested claims, introduce minimum protective guarantees. If these guarantees are present they entail that mutual recognition of such judgments will be a reality in Europe without any possibility of exequatur or other control in the Member State of enforcement. The Legal Aid Directive is arguably also predicated upon mutual recognition of a relative minimum standard.

These crucial features of decentralization, i.e. simplification of procedures, practical and new technology tools, as well as increased information, cooperation, and accessibility, together with mutual recognition and its ancillary minimum procedural standards, have introduced for each of the measures reviewed positive and welcome improvements for litigants caught up in the intersections identified in Chapter 1. In sum, there has undoubtedly been a shift in legislative and political intent and an attempt to address the intersections which were outlined in Chapter 1. More generally the new policy area of judicial cooperation in civil matters has from the perspective of traditional international civil procedure introduced interesting new methodologies. However, as has been identified above for each of the measures separately, there are some features which raise concerns and put in doubt the potential success of the policy area and comprise its weakness and are the source of criticisms.

The first group of measures evidenced the crucial problem of national diversity or fragmentation. First, different levels of court resources and ability are the 'dark side' of decentralization, thereby fostering different treatment in practice in cross-border cases despite the aim of equal treatment. Numerous practical problems were identified in the empirical report on the Service Regulation and evidence the patchy practical results. As could be seen in the report there is no guarantee of speed and efficiency despite specified deadlines. Secondly, reference to national rules or procedures and the mutual recognition of these are further 'dark' characteristics of the kind of decentralization that has been regulated. Accepting diverging national practices vis-à-vis, for example, modes of evidence or type of service means that even though cooperation is perhaps helpful in a specific case, the overall impression is one of diversity and also potential discrimination between jurisdictions rather than coherence.

Following from diversity the inherent total complexity thus introduced is not beneficial for fostering legal certainty for private litigants or businesses and is far from creating a European legal space. As one private person might hypothetically be called as a witness under 25 different evidence regimes, there will inevitably be difficulty in knowing whether privilege exists. Notably also specific measures may introduce significant complexities, which shows that transparency, simplicity, and legal certainty are difficult to achieve in this policy area. For example, the jurisdiction rules for consumer contracts or the rules of lis pendens in the Brussels I Regulation are legally technical and depend on legal interpretation which is by no means transparent and therefore difficult for lay litigants to understand. Perhaps most concern is, however, directed towards the particular risks involved in propagating the mutual recognition of a multitude of different procedures while limiting the possibilities in which to ascertain in practice if the rights of the defence have been protected. As an example the Enforcement Order

Regulation has shown that, if the court of origin is allowed to scrutinize its own standard of service, protection for the defendant might be very weak.

These crucial problems are also starkly evident in the second category of measures. The local resources available to domestic courts are a source of fragmentation and this is evident in the Legal Aid Directive, as regards both procedure and potential qualitative financial support. Similarly, compliance with the Payment Order and Small Claims Regulations might affect the practices and workloads of local courts, put pressure on their resources, and indicate differences between Member States. Carrying out the measures so far in the field of ADR and mediation will also rely on the efforts of private and public actors and therefore also rely heavily on national exigencies and resources. Furthermore, the more technical fragmentation ensuing from minimum standards but mutual recognition of national procedural rules is evident both in the Payment Order Regulation and in the Small Claims Regulation. Therefore, legal certainty, clarity, and transparency are not achieved either at the level of the single case or at the level of implementation across jurisdictions.

The risk of lessened procedural protection, in particular of defendants' rights, is also an element of the payment order and small claims procedures. First, both procedures are schematic as regards scope, which means that a payment order can apply to any amount of liquidated claim which is ostensibly uncontested and a small claim can apply to all claims under 2,000 euros, whatever their complexity. Without safety valves there is the potential for abuse and injustice towards defendants who are not at liberty to choose the form of procedure. Secondly, because mutual recognition entails the abolition of exequatur and the existence of extremely limited possibilities for the defendant to mount an opposition at the stage of recognition and enforcement of judgments following from these two measures, the defendant's protection is reduced. Thirdly, the service rules in both measures allow for service by registered mail, which is efficient in a domestic context, but arguably this method might be extremely uncertain in a cross-border context.

The crucial common themes of the legislative agenda which has been carried through, including the eight procedural mechanisms elaborated in the first and second categories of measures, are potentially affected by the general measures that form the third category, covered in Chapters 14 and 15. The European Judicial Network, the European Judicial Training Network, and the Framework Programme are certainly intended to support the smooth functioning of the policy area. These measures are all in their infancy, and as the Report of the European Judicial Network indicates, there is much room for development and deepening of the structures.

One notable feature is that if the networks are successful in creating interactions, mutual learning, and best practices, there is a potential for convergence and a degree of centralization. Such a development would counter and negate some of the criticisms noted above regarding fragmentation among national practices. Interchanges between judges and training for judges would, as the criticisms point out, be a priority because the local courts are the ones creating day-to-day practice in the policy area and the ones who have to find the means to function, to apply the new tasks, and to deal with the caseload the policy area generates. However, it could be considered that input for citizens or litigants is equally important for the creation of the policy area. The lack of transparency and lack of legal certainty created by fragmentation can be alleviated, for the litigants and the legal profession representing them, by increased information and access to legal assistance. These benefits of the third category of measures are currently still more hypothetical than real.

Nevertheless, there are signs in the Report on the European Judicial Network that information is available to and being accessed by the users and the figures on the European Judicial Training Network website show that the number of judges benefiting from training sessions is increasing annually. The prospects of opening the European Judicial Network to the public and the legal profession are encouraging, as are the prospects for more cohesive and long-term planning of judicial training. However it will take several years for convergence across all jurisdictions to be achieved. In the meantime another structure which would benefit centralization is the emerging case law of the ECJ, which could also contribute to legal certainty and reduced complexity by means of autonomous definitions. ECJ case law could also perhaps address the difficult balance between the rights of the defence and the speed of procedural action such as enforcement, and demarcate the limits to the rights of the defence.

In addition, as we have seen thus far in the cases from the ECJ in relation to judicial cooperation, the dividing line between domestic procedural rules and the uniform application of the legislative instruments of the policy area is in itself a delicate matter and one in which further case law would undoubtedly give needed guidance.[5] Therefore, it is significant and regrettable that this potential is being hampered by the restriction that only courts from

[5] Inter alia case C-443/03 *Götz Leffler v. Berlin Chemie AG* [2005] ECR I-9611.

which there is no appeal are allowed to make preliminary references to the ECJ. It is quite inconceivable and unacceptable that many litigants who might, for example, avail themselves of the order for payment procedure or the small claims procedure would be prepared to and be required to appeal to the highest level in order to be certain of their rights under the relevant legislative measures.

What is Missing?

When reviewing the current regulation one further important approach, in order to obtain a complete picture, is to enquire what is missing. Despite the significant legislative activity taken so far or indeed fuelled by the regulation, one must ask why measures have not yet been taken in certain crucial areas. One such area is procedural sanctions, which domestically function as checks and balances from the legislator to progress proceedings. There are no sanctions for the courts and authorities involved who neglect to meet the deadlines set out in the legislative instruments of judicial cooperation in civil matters.[6] Similarly, there are several questions which might arise regarding situations of procedural default and the correction or sanction that could be imposed for such default by the litigants.[7] This is also an area which commentators have highlighted as one which leads to fragmentation, because domestic rules would appear to fill the gap.

Apart from the issue of sanctions, the most obvious issue, which emerged inevitably after the enactment of the Brussels I, Enforcement Order, Payment Order, and Small Claims regulations, is enforcement procedures, i.e. procedures for execution.[8] It has been realized that the ultimate success of each of the aforementioned measures depends on effective execution, which may take the form of a threat to encourage payment or may be the only tool available to use against recalcitrant debtors. Another issue, which is crucial in transnational litigation and has become more imperative when capital and assets can move very quickly and freely, is that of interim remedies, either at the stage of proceedings or at the stage of judgment awaiting

[6] The possibility of a Member State being held liable either under an infringement procedure brought by the Commission before the ECJ or under a state liability action brought by a private party before a domestic court is of course open. However, the deadlines are often legislated in such a programmatic way that there are difficult issues of proof and discretion to establish before bringing such a claim. Nevertheless, future practice will reveal, if such cases arise, the normative strength of the deadlines.

[7] Mignolet (2003) p. 323f.

[8] Jeuland (2004) p. 113f., who also notes further lacunae, such as rules regarding proof.

execution. Mutual recognition of provisional relief has been called a classic feature of transnational litigation, and the relationship between provisional and protective measures and enforcement of judgments is a vital feature of modern litigation.[9] Both are equally necessary although one may at times duplicate the function of the other.[10] It has been noted that provisional relief is crucial too for reasons of speed, which is inherent in the urgency of the measure, but which can also serve to counter the unfortunate length of proceedings. The transnational nature of a dispute can only accentuate these needs.[11]

For both execution procedures and interim measures a third practical issue is important, namely that of the transparency of the defendant's or debtor's assets. Notably, the Commission has been aware of these issues and in its Communication 'Towards greater efficiency in obtaining and enforcing judgments in the EU' specifically elaborated upon the need for provisional and protective measures, upon the vital need for 'actual enforcement' measures, and upon the importance of transparency of assets.[12] Regarding the state of play the following statements present the problem as the Commission sees it: 'there is no European law-enforcement area but rather a juxtaposition of national systems' and 'there is a risk that assets will escape the enforcement procedure if it is delayed'.[13]

Notwithstanding these statements no measures have yet been enacted in these crucial fields. This is regrettable, though the justifications are easily discerned. The first justification, as could be said of many of the regulated measures, is that of the great diversity between Member States' procedures, which adds complexity to legislative preparation and to the political process.[14] The second justification is that difficult matters of principle would

[9] Andrews (2003) p. 270.

[10] Kennett (2000) p. 23f.

[11] Normand (1998c) p. 1141ff. Note that (p. 1146ff.), despite apparent similarities in domestic interim relief and the aims of these procedures, there are also differences, e.g. some measures are aimed at conservation for a potential judgment, some are aimed rather at ensuring stability between the parties and conserving evidence, whereas some function as a forerunner of the judgment. See further, ibid. pp. 1149–53 for an interesting comparative review of conditions for domestic interim relief.

[12] COM (1997) 609, paras 22–29, 42–7, and 48–54.

[13] Ibid. paras 3 and 5.

[14] Ibid. inter alia para. 46, where the Commission stipulates that it will have to take a cautious and gradual approach to enforcement due to the diversity and complexity of the matter. Kaye (1995) provides information based on collaborative work evidencing the differences between the then 15 EU Member States, with the three different jurisdictions in the UK (and also the Isle of Man and Jersey) shown separately, plus four other European jurisdictions.

arise, which again would complicate the legislative and political processes.[15] The third reason, which links in with the other two, is that these measures relate closely to several other areas of law, e.g. securities, divorce, contract, succession, and taxation, in addition to being closely related to diverging national civil justice structures.[16] For example, a close relationship exists between execution agencies and enforcement proceedings and as these differ considerably between Member States harmonization or mutual recognition is less straightforward.[17] This entails that apart from the existence of complexity and political difficulty there might be intricate questions of competence and legal base and also other strong regulatory concerns such as subsidiarity. Thus, as one comes to the very essence of 'levelling the playing field' for cross-border litigants the 'hard cases' in the regulatory approach emerge.

The institutions have not, however, remained completely inactive. Because diversity in relation to enforcement proper or execution creates an 'enforcement deficit', the question of how to address diversity, by harmonization or by other means, has been studied.[18] And some policy documents have also mentioned that the seizure of bank accounts would be regulated as an initial measure.[19] A study commissioned by the Commission analysed the garnishment of bank accounts and recommended a European Garnishment Order.[20] The Commission has launched a Green Paper on the Attachment of Bank Accounts and the consultation process is in progress.[21] The decision on whether or not to initiate legislation will be subject to an impact assessment and the Green Paper is not intended to prejudice the results of the impact assessment. The Commission nevertheless invites comments on the suggestion that a potential European system for the attachment of bank accounts could either consist of a new stand-alone European procedure or harmonize

[15] Kennett (1997) p. 432f. notes that the transparency of the debtor's assets raises the issue of the balance between the creditor's property expectations and the debtor's right to privacy.

[16] Ibid. p. 424.

[17] Hess (2005a) pp. 31 and 45f. See also Kaye (1995).

[18] Andenas (2005) p. 8. The concept of 'enforcement deficit' is borrowed from the general concept of lack of enforcement of EC law. The debate regarding harmonization of execution measures based on a national comparative study is canvassed in Andenas et al. (eds) (2005), which follows from two projects funded by the Commission.

[19] COM (1997) 609, paragraph 46. Kennett (2000) p. 56 notes that Council Presidency documents suggested when the five year Action Plan was elaborated.

[20] Hess (2005b).

[21] COM (2006) 618.

the rules of the Member States by means of a directive.[22] Irrespective of the type of instrument the Green Paper raises a host of issues that the attachment measure might have to deal with relating, inter alia, to the procedure for obtaining an order, the effects of the order, and procedural safeguards for the defendant.[23] The Commission also raises general policy considerations that juxtapose the need for speed in execution procedures and the need to create a measure that takes into account the speed of bank transfers by the use of modern technology against the need to protect the debtor and to respect proportionality in execution measures.[24] The Study undertaken for the Commission prior to the Green Paper considers that the measure should go further than merely mutual recognition of orders and that it would be valuable to regulate some of the practicalities involved in the collection and distribution of funds without perhaps touching on the structure of the national enforcement agents.[25] In sum, there are several intricate questions including the regulatory scope, and it will be interesting to follow the results of the consultation process and impact assessment as well as any future Commission proposal.

Provisional relief has already been partly regulated by the Brussels I Regulation, Articles 31 and 32, as well as by subsequent significant case law from the ECJ. Article 31 allows for domestic interim measures but does not clearly establish a jurisdiction, which is particularly relevant when some Member States grant extraterritorial protective measures.[26] Regarding these two issues, the ECJ has given some clarification in judging that jurisdiction to order provisional relief is conditional upon a real connecting link, entailing in practice either the court determining the merits or a court where significant assets are located. However, the extent of the 'territorial connection criteria' is still in dispute among commentators and there are still apparently varying national practices.[27] Furthermore, problems have arisen because despite Article 32 of the Regulation, which allows for recognition of provisional measures, the ECJ case law curtails its practical ambit by stipulating

[22] Ibid. p. 3f.; SEC (2006) 1341, p. 7f.

[23] COM (2006) 618 pp. 4–10; SEC (2006) 1341 pp. 10–28.

[24] SEC (2006) 1341, p. 9f.

[25] Hess (2004b) p. 91.

[26] Kerameus (1998b) pp. 1175–81 outlines the varied national practices and options as regards jurisdiction for transnational interim remedies. Further, see pp. 1188–91 regarding the situation in the Brussels and Lugano countries.

[27] Hess (2005b) p. 276f., referring to cases C-391/95 *Van Uden* [1998] ECR I-7091 and C-99/96 *Mietz* [1999] ECR I-3637.

that provisional relief obtained *ex parte* cannot be recognized.[28] Therefore, several commentators have recommended that cross-border protective and provisional measures be regulated with more clarity and detail at the European level.[29]

One suggestion, elaborated by one commentator, would be the creation of a clear system in which the main responsibility would fall to the court judging the merits, when urgently judging the interim relief application *ex parte*.[30] In such a case, the defendant should naturally be heard within a reasonable time and be granted the opportunity to object to the order. An ancillary role should be played by the courts in jurisdictions where assets are located, and they should be able to order ancillary relief if necessary over these assets, but the main court would have the power to suspend or vary such an order. The measures taken by the main court would be recognized in all Member States even though execution proper would be governed by local law. The courts would be under an obligation to cooperate.[31]

Finally, another issue which has been mooted is that of complex or collective litigation at the European level. European-level measures could combat forum shopping and provide procedural economy for the parties as well as contribute to effective realization of substantive policies such as consumer and environmental law. One commentator suggests that the consumer injunction directive should be opened up, i.e. not be limited to consumer protection directives, but should apply to all EC secondary legislation, and considers that Article 65 would provide an adequate legal basis for such a change.[32] Another commentator considers that the associational action model leads to haphazard law enforcement and argues that class actions are more effective.[33] He advocates a class action for Europe, based on a US transplant, which would not be contrary to any principles of the European

[28] Ibid. 278f. See case C-125/79 *Denilauler v. Couchez Frères* [1980] ECR 1553.

[29] Inter alia Hess (2005b).

[30] The urgency, which is often accentuated in transnational procedures, and the potential need to review the *Denilauler* case law to allow *ex parte* provisional relief have also been recognized by other commentators, e.g. Normand (1998c) p. 1165ff.

[31] Hess (2005b) pp. 281–4. Note that the Green Paper on Attachment of Bank Accounts also raises the question of jurisdiction for attachment orders and suggests that there might be a case for enabling the creditor to choose between different fora, i.e. the court deciding the main proceeding, the defendant's domicile, and/or the courts in any Member State in which the bank account is located: COM (2006) 618, p. 6.

[32] Koch (2003) p. 386.

[33] Giussani (2003) pp. 391–7.

civil law systems.[34] However, some other commentators are more sceptical and note that even though class or representative actions are an efficient way to deal with multiple similar claims there are dangers in the mechanism.[35] The very recent development in the Nordic countries is interesting from this perspective because there has been a debate about the potential introduction of collective litigation or class actions, and such mechanisms have inter alia been introduced in Sweden and in a limited form in Finland.[36]

Legitimacy: First Glance

The detailed analysis of the legislative measures and the initial review of the policy area judicial cooperation in civil matters confirm that Community law has many interfaces with and influences on procedural development. It can be seen as a halfway house, creating an interplay with both municipal law and global law.[37] It also confirms that since the Treaty of Amsterdam the EU has in comparison to the other international fora had drive and an unprecedented dynamic approach vis-à-vis judicial cooperation in civil matters, causing some to even envisage a future for a 'Euro judgment' and a 'Euro form of action'.[38] The EC Treaty and the ensuing legislative activity have brought about a paradigm shift, in international and perhaps even domestic procedure, since the goals and needs of the new procedural regulation are formulated from the European perspective.[39] The measures adopted are mostly specific and narrow, aimed at targeting or combating particular procedural obstacles to cross-border trade.[40] Following from these general conclusions and observations, there is a need for a more searching analysis. The question which arises is whether this rapid legislative process and the ensuing regulation are legitimate. Breaking down legitimacy, we can include an evaluation of the functionality of the regulation as well as a discussion of its appropriateness. First, in relation to functionality, if the developing regulation does not work in practice and if there are serious doubts as to whether it

[34] Ibid. pp. 397–400.

[35] Hodges (2003) p. 403ff., who argues that the last 15 years of experience of class action in England and Wales have been 'profoundly unsatisfactory'.

[36] Lindblom (2000c) reviews the emergence and development of multi-party actions, and Oker-Blom (2006) deals with the Finnish debate, relating it to the Swedish one and also to the US situation.

[37] Jessurun D'Oliveira (1992) p. 282f.

[38] Aalto (2000) p. 330f.

[39] Hess (2002a) p. 5.

[40] Normand (1998a) p. 395; Walter and Walther (2001) p. 185.

will achieve its practical aims we do not even get over the hurdle of demonstrating that there is truly a European judicial space. Secondly, once there is at least the beginning of a truly European judicial space, it is pertinent to consider its effects and whether or in which direction we support its further development, i.e. to discuss its appropriateness.

Regarding the first of these questions, functionality, the main issue, which follows from the review of the policy area thus far and which relates back to the debate on the case law of the ECJ, is the inherent tension in Europeanizing through decentralization.[41] Thus, at the fundamental level we have identified that the crucial critique of judicial cooperation in civil matters is that decentralization is likely to cause fragmentation and even discrimination between litigants in the Internal Market. The differing national resources and differing national practices, as separate elements of the fragmentation introduced, have significant and negative effects on functionality. Furthermore, the potential reduction in the protection of defendants can be seen as running counter to the purpose of the policy area, which was intended to create a 'level playing field' for litigants. At the structural level, the unfortunate EC Treaty restrictions on preliminary referrals to the ECJ, which impact on legal certainty and on the uniform interpretation of the regulation, also have a negative impact on functionality. Finally, the missing pieces, in particular and most significantly execution mechanisms and interim remedies, which the policy area does not yet address, affect functionality negatively. The interim conclusion must therefore be that the policy area does not yet fulfil its functional potential and its legitimacy is put into question.

Notwithstanding this critique, the full body of legislative action has not been applied for a considerable period of time, which means that we cannot yet fully gauge its functionality. In addition, the supporting general structures created can have a positive integrating effect. Therefore, one should concede that the beginnings and potential of a truly European judicial space are at hand. The following sections consider its effects and look at whether and in which direction we support its further development, i.e. discuss its appropriateness. First is an analysis that takes an EU or 'inside' perspective, and deals with the constitutional and legal-political background forces shaping the policy area. These background issues constitute the driving force of the policy area and must thus also be linked to and form the natural matrix for the internal evaluation of its legitimacy. Following this analysis subsequent

[41] See Chapter 2.

sections take an outward-looking perspective and examine interactions with procedural trends, international procedure, and procedural functions.

The Inside Perspective: 'How' and 'Why' Regulate?

How? The Constitutional Conundrum

In the debate regarding private law harmonization in the EU, one commentator identifies that competence creep and questioning of the legitimacy of harmonization are among the main lines of criticism.[42] In the area of substantive private law the EU historically had a broad functional reach into policy and the political environment contributed to a broad view or even a subversion of the attribution of competence. However, over time the constitutional objection that the incursion into national autonomy had gone too far gained momentum and culminated in the ECJ's *Tobacco Advertising* judgment. Henceforth and currently there has been a clear imperative in the field of private law to justify legislative measures in more detail and rethink bland generalizations about market efficiency.[43] These observations and this history could be seen to have analogies for the policy area under discussion, in which a somewhat similar development can be seen as evolving, albeit the trend towards caution has been more abrupt.

With the advent of Article 65 of the EC Treaty and the first measures in judicial cooperation in civil matters the attribution of competence was not questioned and the fairly elaborate list of measures in subparagraph (1)(b) made justifying them relatively uncomplicated. However, for every single legislative measure or proposed measure in the second phase, the question of competence and its parameters has been thoroughly canvassed. In particular, the first of the two general limitations of the legal basis, i.e. 'matters having cross-border implications', has become the nexus around which the incursion into national regulatory autonomy has been fought. It is becoming increasingly evident from the policy documents that the Commission would advocate a broad interpretation of this limitation and would include ostensibly domestic litigation. An example is where two parties are domiciled in the same jurisdiction and there is a potential cross-border effect, with the result that there is a need to consider subsequent enforcement against assets

[42] Weatherill (2004b) p. 633f.
[43] Ibid. pp. 634–45.

in another jurisdiction. The Commission would even include completely domestic litigation if the provision of two different regulatory regimes, a domestic and a supranational one, would create discrimination among litigants, e.g. where a claimant might want to bring a simplified European small claims procedure against two defendants one of whom is domiciled locally while the other is domiciled in another Member State. The availability of the measure for the one matter but not for the other might arguably be construed as creating distortions in the European juridical space. However, it is also evident, through the amendments introduced to the Commission proposals, that the Member States in the Council are at present strongly opposed to such a broad interpretation, which might be considered a question of competence creep.

The more the policy area of judicial cooperation in civil matters moves into ancillary structures to procedure, including the make-up of the civil justice system, e.g. the potential future visions of execution procedures, the more these questions will emerge. In relation to the issues of enforcement proper, or execution, commentators argue that Community competence must be interpreted functionally not formally, entailing that enforcement falls within Article 65 of the EC Treaty because it is an integral part of procedure without which the very purpose of civil litigation would be meaningless.[44] The argument made is more pragmatic than technically convincing, but the debate highlights the issue that civil procedures are linked to ancillary structures and that there is a difficult interconnection to be resolved before significant Community progress can be made in certain areas. Another example is the issue of transparency of assets where extraneous factors impact on procedure, and the question is how broad is the competence and how far are the various institutions prepared to go.[45]

The tensions with regard to competence also attest to the very difficult separation between the supranational and domestic procedures, i.e. de facto the levels are not easily distinguishable or separable. In relation to this point the ECJ's first case concerning a legislative measure of the policy area reveals the fine line between national procedural autonomy and the supranational regulation. The Court's judgment in *Götz Leffler* shows the potential it has to become an active player in the policy area and the usefulness, for procedural autonomy and the principle of effectiveness, of the link with its previous case

[44] Andenas and Nazzini (2005), p. 55.

[45] Ibid. p. 56. Note that the Commission proposed that a Green Paper consultation would be launched in 2007 regarding transparency of assets: COM (2006) 618, p. 3.

law.[46] However, it is also noteworthy that no matter how clear the competence demarcation is and how strictly the institutions maintain it, there is a possibility of spillover.[47] As a new and quite quickly elaborated and relatively comprehensive package of legislation, judicial cooperation in civil matters could in the future play the role of a new Europeanized methodology, which would influence even domestic statutory interpretation.[48] In the aftermath of the *Krombach* judgment such a development can be anticipated, the wheel thus potentially coming full circle in the sense that top-down and bottom-up integration are taking place simultaneously.[49]

In relation to structural characteristics the policy area has also generated developments similar to spill-over-type effects. For example, Denmark's desire to participate, despite its clear opt out from the Treaty and despite the difficult domestic legislative procedure necessary for it to accede to the policy area, evidences a concrete increase in strength of the policy area and a further incursion into national regulatory autonomy.[50] Similarly, the Opinion of the ECJ in the *Lugano* matter, which entails a demarcation and clarification that the Community has external competence in the policy field, against the views of many Member States in the Council, evidences the practical reach of the policy into national regulatory autonomy.[51] These developments display a measure of centralization in judicial cooperation in civil matters and demonstrate that despite a more modest or traditional start the policy area is becoming *sui generis* in procedural cooperation.[52] However, particularly since the constitutional debate is not clear-cut, increased

[46] Van Gerven (2004) pp. 113–16 and 121f. notes with regard to the harmonization of private law that the ECJ has not taken a bold and leading role, but rather an incremental approach linking its judgments to the functional interpretation of the rule under discussion here. However, the Court's cautious approach has the potential of leaving room for a more bottom-up judicial convergence. Arguably an analogy or predictions could also be based on this analysis for judicial cooperation in civil matters, but as has been seen in Chapter 6, the ECJ did take a firm approach in the *Götz Leffler* case.

[47] Van Gerven (2006) p. 65ff. elaborates on spillover in the field of private law, e.g. competition law regulation.

[48] Berger (2001) pp. 878–82 makes the argument about spillover and methodology in the field of contract law. Such a spillover effect depends on the persuasiveness of the reference point and on the transparency of comparison on a case-by-case basis.

[49] Muir Watt (2001a) p. 552ff.

[50] See Chapter 4 regarding the Danish situation.

[51] See Chapter 4 regarding the question of external competence and the *Lugano* Opinion.

[52] Normand (1998b) p. 125f. noted at the very beginnings of the policy area that it could be characterized as modest but foresaw its evolution despite the limited legal basis and despite subsidiarity.

centralization will inevitably focus attention in the EU context on the appropriate level of regulation and on suitable methods for regulation.

In this light the background forces of the principles of subsidiarity and proportionality as well as the new governance themes are relevant. As one commentator has admitted, to analyse the approximation of procedural law through judicial cooperation in civil matters solely in terms of Member States' policy discretion is relatively static and does not address the question of the most suitable or desirable regulatory level or methods.[53] The themes of subsidiarity and governance are ones which can help in addressing these very questions. Again, historically, the relevance of these themes for the first phase of measures in judicial cooperation in civil matters was perhaps not apparent since, as they were steeped in the mould of traditional international procedural cooperation, their necessity and regulatory method was not questioned. In contrast, for the measures in the second phase as well as for the general measures, these themes have played a more prominent role in the regulatory debate, in the elaboration of the measures, and in the critique of the measures. In particular, the European Parliament has in its reports, without always specifically referring to these themes, raised the fact that action could perhaps be taken at Member State level or that softer regulatory techniques could be more suitable.[54]

The second group of measures is also the one for which Green Paper consultations have taken place and in which interest organizations, professionals, researchers, and civil society have joined the debate with the institutions and Member State governments on the need for measures and the regulatory form they should take. The results of these consultations, e.g. regarding ADR, have been mixed and there have been diverging views as to which is the most appropriate regulatory level.

For the regulation of judicial cooperation in civil matters, as Article 65 of the EC Treaty created an opportunity to move away from a piecemeal approach, different methods were possible and several regulatory choices could have been made for achieving legal unity. Taking the least intrusive approach could involve the creation of models of law, the creation of mutual concepts and principles, or the exchange of best practices and cooperation

[53] Andersson (2003) pp. 59–62.

[54] This does not mean however that the European Parliament has not supported the measures or even sometimes advocated a further measure of supranational harmonization than the Commission. The Economic and Social Committee (ESC) has also raised similar concerns to the Parliament though still supporting the activity in the policy field.

between authorities.[55] One could even envisage a more structured transplant of the open method of coordination from the substantive fields in which it has been used so far.[56] An interesting ancillary angle is that of legal and business practice at the micro level. At the level of individual transnational legal work, the lawyers involved solve problems and business goes on notwithstanding the absence of a unified supranational policy.[57] Such individual solutions can create a bottom-up kind of harmonization but also show how harmonized law can be challenged by innovative practices and the legal identification of gaps. Global norms are not always in the business interest, i.e. for a key group of players in the market, because they favour the possibility of competitive legal advantage.[58] Nevertheless, despite businesses being able to handle the risks of non-harmonization of procedure, the mosaic of different procedures can be seen as an anomaly in the Internal Market. From the business perspective therefore methods of best practices and functional equivalence have been propagated.[59] The method that has been chosen mirrors these suggestions and opinions, and is arguably fuelled to a large degree by an economic incentive.[60]

The model, as we have observed, displays novel features in the context of international procedural cooperation, but in the Community context is closely linked to the Internal Market logic and the principles of mutual recognition in the field of free movement of goods. Thus, the traditional Internal Market solution – to have a combined framework predicated on the principle of mutual recognition but supplemented by a network of complementary Community legislation – has been transposed to the field of judicial cooperation in civil matters.[61] The principle of mutual recognition,

[55] Rissanen (1999) p. 237f.

[56] Van Gerven (2006) p. 76f.

[57] McBarnet (2002) p. 98f.

[58] Ibid. p. 110ff.

[59] Vincke (2003) p. 23f.

[60] Strömholm (2003) p. 521f. observes a strong economic incentive to the policy area in which political development has been catalysed by EC Treaty revision.

[61] Andenas (2005) p. 11. Further, Meeusen (2004) p. 58f. notes that mutual recognition as a principle of Community law has developed from the *Cassis de Dijon* case, C-120/78, [1979] ECR 649, but today does not concern only the free movement of goods. Recently, we have seen an emanation of the principle in the e-commerce Directive (the country of origin principle), which was also elaborated upon in the *Überseering* case, C-208/00, [2002] ECR I-9919, as a different approach to traditional choice of law questions. Rossi (2004) p. 78ff. further reflects on the development of conflict of law rules via the principle of mutual recognition. The principle also emerges in the first preliminary referral ruling of the ECJ in relation to the Third Pillar, combined cases C-181/01 and C-385/01, *Gözutok and Brugge* [2003] ECR I-1345: 'mutual trust

originating in the *Cassis de Dijon* case and eventually becoming one of the fundamental building blocks of European law in relation to free movement, entailed that a product lawfully produced and marketed in one Member State had to be admitted to the market of any other Member State, and only under very strict conditions were exceptions accepted – i.e. they had to be necessary to satisfy a mandatory requirement, e.g. in relation to public health, consumers, or the environment, and had to be both proportionate and justifiable.

Therefore, ancillary to mutual recognition, or in order to facilitate it, mandatory requirements were harmonized through the introduction of minimum standards of protection.[62] This area can be considered to fall at the intersection between positive and negative integration – retaining regulatory heterogeneity across polities while introducing a single standard across boundaries. However, diverging legal orders generate competition between regulatory systems which progressively encroaches upon the regulatory processes.[63] Consequently, because of negative integration, the legislator shifts attention to so-called 'flanking measures', and deregulation which has initially been favoured is replaced by a mixed approach including framework and specific harmonization measures.[64] Attention is increasingly also focused on information as well as on communication and cooperation between relevant public actors. Paradoxically regulatory structures thus become a European concern. Therefore, notwithstanding national regulatory autonomy, the Member States have to accept strong cooperative mechanisms.[65]

The analogies from the history of the Internal Market can be useful for understanding the tensions emerging in the evolution of judicial cooperation in civil matters, which can be seen to have followed a similar pattern. The central principle of mutual recognition of judgments has entailed the reduction and in certain instances the abolition of the exequatur procedure in order for judgments to move freely unless strictly legislated

in the their criminal justice systems…even when the outcome would be different if its own national law were applied'.

62 Kennett (2003) p. 82f.

63 Ibid. p. 83ff.; Straetmans (2004) p. 299.

64 Ibid. p. 312f.

65 Pipkorn (1981) p. 44f., who was writing generally about market integration as early as 1981. Kennett (2003) p. 86f. makes the analogy specifically to the harmonization of enforcement and the execution of judgments.

exceptions are available.[66] This is particularly evident in the Brussels I Regulation, the Enforcement Order Regulation, and the Payment Order Regulation. However, mutual recognition is also a theme for service of documents and taking of evidence, and influences several measures in the policy area. Minimum standards have been introduced to facilitate and support mutual recognition, e.g. the service rules in the Enforcement Order, Payment Order, and the Small Claims regulations. However, as is clear from the critique of the policy area there are serious concerns at the fragmentation introduced by negative integration. Hence, there are tentative signs that deregulation, which was initially favoured, might be replaced by more detailed and specific harmonization, as can be seen in the Report on the Service Regulation and the Commission's proposal to revise the Service Regulation. Furthermore, as in the field of the free movement of goods, increasing attention has been paid to the provision of information to 'consumers', e.g. litigants and professionals, in order to alleviate negative integration. The European Judicial Network (EJN) and the European Judicial Training Network (EJTN) can in the field of civil justice naturally be perceived as such information structures. Finally, the need for improved administrative cooperation was required for goods and services market integration and the same requirement has also been noted in the civil justice field. The aforementioned structures, EJN and EJTN, which have the potential of evolving into veritable cooperation structures, can be seen as a step towards closer cooperation in order to guarantee efficient mechanisms.

Why? The Driving Forces

Another line of criticism identified in the debate about private law harmonization in the EU is that of cultural diversity. However, moving from a general level to a more detailed one, the commentator finds that in order to be able to evaluate the cultural impact properly one has to seek to identify the values that private law at the European level seeks to promote and evaluate their influence.[67] In setting the scene we identified market integration, citizenship, and fundamental rights as potential driving forces which could constitute such values to justify or propel harmonization of the procedural rules for private law, i.e. civil procedure and judicial cooperation. As one

[66] Meeusen (2004) p. 58 notes that mutual recognition as a leading principle for the Area of Freedom, Security, and Justice, as well as specifically for civil judicial cooperation, was included in Arts I-42 and III-269 of the Constitutional Treaty.

[67] Weatherill (2004b) p. 652f.

commentator has noted, it is extremely difficult to discuss the connection between such objectives and values of the EU and the Europeanization of procedural law, including judicial cooperation in civil matters, as it is in essence a political question.[68] Nevertheless, the attempt should be made since there is no alternative against which to judge the value of retaining national legal cultures and systems, nor can we gauge whether the underlying objectives have been fulfilled internally.

Most evident from the above analysis of the results of the policy area (as indeed from the above close methodological and regulatory analogy with the Internal Market creation of the free movement of goods and services) is the value of market focus and efficiency. In general policies of deregulation, governments have embraced privatization and free competition, and the language and the policies of the marketplace influence the public sphere, including courts and civil procedure.[69] Therefore, it is not surprising that in the Community context such influences are also apparent. In the area of judicial cooperation in civil matters several commentators have emphasized that the most important phenomenon influencing the current development of private international law is market integration and that interest in the economic aspects of policies and concrete rules is growing markedly. Efficiency as an emanation of the market plays the most important role, and is being used as a guiding principle even though its meaning is far from clear.[70]

Heightened economic proximity in the market has also led to an increased acceptance of and an incentive for private international law integration.[71] One of the most obvious and direct references to market forces is visible in the recitals to the European Payment Order Regulation:

> The swift and efficient recovery of outstanding debts over which no legal controversy exists is of paramount importance for economic operators in the European Union, as late payments constitute a major reason for insolvency threatening the survival of businesses, particularly small and medium-sized enterprises, and resulting in numerous job losses.[72]

However, the efficiency argument is also evident in most of the measures; as we have seen combating the delay caused by unnecessary formalities in international procedural cooperation is one of the most frequently recurring

[68] Andersson (2003) p. 63.
[69] Lindblom (1992) p. 199f. notes this development at the national level.
[70] Inter alia Fernández Arroyo (2004) p. 182.
[71] Muir Watt (2001a) p. 540f.
[72] Regulation (EC) No 1896/2006, Recital 5.

themes for a number of legislative measures including the Service Regulation and the Evidence Regulation as well as the Enforcement Order Regulation and the Brussels I Regulation which are intended to speed up enforcement.

Support for the aim and spirit of expedition is also explicit in the *Plumex* case, where the ECJ stated that where there are multiple methods of service the first and most efficient mode of service is the correct one. In addition, market actors welcome the removal of all additional cross-border procedural costs or complexities and the attempt to simplify and clarify the jurisdictional scheme of the Brussels I Regulation must be seen in this light. However, the measures which support ADR also emphasize market interests, since they support qualitative options for out-of-court dispute resolution, which is increasingly an element in businesses' conflict-management strategies. As one commentator has noted, many of the European dispute resolution mechanisms represent an approach to economic and social policy that rejects an adversarial approach and excessive or unnecessary transaction costs but favours conciliation at proportionate costs.[73]

It has to be recognized that 'market interests' are a diverse group and in the particular instance it is relevant to ask which interests are being protected. Difficulties experienced in transnational litigation relate to small businesses, large commercial operators, and consumers.[74] Procedural economy, the fair administration of justice, and legal certainty are certainly beneficial to all these parties.[75] However, part of the introduced procedural mechanisms is specifically targeted at protecting consumers and assisting the perceived weaker parties in litigation, who are considered an important market force too.[76] As an example, a consumer who buys electronic equipment over the Internet for 1,500 euros can potentially benefit from the protective jurisdictional rules in the Brussels I Regulation and in the future potentially bring a European small claims procedure against a producer or seller domiciled in another EU Member State. Thus, the consumer would be allowed to bring the claim in his own jurisdiction, he could avail himself of a standardized form which the court would serve on the defendant, the proceedings

[73] Hodges (2001) p. 327.

[74] Kennett (2000) p. 58.

[75] Boschiero (2003) p. 379 identifies the seemingly neutral theme of good administration of justice in the Enforcement Order Regulation and the Order for Payment Regulation.

[76] Hodges (2001) pp. 339–42 compares this to the United States regulatory model and notes that in Europe there is an emphasis on social cohesion and a pluralistic approach to dispute resolution.

would in most cases be written only, and there would be no obligation for the consumer to have legal representation or legal argument.

These mechanisms that facilitate access to justice touch upon the second value mentioned, namely citizenship. The citizen perspective of civil procedure entails that access to justice should not just be formally valid but also be realized in an equal manner in society. Since society in general is becoming more complex and is simultaneously moving towards a model in which citizens have to fend for themselves in enforcing their rights, the citizenship perspective has been emphasized in the political context of civil procedure and procedural reform.[77] Both the background documents of the Commission and the European Parliament as well as many of the measures themselves can also be viewed in this light. The Legal Aid Directive, which does not apply to legal persons, is solely geared towards assisting citizens in enforcing their rights across borders. In addition both the Payment Order Regulation and the Small Claims Regulation are intended to be constructive tools for citizen claimants to use and facilitate the enforcing of rights across borders. The specific statement in the Small Claims Regulation, that litigants do not have to be represented by counsel and do not have to develop legal argument but should be guided by the active role of the courts and the judge, displays a wish to support lay litigants and contribute to citizen participation in the legal process.

The rights to knowledge of the law, to knowledge of procedure, and to knowledge of the legal help available have been identified as central for the civil rights of citizens.[78] Such aspects receive particular support through the general measures of judicial cooperation in civil matters. The EJN information website is an easily accessible medium of information which is intended to be available in all languages. Any further developments of the EJN to open up to the public would reinforce such a citizen support function. Thus, there is room for considering that citizenship as a value is a driving force behind the policy area, which is a reversal of the orthodox force of state interest apparent in traditional international procedural cooperation.[79]

Market integration and citizenship are thus discernible values justifying and propelling the policy area forward. However, the third value we have identified, fundamental rights, is perhaps less evident. Naturally, the measures which support legal certainty, procedural economy, and the fair

[77] Lindblom (2000b) p. 105f.
[78] White (1993) pp. 236–8.
[79] Hess (2003) p. 221f.

administration of justice also support and realize the goals set forth in Article 6 of the ECHR.[80] However, because these were introduced to serve market integration, the fundamental rights angle seems to be only an ancillary one. This is a matter of concern, since, as commentators have noted, the logic of free commerce is not automatically transferable to all private international law topics and there is an upper limit in the respect for fundamental rights.[81] Applying the mutual recognition principle of Internal Market law to private international law might obfuscate the very detailed, specific choices made in the rules and might perhaps lead to a lower level of protection.[82] Therefore, one commentator warns against the risk of fragmentation and systematic laziness.[83] This is arguably of concern from the point of view of fundamental procedural rights and in particular the protection of the rights of the defence.

One dominant feature of the policy area is the quest for efficiency, clarity, and the realization of rights from the perspective of the claimants, be they businesses or consumers. However, the rights of the defence will in reality perhaps be weaker than those in the previous international regimes or in domestic standards. Due process and the rights of the defence have traditionally been enumerated as one of the principles of the Brussels Convention.[84] In the new framework of judicial cooperation in civil matters several measures do nonetheless curtail the rights of the defence, e.g. the Brussels I Regulation rules for challenging the enforcement of a default judgment, and the streamlining of the certificate of enforceability. Similarly, the complex minimum service standards introduced in the Enforcement Order, Payment Order, and Small Claims regulations raise concerns about the realistic rights of defendants to be aware of proceedings against them and to be able to prepare a defence. These concerns apply to business and consumer litigant defendants alike, but naturally the weaker parties and novice litigants such as consumers or citizens might be more affected by these risks and by the potential failures of justice. Other examples are the Code of Conduct for mediators and the ADR Directive which consumer organizations welcomed, whilst still being aware that the emphasis on self-regulation and

[80] Ibid. p. 236f.
[81] Fernández Arroyo (2004) p. 183.
[82] Strömholm (2003) p. 529f.
[83] Ibid.
[84] Carpi (1998) p. 121f.

the enforcement of consensus might be detrimental to the realization of the rights of weaker parties.[85]

Legitimacy: Second Glance

When dealing with functionality and appropriateness, i.e. legitimacy, from an internal perspective and from the point of view of the regulatory questions 'how' and 'why', the crucial issue that is emerging as complex is that of the constitutional parameters of the policy area. The caution displayed by the Member States in the Council demonstrates a political unwillingness, and the more incursions into national regulatory competence and spillover occur the more tensions will be evident. The constitutional issue does in an essential manner impact negatively on legitimacy. At the time of writing there is no question of re-evaluating the policy area from the point of view of constitutionality, and the careful approach taken by the Council makes a similar scenario to that of *Tobacco advertising* and private law unlikely in the field of judicial cooperation in civil matters. Ironically though, the cautious approach of the Council and the diverging views of the institutions about the parameters of competence weaken the drive of the policy area and can weaken its practical implementation, thereby impacting negatively on legitimacy.

Similarly, the diverging views on regulatory method, together with the subsidiarity and governance concerns broached by the European Parliament and civil society, demonstrate that the supranational policy area can be perceived and received as not appropriate, and this also impacts negatively on legitimacy. The regulatory method identified, analogous to the Internal Market one and based predominantly on an economic incentive, has echoes of fragmentation and in a more theoretical manner demonstrates the difficulty of negative integration. Pure negative integration does, as for the Internal Market, create a further legitimacy hurdle, but flanking or cooperation structures can bridge this gap. The policy area judicial cooperation in civil matters is at the time of writing, after a period of intense legislative activity, between negative and positive integration, which means that it is stretched broadly and has to be consolidated to overcome its legitimacy deficit. Therefore, at present, an evaluation of its functionality and appropriateness, from the perspective of 'how' to regulate, must also be considered negative.

85 ECLG (2004).

From the perspective of 'why' regulate, it has emerged that it is difficult to make absolute assertions and deductions. In the end, the justifying aims and propulsions might be different for the various actors involved in shaping the policy area. The objectives most likely constitute a mixture of the values identified, market integration, citizenship, and fundamental rights, as well as others. Nevertheless, one can arguably discern the market integration value as prevailing. This choice and emphasis does in itself cast some doubts over the legitimacy of the policy area if the paramount value is allowed to curtail the others and negate them. Most commentators would consider that in particular fundamental procedural rights cannot be curtailed by the market integration value. As the *Krombach* judgment has evidenced, procedural rights are moving towards becoming a new kind of mutual *ordre public* standard in Europe. Therefore, it is conceivable that domestic judges and even the ECJ will *in casu* find the legislative measures enacted do not provide enough protection.

This prediction is strengthened by the *Schmidberger* and *Omega* cases, which demonstrate that *in casu* fundamental rights have trumped free movement market rights.[86] The unresolved tension within judicial cooperation in civil matters, where currently fundamental procedural rights are less strong, undoubtedly casts a negative legitimacy shadow over the policy area. Furthermore, all the values intended to be reinforced by the policy area are inevitably weakened if the functionality of the policy area is put into question. As we have seen, the efficiency and 'level playing field' aimed for have not yet been fully attained, and consequently neither the market integration value nor the citizenship values are being fully realized. Hence, the question might be asked whether these values only represent vague discourses and programmatic objectives that do not match reality. This is a question that cannot but further the legitimacy deficit.

Looking Outward: Interaction with Procedural Development

Procedural Trends

After the preceding sections' internal perspective on the Community context and its difficult constitutional and regulatory questions, a change in

[86] See Chapter 5.

perspective might give us further insights and matrices for a holistic evaluation of the policy area. An outward-looking perspective is an external examination from the point of view of developments in the domestic and international procedural orders. The European Community policy area of judicial cooperation in civil matters and its focus on market efficiency as a procedural goal is not taking place in a vacuum. The domestic procedural trends in Europe have for a long time been grappling with what one commentator described in 1970 as 'the "Cape Wrath" where Rapidity and Efficiency have to be combined with Justice'.[87] The reform of civil procedure has been a constant global, and indeed European, feature during the past century.[88] There is a kernel of truth in the statement, 'a sense of crisis in the administration of civil justice is by no means universal, but it is widespread'.[89] Numerous domestic procedural codes or compilations of rules have been reformed and re-reformed to deal with the emerging modern demands of justice. Even in very recent years, since the statement quoted above, reforms have been introduced.[90]

It is possible, on the basis of comparative work, to discern certain trends in reform movements from which we can glean the core procedural issues, which should arguably also influence and interact with the supranational emerging regulation of judicial cooperation in civil matters.[91] It is important to note that in a European context, and even a global one, commentators are increasingly sceptical of creating distinctions between adversarial and inquisitorial jurisdictions, between the civil and the common law legal families, since there are also strong instances of convergence and stark categorizations are unhelpful in identifying these.[92] One study focuses on

[87] Cappelletti (1970–1) p. 886.

[88] Naturally, the specific historical and political background in each European country influences this issue and development in the East European countries, which joined the EU in 2004, has been very different from that in the former Western bloc. However, there are also mutually important events on the Continent. See Van Rhee (ed.) (2005) pp. 3–23, where he traces developments since the 1806 French Code of Civil Procedure; he considers that this code, together with the Austrian Code of 1985 and the Civil Procedure Rules of England and Wales of 1998, form three crucial historical developments in civil procedure on the Continent.

[89] Zuckerman (1999) p. 12.

[90] Examples are the Spanish reform in 2000 and the German and Austrian reforms in 2002: see Trocker and Varano (2005).

[91] Fortunately, the tradition and legacy created by Mauro Cappelletti and others has been continued within the academic community of civil procedure lawyers. Therefore, collected comparative works from which trends can be discerned are available: see Zuckerman (1999), Trocker and Varano (2005), and Van Rhee (2005).

[92] Inter alia Trocker and Varano (2005) p. 244f. and Van Rhee (2005) pp. 5, 21f., and 185. However, this does not mean that the legal family distinctions cannot be useful, nor does it mean that

three dimensions of justice – rectitude of decision, time, and cost – and concludes that the major vices across jurisdictions exist in long delays and high costs.[93] The legal business community in its broad study conducted during the 1990s also identified length of proceedings as the most endemic problem in Europe. Several common causes could be identified, among which were: the behaviour of the players in manipulating proceedings, structural issues such as the lack of premises and the unequal distribution of judges, unnecessarily complex procedures, and the lack of ADR mechanisms.[94] General themes of modern procedural reform therefore unsurprisingly include simplifying the rules or structures of procedure, encouraging ADR, making more resources available, and modernizing court administration.[95]

However, the most common trend appears to be the assertion of judicial control, i.e. an emerging culture of managerial judges, the main idea being that judges have power over the flow of proceedings in order to abate disruptive tactics or just delay on the part of the litigants. This is often coupled with an emphasis on managing litigation in a proportionate manner, entailing that the system of distributing resources to justice be fair, and that each case be allocated resources in line with the value, importance, and complexity of the matter. The advent of more restricted rights of appeal or the more widespread use of summary procedures for undisputed or small claims also displays this novel emphasis on procedural economy. On this point, one study concludes that this shows an indication of a readiness to sacrifice some measure of rectitude of decision in order to achieve more timely resolution of disputes at lower costs.[96]

Several commentators have identified a trend towards case management. An interesting analysis explains its emergence, taking a historical ideological perspective. Thus, the French Civil Procedure Code of 1806, which was very influential on the Continent in the nineteenth century, was based on strong party autonomy which stemmed from the liberal and individualistic ideology of the time.[97] In contrast, the following landmark legislation, the Austrian Code of 1895, marked a change in the ideological landscape and Franz Klein's social function of civil litigation was modern and before

all convergence should be seen as stemming from a common cause or creating an irreversible similarity.

[93] Zuckerman (1999) p. 42.

[94] Platto (1999) p. 137.

[95] Zuckerman (1999) p. 43.

[96] Ibid. p. 47ff.

[97] Van Rhee (2005) p. 6f., and Cappelletti (1970–1) p. 851f.

his time. Thus, he advocated even then giving more powers to the judges to steer litigation.[98] As the final part of this particular analysis, the Civil Procedure Rules of England and Wales of 1998 are also seen as landmark legislation, which conclude the development instigated by the Austrian Code, and which – in emphasizing cooperation between the parties and the judge as well as case management – can be considered a compromise between the liberal and social conceptions of civil litigation.[99] Hence, in the reforms and reform debates, the reform of civil procedure can be perceived as creating its own dialectic or pendulum swing.[100]

Another commentator has also observed this common modern European core when comparing the various reform debates in the Nordic countries to the English reform of 1998. Thus, there is emerging a common trend towards more flexibility and an active role and responsibility for both the parties and the judge in order attain the international standards of fair trial at reasonable cost. With the modernization of the machinery of justice the perspective of citizenship is emphasized, in parallel with an increasingly predominant quest for efficiency.[101] Finally, another recent study identifies as one of the main current trends increasing flexibility of procedural rules and the need for models of procedure to be adapted to meet the particularities of cases. Flexibility is enhanced by the rhythm of procedure and procedural deadlines being adapted depending on the case and steered by judges. Another facet of flexibility and efficiency is the active case management by the judge, particularly at the pre-trial stage.[102] Further trends identified are an emphasis on the development of ADR mechanisms, court sponsored or not, and an emphasis on all participants in the legal machinery as contributors to justice; this includes a focus on the bar and its personnel as well as on the courts, their personnel, and their practical technological resources.[103]

These trends and common issues are indeed reflected at the supranational level. The sense of crisis and the modern demands on civil procedure are naturally the same in cross-border litigation as in domestic litigation. Furthermore, the careful balancing of the rectitude of a decision against the time and cost of proceedings is obviously even more difficult in the cross-border context, as has very pragmatically been realized and brought forward by the

[98] Van Rhee (2005) p. 11f. See also Cappelletti (1970–1) pp. 857f. and 879ff.
[99] Van Rhee (2005) p. 21f.
[100] Lindblom (2000b) p. 116.
[101] Ibid. p. 114.
[102] Trocker and Varano (2005) pp. 247–54.
[103] Ibid. pp. 259–64.

European institutions espousing the development of judicial cooperation in civil matters. Therefore, the proposed judicial cooperation measures as solutions to the problems mirror the recent domestic reform efforts. The first example is the general effort in all the measures of judicial cooperation in civil matters to simplify both the procedural rules and the structures for their application. The desire in inter alia the Service and Evidence Regulations to avoid unnecessary procedural steps, to streamline the practical action involved, and to synthesize the underlying legal parameters as far as possible forms a clear policy aim and a challenge to the complex, obviously outdated structures and rules previously in force.

The second related example is that of encouraging the use of technical innovation to assist courts and litigants to progress proceedings more quickly and in a less cumbersome manner. This can be seen in several measures, amongst others the Evidence Regulation and potentially the Payment Order Regulation. As with the domestic efforts, these examples underline the aim of achieving quicker and cheaper access to justice. This aim of procedural economy and the proper allocation of court resources is also a paramount goal underlying the payment order and the small claims procedures, which are intended to resolve liquidated, uncontested, and small claims as proportionately as possible. Another modern trend, which is linked to the vision of proportionate use of court resources and procedural economy for litigants, is the encouragement to use ADR, which is also reinforced at the supranational level by the Commission's endeavours under the auspices of judicial cooperation in civil matters.

Judicial control over proceedings, embodied in case-management rules, is also reflected in the decentralization characteristic of all measures of judicial cooperation in civil matters. The belief that the local judge seized of the case is the best to deal with inter alia cross-border service or a certificate of enforcement can be seen as reinforcing judicial control. In particular as the regulations even recommend time spans within which the local courts are to deal with the relevant regulated cross-border procedural issues, far from removing judicial control these strict and rigorous rules actually assist the judges in maintaining control and in carrying out their case-management duties. In sum, a comparison between the supranational measures of judicial cooperation in civil matters and the domestic reform trends demonstrates that there is a certain harmony between them. There is a clear interaction, which at first was only one-way, with domestic trends being carried over to the supranational level. However, with the rapid expansion of the policy area, it may speed ahead of domestic reform processes and become the source for the domestic level of the goals of simplification and procedural economy and may create spillover potential in the aims as well as in the elaborated rules.

International Procedure

The supranational rules within the EU are not the only emanation of international procedural development that mirrors the trends and themes of domestic procedural reform. The Principles of Transnational Civil Procedure, developed cooperatively by the American Law Institute and UNIDROIT through a process of consultation between the legal communities, constitute a formidable attempt to resolve and address issues of cross-border judicial cooperation in a global arena.[104] Despite the various opinions including critique voiced during the consultation process and debate, the ALI/UNIDROIT principles merit attention.[105] Similarly, it should not be forgotten that behind the development of the EU policy area judicial cooperation in civil matters there is a broader background context of international procedural cooperation, which had taken place outside the EU context on multilateral levels, 'regionally' such as between the Nordic countries and the Benelux countries, and 'globally' particularly under the auspices of the Hague Conference on Private International Law.[106] Within the latter international organization cooperation has been carried on since and the most recent convention in the civil procedural field is the Choice of Court Convention.

The ALI/UNIDROIT Principles of Transnational Procedure (the 'Principles') were adopted by both organizations in 2004 after a process of review and consultation in the global legal community. Ancillary to the Principles a set of more detailed Rules was also developed. However, UNIDROIT only promotes promulgation of the Principles, and the Rules are viewed as a model implementation of the Principles. This being the case, only the Principles will be dealt with here.[107] The Principles aim to reconcile national procedural rules, taking into account the peculiarity of transnational disputes. The intention is that they will set standards for adjudication that can be adopted in dispute resolution or form the basis for future reforms of civil

[104] The Principles are available inter alia at: http://www.unidroit.org/english/principles/civilprocedure/main.htm (visited 23.8.2007).

[105] Debates during the consultation process are in Fouchard (ed.) (2001) and Zuckerman (2002). See above Chapter 2 and further McAuley (2004).

[106] Kennett (2000) p. 25ff.

[107] McAuley (2004) p. 239.

procedure. There are three categories of general principles – fundamental, leading, and incidental principles. The fundamental principles encompass guarantees of fair trial such as judicial independence and impartiality, the leading principles deal with matters such as the responsibilities of the parties and access to evidence, whereas the incidental principles deal with matters such as jurisdiction, costs, and appeal.[108] Despite being general the Principles provide a succinct and clear set of guidelines together with commentary. Although there are only 31 in number they cover the essential steps of civil procedure from the start of proceedings up to appeal, enforceability, and recognition. Hence, they form a holistic and balanced entity that although general still manages to deal with issues. The Principles are remarkable in that they not only specify aspects of procedural law but cover the field of civil procedure.[109]

The trends of procedural law analysed above are evident in the Principles. Case management and the role of both the courts and the parties in progressing proceedings are dealt with in Principles 7, 11, and 14. The court has the responsibility for actively managing proceedings in order to achieve fairness and efficiency at reasonable speed. The court should in general consult with the parties, take the potential transnational character of the dispute into account, and give fixed directions including a timetable.[110] The parties share responsibility with the court and must in good faith cooperate to achieve fair and efficient proceedings at reasonable speed. In particular procedural abuse is not allowed.[111] In addition the court is required to resolve the dispute and render justice within a reasonable time and the parties might be sanctioned if they do not cooperate or fulfil their tasks within reasonably set deadlines.[112] Hence, the Principles follow the trend of an emphasis on an active role and responsibility for both the parties and the judge in order to attain the international standard of a fair trial at reasonable cost.

Regarding other streamlining and procedural efficiencies the Principles with commentary note that due notice may with court approval or as a forum law requirement be effected through expedited means of communication, e.g. telecommunications.[113] Similarly, oral and written presentations of evidence may by permission of the court or as a requirement under forum law be

[108] Zuckerman (2002) p. 323.
[109] McAuley (2004) p. 233f.
[110] Principle 14.
[111] Principle 11(2).
[112] Principle 7.
[113] Principle 5(7), commentary 5F.

made via telecommunication means.[114] Hence the principles provide room for encouraging the use of technical innovation to assist courts and litigants in managing to progress proceedings more quickly and in a less cumbersome manner whilst being sensitive to local requirements and possibilities. The Principles also include an obligation on the court to encourage settlement between the parties and to facilitate ADR as well as an obligation on the parties to cooperate in attempting to reach settlement both before and after commencement of proceedings.[115] They thereby support and provide evidence of another procedural trend of using alternative justice mechanisms where appropriate to relieve the burden of the court system and assist litigants in reaching a solution more quickly and at a lower cost.

At a regulatory level the ALI/UNIDROIT project demonstrates the potential of bottom-up 'soft' forms of cooperation and coordination and shows that such processes can yield results in a global context. As one commentator notes, the process of trying to distil common principles of different procedural systems has in itself as a process been 'illuminating and enriching'.[116] Therefore, notwithstanding whatever effect the Principles may have in the future, the debate generated and the experience of the parties involved in or following the debate are likely to have resulted in mutual learning and trust.[117] The process thereby displays benchmarking and the sharing of best practices reminiscent of governance mechanisms. The participatory element in the process has also been remarkable, involving procedural actors, lawyers, and judges, apart from the academics and drafters of the Principles. The process thereby fulfils and supports the modern procedural trend to emphasize all participants in the legal machinery as contributors to justice, including the bar and its professionals and the courts and their professionals. Hence the process also displays a significant feature of governance, which is the participatory element.

One commentator analysing the effect of globalization on dispute resolution has noted that inter alia informal justice mechanisms, i.e. ADR and arbitration procedures, have burgeoned successfully in the western world as a result of accelerated means of communication and increased international

[114] Principle 19, commentary 19B.

[115] Principle 24.

[116] Zuckerman (2002) p. 325.

[117] McAuley (2004) pp. 246–9 and 252 notes that the success of the project depends on its being implemented in national procedures, and notes that in Lithuania the reform of civil procedure reflects the Principles; but he also notes that quite apart from their implementation the Principles have reinvigorated discussions on effective dispute resolution.

trade, i.e. globalization.[118] They evidence the potential of bottom-up or 'soft' forms of justice regulation that stem from the actors in the field.[119] They also evidence the potential global reach of mechanisms. The commentator also noted that globalization puts pressure on substantive justice mechanisms, apparently meaning legislative measures, and their development at national, regional, and multilateral levels.[120] The ALI/UNIDROIT project can be seen as falling within the framework of these observations. The Principles are a global form of informal justice and may for example even be used in arbitral proceedings. The Principles are also elaborated in the informal justice field and have a global scope stemming from the transnational procedural actors and organizations themselves. However, because the Principles form a complete set intended to apply to civil procedure rules they also resemble a multilateral substantive justice mechanism, albeit without legally binding force, and evidence the pressure and need for such mechanisms. The Choice of Court Convention that will be dealt with below is precisely such a multilateral form of substantive justice.

The Choice of Court Convention was signed at the Hague Conference on Private International Law (the 'Hague Conference') in June 2005.[121] The Convention stems from previous endeavours and from a more ambitious project.[122] Nevertheless, the aim of the Convention is to emulate the success of the New York Convention on the Recognition and Enforcement of Foreign Arbitral Awards of 1958. Many legal systems recognize choice of court agreements. However, the cross-border recognition of such clauses in contracts and the subsequent international enforcement of judgments emanating from courts whose jurisdiction is based on such clauses are not comprehensively regulated.[123] Therefore, for commercial disputes involving transnational commercial businesses the first alternative has been arbitration proceedings, backed up by the promise of enforcement of the arbitral award under the New York Convention. The expectation is that commercial

[118] Glenn (2000) pp. 137–41.

[119] Ibid. p. 140. National arbitration laws are naturally state sponsored but the pressure has come from the business and legal communities that have also supported the proliferation of international arbitration institutions.

[120] Ibid. p. 150f.

[121] Convention on Choice of Court Agreements, Convention No. 37, and 'Explanatory Report on the 2005 Hague Choice of Court Agreements Convention' by Trevor Hartley and Masato Dogauchi (2007), available at: http://www.hcch.net/index_en.php (visited 29.8.2007).

[122] O'Brien (2003) pp. 498–509, McClean (2002b) pp. 257–67, Hartley (2006) p. 414f.

[123] Ibid. p. 424. The Brussels I Regulation gives effect to choice of court agreements if the chosen court is in a Member State.

actors will have an alternative to arbitration in their contractual clauses when the Choice of Court Convention enters into force.[124]

The Choice of Court Convention applies to exclusive choice of court agreements in international business-to-business contracts of a civil or commercial law nature.[125] A case is international for jurisdictional purposes unless the parties are resident in the same Contracting State and for recognition and enforcement purposes where an application concerns a foreign judgment.[126] The choice of court must be in writing or other form accessible for subsequent reference and without any specification the choice will be presumed to be exclusive.[127] The three basic principles of the Convention are the obligation of the chosen court to assume jurisdiction, the obligation of other courts to refrain from taking jurisdiction, and the obligation of other courts to recognize and enforce the resulting judgment.[128]

The Choice of Court Convention has not yet entered into force, since it appears that not enough ratifications have yet been deposited.[129] Commentators seem to consider that the EC has competence in relation to the Choice of Court Convention.[130] The Convention includes the possibility for a regional organization to sign it and, as since April 2007 the EU has been a member of the Hague Conference, for the Community to do so.[131] Therefore, there is a possibility that ratification by the EU will take place in lieu of separate ratifications by the Member States. The success of the Convention and the generation of benefits for commercial parties depend on ratification of the Convention globally by as many States as possible, a success that

[124] Kruger (2006) p. 447.

[125] Art. 2 limits the material scope. Choice of court clauses in consumer and employment contracts are excluded as are a host of other matters, inter alia matters of a family law nature, antitrust matters, non-contractual tort, and the validity and infringement of intellectual property rights other than copyright. See Art. 2(2)(a)–(p) for the complete list.

[126] Art. 1.

[127] Art. 3.

[128] Arts 5, 6, 8, 9, and 11. All the three main rules are qualified by certain exceptions or circumstances set out in the provisions: Kruger (2006) p. 451f. Note specifically Hartley (2006), p. 415ff., who points out that difficult negotiations resulted in Art. 11, under which recognition and enforcement of a judgment may be refused if and to the extent that damages awarded are exemplary or punitive, i.e. do not compensate for an actual loss or harm suffered.

[129] According to information obtained on the website of the Hague Conference, http://www.hcch.net/index_en.php (visited 29.8.2007). Art. 31 regulates entry into force.

[130] Wilderspin and Rouchaud-Joët (2004) p. 34 and Hess (2004) p. 93 consider the EC has exclusive competence.

[131] Arts 29–30.

remains to be realized although it is hoped that it will be achieved in the next few years.[132]

The Choice of Court Convention is not the only international procedural convention agreed under the auspices of the Hague Conference. Others include the Service Convention of 1965 and the Evidence Convention of 1970. These have in part inspired the EU into action in the same fields within the policy area of judicial cooperation in civil matters. In addition, despite the Commission's argument that the procedures set out in the Hague Conventions are cumbersome and that there is a need for more streamlined procedures within the EU, the Hague mechanisms and the solutions that were debated and agreed on at international level can be seen as significant developments and successful models. For example one commentator notes in relation to the Service Convention that it produced an orderly framework for cross-border service as well as a successful and well-used mechanism.[133] Furthermore, the fact that it copes with diversity and offers procedures acceptable to all State are perceived as the strengths of the Service Convention.[134] The mechanism referred to is the system by which requests for judicial cooperation are transmitted via designated central authorities in each State. As a mechanism it is much more centralized than the highly decentralized model adopted within the EU, in inter alia the Service Regulation. As the new judicial cooperation mechanisms within the EU are still at the start of their practical implementation one cannot yet say that the decentralized model has proven successful. Only after a longer period of time, and in particular through the development of judicial training, can the decentralized model be evaluated; depending on the outcome some form of centralization might potentially have to be introduced.[135]

Both the ALI/UNIDROIT Principles and the Hague Conventions demonstrate that there is a global arena for international procedure or judicial cooperation. The regional development of judicial cooperation in civil matters in the EU should not hamper or obfuscate the multilateral level of development. Concern has been raised about procedural cooperation and the consequences of Community action and the effects on the diversity and quality of the comparative debate and ensuing work within international

[132] Hartley (2006) pp. 414 and 424; Kruger (2006) p. 455.

[133] McClean (2002a) p. 55 also provides some figures: 5,433 requests for service were received by the US central authority in the fiscal year of 1987 and the German central authority received 661 requests solely from the USA in 1986.

[134] Ibid.

[135] See Chapter 6 on the Service Regulation and the report on its functioning.

and multilateral fora.[136] There has also been concern about the favouring of the regional or European approach, which thus becomes entrenched at the expense of looking to the more universal or global needs for judicial cooperation.[137] As noted in Chapter 4, there is a risk that the phrase 'fortress Europe' might in the future also be applicable to the field of procedural law, since the Community can be a source of paralysis in international negotiations; 'fortress Europe' could also suggest that the Community is more interested in removing barriers within its own free trade area than in ensuring fair jurisdiction rules for third parties.[138] Only very recently, following upon the mention of the international legal order and the aim of synergy with other international organizations in the Hague Programme of 2004, has the global or extra-EU dimension surfaced in the policy documents regarding judicial cooperation in civil matters.[139] The EU's membership of the Hague Conference from April 2007 might also be seen as a step in the direction of a global awareness and greater coordination with the multilateral level.[140]

Procedural Functions

Besides the practical trends of civil procedure reform, which today are bridging the orthodox legal family gap, and which can be affected by the new European and supranational regulation and interact with it, there is the question of the functions of procedure in society. This relates to the purpose behind the reforms and the political or societal aspirations underlying civil procedure. Indeed these functions, objectives, or purposes are interlinked with the formation of the rules and with the way that the legal community approaches and interprets them. In the Nordic legal doctrine, here mainly focusing on those of Sweden and Finland, there has been an extensive debate about the functions of civil procedure. This debate is conducted from a legal analytical perspective, e.g. it is a debate among those with different views upon what should be the function and tasks of procedural law as a public institution and how this can influence how the rules are enacted. Thus, the point of view does not follow from society at large or from sociological facts

[136] See the discussion of external relations at the end of Chapter 4. See also, inter alia, Boele-Woelki (2000) p. 75; Gillies (2003) pp. 364 and 373f.; and Beaumont (2002) p. 14.

[137] Boele-Woelki (2000) p. 76; Gillies (2003) p. 380ff.; and Aalto (2000) p. 333f.

[138] Beaumont (2002) pp. 14, 26–9.

[139] An example is provided by COM (2006) 356, p. 9, where the Commission notes that in the area of judicial training the strategy should also move beyond the borders of the EU.

[140] (EC) No 719/2006 Council Decision of 5 October 2006 on the accession of the Community to the Hague Conference on Private International Law. See Chapter 4.

of how the procedural rules are perceived or function in an empirical sense.[141] The doctrinal debate is admittedly an ideological or normative meta-theory, which may be considered as having a limited perspective.[142] However, for the purpose of this analysis the doctrine can be useful in its legalistic trappings, particularly since there is little alternative empirical information available yet. Naturally, it is also important to observe that the functions can be viewed differently if the perspective is that of the citizenry, the courts, legal professionals, or legislators.[143] However, the main functions can still be identified in general terms, and no particular perspective is excluded.

German influence in the late nineteenth century historically led to the establishment of a traditional view in Finland that the central purpose of civil procedure is to provide legal protection and the realization of private rights. The focus of this vision is on the legal substantive relationship between the parties and on the goal of rectitude of decision.[144] This functional view has not been challenged *per se* but has been considered one-dimensional in attempts to elaborate the functions of procedural rules more precisely. Hence, the first seeds of debate were sown by the introduction by one commentator of a vision of the procedural system as machinery to exercise social control and reinforce the moral values of society, a 'behaviour modification model'. According to this model, proceedings in an individual case not only provide effective protection of rights, but also influence others so that they honour their obligations.[145] On the macro level procedure thus becomes a tool of prevention and the functional focus is prospective and on the defendant.[146]

The social control function was subsequently criticized and a conflict resolution function was introduced into the debate, a 'conflict resolution model'. The vision of the latter model is similar to that of protection of rights, but

[141] Virolainen (2003) p. 60.

[142] Ervasti (2002) pp. 47–52 notes that the functions of procedural law in society can be analysed from varied points of view, e.g. empirical sociology, legal anthropology, and political science. He finds that the Nordic doctrine has been centred on an ideological and normative meta-theory, which is narrow and does not take into account broader approaches.

[143] Ibid. pp. 54–67 divides the perspectives into five levels: society, politics, legal community, court system, and citizenry.

[144] Knuts (2005) p. 36; and Virolainen (2003) p. 61.

[145] Lindell (2003) pp. 92–4. Virolainen (2003) p. 61ff. states that the Uppsala school of legal theory influenced Ekelöf. The commentator further notes that several prominent Swedish commentators even today subscribe to the view that 'behaviour modification' is the most important function of procedural law.

[146] Lindblom (2004) p. 240.

rectitude of decision is not emphasized; the key aim is actual resolution of the dispute. This model hence aims at reparation and compensation; it is retrospective as well as focused on the claimant.[147] Furthermore, the citizen perspective has been included in this function, i.e. civil procedure is seen as a dispute resolution service for the parties.[148] It has been suggested that the classic legal protection function is an emanation of the rule of law ideal, that the 'behaviour modification' function is an emanation of the welfare state ideal, and that the 'conflict resolution' function mirrors the neo-liberal society of today.[149] The two main views in the debate, 'behaviour modification' and 'conflict resolution', have previously been seen as opposites, but later commentators have acknowledged that in reality they interact; ideally they are indeed attained in parallel or in tandem.[150] Thus, one commentator sees the two central functions as tools of substantive law, ensuring enforcement of the substantive law at both the general and the individual level.[151]

However, another commentator notes that in a modern context the term 'steering function' sounds very intrusive and since both theories are based on an ideological choice of what is best for society there is a practical implication of choice of one view rather than the other. This will influence how the conflict between the parties is resolved as well as what role and capacities are given to courts.[152] Therefore, he sees the courts as adapting rather then steering and chooses an individual rather than a collective view of procedure.[153] This is significant, because here similarities may be identified with debates in jurisdictions that belong to a different legal family, namely the common law one. We also see how the themes sometimes move in reverse. A common law commentator notes that the nature of procedural rules propounds the logic that civil litigation should be seen as primarily a process for the resolution of disputes. However, the importance of achieving justice between individual litigants is in no way diminished by recognition that the process of litigation, considered as a whole, serves other ends, one of which is to demonstrate the effectiveness of law. This effectiveness function embodies the idea of civil litigation as civilization's substitute for injustice.

[147] Ibid. p. 241.
[148] Knuts (2005) p. 37.
[149] Virolainen (2003) p. 65; and Leppänen (1998) p. 828ff.
[150] Lindell (2003) p. 94; Lindblom (2004) p. 240.
[151] Ibid.
[152] Lindell (2003) p. 95f
[153] Ibid. pp. 96–100.

In order to fulfil these functions the elaborators of procedural rules must try to create a balance between incentives and disincentives to litigation.[154] Furthermore, if it is recognized that there are other purposes than vindication of individual rights then the allocation of the power of choice between the parties and the court becomes different. The allocation of power is thus based on tradition but should also be based on prevailing conscious views of policy, i.e. it certainly does not stem from some elusive 'nature of things' which cannot be changed.[155] Therefore, it is clear that even the modern common law procedure can start from somewhere beyond the parties' interests and itself emphasize a benefit in the law to which these interests are subordinated, as such courts are more than mere dispute solvers.[156]

Besides these two main procedural functions, behaviour modification and conflict resolution, two further functions arise quite naturally in the course of judicial proceedings and from the civil justice system. The first of these is interpreting, clarifying, and developing the law. This function arises in part through precedent created by higher courts but also in lower courts where there is a gap in the law. Precedent is of course not always pure lawmaking but can be merely clarifying, which could rather be seen as an element of the first two functions.[157] In practice, depending on the emphasis given to this function, procedural rules can be elaborated very differently, e.g. in relation to access to appellate courts. Secondly, civil procedure can have a control function, e.g. as a forum for judicial review of both the legislative and executive branches of power. The main object is of course to uphold the constitutional guarantees and achieve the maximum enforcement of the values inherent in higher laws, but this takes place at the expense of, i.e. causes the failure of, the legislative or executive branch.[158] In the past few decades these two latter functions, 'developing the law' and the 'control function', have progressively grown stronger, and with them belief in the general preventative

[154] Jolowicz (1990) pp. 36–9.

[155] Ibid. p. 43ff.

[156] Jolowicz (1993) p. 145f.

[157] From the Swedish perspective Lindblom (2004) p. 242; Knuts (2005) p. 40 and Virolainen (2003) p. 67f., from a Finnish perspective. This function might in certain emanations and in certain jurisdictions be considered problematic in terms of the separation of powers and democratic legitimacy. For a common law perspective see Jolowicz (1990) pp. 39–43.

[158] Lindblom (2004) p. 241f. Notably in countries which have a separate administrative procedure, judicial review of the executive branch of power will very rarely arise in civil proceedings. Knuts (2005) p. 39 notes that in the Nordic countries such a control function is a relatively new phenomenon, due to a strict or particular interpretation of the separation of powers.

influence has increased.[159] For civil procedure itself and the development of the procedural rules this is a great challenge, in particular since the individual reparative function has also increased in importance.

Besides the clearly elaborated and identified main functions, other values can be discerned. As one commentator notes, these purposes are not necessarily novel but rather represent a resurgence of certain impulses in civil procedural development.[160] First, civil procedure has become an instrument for satisfying the democratic and psychological expectations of citizens and citizenship. This 'participation or dignity value' emphasizes the importance of principles of procedural fairness which guide the progress of litigation and which become as important as the outcome. Secondly, the courts and procedure itself are used as instruments of communication and debate, e.g. in raising awareness and trying to influence legal reform. This 'politico-legal debate function', using procedure as one forum or stage for debate and dialogue in society, also influences the procedure, e.g. fuels the need for more hands-on case management by judges.[161]

Thirdly, the vision of procedure as a means of solving human conflicts with the novel element of therapeutic considerations has emerged. The vision entails that judges are expected to take into account the social and psychological effects of conflict resolution in the progress of the procedure. In this 'therapeutic function' it is recognized, albeit critically, that judges increasingly have to adopt a consequential perspective and apply the law in a multidisciplinary fashion, which demands sociological and psychological and societal empirical knowledge.[162] Finally, the same commentator identifies an 'integration function', which stems from membership of the EU and other international obligations and which creates in the procedure rules as well as in the judicial function an impulse to contribute to the smooth implementation and enforcement of the mutual programmatic values, e.g. the Internal Market.[163]

This exposé gives us a final matrix in which to evaluate and pitch judicial cooperation in civil matters. One commentator suggests that ultimately any judgment of a procedural system should go beyond its average speed, cheapness, and accuracy and consider what it is intended to foster or discourage.

[159] Virolainen (2003) p. 67 ff. notes that this development is in part fuelled by European law and its teleological interpretation and important judicial review of national norms.

[160] Lindblom (2004) p. 251.

[161] Ibid. pp. 252–6.

[162] Ibid. p. 256ff.

[163] Ibid. p. 252.

Procedural reform must have a vision of procedural and social justice; it cannot be talked about as simply a matter of increased judicial efficiency.[164] However, when evaluating the policy area of judicial cooperation in civil matters in light of the spectrum of procedural functions it seems as if procedural economy and efficiency are paramount. This realization, which follows from the first measure, the Service Regulation, to the last one, the Small Claims Regulation, can in one sense be considered close to the conflict resolution function. The aim of achieving speedy resolution of conflicts for market actors, consumers, SMEs, and multinational corporations, can easily be aligned with the functional vision that focuses on the claimant and aims at reparation and compensation. In addition, the citizen perspective of the conflict resolution function entails that judicial cooperation in civil matters, which is also trumpeted as a dispute resolution service for these litigants, fits well with this vision.

It is perhaps not surprising that an EU endeavour in the field of procedural law resonates with a functional analysis that has been identified as characteristically 'neo-liberal'. Nevertheless, as has been noted in the functional debate, the conflict resolution function and the behaviour modification function can appear simultaneously and reflect two sides of efficiency. Indeed, even though judicial cooperation in civil matters initially seems more attuned to the conflict resolution function, it is not unreasonable to consider that this individual efficiency drive can also be a positive influence in a broader context, e.g. prospectively focus on the defendants. By achieving economy and efficiency a threat can be created to modify the behaviour of potential defendants and thus increase the general efficiency and enforcement of legislation. This is also desirable from the perspective of judicial cooperation in civil matters.

Considering other aspects of the function spectrum, the function of interpreting and developing the law and the function of control are procedural functions which are very well known and established in the Community Court context.[165] To a certain extent they are also reinforced at the local court level in cross-border litigation by judicial cooperation in civil matters. For the courts to be able to give interpretative or legality review rulings in cross-border cases, it must be possible to bring and pursue these cases. The efficiency drive of the policy area can therefore support pragmatically

[164] Leubsdorf (1999) p. 67.

[165] Two of the central tasks of the ECJ are to give preliminary rulings under Art. 234 of the EC Treaty and to review legality under Art. 230 of the EC Treaty.

the conditions for the interpretation and control functions. Nevertheless, the strong emphasis on conflict resolution and procedural economy does not provide significant support for an ethos or an ideal of developing the law or reviewing legality. Similarly, the participatory dignity function, the political-legal debate function, and the therapeutic function appear to be absent from the functional visions behind judicial cooperation in civil matters. Because procedural economy is paramount and the principle of mutual recognition from the field of economic freedoms is emphasized, the rights of the defence are being strictly curtailed to the minimum and the important horizontal functions which make 'civil procedure' into 'civil procedure', e.g. the important adversarial process nature of dispute resolution, seem to play a secondary role.

Legitimacy: Third Glance

The outward-looking perspective thus contributes additional important and interesting procedural themes with which to evaluate judicial cooperation in civil matters and the legitimacy of the policy area. First, the modern trends of procedural reform show that the policy area is definitely not taking place in a void. The harmony between the supranational and local levels of regulation as regards the perceived political concerns and the legislative solutions to address these identifies additional currents which are shaping the policy area at the European level. This harmony also demonstrates the strength that certain themes and conceptions currently have in the civil procedural field. The harmony finally undoubtedly increases the political legitimacy and acceptance of supranational action. It can also potentially alleviate the political regulatory concerns of competence creep and subsidiarity. However, it is to be remembered that, for both the domestic and the supranational level, only the success of the enacted measures in achieving the projected political goals can truly contribute to legitimacy, i.e. functionality is still a major issue.

The general trends of procedure and globalization together also highlight the fact that the policy area of judicial cooperation in civil matters is not the only potential level of regulation. On the contrary, economic actors are increasingly mobile globally and regional cooperation should at the very least be coordinated with multilateral development. The ALI/UNIDROIT project as well as the Choice of Court Convention, emanations of modern international procedural debate, show the need for global learning, cooperation, and development. The functionality of judicial cooperation in civil matters should not be solely Eurocentric and needs to be reviewed also in the light of this broader development, and the legitimacy analysis needs to encompass the international perspective and context. In particular the ALI/UNIDROIT project demonstrates an alternative to the piecemeal and top-down regulation of judicial cooperation in civil matters; and it is to be hoped that the Choice of Court Convention will, when ratified, demonstrate that the apparently limited focus on and regulation of one very specific aspect of procedure may after all have a significant and pervasive global market impact.

Furthermore, a more in-depth functional debate regarding the core procedural rationale reveals that appropriateness does not hinge only upon the current trend of efficiency. On the contrary, the functional analysis shows an ideological or visionary weakness in judicial cooperation in civil matters. Particularly in the EU context the fact that the functions of developing the law and reviewing legality are less supported by the policy area raises a legitimacy issue. The balance between procedural expediency and other functional aims is always a difficult one. However, it is arguably a crucial balance and deserves to be considered seriously. The function of dignity and participation, as well as the political legal debate function, underscore procedural human rights and the importance of the adversarial process itself in upholding certain values and resolving disputes in a larger sense than just the case at hand. These concerns as well as a more searching concern for consumers of the civil justice system are reinforced in the therapeutic function. Until such perspectives are incorporated into the functional balance of judicial cooperation in civil matters the legitimacy of the policy area is put into question.

17

Conclusion: The Way Forward

Legitimacy Crisis

Following on from the enquiry in Chapter 16 into the character and role of the 'Brave New World' created by judicial cooperation in civil matters within the traditional procedural landscape, this concluding chapter makes some proposals on the way forward. Since the 1970s local judges and domestic civil procedures have been slowly orienting themselves towards a more international perspective and towards Communitarian awareness.[1] The internationalization of procedure seems to be an unstoppable feature in the world of globalization.[2] However, it is significant that the tripartite analysis in Chapter 16 of the evaluation and legitimacy of a conscious attempt, in the form of judicial cooperation in civil matters, to create a more permanent and comprehensive transnational procedural model comes close to identifying and predicting a legitimacy crisis. Therefore there is not a clear-cut way forward towards ever deepening integration; perhaps we have to stem or redirect the tide.[3]

The legitimacy analysis in Chapter 16 identified first that the crucial decentralization feature, characteristic of several of the instruments of judicial cooperation in civil matters, may lead to worrying forms of fragmentation and potential discrimination, thereby countering the underlying purpose of creating an equal judicial space and legal certainty for cross-border litigants. Secondly, the legitimacy analysis identified the

[1] Cappelletti (1970–1) pp. 867–70.

[2] Weatherill (2004b) p. 695f.

[3] Storskrubb (2006) p. 30. The tide metaphor refers to a quote from Lord Denning: 'No longer is European law an incoming tide flowing up the estuaries of England. It is like a tidal wave bringing down our sea walls and flowing inland over our fields and houses – to the dismay of all' (Denning, 1990).

constitutional conundrum constituting the lack of clarity with regard to the scope of legislative competence and the parameters of the legal basis, a conundrum potentially resulting in complexity and discrimination through instruments that create a separate level of regulation. In addition, negative integration through mutual recognition and abolition of the exequatur has generated widespread concerns about the regulatory method which, it is feared, might not satisfactorily protect procedural rights. Thirdly, the legitimacy analysis identified the tension between the emphasis on market integration and the rhetoric about citizenship and fundamental human rights. The final part of the legitimacy analysis examined the ideological weakness of emphasizing procedural efficiency without considering other functions of procedural law, and suggested international development as an alternative to a piecemeal accumulation of measures.

The legitimacy analysis did uncover several areas of concern and critique from which it may be warranted to deduce a legitimacy crisis. Some of the diverse concrete concerns in the perceived legitimacy crisis may be addressed in a practical manner. For example, the structural problems created by the Danish opt-out and by the anomalous role of the European Court of Justice (ECJ) can be and have in certain parts been resolved through distinct EC Treaty or legislative amendments.[4] Similarly, the 'missing' legislative projects of execution measures and regulation of interim relief can be addressed by distinct legislative proposals.[5] In contrast, the central feature of decentralization in the policy area, which gives rise to concerns about fragmentation and discrimination, cannot be perfunctorily addressed. A move in the opposite direction, towards centralization, is difficult to envisage, since this might run into even deeper constitutional and regulatory issues than the current choice of regulatory method has faced. Hence, within the current parameters of political conflict about the 'cross-border' issue and the possibility of fragmented implementation, the first suitable key future strategy for the policy area would seem to be consolidation.

However, the concern about decentralization coupled with the concern about the emphasis on procedural efficiency and market integration, possibly at the cost of procedural rights, entails that some form of centralization might be necessary. Since procedural law and judicial cooperation should take into account a broader view of functions and are inherently supposed

[4] See Chapters 3 and 4.

[5] Inter alia the pending consultation: Green Paper on the Attachment of Bank Accounts, COM (2006) 618.

to protect procedural rights, it might be necessary for negative integration through mutual recognition to be supported by further positive strengthening integration. Therefore, a second proposed future strategy includes scrutiny of the minimum standards introduced and a debate on the procedural rights and functions.[6] In addition, the outward-looking perspective raises concerns that multilateral strategies and issues are not being taken into account. Therefore, an additional proposal for future strategy encompasses broadening the horizon.

Consolidation and Coherence

The proposed consolidation strategy entails active and proactive measures to counteract fragmented implementation. Thus the intention is to ensure consistency in implementation and to apply a programme of constructive judicial cooperation across all measures and in all Member States.[7] Such a strategy was recognized in the Hague Programme but needs to be backed up by concrete measures. The commitment to the development of the measures of our third category, networks and training, i.e. the European Judicial Network (EJN) and the European Judicial Training Network (EJTN), supports such a strategy.[8] Arguably, the emergence of a genuine common judicial culture and a more open role for the members of the EJN could alleviate the legitimacy deficit and have a crucial impact on the implementation of the policy area. This strategy does however present a challenge in terms of implementation. For the supranational regulator to reach out and influence local actors it is necessary for the training structure and the EJN to be developed. In addition, a certain measure of patience needs to be adopted and a long-term vision and effort need to be sustained.

The Communication on judicial training is notable in this respect because the focus of financial assistance from the Community is more a measure of support than a form of steering. Several commentators have noted that it is the judicial cooperation actors who have a central role.[9] One commentator has also noted that the 'free movement' of legal practice and openness

[6] Storskrubb (2006) pp. 30–3, which includes a review of the two strategies, consolidation and debate.

[7] Liukkunen (2006) p. 72 urges the same strategy in relation to conflict of law rules.

[8] The Hague Programme, Presidency conclusions 1492/04, Annex I, pp. 36f. and 41.

[9] From a multilateral perspective see inter alia McAuley (2004) p. 252.

for cross-border impacts can be much more effective through interaction among legal actors at all levels than rigid and static harmonization measures, and may contribute more deeply to Europeanization.[10] Another commentator notes that the coherence of the European judicial space remains an open question and if the Member States are to retain their identity but accept solidarity a legal community must develop.[11]

The Hague Programme also emphasizes the need to ensure coherence and quality of legislation. As part of the consolidation strategy most of the measures of judicial cooperation in civil matters include crucial review clauses that require the Commission to evaluate the measures and if necessary propose revisions. Such evaluation processes have already been carried out for the Service Regulation and the EJN and evaluation reports are due to be published for the Evidence Regulation and the Brussels I Regulation. The commitment to conduct empirical research and reassess each measure after five years, as well as address its functioning, should highlight any lacunae and problems.

These evaluations should also be linked to judicial training and to the EJN in order to create a synergy between the practical and the legislative level. Hence, no matter what the nature of problems identified these could be addressed not only 'formally' through 'hard law' regulation, but potentially also 'informally' through 'softer' methods of governance. The measure-specific evaluations have also been included in the Commission's communication on the Area of Freedom, Security, and Justice and the proposed regular general evaluations of this area.[12] An interesting proposal to secure coherence and further transparency has been suggested, namely to consolidate the various measures into a 'code', which might counter the piecemeal nature of the numerous existing legislative measures and therefore be more accessible to users.[13]

Another key aspect of consolidation is that of regulatory and constitutional sensitivity. The Member States seem to have reached a compromise regarding the definition of 'cross-border' as evidenced by the legislative processes for the Payment Order and Small Claims Regulations. However the cross-border issue and the difficult issues of subsidiarity and proportionality

[10] Wilhelmsson (2001) p. 30ff.

[11] Labayle (2004) p. 30.

[12] COM (2006) 332, inter alia p. 2.

[13] Jeuland (2004) p. 115f. proposes further coherence by means of interactions between actors, e.g. through the EJN and even a code to integrate all the procedural measures of the policy area and include inter alia the relevant provisions of the Charter of Fundamental Rights.

underlying the debate will now surface at the domestic level. Domestic court systems will in the coming years have to test their resources and the capacity of the local procedural system to adapt, a test that will reveal the functionality of the supranational regulation. Private litigants will test the efficiency of and the protection offered by the measures introduced, a test that will ultimately indicate how suitable they are.

Commentators note that the cross-border conundrum has created two parallel systems with resulting practical problems at the domestic level, causing delay and confusion. These problems are difficult to resolve *in casu* as well as generically and awkward to promote with certainty.[14] Therefore, there should be an openness to review the chosen regulatory path and constantly to consider the remits of the constitutional limits. The regulatory and constitutional sensitivity also supports a 'consolidation' strategy, the projected direction of the policy area emphasizing mutual understanding, the flexible development of common procedural rules, and the importance of simultaneously developing a common legal culture and education.[15]

Scrutiny and Debate

At present when nearly all the legislative measures of the second group of judicial cooperation in civil matters have been enacted and are set to enter into force it is evident that a certain crossroads has been reached, the crossroads of mutual recognition and mutual trust. The introduction of the principle of mutual recognition in the field of procedural law, entailing the abolition of the exequatur for uncontested claims, payment orders, and small claims, as well as the limiting or removal of *ordre public* clauses in several instances where it would be customary in judicial cooperation, constitutes a significant development and a crossroads. It has been noted that 'opening the door', i.e. adopting mutual recognition as a regulatory strategy and leaving ancillary procedures to be decided at the domestic level, augments uncertainty and indicates shortcomings.[16] However, mutual recognition might also function in practice, and judgments are probably being recognized all

[14] Andersson (2005b) p. 246.

[15] See Chapter 2 and inter alia Lindblom (1997a) pp. 26f. and 45f.; Niemi-Kiesiläinen (1999) p. 254ff.; Kerameus (1995) p. 405, Kötz (1992) p. 34ff.; and Biavati (2001) p. 100f.

[16] Andenas (2005) p. 20.

over Europe at this very minute. However, the legitimacy of the principle and its core implications has to be evaluated now.[17]

Several commentators have been sceptical about the minimum standards introduced in the Enforcement Order, Payment Order, and Small Claims Regulations. When these measures are implemented and applied at the domestic level further issues will no doubt arise. The removal of *ordre public* has been considered a key issue of the policy area. Some argue that it should only have been removed at the end of the harmonization process rather than in this initial stage of introducing completely novel measures. The removal of *ordre public* might even, instead of creating efficiency, cause litigants to lose trust in the courts.[18] And the existence of an order public clause has, on the basis of experience from the Brussels Convention and the Brussels I Regulation, been considered to act as a buttress for mutual debate and trust.[19] Therefore, the second proposed strategy is one of scrutiny of the minimum standards and the system developed and a debate on the minimum standards.

Interestingly, a similar scrutiny and debate is evident in the field of criminal cooperation in the EU. In the criminal law arena the principle of mutual recognition is also at the centre of the development of the policy area. As a logical step from the principle of free movement, criminal matters also gain a cross-border angle, and the need for speed and efficiency in legal protection for crime victims necessitates cross-border cooperation and mutual recognition.[20] The legislative instruments so far enacted in the policy area concern specific measures, such as the European arrest warrant, freezing orders, and financial penalties, and other measures are in progress.[21] Efforts have also been focused on supporting the mutual recognition of decisions and judgments by the substantive approximation of criminal law.[22] However, the focus is increasingly on the harmonization of criminal procedure and in

[17] See Suominen (2006) p. 612 for an analogous point in relation to criminal cooperation.

[18] Stadler (2005) p. 1659f.

[19] Boytha (2006) p. 646f.

[20] Frände (2006) p. 38.

[21] Council Framework Decision 2002/584/JHA of 13 June 2002 on the European arrest warrant and the surrender procedures between Member States; Council Framework Decision 2003/577/JHA of 22 July 2003, on the execution in the European Union of orders freezing property or evidence; and Council Framework Decision 2005/214/JHA of 24 February 2005 on the application of the principle of mutual recognition to financial penalties. For further measures see: http://europa.eu/scadplus/leg/en/s22006.htm (visited 28.8.2007).

[22] Frände (2006) pp. 40–3.

particular procedural rights and a recognition that such an approximation is required for mutual recognition to move forward.[23]

The proposals and the measures adopted are considered insufficient to provide for the effective defence of suspects. Although the ECHR affords a common standard, realizing an effective defence is challenging in this new context. A suspect might have to arrange a defence abroad, or in parallel proceedings in several Member States, with investigations including evidence and property seizures taking place at increased speed across borders.[24] The debate, as well as examining the approximation of procedural defence standards, has also generated proposals for structural support and centralized coordination, e.g. for an ombudsman like Eurodefensor.[25] In the criminal law debate the questions that are openly raised are whether the Member States have mutual trust in each other's legal and procedural systems and whether the applicability of the ECHR in all Member States offers sufficient guarantees.[26] In particular mutual trust is seen as necessary at the 'deep level' of law.[27]

These observations can be transposed to the civil cooperation arena where a commentator notes that mutual trust cannot be created on demand. Initial distrust can be alleviated by information and communication about national minimum standards, and by adopting minimum standards that do not allow too many legal variations. Such actions may foster certainty and trust, but distrust can still exist in practice.[28] One commentator notes that mutual recognition and harmonization are twin strategies and considers that the Tampere conclusions evidence an intention to maintain these in parallel.[29] Therefore, some form of harmonization of rights of the defence or centralization may, in parallel with mutual recognition, be the way forward.[30] As in the criminal field the first question to answer is whether harmonization is required before different procedural systems can communicate.[31] The principle of judicial protection elaborated by the Court of Justice in its case law, which precipitated judicial cooperation in civil matters and which

[23] Ibid. p. 47.
[24] Ibid. pp. 38f., 43, and 47ff.
[25] Ibid. p. 49.
[26] Suominen (2006) p. 610f.
[27] Ibid. p. 611f.
[28] Andenas (2005) p. 7.
[29] Boytha (2006) p. 631.
[30] Andersson (2005b) p. 249ff.
[31] Andenas (2005) p. 7.

constituted an important part of our background analysis, might be considered to create a common standard which should foster mutual trust.[32] Additionally, Article 6 of the ECHR, together with the case law of the European Court of Human Rights, represents a common standard which should foster mutual trust. These are indeed important forces shaping the development of procedural rules and conclusively instituting significant standards.

However, as in criminal cooperation, judicial cooperation in civil matters, with its central idea of mutual recognition, presents litigants and courts with completely different challenges when they encounter one another's procedural rules and local court practices. When confronted with, inter alia, modes of evidence, methods of service, payment orders, and jurisdiction decisions litigants and courts are directly implicated in a practical context of minimum procedural guarantees. Similarly, when local judges or mediators are confronted, perhaps daily, with applying a European small claims procedure or the Code of Conduct the issue of a mutual procedural standard is confronted regularly and concretely. The practical and effective rights of the defence and the requirements of access to justice should be addressed in the policy area that has been created. Consequently a scrutiny and debate on the minimum standards and their functioning has to take place. Only through such a scrutiny can the legitimacy concerns be addressed. The results of the debate should be linked to the elaborated strategy of consolidation and coherence. Hence, regulatory sensitivity should allow a departure from the chosen method if it does not work and innovative solutions might have to be envisaged, such as the Eurodefensor in criminal matters, referred to above.

Broader Horizons

The global perspective that has been somewhat neglected in the development of judicial cooperation in civil matters can be counteracted by the specific aim of synergy with other international organizations in the field of international procedure. The promise of such coordination in the Hague Programme is the first sign of a response to the critical concern about the external dimension of Community development. If there is a genuine intention to support the quality of the comparative debate within international fora as well as to consider the global needs for cooperation, a broader horizon

[32] See Chapter 2.

might emerge. The strategies of coherence and scrutiny discussed above should also take the multilateral perspective into account. A commentator has noted that it has been argued in the field of choice of law rules that the maximization of universal rules is desirable and that regional rules should only be adopted when there is a particular necessity.[33] Therefore, it is not impossible that regulatory sensitivity might lead to the conclusion that global measures of civil procedural cooperation are preferable; further scrutiny might identify difficult interactions between regional and global regulation that should be avoided.

Finally the perceived legitimacy crisis should be seen as an opportunity for the policy area of judicial cooperation in civil matters to mature and find its role. Without being Eurocentric a constructive approach should be taken to find strategies and to execute these. The focus should not be on the institutional drive within the policy area but be directed towards involving the real actors in transnational litigation and their needs and capacity to steer the tide. The direction should not be one that forgets the procedural achievements and themes of the twentieth century – fair trial and access to justice – but one that fosters and progresses these. That efficiency of procedures is important for private individuals and businesses involved in litigation is true in most cases. However, there is an equally important assumption underlying the desire for efficiency: that the procedures as a *sine qua non* respect fundamental rights. In addition, procedures might have other functions than solely providing quick dispute resolution. In conclusion, the Brave New World created by judicial cooperation in civil matters does reflect tendencies of dystopia but has the potential to break free from its schematic premises and might with other influences from the 'savage' world move towards Utopia.

[33] Liukkunen (2006) p. 70f.

Tampere European Council: Presidency Conclusions 15th and 16th October 1999

...

B. A GENUINE EUROPEAN AREA OF JUSTICE

28. In a genuine European Area of Justice individuals and businesses should not be prevented or discouraged from exercising their rights by the incompatibility or complexity of legal and administrative systems in the Member States.

V. Better access to justice in Europe

29. In order to facilitate access to justice the European Council invites the Commission, in cooperation with other relevant forums, such as the Council of Europe, to launch an information campaign and to publish appropriate 'user guides' on judicial cooperation within the Union and on the legal systems of the Member States. It also calls for the establishment of an easily accessible information system to be maintained and up-dated by a network of competent national authorities.

30. The European Council invites the Council, on the basis of proposals by the Commission, to establish minimum standards ensuring an adequate level of legal aid in cross-border cases throughout the Union as well as special common procedural rules for simplified and accelerated cross-border litigation on small consumer and commercial claims, as well as maintenance claims, and on uncontested claims. Alternative, extra-judicial procedures should also be created by Member States.

31. Common minimum standards should be set for multilingual forms or documents to be used in cross-border court cases throughout the Union. Such documents or forms should then be accepted mutually as valid documents in all legal proceedings in the Union.

32. Having regard to the Commission's communication, minimum standards should be drawn up on the protection of the victims of crime, in particular on crime victims' access to justice and on their rights to compensation for damages, including legal costs. In addition, national programmes should be set up to finance measures, public and non-governmental, for assistance to and protection of victims.

VI. Mutual recognition of judicial decisions

33. Enhanced mutual recognition of judicial decisions and judgments and the necessary approximation of legislation would facilitate cooperation between authorities and the judicial protection of individual rights. The European Council therefore endorses the principle of mutual recognition which, in its view, should become the cornerstone of judicial cooperation in both civil and criminal matters within the Union. The principle should apply both to judgments and to other decisions of judicial authorities.

34. In civil matters the European Council calls upon the Commission to make a proposal for further reduction of the intermediate measures which are still required to enable the recognition and enforcement of a decision or judgment in the requested State. As a first step these intermediate procedures should be abolished for titles in respect of small consumer or commercial claims and for certain judgments in the field of family litigation (e.g. on maintenance claims and visiting rights). Such decisions would be automatically recognised throughout the Union without any intermediate proceedings or grounds for refusal of enforcement. This could be accompanied by the setting of minimum standards on specific aspects of civil procedural law.

35. With respect to criminal matters, the European Council urges Member States to speedily ratify the 1995 and 1996 EU Conventions on extradition. It considers that the formal extradition procedure should be abolished among the Member States as far as persons are concerned who are fleeing from justice after having been finally sentenced, and replaced by a simple transfer of such persons, in compliance with Article 6 TEU. Consideration should also be given to fast track extradition procedures, without prejudice to the principle of fair trial. The European Council invites the Commission to make proposals on this matter in the light of the Schengen Implementing Agreement.

36. The principle of mutual recognition should also apply to pre-trial orders, in particular to those which would enable competent authorities quickly to secure evidence and to seize assets which are easily movable; evidence lawfully gathered by one Member State's authorities should be admissible before the courts of other Member States, taking into account the standards that apply there.

37. The European Council asks the Council and the Commission to adopt, by December 2000, a programme of measures to implement the principle of mutual recognition. In this programme, work should also be launched on a European Enforcement Order and on those aspects of procedural law on which common minimum standards are considered necessary in order to facilitate the application of the principle of mutual recognition, respecting the fundamental legal principles of Member States.

VII. Greater convergence in civil law

38. The European Council invites the Council and the Commission to prepare new procedural legislation in cross-border cases, in particular on those elements

which are instrumental to smooth judicial cooperation and to enhanced access to law, e.g. provisional measures, taking of evidence, orders for money payment and time limits.

39. As regards substantive law, an overall study is requested on the need to approximate Member States' legislation in civil matters in order to eliminate obstacles to the good functioning of civil proceedings. The Council should report back by 2001.

Draft programme of measures for implementation of the principle of mutual recognition of decisions in civil and commercial matters

(2001/C 12/01)

INTRODUCTION

The Treaty of Amsterdam inserted into the Treaty establishing the European Community a new Title IV containing specific provisions on judicial cooperation in civil matters.

In order to lend impetus to this cooperation and to set precise guidelines therefor, the European Council meeting in Tampere on 15 and 16 October 1999 held that 'enhanced mutual recognition of judicial decisions and judgments and the necessary approximation of legislation would facilitate cooperation between authorities and the judicial protection of individual rights'. It approved the principle of mutual recognition, which should become 'the cornerstone of judicial cooperation in both civil and criminal matters within the Union'.

In civil matters, the Tampere European Council advocated 'further reduction of the intermediate measures which are still required to enable the recognition and enforcement of a decision or judgment in the requested State'. 'As a first step these intermediate procedures should be abolished for titles in respect of small consumer or commercial claims and for certain judgments in the field of family litigation (e.g. on maintenance claims and visiting rights). Such decisions would be automatically recognised throughout the Union without any intermediate proceedings or grounds for refusal of enforcement. This could be accompanied by the setting of minimum standards on specific aspects of civil procedural law'.

It asked the Council and the Commission to adopt, by the end of 2000, a programme of measures to implement the principle of mutual recognition, and added that 'in this programme, work should also be launched on a European Enforcement Order and on those aspects of procedural law on which common minimum standards are considered necessary in order to facilitate the application of the principle of mutual recognition, respecting the fundamental legal principles of Member States'.

The Brussels Convention of 27 September 1968 lays down rules on jurisdiction and the recognition and enforcement of judgments in civil and commercial matters. This

Convention has undergone several amendments with the accession of new States to the Community[1] and is now in the process of being converted into a regulation.[2]

The Community has other major achievements to its credit: the 'Brussels II' Regulation on jurisdiction and the recognition and enforcement of judgments in matrimonial matters and in matters of parental responsibility for children of both spouses, and the Regulation on insolvency proceedings.[3]

The principle of mutual recognition of civil and commercial judgments between Member States is therefore not new. However, its implementation has had limited effect to date, for two main reasons. The first relates to the fact that many areas of private law do not come within the ambit of the existing instruments. This applies, for example, to family situations arising through relationships other than marriage, rights in property arising out of a matrimonial relationship, and succession.

The second reason lies with the fact that the existing texts retain certain barriers to the free movement of judicial decisions. The intermediate procedures enabling a ruling handed down in one Member State to be enforced in another are still too restrictive. Thus, despite the changes and simplifications it makes with regard to recognition and enforcement of judgments, the future Brussels I Regulation does not remove all the obstacles to the unhindered movement of judgments within the European Union.

Discussions on the subject were held at the informal meeting of Justice and Home Affairs Ministers in Marseilles on 28 and 29 July 2000.

The current programme of measures establishes objectives and stages for the work to be undertaken within the Union in the coming years to implement the principle of mutual recognition. It advocates the adoption of measures that can facilitate both the activity of economic agents and the everyday lives of citizens.

This programme contains measures that concern the recognition and enforcement in one Member State of a decision taken in another Member State, which implies that harmonised jurisdiction rules should be adopted, as was the case in the Brussels Convention and the Brussels II Regulation. It in no way prejudges work that will be undertaken in other areas under judicial cooperation in civil matters, particularly with regard to conflicts of law. The measures relating to harmonisation of conflict-of-law rules, which may sometimes be incorporated in the same instruments as those relating to jurisdiction, recognition and enforcement of judgments, actually do help facilitate the mutual recognition of judgments.

[1] A consolidated version of the Brussels Convention was published in OJ C 27 of 26 January 1998.

[2] Usually referred to as the 'Brussels I' Regulation.

[3] Council Regulations (EC) No 1347/2000 and (EC) No 1346/2000 of 29 May 2000 (OJ L 160, 30.6.2000).

In the implementation of the measures advocated, account will be taken of the instruments adopted and ongoing work in other international forums.

The approach adopted to establish the programme is threefold:

— identifying the areas in which progress should be made,
— determining the nature, detailed procedures and scope of potential progress,
— fixing the stages for the progress to be made.

I. AREAS OF MUTUAL RECOGNITION

STATE OF PLAY

The 1968 Brussels Convention is the basic instrument. It covers all areas of civil and commercial law except for those which are expressly excluded from its scope, which are listed exhaustively in the text: the status or legal capacity of natural persons, rights in property arising out of a matrimonial relationship, wills and succession; bankruptcy; social security; and arbitration. The scope will not be changed by the future Brussels I Regulation, which is to replace the Brussels Convention.

Supplementary instruments: the areas excluded from the scope of the Brussels Convention are not yet all covered by instruments supplementing the 1968 provisions.

The Brussels II Regulation of 29 May 2000 applies to civil proceedings relating to divorce, legal separation or marriage annulment and to civil proceedings relating to parental responsibility for the children of both spouses on the occasion of such matrimonial proceedings.

The following are therefore not covered, and remain outside the ambit of any instrument applicable between the Member States:

— certain aspects of divorce litigation or legal separation that are not covered by the Brussels II Regulation (particularly decisions concerning parental responsibility amending decisions taken at the time of the divorce or legal separation),
— family situations arising through relationships other than marriage,
— rights in property arising out of a matrimonial relationship,
— wills and succession.

The Regulation of 29 May 2000 on insolvency proceedings applies to collective proceedings which entail the partial or total divestment of the debtor and the appointment of a liquidator.[4]

[4] This excludes insolvency proceedings concerning insurance undertakings, credit institutions, investment undertakings which provide services involving the holding of funds or securities for third parties, and collective investment undertakings.

PROPOSALS

A. IN AREAS NOT YET COVERED BY EXISTING INSTRUMENTS

It is mainly in the area of family law that progress is needed. Legal instruments will be drawn up in both the following areas.

1. International jurisdiction, recognition and enforcement of judgments relating to the dissolution of rights in property arising out of a matrimonial relationship, to property consequences of the separation of unmarried couples and to succession

Rights in property arising out of a matrimonial relationship and succession were already featured among the priorities of the Vienna action plan (December 1998). The economic consequences of judgments delivered when matrimonial ties are loosened or dissolved, during the lifetime of the spouses, or on the death of a spouse, are clearly of major interest in the creation of a European Judicial Area. In this context it is possible that, when drawing up instruments, a distinction needs to be drawn between rights in property arising out of a matrimonial relationship and succession. In this respect the relationship existing in Member States' law between rights in property arising out of a matrimonial relationship and succession will be examined.

The question of property consequences of the separation of unmarried couples will also be dealt with, so that all property aspects of family law can be examined.

2. International jurisdiction, recognition and enforcement of judgments relating to parental responsibility and other non-property aspects of the separation of couples

(a) *Family situations arising through relationships other than marriage*

Here it is a matter of supplementing the area covered by the Brussels II Regulation to take account of sociological reality: increasingly, couples are choosing to dispense with any matrimonial formalities, and there is a marked rise in the number of children born out of wedlock.

In order to take this new social reality into consideration, the scope of the Brussels II Regulation should be extended, by means of a separate instrument if necessary, notably to judgments concerning the exercise of parental responsibility with regard to the children of unmarried couples.

(b) *Judgments on parental responsibility other than those taken at the time of the divorce or separation*

The provisions of the Brussels II Regulation relate only to judgments in matrimonial proceedings. In view of the frequency and importance of judgments that are made subsequently and may modify the conditions under which parental responsibility is exercised, as fixed in judgments made at the time of the divorce or separation, it is necessary to apply to them the rules governing jurisdiction, recognition and enforcement contained in the Brussels II Regulation. This development must relate both to judgments concerning married couples and to those made in the context of the separation of unmarried couples.

In these new areas, which are not at present covered by any instrument, it will be useful to examine the legal situation in Member States' national law, as well as existing international instruments, in order to gauge the scope that should be given to any instruments that might be drawn up.

B. IN AREAS ALREADY COVERED BY EXISTING INSTRUMENTS

Here, the aim is to make the existing machinery work better by reducing or abolishing obstacles to the free movement of judicial decisions. The Tampere conclusions refer generally to all 'civil matters', but also stress that as a first step these intermediate procedures should be abolished for titles in respect of small consumer or commercial claims and for certain judgments in the field of family litigation (e.g. on maintenance claims and rights of access).

Thus, two areas are involved: family law on the one hand, more especially rights of access and maintenance claims, and commercial and consumer law on the other. These areas are thus identified as being priorities.

1. Rights of access

France has already tabled an initiative. It is designed to abolish the exequatur procedure for the cross-border exercise of rights of access arising from a judgment falling within the scope of the Brussels II Regulation.

2. Maintenance claims

This matter, expressly mentioned in the conclusions of the Tampere European Council, directly concerns the everyday lives of citizens in the same way as the previous matter. Although the guarantee of effective and rapid recovery of maintenance claims is indeed essential to the welfare of very large numbers of people in Europe, this does not necessarily imply that a separate legal instrument has to be drawn up. Maintenance creditors are already covered by provisions of the Brussels Convention and of the future Brussels I Regulation, but it would also be advisable in the long term to abolish the exequatur procedure for maintenance creditors, thus boosting the effectiveness of the means by which they safeguard their rights.

3. Uncontested claims

The abolition of exequatur for uncontested claims should feature among the Community's priorities.

The substance of the concept of 'uncontested claims' will be specified when the limits of the instruments drawn up in application of the programme are defined. At present, that concept generally covers situations in which a creditor, given the verifiable absence of any dispute by the debtor over the nature or extent of the debt, has obtained an enforcement order against that debtor.

The fact that an exequatur procedure can delay the enforcement of judgments concerning uncontested claims is a contradiction in terms. It fully justifies this area being the first in which exequatur is abolished. Rapid recovery of outstanding payments is an absolute necessity for business and is a constant concern for the economic sectors whose interest lies in the proper operation of the internal market.

4. Litigation on small claims

The concept of litigation on small claims referred to by the Tampere European Council covers various situations of varying degrees of importance that give rise to different procedures according to the Member State concerned. Discussions on simplifying and speeding up the settlement of cross-border litigation on small claims, in line with the Tampere conclusions, will also, through the establishment of specific common rules of procedure or minimum standards, facilitate the recognition and enforcement of judgments.[5]

II. DEGREES OF MUTUAL RECOGNITION

STATE OF PLAY

Current degrees of mutual recognition

In areas not covered by existing instruments, recognition and enforcement of foreign judgments is governed by the law of the requested State and by existing international, bilateral or multilateral agreements on the subject.

In areas already covered, there are two degrees of mutual recognition.

The first degree still features today in the 1968 Brussels Convention and the Brussels II Regulation: recognition is automatic unless contested; a declaration of enforceability (exequatur) may be obtained upon application and can be refused on one of the grounds on the exhaustive list in the relevant instrument. This exequatur procedure is therefore less complex than would generally result from the application of national law.

The second degree resulted from the review of the Brussels and Lugano Conventions and will be implemented following adoption of the Brussels I Regulation, which is due to replace the 1968 Brussels Convention: the procedure for obtaining a declaration of enforceability is considerably streamlined; it is obtained on completion of certain formalities and can only be contested by the other party at the second

[5] The Commission is preparing a comparative study of law in the area, based on a questionnaire addressed to the Member States.

stage (system of 'reversing the responsibility for action'). This streamlined exequatur will apply to all areas covered by the current 1968 Brussels Convention and to insolvency procedures covered by the Regulation of 29 May 2000.

PROPOSALS

Achieving further degrees of mutual recognition

A. MEASURES DIRECTLY AFFECTING MUTUAL RECOGNITION

1. Areas not covered by the existing instruments

The approach must be to follow a gradual method to reach the degree of mutual recognition currently achieved by the Brussels II Regulation, before attaining the degree achieved by the future Brussels I Regulation, and then to progress beyond it. However, it will be possible in certain cases to reach new degrees of mutual recognition directly, without any intermediate step.

2. Areas already covered by the existing instruments

In these areas, further progress should be made, with two series of measures.

(a) *First series of measures: further streamlining of intermediate measures and strengthening the effects in the requested State of judgments made in the State of origin*

(i) Limiting the reasons which can be given for challenging recognition or enforcement of a foreign judgment (for example, removal of the test of public policy, taking account of cases in which this reason is currently used by the Member States' courts).

(ii) Establishing provisional enforcement: the decision stating enforceability in the requested country would thus be enforceable on a provisional basis, despite the possibility of appeal.

Such a development requires an amendment of Article 47(3) of the draft Brussels I Regulation (Article 39(1) of the Brussels Convention).

(iii) Establishing protective measures at European level will enable a decision given in one Member State to embrace the authorisation to take protective measures against the debtor's assets in the whole territory of the Union.

This possibility, which is currently not afforded by the draft Brussels I Regulation, would, for example, enable a person who has obtained judgment against a debtor in one Member State, in the event of the latter challenging recovery of his debt, to have the debtor's property forthwith frozen in another Member State as a protective measure, without recourse to a further procedure. These measures would be without prejudice to the fact that certain types of property may not be seized under domestic law.

(iv) Improving attachment measures concerning banks, e.g. by establishing a European system for the attachment of bank accounts: with a judgment certified as enforceable in the Member State of origin, measures could be taken in any other Member State, without exequatur and *ipso jure*, for attachment of the debtor's bank accounts. The judgment would become enforceable in the country of attachment, at least for the purposes of the latter, unless contested by the debtor.

(b) *Second series of measures: abolition of intermediate measures*

Abolition, pure and simple, of any checks on the foreign judgment by courts in the requested country allows national judgments to move freely throughout the Community. Each requested State treats these national judgments as if they had been delivered by one of its own courts.

In some areas, abolition of the exequatur might take the form of establishing a true European enforcement order, obtained following a specific, uniform and harmonised procedure[6] laid down within the Community.

B. MEASURES ANCILLARY TO MUTUAL RECOGNITION

1. Minimum standards for certain aspects of civil procedure

It will sometimes be necessary, or even essential, to lay down a number of procedural rules at European level, which will constitute common minimum guarantees intended to strengthen mutual trust between the Member States' legal systems. These guarantees will make it possible, *inter alia*, to ensure that the requirements for a fair trial are strictly observed, in keeping with the European Convention for the Protection of Human Rights and Fundamental Freedoms.

For each measure under consideration, the question of drawing up some of these minimum guarantees will be examined, in order to determine their usefulness and their role. In certain areas, and particularly where abolition of the exequatur is planned, drawing up such minimum guarantees may be a precondition for the desired progress.

If the establishment of minimum guarantees appears to be insufficient, discussions should be directed towards a certain degree of harmonisation of the procedures.

In order to take into account the fundamental principles of law recognised by Member States, measures aiming at the establishment of minimum guarantees or at a certain degree of harmonisation of procedures will be sought most particularly in the case of the mutual recognition of decisions relating to parental responsibility (including those concerning rights of access). Questions relating to the child's best interests and the child's place in the procedure will, *inter alia*, be discussed in this context.

In order to increase the certainty, efficiency and rapidity of service of legal documents, which is clearly one of the foundations of mutual trust between national legal

[6] This might be either a uniform procedure laid down in a regulation, or a harmonised procedure set up by each Member State pursuant to a directive.

systems, consideration will be given to harmonising the applicable rules or setting minimum standards.

If the parties to proceedings are able to adduce their arguments in a manner recognised as valid by all the Member States, this clearly increases confidence in the proper administration of justice at an early stage in the proceedings, making it easier to dispense with checks later on.

Such a development will take duly into account progress already made on account of the entry into force of Council Regulation (EC) No 1348/2000 of 29 May 2000 on the service in the Member States of judicial and extrajudicial documents in civil or commercial matters.

2. Efficiency of measures providing for improved enforcement of decisions

Another series of ancillary measures would consist in seeking to make more efficient the enforcement, in the requested State, of judgments delivered in another Member State.

Some of these measures could concern more specifically debtors' assets. It would in fact be much easier to enforce judgments within the European Union if it were possible to obtain accurate information on the debtor's financial position. Measures could therefore be taken to enable precise identification of a debtor's assets in the territory of the Member States.

When devising measures of this kind, account should be taken of the impact they could have on data protection and the confidential nature of certain information as provided for in Member States' domestic law or in international law.

3. Improving judicial cooperation on civil matters in general

These would include measures conducive to implementation of the principle of mutual recognition, i.e. which would make for a climate of improved cooperation between national judicial authorities.

The establishment of the European Judicial Network on civil and commercial matters should accordingly feature in the programme of measures, as an ancillary measure.[7]

Mention should also be made of an instrument for enhancing cooperation between Member States' courts on the taking of evidence in civil and commercial matters.[8]

Similarly, the programme includes the development of measures giving easier access to justice. Here, account will be taken of the follow-up to the Green Paper on legal aid submitted by the Commission in February 2000, with a view to taking initiatives with regard to legal aid in cross-border cases.

[7] On 25 September 2000, the Commission submitted a proposal for a decision establishing a European Judicial Network in civil and commercial matters.

[8] Germany has submitted a draft Regulation in this area.

Likewise, it would seem particularly useful to make the public better informed on the rules on mutual recognition.[9]

Lastly, implementation of the mutual recognition principle may be facilitated through harmonisation of conflict-of-law rules.

III. STAGES

METHOD

It is always difficult to set deadlines for work to be achieved in the Community: deadlines which are too short are unrealistic, while those set too far ahead do not provide sufficient incentive for States. Progress should be made in stages, without any precise deadlines, but simply some broad guidelines.

1. The programme will be put in hand as from adoption of the Brussels I Regulation, which is the basic instrument for mutual recognition.
2. The programme distinguishes between the following four areas of action:
   — areas of civil and commercial law covered by the Brussels I Regulation,
   — areas of family law covered by the Brussels II Regulation, and family situations arising through relationships other than marriage,
   — rights in property arising out of a matrimonial relationship and the property consequences of the separation of unmarried couples,
   — wills and succession.
3. In each area stages are established with a view to making gradual progress. A stage is begun when the previous one has ended, at least as regards essentials (for example, Council agreement on an instrument, even if it has not yet been formally adopted for technical reasons); however, this requirement must not prohibit more rapid progress from being made in certain subjects.
4. Several initiatives may be taken at the same time in several areas.
5. Ancillary measures mentioned in the programme are taken whenever they seem necessary, in all areas and at all stages of the programme.

PROPOSALS

A. AREAS COVERED BY THE BRUSSELS I REGULATION

First stage

— European enforcement order for uncontested claims.

— Simplifying and speeding up the settlement of cross-border litigation on small claims.

— Abolition of exequatur for maintenance claims.

[9] Provisions on information to the public are contained in the Commission's proposal on the establishment of the European Judicial Network in civil and commercial matters.

Second stage

Revision of the Brussels I Regulation:

— incorporation of previous developments,
— abolition of exequatur in other areas,
— measures to strengthen the effects in the requested State of judgments made in the State of origin (provisional enforcement, protective measures, including the attachment of bank accounts).

Third stage

Abolition of exequatur in the areas covered by the Brussels I Regulation.

B. AREA OF FAMILY LAW (BRUSSELS II AND FAMILY SITUATIONS ARISING THROUGH RELATIONSHIPS OTHER THAN MARRIAGE)[10]

First stage

— Abolition of exequatur for judgments on rights of access.[11]
— Instrument relating to family situations arising through relationships other than marriage: adoption of the Brussels II Regulation's machinery. This may be a new instrument or a revision of the Brussels II Regulation, through extension of the latter's scope.
— Extending the scope of any instrument(s) adopted earlier to judgments modifying the conditions under which parental responsibility is exercised, as fixed in judgments made at the time of the divorce or separation.

Second stage

For every previously adopted instrument:

— application of the simplified procedures for recognition and enforcement of the Brussels I Regulation,
— measures to strengthen the effects in the requested State of the judgments made in the State of origin (provisional enforcement and protective measures).

Third stage

Abolition of exequatur for the areas covered by the Brussels II Regulation and for family situations arising through relationships other than marriage.

[10] It being specified that, with regard to measures concerning judgments on parental responsibility (including judgments on rights of access), the ancillary measures referred to in point II(B)(1) concerning consideration of the child's best interests and the child's place in the procedure should be taken into account.

[11] Initiative already presented by France.

C. DISSOLUTION OF RIGHTS IN PROPERTY ARISING OUT OF A MATRIMONIAL RELATIONSHIP AND THE PROPERTY CONSEQUENCES OF THE SEPARATION OF UNMARRIED COUPLES

First stage

Drawing up of one or more instruments on jurisdiction, recognition and enforcement of judgments relating to rights in property arising out of a matrimonial relationship and the property consequences of the separation of unmarried couples: adoption of the Brussels II Regulation's machinery.

Second stage

Revision of the instrument(s) drawn up at the first stage:

— application of the simplified procedures for recognition and enforcement of the Brussels I Regulation,
— measures to strengthen the effects in the requested State of the judgments made in the State of origin (provisional enforcement and protective measures).

Third stage

Abolition of exequatur for the areas covered by the instrument(s) drawn up.

D. WILLS AND SUCCESSION

First stage

Drawing up of an instrument on jurisdiction, recognition and enforcement of judgments relating to wills and succession: adoption of the Brussels II Regulation's machinery.

Second stage

Revision of the instrument drawn up at the first stage:

— application of the simplified procedures for recognition and enforcement of the Brussels I Regulation,
— measures to strengthen the effects in the requested State of the judgments made in the State of origin (provisional enforcement and protective measures).

Third stage

Abolition of exequatur for the areas covered by the instrument drawn up.

E. ANCILLARY MEASURES

Two measures have already been proposed: their adoption would seem to be necessary as soon as the programme is launched:

— instrument on the taking of evidence;
— establishment of the European Judicial Network on civil and commercial matters.

Furthermore, for each area of the programme and at each stage, the following ancillary measures could be considered:

— minimum standards for civil procedure;
— harmonisation of rules on, or minimum standards for, the service of judicial documents;
— measures to facilitate the enforcement of judgments, including those allowing identification of a debtor's assets;
— measures for easier access to justice;
— measures for easier provision of information to the public;
— measures relating to harmonisation of conflict-of-law rules.

LAUNCHING, MONITORING AND COMPLETION OF THE PROGRAMME

The programme starts with the launching of work on the first stage in one or more areas. It continues by following the order of stages in each area, on the understanding that progress may be achieved more rapidly in one area than in another.

Five years after adoption of the programme, the Commission will submit to the Council and the Parliament a report on its implementation. The Commission will make any recommendations to the Council that it deems useful for the proper execution of the programme, indicating in particular those areas in which it considers that special efforts should be made.

The monitoring report drawn up by the Commission may also contain recommendations concerning measures which were not initially planned in the programme but which it seemed necessary to adopt subsequently.

The programme of measures is completed by the general abolition of exequatur.

Areas	Brussels I	Brussels II and family situations arising through relationships other than marriage	Rights in property arising out of a matrimonial relationship and the property consequences of the separation of an unmarried couple	Wills and succession	Ancillary measures
Measures	**First stage:** European enforcement order for uncontested claims Small claims Abolition of exequatur for maintenance claims	**First stage:** Abolition of exequatur for judgments on rights of access Instrument on family situations arising through relationships other than marriage (separate instrument or revision of Brussels II) Extension of the scope of any instrument(s) adopted to judgments modifying the conditions under which parental responsibility is exercised, as fixed in judgments made at the time of the divorce or separation	**First stage:** Drafting of one or more instruments on mutual recognition with regard to rights in property arising out of a matrimonial relationship and the property consequences of the separation of unmarried couples: adoption of the Brussels II machinery	**First stage:** Drafting of an instrument on mutual recognition with regard to wills and succession: adoption of the Brussels II machinery	**Instrument on the taking of evidence** Establishment of the European Judicial Network on civil and commercial matters Minimum standards of civil procedure Harmonisation of rules on, or minimum standards for, the service of judicial documents Measures to facilitate the enforcement of judgments, including those allowing identification of a debtor's assets Measures for easier access to justice Measures for easier provision of information to the public Measures relating to harmonisation of conflict-of-law rules

	Second stage: Revision of the Brussels I Regulation: — incorporation of previous developments — extension of abolition of exequatur — measures to strengthen the effects in the requested State of judgments made in the State of origin (provisional enforcement, protective measures, including the attachment of bank accounts)	**Second stage:** For every previously adopted instrument: — application of simplified recognition and enforcement procedures in the Brussels I Regulation — measures to strengthen the effects in the requested State of judgments made in the State of origin (provisional enforcement and protective measures)	**Second stage:** Revision of the instrument(s) drawn up at the first stage: — application of simplified recognition and enforcement procedures in the Brussels I Regulation — measures to strengthen the effects in the requested State of judgments made in the State of origin (provisional enforcement and protective measures)	**Second stage:** Revision of the instrument(s) drawn up at the first stage: — application of simplified recognition and enforcement procedures in the Brussels I Regulation — measures to strengthen the effects in the requested State of judgments made in the State of origin (provisional enforcement and protective measures)	
	Third stage: Abolition of exequatur for all the areas covered by the Brussels I Regulation	**Third stage:** Abolition of exequatur for the areas covered by the Brussels II Regulation and for family situations arising through relationships other than marriage	**Third stage:** Abolition of exequatur for the areas covered by the instrument(s) drawn up	**Third stage:** Abolition of exequatur for the areas covered by the instrument drawn up	

Brussels European Council: Presidency Conclusions, 4th and 5th November 2004

Annex 1

...

3. STRENGTHENING JUSTICE

The European Council underlines the need further to enhance work on the creation of a Europe for citizens and the essential role that the setting up of a European Area for Justice will play in this respect. A number of measures have already been carried out. Further efforts should be made to facilitate access to justice and judicial cooperation as well as the full employment of mutual recognition. It is of particular importance that borders between countries in Europe no longer constitute an obstacle to the settlement of civil law matters or to the bringing of court proceedings and the enforcement of decisions in civil matters.

3.1 European Court of Justice

The European Council underlines the importance of the European Court of Justice in the relatively new area of freedom, security and justice and is satisfied that the Constitutional Treaty greatly increases the powers of the European Court of Justice in that area.

To ensure, both for European citizens and for the functioning of the area of freedom, security and justice, that questions on points of law brought before the Court are answered quickly, it is necessary to enable the Court to respond quickly as required by Article III-369 of the Constitutional Treaty.

In this context and with the Constitutional Treaty in prospect, thought should be given to creating a solution for the speedy and appropriate handling of requests for preliminary rulings concerning the area of freedom, security and justice, where appropriate, by amending the Statutes of the Court. The Commission is invited to bring forward – after consultation of the Court of Justice – a proposal to that effect.

3.2 Confidence-building and mutual trust

Judicial cooperation both in criminal and civil matters could be further enhanced by strengthening mutual trust and by progressive development of a European judicial culture based on diversity of the legal systems of the Member States and unity through European law. In an enlarged European Union, mutual confidence shall be based on the certainty that all European citizens have access to a judicial system meeting high standards of quality. In order to facilitate full implementation of the principle of mutual recognition, a system providing for objective and impartial evaluation of the implementation of EU policies in the field of justice, while fully respecting the independence of the judiciary and consistent with all the existing European mechanisms, must be established.

Strengthening mutual confidence requires an explicit effort to improve mutual understanding among judicial authorities and different legal systems. In this regard, networks of judicial organisations and institutions, such as the network of the Councils for the Judiciary, the European Network of Supreme Courts and the European Judicial Training Network, should be supported by the Union.

Exchange programmes for judicial authorities will facilitate cooperation and help develop mutual trust. An EU component should be systematically included in the training of judicial authorities. The Commission is invited to prepare as soon as possible a proposal aimed at creating, from the existing structures, an effective European training network for judicial authorities for both civil and criminal matters, as envisaged by Articles III-269 and III-270 of the Constitutional Treaty.

...

3.4 Judicial cooperation in civil matters

3.4.1 Facilitating civil law procedure across borders

Civil law, including family law, concerns citizens in their everyday lives. The European Council therefore attaches great importance to the continued development of judicial cooperation in civil matters and full completion of the programme of mutual recognition adopted in 2000. The main policy objective in this area is that borders between countries in Europe should no longer constitute an obstacle to the settlement of civil law matters or to the bringing of court proceedings and the enforcement of decisions in civil matters.

3.4.2 Mutual recognition of decisions

Mutual recognition of decisions is an effective means of protecting citizens' rights and securing the enforcement of such rights across European borders.

Continued implementation of the programme of measures on mutual recognition[1] must therefore be a main priority in the coming years to ensure its completion by 2011. Work concerning the following projects should be actively pursued: the conflict of laws regarding non-contractual obligations ('Rome II') and contractual

[1] OJ C 12, 15.1.2001, pages 1-9.

obligations ('Rome I'), a European Payment Order and instruments concerning alternative dispute resolution and concerning small claims. In timing the completion of these projects, due regard should be given to current work in related areas.

The effectiveness of existing instruments on mutual recognition should be increased by standardising procedures and documents and developing minimum standards for aspects of procedural law, such as the service of judicial and extra-judicial documents, the commencement of proceedings, enforcement of judgments and transparency of costs.

Regarding family and succession law, the Commission is invited to submit the following proposals:

- a draft instrument on the recognition and enforcement of decisions on maintenance, including precautionary measures and provisional enforcement in 2005;
- a green paper on the conflict of laws in matters of succession, including the question of jurisdiction, mutual recognition and enforcement of decisions in this area, a European certificate of inheritance and a mechanism allowing precise knowledge of the existence of last wills and testaments of residents of European Union in 2005; and
- a green paper on the conflict of laws in matters concerning matrimonial property regimes, including the question of jurisdiction and mutual recognition in 2006;
- a green paper on the conflict of laws in matters relating to divorce (Rome III) in 2005.

Instruments in these areas should be completed by 2011. Such instruments should cover matters of private international law and should not be based on harmonised concepts of 'family', 'marriage', or other. Rules of uniform substantive law should only be introduced as an accompanying measure, whenever necessary to effect mutual recognition of decisions or to improve judicial cooperation in civil matters.

Implementation of the programme of mutual recognition should be accompanied by a careful review of the operation of instruments that have recently been adopted. The outcome of such reviews should provide the necessary input for the preparation of new measures.

3.4.3 Enhancing cooperation

With a view to achieving smooth operation of instruments involving cooperation of judicial or other bodies, Member States should be required to designate liaison judges or other competent authorities based in their own country. Where appropriate they could use their national contact point within the European Judicial Network in civil matters. The Commission is invited to organise EU workshops on the application of EU law and promote cooperation between members of the legal professions (such as bailiffs and notaries public) with a view to establishing best practice.

3.4.4 Ensuring coherence and upgrading the quality of EU legislation

In matters of contract law, the quality of existing and future Community law should be improved by measures of consolidation, codification and rationalisation of legal instruments in force and by developing a common frame of reference. A framework should be set up to explore the possibilities to develop EU-wide standard terms and conditions of contract law which could be used by companies and trade associations in the Union.

Measures should be taken to enable the Council to effect a more systematic scrutiny of the quality and coherence of all Community law instruments relating to cooperation on civil law matters.

3.4.5 International legal order

The Commission and the Council are urged to ensure coherence between the EU and the international legal order and continue to engage in closer relations and cooperation with international organisations such as The Hague Conference on Private International Law and the Council of Europe, particularly in order to coordinate initiatives and to maximise synergies between these organisations' activities and instruments and the EU instruments. Accession of the Community to the Hague Conference should be concluded as soon as possible.

...

Council Regulation (EC) No 1348/2000

of 29 May 2000

on the service in the Member States of judicial and extrajudicial documents in civil or commercial matters

THE COUNCIL OF THE EUROPEAN UNION,

Having regard to the Treaty establishing the European Community, and in particular Article 61(c) and Article 67(1) thereof,

Having regard to the proposal from the Commission,[1]

Having regard to the opinion of the European Parliament,[2]

Having regard to the opinion of the Economic and Social Committee,[3]

Whereas:

(1) The Union has set itself the objective of maintaining and developing the Union as an area of freedom, security and justice, in which the free movement of persons is assured. To establish such an area, the Community is to adopt, among others, the measures relating to judicial cooperation in civil matters needed for the proper functioning of the internal market.

(2) The proper functioning of the internal market entails the need to improve and expedite the transmission of judicial and extrajudicial documents in civil or commercial matters for service between the Member States.

(3) This is a subject now falling within the ambit of Article 65 of the Treaty.

(4) In accordance with the principles of subsidiarity and proportionality as set out in Article 5 of the Treaty, the objectives of this Regulation cannot be sufficiently achieved by the Member States and can therefore be better achieved by the Community. This Regulation does not go beyond what is necessary to achieve those objectives.

(5) The Council, by an Act dated 26 May 1997[4], drew up a Convention on the service in the Member States of the European Union of judicial and extrajudicial documents in civil or commercial matters and recommended it for adoption

[1] OJ C 247 E, 31.8.1999, p. 11.

[2] Opinion of 17 November 1999 (not yet published in the Official Journal).

[3] OJ C 368, 20.12.1999, p. 47.

by the Member States in accordance with their respective constitutional rules. That Convention has not entered into force. Continuity in the results of the negotiations for conclusion of the Convention should be ensured. The main content of this Regulation is substantially taken over from it.

(6) Efficiency and speed in judicial procedures in civil matters means that the transmission of judicial and extrajudicial documents is to be made direct and by rapid means between local bodies designated by the Member States. However, the Member States may indicate their intention of designating only one transmitting or receiving agency or one agency to perform both functions for a period of five years. This designation may, however, be renewed every five years.

(7) Speed in transmission warrants the use of all appropriate means, provided that certain conditions as to the legibility and reliability of the document received are observed. Security in transmission requires that the document to be transmitted be accompanied by a pre-printed form, to be completed in the language of the place where service is to be effected, or in another language accepted by the Member State in question.

(8) To secure the effectiveness of this Regulation, the possibility of refusing service of documents is confined to exceptional situations.

(9) Speed of transmission warrants documents being served within days of reception of the document. However, if service has not been effected after one month has elapsed, the receiving agency should inform the transmitting agency. The expiry of this period should not imply that the request be returned to the transmitting agency where it is clear that service is feasible within a reasonable period.

(10) For the protection of the addressee's interests, service should be effected in the official language or one of the official languages of the place where it is to be effected or in another language of the originating Member State which the addressee understands.

(11) Given the differences between the Member States as regards their rules of procedure, the material date for the purposes of service varies from one Member State to another. Having regard to such situations and the possible difficulties that may arise, this Regulation should provide for a system where it is the law of the receiving Member State which determines the date of service. However, if the relevant documents in the context of proceedings to be brought or pending in the Member State of origin are to be served within a specified period, the date to be taken into consideration with respect to the applicant shall be that determined according to the law of the Member State of origin. A Member State is, however, authorised to derogate from the aforementioned provisions for a transitional period of five years, for appropriate reasons. Such a derogation may be renewed by a Member State at five-year intervals due to reasons related to its legal system.

[4] OJ C 261, 27.8.1997, p. 1. On the same day as the Convention was drawn up the Council took note of the explanatory report on the Convention which is set out on page 26 of the aforementioned Official Journal.

(12) This Regulation prevails over the provisions contained in bilateral or multilateral agreements or arrangements having the same scope, concluded by the Member States, and in particular the Protocol annexed to the Brussels Convention of 27 September 1968[5] and the Hague Convention of 15 November 1965 in relations between the Member States party thereto. This Regulation does not preclude Member States from maintaining or concluding agreements or arrangements to expedite or simplify the transmission of documents, provided that they are compatible with the Regulation.

(13) The information transmitted pursuant to this Regulation should enjoy suitable protection. This matter falls within the scope of Directive 95/46/EC of the European Parliament and of the Council of 24 October 1995 on the protection of individuals with regard to the processing of personal data and on the free movement of such data,[6] and of Directive 97/66/EC of the European Parliament and of the Council of 15 December 1997 concerning the processing of personal data and the protection of privacy in the telecommunications sector.[7]

(14) The measures necessary for the implementation of this Regulation should be adopted in accordance with Council Decision 1999/468/EC of 28 June 1999 laying down the procedures for the exercise of implementing powers conferred on the Commission.[8]

(15) These measures also include drawing up and updating the manual using appropriate modern means.

(16) No later than three years after the date of entry into force of this Regulation, the Commission should review its application and propose such amendments as may appear necessary.

(17) The United Kingdom and Ireland, in accordance with Article 3 of the Protocol on the position of the United Kingdom and Ireland annexed to the Treaty on European Union and the Treaty establishing the European Community, have given notice of their wish to take part in the adoption and application of this Regulation.

(18) Denmark, in accordance with Articles 1 and 2 of the Protocol on the position of Denmark annexed to the Treaty on European Union and the Treaty establishing the European Community, is not participating in the adoption of this Regulation, and is therefore not bound by it nor subject to its application,

[5] Brussels Convention of 27 September 1968 on Jurisdiction and the Enforcement of Judgments in Civil and Commercial Matters (OJ L 299, 13.12.1972, p. 32; consolidated version, OJ C 27, 26.1.1998, p. 1).

[6] OJ L 281, 23.11.1995, p. 31.

[7] OJ L 24, 30.1.1998, p. 1.

[8] OJ L 184, 17.7.1999, p. 23.

HAS ADOPTED THIS REGULATION:

CHAPTER I
GENERAL PROVISIONS

Article 1
Scope

1. This Regulation shall apply in civil and commercial matters where a judicial or extrajudicial document has to be transmitted from one Member State to another for service there.
2. This Regulation shall not apply where the address of the person to be served with the document is not known.

Article 2
Transmitting and receiving agencies

1. Each Member State shall designate the public officers, authorities or other persons, hereinafter referred to as 'transmitting agencies', competent for the transmission of judicial or extrajudicial documents to be served in another Member State.
2. Each Member State shall designate the public officers, authorities or other persons, hereinafter referred to as 'receiving agencies', competent for the receipt of judicial or extrajudicial documents from another Member State.
3. A Member State may designate one transmitting agency and one receiving agency or one agency to perform both functions. A federal State, a State in which several legal systems apply or a State with autonomous territorial units shall be free to designate more than one such agency. The designation shall have effect for a period of five years and may be renewed at five-year intervals.
4. Each Member State shall provide the Commission with the following information:
   (a) the names and addresses of the receiving agencies referred to in paragraphs 2 and 3;
   (b) the geographical areas in which they have jurisdiction;
   (c) the means of receipt of documents available to them; and
   (d) the languages that may be used for the completion of the standard form in the Annex.

   Member States shall notify the Commission of any subsequent modification of such information.

Article 3
Central body

Each Member State shall designate a central body responsible for:

(a) supplying information to the transmitting agencies;

(b) seeking solutions to any difficulties which may arise during transmission of documents for service;
(c) forwarding, in exceptional cases, at the request of a transmitting agency, a request for service to the competent receiving agency.

A federal State, a State in which several legal systems apply or a State with autonomous territorial units shall be free to designate more than one central body.

CHAPTER II
JUDICIAL DOCUMENTS

Section 1
Transmission and service of judicial documents

Article 4
Transmission of documents

1. Judicial documents shall be transmitted directly and as soon as possible between the agencies designated on the basis of Article 2.
2. The transmission of documents, requests, confirmations, receipts, certificates and any other papers between transmitting agencies and receiving agencies may be carried out by any appropriate means, provided that the content of the document received is true and faithful to that of the document forwarded and that all information in it is easily legible.
3. The document to be transmitted shall be accompanied by a request drawn up using the standard form in the Annex. The form shall be completed in the official language of the Member State addressed or, if there are several official languages in that Member State, the official language or one of the official languages of the place where service is to be effected, or in another language which that Member State has indicated it can accept. Each Member State shall indicate the official language or languages of the European Union other than its own which is or are acceptable to it for completion of the form.
4. The documents and all papers that are transmitted shall be exempted from legalisation or any equivalent formality.
5. When the transmitting agency wishes a copy of the document to be returned together with the certificate referred to in Article 10, it shall send the document in duplicate.

Article 5
Translation of documents

1. The applicant shall be advised by the transmitting agency to which he or she forwards the document for transmission that the addressee may refuse to accept it if it is not in one of the languages provided for in Article 8.

2. The applicant shall bear any costs of translation prior to the transmission of the document, without prejudice to any possible subsequent decision by the court or competent authority on liability for such costs.

Article 6

Receipt of documents by receiving agency

1. On receipt of a document, a receiving agency shall, as soon as possible and in any event within seven days of receipt, send a receipt to the transmitting agency by the swiftest possible means of transmission using the standard form in the Annex.
2. Where the request for service cannot be fulfilled on the basis of the information or documents transmitted, the receiving agency shall contact the transmitting agency by the swiftest possible means in order to secure the missing information or documents.
3. If the request for service is manifestly outside the scope of this Regulation or if non-compliance with the formal conditions required makes service impossible, the request and the documents transmitted shall be returned, on receipt, to the transmitting agency, together with the notice of return in the standard form in the Annex.
4. A receiving agency receiving a document for service but not having territorial jurisdiction to serve it shall forward it, as well as the request, to the receiving agency having territorial jurisdiction in the same Member State if the request complies with the conditions laid down in Article 4(3) and shall inform the transmitting agency accordingly, using the standard form in the Annex. That receiving agency shall inform the transmitting agency when it receives the document, in the manner provided for in paragraph 1.

Article 7

Service of documents

1. The receiving agency shall itself serve the document or have it served, either in accordance with the law of the Member State addressed or by a particular form requested by the transmitting agency, unless such a method is incompatible with the law of that Member State.
2. All steps required for service of the document shall be effected as soon as possible. In any event, if it has not been possible to effect service within one month of receipt, the receiving agency shall inform the transmitting agency by means of the certificate in the standard form in the Annex, which shall be drawn up under the conditions referred to in Article 10(2). The period shall be calculated in accordance with the law of the Member State addressed.

Article 8

Refusal to accept a document

1. The receiving agency shall inform the addressee that he or she may refuse to accept the document to be served if it is in a language other than either of the following languages:
   (a) the official language of the Member State addressed or, if there are several official languages in that Member State, the official language or one of the official languages of the place where service is to be effected; or
   (b) a language of the Member State of transmission which the addressee understands.
2. Where the receiving agency is informed that the addressee refuses to accept the document in accordance with paragraph 1, it shall immediately inform the transmitting agency by means of the certificate provided for in Article 10 and return the request and the documents of which a translation is requested.

Article 9

Date of service

1. Without prejudice to Article 8, the date of service of a document pursuant to Article 7 shall be the date on which it is served in accordance with the law of the Member State addressed.
2. However, where a document shall be served within a particular period in the context of proceedings to be brought or pending in the Member State of origin, the date to be taken into account with respect to the applicant shall be that fixed by the law of that Member State.
3. A Member State shall be authorised to derogate from the provisions of paragraphs 1 and 2 for a transitional period of five years, for appropriate reasons.

   This transitional period may be renewed by a Member State at five-yearly intervals due to reasons related to its legal system. That Member State shall inform the Commission of the content of such a derogation and the circumstances of the case.

Article 10

Certificate of service and copy of the document served

1. When the formalities concerning the service of the document have been completed, a certificate of completion of those formalities shall be drawn up in the standard form in the Annex and addressed to the transmitting agency, together with, where Article 4(5) applies, a copy of the document served.
2. The certificate shall be completed in the official language or one of the official languages of the Member State of origin or in another language which the

Member State of origin has indicated that it can accept. Each Member State shall indicate the official language or languages of the European Union other than its own which is or are acceptable to it for completion of the form.

Article 11

Costs of service

1. The service of judicial documents coming from a Member State shall not give rise to any payment or reimbursement of taxes or costs for services rendered by the Member State addressed.
2. The applicant shall pay or reimburse the costs occasioned by:
   (a) the employment of a judicial officer or of a person competent under the law of the Member State addressed;
   (b) the use of a particular method of service.

Section 2

Other means of transmission and service of judicial documents

Article 12

Transmission by consular or diplomatic channels

Each Member State shall be free, in exceptional circumstances, to use consular or diplomatic channels to forward judicial documents, for the purpose of service, to those agencies of another Member State which are designated pursuant to Article 2 or 3.

Article 13

Service by diplomatic or consular agents

1. Each Member State shall be free to effect service of judicial documents on persons residing in another Member State, without application of any compulsion, directly through its diplomatic or consular agents.
2. Any Member State may make it known, in accordance with Article 23(1), that it is opposed to such service within its territory, unless the documents are to be served on nationals of the Member State in which the documents originate.

Article 14

Service by post

1. Each Member State shall be free to effect service of judicial documents directly by post to persons residing in another Member State.
2. Any Member State may specify, in accordance with Article 23(1), the conditions under which it will accept service of judicial documents by post.

Article 15

Direct service

1. This Regulation shall not interfere with the freedom of any person interested in a judicial proceeding to effect service of judicial documents directly through the judicial officers, officials or other competent persons of the Member State addressed.
2. Any Member State may make it known, in accordance with Article 23(1), that it is opposed to the service of judicial documents in its territory pursuant to paragraph 1.

CHAPTER III
EXTRAJUDICIAL DOCUMENTS

Article 16

Transmission

Extrajudicial documents may be transmitted for service in another Member State in accordance with the provisions of this Regulation.

CHAPTER IV
FINAL PROVISIONS

Article 17

Implementing rules

The measures necessary for the implementation of this Regulation relating to the matters referred to below shall be adopted in accordance with the advisory procedure referred to in Article 18(2):

(a) drawing up and annually updating a manual containing the information provided by Member States in accordance with Article 2(4);
(b) drawing up a glossary in the official languages of the European Union of documents which may be served under this Regulation;
(c) updating or making technical amendments to the standard form set out in the Annex.

Article 18

Committee

1. The Commission shall be assisted by a committee.
2. Where reference is made to this paragraph, Articles 3 and 7 of Decision 1999/468/EC shall apply.
3. The Committee shall adopt its rules of procedure.

Article 19

Defendant not entering an appearance

1. Where a writ of summons or an equivalent document has had to be transmitted to another Member State for the purpose of service, under the provisions of this Regulation, and the defendant has not appeared, judgment shall not be given until it is established that:
   (a) the document was served by a method prescribed by the internal law of the Member State addressed for the service of documents in domestic actions upon persons who are within its territory; or
   (b) the document was actually delivered to the defendant or to his residence by another method provided for by this Regulation;

   and that in either of these cases the service or the delivery was effected in sufficient time to enable the defendant to defend.
2. Each Member State shall be free to make it known, in accordance with Article 23(1), that the judge, notwithstanding the provisions of paragraph 1, may give judgment even if no certificate of service or delivery has been received, if all the following conditions are fulfilled:
   (a) the document was transmitted by one of the methods provided for in this Regulation;
   (b) a period of time of not less than six months, considered adequate by the judge in the particular case, has elapsed since the date of the transmission of the document;
   (c) no certificate of any kind has been received, even though every reasonable effort has been made to obtain it through the competent authorities or bodies of the Member State addressed.
3. Notwithstanding paragraphs 1 and 2, the judge may order, in case of urgency, any provisional or protective measures.
4. When a writ of summons or an equivalent document has had to be transmitted to another Member State for the purpose of service, under the provisions of this Regulation, and a judgment has been entered against a defendant who has not appeared, the judge shall have the power to relieve the defendant from the effects of the expiration of the time for appeal from the judgment if the following conditions are fulfilled:
   (a) the defendant, without any fault on his part, did not have knowledge of the document in sufficient time to defend, or knowledge of the judgment in sufficient time to appeal; and
   (b) the defendant has disclosed a prima facie defence to the action on the merits.

   An application for relief may be filed only within a reasonable time after the defendant has knowledge of the judgment.

   Each Member State may make it known, in accordance with Article 23(1), that such application will not be entertained if it is filed after the expiration of a time to be stated by it in that communication, but which shall in no case be less than one year following the date of the judgment.

5. Paragraph 4 shall not apply to judgments concerning status or capacity of persons.

Article 20

Relationship with agreements or arrangements to which Member States are Parties

1. This Regulation shall, in relation to matters to which it applies, prevail over other provisions contained in bilateral or multilateral agreements or arrangements concluded by the Member States, and in particular Article IV of the Protocol to the Brussels Convention of 1968 and the Hague Convention of 15 November 1965.
2. This Regulation shall not preclude individual Member States from maintaining or concluding agreements or arrangements to expedite further or simplify the transmission of documents, provided that they are compatible with this Regulation.
3. Member States shall send to the Commission:
   (a) a copy of the agreements or arrangements referred to in paragraph 2 concluded between the Member States as well as drafts of such agreements or arrangements which they intend to adopt;
   and
   (b) any denunciation of, or amendments to, these agreements or arrangements.

Article 21

Legal aid

This Regulation shall not affect the application of Article 23 of the Convention on Civil Procedure of 17 July 1905, Article 24 of the Convention on Civil Procedure of 1 March 1954 or Article 13 of the Convention on International Access to Justice of 25 October 1980 between the Member States Parties to these Conventions.

Article 22

Protection of information transmitted

1. Information, including in particular personal data, transmitted under this Regulation shall be used by the receiving agency only for the purpose for which it was transmitted.
2. Receiving agencies shall ensure the confidentiality of such information, in accordance with their national law.
3. Paragraphs 1 and 2 shall not affect national laws enabling data subjects to be informed of the use made of information transmitted under this Regulation.

4. This Regulation shall be without prejudice to Directives 95/46/EC and 97/66/EC.

Article 23

Communication and publication

1. Member States shall communicate to the Commission the information referred to in Articles 2, 3, 4, 9, 10, 13, 14, 15, 17(a) and 19.
2. The Commission shall publish in the *Official Journal of the European Communities* the information referred to in paragraph 1.

Article 24

Review

No later than 1 June 2004, and every five years thereafter, the Commission shall present to the European Parliament, the Council and the Economic and Social Committee a report on the application of this Regulation, paying special attention to the effectiveness of the bodies designated pursuant to Article 2 and to the practical application of point (c) of Article 3 and Article 9. The report shall be accompanied if need be by proposals for adaptations of this Regulation in line with the evolution of notification systems.

Article 25

Entry into force

This Regulation shall enter into force on 31 May 2001.

This Regulation shall be binding in its entirety and directly applicable in the Member States in accordance with the Treaty establishing the European Community.

Done at Brussels, 29 May 2000.

For the Council
The President
A. COSTA

[Note that annexes have been removed from this appendix. Note also that the Service Regulation as of 13 November 2008 will be replaced by Council Regulation (EC) No 1393/2007.]

Council Regulation (EC) No 1206/2001

of 28 May 2001

on cooperation between the courts of the Member States in the taking of evidence in civil or commercial matters

THE COUNCIL OF THE EUROPEAN UNION,

Having regard to the Treaty establishing the European Community, and in particular Article 61(c) and Article 67(1) thereof,

Having regard to the initiative of the Federal Republic of Germany,[1]

Having regard to the opinion of the European Parliament,[2]

Having regard to the opinion of the Economic and Social Committee,[3]

Whereas:

(1) The European Union has set itself the objective of maintaining and developing the European Union as an area of freedom, security and justice in which the free movement of persons is ensured. For the gradual establishment of such an area, the Community is to adopt, among others, the measures relating to judicial cooperation in civil matters needed for the proper functioning of the internal market.

(2) For the purpose of the proper functioning of the internal market, cooperation between courts in the taking of evidence should be improved, and in particular simplified and accelerated.

(3) At its meeting in Tampere on 15 and 16 October 1999, the European Council recalled that new procedural legislation in cross-border cases, in particular on the taking of evidence, should be prepared.

(4) This area falls within the scope of Article 65 of the Treaty.

(5) The objectives of the proposed action, namely the improvement of cooperation between the courts on the taking of evidence in civil or commercial matters, cannot be sufficiently achieved by the Member States and can therefore be better achieved at Community level. The Community may adopt measures in accordance with the principle of subsidiarity as set out in Article 5 of the

[1] OJ C 314, 3.11.2000, p. 2.

[2] Opinion delivered on 14 March 2001 (not yet published in the Official Journal).

[3] Opinion delivered on 28 February 2001 (not yet published in the Official Journal).

Treaty. In accordance with the principle of proportionality, as set out in that Article, this Regulation does not go beyond what is necessary to achieve those objectives.

(6) To date, there is no binding instrument between all the Member States concerning the taking of evidence. The Hague Convention of 18 March 1970 on the taking of evidence abroad in civil or commercial matters applies between only 11 Member States of the European Union.

(7) As it is often essential for a decision in a civil or commercial matter pending before a court in a Member State to take evidence in another Member State, the Community's activity cannot be limited to the field of transmission of judicial and extrajudicial documents in civil or commercial matters which falls within the scope of Council Regulation (EC) No 1348/2000 of 29 May 2000 on the serving in the Member States of judicial and extrajudicial documents in civil or commercial matters.[4] It is therefore necessary to continue the improvement of cooperation between courts of Member States in the field of taking of evidence.

(8) The efficiency of judicial procedures in civil or commercial matters requires that the transmission and execution of requests for the performance of taking of evidence is to be made directly and by the most rapid means possible between Member States' courts.

(9) Speed in transmission of requests for the performance of taking of evidence warrants the use of all appropriate means, provided that certain conditions as to the legibility and reliability of the document received are observed. So as to ensure the utmost clarity and legal certainty the request for the performance of taking of evidence must be transmitted on a form to be completed in the language of the Member State of the requested court or in another language accepted by that State. For the same reasons, forms should also be used as far as possible for further communication between the relevant courts.

(10) A request for the performance of the taking of evidence should be executed expeditiously. If it is not possible for the request to be executed within 90 days of receipt by the requested court, the latter should inform the requesting court accordingly, stating the reasons which prevent the request from being executed swiftly.

(11) To secure the effectiveness of this Regulation, the possibility of refusing to execute the request for the performance of taking of evidence should be confined to strictly limited exceptional situations.

(12) The requested court should execute the request in accordance with the law of its Member State.

(13) The parties and, if any, their representatives, should be able to be present at the performance of the taking of evidence, if that is provided for by the law

[4] OJ L 160, 30.6.2000, p. 37.

of the Member State of the requesting court, in order to be able to follow the proceedings in a comparable way as if evidence were taken in the Member State of the requesting court. They should also have the right to request to participate in order to have a more active role in the performance of the taking of evidence. However, the conditions under which they may participate should be determined by the requested court in accordance with the law of its Member State.

(14) The representatives of the requesting court should be able to be present at the performance of the taking of evidence, if that is compatible with the law of the Member State of the requesting court, in order to have an improved possibility of evaluation of evidence. They should also have the right to request to participate, under the conditions laid down by the requested court in accordance with the law of its Member State, in order to have a more active role in the performance of the taking of evidence.

(15) In order to facilitate the taking of evidence it should be possible for a court in a Member State, in accordance with the law of its Member State, to take evidence directly in another Member State, if accepted by the latter, and under the conditions determined by the central body or competent authority of the requested Member State.

(16) The execution of the request, according to Article 10, should not give rise to a claim for any reimbursement of taxes or costs. Nevertheless, if the requested court requires reimbursement, the fees paid to experts and interpreters, as well as the costs occasioned by the application of Article 10(3) and (4), should not be borne by that court. In such a case, the requesting court is to take the necessary measures to ensure reimbursement without delay. Where the opinion of an expert is required, the requested court may, before executing the request, ask the requesting court for an adequate deposit or advance towards the costs.

(17) This Regulation should prevail over the provisions applying to its field of application, contained in international conventions concluded by the Member States. Member States should be free to adopt agreements or arrangements to further facilitate cooperation in the taking of evidence.

(18) The information transmitted pursuant to this Regulation should enjoy protection. Since Directive 95/46/EC of the European Parliament and of the Council of 24 October 1995 on the protection of individuals with regard to the processing of personal data and on the free movement of such data,[5] and Directive 97/66/EC of the European Parliament and of the Council of 15 December 1997 concerning the processing of personal data and the protection of privacy in the telecommunications sector,[6] are applicable, there is no need for specific provisions on data protection in this Regulation.

[5] OJ L 281, 23.11.1995, p. 31.
[6] OJ L 24, 30.1.1998, p. 1.

(19) The measures necessary for the implementation of this Regulation should be adopted in accordance with Council Decision 1999/468/EC of 28 June 1999[7] laying down the procedures for the exercise of implementing powers conferred on the Commission.

(20) For the proper functioning of this Regulation, the Commission should review its application and propose such amendments as may appear necessary.

(21) The United Kingdom and Ireland, in accordance with Article 3 of the Protocol on the position of the United Kingdom and Ireland annexed to the Treaty on the European Union and to the Treaty establishing the European Community, have given notice of their wish to take part in the adoption and application of this Regulation.

(22) Denmark, in accordance with Articles 1 and 2 of the Protocol on the position of Denmark annexed to the Treaty on European Union and to the Treaty establishing the European Community, is not participating in the adoption of this Regulation, and is therefore not bound by it nor subject to its application,

HAS ADOPTED THIS REGULATION:

CHAPTER I
GENERAL PROVISIONS

Article 1
Scope

1. This Regulation shall apply in civil or commercial matters where the court of a Member State, in accordance with the provisions of the law of that State, requests:
   (a) the competent court of another Member State to take evidence; or
   (b) to take evidence directly in another Member State.
2. A request shall not be made to obtain evidence which is not intended for use in judicial proceedings, commenced or contemplated.
3. In this Regulation, the term 'Member State' shall mean Member States with the exception of Denmark.

Article 2
Direct transmission between the courts

1. Requests pursuant to Article 1(1)(a), hereinafter referred to as 'requests', shall be transmitted by the court before which the proceedings are commenced

[7] OJ L 184, 17.7.1999, p. 23.

or contemplated, hereinafter referred to as the 'requesting court', directly to the competent court of another Member State, hereinafter referred to as the 'requested court', for the performance of the taking of evidence.

2. Each Member State shall draw up a list of the courts competent for the performance of taking of evidence according to this Regulation. The list shall also indicate the territorial and, where appropriate, the special jurisdiction of those courts.

Article 3

Central body

1. Each Member State shall designate a central body responsible for:
   (a) supplying information to the courts;
   (b) seeking solutions to any difficulties which may arise in respect of a request;
   (c) forwarding, in exceptional cases, at the request of a requesting court, a request to the competent court.
2. A federal State, a State in which several legal systems apply or a State with autonomous territorial entities shall be free to designate more than one central body.
3. Each Member State shall also designate the central body referred to in paragraph 1 or one or several competent authority(ies) to be responsible for taking decisions on requests pursuant to Article 17.

CHAPTER II
TRANSMISSION AND EXECUTION OF REQUESTS

Section 1

Transmission of the request

Article 4

Form and content of the request

1. The request shall be made using form A or, where appropriate, form I in the Annex. It shall contain the following details:
   (a) the requesting and, where appropriate, the requested court;
   (b) the names and addresses of the parties to the proceedings and their representatives, if any;
   (c) the nature and subject matter of the case and a brief statement of the facts;
   (d) a description of the taking of evidence to be performed;
   (e) where the request is for the examination of a person:

— the name(s) and address(es) of the person(s) to be examined,
— the questions to be put to the person(s) to be examined or a statement of the facts about which he is (they are) to be examined,
— where appropriate, a reference to a right to refuse to testify under the law of the Member State of the requesting court,
— any requirement that the examination is to be carried out under oath or affirmation in lieu thereof, and any special form to be used,
— where appropriate, any other information that the requesting court deems necessary;

(f) where the request is for any other form of taking of evidence, the documents or other objects to be inspected;

(g) where appropriate, any request pursuant to Article 10(3) and (4), and Articles 11 and 12 and any information necessary for the application thereof.

2. The request and all documents accompanying the request shall be exempted from authentication or any equivalent formality.
3. Documents which the requesting court deems it necessary to enclose for the execution of the request shall be accompanied by a translation into the language in which the request was written.

Article 5
Language

The request and communications pursuant to this Regulation shall be drawn up in the official language of the requested Member State or, if there are several official languages in that Member State, in the official language or one of the official languages of the place where the requested taking of evidence is to be performed, or in another language which the requested Member State has indicated it can accept. Each Member State shall indicate the official language or languages of the institutions of the European Community other than its own which is or are acceptable to it for completion of the forms.

Article 6
Transmission of requests and other communications

Requests and communications pursuant to this Regulation shall be transmitted by the swiftest possible means, which the requested Member State has indicated it can accept. The transmission may be carried out by any appropriate means, provided that the document received accurately reflects the content of the document forwarded and that all information in it is legible.

Section 2
Receipt of request

Article 7
Receipt of request

1. Within seven days of receipt of the request, the requested competent court shall send an acknowledgement of receipt to the requesting court using form B in the Annex. Where the request does not comply with the conditions laid down in Articles 5 and 6, the requested court shall enter a note to that effect in the acknowledgement of receipt.
2. Where the execution of a request made using form A in the Annex, which complies with the conditions laid down in Article 5, does not fall within the jurisdiction of the court to which it was transmitted, the latter shall forward the request to the competent court of its Member State and shall inform the requesting court thereof using form A in the Annex.

Article 8
Incomplete request

1. If a request cannot be executed because it does not contain all of the necessary information pursuant to Article 4, the requested court shall inform the requesting court thereof without delay and, at the latest, within 30 days of receipt of the request using form C in the Annex, and shall request it to send the missing information, which should be indicated as precisely as possible.
2. If a request cannot be executed because a deposit or advance is necessary in accordance with Article 18(3), the requested court shall inform the requesting court thereof without delay and, at the latest, within 30 days of receipt of the request using form C in the Annex and inform the requesting court how the deposit or advance should be made. The requested Court shall acknowledge receipt of the deposit or advance without delay, at the latest within 10 days of receipt of the deposit or the advance using form D.

Article 9
Completion of the request

1. If the requested court has noted on the acknowledgement of receipt pursuant to Article 7(1) that the request does not comply with the conditions laid down in Articles 5 and 6 or has informed the requesting court pursuant to Article 8 that the request cannot be executed because it does not contain all of the necessary information pursuant to Article 4, the time limit pursuant to Article 10 shall begin to run when the requested court received the request duly completed.

2. Where the requested court has asked for a deposit or advance in accordance with Article 18(3), this time limit shall begin to run when the deposit or the advance is made.

Section 3
Taking of evidence by the requested court

Article 10
General provisions on the execution of the request

1. The requested court shall execute the request without delay and, at the latest, within 90 days of receipt of the request.
2. The requested court shall execute the request in accordance with the law of its Member State.
3. The requesting court may call for the request to be executed in accordance with a special procedure provided for by the law of its Member State, using form A in the Annex. The requested court shall comply with such a requirement unless this procedure is incompatible with the law of the Member State of the requested court or by reason of major practical difficulties. If the requested court does not comply with the requirement for one of these reasons it shall inform the requesting court using form E in the Annex.
4. The requesting court may ask the requested court to use communications technology at the performance of the taking of evidence, in particular by using video conference and teleconference.
   The requested court shall comply with such a requirement unless this is incompatible with the law of the Member State of the requested court or by reason of major practical difficulties.
   If the requested court does not comply with the requirement for one of these reasons, it shall inform the requesting court, using form E in the Annex.
   If there is no access to the technical means referred to above in the requesting or in the requested court, such means may be made available by the courts by mutual agreement.

Article 11
Performance with the presence and participation of the parties

1. If it is provided for by the law of the Member State of the requesting court, the parties and, if any, their representatives, have the right to be present at the performance of the taking of evidence by the requested court.
2. The requesting court shall, in its request, inform the requested court that the parties and, if any, their representatives, will be present and, where appropriate,

that their participation is requested, using form A in the Annex. This information may also be given at any other appropriate time.

3. If the participation of the parties and, if any, their representatives, is requested at the performance of the taking of evidence, the requested court shall determine, in accordance with Article 10, the conditions under which they may participate.
4. The requested court shall notify the parties and, if any, their representatives, of the time when, the place where, the proceedings will take place, and, where appropriate, the conditions under which they may participate, using form F in the Annex.
5. Paragraphs 1 to 4 shall not affect the possibility for the requested court of asking the parties and, if any, their representatives, to be present at or to participate in the performance of the taking of evidence if that possibility is provided for by the law of its Member State.

Article 12

Performance with the presence and participation of representatives of the requesting court

1. If it is compatible with the law of the Member State of the requesting court, representatives of the requesting court have the right to be present in the performance of the taking of evidence by the requested court.
2. For the purpose of this Article, the term 'representative' shall include members of the judicial personnel designated by the requesting court, in accordance with the law of its Member State. The requesting court may also designate, in accordance with the law of its Member State, any other person, such as an expert.
3. The requesting court shall, in its request, inform the requested court that its representatives will be present and, where appropriate, that their participation is requested, using form A in the Annex. This information may also be given at any other appropriate time.
4. If the participation of the representatives of the requesting court is requested in the performance of the taking of evidence, the requested court shall determine, in accordance with Article 10, the conditions under which they may participate.
5. The requested court shall notify the requesting court, of the time when, and the place where, the proceedings will take place, and, where appropriate, the conditions under which the representatives may participate, using form F in the Annex.

Article 13

Coercive measures

Where necessary, in executing a request the requested court shall apply the appropriate coercive measures in the instances and to the extent as are provided for by the law of the Member State of the requested court for the execution of a request made for the same purpose by its national authorities or one of the parties concerned.

Article 14

Refusal to execute

1. A request for the hearing of a person shall not be executed when the person concerned claims the right to refuse to give evidence or to be prohibited from giving evidence,
   (a) under the law of the Member State of the requested court; or
   (b) under the law of the Member State of the requesting court, and such right has been specified in the request, or, if need be, at the instance of the requested court, has been confirmed by the requesting court.
2. In addition to the grounds referred to in paragraph 1, the execution of a request may be refused only if:
   (a) the request does not fall within the scope of this Regulation as set out in Article 1; or
   (b) the execution of the request under the law of the Member State of the requested court does not fall within the functions of the judiciary; or
   (c) the requesting court does not comply with the request of the requested court to complete the request pursuant to Article 8 within 30 days after the requested court asked it to do so; or
   (d) a deposit or advance asked for in accordance with Article 18(3) is not made within 60 days after the requested court asked for such a deposit or advance.
3. Execution may not be refused by the requested court solely on the ground that under the law of its Member State a court of that Member State has exclusive jurisdiction over the subject matter of the action or that the law of that Member State would not admit the right of action on it.
4. If execution of the request is refused on one of the grounds referred to in paragraph 2, the requested court shall notify the requesting court thereof within 60 days of receipt of the request by the requested court using form H in the Annex.

Article 15

Notification of delay

If the requested court is not in a position to execute the request within 90 days of receipt, it shall inform the requesting court thereof, using form G in the Annex. When it does so, the grounds for the delay shall be given as well as the estimated time that the requested court expects it will need to execute the request.

Article 16

Procedure after execution of the request

The requested court shall send without delay to the requesting court the documents establishing the execution of the request and, where appropriate, return the documents received from the requesting court. The documents shall be accompanied by a confirmation of execution using form H in the Annex.

Section 4
Direct taking of evidence by the requesting court

Article 17

1. Where a court requests to take evidence directly in another Member State, it shall submit a request to the central body or the competent authority referred to in Article 3(3) in that State, using form I in the Annex.
2. Direct taking of evidence may only take place if it can be performed on a voluntary basis without the need for coercive measures.
   Where the direct taking of evidence implies that a person shall be heard, the requesting court shall inform that person that the performance shall take place on a voluntary basis.
3. The taking of evidence shall be performed by a member of the judicial personnel or by any other person such as an expert, who will be designated, in accordance with the law of the Member State of the requesting court.
4. Within 30 days of receiving the request, the central body or the competent authority of the requested Member State shall inform the requesting court if the request is accepted and, if necessary, under what conditions according to the law of its Member State such performance is to be carried out, using form J.
   In particular, the central body or the competent authority may assign a court of its Member State to take part in the performance of the taking of evidence in order to ensure the proper application of this Article and the conditions that have been set out.
   The central body or the competent authority shall encourage the use of communications technology, such as videoconferences and teleconferences.
5. The central body or the competent authority may refuse direct taking of evidence only if:
   (a) the request does not fall within the scope of this Regulation as set out in Article 1;
   (b) the request does not contain all of the necessary information pursuant to Article 4; or
   (c) the direct taking of evidence requested is contrary to fundamental principles of law in its Member State.
6. Without prejudice to the conditions laid down in accordance with paragraph 4, the requesting court shall execute the request in accordance with the law of its Member State.

Section 5
Costs

Article 18

1. The execution of the request, in accordance with Article 10, shall not give rise to a claim for any reimbursement of taxes or costs.

2. Nevertheless, if the requested court so requires, the requesting court shall ensure the reimbursement, without delay, of:
   — the fees paid to experts and interpreters, and
   — the costs occasioned by the application of Article 10(3) and(4).
   The duty for the parties to bear these fees or costs shall be governed by the law of the Member State of the requesting court.
3. Where the opinion of an expert is required, the requested court may, before executing the request, ask the requesting court for an adequate deposit or advance towards the requested costs. In all other cases, a deposit or advance shall not be a condition for the execution of a request.
   The deposit or advance shall be made by the parties if that is provided for by the law of the Member State of the requesting court.

CHAPTER III
FINAL PROVISIONS

Article 19
Implementing rules

1. The Commission shall draw up and regularly update a manual, which shall also be available electronically, containing the information provided by the Member States in accordance with Article 22 and the agreements or arrangements in force, according to Article 21.
2. The updating or making of technical amendments to the standard forms set out in the Annex shall be carried out in accordance with the advisory procedure set out in Article 20(2).

Article 20
Committee

1. The Commission shall be assisted by a Committee.
2. Where reference is made to this paragraph, Articles 3 and 7 of Decision 1999/468/EC shall apply.
3. The Committee shall adopt its Rules of Procedure.

Article 21
Relationship with existing or future agreements or arrangements between Member States

1. This Regulation shall, in relation to matters to which it applies, prevail over other provisions contained in bilateral or multilateral agreements or arrangements concluded by the Member States and in particular the Hague Convention of 1 March 1954 on Civil Procedure and the Hague Convention of 18 March 1970

on the Taking of Evidence Abroad in Civil or Commercial Matters, in relations between the Member States party thereto.

2. This Regulation shall not preclude Member States from maintaining or concluding agreements or arrangements between two or more of them to further facilitate the taking of evidence, provided that they are compatible with this Regulation.
3. Member States shall send to the Commission:
   (a) by 1 July 2003, a copy of the agreements or arrangements maintained between the Member States referred to in paragraph 2;
   (b) a copy of the agreements or arrangements concluded between the Member States referred to in paragraph 2 as well as drafts of such agreements or arrangements which they intend to adopt; and
   (c) any denunciation of, or amendments to, these agreements or arrangements.

Article 22
Communication

By 1 July 2003 each Member State shall communicate to the Commission the following:

(a) the list pursuant to Article 2(2) indicating the territorial and, where appropriate, the special jurisdiction of the courts;
(b) the names and addresses of the central bodies and competent authorities pursuant to Article 3, indicating their territorial jurisdiction;
(c) the technical means for the receipt of requests available to the courts on the list pursuant to Article 2(2);
(d) the languages accepted for the requests as referred to in Article 5.

Member States shall inform the Commission of any subsequent changes to this information.

Article 23
Review

No later than 1 January 2007, and every five years thereafter, the Commission shall present to the European Parliament, the Council and the Economic and Social Committee a report on the application of this Regulation, paying special attention to the practical application of Article 3(1)(c) and 3, and Articles 17 and 18.

Article 24
Entry into force

1. This Regulation shall enter into force on 1 July 2001.
2. This Regulation shall apply from 1 January 2004, except for Articles 19, 21 and 22, which shall apply from 1 July 2001.

This Regulation shall be binding in its entirety and directly applicable in the Member States in accordance with the Treaty establishing the European Community.

Done at Brussels, 28 May 2001.

For the Council
The President
T. BODSTROM

[Note that annexes have been removed from this appendix.]

Council Regulation (EC) No 44/2001

of 22 December 2000

on jurisdiction and the recognition and enforcement of judgments in civil and commercial matters

THE COUNCIL OF THE EUROPEAN UNION,

Having regard to the Treaty establishing the European Community, and in particular Article 61(c) and Article 67(1) thereof,

Having regard to the proposal from the Commission,[1]

Having regard to the opinion of the European Parliament,[2]

Having regard to the opinion of the Economic and Social Committee,[3]

Whereas:

(1) The Community has set itself the objective of maintaining and developing an area of freedom, security and justice, in which the free movement of persons is ensured. In order to establish progressively such an area, the Community should adopt, amongst other things, the measures relating to judicial cooperation in civil matters which are necessary for the sound operation of the internal market.

(2) Certain differences between national rules governing jurisdiction and recognition of judgments hamper the sound operation of the internal market. Provisions to unify the rules of conflict of jurisdiction in civil and commercial matters and to simplify the formalities with a view to rapid and simple recognition and enforcement of judgments from Member States bound by this Regulation are essential.

(3) This area is within the field of judicial cooperation in civil matters within the meaning of Article 65 of the Treaty.

[1] OJ C 376, 28.12.1999, p. 1.

[2] Opinion delivered on 21 September 2000 (not yet published in the Official Journal).

[3] OJ C 117, 26.4.2000, p. 6.

(4) In accordance with the principles of subsidiarity and proportionality as set out in Article 5 of the Treaty, the objectives of this Regulation cannot be sufficiently achieved by the Member States and can therefore be better achieved by the Community. This Regulation confines itself to the minimum required in order to achieve those objectives and does not go beyond what is necessary for that purpose.

(5) On 27 September 1968 the Member States, acting under Article 293, fourth indent, of the Treaty, concluded the Brussels Convention on Jurisdiction and the Enforcement of Judgments in Civil and Commercial Matters, as amended by Conventions on the Accession of the New Member States to that Convention (hereinafter referred to as the 'Brussels Convention').[4] On 16 September 1988 Member States and EFTA States concluded the Lugano Convention on Jurisdiction and the Enforcement of Judgments in Civil and Commercial Matters, which is a parallel Convention to the 1968 Brussels Convention. Work has been undertaken for the revision of those Conventions, and the Council has approved the content of the revised texts. Continuity in the results achieved in that revision should be ensured.

(6) In order to attain the objective of free movement of judgments in civil and commercial matters, it is necessary and appropriate that the rules governing jurisdiction and the recognition and enforcement of judgments be governed by a Community legal instrument which is binding and directly applicable.

(7) The scope of this Regulation must cover all the main civil and commercial matters apart from certain well-defined matters.

(8) There must be a link between proceedings to which this Regulation applies and the territory of the Member States bound by this Regulation. Accordingly common rules on jurisdiction should, in principle, apply when the defendant is domiciled in one of those Member States.

(9) A defendant not domiciled in a Member State is in general subject to national rules of jurisdiction applicable in the territory of the Member State of the court seised, and a defendant domiciled in a Member State not bound by this Regulation must remain subject to the Brussels Convention.

(10) For the purposes of the free movement of judgments, judgments given in a Member State bound by this Regulation should be recognised and enforced in another Member State bound by this Regulation, even if the judgment debtor is domiciled in a third State.

(11) The rules of jurisdiction must be highly predictable and founded on the principle that jurisdiction is generally based on the defendant's domicile and

[4] OJ L 299, 31.12.1972, p. 32. OJ L 304, 30.10.1978, p. 1. OJ L 388, 31.12.1982, p. 1. OJ L 285, 3.10.1989, p. 1. OJ C 15, 15.1.1997, p. 1.

jurisdiction must always be available on this ground save in a few well-defined situations in which the subject-matter of the litigation or the autonomy of the parties warrants a different linking factor. The domicile of a legal person must be defined autonomously so as to make the common rules more transparent and avoid conflicts of jurisdiction.

(12) In addition to the defendant's domicile, there should be alternative grounds of jurisdiction based on a close link between the court and the action or in order to facilitate the sound administration of justice.

(13) In relation to insurance, consumer contracts and employment, the weaker party should be protected by rules of jurisdiction more favourable to his interests than the general rules provide for.

(14) The autonomy of the parties to a contract, other than an insurance, consumer or employment contract, where only limited autonomy to determine the courts having jurisdiction is allowed, must be respected subject to the exclusive grounds of jurisdiction laid down in this Regulation.

(15) In the interests of the harmonious administration of justice it is necessary to minimise the possibility of concurrent proceedings and to ensure that irreconcilable judgments will not be given in two Member States. There must be a clear and effective mechanism for resolving cases of lis pendens and related actions and for obviating problems flowing from national differences as to the determination of the time when a case is regarded as pending. For the purposes of this Regulation that time should be defined autonomously.

(16) Mutual trust in the administration of justice in the Community justifies judgments given in a Member State being recognised automatically without the need for any procedure except in cases of dispute.

(17) By virtue of the same principle of mutual trust, the procedure for making enforceable in one Member State a judgment given in another must be efficient and rapid. To that end, the declaration that a judgment is enforceable should be issued virtually automatically after purely formal checks of the documents supplied, without there being any possibility for the court to raise of its own motion any of the grounds for non-enforcement provided for by this Regulation.

(18) However, respect for the rights of the defence means that the defendant should be able to appeal in an adversarial procedure, against the declaration of enforceability, if he considers one of the grounds for non-enforcement to be present. Redress procedures should also be available to the claimant where his application for a declaration of enforceability has been rejected.

(19) Continuity between the Brussels Convention and this Regulation should be ensured, and transitional provisions should be laid down to that end. The same need for continuity applies as regards the interpretation of the Brussels Convention by the Court of Justice of the European Communities and the 1971

Protocol[5] should remain applicable also to cases already pending when this Regulation enters into force.

(20) The United Kingdom and Ireland, in accordance with Article 3 of the Protocol on the position of the United Kingdom and Ireland annexed to the Treaty on European Union and to the Treaty establishing the European Community, have given notice of their wish to take part in the adoption and application of this Regulation.

(21) Denmark, in accordance with Articles 1 and 2 of the Protocol on the position of Denmark annexed to the Treaty on European Union and to the Treaty establishing the European Community, is not participating in the adoption of this Regulation, and is therefore not bound by it nor subject to its application.

(22) Since the Brussels Convention remains in force in relations between Denmark and the Member States that are bound by this Regulation, both the Convention and the 1971 Protocol continue to apply between Denmark and the Member States bound by this Regulation.

(23) The Brussels Convention also continues to apply to the territories of the Member States which fall within the territorial scope of that Convention and which are excluded from this Regulation pursuant to Article 299 of the Treaty.

(24) Likewise for the sake of consistency, this Regulation should not affect rules governing jurisdiction and the recognition of judgments contained in specific Community instruments.

(25) Respect for international commitments entered into by the Member States means that this Regulation should not affect conventions relating to specific matters to which the Member States are parties.

(26) The necessary flexibility should be provided for in the basic rules of this Regulation in order to take account of the specific procedural rules of certain Member States. Certain provisions of the Protocol annexed to the Brussels Convention should accordingly be incorporated in this Regulation.

(27) In order to allow a harmonious transition in certain areas which were the subject of special provisions in the Protocol annexed to the Brussels Convention, this Regulation lays down, for a transitional period, provisions taking into consideration the specific situation in certain Member States.

(28) No later than five years after entry into force of this Regulation the Commission will present a report on its application and, if need be, submit proposals for adaptations.

(29) The Commission will have to adjust Annexes I to IV on the rules of national jurisdiction, the courts or competent authorities and redress procedures available on the basis of the amendments forwarded by the Member State concerned; amendments made to Annexes V and VI should be adopted in accordance with

[5] OJ L 204, 2.8.1975, p. 28. OJ L 304, 30.10.1978, p. 1. OJ L 388, 31.12.1982, p. 1. OJ L 285, 3.10.1989, p. 1. OJ C 15, 15.1.1997, p. 1. For a consolidated text see OJ C 27, 26.1.1998, p. 28.

Council Decision 1999/468/EC of 28 June 1999 laying down the procedures for the exercise of implementing powers conferred on the Commission,[6]

HAS ADOPTED THIS REGULATION:

CHAPTER I
SCOPE

Article 1

1. This Regulation shall apply in civil and commercial matters whatever the nature of the court or tribunal. It shall not extend, in particular, to revenue, customs or administrative matters.
2. The Regulation shall not apply to:
   (a) the status or legal capacity of natural persons, rights in property arising out of a matrimonial relationship, wills and succession;
   (b) bankruptcy, proceedings relating to the winding-up of insolvent companies or other legal persons, judicial arrangements, compositions and analogous proceedings;
   (c) social security;
   (d) arbitration.
3. In this Regulation, the term 'Member State' shall mean Member States with the exception of Denmark.

CHAPTER II
JURISDICTION

Section 1
General Provisions

Article 2

1. Subject to this Regulation, persons domiciled in a Member State shall, whatever their nationality, be sued in the courts of that Member State.
2. Persons who are not nationals of the Member State in which they are domiciled shall be governed by the rules of jurisdiction applicable to nationals of that State.

Article 3

1. Persons domiciled in a Member State may be sued in the courts of another Member State only by virtue of the rules set out in Sections 2 to 7 of this Chapter.

[6] OJ L 184, 17.7.1999, p. 23.

2. In particular the rules of national jurisdiction set out in Annex I shall not be applicable as against them.

Article 4

1. If the defendant is not domiciled in a Member State, the jurisdiction of the courts of each Member State shall, subject to Articles 22 and 23, be determined by the law of that Member State.
2. As against such a defendant, any person domiciled in a Member State may, whatever his nationality, avail himself in that State of the rules of jurisdiction there in force, and in particular those specified in Annex I, in the same way as the nationals of that State.

Section 2
Special jurisdiction

Article 5

A person domiciled in a Member State may, in another Member State, be sued:

1. (a) in matters relating to a contract, in the courts for the place of performance of the obligation in question;
   (b) for the purpose of this provision and unless otherwise agreed, the place of performance of the obligation in question shall be:
   — in the case of the sale of goods, the place in a Member State where, under the contract, the goods were delivered or should have been delivered,
   — in the case of the provision of services, the place in a Member State where, under the contract, the services were provided or should have been provided,
   (c) if subparagraph (b) does not apply then subparagraph (a) applies;
2. in matters relating to maintenance, in the courts for the place where the maintenance creditor is domiciled or habitually resident or, if the matter is ancillary to proceedings concerning the status of a person, in the court which, according to its own law, has jurisdiction to entertain those proceedings, unless that jurisdiction is based solely on the nationality of one of the parties;
3. in matters relating to tort, delict or quasi-delict, in the courts for the place where the harmful event occurred or may occur;
4. as regards a civil claim for damages or restitution which is based on an act giving rise to criminal proceedings, in the court seised of those proceedings, to the extent that that court has jurisdiction under its own law to entertain civil proceedings;
5. as regards a dispute arising out of the operations of a branch, agency or other establishment, in the courts for the place in which the branch, agency or other establishment is situated;

6. as settlor, trustee or beneficiary of a trust created by the operation of a statute, or by a written instrument, or created orally and evidenced in writing, in the courts of the Member State in which the trust is domiciled;
7. as regards a dispute concerning the payment of remuneration claimed in respect of the salvage of a cargo or freight, in the court under the authority of which the cargo or freight in question:
   (a) has been arrested to secure such payment, or
   (b) could have been so arrested, but bail or other security has been given;
   provided that this provision shall apply only if it is claimed that the defendant has an interest in the cargo or freight or had such an interest at the time of salvage.

Article 6

A person domiciled in a Member State may also be sued:

1. where he is one of a number of defendants, in the courts for the place where any one of them is domiciled, provided the claims are so closely connected that it is expedient to hear and determine them together to avoid the risk of irreconcilable judgments resulting from separate proceedings;
2. as a third party in an action on a warranty or guarantee or in any other third party proceedings, in the court seised of the original proceedings, unless these were instituted solely with the object of removing him from the jurisdiction of the court which would be competent in his case;
3. on a counter-claim arising from the same contract or facts on which the original claim was based, in the court in which the original claim is pending;
4. in matters relating to a contract, if the action may be combined with an action against the same defendant in matters relating to rights *in rem* in immovable property, in the court of the Member State in which the property is situated.

Article 7

Where by virtue of this Regulation a court of a Member State has jurisdiction in actions relating to liability from the use or operation of a ship, that court, or any other court substituted for this purpose by the internal law of that Member State, shall also have jurisdiction over claims for limitation of such liability.

Section 3
Jurisdiction in matters relating to insurance

Article 8

In matters relating to insurance, jurisdiction shall be determined by this Section, without prejudice to Article 4 and point 5 of Article 5.

Article 9

1. An insurer domiciled in a Member State may be sued:
   (a) in the courts of the Member State where he is domiciled, or
   (b) in another Member State, in the case of actions brought by the policyholder, the insured or a beneficiary, in the courts for the place where the plaintiff is domiciled,
   (c) if he is a co-insurer, in the courts of a Member State in which proceedings are brought against the leading insurer.
2. An insurer who is not domiciled in a Member State but has a branch, agency or other establishment in one of the Member States shall, in disputes arising out of the operations of the branch, agency or establishment, be deemed to be domiciled in that Member State.

Article 10

In respect of liability insurance or insurance of immovable property, the insurer may in addition be sued in the courts for the place where the harmful event occurred. The same applies if movable and immovable property are covered by the same insurance policy and both are adversely affected by the same contingency.

Article 11

1. In respect of liability insurance, the insurer may also, if the law of the court permits it, be joined in proceedings which the injured party has brought against the insured.
2. Articles 8, 9 and 10 shall apply to actions brought by the injured party directly against the insurer, where such direct actions are permitted.
3. If the law governing such direct actions provides that the policyholder or the insured may be joined as a party to the action, the same court shall have jurisdiction over them.

Article 12

1. Without prejudice to Article 11(3), an insurer may bring proceedings only in the courts of the Member State in which the defendant is domiciled, irrespective of whether he is the policyholder, the insured or a beneficiary.
2. The provisions of this Section shall not affect the right to bring a counter-claim in the court in which, in accordance with this Section, the original claim is pending.

Article 13

The provisions of this Section may be departed from only by an agreement:

1. which is entered into after the dispute has arisen, or

2. which allows the policyholder, the insured or a beneficiary to bring proceedings in courts other than those indicated in this Section, or
3. which is concluded between a policyholder and an insurer, both of whom are at the time of conclusion of the contract domiciled or habitually resident in the same Member State, and which has the effect of conferring jurisdiction on the courts of that State even if the harmful event were to occur abroad, provided that such an agreement is not contrary to the law of that State, or
4. which is concluded with a policyholder who is not domiciled in a Member State, except in so far as the insurance is compulsory or relates to immovable property in a Member State, or
5. which relates to a contract of insurance in so far as it covers one or more of the risks set out in Article 14.

Article 14

The following are the risks referred to in Article 13(5):

1. any loss of or damage to:
   (a) seagoing ships, installations situated offshore or on the high seas, or aircraft, arising from perils which relate to their use for commercial purposes;
   (b) goods in transit other than passengers' baggage where the transit consists of or includes carriage by such ships or aircraft;
2. any liability, other than for bodily injury to passengers or loss of or damage to their baggage:
   (a) arising out of the use or operation of ships, installations or aircraft as referred to in point 1(a) in so far as, in respect of the latter, the law of the Member State in which such aircraft are registered does not prohibit agreements on jurisdiction regarding insurance of such risks;
   (b) for loss or damage caused by goods in transit as described in point 1(b);
3. any financial loss connected with the use or operation of ships, installations or aircraft as referred to in point 1(a), in particular loss of freight or charter-hire;
4. any risk or interest connected with any of those referred to in points 1 to 3;
5. notwithstanding points 1 to 4, all 'large risks' as defined in Council Directive 73/239/EEC[7] as amended by Council Directives 88/357/EEC[8] and 90/618/EEC,[9] as they may be amended.

[7] OJ L 228, 16.8.1973, p. 3. Directive as last amended by Directive 2000/26/EC of the European Parliament and of the Council (OJ L 181, 20.7.2000, p. 65).

[8] OJ L 172, 4.7.1988, p. 1. Directive as last amended by Directive 2000/26/EC.

[9] OJ L 330, 29.11.1990, p. 44.

Section 4
Jurisdiction over consumer contracts

Article 15

1. In matters relating to a contract concluded by a person, the consumer, for a purpose which can be regarded as being outside his trade or profession, jurisdiction shall be determined by this Section, without prejudice to Article 4 and point 5 of Article 5, if:
   (a) it is a contract for the sale of goods on instalment credit terms; or
   (b) it is a contract for a loan repayable by instalments, or for any other form of credit, made to finance the sale of goods; or
   (c) in all other cases, the contract has been concluded with a person who pursues commercial or professional activities in the Member State of the consumer's domicile or, by any means, directs such activities to that Member State or to several States including that Member State, and the contract falls within the scope of such activities.
2. Where a consumer enters into a contract with a party who is not domiciled in the Member State but has a branch, agency or other establishment in one of the Member States, that party shall, in disputes arising out of the operations of the branch, agency or establishment, be deemed to be domiciled in that State.
3. This Section shall not apply to a contract of transport other than a contract which, for an inclusive price, provides for a combination of travel and accommodation.

Article 16

1. A consumer may bring proceedings against the other party to a contract either in the courts of the Member State in which that party is domiciled or in the courts for the place where the consumer is domiciled.
2. Proceedings may be brought against a consumer by the other party to the contract only in the courts of the Member State in which the consumer is domiciled.
3. This Article shall not affect the right to bring a counter-claim in the court in which, in accordance with this Section, the original claim is pending.

Article 17

The provisions of this Section may be departed from only by an agreement:

1. which is entered into after the dispute has arisen; or
2. which allows the consumer to bring proceedings in courts other than those indicated in this Section; or
3. which is entered into by the consumer and the other party to the contract, both of whom are at the time of conclusion of the contract domiciled or habitually

resident in the same Member State, and which confers jurisdiction on the courts of that Member State, provided that such an agreement is not contrary to the law of that Member State.

Section 5
Jurisdiction over individual contracts of employment

Article 18

1. In matters relating to individual contracts of employment, jurisdiction shall be determined by this Section, without prejudice to Article 4 and point 5 of Article 5.
2. Where an employee enters into an individual contract of employment with an employer who is not domiciled in a Member State but has a branch, agency or other establishment in one of the Member States, the employer shall, in disputes arising out of the operations of the branch, agency or establishment, be deemed to be domiciled in that Member State.

Article 19

An employer domiciled in a Member State may be sued:

1. in the courts of the Member State where he is domiciled; or
2. in another Member State:
   (a) in the courts for the place where the employee habitually carries out his work or in the courts for the last place where he did so, or
   (b) if the employee does not or did not habitually carry out his work in any one country, in the courts for the place where the business which engaged the employee is or was situated.

Article 20

1. An employer may bring proceedings only in the courts of the Member State in which the employee is domiciled.
2. The provisions of this Section shall not affect the right to bring a counter-claim in the court in which, in accordance with this Section, the original claim is pending.

Article 21

The provisions of this Section may be departed from only by an agreement on jurisdiction:

1. which is entered into after the dispute has arisen; or
2. which allows the employee to bring proceedings in courts other than those indicated in this Section.

Section 6
Exclusive jurisdiction

Article 22

The following courts shall have exclusive jurisdiction, regardless of domicile:

1. in proceedings which have as their object rights *in rem* in immovable property or tenancies of immovable property, the courts of the Member State in which the property is situated.
   However, in proceedings which have as their object tenancies of immovable property concluded for temporary private use for a maximum period of six consecutive months, the courts of the Member State in which the defendant is domiciled shall also have jurisdiction, provided that the tenant is a natural person and that the landlord and the tenant are domiciled in the same Member State;
2. in proceedings which have as their object the validity of the constitution, the nullity or the dissolution of companies or other legal persons or associations of natural or legal persons, or of the validity of the decisions of their organs, the courts of the Member State in which the company, legal person or association has its seat. In order to determine that seat, the court shall apply its rules of private international law;
3. in proceedings which have as their object the validity of entries in public registers, the courts of the Member State in which the register is kept;
4. in proceedings concerned with the registration or validity of patents, trade marks, designs, or other similar rights required to be deposited or registered, the courts of the Member State in which the deposit or registration has been applied for, has taken place or is under the terms of a Community instrument or an international convention deemed to have taken place.
   Without prejudice to the jurisdiction of the European Patent Office under the Convention on the Grant of European Patents, signed at Munich on 5 October 1973, the courts of each Member State shall have exclusive jurisdiction, regardless of domicile, in proceedings concerned with the registration or validity of any European patent granted for that State;
5. in proceedings concerned with the enforcement of judgments, the courts of the Member State in which the judgment has been or is to be enforced.

Section 7
Prorogation of jurisdiction

Article 23

1. If the parties, one or more of whom is domiciled in a Member State, have agreed that a court or the courts of a Member State are to have jurisdiction to settle any

disputes which have arisen or which may arise in connection with a particular legal relationship, that court or those courts shall have jurisdiction. Such jurisdiction shall be exclusive unless the parties have agreed otherwise. Such an agreement conferring jurisdiction shall be either:

(a) in writing or evidenced in writing; or
(b) in a form which accords with practices which the parties have established between themselves; or
(c) in international trade or commerce, in a form which accords with a usage of which the parties are or ought to have been aware and which in such trade or commerce is widely known to, and regularly observed by, parties to contracts of the type involved in the particular trade or commerce concerned.

2. Any communication by electronic means which provides a durable record of the agreement shall be equivalent to 'writing'.
3. Where such an agreement is concluded by parties, none of whom is domiciled in a Member State, the courts of other Member States shall have no jurisdiction over their disputes unless the court or courts chosen have declined jurisdiction.
4. The court or courts of a Member State on which a trust instrument has conferred jurisdiction shall have exclusive jurisdiction in any proceedings brought against a settlor, trustee or beneficiary, if relations between these persons or their rights or obligations under the trust are involved.
5. Agreements or provisions of a trust instrument conferring jurisdiction shall have no legal force if they are contrary to Articles 13, 17 or 21, or if the courts whose jurisdiction they purport to exclude have exclusive jurisdiction by virtue of Article 22.

Article 24

Apart from jurisdiction derived from other provisions of this Regulation, a court of a Member State before which a defendant enters an appearance shall have jurisdiction. This rule shall not apply where appearance was entered to contest the jurisdiction, or where another court has exclusive jurisdiction by virtue of Article 22.

Section 8
Examination as to jurisdiction and admissibility

Article 25

Where a court of a Member State is seised of a claim which is principally concerned with a matter over which the courts of another Member State have exclusive jurisdiction by virtue of Article 22, it shall declare of its own motion that it has no jurisdiction.

Article 26

1. Where a defendant domiciled in one Member State is sued in a court of another Member State and does not enter an appearance, the court shall declare of its own motion that it has no jurisdiction unless its jurisdiction is derived from the provisions of this Regulation.
2. The court shall stay the proceedings so long as it is not shown that the defendant has been able to receive the document instituting the proceedings or an equivalent document in sufficient time to enable him to arrange for his defence, or that all necessary steps have been taken to this end.
3. Article 19 of Council Regulation (EC) No 1348/2000 of 29 May 2000 on the service in the Member States of judicial and extrajudicial documents in civil or commercial matters[10] shall apply instead of the provisions of paragraph 2 if the document instituting the proceedings or an equivalent document had to be transmitted from one Member State to another pursuant to this Regulation.
4. Where the provisions of Regulation (EC) No 1348/2000 are not applicable, Article 15 of the Hague Convention of 15 November 1965 on the Service Abroad of Judicial and Extrajudicial Documents in Civil or Commercial Matters shall apply if the document instituting the proceedings or an equivalent document had to be transmitted pursuant to that Convention.

Section 9
Lis pendens—related actions

Article 27

1. Where proceedings involving the same cause of action and between the same parties are brought in the courts of different Member States, any court other than the court first seised shall of its own motion stay its proceedings until such time as the jurisdiction of the court first seised is established.
2. Where the jurisdiction of the court first seised is established, any court other than the court first seised shall decline jurisdiction in favour of that court.

Article 28

1. Where related actions are pending in the courts of different Member States, any court other than the court first seised may stay its proceedings.
2. Where these actions are pending at first instance, any court other than the court first seised may also, on the application of one of the parties, decline jurisdiction if the court first seised has jurisdiction over the actions in question and its law permits the consolidation thereof.

[10] OJ L 160, 30.6.2000, p. 37.

3. For the purposes of this Article, actions are deemed to be related where they are so closely connected that it is expedient to hear and determine them together to avoid the risk of irreconcilable judgments resulting from separate proceedings.

Article 29

Where actions come within the exclusive jurisdiction of several courts, any court other than the court first seised shall decline jurisdiction in favour of that court.

Article 30

For the purposes of this Section, a court shall be deemed to be seised:

1. at the time when the document instituting the proceedings or an equivalent document is lodged with the court, provided that the plaintiff has not subsequently failed to take the steps he was required to take to have service effected on the defendant, or
2. if the document has to be served before being lodged with the court, at the time when it is received by the authority responsible for service, provided that the plaintiff has not subsequently failed to take the steps he was required to take to have the document lodged with the court.

Section 10
Provisional, including protective, measures

Article 31

Application may be made to the courts of a Member State for such provisional, including protective, measures as may be available under the law of that State, even if, under this Regulation, the courts of another Member State have jurisdiction as to the substance of the matter.

CHAPTER III
RECOGNITION AND ENFORCEMENT

Article 32

For the purposes of this Regulation, 'judgment' means any judgment given by a court or tribunal of a Member State, whatever the judgment may be called, including a decree, order, decision or writ of execution, as well as the determination of costs or expenses by an officer of the court.

Section 1
Recognition

Article 33

1. A judgment given in a Member State shall be recognised in the other Member States without any special procedure being required.
2. Any interested party who raises the recognition of a judgment as the principal issue in a dispute may, in accordance with the procedures provided for in Sections 2 and 3 of this Chapter, apply for a decision that the judgment be recognised.
3. If the outcome of proceedings in a court of a Member State depends on the determination of an incidental question of recognition that court shall have jurisdiction over that question.

Article 34

A judgment shall not be recognised:

1. if such recognition is manifestly contrary to public policy in the Member State in which recognition is sought;
2. where it was given in default of appearance, if the defendant was not served with the document which instituted the proceedings or with an equivalent document in sufficient time and in such a way as to enable him to arrange for his defence, unless the defendant failed to commence proceedings to challenge the judgment when it was possible for him to do so;
3. if it is irreconcilable with a judgment given in a dispute between the same parties in the Member State in which recognition is sought;
4. if it is irreconcilable with an earlier judgment given in another Member State or in a third State involving the same cause of action and between the same parties, provided that the earlier judgment fulfils the conditions necessary for its recognition in the Member State addressed.

Article 35

1. Moreover, a judgment shall not be recognised if it conflicts with Sections 3, 4 or 6 of Chapter II, or in a case provided for in Article 72.
2. In its examination of the grounds of jurisdiction referred to in the foregoing paragraph, the court or authority applied to shall be bound by the findings of fact on which the court of the Member State of origin based its jurisdiction.
3. Subject to the paragraph 1, the jurisdiction of the court of the Member State of origin may not be reviewed. The test of public policy referred to in point 1 of Article 34 may not be applied to the rules relating to jurisdiction.

Article 36

Under no circumstances may a foreign judgment be reviewed as to its substance.

Article 37

1. A court of a Member State in which recognition is sought of a judgment given in another Member State may stay the proceedings if an ordinary appeal against the judgment has been lodged.
2. A court of a Member State in which recognition is sought of a judgment given in Ireland or the United Kingdom may stay the proceedings if enforcement is suspended in the State of origin, by reason of an appeal.

Section 2
Enforcement

Article 38

1. A judgment given in a Member State and enforceable in that State shall be enforced in another Member State when, on the application of any interested party, it has been declared enforceable there.
2. However, in the United Kingdom, such a judgment shall be enforced in England and Wales, in Scotland, or in Northern Ireland when, on the application of any interested party, it has been registered for enforcement in that part of the United Kingdom.

Article 39

1. The application shall be submitted to the court or competent authority indicated in the list in Annex II.
2. The local jurisdiction shall be determined by reference to the place of domicile of the party against whom enforcement is sought, or to the place of enforcement.

Article 40

1. The procedure for making the application shall be governed by the law of the Member State in which enforcement is sought.
2. The applicant must give an address for service of process within the area of jurisdiction of the court applied to. However, if the law of the Member State in which enforcement is sought does not provide for the furnishing of such an address, the applicant shall appoint a representative *ad litem*.
3. The documents referred to in Article 53 shall be attached to the application.

Article 41

The judgment shall be declared enforceable immediately on completion of the formalities in Article 53 without any review under Articles 34 and 35. The party against whom enforcement is sought shall not at this stage of the proceedings be entitled to make any submissions on the application.

Article 42

1. The decision on the application for a declaration of enforceability shall forthwith be brought to the notice of the applicant in accordance with the procedure laid down by the law of the Member State in which enforcement is sought.
2. The declaration of enforceability shall be served on the party against whom enforcement is sought, accompanied by the judgment, if not already served on that party.

Article 43

1. The decision on the application for a declaration of enforceability may be appealed against by either party.
2. The appeal is to be lodged with the court indicated in the list in Annex III.
3. The appeal shall be dealt with in accordance with the rules governing procedure in contradictory matters.
4. If the party against whom enforcement is sought fails to appear before the appellate court in proceedings concerning an appeal brought by the applicant, Article 26(2) to (4) shall apply even where the party against whom enforcement is sought is not domiciled in any of the Member States.
5. An appeal against the declaration of enforceability is to be lodged within one month of service thereof. If the party against whom enforcement is sought is domiciled in a Member State other than that in which the declaration of enforceability was given, the time for appealing shall be two months and shall run from the date of service, either on him in person or at his residence. No extension of time may be granted on account of distance.

Article 44

The judgment given on the appeal may be contested only by the appeal referred to in Annex IV.

Article 45

1. The court with which an appeal is lodged under Article 43 or Article 44 shall refuse or revoke a declaration of enforceability only on one of the grounds specified in Articles 34 and 35. It shall give its decision without delay.

2. Under no circumstances may the foreign judgment be reviewed as to its substance.

Article 46

1. The court with which an appeal is lodged under Article 43 or Article 44 may, on the application of the party against whom enforcement is sought, stay the proceedings if an ordinary appeal has been lodged against the judgment in the Member State of origin or if the time for such an appeal has not yet expired; in the latter case, the court may specify the time within which such an appeal is to be lodged.
2. Where the judgment was given in Ireland or the United Kingdom, any form of appeal available in the Member State of origin shall be treated as an ordinary appeal for the purposes of paragraph 1.
3. The court may also make enforcement conditional on the provision of such security as it shall determine.

Article 47

1. When a judgment must be recognised in accordance with this Regulation, nothing shall prevent the applicant from availing himself of provisional, including protective, measures in accordance with the law of the Member State requested without a declaration of enforceability under Article 41 being required.
2. The declaration of enforceability shall carry with it the power to proceed to any protective measures.
3. During the time specified for an appeal pursuant to Article 43(5) against the declaration of enforceability and until any such appeal has been determined, no measures of enforcement may be taken other than protective measures against the property of the party against whom enforcement is sought.

Article 48

1. Where a foreign judgment has been given in respect of several matters and the declaration of enforceability cannot be given for all of them, the court or competent authority shall give it for one or more of them.
2. An applicant may request a declaration of enforceability limited to parts of a judgment.

Article 49

A foreign judgment which orders a periodic payment by way of a penalty shall be enforceable in the Member State in which enforcement is sought only if the amount of the payment has been finally determined by the courts of the Member State of origin.

Article 50

An applicant who, in the Member State of origin has benefited from complete or partial legal aid or exemption from costs or expenses, shall be entitled, in the procedure provided for in this Section, to benefit from the most favourable legal aid or the most extensive exemption from costs or expenses provided for by the law of the Member State addressed.

Article 51

No security, bond or deposit, however described, shall be required of a party who in one Member State applies for enforcement of a judgment given in another Member State on the ground that he is a foreign national or that he is not domiciled or resident in the State in which enforcement is sought.

Article 52

In proceedings for the issue of a declaration of enforceability, no charge, duty or fee calculated by reference to the value of the matter at issue may be levied in the Member State in which enforcement is sought.

Section 3
Common provisions

Article 53

1. A party seeking recognition or applying for a declaration of enforceability shall produce a copy of the judgment which satisfies the conditions necessary to establish its authenticity.
2. A party applying for a declaration of enforceability shall also produce the certificate referred to in Article 54, without prejudice to Article 55.

Article 54

The court or competent authority of a Member State where a judgment was given shall issue, at the request of any interested party, a certificate using the standard form in Annex V to this Regulation.

Article 55

1. If the certificate referred to in Article 54 is not produced, the court or competent authority may specify a time for its production or accept an equivalent document or, if it considers that it has sufficient information before it, dispense with its production.

2. If the court or competent authority so requires, a translation of the documents shall be produced. The translation shall be certified by a person qualified to do so in one of the Member States.

Article 56

No legalisation or other similar formality shall be required in respect of the documents referred to in Article 53 or Article 55(2), or in respect of a document appointing a representative *ad litem*.

CHAPTER IV
AUTHENTIC INSTRUMENTS AND COURT SETTLEMENTS

Article 57

1. A document which has been formally drawn up or registered as an authentic instrument and is enforceable in one Member State shall, in another Member State, be declared enforceable there, on application made in accordance with the procedures provided for in Articles 38, et seq. The court with which an appeal is lodged under Article 43 or Article 44 shall refuse or revoke a declaration of enforceability only if enforcement of the instrument is manifestly contrary to public policy in the Member State addressed.
2. Arrangements relating to maintenance obligations concluded with administrative authorities or authenticated by them shall also be regarded as authentic instruments within the meaning of paragraph 1.
3. The instrument produced must satisfy the conditions necessary to establish its authenticity in the Member State of origin.
4. Section 3 of Chapter III shall apply as appropriate. The competent authority of a Member State where an authentic instrument was drawn up or registered shall issue, at the request of any interested party, a certificate using the standard form in Annex VI to this Regulation.

Article 58

A settlement which has been approved by a court in the course of proceedings and is enforceable in the Member State in which it was concluded shall be enforceable in the State addressed under the same conditions as authentic instruments. The court or competent authority of a Member State where a court settlement was approved shall issue, at the request of any interested party, a certificate using the standard form in Annex V to this Regulation.

CHAPTER V
GENERAL PROVISIONS

Article 59

1. In order to determine whether a party is domiciled in the Member State whose courts are seised of a matter, the court shall apply its internal law.
2. If a party is not domiciled in the Member State whose courts are seised of the matter, then, in order to determine whether the party is domiciled in another Member State, the court shall apply the law of that Member State.

Article 60

1. For the purposes of this Regulation, a company or other legal person or association of natural or legal persons is domiciled at the place where it has its:
   (a) statutory seat, or
   (b) central administration, or
   (c) principal place of business.
2. For the purposes of the United Kingdom and Ireland 'statutory seat' means the registered office or, where there is no such office anywhere, the place of incorporation or, where there is no such place anywhere, the place under the law of which the formation took place.
3. In order to determine whether a trust is domiciled in the Member State whose courts are seised of the matter, the court shall apply its rules of private international law.

Article 61

Without prejudice to any more favourable provisions of national laws, persons domiciled in a Member State who are being prosecuted in the criminal courts of another Member State of which they are not nationals for an offence which was not intentionally committed may be defended by persons qualified to do so, even if they do not appear in person. However, the court seised of the matter may order appearance in person; in the case of failure to appear, a judgment given in the civil action without the person concerned having had the opportunity to arrange for his defence need not be recognised or enforced in the other Member States.

Article 62

In Sweden, in summary proceedings concerning orders to pay (*betalningsfdreldggande*) and assistance (*handrdckning*), the expression 'court' includes the 'Swedish enforcement service' (*kronofogdemyndighet*).

Article 63

1. A person domiciled in the territory of the Grand Duchy of Luxembourg and sued in the court of another Member State pursuant to Article 5(1) may refuse to submit to the jurisdiction of that court if the final place of delivery of the goods or provision of the services is in Luxembourg.
2. Where, under paragraph 1, the final place of delivery of the goods or provision of the services is in Luxembourg, any agreement conferring jurisdiction must, in order to be valid, be accepted in writing or evidenced in writing within the meaning of Article 23(1)(a).
3. The provisions of this Article shall not apply to contracts for the provision of financial services.
4. The provisions of this Article shall apply for a period of six years from entry into force of this Regulation.

Article 64

1. In proceedings involving a dispute between the master and a member of the crew of a seagoing ship registered in Greece or in Portugal, concerning remuneration or other conditions of service, a court in a Member State shall establish whether the diplomatic or consular officer responsible for the ship has been notified of the dispute. It may act as soon as that officer has been notified.
2. The provisions of this Article shall apply for a period of six years from entry into force of this Regulation.

Article 65

1. The jurisdiction specified in Article 6(2), and Article 11 in actions on a warranty of guarantee or in any other third party proceedings may not be resorted to in Germany and Austria. Any person domiciled in another Member State may be sued in the courts:
   (a) of Germany, pursuant to Articles 68 and 72 to 74 of the Code of Civil Procedure *(Zivilprozessordnung)* concerning third-party notices,
   (b) of Austria, pursuant to Article 21 of the Code of Civil Procedure *(Zivilprozessordnung)* concerning third-party notices.
2. Judgments given in other Member States by virtue of Article 6(2), or Article 11 shall be recognised and enforced in Germany and Austria in accordance with Chapter III. Any effects which judgments given in these States may have on third parties by application of the provisions in paragraph 1 shall also be recognised in the other Member States.

CHAPTER VI
TRANSITIONAL PROVISIONS

Article 66

1. This Regulation shall apply only to legal proceedings instituted and to documents formally drawn up or registered as authentic instruments after the entry into force thereof.
2. However, if the proceedings in the Member State of origin were instituted before the entry into force of this Regulation, judgments given after that date shall be recognised and enforced in accordance with Chapter III,
   (a) if the proceedings in the Member State of origin were instituted after the entry into force of the Brussels or the Lugano Convention both in the Member State or origin and in the Member State addressed;
   (b) in all other cases, if jurisdiction was founded upon rules which accorded with those provided for either in Chapter II or in a convention concluded between the Member State of origin and the Member State addressed which was in force when the proceedings were instituted.

CHAPTER VII
RELATIONS WITH OTHER INSTRUMENTS

Article 67

This Regulation shall not prejudice the application of provisions governing jurisdiction and the recognition and enforcement of judgments in specific matters which are contained in Community instruments or in national legislation harmonised pursuant to such instruments.

Article 68

1. This Regulation shall, as between the Member States, supersede the Brussels Convention, except as regards the territories of the Member States which fall within the territorial scope of that Convention and which are excluded from this Regulation pursuant to Article 299 of the Treaty.
2. In so far as this Regulation replaces the provisions of the Brussels Convention between Member States, any reference to the Convention shall be understood as a reference to this Regulation.

Article 69

Subject to Article 66(2) and Article 70, this Regulation shall, as between Member States, supersede the following conventions and treaty concluded between two or more of them:

— the Convention between Belgium and France on Jurisdiction and the Validity and Enforcement of Judgments, Arbitration Awards and Authentic Instruments, signed at Paris on 8 July 1899,
— the Convention between Belgium and the Netherlands on Jurisdiction, Bankruptcy, and the Validity and Enforcement of Judgments, Arbitration Awards and Authentic Instruments, signed at Brussels on 28 March 1925,
— the Convention between France and Italy on the Enforcement of Judgments in Civil and Commercial Matters, signed at Rome on 3 June 1930,
— the Convention between Germany and Italy on the Recognition and Enforcement of Judgments in Civil and Commercial Matters, signed at Rome on 9 March 1936,
— the Convention between Belgium and Austria on the Reciprocal Recognition and Enforcement of Judgments and Authentic Instruments relating to Maintenance Obligations, signed at Vienna on 25 October 1957,
— the Convention between Germany and Belgium on the Mutual Recognition and Enforcement of Judgments, Arbitration Awards and Authentic Instruments in Civil and Commercial Matters, signed at Bonn on 30 June 1958,
— the Convention between the Netherlands and Italy on the Recognition and Enforcement of Judgments in Civil and Commercial Matters, signed at Rome on 17 April 1959,
— the Convention between Germany and Austria on the Reciprocal Recognition and Enforcement of Judgments, Settlements and Authentic Instruments in Civil and Commercial Matters, signed at Vienna on 6 June 1959,
— the Convention between Belgium and Austria on the Reciprocal Recognition and Enforcement of Judgments, Arbitral Awards and Authentic Instruments in Civil and Commercial Matters, signed at Vienna on 16 June 1959,
— the Convention between Greece and Germany for the Reciprocal Recognition and Enforcement of Judgments, Settlements and Authentic Instruments in Civil and Commercial Matters, signed in Athens on 4 November 1961,
— the Convention between Belgium and Italy on the Recognition and Enforcement of Judgments and other Enforceable Instruments in Civil and Commercial Matters, signed at Rome on 6 April 1962,
— the Convention between the Netherlands and Germany on the Mutual Recognition and Enforcement of Judgments and Other Enforceable Instruments in Civil and Commercial Matters, signed at The Hague on 30 August 1962,
— the Convention between the Netherlands and Austria on the Reciprocal Recognition and Enforcement of Judgments and Authentic Instruments in Civil and Commercial Matters, signed at The Hague on 6 February 1963,
— the Convention between France and Austria on the Recognition and Enforcement of Judgments and Authentic Instruments in Civil and Commercial Matters, signed at Vienna on 15 July 1966,
— the Convention between Spain and France on the Recognition and Enforcement of Judgment Arbitration Awards in Civil and Commercial Matters, signed at Paris on 28 May 1969,

— the Convention between Luxembourg and Austria on the Recognition and Enforcement of Judgments and Authentic Instruments in Civil and Commercial Matters, signed at Luxembourg on 29 July 1971,
— the Convention between Italy and Austria on the Recognition and Enforcement of Judgments in Civil and Commercial Matters, of Judicial Settlements and of Authentic Instruments, signed at Rome on 16 November 1971,
— the Convention between Spain and Italy regarding Legal Aid and the Recognition and Enforcement of Judgments in Civil and Commercial Matters, signed at Madrid on 22 May 1973,
— the Convention between Finland, Iceland, Norway, Sweden and Denmark on the Recognition and Enforcement of Judgments in Civil Matters, signed at Copenhagen on 11 October 1977,
— the Convention between Austria and Sweden on the Recognition and Enforcement of Judgments in Civil Matters, signed at Stockholm on 16 September 1982,
— the Convention between Spain and the Federal Republic of Germany on the Recognition and Enforcement of Judgments, Settlements and Enforceable Authentic Instruments in Civil and Commercial Matters, signed at Bonn on 14 November 1983,
— the Convention between Austria and Spain on the Recognition and Enforcement of Judgments, Settlements and Enforceable Authentic Instruments in Civil and Commercial Matters, signed at Vienna on 17 February 1984,
— the Convention between Finland and Austria on the Recognition and Enforcement of Judgments in Civil Matters, signed at Vienna on 17 November 1986, and
— the Treaty between Belgium, the Netherlands and Luxembourg in Jurisdiction, Bankruptcy, and the Validity and Enforcement of Judgments, Arbitration Awards and Authentic Instruments, signed at Brussels on 24 November 1961, in so far as it is in force.

Article 70

1. The Treaty and the Conventions referred to in Article 69 shall continue to have effect in relation to matters to which this Regulation does not apply.
2. They shall continue to have effect in respect of judgments given and documents formally drawn up or registered as authentic instruments before the entry into force of this Regulation.

Article 71

1. This Regulation shall not affect any conventions to which the Member States are parties and which in relation to particular matters, govern jurisdiction or the recognition or enforcement of judgments.
2. With a view to its uniform interpretation, paragraph 1 shall be applied in the following manner:

(a) this Regulation shall not prevent a court of a Member State, which is a party to a convention on a particular matter, from assuming jurisdiction in accordance with that convention, even where the defendant is domiciled in another Member State which is not a party to that convention. The court hearing the action shall, in any event, apply Article 26 of this Regulation;

(b) judgments given in a Member State by a court in the exercise of jurisdiction provided for in a convention on a particular matter shall be recognised and enforced in the other Member States in accordance with this Regulation.

Where a convention on a particular matter to which both the Member State of origin and the Member State addressed are parties lays down conditions for the recognition or enforcement of judgments, those conditions shall apply. In any event, the provisions of this Regulation which concern the procedure for recognition and enforcement of judgments may be applied.

Article 72

This Regulation shall not affect agreements by which Member States undertook, prior to the entry into force of this Regulation pursuant to Article 59 of the Brussels Convention, not to recognise judgments given, in particular in other Contracting States to that Convention, against defendants domiciled or habitually resident in a third country where, in cases provided for in Article 4 of that Convention, the judgment could only be founded on a ground of jurisdiction specified in the second paragraph of Article 3 of that Convention.

CHAPTER VIII
FINAL PROVISIONS

Article 73

No later than five years after the entry into force of this Regulation, the Commission shall present to the European Parliament, the Council and the Economic and Social Committee a report on the application of this Regulation. The report shall be accompanied, if need be, by proposals for adaptations to this Regulation.

Article 74

1. The Member States shall notify the Commission of the texts amending the lists set out in Annexes I to IV. The Commission shall adapt the Annexes concerned accordingly.
2. The updating or technical adjustment of the forms, specimens of which appear in Annexes V and VI, shall be adopted in accordance with the advisory procedure referred to in Article 75(2).

Article 75

1. The Commission shall be assisted by a committee.
2. Where reference is made to this paragraph, Articles 3 and 7 of Decision 1999/468/EC shall apply.
3. The Committee shall adopt its rules of procedure.

Article 76

This Regulation shall enter into force on 1 March 2002.

This Regulation is binding in its entirety and directly applicable in the Member States in accordance with the Treaty establishing the European Community.

Done at Brussels, 22 December 2000.

For the Council
The President
C. PIERRET

[Note that annexes have been removed from the appendix. Note that Articles 65 and 69 of the Brussels I Regulation as well as its annexes have been corrected and amended since the original publication, see OJ L 307, 24 November 2001, p. 28; OJ L 236, 23 September 2003, p. 33; OJ L 225, 22 August 2002, p. 13; OJ L 334, 10 November 2004, p. 3; OJ L 381, 28 December 2004, p. 10; OJ L 363, 20 December 2006, p. 1. These corrections and amendments have not been consolidated into the appendix, which is therefore not up to date with regard to Articles 65 and 69.]

Regulation (EC) No 805/2004 of the European Parliament and of the Council

of 21 April 2004

creating a European Enforcement Order for uncontested claims

THE EUROPEAN PARLIAMENT AND THE COUNCIL OF THE EUROPEAN UNION,

Having regard to the Treaty establishing the European Community, and in particular Articles 61(c) and the second indent of Article 67(5) thereof,

Having regard to the proposal from the Commission,[1]

Having regard to the Opinion of the European Economic and Social Committee,[2]

Acting in accordance with the procedure laid down in Article 251 of the Treaty,[3]

Whereas:

(1) The Community has set itself the objective of maintaining and developing an area of freedom, security and justice, in which the free movement of persons is ensured. To this end, the Community is to adopt, *inter alia*, measures in the field of judicial cooperation in civil matters that are necessary for the proper functioning of the internal market.

(2) On 3 December 1998, the Council adopted an Action Plan of the Council and the Commission on how best to implement the provisions of the Treaty of Amsterdam on an area of freedom, security and justice[4] (the Vienna Action Plan).

[1] OJ C 203 E, 27.8.2002, p. 86.

[2] OJ C 85, 8.4.2003, p. 1.

[3] Opinion of the European Parliament of 8 April 2003 (OJ C 64 E, 12.3.2004, p. 79), Council Common Position of 6.2.2004 (not yet published in the Official Journal) and Position of the European Parliament of 30.3.2004 (not yet published in the Official Journal).

[4] OJ C 19, 23.1.1999, p. 1.

(3) The European Council meeting in Tampere on 15 and 16 October 1999 endorsed the principle of mutual recognition of judicial decisions as the cornerstone for the creation of a genuine judicial area.
(4) On 30 November 2000, the Council adopted a programme of measures for implementation of the principle of mutual recognition of decisions in civil and commercial matters.[5] This programme includes in its first stage the abolition of exequatur, that is to say, the creation of a European Enforcement Order for uncontested claims.
(5) The concept of 'uncontested claims' should cover all situations in which a creditor, given the verified absence of any dispute by the debtor as to the nature or extent of a pecuniary claim, has obtained either a court decision against that debtor or an enforceable document that requires the debtor's express consent, be it a court settlement or an authentic instrument.
(6) The absence of objections from the debtor as stipulated in Article 3(1)(b) can take the shape of default of appearance at a court hearing or of failure to comply with an invitation by the court to give written notice of an intention to defend the case.
(7) This Regulation should apply to judgments, court settlements and authentic instruments on uncontested claims and to decisions delivered following challenges to judgments, court settlements and authentic instruments certified as European Enforcement Orders.
(8) In its Tampere conclusions, the European Council considered that access to enforcement in a Member State other than that in which the judgment has been given should be accelerated and simplified by dispensing with any intermediate measures to be taken prior to enforcement in the Member State in which enforcement is sought. A judgment that has been certified as a European Enforcement Order by the court of origin should, for enforcement purposes, be treated as if it had been delivered in the Member State in which enforcement is sought. In the United Kingdom, for example, the registration of a certified foreign judgment will therefore follow the same rules as the registration of a judgment from another part of the United Kingdom and is not to imply a review as to the substance of the foreign judgment. Arrangements for the enforcement of judgments should continue to be governed by national law.
(9) Such a procedure should offer significant advantages as compared with the exequatur procedure provided for in Council Regulation (EC) No 44/2001 of 22 December 2000 on jurisdiction and the recognition and enforcement of judgments in civil and commercial matters,[6] in that there is no need for approval by the judiciary in a second Member State with the delays and expenses that this entails.

[5] OJ C 12, 15.1.2001, p. 1.

[6] OJ L 12, 16.1.2001, p. 1. Regulation as last amended by Commission Regulation (EC) No 1496/2002 (OJ L 225, 22.8.2002, p. 13).

(10) Where a court in a Member State has given judgment on an uncontested claim in the absence of participation of the debtor in the proceedings, the abolition of any checks in the Member State of enforcement is inextricably linked to and dependent upon the existence of a sufficient guarantee of observance of the rights of the defence.

(11) This Regulation seeks to promote the fundamental rights and takes into account the principles recognised in particular by the Charter of Fundamental Rights of the European Union. In particular, it seeks to ensure full respect for the right to a fair trial as recognised in Article 47 of the Charter.

(12) Minimum standards should be established for the proceedings leading to the judgment in order to ensure that the debtor is informed about the court action against him, the requirements for his active participation in the proceedings to contest the claim and the consequences of his non-participation in sufficient time and in such a way as to enable him to arrange for his defence.

(13) Due to differences between the Member States as regards the rules of civil procedure and especially those governing the service of documents, it is necessary to lay down a specific and detailed definition of those minimum standards. In particular, any method of service that is based on a legal fiction as regards the fulfilment of those minimum standards cannot be considered sufficient for the certification of a judgment as a European Enforcement Order.

(14) All the methods of service listed in Articles 13 and 14 are characterised by either full certainty (Article 13) or a very high degree of likelihood (Article 14) that the document served has reached its addressee. In the second category, a judgment should only be certified as a European Enforcement Order if the Member State of origin has an appropriate mechanism in place enabling the debtor to apply for a full review of the judgment under the conditions set out in Article 19 in those exceptional cases where, in spite of compliance with Article 14, the document has not reached the addressee.

(15) Personal service on certain persons other than the debtor himself pursuant to Article 14(1)(a) and (b) should be understood to meet the requirements of those provisions only if those persons actually accepted/received the document in question.

(16) Article 15 should apply to situations where the debtor cannot represent himself in court, as in the case of a legal person, and where a person to represent him is determined by law as well as situations where the debtor has authorised another person, in particular a lawyer, to represent him in the specific court proceedings at issue.

(17) The courts competent for scrutinising full compliance with the minimum procedural standards should, if satisfied, issue a standardised European Enforcement Order certificate that makes that scrutiny and its result transparent.

(18) Mutual trust in the administration of justice in the Member States justifies the assessment by the court of one Member State that all conditions for certification as a European Enforcement Order are fulfilled to enable a judgment to be enforced in all other Member States without judicial review of the proper application of the minimum procedural standards in the Member State where the judgment is to be enforced.
(19) This Regulation does not imply an obligation for the Member States to adapt their national legislation to the minimum procedural standards set out herein. It provides an incentive to that end by making available a more efficient and rapid enforceability of judgments in other Member States only if those minimum standards are met.
(20) Application for certification as a European Enforcement Order for uncontested claims should be optional for the creditor, who may instead choose the system of recognition and enforcement under Regulation (EC) No 44/2001 or other Community instruments.
(21) When a document has to be sent from one Member State to another for service there, this Regulation and in particular the rules on service set out herein should apply together with Council Regulation (EC) No 1348/2000 of 29 May 2000 on the service in the Member States of judicial and extrajudicial documents in civil or commercial matters,[7] and in particular Article 14 thereof in conjunction with Member States declarations made under Article 23 thereof.
(22) Since the objectives of the proposed action cannot be sufficiently achieved by the Member States and can therefore, by reason of the scale or effects of the action, be better achieved at Community level, the Community may adopt measures, in accordance with the principle of subsidiarity as set out in Article 5 of the Treaty. In accordance with the principle of proportionality, as set out in that Article, this Regulation does not go beyond what is necessary in order to achieve those objectives.
(23) The measures necessary for the implementation of this Regulation should be adopted in accordance with Council Decision 1999/468/EC of 28 June 1999 laying down the procedures for the exercise of implementing powers conferred on the Commission.[8]
(24) In accordance with Article 3 of the Protocol on the position of the United Kingdom and Ireland annexed to the Treaty on European Union and the Treaty establishing the European Community, the United Kingdom and Ireland have notified their wish to take part in the adoption and application of this Regulation.
(25) In accordance with Articles 1 and 2 of the Protocol on the position of Denmark annexed to the Treaty on European Union and the Treaty establishing the European Community, Denmark does not take part in the adoption of this Regulation, and is therefore not bound by it or subject to its application.

[7] OJ L 160, 30.6.2000, p. 37.
[8] OJ L 184, 17.7.1999, p. 23.

(26) Pursuant to the second indent of Article 67(5) of the Treaty, the codecision procedure is applicable from 1 February 2003 for the measures laid down in this Regulation,

HAVE ADOPTED THIS REGULATION:

CHAPTER I
SUBJECT MATTER, SCOPE AND DEFINITIONS

Article 1

Subject matter

The purpose of this Regulation is to create a European Enforcement Order for uncontested claims to permit, by laying down minimum standards, the free circulation of judgments, court settlements and authentic instruments throughout all Member States without any intermediate proceedings needing to be brought in the Member State of enforcement prior to recognition and enforcement.

Article 2

Scope

1. This Regulation shall apply in civil and commercial matters, whatever the nature of the court or tribunal. It shall not extend, in particular, to revenue, customs or administrative matters or the liability of the State for acts and omissions in the exercise of State authority ('acta iure imperii').
2. This Regulation shall not apply to:
   (a) the status or legal capacity of natural persons, rights in property arising out of a matrimonial relationship, wills and succession;
   (b) bankruptcy, proceedings relating to the winding-up of insolvent companies or other legal persons, judicial arrangements, compositions and analogous proceedings;
   (c) social security;
   (d) arbitration.
3. In this Regulation, the term 'Member State' shall mean Member States with the exception of Denmark.

Article 3

Enforcement titles to be certified as a European Enforcement Order

1. This Regulation shall apply to judgments, court settlements and authentic instruments on uncontested claims.
   A claim shall be regarded as uncontested if:
   (a) the debtor has expressly agreed to it by admission or by means of a settlement which has been approved by a court or concluded before a court in the course of proceedings; or

(b) the debtor has never objected to it, in compliance with the relevant procedural requirements under the law of the Member State of origin, in the course of the court proceedings; or
(c) the debtor has not appeared or been represented at a court hearing regarding that claim after having initially objected to the claim in the course of the court proceedings, provided that such conduct amounts to a tacit admission of the claim or of the facts alleged by the creditor under the law of the Member State of origin; or
(d) the debtor has expressly agreed to it in an authentic instrument.

2. This Regulation shall also apply to decisions delivered following challenges to judgments, court settlements or authentic instruments certified as European Enforcement Orders.

Article 4
Definitions

For the purposes of this Regulation, the following definitions shall apply:

1. 'judgment': any judgment given by a court or tribunal of a Member State, whatever the judgment may be called, including a decree, order, decision or writ of execution, as well as the determination of costs or expenses by an officer of the court;
2. 'claim': a claim for payment of a specific sum of money that has fallen due or for which the due date is indicated in the judgment, court settlement or authentic instrument;
3. 'authentic instrument':
   (a) a document which has been formally drawn up or registered as an authentic instrument, and the authenticity of which:
      (i) relates to the signature and the content of the instrument; and
      (ii) has been established by a public authority or other authority empowered for that purpose by the Member State in which it originates;
   or
   (b) an arrangement relating to maintenance obligations concluded with administrative authorities or authenticated by them;
4. 'Member State of origin': the Member State in which the judgment has been given, the court settlement has been approved or concluded or the authentic instrument has been drawn up or registered, and is to be certified as a European Enforcement Order;
5. 'Member State of enforcement': the Member State in which enforcement of the judgment, court settlement or authentic instrument certified as a European Enforcement Order is sought;
6. 'court of origin': the court or tribunal seised of the proceedings at the time of fulfilment of the conditions set out in Article 3(1)(a), (b) or (c);

7. in Sweden, in summary proceedings concerning orders to pay (betalningsforclaggande), the expression 'court' includes the Swedish enforcement service (kronofogdemyndighet).

CHAPTER II
EUROPEAN ENFORCEMENT ORDER

Article 5
Abolition of exequatur

A judgment which has been certified as a European Enforcement Order in the Member State of origin shall be recognised and enforced in the other Member States without the need for a declaration of enforceability and without any possibility of opposing its recognition.

Article 6
Requirements for certification as a European Enforcement Order

1. A judgment on an uncontested claim delivered in a Member State shall, upon application at any time to the court of origin, be certified as a European Enforcement Order if:
   (a) the judgment is enforceable in the Member State of origin; and
   (b) the judgment does not conflict with the rules on jurisdiction as laid down in sections 3 and 6 of Chapter II of Regulation (EC) No 44/2001; and
   (c) the court proceedings in the Member State of origin met the requirements as set out in Chapter III where a claim is uncontested within the meaning of Article 3(1)(b) or (c); and
   (d) the judgment was given in the Member State of the debtor's domicile within the meaning of Article 59 of Regulation (EC) No 44/2001, in cases where
   — a claim is uncontested within the meaning of Article 3(1)(b) or (c); and
   — it relates to a contract concluded by a person, the consumer, for a purpose which can be regarded as being outside his trade or profession; and
   — the debtor is the consumer.
2. Where a judgment certified as a European Enforcement Order has ceased to be enforceable or its enforceability has been suspended or limited, a certificate indicating the lack or limitation of enforceability shall, upon application at any time to the court of origin, be issued, using the standard form in Annex IV.
3. Without prejudice to Article 12(2), where a decision has been delivered following a challenge to a judgment certified as a European Enforcement Order in accordance with paragraph 1 of this Article, a replacement certificate shall, upon application at any time, be issued, using the standard form in Annex V, if that decision on the challenge is enforceable in the Member State of origin.

Article 7
Costs related to court proceedings

Where a judgment includes an enforceable decision on the amount of costs related to the court proceedings, including the interest rates, it shall be certified as a European Enforcement Order also with regard to the costs unless the debtor has specifically objected to his obligation to bear such costs in the course of the court proceedings, in accordance with the law of the Member State of origin.

Article 8
Partial European Enforcement Order certificate

If only parts of the judgment meet the requirements of this Regulation, a partial European Enforcement Order certificate shall be issued for those parts.

Article 9
Issue of the European Enforcement Order certificate

1. The European Enforcement Order certificate shall be issued using the standard form in Annex I.
2. The European Enforcement Order certificate shall be issued in the language of the judgment.

Article 10
Rectification or withdrawal of the European Enforcement Order certificate

1. The European Enforcement Order certificate shall, upon application to the court of origin, be
   (a) rectified where, due to a material error, there is a discrepancy between the judgment and the certificate;
   (b) withdrawn where it was clearly wrongly granted, having regard to the requirements laid down in this Regulation.
2. The law of the Member State of origin shall apply to the rectification or withdrawal of the European Enforcement Order certificate.
3. An application for the rectification or withdrawal of a European Enforcement Order certificate may be made using the standard form in Annex VI.
4. No appeal shall lie against the issuing of a European Enforcement Order certificate.

Article 11
Effect of the European Enforcement Order certificate

The European Enforcement Order certificate shall take effect only within the limits of the enforceability of the judgment.

CHAPTER III
MINIMUM STANDARDS FOR UNCONTESTED CLAIMS PROCEDURES

Article 12
Scope of application of minimum standards

1. A judgment on a claim that is uncontested within the meaning of Article 3(1)(b) or (c) can be certified as a European Enforcement Order only if the court proceedings in the Member State of origin met the procedural requirements as set out in this Chapter.
2. The same requirements shall apply to the issuing of a European Enforcement Order certificate or a replacement certificate within the meaning of Article 6(3) for a decision following a challenge to a judgment where, at the time of that decision, the conditions of Article 3(1)(b) or (c) are fulfilled.

Article 13
Service with proof of receipt by the debtor

1. The document instituting the proceedings or an equivalent document may have been served on the debtor by one of the following methods:
   (a) personal service attested by an acknowledgement of receipt, including the date of receipt, which is signed by the debtor;
   (b) personal service attested by a document signed by the competent person who effected the service stating that the debtor has received the document or refused to receive it without any legal justification, and the date of the service;
   (c) postal service attested by an acknowledgement of receipt including the date of receipt, which is signed and returned by the debtor;
   (d) service by electronic means such as fax or e-mail, attested by an acknowledgement of receipt including the date of receipt, which is signed and returned by the debtor.
2. Any summons to a court hearing may have been served on the debtor in compliance with paragraph 1 or orally in a previous court hearing on the same claim and stated in the minutes of that previous court hearing.

Article 14
Service without proof of receipt by the debtor

1. Service of the document instituting the proceedings or an equivalent document and any summons to a court hearing on the debtor may also have been effected by one of the following methods:
   (a) personal service at the debtor's personal address on persons who are living in the same household as the debtor or are employed there;

(b) in the case of a self-employed debtor or a legal person, personal service at the debtor's business premises on persons who are employed by the debtor;
(c) deposit of the document in the debtor's mailbox;
(d) deposit of the document at a post office or with competent public authorities and the placing in the debtor's mailbox of written notification of that deposit, provided that the written notification clearly states the character of the document as a court document or the legal effect of the notification as effecting service and setting in motion the running of time for the purposes of time limits;
(e) postal service without proof pursuant to paragraph 3 where the debtor has his address in the Member State of origin;
(f) electronic means attested by an automatic confirmation of delivery, provided that the debtor has expressly accepted this method of service in advance.

2. For the purposes of this Regulation, service under paragraph 1 is not admissible if the debtor's address is not known with certainty.
3. Service pursuant to paragraph 1, (a) to (d), shall be attested by:
   (a) a document signed by the competent person who effected the service, indicating:
      (i) the method of service used; and
      (ii) the date of service; and
      (iii) where the document has been served on a person other than the debtor, the name of that person and his relation to the debtor,

   or
   (b) an acknowledgement of receipt by the person served, for the purposes of paragraphs 1(a) and (b).

Article 15

Service on the debtor's representatives

Service pursuant to Articles 13 or 14 may also have been effected on a debtor's representative.

Article 16

Provision to the debtor of due information about the claim

In order to ensure that the debtor was provided with due information about the claim, the document instituting the proceedings or the equivalent document must have contained the following:

(a) the names and the addresses of the parties;
(b) the amount of the claim;

(c) if interest on the claim is sought, the interest rate and the period for which interest is sought unless statutory interest is automatically added to the principal under the law of the Member State of origin;
(d) a statement of the reason for the claim.

Article 17

Provision to the debtor of due information about the procedural steps necessary to contest the claim

The following must have been clearly stated in or together with the document instituting the proceedings, the equivalent document or any summons to a court hearing:

(a) the procedural requirements for contesting the claim, including the time limit for contesting the claim in writing or the time for the court hearing, as applicable, the name and the address of the institution to which to respond or before which to appear, as applicable, and whether it is mandatory to be represented by a lawyer;
(b) the consequences of an absence of objection or default of appearance, in particular, where applicable, the possibility that a judgment may be given or enforced against the debtor and the liability for costs related to the court proceedings.

Article 18

Cure of non-compliance with minimum standards

1. If the proceedings in the Member State of origin did not meet the procedural requirements as set out in Articles 13 to 17, such non-compliance shall be cured and a judgment may be certified as a European Enforcement Order if:
   (a) the judgment has been served on the debtor in compliance with the requirements pursuant to Article 13 or Article 14; and
   (b) it was possible for the debtor to challenge the judgment by means of a full review and the debtor has been duly informed in or together with the judgment about the procedural requirements for such a challenge, including the name and address of the institution with which it must be lodged and, where applicable, the time limit for so doing; and
   (c) the debtor has failed to challenge the judgment in compliance with the relevant procedural requirements.
2. If the proceedings in the Member State of origin did not comply with the procedural requirements as set out in Article 13 or Article 14, such non-compliance shall be cured if it is proved by the conduct of the debtor in the court proceedings that he has personally received the document to be served in sufficient time to arrange for his defence.

Article 19

Minimum standards for review in exceptional cases

1. Further to Articles 13 to 18, a judgment can only be certified as a European Enforcement Order if the debtor is entitled, under the law of the Member State of origin, to apply for a review of the judgment where:
   (a) (i) the document instituting the proceedings or an equivalent document or, where applicable, the summons to a court hearing, was served by one of the methods provided for in Article 14; and
   (ii) service was not effected in sufficient time to enable him to arrange for his defence, without any fault on his part;

   or

   (b) the debtor was prevented from objecting to the claim by reason of *force majeure*, or due to extraordinary circumstances without any fault on his part,

   provided in either case that he acts promptly.
2. This Article is without prejudice to the possibility for Member States to grant access to a review of the judgment under more generous conditions than those mentioned in paragraph 1.

CHAPTER IV
ENFORCEMENT

Article 20

Enforcement procedure

1. Without prejudice to the provisions of this Chapter, the enforcement procedures shall be governed by the law of the Member State of enforcement.

   A judgment certified as a European Enforcement Order shall be enforced under the same conditions as a judgment handed down in the Member State of enforcement.
2. The creditor shall be required to provide the competent enforcement authorities of the Member State of enforcement with:
   (a) a copy of the judgment which satisfies the conditions necessary to establish its authenticity; and
   (b) a copy of the European Enforcement Order certificate which satisfies the conditions necessary to establish its authenticity; and
   (c) where necessary, a transcription of the European Enforcement Order certificate or a translation thereof into the official language of the Member State of enforcement or, if there are several official languages in that

Member State, the official language or one of the official languages of court proceedings of the place where enforcement is sought, in conformity with the law of that Member State, or into another language that the Member State of enforcement has indicated it can accept. Each Member State may indicate the official language or languages of the institutions of the European Community other than its own which it can accept for the completion of the certificate. The translation shall be certified by a person qualified to do so in one of the Member States.

3. No security, bond or deposit, however described, shall be required of a party who in one Member State applies for enforcement of a judgment certified as a European Enforcement Order in another Member State on the ground that he is a foreign national or that he is not domiciled or resident in the Member State of enforcement.

Article 21

Refusal of enforcement

1. Enforcement shall, upon application by the debtor, be refused by the competent court in the Member State of enforcement if the judgment certified as a European Enforcement Order is irreconcilable with an earlier judgment given in any Member State or in a third country, provided that:
   (a) the earlier judgment involved the same cause of action and was between the same parties; and
   (b) the earlier judgment was given in the Member State of enforcement or fulfils the conditions necessary for its recognition in the Member State of enforcement; and
   (c) the irreconcilability was not and could not have been raised as an objection in the court proceedings in the Member State of origin.
2. Under no circumstances may the judgment or its certification as a European Enforcement Order be reviewed as to their substance in the Member State of enforcement.

Article 22

Agreements with third countries

This Regulation shall not affect agreements by which Member States undertook, prior to the entry into force of Regulation (EC) No 44/2001, pursuant to Article 59 of the Brussels Convention on jurisdiction and the enforcement of judgments in civil and commercial matters, not to recognise judgments given, in particular in other Contracting States to that Convention, against defendants domiciled or habitually resident in a third country where, in cases provided for in Article 4 of that Convention, the judgment could only be founded on a ground of jurisdiction specified in the second paragraph of Article 3 of that Convention.

Article 23
Stay or limitation of enforcement

Where the debtor has

— challenged a judgment certified as a European Enforcement Order, including an application for review within the meaning of Article 19, or
— applied for the rectification or withdrawal of a European Enforcement Order certificate in accordance with Article 10,

the competent court or authority in the Member State of enforcement may, upon application by the debtor:

(a) limit the enforcement proceedings to protective measures; or
(b) make enforcement conditional on the provision of such security as it shall determine; or
(c) under exceptional circumstances, stay the enforcement proceedings.

CHAPTER V
COURT SETTLEMENTS AND AUTHENTIC INSTRUMENTS

Article 24
Court settlements

1. A settlement concerning a claim within the meaning of Article 4(2) which has been approved by a court or concluded before a court in the course of proceedings and is enforceable in the Member State in which it was approved or concluded shall, upon application to the court that approved it or before which it was concluded, be certified as a European Enforcement Order using the standard form in Annex II.
2. A settlement which has been certified as a European Enforcement Order in the Member State of origin shall be enforced in the other Member States without the need for a declaration of enforceability and without any possibility of opposing its enforceability.
3. The provisions of Chapter II, with the exception of Articles 5, 6(1) and 9(1), and of Chapter IV, with the exception of Articles 21(1) and 22, shall apply as appropriate.

Article 25
Authentic instruments

1. An authentic instrument concerning a claim within the meaning of Article 4(2) which is enforceable in one Member State shall, upon application to the authority designated by the Member State of origin, be certified as a European Enforcement Order, using the standard form in Annex III.

2. An authentic instrument which has been certified as a European Enforcement Order in the Member State of origin shall be enforced in the other Member States without the need for a declaration of enforceability and without any possibility of opposing its enforceability.
3. The provisions of Chapter II, with the exception of Articles 5, 6(1) and 9(1), and of Chapter IV, with the exception of Articles 21(1) and 22, shall apply as appropriate.

CHAPTER VI
TRANSITIONAL PROVISION

Article 26

Transitional provision

This Regulation shall apply only to judgments given, to court settlements approved or concluded and to documents formally drawn up or registered as authentic instruments after the entry into force of this Regulation.

CHAPTER VII
RELATIONSHIP WITH OTHER COMMUNITY INSTRUMENTS

Article 27

Relationship with Regulation (EC) No 44/2001

This Regulation shall not affect the possibility of seeking recognition and enforcement, in accordance with Regulation (EC) No 44/2001, of a judgment, a court settlement or an authentic instrument on an uncontested claim.

Article 28

Relationship with Regulation (EC) No 1348/2000

This Regulation shall not affect the application of Regulation (EC) No 1348/2000.

CHAPTER VIII
GENERAL AND FINAL PROVISIONS

Article 29

Information on enforcement procedures and authorities

The Member States shall cooperate to provide the general public and professional circles with information on:

(a) the methods and procedures of enforcement in the Member States; and
(b) the competent authorities for enforcement in the Member States,

in particular via the European Judicial Network in civil and commercial matters established in accordance with Decision 2001/470/EC.[9]

Article 30

Information relating to redress procedures, languages and authorities

1. The Member States shall notify the Commission of:
   (a) the procedures for rectification and withdrawal referred to in Article 10(2) and for review referred to in Article 19(1);
   (b) the languages accepted pursuant to Article 20(2)(c);
   (c) the lists of the authorities referred to in Article 25;

   and any subsequent changes thereof.
2. The Commission shall make the information notified in accordance with paragraph 1 publicly available through publication in the Official Journal of the European Union and through any other appropriate means.

Article 31

Amendments to the Annexes

Any amendment to the standard forms in the Annexes shall be adopted in accordance with the advisory procedure referred to in Article 32(2).

Article 32

Committee

1. The Commission shall be assisted by the committee provided for by Article 75 of Regulation (EC) No 44/2001.
2. Where reference is made to this paragraph, Articles 3 and 7 of Decision 1999/468/EC shall apply, having regard to the provisions of Article 8 thereof.
3. The Committee shall adopt its Rules of Procedure.

Article 33

Entry into force

This Regulation shall enter into force on 21 January 2005.

It shall apply from 21 October 2005, with the exception of Articles 30, 31 and 32, which shall apply from 21 January 2005.

[9] OJ L 174, 27.6.2001, p. 25.

This Regulation shall be binding in its entirety and directly applicable in the Member States in accordance with the Treaty establishing the European Community.

Done at Strasbourg, 21 April 2004.

For the European Parliament	*For the Council*
The President	*The President*
P. COX	D. ROCHE

[Note that annexes have been removed from this appendix. Note also that annexes have been updated since the original publication, see OJ L 300, 17 November 2005, p. 6.]

Council Directive 2003/8/EC

of 27 January 2003

to improve access to justice in cross-border disputes by establishing minimum common rules relating to legal aid for such disputes

THE COUNCIL OF THE EUROPEAN UNION,

Having regard to the Treaty establishing the European Community, and in particular Articles 61(c) and 67 thereof,

Having regard to the proposal from the Commission,[1]

Having regard to the opinion of the European Parliament,[2]

Having regard to the opinion of the Economic and Social Committee,[3]

Whereas:

(1) The European Union has set itself the objective of maintaining and developing an area of freedom, security and justice in which the free movement of persons is ensured. For the gradual establishment of such an area, the Community is to adopt, among others, the measures relating to judicial cooperation in civil matters having cross-border implications and needed for the proper functioning of the internal market.

(2) According to Article 65(c) of the Treaty, these measures are to include measures eliminating obstacles to the good functioning of civil proceedings, if necessary by promoting the compatibility of the rules on civil procedure applicable in the Member States.

(3) The Tampere European Council on 15 and 16 October 1999 called on the Council to establish minimum standards ensuring an adequate level of legal aid in cross-border cases throughout the Union.

[1] OJ C 103 E, 30.4.2002, p. 368.

[2] Opinion delivered on 25 September 2002 (not yet published in the Official Journal).

[3] OJ C 221, 17.9.2002, p. 64.

(4) All Member States are contracting parties to the European Convention for the Protection of Human Rights and Fundamental Freedom of 4 November 1950. The matters referred to in this Directive shall be dealt with in compliance with that Convention and in particular the respect of the principle of equality of both parties in a dispute.

(5) This Directive seeks to promote the application of legal aid in cross-border disputes for persons who lack sufficient resources where aid is necessary to secure effective access to justice. The generally recognised right to access to justice is also reaffirmed by Article 47 of the Charter of Fundamental Rights of the European Union.

(6) Neither the lack of resources of a litigant, whether acting as claimant or as defendant, nor the difficulties flowing froma dispute's cross-border dimension should be allowed to hamper effective access to justice.

(7) Since the objectives of this Directive cannot be sufficiently achieved by the Member States acting alone and can therefore be better achieved at Community level, the Community may adopt measures, in accordance with the principle of subsidiarity as set out in Article 5 of the Treaty. In accordance with the principle of proportionality, as set out in that Article, this Directive does not go beyond what is necessary in order to achieve those objectives.

(8) The main purpose of this Directive is to guarantee an adequate level of legal aid in cross-border disputes by laying down certain minimum common standards relating to legal aid in such disputes. A Council directive is the most suitable legislative instrument for this purpose.

(9) This Directive applies in cross-border disputes, to civil and commercial matters.

(10) All persons involved in a civil or commercial dispute within the scope of this Directive must be able to assert their rights in the courts even if their personal financial situation makes it impossible for them to bear the costs of the proceedings. Legal aid is regarded as appropriate when it allows the recipient effective access to justice under the conditions laid down in this Directive.

(11) Legal aid should cover pre-litigation advice with a view to reaching a settlement prior to bringing legal proceedings, legal assistance in bringing a case before a court and representation in court and assistance with or exemption from the cost of proceedings.

(12) It shall be left to the law of the Member State in which the court is sitting or where enforcement is sought whether the costs of proceedings may include the costs of the opponent imposed on the recipient of legal aid.

(13) All Union citizens, wherever they are domiciled or habitually resident in the territory of a Member State, must be eligible for legal aid in cross-border disputes if they meet the conditions provided for by this Directive. The same applies to third-country nationals who habitually and lawfully reside in a Member State.

(14) Member States should be left free to define the threshold above which a person would be presumed able to bear the costs of proceedings, in the conditions defined in this Directive. Such thresholds are to be defined in the light of various objective factors such as income, capital or family situation.

(15) The objective of this Directive could not, however, be attained if legal aid applicants did not have the possibility of proving that they cannot bear the costs of proceedings even if their resources exceed the threshold defined by the Member State where the court is sitting. When making the assessment of whether legal aid is to be granted on this basis, the authorities in the Member State where the court is sitting may take into account information as to the fact that the applicant satisfies criteria in respect of financial eligibility in the Member State of domicile or habitual residence.

(16) The possibility in the instant case of resorting to other mechanisms to ensure effective access to justice is not a form of legal aid. But it can warrant a presumption that the person concerned can bear the costs of the procedure despite his/her unfavourable financial situation.

(17) Member States should be allowed to reject applications for legal aid in respect of manifestly unfounded actions or on grounds related to the merits of the case in so far as pre-litigation advice is offered and access to justice is guaranteed. When taking a decision on the merits of an application, Member States may reject legal aid applications when the applicant is claiming damage to his or her reputation, but has suffered no material or financial loss or the application concerns a claim arising directly out of the applicant's trade or self-employed profession.

(18) The complexity of and differences between the legal systems of the Member States and the costs inherent in the cross-border dimension of a dispute should not preclude access to justice. Legal aid should accordingly cover costs directly connected with the cross-border dimension of a dispute.

(19) When considering if the physical presence of a person in court is required, the courts of a Member State should take into consideration the full advantage of the possibilities offered by Council Regulation (EC) No 1206/2001 of 28 May 2001 on cooperation between the courts of the Member States in the taking of evidence in civil or commercial matters.[4]

(20) If legal aid is granted, it must cover the entire proceeding, including expenses incurred in having a judgment enforced; the recipient should continue receiving this aid if an appeal is brought either against or by the recipient in so far as the conditions relating to the financial resources and the substance of the dispute remain fulfilled.

[4] OJ L 174, 27.6.2001, p. 1.

(21) Legal aid is to be granted on the same terms both for conventional legal proceedings and for out-of-court procedures such as mediation, where recourse to them is required by the law, or ordered by the court.

(22) Legal aid should also be granted for the enforcement of authentic instruments in another Member State under the conditions defined in this Directive.

(23) Since legal aid is given by the Member State in which the court is sitting or where enforcement is sought, except pre-litigation assistance if the legal aid applicant is not domiciled or habitually resident in the Member State where the court is sitting, that Member State must apply its own legislation, in compliance with the principles of this Directive.

(24) It is appropriate that legal aid is granted or refused by the competent authority of the Member State in which the court is sitting or where a judgment is to be enforced. This is the case both when that court is trying the case in substance and when it first has to decide whether it has jurisdiction.

(25) Judicial cooperation in civil matters should be organised between Member States to encourage information for the public and professional circles and to simplify and accelerate the transmission of legal aid applications between Member States.

(26) The notification and transmission mechanisms provided for by this Directive are inspired directly by those of the European Agreement on the transmission of applications for legal aid, signed in Strasbourg on 27 January 1977, hereinafter referred to as '1977 Agreement'. A time limit, not provided for by the 1977 Agreement, is set for the transmission of legal aid applications. A relatively short time limit contributes to the smooth operation of justice.

(27) The information transmitted pursuant to this Directive should enjoy protection. Since Directive 95/46/EC of the European Parliament and of the Council of 24 October 1995 on the protection of individuals with regard to the processing of personal data and on the free movement of such data,[5] and Directive 97/66/EC of the European Parliament and of the Council of 15 December 1997 concerning the processing of personal data and the protection of privacy in the telecommunications sector,[6] are applicable, there is no need for specific provisions on data protection in this Directive.

(28) The establishment of a standard form for legal aid applications and for the transmission of legal aid applications in the event of cross-border litigation will make the procedures easier and faster.

(29) Moreover, these application forms, as well as national application forms, should be made available on a European level through the information system of the

[5] OJ L 281, 23.11.1995, p. 31.

[6] OJ L 24, 30.1.1998, p. 1.

European Judicial Network, established in accordance with Decision 2001/470/EC.[7]

(30) The measures necessary for the implementation of this Directive should be adopted in accordance with Council Decision 1999/468/EC of 28 June 1999 laying down the procedures for the exercise of implementing powers conferred on the Commission.[8]

(31) It should be specified that the establishment of minimum standards in cross-border disputes does not prevent Member States from making provision for more favourable arrangements for legal aid applicants and recipients.

(32) The 1977 Agreement and the additional Protocol to the European Agreement on the transmission of applications for legal aid, signed in Moscow in 2001, remain applicable to relations between Member States and third countries that are parties to the 1977 Agreement or the Protocol. But this Directive takes precedence over provisions contained in the 1977 Agreement and the Protocol in relations between Member States.

(33) The United Kingdom and Ireland have given notice of their wish to participate in the adoption of this Directive in accordance with Article 3 of the Protocol on the position of the United Kingdom and Ireland annexed to the Treaty on European Union and to the Treaty establishing the European Community.

(34) In accordance with Articles 1 and 2 of the Protocol on the position of Denmark annexed to the Treaty on European Union and to the Treaty establishing the European Community, Denmark is not taking part in the adoption of this Directive and is not bound by it or subject to its application,

HAS ADOPTED THIS DIRECTIVE:

CHAPTER I
SCOPE AND DEFINITIONS

Article 1

Aims and scope

1. The purpose of this Directive is to improve access to justice in cross-border disputes by establishing minimum common rules relating to legal aid in such disputes.
2. It shall apply, in cross-border disputes, to civil and commercial matters whatever the nature of the court or tribunal. It shall not extend, in particular, to revenue, customs or administrative matters.

[7] OJ L 174, 27.6.2001, p. 25.
[8] OJ L 184, 17.7.1999, p. 23.

3. In this Directive, 'Member State' shall mean Member States with the exception of Denmark.

Article 2

Cross-border disputes

1. For the purposes of this Directive, a cross-border dispute is one where the party applying for legal aid in the context of this Directive is domiciled or habitually resident in a Member State other than the Member State where the court is sitting or where the decision is to be enforced.
2. The Member State in which a party is domiciled shall be determined in accordance with Article 59 of Council Regulation (EC) No 44/2001 of 22 December 2000 on jurisdiction and the recognition and enforcement of judgments in civil and commercial matters.[9]
3. The relevant moment to determine if there is a cross-border dispute is the time when the application is submitted, in accordance with this Directive.

CHAPTER II
RIGHT TO LEGAL AID

Article 3

Right to legal aid

1. Natural persons involved in a dispute covered by this Directive shall be entitled to receive appropriate legal aid in order to ensure their effective access to justice in accordance with the conditions laid down in this Directive.
2. Legal aid is considered to be appropriate when it guarantees:
   (a) pre-litigation advice with a view to reaching a settlement prior to bringing legal proceedings;
   (b) legal assistance and representation in court, and exemption from, or assistance with, the cost of proceedings of the recipient, including the costs referred to in Article 7 and the fees to persons mandated by the court to perform acts during the proceedings.

   In Member States in which a losing party is liable for the costs of the opposing party, if the recipient loses the case, the legal aid shall cover the costs incurred by the opposing party, if it would have covered such costs had the recipient been domiciled or habitually resident in the Member State in which the court is sitting.
3. Member States need not provide legal assistance or representation in the courts or tribunals in proceedings especially designed to enable litigants to

[9] OJ L 12, 16.1.2001, p. 1; Regulation as amended by Commission Regulation (EC) No 1496/2002 (OJ L 225, 22.8.2002, p.13).

make their case in person, except when the courts or any other competent authority otherwise decide in order to ensure equality of parties or in view of the complexity of the case.

4. Member States may request that legal aid recipients pay reasonable contributions towards the costs of proceedings taking into account the conditions referred to in Article 5.
5. Member States may provide that the competent authority may decide that recipients of legal aid must refund it in whole or in part if their financial situation has substantially improved or if the decision to grant legal aid had been taken on the basis of inaccurate information given by the recipient.

Article 4

Non-discrimination

Member States shall grant legal aid without discrimination to Union citizens and third-country nationals residing lawfully in a Member State.

CHAPTER III

CONDITIONS AND EXTENT OF LEGAL AID

Article 5

Conditions relating to financial resources

1. Member States shall grant legal aid to persons referred to in Article 3(1) who are partly or totally unable to meet the costs of proceedings referred to in Article 3(2) as a result of their economic situation, in order to ensure their effective access to justice.
2. The economic situation of a person shall be assessed by the competent authority of the Member State in which the court is sitting, in the light of various objective factors such as income, capital or family situation, including an assessment of the resources of persons who are financially dependant on the applicant.
3. Member States may define thresholds above which legal aid applicants are deemed partly or totally able to bear the costs of proceedings set out in Article 3(2). These thresholds shall be defined on the basis of the criteria defined in paragraph 2 of this Article.
4. Thresholds defined according to paragraph 3 of this Article may not prevent legal aid applicants who are above the thresholds from being granted legal aid if they prove that they are unable to pay the cost of the proceedings referred to in Article 3(2) as a result of differences in the cost of living between the Member States of domicile or habitual residence and of the forum.
5. Legal aid does not need to be granted to applicants in so far as they enjoy, in the instant case, effective access to other mechanisms that cover the cost of proceedings referred to in Article 3(2).

Article 6

Conditions relating to the substance of disputes

1. Member States may provide that legal aid applications for actions which appear to be manifestly unfounded may be rejected by the competent authorities.
2. If pre-litigation advice is offered, the benefit of further legal aid may be refused or cancelled on grounds related to the merits of the case in so far as access to justice is guaranteed.
3. When taking a decision on the merits of an application and without prejudice to Article 5, Member States shall consider the importance of the individual case to the applicant but may also take into account the nature of the case when the applicant is claiming damage to his or her reputation but has suffered no material or financial loss or when the application concerns a claim arising directly out of the applicant's trade or self-employed profession.

Article 7

Costs related to the cross-border nature of the dispute

Legal aid granted in the Member State in which the court is sitting shall cover the following costs directly related to the cross-border nature of the dispute:

(a) interpretation;
(b) translation of the documents required by the court or by the competent authority and presented by the recipient which are necessary for the resolution of the case; and
(c) travel costs to be borne by the applicant where the physical presence of the persons concerned with the presentation of the applicant's case is required in court by the law or by the court of that Member State and the court decides that the persons concerned cannot be heard to the satisfaction of the court by any other means.

Article 8

Costs covered by the Member State of the domicile or habitual residence

The Member State in which the legal aid applicant is domiciled or habitually resident shall provide legal aid, as referred to in Article 3(2), necessary to cover:

(a) costs relating to the assistance of a local lawyer or any other person entitled by the law to give legal advice, incurred in that Member State until the application for legal aid has been received, in accordance with this Directive, in the Member State where the court is sitting;
(b) the translation of the application and of the necessary supporting documents when the application is submitted to the authorities in that Member State.

Article 9

Continuity of legal aid

1. Legal aid shall continue to be granted totally or partially to recipients to cover expenses incurred in having a judgment enforced in the Member State where the court is sitting.
2. A recipient who in the Member State where the court is sitting has received legal aid shall receive legal aid provided for by the law of the Member State where recognition or enforcement is sought.
3. Legal aid shall continue to be available if an appeal is brought either against or by the recipient, subject to Articles 5 and 6.
4. Member States may make provision for the re-examination of the application at any stage in the proceedings on the grounds set out in Articles 3(3) and (5), 5 and 6, including proceedings referred to in paragraphs 1 to 3 of this Article.

Article 10

Extrajudicial procedures

Legal aid shall also be extended to extrajudicial procedures, under the conditions defined in this Directive, if the law requires the parties to use them, or if the parties to the dispute are ordered by the court to have recourse to them.

Article 11

Authentic instruments

Legal aid shall be granted for the enforcement of authentic instruments in another Member State under the conditions defined in this Directive.

CHAPTER IV

PROCEDURE

Article 12

Authority granting legal aid

Legal aid shall be granted or refused by the competent authority of the Member State in which the court is sitting, without prejudice to Article 8.

Article 13

Introduction and transmission of legal aid applications

1. Legal aid applications may be submitted to either:
   (a) the competent authority of the Member State in which the applicant is domiciled or habitually resident (transmitting authority); or
   (b) the competent authority of the Member State in which the court is sitting or where the decision is to be enforced (receiving authority).

2. Legal aid applications shall be completed in, and supporting documents translated into:
   (a) the official language or one of the languages of the Member State of the competent receiving authority which corresponds to one of the languages of the Community institutions; or
   (b) another language which that Member State has indicated it can accept in accordance with Article 14(3).
3. The competent transmitting authorities may decide to refuse to transmit an application if it is manifestly:
   (a) unfounded; or
   (b) outside the scope of this Directive.

   The conditions referred to in Article 15(2) and (3) apply to such decisions.
4. The competent transmitting authority shall assist the applicant in ensuring that the application is accompanied by all the supporting documents known by it to be required to enable the application to be determined. It shall also assist the applicant in providing any necessary translation of the supporting documents, in accordance with Article 8(b).

   The competent transmitting authority shall transmit the application to the competent receiving authority in the other Member State within 15 days of the receipt of the application duly completed in one of the languages referred to in paragraph 2, and the supporting documents, translated, where necessary, into one of those languages.
5. Documents transmitted under this Directive shall be exempt from legalisation or any equivalent formality.
6. The Member States may not charge for services rendered in accordance with paragraph 4. Member States in which the legal aid applicant is domiciled or habitually resident may lay down that the applicant must repay the costs of translation borne by the competent transmitting authority if the application for legal aid is rejected by the competent authority.

Article 14

Competent authorities and language

1. Member States shall designate the authority or authorities competent to send (transmitting authorities) and receive (receiving authorities) the application.
2. Each Member State shall provide the Commission with the following information:
   — the names and addresses of the competent receiving or transmitting authorities referred to in paragraph 1,
   — the geographical areas in which they have jurisdiction,
   — the means by which they are available to receive applications, and
   — the languages that may be used for the completion of the application.
3. Member States shall notify the Commission of the official language or languages of the Community institutions other than their own which is or are acceptable to

the competent receiving authority for completion of the legal aid applications to be received, in accordance with this Directive.

4. Member States shall communicate to the Commission the information referred to in paragraphs 2 and 3 before 30 November 2004. Any subsequent modification of such information shall be notified to the Commission no later than two months before the modification enters into force in that Member State.
5. The information referred to in paragraphs 2 and 3 shall be published in the *Official Journal of the European Communities.*

Article 15

Processing of applications

1. The national authorities empowered to rule on legal aid applications shall ensure that the applicant is fully informed of the processing of the application.
2. Where applications are totally or partially rejected, the reasons for rejection shall be given.
3. Member States shall make provision for review of or appeals against decisions rejecting legal aid applications. Member States may exempt cases where the request for legal aid is rejected by a court or tribunal against whose decision on the subject of the case there is no judicial remedy under national law or by a court of appeal.
4. When the appeals against a decision refusing or cancelling legal aid by virtue of Article 6 are of an administrative nature, they shall always be ultimately subject to judicial review.

Article 16

Standard form

1. To facilitate transmission, a standard form for legal aid applications and for the transmission of such applications shall be established in accordance with the procedure set out in Article 17(2).
2. The standard form for the transmission of legal aid applications shall be established at the latest by 30 May 2003.
   The standard form for legal aid applications shall be established at the latest by 30 November 2004.

CHAPTER V

FINAL PROVISIONS

Article 17

Committee

1. The Commission shall be assisted by a Committee.
2. Where reference is made to this paragraph, Articles 3 and 7 of Decision 1999/468/EC shall apply.
3. The Committee shall adopt its Rules of Procedure.

Article 18
Information

The competent national authorities shall cooperate to provide the general public and professional circles with information on the various systems of legal aid, in particular via the European Judicial Network, established in accordance with Decision 2001/470/EC.

Article 19
More favourable provisions

This Directive shall not prevent the Member States from making provision for more favourable arrangements for legal aid applicants and recipients.

Article 20
Relation with other instruments

This Directive shall, as between the Member States, and in relation to matters to which it applies, take precedence over provisions contained in bilateral and multilateral agreements concluded by Member States including:

(a) the European Agreement on the transmission of applications for legal aid, signed in Strasbourg on 27 January 1977, as amended by the additional Protocol to the European Agreement on the transmission of applications for legal aid, signed in Moscow in 2001;
(b) the Hague Convention of 25 October 1980 on International Access to Justice.

Article 21
Transposition into national law

1. Member States shall bring into force the laws, regulations and administrative provisions necessary to comply with this Directive no later than 30 November 2004 with the exception of Article 3(2)(a) where the transposition of this Directive into national law shall take place no later than 30 May 2006. They shall forthwith inform the Commission thereof.

   When Member States adopt these measures, they shall contain a reference to this Directive or shall be accompanied by such a reference on the occasion of their official publication. The methods of making such a reference shall be laid down by Member States.
2. Member States shall communicate to the Commission the text of the main provisions of national law which they adopt in the field covered by this Directive.

Article 22

Entry into force

This Directive shall enter into force on the date of its publication in the *Official Journal of the European Communities.*

Article 23

Addressees

This Directive is addressed to the Member States in accordance with the Treaty establishing the European Community.

Done at Brussels, 27 January 2003.

For the Council
The President
G. PAPANDREOU

European code of conduct for mediators*

This code of conduct sets out a number of principles to which individual mediators can voluntarily decide to commit, under their own responsibility. It is intended to be applicable to all kinds of mediation in civil and commercial matters.

Organisations providing mediation services can also make such a commitment, by asking mediators acting under the auspices of their organisation to respect the code. Organisations have the opportunity to make available information on the measures they are taking to support the respect of the code by individual mediators through, for example, training, evaluation and monitoring.

For the purposes of the code mediation is defined as any process where two or more parties agree to the appointment of a third-party—hereinafter 'the mediator'—to help the parties to solve a dispute by reaching an agreement without adjudication and regardless of how that process may be called or commonly referred to in each Member State.

Adherence to the code is without prejudice to national legislation or rules regulating individual professions.

Organisations providing mediation services may wish to develop more detailed codes adapted to their specific context or the types of mediation services they offer, as well as with regard to specific areas such as family mediation or consumer mediation.

1. COMPETENCE AND APPOINTMENT OF MEDIATORS

1.1 Competence

Mediators shall be competent and knowledgeable in the process of mediation. Relevant factors shall include proper training and continuous updating of their education and practice in mediation skills, having regard to any relevant standards or accreditation schemes.

1.2 Appointment

The mediator will confer with the parties regarding suitable dates on which the mediation may take place. The mediator shall satisfy him/herself as to his/her background and competence to conduct the mediation before accepting the

* Located at http://ec.europa.eu/civiljustice/adr/adr_ec_code_conduct_en.htm

appointment and, upon request, disclose information concerning his/her background and experience to the parties.

1.3 Advertising/promotion of the mediator's services

Mediators may promote their practice, in a professional, truthful and dignified way.

2. INDEPENDENCE AND IMPARTIALITY

2.1 Independence and neutrality

The mediator must not act, or, having started to do so, continue to act, before having disclosed any circumstances that may, or may be seen to, affect his or her independence or conflict of interests. The duty to disclose is a continuing obligation throughout the process.

Such circumstances shall include

- any personal or business relationship with one of the parties,
- any financial or other interest, direct or indirect, in the outcome of the mediation, or
- the mediator, or a member of his or her firm, having acted in any capacity other than mediator for one of the parties.

In such cases the mediator may only accept or continue the mediation provided that he/she is certain of being able to carry out the mediation with full independence and neutrality in order to guarantee full impartiality and that the parties explicitly consent.

2.2 Impartiality

The mediator shall at all times act, and endeavour to be seen to act, with impartiality towards the parties and be committed to serve all parties equally with respect to the process of mediation.

3. THE MEDIATION AGREEMENT, PROCESS, SETTLEMENT AND FEES

3.1 Procedure

The mediator shall satisfy himself/herself that the parties to the mediation understand the characteristics of the mediation process and the role of the mediator and the parties in it.

The mediator shall in particular ensure that prior to commencement of the mediation the parties have understood and expressly agreed the terms and conditions of the mediation agreement including in particular any applicable provisions relating to obligations of confidentiality on the mediator and on the parties.

The mediation agreement shall, upon request of the parties, be drawn up in writing.

The mediator shall conduct the proceedings in an appropriate manner, taking into account the circumstances of the case, including possible power imbalances and the rule of law, any wishes the parties may express and the need for a prompt settlement of the dispute. The parties shall be free to agree with the mediator, by reference to a set of rules or otherwise, on the manner in which the mediation is to be conducted.

The mediator, if he/she deems it useful, may hear the parties separately.

3.2 Fairness of the process

The mediator shall ensure that all parties have adequate opportunities to be involved in the process.

The mediator if appropriate shall inform the parties, and may terminate the mediation, if:

— a settlement is being reached that for the mediator appears unenforceable or illegal, having regard to the circumstances of the case and the competence of the mediator for making such an assessment, or

— the mediator considers that continuing the mediation is unlikely to result in a settlement.

3.3 The end of the process

The mediator shall take all appropriate measures to ensure that any understanding is reached by all parties through knowing and informed consent, and that all parties understand the terms of the agreement.

The parties may withdraw from the mediation at any time without giving any justification.

The mediator may, upon request of the parties and within the limits of his or her competence, inform the parties as to how they may formalise the agreement and as to the possibilities for making the agreement enforceable.

3.4 Fees

Where not already provided, the mediator must always supply the parties with complete information on the mode of remuneration which he intends to apply. He/she shall not accept a mediation before the principles of his/her remuneration have been accepted by all parties concerned.

4. CONFIDENTIALITY

The mediator shall keep confidential all information, arising out of or in connection with the mediation, including the fact that the mediation is to take place or has taken place, unless compelled by law or public policy grounds. Any information disclosed in confidence to mediators by one of the parties shall not be disclosed to the other parties without permission or unless compelled by law.

Proposal for a Directive of the European Parliament and of the Council

on certain aspects of mediation in civil and commercial matters
{SEC(2004) 1314}
(presented by the Commission)

Explanatory Memorandum

1. SCOPE AND OBJECTIVES OF THE PROPOSAL

1.1. Objective

1.1.1. Ensuring better access to justice

Better access to justice is one of the key objectives of the EU's policy to establish an area of freedom, security and justice, where individuals and businesses should not be prevented or discouraged from exercising their rights by the incompatibility or complexity of legal and administrative systems in the Member States. The concept of access to justice should, in this context, include promoting access to adequate dispute resolution processes for individuals and business, and not just access to the judicial system.

The proposed directive contributes to this objective by facilitating access to dispute resolution through two types of provisions: first, provisions that aim at ensuring a sound relationship between mediation and judicial proceedings, by establishing minimum common rules in the Community on a number of key aspects of civil procedure. Secondly, by providing the necessary tools for the courts of the Member States to actively promote the use of mediation, without nevertheless making mediation compulsory or subject to specific sanctions.

Provisions touching the mediation process or the appointment or accreditation of mediators have been excluded from the proposed directive. Having regard to the reactions to the Green Paper of 2002 and current developments at national level, it is not clear that legislation is the preferred policy option as regards this type of provision. While excluding regulatory measures concerning the mediation procedure itself from this proposal the Commission has instead sought to encourage self-regulatory initiatives and is seeking to continue to do so through the proposed directive also.

In the consultations on the preliminary draft of this proposal most respondents endorsed the overall approach of the draft concerning the issues covered as well as the issues excluded from it. Compared to the preliminary draft certain changes, mainly of a technical nature, have been made to specific provisions and are further explained in the annex.

1.1.2. A sound relationship between mediation and civil proceedings

What have been retained for this proposal are essentially matters which cannot be adequately addressed through market-based solutions. This concerns notably civil procedural rules which may impact on the use of mediation as well as on its effectiveness. The interaction between mediation and traditional civil proceedings can take place at several occasions, for example:

— The parties consider use of mediation immediately after the dispute has arisen, as an alternative to launching civil proceedings; if the parties do choose to use mediation and fail to reach a settlement agreement, civil proceedings are launched after the termination of the mediation;

— If a settlement agreement is reached through mediation, one of the parties may fail to honour the agreement, calling for civil proceedings to be launched anyway;

— The parties launch civil proceedings immediately after the dispute has arisen, without having (yet) considered the possibility of mediation.

At present the interaction between mediation and civil proceedings presents a number of uncertain elements, due to the absence of or discrepancies between national procedural laws, elements which make themselves known with particular force in situations involving cross-border elements. Even if mediation may be the most suitable form of dispute resolution in a given case the parties may therefore opt for traditional civil proceedings in view of these uncertainties. A stable and predictable legal framework should contribute to putting mediation on an equal footing with judicial proceedings where factors related to the specific dispute play the most significant role for the parties in determining their choice of dispute resolution method. Such a framework should also help to preserve the possibility for the parties to solve their dispute through judicial proceedings even if mediation is attempted.

1.1.3. Promoting the use of mediation

The value of increasing the use of mediation rests principally in the advantages of the dispute resolution mechanism itself: a quicker, simpler and more cost-efficient way to solve disputes, which allows for taking into account a wider range of interests of the parties, with a greater chance of reaching an agreement which will be voluntarily respected, and which preserves an amicable and sustainable relationship between them. The Commission believes that mediation holds an untapped potential as a dispute resolution method and as a means of providing access to justice for individuals and business.

The role of the Community in directly promoting mediation is however by necessity limited and the only concrete measure to promote mediation contained in the proposal is the obligation for Member States to allow courts to suggest mediation to the parties. Ensuring a sound relationship between mediation and judicial proceedings will however indirectly contribute to promoting mediation also.

The pursuit of the objectives of this proposal can not take in place in isolation without regard to the very provision of mediation services. The question of quality of mediation services must therefore be addressed together with, and as a function of, the other provisions of the proposed directive which must operate with a sufficient level of mutual trust between the Member States in cross-border situations.

1.1.4. The relationship with the organisation of the judicial systems of the Member States

One of the often quoted benefits of mediation is that its increased use can offload pressure on the court system, thereby reducing what are often long delays in case-handling and possibly allowing for savings of public resources. As the proposed directive seeks to promote the use of mediation, it could indeed have a positive impact in this sense. This is however not pursued as an independent objective, for several reasons. First, the organisation of the judicial system is the sole competence of the Member States. Secondly, and most importantly, mediation has a value in itself as a dispute resolution method, to which citizens and business should have easy access and which deserves to be promoted independently of its value in off-loading pressure on the court system. The Commission does not see mediation as an alternative to court proceedings; it is rather one of several dispute resolution methods available in a modern society and which may be the most suited for some, but certainly not all, disputes. Moreover, it should be stressed that the availability of ADRs in general can not in any way detract from the obligation of Member States to maintain an effective and fair legal system that meets the requirements of the European Convention of Human Rights, which forms one of the central pillars of a democratic society.

1.1.5. Impact assessment

A preliminary impact assessment of this proposal was carried out in the context of the Commission's annual policy strategy for 2004. The proposal has not been selected for an extended impact assessment. The proposed directive aims at increasing the use of mediation in the EU, which will have beneficial economic effects by lowering transaction costs for individuals and business, through a quicker and more cost-efficient resolution of disputes. Mediation can also contribute to more sustainable economic and social trends in preserving the relationship between the parties after the dispute has been solved, in contrast to the often disruptive effects of solving a dispute through an adjudicatory process. The consultation process and other preparatory steps are described in the annex. In terms of alternative policy options the proposed directive contains mainly rules on civil procedure, and the results cannot be achieved using another policy instrument.

1.2. Legal basis

The objective and content of this proposed directive fall squarely within the scope of Article 65 TEC since it concerns civil procedural rules, where the provision on quality and training in Article 4 is ancillary to the other provisions. The proposed directive is necessary for the proper functioning of the internal market in view of the need to ensure access to dispute resolution mechanisms for individuals and business exercising the four freedoms and in view of the need to ensure the freedom to provide and to receive mediation services.

As has been stressed in the description of the objectives of the proposal the need for Community action in this field stems from the need to ensure legal certainty throughout the duration of a dispute regardless of the presence of cross-border elements at one stage or another. To ensure a coherent legal framework it is therefore necessary to address key aspects of the whole chain of possible events that can follow after the dispute has arisen, having regard to any possible scenario (success/failure of the mediation, settlement agreement followed by both parties or not, etc).

In the context of ADR the impact of cross-border elements is potentially greater than when considering measures relating to civil proceedings in isolation, since it is necessary to have regard to relevant factors at the time of the mediation as well as at the time of any subsequent civil proceedings, including the circumstance that these factors may change in the meantime. For example, cross-border elements may come from the domicile or place of business of one or both of the parties, the place of the mediation, or the place of the competent court. The agreement to mediate may in itself be governed by a different law than that which governs the original legal or contractual relationship between the parties, and an ensuing settlement agreement may be governed by the law of yet another third country. The settlement agreement may have to be enforced in yet another Member State depending on, for example, the location of the debtor's assets at the time when enforcement is sought.

However, it would not be feasible to restrict the scope of the proposal so as to only aim at removing obstacles created by cross-border elements or to ease the resolution of only those disputes displaying a cross-border element, however defined.

In assessing the suitability of mediation as a dispute resolution method for a given dispute, cross-border elements make up for only one of several relevant circumstances to be taken into account. Other circumstances include the nature of the dispute and the merits of the case as well as factors related to costs, delay and prospects of success. Promoting mediation in relation to those disputes that display a cross-border element only would therefore be arbitrary and create a risk of discriminatory effects, since the courts would suggest mediation to some parties only depending on their place of residence. A restriction of this type will undoubtedly entail a substantial reduction in the practical impact of the proposed directive also. Making the applicability of the civil procedural rules contained in the proposed directive subject to the presence of cross-border elements would rather lead to increased legal uncertainty. Alternatively such a restriction in scope may leave the applicability of the directive in the hands of the parties, who could introduce cross-border elements through their choice of mediator or court for the dispute in order to benefit from the rules laid down by the directive.

The proposed directive will form an important part of the legal framework for mediation services in the Community, as concerns the freedom to provide services in another Member State as well as the freedom to receive services. A limitation in scope to cross-border situations would lead to the creation of two parallel legal regimes, possibly even different standards as concern the provision and receipt of mediation services, with a risk of discriminatory effects for users as well as providers of mediation services. Such effects run counter to the principles of the internal market as well as the efforts of the Community to simplify the regulatory framework for individuals and business.

In conclusion the Commission considers that introducing an explicit condition of cross-border implications would invalidate the objectives of the proposed directive and be counterproductive to the proper functioning of the internal market. The directive must therefore apply to all situations regardless of the presence of cross-border elements at the time of the mediation or at the time of the judicial proceedings.

1.3. Subsidiarity and proportionality

In view of the need for legal certainty and predictability in situations involving the relationship between mediation and civil proceedings in situations displaying a cross-border element and the need to ensure the proper functioning of the internal market for the provision of and receipt of mediation services the objectives of this proposal cannot be sufficiently accomplished by the Member States. Measures taken at Community level will be more effective compared to individual initiatives taken by each Member State, for reasons of coherence and reasons of providing certain basic uniform rules applicable in cross-border situations as well as in domestic cases.

The provisions of the proposal are strictly limited to what is necessary to reach the objectives. A directive has been chosen as the most appropriate instrument since the provisions are designed to achieve certain specific objectives while leaving the means for how to reach those objectives to Member States' discretion. The proposal also confines itself to issues which can only be solved through legislation while inversely issues where market-based solutions are feasible have been excluded from the scope.

2. BACKGROUND TO THE PROPOSAL, CONSULTATION WITH INTERESTED PARTIES, AND COMMENTS ON MAIN PROVISIONS

The staff working paper annexed to this proposal provides further information on these issues.

Proposal for a Directive of the European Parliament and of the Council

on certain aspects of mediation in civil and commercial matters

THE EUROPEAN PARLIAMENT AND THE COUNCIL OF THE EUROPEAN UNION,

Having regard to the Treaty establishing the European Community, and in particular Article 61 (c) and the second indent of Article 67(5) thereof,

Having regard to the proposal from the Commission,[1]

Having regard to the opinion of the European Economic and Social Committee,[2]

Acting in accordance with the procedure laid down in Article 251 of the Treaty,[3]

Whereas:

(1) The Community has set itself the objective of maintaining and developing an area of freedom, security and justice, in which the free movement of persons is ensured. To this end, the Community is to adopt, *inter alia*, measures in the

[1] OJ C , , p. .
[2] OJ C , , p. .
[3] OJ C , , p. .

field of judicial cooperation in civil matters that are necessary for the proper functioning of the internal market.

(2) The European Council meeting in Tampere on 15 and 16 October 1999 called for, in relation to better access to justice in Europe, for alternative, extrajudicial procedures to be created by Member States.

(3) The Council adopted conclusions on alternative methods of settling disputes under civil and commercial law in 2000, stating that the establishment of basic principles in this area is an essential step towards enabling the appropriate development and operation of extrajudicial procedures for the settlement of disputes in civil and commercial matters so as to simplify and improve access to justice.

(4) The European Commission presented a Green Paper in 2002, taking stock of the existing situation as concerns ADRs in Europe and initiating widespread consultations with Member States and interested parties on possible measures to promote the use of mediation.

(5) The objective of ensuring better access to justice, as part of the policy of the European Union to establish an area of freedom, security and justice should encompass access to judicial as well as extrajudicial dispute resolution methods. This directive should contribute to the proper functioning of the internal market, in particular as concerns the provision and receipt of mediation services.

(6) Mediation can provide a cost-efficient and quick extrajudicial resolution of disputes in civil and commercial matters through processes tailored to the needs of the parties. Settlement agreements reached through mediation are more likely to be enforced voluntarily and are more likely to preserve an amicable and sustainable relationship between the parties. These benefits become even more pronounced in situations displaying cross-border elements.

(7) Framework legislation, addressing key aspects of civil procedure in particular, is therefore necessary to promote the further use of mediation and to ensure that parties having recourse to mediation can rely on a predictable legal framework.

(8) This directive should cover processes where two or more parties to a dispute are assisted by a mediator to reach an amicable agreement on the settlement of the dispute, but exclude processes of an adjudicatory nature such as arbitration, ombudsmen schemes, consumer complaint schemes, expert determination or processes administered by bodies issuing a formal recommendation, be it legally binding or not, as to the resolution of the dispute.

(9) A minimum degree of compatibility of civil procedural rules is necessary as concerns the effect of mediation on limitation periods and how the confidentiality of the mediator will be protected in any subsequent judicial proceedings. The possibility for the court to refer the parties to mediation should also be covered, while retaining the principle that mediation is a voluntary process.

(10) Mediation should not be regarded as a poorer alternative to judicial proceedings in the sense that settlement agreements are dependant on the good will of the parties for their enforcement. It is therefore necessary to ensure that all Member States provide for a procedure whereby a settlement agreement can be confirmed in a judgment, decision or authentic instrument by a court or public authority.

(11) Such a possibility will allow for a settlement agreement to be recognised and enforced across the Union, under the conditions laid down by Community instruments on mutual recognition and enforcement of judgments and decisions.

(12) To ensure the necessary trust between the Member States in the respect of confidentiality, suspension of limitation periods, and recognition and enforcement of settlement agreements, effective quality control mechanisms must be put in place concerning the provision of mediation services and training of mediators.

(13) These mechanisms and measures, which shall be defined by the Member States and may include having recourse to market-based solutions, should aim at preserving the flexibility of the mediation process and the private autonomy of the parties. The Commission shall encourage self-regulatory measures at Community level through, for example, development of a European code of conduct addressing key aspects of the mediation process.

(14) In the field of consumer protection, the Commission adopted in 2001 a formal recommendation[4] which establishes minimum quality criteria that out-of-court bodies involved in the consensual resolution of consumer disputes should offer to their users. It is advisable that any mediators or organisation concerned by the recommendation respect its principles. In order to ensure the dissemination of information concerning these bodies, the Commission is setting up a database of out-of-court schemes that Member States consider as respecting the principles of the recommendation.

(15) This directive respects the fundamental rights and observes the principles recognised in particular by the Charter of Fundamental Rights of the European Union. In particular, it seeks to ensure full respect for the right to a fair trial as recognised in Article 47 of the Charter.

(16) Since the objectives of this directive cannot be sufficiently achieved by the Member States and can therefore, by reason of the scale of effects of the action, be better achieved at Community level, the Community may adopt measures in accordance with the principle of subsidiarity as set out in Article 5 of the Treaty. / In accordance with the principle of proportionality, as set out in that Article, this Directive does not go beyond what is necessary in order to achieve those objectives.

[4] Commission Recommendation of 4 April 2001 on the principles for out-of-court bodies in the consensual resolution of consumer disputes (OJ L 109, 19.4.2001, p. 56).

(17) [In accordance with Article 3 of the Protocol on the position of the United Kingdom and Ireland, annexed to the Treaty on European Union and the Treaty establishing the European Community, the United Kingdom and Ireland have notified their wish to take part in the adoption and application of this Directive. / In accordance with Articles 1 and 2 of the Protocol on the position of the United Kingdom and Ireland, annexed to the Treaty on European Union and the Treaty establishing the European Community, the United Kingdom and Ireland do not take part in the adoption of this Directive, which is therefore not binding on those Member States.]

(18) In accordance with Articles 1 and 2 of the Protocol on the position of Denmark annexed to the Treaty on European Union and the Treaty establishing the European Community, Denmark does not take part in the adoption of this Directive, and is therefore not bound by it or subject to its application,

HAVE ADOPTED THIS DIRECTIVE:

Article 1—Objective and scope

1. The objective of this directive is to facilitate access to dispute resolution by promoting the use of mediation and by ensuring a sound relationship between mediation and judicial proceedings.
2. This directive shall apply in civil and commercial matters.
3. In this directive, 'Member State' shall mean Member States with the exception of Denmark.

Article 2—Definitions

For the purposes of this Directive the following definitions shall apply:

(a) 'Mediation' shall mean any process, however named or referred to, where two or more parties to a dispute are assisted by a third party to reach an agreement on the settlement of the dispute, and regardless of whether the process is initiated by the parties, suggested or ordered by a court or prescribed by the national law of a Member State.

It shall not include attempts made by the judge to settle a dispute within the course of judicial proceedings concerning that dispute.

(b) 'Mediator' shall mean any third party conducting a mediation, regardless of the denomination or profession of that third party in the Member State concerned and of the way the third party has been appointed or requested to conduct the mediation.

Article 3—Referral to mediation

1. A court before which an action is brought may, when appropriate and having regard to all circumstances of the case, invite the parties to use mediation in

order to settle the dispute. The court may in any event require the parties to attend an information session on the use of mediation.

2. This directive is without prejudice to national legislation making the use of mediation compulsory or subject to incentives or sanctions, whether before or after judicial proceedings have started, provided that such legislation does not impede on the right of access to the judicial system, in particular in situations where one of the parties is resident in a Member State other than that of the court.

Article 4—Ensuring the quality of mediation

1. The Commission and the Member States shall promote and encourage the development of and adherence to voluntary codes of conduct by mediators and organisations providing mediation services, at Community as well as at national level, as well as other effective quality control mechanisms concerning the provision of mediation services.
2. Member States shall promote and encourage the training of mediators in order to allow parties in dispute to choose a mediator who will be able to effectively conduct a mediation in the manner expected by the parties.

Article 5—Enforcement of settlement agreements

1. Member States shall ensure that, upon request of the parties, a settlement agreement reached as a result of a mediation can be confirmed in a judgment, decision, authentic instrument or any other form by a court or public authority that renders the agreement enforceable in a similar manner as a judgment under national law, provided that the agreement is not contrary to European law or to national law in the Member State where the request is made.
2. Member States shall inform the Commission of the courts or public authorities that are competent for receiving a request in accordance with paragraph 1.

Article 6—Admissibility of evidence in civil judicial proceedings

1. Mediators, as well as any person involved in the administration of mediation services, shall not in civil judicial proceedings give testimony or evidence regarding any of the following:
   (a) An invitation by a party to engage in mediation or the fact that a party was willing to participate in mediation;
   (b) Views expressed or suggestions made by a party in a mediation in respect of a possible settlement of the dispute;
   (c) Statements or admissions made by a party in the course of the mediation;
   (d) Proposals made by the mediator;
   (e) The fact that a party had indicated its willingness to accept a proposal for a settlement made by the mediator;

(f) A document prepared solely for purposes of the mediation.

2. Paragraph 1 shall apply irrespective of the form of the information or evidence referred to therein.
3. The disclosure of the information referred to in paragraph 1 shall not be ordered by a court or other judicial authority in civil judicial proceedings and, if such information is offered as evidence in contravention of paragraph 1, that evidence shall be treated as inadmissible. Nevertheless, such information may be disclosed or admitted in evidence
   (a) to the extent required for the purposes of implementation or enforcement of a settlement agreement reached as a direct result of the mediation,
   (b) for overriding considerations of public policy, in particular when required to ensure the protection of children or to prevent harm to the physical or psychological integrity of a person, or
   (c) if the mediator and the parties agree thereto.
4. The provisions of paragraphs 1, 2 and 3 shall apply whether or not the judicial proceedings relate to the dispute that is or was the subject matter of the mediation.
5. Subject to paragraph 1, evidence that is otherwise admissible in judicial proceedings does not become inadmissible as a consequence of having been used in a mediation.

Article 7—Suspension of limitation periods

1. The running of any period of prescription or limitation regarding the claim that is the subject matter of the mediation shall be suspended as of when, after the dispute has arisen:
   (a) the parties agree to use mediation,
   (b) the use of mediation is ordered by a court, or
   (c) an obligation to use mediation arises under the national law of a Member State.
2. Where the mediation has ended without a settlement agreement, the period resumes running from the time the mediation ended without a settlement agreement, counting from the date when one or both of the parties or the mediator declares that the mediation is terminated or effectively withdraws from it. The period shall in any event extend for at least one month from the date when it resumes running, except when it concerns a period within which an action must be brought to prevent that a provisional or similar measure ceases to have effect or is revoked.

Article 8—Implementing provisions

The Commission shall publish information on the competent courts and authorities communicated by the Member States pursuant to Article 5(2).

Article 9—Transposition

1. Member States shall bring into force the laws, regulations and administrative provisions necessary to comply with this Directive by 1 September 2007 at the latest. They shall forthwith inform the Commission thereof.
2. When Member States adopt those provisions, they shall contain a reference to this Directive or be accompanied by such a reference on the occasion of their official publication. Member States shall determine how such reference is to be made.

Article 10—Entry into force

This Directive shall enter into force on the twentieth day following that of its publication in the *Official Journal of the European Union*.

Article 11—Addressees

This Directive is addressed to the Member States.

Done at Brussels,

For the European Parliament	*For the Council*
The President	*The President*

Regulation (EC) No 1896/2006 of the European Parliament and of the Council

of 12 December 2006

creating a European order for payment procedure

THE EUROPEAN PARLIAMENT AND THE COUNCIL OF THE EUROPEAN UNION,

Having regard to the Treaty establishing the European Community, and in particular Article 61(c) thereof,

Having regard to the proposal from the Commission,

Having regard to the Opinion of the European Economic and Social Committee,[1]

Acting in accordance with the procedure laid down in Article 251 of the Treaty,[2]

Whereas:

(1) The Community has set itself the objective of maintaining and developing an area of freedom, security and justice in which the free movement of persons is ensured. For the gradual establishment of such an area, the Community is to adopt, *inter alia*, measures in the field of judicial cooperation in civil matters having cross-border implications and needed for the proper functioning of the internal market.

(2) According to Article 65(c) of the Treaty, these measures are to include measures eliminating obstacles to the good functioning of civil proceedings, if necessary by promoting the compatibility of the rules on civil procedure applicable in the Member States.

(3) The European Council meeting in Tampere on 15 and 16 October 1999 invited the Council and the Commission to prepare new legislation on issues that are instrumental to smooth judicial cooperation and to enhanced access to law and specifically made reference, in that context, to orders for money payment.

[1] OJ C 221, 8.9.2005, p. 77.

[2] Opinion of the European Parliament of 13 December 2005 (not yet published in the Official Journal), Council Common Position of 30 June 2006 (not yet published in the Official Journal) and Position of the European Parliament of 25 October 2006. Council Decision of 11 December 2006.

(4) On 30 November 2000, the Council adopted a joint Commission and Council programme of measures for implementation of the principle of mutual recognition of decisions in civil and commercial matters.[3] The programme envisages the possibility of a specific, uniform or harmonised procedure laid down within the Community to obtain a judicial decision in specific areas including that of uncontested claims. This was taken forward by the Hague Programme, adopted by the European Council on 5 November 2004, which called for work to be actively pursued on the European order for payment.

(5) The Commission adopted a Green Paper on a European order for payment procedure and on measures to simplify and speed up small claims litigation on 20 December 2002. The Green Paper launched consultations on the possible objectives and features of a uniform or harmonised European procedure for the recovery of uncontested claims.

(6) The swift and efficient recovery of outstanding debts over which no legal controversy exists is of paramount importance for economic operators in the European Union, as late payments constitute a major reason for insolvency threatening the survival of businesses, particularly small and medium-sized enterprises, and resulting in numerous job losses.

(7) All Member States are trying to tackle the issue of mass recovery of uncontested claims, in the majority of States by means of a simplified order for payment procedure, but both the content of national legislation and the performance of domestic procedures vary substantially. Furthermore, the procedures currently in existence are frequently either inadmissible or impracticable in cross-border cases.

(8) The resulting impediments to access to efficient justice in cross-border cases and the distortion of competition within the internal market due to imbalances in the functioning of procedural means afforded to creditors in different Member States necessitate Community legislation guaranteeing a level playing field for creditors and debtors throughout the European Union.

(9) The purpose of this Regulation is to simplify, speed up and reduce the costs of litigation in cross-border cases concerning uncontested pecuniary claims by creating a European order for payment procedure, and to permit the free circulation of European orders for payment throughout the Member States by laying down minimum standards, compliance with which renders unnecessary any intermediate proceedings in the Member State of enforcement prior to recognition and enforcement.

(10) The procedure established by this Regulation should serve as an additional and optional means for the claimant, who remains free to resort to a procedure provided for by national law. Accordingly, this Regulation neither replaces nor harmonises the existing mechanisms for the recovery of uncontested claims under national law.

[3] OJ C 12, 15.1.2001, p. 1.

(11) The procedure should be based, to the largest extent possible, on the use of standard forms in any communication between the court and the parties in order to facilitate its administration and enable the use of automatic data processing.
(12) When deciding which courts are to have jurisdiction to issue a European order for payment, Member States should take due account of the need to ensure access to justice.
(13) In the application for a European order for payment, the claimant should be obliged to provide information that is sufficient to clearly identify and support the claim in order to place the defendant in a position to make a well-informed choice either to oppose the claim or to leave it uncontested.
(14) In that context, it should be compulsory for the claimant to include a description of evidence supporting the claim. For that purpose the application form should include as exhaustive a list as possible of types of evidence that are usually produced in support of pecuniary claims.
(15) The lodging of an application for a European order for payment should entail the payment of any applicable court fees.
(16) The court should examine the application, including the issue of jurisdiction and the description of evidence, on the basis of the information provided in the application form. This would allow the court to examine prima facie the merits of the claim and *inter alia* to exclude clearly unfounded claims or inadmissible applications. The examination should not need to be carried out by a judge.
(17) There is to be no right of appeal against the rejection of the application. This does not preclude, however, a possible review of the decision rejecting the application at the same level of jurisdiction in accordance with national law.
(18) The European order for payment should apprise the defendant of his options to pay the amount awarded to the claimant or to send a statement of opposition within a time limit of 30 days if he wishes to contest the claim. In addition to being provided with full information concerning the claim as supplied by the claimant, the defendant should be advised of the legal significance of the European order for payment and in particular of the consequences of leaving the claim uncontested.
(19) Due to differences between Member States' rules of civil procedure and especially those governing the service of documents, it is necessary to lay down a specific and detailed definition of minimum standards that should apply in the context of the European order for payment procedure. In particular, as regards the fulfilment of those standards, any method based on legal fiction should not be considered sufficient for the service of the European order for payment.
(20) All the methods of service listed in Articles 13 and 14 are characterised by either complete certainty (Article 13) or a very high degree of likelihood (Article 14) that the document served has reached its addressee.

(21) Personal service on certain persons other than the defendant himself pursuant to Article 14(1)(a) and (b) should be deemed to meet the requirements of those provisions only if those persons actually accepted/received the European order for payment.

(22) Article 15 should apply to situations where the defendant cannot represent himself in court, as in the case of a legal person, and where a person authorised to represent him is determined by law, as well as to situations where the defendant has authorised another person, in particular a lawyer, to represent him in the specific court proceedings at issue.

(23) The defendant may submit his statement of opposition using the standard form set out in this Regulation. However, the courts should take into account any other written form of opposition if it is expressed in a clear manner.

(24) A statement of opposition filed within the time limit should terminate the European order for payment procedure and should lead to an automatic transfer of the case to ordinary civil proceedings unless the claimant has explicitly requested that the proceedings be terminated in that event. For the purposes of this Regulation the concept of ordinary civil proceedings should not necessarily be interpreted within the meaning of national law.

(25) After the expiry of the time limit for submitting the statement of opposition, in certain exceptional cases the defendant should be entitled to apply for a review of the European order for payment. Review in exceptional cases should not mean that the defendant is given a second opportunity to oppose the claim. During the review procedure the merits of the claim should not be evaluated beyond the grounds resulting from the exceptional circumstances invoked by the defendant. The other exceptional circumstances could include a situation where the European order for payment was based on false information provided in the application form.

(26) Court fees covered by Article 25 should not include for example lawyers' fees or costs of service of documents by an entity other than a court.

(27) A European order for payment issued in one Member State which has become enforceable should be regarded for the purposes of enforcement as if it had been issued in the Member State in which enforcement is sought. Mutual trust in the administration of justice in the Member States justifies the assessment by the court of one Member State that all conditions for issuing a European order for payment are fulfilled to enable the order to be enforced in all other Member States without judicial review of the proper application of minimum procedural standards in the Member State where the order is to be enforced. Without prejudice to the provisions of this Regulation, in particular the minimum standards laid down in Article 22(1) and (2) and Article 23, the procedures for the enforcement of the European order for payment should continue to be governed by national law.

(28) For the purposes of calculating time limits, Regulation (EEC, Euratom) No 1182/71 of the Council of 3 June 1971 determining the rules applicable to

periods, dates and time limits[4] should apply. The defendant should be advised of this and should be informed that account will be taken of the public holidays of the Member State in which the court issuing the European order for payment is situated.

(29) Since the objective of this Regulation, namely to establish a uniform rapid and efficient mechanism for the recovery of uncontested pecuniary claims throughout the European Union, cannot be sufficiently achieved by the Member States and can therefore, by reason of the scale and effects of the Regulation, be better achieved at Community level, the Community may adopt measures in accordance with the principle of subsidiarity as set out in Article 5 of the Treaty. In accordance with the principle of proportionality as set out in that Article, this Regulation does not go beyond what is necessary in order to achieve that objective.

(30) The measures necessary for the implementation of this Regulation should be adopted in accordance with Council Decision 1999/468/EC of 28 June 1999 laying down the procedures for the exercise of implementing powers conferred on the Commission.[5]

(31) The United Kingdom and Ireland, in accordance with Article 3 of the Protocol on the position of the United Kingdom and Ireland annexed to the Treaty on European Union and the Treaty establishing the European Community, have given notice of their wish to take part in the adoption and application of this Regulation.

(32) In accordance with Articles 1 and 2 of the Protocol on the position of Denmark annexed to the Treaty on European Union and the Treaty establishing the European Community, Denmark does not take part in the adoption of this Regulation, and is not bound by it or subject to its application,

HAVE ADOPTED THIS REGULATION:

Article 1

Subject matter

1. The purpose of this Regulation is:
   (a) to simplify, speed up and reduce the costs of litigation in cross-border cases concerning uncontested pecuniary claims by creating a European order for payment procedure;
   and
   (b) to permit the free circulation of European orders for payment throughout the Member States by laying down minimum standards, compliance with which

[4] OJ L 124, 8.6.1971, p. 1.

[5] OJ L 184, 17.7.1999, p. 23. Decision as amended by Decision 2006/512/EC (OJ L 200, 22.7.2006, p. 11).

renders unnecessary any intermediate proceedings in the Member State of enforcement prior to recognition and enforcement.

2. This Regulation shall not prevent a claimant from pursuing a claim within the meaning of Article 4 by making use of another procedure available under the law of a Member State or under Community law.

Article 2

Scope

1. This Regulation shall apply to civil and commercial matters in cross-border cases, whatever the nature of the court or tribunal. It shall not extend, in particular, to revenue, customs or administrative matters or the liability of the State for acts and omissions in the exercise of State authority ('acta iure imperii').
2. This Regulation shall not apply to:
   (a) rights in property arising out of a matrimonial relationship, wills and succession;
   (b) bankruptcy, proceedings relating to the winding-up of insolvent companies or other legal persons, judicial arrangements, compositions and analogous proceedings;
   (c) social security;
   (d) claims arising from non-contractual obligations, unless:
      (i) they have been the subject of an agreement between the parties or there has been an admission of debt,
      or
      (ii) they relate to liquidated debts arising from joint ownership of property.
3. In this Regulation, the term 'Member State' shall mean Member States with the exception of Denmark.

Article 3

Cross-border cases

1. For the purposes of this Regulation, a cross-border case is one in which at least one of the parties is domiciled or habitually resident in a Member State other than the Member State of the court seised.
2. Domicile shall be determined in accordance with Articles 59 and 60 of Council Regulation (EC) No 44/2001 of 22 December 2000 on jurisdiction and the recognition and enforcement of judgments in civil and commercial matters.[6]
3. The relevant moment for determining whether there is a cross-border case shall be the time when the application for a European order for payment is submitted in accordance with this Regulation.

[6] OJ L 12, 16.1.2001, p. 1. Regulation as last amended by Commission Regulation (EC) No 2245/2004 (OJ L 381, 28.12.2004, p. 10).

Article 4
European order for payment procedure

The European order for payment procedure shall be established for the collection of pecuniary claims for a specific amount that have fallen due at the time when the application for a European order for payment is submitted.

Article 5
Definitions

For the purposes of this Regulation, the following definitions shall apply:

1) 'Member State of origin' means the Member State in which a European order for payment is issued;
2) 'Member State of enforcement' means the Member State in which enforcement of a European order for payment is sought;
3) 'court' means any authority in a Member State with competence regarding European orders for payment or any other related matters;
4) 'court of origin' means the court which issues a European order for payment.

Article 6
Jurisdiction

1. For the purposes of applying this Regulation, jurisdiction shall be determined in accordance with the relevant rules of Community law, in particular Regulation (EC) No 44/2001.
2. However, if the claim relates to a contract concluded by a person, the consumer, for a purpose which can be regarded as being outside his trade or profession, and if the defendant is the consumer, only the courts in the Member State in which the defendant is domiciled, within the meaning of Article 59 of Regulation (EC) No 44/2001, shall have jurisdiction.

Article 7
Application for a European order for payment

1. An application for a European order for payment shall be made using standard form A as set out in Annex I.
2. The application shall state:
   (a) the names and addresses of the parties, and, where applicable, their representatives, and of the court to which the application is made;
   (b) the amount of the claim, including the principal and, where applicable, interest, contractual penalties and costs;
   (c) if interest on the claim is demanded, the interest rate and the period of time for which that interest is demanded unless statutory interest is automatically added to the principal under the law of the Member State of origin;

(d) the cause of the action, including a description of the circumstances invoked as the basis of the claim and, where applicable, of the interest demanded;
(e) a description of evidence supporting the claim;
(f) the grounds for jurisdiction;
and
(g) the cross-border nature of the case within the meaning of Article 3.

3. In the application, the claimant shall declare that the information provided is true to the best of his knowledge and belief and shall acknowledge that any deliberate false statement could lead to appropriate penalties under the law of the Member State of origin.
4. In an Appendix to the application the claimant may indicate to the court that he opposes a transfer to ordinary civil proceedings within the meaning of Article 17 in the event of opposition by the defendant. This does not prevent the claimant from informing the court thereof subsequently, but in any event before the order is issued.
5. The application shall be submitted in paper form or by any other means of communication, including electronic, accepted by the Member State of origin and available to the court of origin.
6. The application shall be signed by the claimant or, where applicable, by his representative. Where the application is submitted in electronic form in accordance with paragraph 5, it shall be signed in accordance with Article 2(2) of Directive 1999/93/EC of the European Parliament and of the Council of 13 December 1999 on a Community framework for electronic signatures.[7] The signature shall be recognised in the Member State of origin and may not be made subject to additional requirements.

However, such electronic signature shall not be required if and to the extent that an alternative electronic communications system exists in the courts of the Member State of origin which is available to a certain group of pre-registered authenticated users and which permits the identification of those users in a secure manner. Member States shall inform the Commission of such communications systems.

Article 8

Examination of the application

The court seised of an application for a European order for payment shall examine, as soon as possible and on the basis of the application form, whether the requirements set out in Articles 2, 3, 4, 6 and 7 are met and whether the claim appears to be founded. This examination may take the form of an automated procedure.

[7] OJ L 13, 19.1.2000, p. 12.

Article 9
Completion and rectification

1. If the requirements set out in Article 7 are not met and unless the claim is clearly unfounded or the application is inadmissible, the court shall give the claimant the opportunity to complete or rectify the application. The court shall use standard form B as set out in Annex II.
2. Where the court requests the claimant to complete or rectify the application, it shall specify a time limit it deems appropriate in the circumstances. The court may at its discretion extend that time limit.

Article 10
Modification of the application

1. If the requirements referred to in Article 8 are met for only part of the claim, the court shall inform the claimant to that effect, using standard form C as set out in Annex III. The claimant shall be invited to accept or refuse a proposal for a European order for payment for the amount specified by the court and shall be informed of the consequences of his decision. The claimant shall reply by returning standard form C sent by the court within a time limit specified by the court in accordance with Article 9(2).
2. If the claimant accepts the court's proposal, the court shall issue a European order for payment, in accordance with Article 12, for that part of the claim accepted by the claimant. The consequences with respect to the remaining part of the initial claim shall be governed by national law.
3. If the claimant fails to send his reply within the time limit specified by the court or refuses the court's proposal, the court shall reject the application for a European order for payment in its entirety.

Article 11
Rejection of the application

1. The court shall reject the application if:
   (a) the requirements set out in Articles 2, 3, 4, 6 and 7 are not met;
   or
   (b) the claim is clearly unfounded;
   or
   (c) the claimant fails to send his reply within the time limit specified by the court under Article 9(2);
   or
   (d) the claimant fails to send his reply within the time limit specified by the court or refuses the court's proposal, in accordance with Article 10.

   The claimant shall be informed of the grounds for the rejection by means of standard form D as set out in Annex IV.

2. There shall be no right of appeal against the rejection of the application.
3. The rejection of the application shall not prevent the claimant from pursuing the claim by means of a new application for a European order for payment or of any other procedure available under the law of a Member State.

Article 12

Issue of a European order for payment

1. If the requirements referred to in Article 8 are met, the court shall issue, as soon as possible and normally within 30 days of the lodging of the application, a European order for payment using standard form E as set out in Annex V.

   The 30-day period shall not include the time taken by the claimant to complete, rectify or modify the application.
2. The European order for payment shall be issued together with a copy of the application form. It shall not comprise the information provided by the claimant in Appendices 1 and 2 to form A.
3. In the European order for payment, the defendant shall be advised of his options to:
   (a) pay the amount indicated in the order to the claimant;
   or
   (b) oppose the order by lodging with the court of origin a statement of opposition, to be sent within 30 days of service of the order on him.
4. In the European order for payment, the defendant shall be informed that:
   (a) the order was issued solely on the basis of the information which was provided by the claimant and was not verified by the court;
   (b) the order will become enforceable unless a statement of opposition has been lodged with the court in accordance with Article 16;
   (c) where a statement of opposition is lodged, the proceedings shall continue before the competent courts of the Member State of origin in accordance with the rules of ordinary civil procedure unless the claimant has explicitly requested that the proceedings be terminated in that event.
5. The court shall ensure that the order is served on the defendant in accordance with national law by a method that shall meet the minimum standards laid down in Articles 13, 14 and 15.

Article 13

Service with proof of receipt by the defendant

The European order for payment may be served on the defendant in accordance with the national law of the State in which the service is to be effected, by one of the following methods:

(a) personal service attested by an acknowledgement of receipt, including the date of receipt, which is signed by the defendant;

(b) personal service attested by a document signed by the competent person who effected the service stating that the defendant has received the document or refused to receive it without any legal justification, and the date of service;
(c) postal service attested by an acknowledgement of receipt, including the date of receipt, which is signed and returned by the defendant;
(d) service by electronic means such as fax or e-mail, attested by an acknowledgement of receipt, including the date of receipt, which is signed and returned by the defendant.

Article 14

Service without proof of receipt by the defendant

1. The European order for payment may also be served on the defendant in accordance with the national law of the State in which service is to be effected, by one of the following methods:
   (a) personal service at the defendant's personal address on persons who are living in the same household as the defendant or are employed there;
   (b) in the case of a self-employed defendant or a legal person, personal service at the defendant's business premises on persons who are employed by the defendant;
   (c) deposit of the order in the defendant's mailbox;
   (d) deposit of the order at a post office or with competent public authorities and the placing in the defendant's mailbox of written notification of that deposit, provided that the written notification clearly states the character of the document as a court document or the legal effect of the notification as effecting service and setting in motion the running of time for the purposes of time limits;
   (e) postal service without proof pursuant to paragraph 3 where the defendant has his address in the Member State of origin;
   (f) electronic means attested by an automatic confirmation of delivery, provided that the defendant has expressly accepted this method of service in advance.
2. For the purposes of this Regulation, service under paragraph 1 is not admissible if the defendant's address is not known with certainty.
3. Service pursuant to paragraph 1(a), (b), (c) and (d) shall be attested by:
   (a) a document signed by the competent person who effected the service, indicating:
      (i) the method of service used;
      and
      (ii) the date of service;
      and
      (iii) where the order has been served on a person other than the defendant, the name of that person and his relation to the defendant;
   or

(b) an acknowledgement of receipt by the person served, for the purposes of paragraphs (1)(a) and (b).

Article 15

Service on a representative

Service pursuant to Articles 13 or 14 may also be effected on a defendant's representative.

Article 16

Opposition to the European order for payment

1. The defendant may lodge a statement of opposition to the European order for payment with the court of origin using standard form F as set out in Annex VI, which shall be supplied to him together with the European order for payment.
2. The statement of opposition shall be sent within 30 days of service of the order on the defendant.
3. The defendant shall indicate in the statement of opposition that he contests the claim, without having to specify the reasons for this.
4. The statement of opposition shall be submitted in paper form or by any other means of communication, including electronic, accepted by the Member State of origin and available to the court of origin.
5. The statement of opposition shall be signed by the defendant or, where applicable, by his representative. Where the statement of opposition is submitted in electronic form in accordance with paragraph 4, it shall be signed in accordance with Article 2(2) of Directive 1999/93/EC. The signature shall be recognised in the Member State of origin and may not be made subject to additional requirements.
   However, such electronic signature shall not be required if and to the extent that an alternative electronic communications system exists in the courts of the Member State of origin which is available to a certain group of pre-registered authenticated users and which permits the identification of those users in a secure manner. Member States shall inform the Commission of such communications systems.

Article 17

Effects of the lodging of a statement of opposition

1. If a statement of opposition is entered within the time limit laid down in Article 16(2), the proceedings shall continue before the competent courts of the Member State of origin in accordance with the rules of ordinary civil procedure unless the claimant has explicitly requested that the proceedings be terminated in that event.

Where the claimant has pursued his claim through the European order for payment procedure, nothing under national law shall prejudice his position in subsequent ordinary civil proceedings.

2. The transfer to ordinary civil proceedings within the meaning of paragraph 1 shall be governed by the law of the Member State of origin.
3. The claimant shall be informed whether the defendant has lodged a statement of opposition and of any transfer to ordinary civil proceedings.

Article 18

Enforceability

1. If within the time limit laid down in Article 16(2), taking into account an appropriate period of time to allow a statement to arrive, no statement of opposition has been lodged with the court of origin, the court of origin shall without delay declare the European order for payment enforceable using standard form G as set out in Annex VII. The court shall verify the date of service.
2. Without prejudice to paragraph 1, the formal requirements for enforceability shall be governed by the law of the Member State of origin.
3. The court shall send the enforceable European order for payment to the claimant.

Article 19

Abolition of exequatur

A European order for payment which has become enforceable in the Member State of origin shall be recognised and enforced in the other Member States without the need for a declaration of enforceability and without any possibility of opposing its recognition.

Article 20

Review in exceptional cases

1. After the expiry of the time limit laid down in Article 16(2) the defendant shall be entitled to apply for a review of the European order for payment before the competent court in the Member State of origin where:
   (a) (i) the order for payment was served by one of the methods provided for in Article 14,

   and

   (ii) service was not effected in sufficient time to enable him to arrange for his defence, without any fault on his part,

   or

   (b) the defendant was prevented from objecting to the claim by reason of *force majeure* or due to extraordinary circumstances without any fault on his part,

   provided in either case that he acts promptly.

2. After expiry of the time limit laid down in Article 16(2) the defendant shall also be entitled to apply for a review of the European order for payment before the competent court in the Member State of origin where the order for payment was clearly wrongly issued, having regard to the requirements laid down in this Regulation, or due to other exceptional circumstances.
3. If the court rejects the defendant's application on the basis that none of the grounds for review referred to in paragraphs 1 and 2 apply, the European order for payment shall remain in force.

   If the court decides that the review is justified for one of the reasons laid down in paragraphs 1 and 2, the European order for payment shall be null and void.

Article 21

Enforcement

1. Without prejudice to the provisions of this Regulation, enforcement procedures shall be governed by the law of the Member State of enforcement.

   A European order for payment which has become enforceable shall be enforced under the same conditions as an enforceable decision issued in the Member State of enforcement.
2. For enforcement in another Member State, the claimant shall provide the competent enforcement authorities of that Member State with:
   (a) a copy of the European order for payment, as declared enforceable by the court of origin, which satisfies the conditions necessary to establish its authenticity;
   and
   (b) where necessary, a translation ofthe European order for payment into the official language of the Member State of enforcement or, if there are several official languages in that Member State, the official language or one of the official languages of court proceedings of the place where enforcement is sought, in conformity with the law of that Member State, or into another language that the Member State of enforcement has indicated it can accept. Each Member State may indicate the official language or languages of the institutions of the European Union other than its own which it can accept for the European order for payment. The translation shall be certified by a person qualified to do so in one of the Member States.
3. No security, bond or deposit, however described, shall be required of a claimant who in one Member State applies for enforcement of a European order for payment issued in another Member State on the ground that he is a foreign national or that he is not domiciled or resident in the Member State of enforcement.

Article 22

Refusal of enforcement

1. Enforcement shall, upon application by the defendant, be refused by the competent court in the Member State of enforcement if the European order for payment is irreconcilable with an earlier decision or order previously given in any Member State or in a third country, provided that:
   (a) the earlier decision or order involved the same cause of action between the same parties;
   and
   (b) the earlier decision or order fulfils the conditions necessary for its recognition in the Member State of enforcement;
   and
   (c) the irreconcilability could not have been raised as an objection in the court proceedings in the Member State of origin.
2. Enforcement shall, upon application, also be refused if and to the extent that the defendant has paid the claimant the amount awarded in the European order for payment.
3. Undcr no circumstances may the European order for payment be reviewed as to its substance in the Member State of enforcement.

Article 23

Stay or limitation of enforcement

Where the defendant has applied for a review in accordance with Article 20, the competent court in the Member State of enforcement may, upon application by the defendant:

(a) limit the enforcement proceedings to protective measures;
or
(b) make enforcement conditional on the provision of such security as it shall determine;
or
(c) under exceptional circumstances, stay the enforcement proceedings.

Article 24

Legal representation

Representation by a lawyer or another legal professional shall not be mandatory:

(a) for the claimant in respect of the application for a European order for payment;
(b) for the defendant in respect of the statement of opposition to a European order for payment.

Article 25

Court fees

1. The combined court fees of a European order for payment procedure and of the ordinary civil proceedings that ensue in the event of a statement of opposition to a European order for payment in a Member State shall not exceed the court fees of ordinary civil proceedings without a preceding European order for payment procedure in that Member State.
2. For the purposes of this Regulation, court fees shall comprise fees and charges to be paid to the court, the amount of which is fixed in accordance with national law.

Article 26

Relationship with national procedural law

All procedural issues not specifically dealt with in this Regulation shall be governed by national law.

Article 27

Relationship with Regulation (EC) No 1348/2000

This Regulation shall not affect the application of Council Regulation (EC) No 1348/2000 of 29 May 2000 on the service in the Member States of judicial and extrajudicial documents in civil and commercial matters.[8]

Article 28

Information relating to service costs and enforcement

Member States shall cooperate to provide the general public and professional circles with information on:

(a) costs of service of documents;
 and
(b) which authorities have competence with respect to enforcement for the purposes of applying Articles 21, 22 and 23,

in particular via the European Judicial Network in civil and commercial matters established in accordance with Council Decision 2001/470/EC.[9]

Article 29

Information relating to jurisdiction, review procedures, means of communication and languages

1. By 12 June 2008, Member States shall communicate to the Commission:
   (a) which courts have jurisdiction to issue a European order for payment;

[8] OJ L 160, 30.6.2000, p. 37.
[9] OJ L 174, 27.6.2001, p. 25.

(b) the review procedure and the competent courts for the purposes of the application of Article 20;
(c) the means of communication accepted for the purposes of the European order for payment procedure and available to the courts;
(d) languages accepted pursuant to Article 21(2)(b).

Member States shall apprise the Commission of any subsequent changes to this information.

2. The Commission shall make the information notified in accordance with paragraph 1 publicly available through publication in the *Official Journal of the European Union* and through any other appropriate means.

Article 30
Amendments to the Annexes

The standard forms set out in the Annexes shall be updated or technically adjusted, ensuring full conformity with the provisions of this Regulation, in accordance with the procedure referred to in Article 31(2).

Article 31
Committee

1. The Commission shall be assisted by the committee established by Article 75 of Regulation (EC) No 44/2001.
2. Where reference is made to this paragraph, Article 5a(1)–(4) and Article 7 of Decision 1999/468/EC shall apply, having regard to the provisions of Article 8 thereof.
3. The Committee shall adopt its Rules of Procedure.

Article 32
Review

By 12 December 2013, the Commission shall present to the European Parliament, the Council and the European Economic and Social Committee a detailed report reviewing the operation of the European order for payment procedure. That report shall contain an assessment of the procedure as it has operated and an extended impact assessment for each Member State.

To that end, and in order to ensure that best practice in the European Union is duly taken into account and reflects the principles of better legislation, Member States shall provide the Commission with information relating to the cross-border operation of the European order for payment. This information shall cover court fees, speed of the procedure, efficiency, ease of use and the internal payment order procedures of the Member States.

The Commission's report shall be accompanied, if appropriate, by proposals for adaptation.

Article 33

Entry into force

This Regulation shall enter into force on the day following the date of its publication in the *Official Journal of the European Union.*

It shall apply from 12 December 2008, with the exception of Articles 28, 29, 30 and 31 which shall apply from 12 June 2008.

This Regulation shall be binding in its entirety and directly applicable in the Member States in accordance with the Treaty establishing the European Community.

Done at Strasbourg, 12 December 2006.

For the European Parliament
The President
J. BORRELL FONTELLES

For the Council
The President
M. PEKKARINEN

[Note that annexes have been removed from the appendix. Note also that annexes have been updated since the original publication, see OJ L 18, 25 January 2007, p. 11.]

Regulation (EC) No 861/2007 of the European Parliament and of the Council

of 11 July 2007

establishing a European Small Claims Procedure

THE EUROPEAN PARLIAMENT AND THE COUNCIL OF THE EUROPEAN UNION,

Having regard to the Treaty establishing the European Community, and in particular Article 61(c) and Article 67 thereof,

Having regard to the proposal from the Commission,

Having regard to the opinion of the European Economic and Social Committee,[1]

Acting in accordance with the procedure laid down in Article 251 of the Treaty,[2]

Whereas:

(1) The Community has set itself the objective of maintaining and developing an area of freedom, security and justice in which the free movement of persons is ensured. For the gradual establishment of such an area, the Community is to adopt, *inter alia*, measures in the field of judicial cooperation in civil matters having cross-border implications and needed for the proper functioning of the internal market.

(2) According to Article 65(c) of the Treaty, those measures are to include those eliminating obstacles to the good functioning of civil proceedings, if necessary by promoting the compatibility of the rules on civil procedure applicable in the Member States.

(3) In this respect, the Community has, among other measures, already adopted Council Regulation (EC) No 1348/2000 of 29 May 2000 on the service in the Member States of judicial and extrajudicial documents in civil or commercial matters,[3] Council Regulation (EC) No 44/2001 of 22 December 2000 on

[1] OJ C 88, 11.4.2006, p. 61.

[2] Opinion of the European Parliament of 14 December 2006 (not yet published in the Official Journal) and Council Decision of 13 June 2007.

[3] OJ L 160, 30.6.2000, p. 37.

jurisdiction and the recognition and enforcement of judgments in civil and commercial matters,[4] Council Decision 2001/470/EC of 28 May 2001 establishing a European Judicial Network in civil and commercial matters,[5] Regulation (EC) No 805/2004 of the European Parliament and of the Council of 21 April 2004 creating a European Enforcement Order for uncontested claims[6] and Regulation (EC) No 1896/2006 of the European Parliament and of the Council of 12 December 2006 creating a European order for payment procedure.[7]

(4) The European Council meeting in Tampere on 15 and 16 October 1999 invited the Council and the Commission to establish common procedural rules for simplified and accelerated cross-border litigation on small consumer and commercial claims.

(5) On 30 November 2000, the Council adopted a joint programme of the Commission and the Council of measures for the implementation of the principle of mutual recognition of decisions in civil and commercial matters.[8] The programme refers to simplifying and speeding up the settlement of cross-border litigation on small claims. This was taken forward by the Hague Programme,[9] adopted by the European Council on 5 November 2004, which called for work on small claims to be actively pursued.

(6) On 20 December 2002, the Commission adopted a Green Paper on a European order for payment procedure and on measures to simplify and speed up small claims litigation. The Green Paper launched a consultation on measures concerning the simplification and the speeding up of small claims litigation.

(7) Many Member States have introduced simplified civil procedures for small claims since costs, delays and complexities connected with litigation do not necessarily decrease proportionally with the value of the claim. The obstacles to obtaining a fast and inexpensive judgment are exacerbated in cross-border cases. It is therefore necessary to establish a European procedure for small claims (European Small Claims Procedure). The objective of such a procedure should be to facilitate access to justice. The distortion of competition within the internal market due to imbalances with regard to the functioning of the procedural means afforded to creditors in different Member States entails the need for Community legislation that guarantees a level playing-field for creditors and debtors throughout the European Union. It should be necessary to have regard to the principles of simplicity, speed and proportionality when setting the costs of dealing with a claim under the European Small Claims Procedure.

[4] OJ L 12, 16.1.2001, p. 1. Regulation as amended by Regulation (EC) No 1791/2006 (OJ L 363, 20.12.2006, p. 1).

[5] OJ L 174, 27.6.2001, p. 25.

[6] OJ L 143, 30.4.2004, p. 15. Regulation as amended by Commission Regulation (EC) No 1869/2005 (OJ L 300, 17.11.2005, p. 6).

[7] OJ L 399, 30.12.2006, p. 1.

[8] OJ C 12, 15.1.2001, p. 1.

[9] OJ C 53, 3.3.2005, p. 1.

It is appropriate that details of the costs to be charged be made public, and that the means of setting any such costs be transparent.

(8) The European Small Claims Procedure should simplify and speed up litigation concerning small claims in cross-border cases, whilst reducing costs, by offering an optional tool in addition to the possibilities existing under the laws of the Member States, which will remain unaffected. This Regulation should also make it simpler to obtain the recognition and enforcement of a judgment given in the European Small Claims Procedure in another Member State.

(9) This Regulation seeks to promote fundamental rights and takes into account, in particular, the principles recognised by the Charter of Fundamental Rights of the European Union. The court or tribunal should respect the right to a fair trial and the principle of an adversarial process, in particular when deciding on the necessity of an oral hearing and on the means of taking evidence and the extent to which evidence is to be taken.

(10) For the purposes of facilitating calculation of the value of a claim, all interest, expenses and disbursements should be disregarded. This should affect neither the power of the court or tribunal to award these in its judgment nor the national rules on the calculation of interest.

(11) In order to facilitate the commencement of the European Small Claims Procedure, the claimant should make an application by filling in a standard claim form and lodging it with the court or tribunal. The claim form should be submitted only to a court or tribunal that has jurisdiction.

(12) The claim form should be accompanied, where appropriate, by any relevant supporting documents. However, this does not prevent the claimant from submitting, where appropriate, further evidence during the procedure. The same principle should apply to the response by the defendant.

(13) The concepts of 'clearly unfounded' in the context of the dismissal of a claim and of 'inadmissible' in the context of the dismissal of an application should be determined in accordance with national law.

(14) The European Small Claims Procedure should be a written procedure, unless an oral hearing is considered necessary by the court or tribunal or a party so requests. The court or tribunal may refuse such a request. Such refusal may not be contested separately.

(15) The parties should not be obliged to be represented by a lawyer or another legal professional.

(16) The concept of 'counterclaim' should be interpreted within the meaning of Article 6(3) of Regulation (EC) No 44/2001 as arising from the same contract or facts on which the original claim was based. Articles 2 and 4 as well as Article 5(3), (4) and (5) should apply, *mutatis mutandis*, to counterclaims.

(17) In cases where the defendant invokes a right of set-off during the proceedings, such claim should not constitute a counterclaim for the purposes of this Regulation. Therefore, the defendant should not be obliged to use standard Form A, as set out in Annex I, for invoking such a right.

(18) The Member State addressed for the purposes of the application of Article 6 is the Member State where service is to be effected or to where the document is to be dispatched. In order to reduce costs and delays, documents should be served on the parties primarily by postal service attested by an acknowledgement of receipt, including the date of receipt.

(19) A party may refuse to accept a document at the time of service or by returning the document within one week if it is not written in, or accompanied by a translation into, the official language of the Member State addressed (or, if there are several official languages in that Member State, the official language or one of the official languages of the place where service is to be effected or to where the document is to be dispatched) or a language which the addressee understands.

(20) In the context of oral hearings and the taking of evidence, the Member States should encourage the use of modern communication technology subject to the national law of the Member State where the court or tribunal is situated. The court or tribunal should use the simplest and least costly method of taking evidence.

(21) The practical assistance to be made available to the parties should include technical information concerning the availability and the filling in of the forms.

(22) The information about procedural questions can also be given by the court or tribunal staff in accordance with national law.

(23) As the objective of this Regulation is to simplify and speed up litigation concerning small claims in cross-border cases, the court or tribunal should act as soon as possible even when this Regulation does not prescribe any time limit for a specific phase of the procedure.

(24) For the purposes of calculating time limits as provided for in this Regulation, Regulation (EEC, Euratom) No 1182/71 of the Council of 3 June 1971 determining the rules applicable to periods, dates and time limits[10] should apply.

(25) In order to speed up the recovery of small claims, the judgment should be enforceable notwithstanding any possible appeal and without the condition of the provision of a security except as provided for in this Regulation.

(26) Any reference in this Regulation to an appeal should include any possible means of appeal available under national law.

(27) The court or tribunal must include a person qualified to serve as a judge in accordance with national law.

(28) Whenever the court or tribunal is required to set a time limit, the party concerned should be informed of the consequences of not complying with it.

(29) The unsuccessful party should bear the costs of the proceedings. The costs of the proceedings should be determined in accordance with national law. Having regard to the objectives of simplicity and cost-effectiveness, the court or tribunal should order that an unsuccessful party be obliged to pay only the costs of the proceedings, including for example any costs resulting from the fact that

[10] OJ L 124, 8.6.1971, p. 1.

the other party was represented by a lawyer or another legal professional, or any costs arising from the service or translation of documents, which are proportionate to the value of the claim or which were necessarily incurred.

(30) In order to facilitate recognition and enforcement, a judgment given in a Member State in the European Small Claims Procedure should be recognised and enforceable in another Member State without the need for a declaration of enforceability and without any possibility of opposing its recognition.

(31) There should be minimum standards for the review of a judgment in situations where the defendant was not able to contest the claim.

(32) Having regard to the objectives of simplicity and cost-effectiveness, the party seeking enforcement shall not be required to have an authorised representative or a postal address in the Member State of enforcement, other than with agents having competence for the enforcement procedure in accordance with the national law of that Member State.

(33) Chapter III of this Regulation should also apply to the determination of costs and expenses made by officers of the court or tribunal due to a judgment given pursuant to the procedure specified in this Regulation.

(34) The measures necessary for the implementation of this Regulation should be adopted in accordance with Council Decision 1999/468/EC of 28 June 1999 laying down the procedures for the exercise of implementing powers conferred on the Commission.[11]

(35) In particular, power should be conferred on the Commission to adopt measures necessary to update or make technical amendments to the forms set out in the Annexes. Since those measures are of general scope and are designed to amend non-essential elements of this Regulation and/or to supplement this Regulation by the addition of new non-essential elements, they should be adopted in accordance with the regulatory procedure with scrutiny provided for in Article 5a of Decision 1999/468/EC.

(36) Since the objectives of this Regulation, namely, the establishment of a procedure to simplify and speed up litigation concerning small claims in cross-border cases, and to reduce costs, cannot be sufficiently achieved by the Member States and can therefore, by reason of the scale and effects of this Regulation, be better achieved at Community level, the Community may adopt measures in accordance with the principle of subsidiarity as set out in Article 5 of the Treaty. In accordance with the principle of proportionality, as set out in that Article, this Regulation does not go beyond what is necessary to achieve those objectives.

(37) In accordance with Article 3 of the Protocol on the position of the United Kingdom and Ireland annexed to the Treaty on European Union and to the Treaty establishing the European Community, the United Kingdom and

[11] OJ L 184, 17.7.1999, p. 23. Decision as amended by Decision 2006/512/EC (OJ L 200, 22.7.2006, p. 11).

Ireland have given notice of their wish to take part in the adoption and application of this Regulation.

(38) In accordance with Articles 1 and 2 of the Protocol on the position of Denmark annexed to the Treaty on European Union and to the Treaty establishing the European Community, Denmark does not take part in the adoption of this Regulation and is not bound by it or subject to its application,

HAVE ADOPTED THIS REGULATION:

CHAPTER I
SUBJECT MATTER AND SCOPE

Article 1
Subject matter

This Regulation establishes a European procedure for small claims (hereinafter referred to as the European Small Claims Procedure), intended to simplify and speed up litigation concerning small claims in cross-border cases, and to reduce costs. The European Small Claims Procedure shall be available to litigants as an alternative to the procedures existing under the laws of the Member States.

This Regulation also eliminates the intermediate proceedings necessary to enable recognition and enforcement, in other Member States, of judgments given in one Member State in the European Small Claims Procedure.

Article 2
Scope

1. This Regulation shall apply, in cross-border cases, to civil and commercial matters, whatever the nature of the court or tribunal, where the value of a claim does not exceed EUR 2 000 at the time when the claim form is received by the court or tribunal with jurisdiction, excluding all interest, expenses and disbursements. It shall not extend, in particular, to revenue, customs or administrative matters or to the liability of the State for acts and omissions in the exercise of State authority (*acta jure imperii*).
2. This Regulation shall not apply to matters concerning:
   (a) the status or legal capacity of natural persons;
   (b) rights in property arising out of a matrimonial relationship, maintenance obligations, wills and succession;
   (c) bankruptcy, proceedings relating to the winding-up of insolvent companies or other legal persons, judicial arrangements, compositions and analogous proceedings;

(d) social security;
(e) arbitration;
(f) employment law;
(g) tenancies of immovable property, with the exception of actions on monetary claims; or
(h) violations of privacy and of rights relating to personality, including defamation.
3. In this Regulation, the term 'Member State' shall mean Member States with the exception of Denmark.

Article 3

Cross-border cases

1. For the purposes of this Regulation, a cross-border case is one in which at least one of the parties is domiciled or habitually resident in a Member State other than the Member State of the court or tribunal seised.
2. Domicile shall be determined in accordance with Articles 59 and 60 of Regulation (EC) No 44/2001.
3. The relevant moment for determining whether there is a cross-border case is the date on which the claim form is received by the court or tribunal with jurisdiction.

CHAPTER II
THE EUROPEAN SMALL CLAIMS PROCEDURE

Article 4

Commencement of the Procedure

1. The claimant shall commence the European Small Claims Procedure by filling in standard claim Form A, as set out in Annex I, and lodging it with the court or tribunal with jurisdiction directly, by post or by any other means of communication, such as fax or e-mail, acceptable to the Member State in which the procedure is commenced. The claim form shall include a description of evidence supporting the claim and be accompanied, where appropriate, by any relevant supporting documents.
2. Member States shall inform the Commission which means of communication are acceptable to them. The Commission shall make such information publicly available.
3. Where a claim is outside the scope of this Regulation, the court or tribunal shall inform the claimant to that effect. Unless the claimant withdraws the claim, the court or tribunal shall proceed with it in accordance with the relevant procedural law applicable in the Member State in which the procedure is conducted.

4. Where the court or tribunal considers the information provided by the claimant to be inadequate or insufficiently clear or if the claim form is not filled in properly, it shall, unless the claim appears to be clearly unfounded or the application inadmissible, give the claimant the opportunity to complete or rectify the claim form or to supply supplementary information or documents or to withdraw the claim, within such period as it specifies. The court or tribunal shall use standard Form B, as set out in Annex II, for this purpose.
   Where the claim appears to be clearly unfounded or the application inadmissible or where the claimant fails to complete or rectify the claim form within the time specified, the application shall be dismissed.
5. Member States shall ensure that the claim form is available at all courts and tribunals at which the European Small Claims Procedure can be commenced.

Article 5

Conduct of the Procedure

1. The European Small Claims Procedure shall be a written procedure. The court or tribunal shall hold an oral hearing if it considers this to be necessary or if a party so requests. The court or tribunal may refuse such a request if it considers that with regard to the circumstances of the case, an oral hearing is obviously not necessary for the fair conduct of the proceedings. The reasons for refusal shall be given in writing. The refusal may not be contested separately.
2. After receiving the properly filled in claim form, the court or tribunal shall fill in Part I of the standard answer Form C, as set out in Annex III.
   A copy of the claim form, and, where applicable, of the supporting documents, together with the answer form thus filled in, shall be served on the defendant in accordance with Article 13. These documents shall be dispatched within 14 days of receiving the properly filled in claim form.
3. The defendant shall submit his response within 30 days of service of the claim form and answer form, by filling in Part II of standard answer Form C, accompanied, where appropriate, by any relevant supporting documents, and returning it to the court or tribunal, or in any other appropriate way not using the answer form.
4. Within 14 days of receipt of the response from the defendant, the court or tribunal shall dispatch a copy thereof, together with any relevant supporting documents to the claimant.
5. If, in his response, the defendant claims that the value of a non-monetary claim exceeds the limit set out in Article 2(1), the court or tribunal shall decide within 30 days of dispatching the response to the claimant, whether the claim is within the scope of this Regulation. Such decision may not be contested separately.
6. Any counterclaim, to be submitted using standard Form A, and any relevant supporting documents shall be served on the claimant in accordance with Article 13. Those documents shall be dispatched within 14 days of receipt.

The claimant shall have 30 days from service to respond to any counterclaim.

7. If the counterclaim exceeds the limit set out in Article 2(1), the claim and counterclaim shall not proceed in the European Small Claims Procedure but shall be dealt with in accordance with the relevant procedural law applicable in the Member State in which the procedure is conducted.
Articles 2 and 4 as well as paragraphs 3, 4 and 5 of this Article shall apply, *mutatis mutandis*, to counterclaims.

Article 6
Languages

1. The claim form, the response, any counterclaim, any response to a counterclaim and any description of relevant supporting documents shall be submitted in the language or one of the languages of the court or tribunal.
2. If any other document received by the court or tribunal is not in the language in which the proceedings are conducted, the court or tribunal may require a translation of that document only if the translation appears to be necessary for giving the judgment.
3. Where a party has refused to accept a document because it is not in either of the following languages:
   (a) the official language of the Member State addressed, or, if there are several official languages in that Member State, the official language or one of the official languages of the place where service is to be effected or to where the document is to be dispatched; or
   (b) a language which the addressee understands,

   the court or tribunal shall so inform the other party with a view to that party providing a translation of the document.

Article 7
Conclusion of the Procedure

1. Within 30 days of receipt of the response from the defendant or the claimant within the time limits laid down in Article 5(3) or (6), the court or tribunal shall give a judgment, or:
   (a) demand further details concerning the claim from the parties within a specified period of time, not exceeding 30 days;
   (b) take evidence in accordance with Article 9; or
   (c) summon the parties to an oral hearing to be held within 30 days of the summons.
2. The court or tribunal shall give the judgment either within 30 days of any oral hearing or after having received all information necessary for giving the judgment. The judgment shall be served on the parties in accordance with Article 13.

3. If the court or tribunal has not received an answer from the relevant party within the time limits laid down in Article 5(3) or (6), it shall give a judgment on the claim or counterclaim.

Article 8
Oral hearing

The court or tribunal may hold an oral hearing through video conference or other communication technology if the technical means are available.

Article 9
Taking of evidence

1. The court or tribunal shall determine the means of taking evidence and the extent of the evidence necessary for its judgment under the rules applicable to the admissibility of evidence. The court or tribunal may admit the taking of evidence through written statements of witnesses, experts or parties. It may also admit the taking of evidence through video conference or other communication technology if the technical means are available.
2. The court or tribunal may take expert evidence or oral testimony only if it is necessary for giving the judgment. In making its decision, the court or tribunal shall take costs into account.
3. The court or tribunal shall use the simplest and least burdensome method of taking evidence.

Article 10
Representation of parties

Representation by a lawyer or another legal professional shall not be mandatory.

Article 11
Assistance for the parties

The Member States shall ensure that the parties can receive practical assistance in filling in the forms.

Article 12
Remit of the court or tribunal

1. The court or tribunal shall not require the parties to make any legal assessment of the claim.
2. If necessary, the court or tribunal shall inform the parties about procedural questions.
3. Whenever appropriate, the court or tribunal shall seek to reach a settlement between the parties.

Article 13

Service of documents

1. Documents shall be served by postal service attested by an acknowledgement of receipt including the date of receipt.
2. If service in accordance with paragraph 1 is not possible, service may be effected by any of the methods provided for in Articles 13 or 14 of Regulation (EC) No 805/2004.

Article 14

Time limits

1. Where the court or tribunal sets a time limit, the party concerned shall be informed of the consequences of not complying with it.
2. The court or tribunal may extend the time limits provided for in Article 4(4), Article 5(3) and (6) and Article 7(1), in exceptional circumstances, if necessary in order to safeguard the rights of the parties.
3. If, in exceptional circumstances, it is not possible for the court or tribunal to respect the time limits provided for in Article 5(2) to (6) and Article 7, it shall take the steps required by those provisions as soon as possible.

Article 15

Enforceability of the judgment

1. The judgment shall be enforceable notwithstanding any possible appeal. The provision of a security shall not be required.
2. Article 23 shall also apply in the event that the judgment is to be enforced in the Member State where the judgment was given.

Article 16

Costs

The unsuccessful party shall bear the costs of the proceedings. However, the court or tribunal shall not award costs to the successful party to the extent that they were unnecessarily incurred or are disproportionate to the claim.

Article 17

Appeal

1. Member States shall inform the Commission whether an appeal is available under their procedural law against a judgment given in the European Small Claims Procedure and within what time limit such appeal shall be lodged. The Commission shall make that information publicly available.
2. Article 16 shall apply to any appeal.

Article 18

Minimum standards for review of the judgment

1. The defendant shall be entitled to apply for a review of the judgment given in the European Small Claims Procedure before the court or tribunal with jurisdiction of the Member State where the judgment was given where:
   (a) (i) the claim form or the summons to an oral hearing were served by a method without proof of receipt by him personally, as provided for in Article 14 of Regulation (EC) No 805/2004; and
   (ii) service was not effected in sufficient time to enable him to arrange for his defence without any fault on his part,

   or

   (b) the defendant was prevented from objecting to the claim by reason of *force majeure*, or due to extraordinary circumstances without any fault on his part,

   provided in either case that he acts promptly.
2. If the court or tribunal rejects the review on the basis that none of the grounds referred to in paragraph 1 apply, the judgment shall remain in force.
   If the court or tribunal decides that the review is justified for one of the reasons laid down in paragraph 1, the judgment given in the European Small Claims Procedure shall be null and void.

Article 19

Applicable procedural law

Subject to the provisions of this Regulation, the European Small Claims Procedure shall be governed by the procedural law of the Member State in which the procedure is conducted.

CHAPTER III
RECOGNITION AND ENFORCEMENT IN ANOTHER MEMBER STATE

Article 20

Recognition and enforcement

1. A judgment given in a Member State in the European Small Claims Procedure shall be recognised and enforced in another Member State without the need for a declaration of enforceability and without any possibility of opposing its recognition.
2. At the request of one of the parties, the court or tribunal shall issue a certificate concerning a judgment in the European Small Claims Procedure using standard Form D, as set out in Annex IV, at no extra cost.

Article 21

Enforcement procedure

1. Without prejudice to the provisions of this Chapter, the enforcement procedures shall be governed by the law of the Member State of enforcement.
   Any judgment given in the European Small Claims Procedure shall be enforced under the same conditions as a judgment given in the Member State of enforcement.
2. The party seeking enforcement shall produce:
   (a) a copy of the judgment which satisfies the conditions necessary to establish its authenticity; and
   (b) a copy of the certificate referred to in Article 20(2) and, where necessary, the translation thereof into the official language of the Member State of enforcement or, if there are several official languages in that Member State, the official language or one of the official languages of court or tribunal proceedings of the place where enforcement is sought in conformity with the law of that Member State, or into another language that the Member State of enforcement has indicated it can accept. Each Member State may indicate the official language or languages of the institutions of the European Union other than its own which it can accept for the European Small Claims Procedure. The content of Form D shall be translated by a person qualified to make translations in one of the Member States.
3. The party seeking the enforcement of a judgment given in the European Small Claims Procedure in another Member State shall not be required to have:
   (a) an authorised representative; or
   (b) a postal address

   in the Member State of enforcement, other than with agents having competence for the enforcement procedure.
4. No security, bond or deposit, however described, shall be required of a party who in one Member State applies for enforcement of a judgment given in the European Small Claims Procedure in another Member State on the ground that he is a foreign national or that he is not domiciled or resident in the Member State of enforcement.

Article 22

Refusal of enforcement

1. Enforcement shall, upon application by the person against whom enforcement is sought, be refused by the court or tribunal with jurisdiction in the Member State of enforcement if the judgment given in the European Small Claims Procedure is irreconcilable with an earlier judgment given in any Member State or in a third country, provided that:
   (a) the earlier judgment involved the same cause of action and was between the same parties;

(b) the earlier judgment was given in the Member State of enforcement or fulfils the conditions necessary for its recognition in the Member State of enforcement; and
(c) the irreconcilability was not and could not have been raised as an objection in the court or tribunal proceedings in the Member State where the judgment in the European Small Claims Procedure was given.

2. Under no circumstances may a judgment given in the European Small Claims Procedure be reviewed as to its substance in the Member State of enforcement.

Article 23
Stay or limitation of enforcement

Where a party has challenged a judgment given in the European Small Claims Procedure or where such a challenge is still possible, or where a party has made an application for review within the meaning of Article 18, the court or tribunal with jurisdiction or the competent authority in the Member State of enforcement may, upon application by the party against whom enforcement is sought:

(a) limit the enforcement proceedings to protective measures;
(b) make enforcement conditional on the provision of such security as it shall determine; or
(c) under exceptional circumstances, stay the enforcement proceedings.

CHAPTER IV
FINAL PROVISIONS

Article 24
Information

The Member States shall cooperate to provide the general public and professional circles with information on the European Small Claims Procedure, including costs, in particular by way of the European Judicial Network in Civil and Commercial Matters established in accordance with Decision 2001/470/EC.

Article 25
Information relating to jurisdiction, means of communication and appeals

1. By 1 January 2008 the Member States shall communicate to the Commission:
   (a) which courts or tribunals have jurisdiction to give a judgment in the European Small Claims Procedure;
   (b) which means of communication are accepted for the purposes of the European Small Claims Procedure and available to the courts or tribunals in accordance with Article 4(1);

(c) whether an appeal is available under their procedural law in accordance with Article 17 and with which court or tribunal this may be lodged;
(d) which languages are accepted pursuant to Article 21(2)(b); and
(e) which authorities have competence with respect to enforcement and which authorities have competence for the purposes of the application of Article 23.

Member States shall apprise the Commission of any subsequent changes to this information.

2. The Commission shall make the information notified in accordance with paragraph 1 publicly available through publication in the *Official Journal of the European Union* and through any other appropriate means.

Article 26
Implementing measures

The measures designed to amend non-essential elements of this Regulation, including by supplementing it, relating to updates or technical amendments to the forms in the Annexes shall be adopted in accordance with the regulatory procedure with scrutiny referred to in Article 27(2).

Article 27
Committee

1. The Commission shall be assisted by a Committee.
2. Where reference is made to this paragraph, Article 5a(1) to (4), and Article 7 of Decision 1999/468/EC shall apply, having regard to the provisions of Article 8 thereof.

Article 28
Review

By 1 January 2014, the Commission shall present to the European Parliament, the Council and the European Economic and Social Committee a detailed report reviewing the operation of the European Small Claims Procedure, including the limit of the value of the claim referred to in Article 2(1). That report shall contain an assessment of the procedure as it has operated and an extended impact assessment for each Member State.

To that end and in order to ensure that best practice in the European Union is duly taken into account and reflects the principles of better legislation, Member States shall provide the Commission with information relating to the cross-border operation of the European Small Claims Procedure. This information shall cover court fees, speed of the procedure, efficiency, ease of use and the internal small claims procedures of the Member States.

The Commission's report shall be accompanied, if appropriate, by proposals for adaptation.

Article 29
Entry into force

This Regulation shall enter into force on the day following its publication in the *Official Journal of the European Union.*

It shall apply from 1 January 2009, with the exception of Article 25, which shall apply from 1 January 2008.

This Regulation shall be binding in its entirety and directly applicable in the Member States in accordance with the Treaty establishing the European Community.

Done at Strasbourg, 11 July 2007.

For the European Parliament
The President
H.-G. POTTERING
For the Council
The President
M. LOBO ANTUNES

Council Decision

of 28 May 2001

establishing a European Judicial Network in civil and commercial matters

(2001/470/EC)

THE COUNCIL OF THE EUROPEAN UNION,

Having regard to the Treaty establishing the European Community, and in particular Articles 61(c) and (d), 66 and 67(1) thereof,

Having regard to the proposal from the Commission,[1]

Having regard to the opinion of the European Parliament,[2]

Having regard to the opinion of the Economic and Social Committee,[3]

Whereas:

(1) The European Union has set itself the objective of maintaining and developing the European Union as an area of freedom, security and justice, in which the free movement of persons is assured.

(2) The gradual establishment of this area and the sound operation of the internal market entails the need to improve, simplify and expedite effective judicial cooperation between the Member States in civil and commercial matters.

(3) The action plan of the Council and the Commission on how best to implement the provisions of the Treaty of Amsterdam on an area of freedom, security and justice[4] which was adopted by the Council on 3 December 1998 and approved by the European Council on 11 and 12 December 1998 acknowledges that reinforcement of judicial cooperation in civil matters represents a fundamental stage in the creation of a European judicial area which will bring tangible benefits for every European Union citizen.

[1] OJ C 29 E, 30.1.2001, p. 281.
[2] Opinion delivered on 5 April 2001 (not yet published in the Official Journal).
[3] OJ C 139, 11.5.2001, p. 6.
[4] OJ C 19, 23.1.1999, p. 1.

(4) One of the measures provided for in paragraph 40 of the action plan is to examine the possibility of extending the concept of the European Judicial Network in criminal matters to embrace civil proceedings.
(5) The conclusions of the special European Council held at Tampere on 15 and 16 October 1999 recommend the establishment of an easily accessible information system, to be maintained and updated by a Network of competent national authorities.
(6) In order to improve, simplify and expedite effective judicial cooperation between the Member States in civil and commercial matters, it is necessary to establish at Community level a network cooperation structure—the European Judicial Network in civil and commercial matters.
(7) This is a subject falling within the ambit of Articles 65 and 66 of the Treaty, and the measures are to be adopted in accordance with Article 67.
(8) To ensure the attainment of the objectives of the European Judicial Network in civil and commercial matters, the rules governing its establishment should be laid down in a mandatory instrument of Community law.
(9) The objectives of the proposed action, namely to improve effective judicial cooperation between the Member States and effective access to justice for persons engaging in cross-border litigation cannot be sufficiently achieved by the Member States and can therefore by reason of the scale or effects of the action be better achieved at Community level, the Community may adopt measures in accordance with the principle of subsidiarity as set out in Article 5 of the Treaty. In accordance with the principle of proportionality as set out in that Article, this Decision does not go beyond what is necessary in order to achieve those objectives.
(10) The European Judicial Network in civil and commercial matters established by this Decision seeks to facilitate judicial cooperation between the Member States in civil and commercial matters both in areas to which existing instruments apply and in those where no instrument is currently applicable.
(11) In certain specific areas, Community or international instruments relating to judicial cooperation in civil and commercial matters already provide for cooperation mechanisms. The European Judicial Network in civil and commercial matters does not set out to replace these mechanisms, and it must operate in full compliance with them. This Decision will consequently be without prejudice to Community or international instruments relating to judicial cooperation in civil or commercial matters.
(12) The European Judicial Network in civil and commercial matters should be established in stages on the basis of the closest cooperation between the Commission and the Member States. It should be able to take advantage of modern communication and information technologies.

(13) To attain its objectives, the European Judicial Network in civil and commercial matters needs to be supported by contact points designated by the Member States and to be sure of the participation of their authorities with specific responsibilities for judicial cooperation in civil and commercial matters. Contacts between them and periodic meetings are essential to the operation of the Network.

(14) It is essential that efforts to establish an area of freedom, security and justice produce tangible benefits for persons engaging in cross-border litigation. It is accordingly necessary for the European Judicial Network in civil and commercial matters to promote access to justice. To this end, using the information supplied and updated by the contact points, the Network should progressively establish an information system that is accessible to the public, both the general public and specialists.

(15) This Decision does not preclude the provision of other information than that which is provided for herein, within the European Judicial Network in civil and commercial matters and to the public. The enumeration in Title III is accordingly not to be regarded as exhaustive.

(16) Processing of information and data should take place in compliance with Directive 95/46/EC of the European Parliament and of the Council of 24 October 1995 on the protection of individuals with regard to the processing of personal data and of the free movement of such data[5] and Directive 97/66/EC of the European Parliament and of the Council of 15 December 1997 concerning the processing of personal data and the protection of privacy in the telecommunications sector.[6]

(17) To ensure that the European Judicial Network in civil and commercial matters remains an effective instrument, incorporates the best practice in judicial cooperation and internal operation and meets the public's expectations, provision should be made for periodic evaluations and for proposals for such changes as may be found necessary.

(18) The United Kingdom and Ireland, in accordance with Article 3 of the Protocol on the position of the United Kingdom and Ireland annexed to the Treaty on European Union and to the Treaty establishing the European Community, have given notice of their wish to take part in the adoption and application of this Decision.

(19) Denmark, in accordance with Articles 1 and 2 of the Protocol on the position of Denmark, annexed to the Treaty on European Union and to the Treaty establishing the European Community, is not participating in the adoption of this Decision and is therefore not bound by it nor subject to its application,

[5] OJ L 281, 23.11.1995, p. 31.

[6] OJ L 24, 30.1.1998, p. 1.

HAS ADOPTED THIS DECISION:

TITLE I

PRINCIPLES OF THE EUROPEAN JUDICIAL NETWORK IN CIVIL AND COMMERCIAL MATTERS

Article 1

Establishment

1. A European Judicial Network in civil and commercial matters ('the Network') is hereby established among the Member States.
2. In this Decision, the term 'Member State' shall mean Member States with the exception of Denmark.

Article 2

Composition

1. The Network shall be composed of:
   (a) contact points designated by the Member States, in accordance with paragraph 2;
   (b) central bodies and central authorities provided for in Community instruments, instruments of international law to which the Member States are parties or rules of domestic law in the area of judicial cooperation in civil and commercial matters;
   (c) the liaison magistrates to whom Joint Action 96/277/JAI of 22 April 1996 concerning a framework for the exchange of liaison magistrates to improve judicial cooperation between the Member States of the European Union[7] applies, where they have responsibilities in cooperation in civil and commercial matters;
   (d) any other appropriate judicial or administrative authority with responsibilities for judicial cooperation in civil and commercial matters whose membership of the Network is considered to be useful by the Member State to which it belongs.
2. Each Member State shall designate a contact point. Each Member State may, however, designate a limited number of other contact points if they consider this necessary on the basis of the existence of separate legal systems, the domestic distribution of jurisdiction, the tasks to be entrusted to the contact points or in order to associate judicial bodies that frequently deal with cross-border litigation directly with the activities of the contact points.

   Where a Member State designates several contact points, it shall ensure that appropriate coordination mechanisms apply between them.

[7] OJ L 105, 27.4.1996, p. 1.

3. The Member States shall identify the authorities mentioned at points (b) and (c) of paragraph 1.
4. The Member States shall designate the authorities mentioned at point (d) of paragraph 1.
5. The Member States shall notify the Commission, in accordance with Article 20, of the names and full addresses of the authorities referred to in paragraph 1, specifying:
   (a) the communication facilities available to them;
   (b) their knowledge of languages; and
   (c) where appropriate, their specific functions in the Network.

Article 3

Tasks and activities of the Network

1. The Network shall be responsible for:
   (a) facilitating judicial cooperation between the Member States in civil and commercial matters, including devising, progressively establishing and updating an information system for the members of the Network;
   (b) devising, progressively establishing and updating an information system that is accessible to the public.
2. Without prejudice to other Community or international instruments relating to judicial cooperation in civil or commercial matters, the Network shall develop its activities for the following purposes in particular:
   (a) the smooth operation of procedures having a cross-border impact and the facilitation of requests for judicial cooperation between the Member States, in particular where no Community or international instrument is applicable;
   (b) the effective and practical application of Community instruments or conventions in force between two or more Member States;
   (c) the establishment and maintenance of an information system for the public on judicial cooperation in civil and commercial matters in the European Union, relevant Community and international instruments and the domestic law of the Member States, with particular reference to access to justice.

Article 4

Modus operandi of the Network

The Network shall accomplish its tasks in particular by the following means:
1. it shall facilitate appropriate contacts between the authorities of the Member States mentioned in Article 2(1) for the accomplishment of the tasks provided for by Article 3;
2. it shall organise periodic meetings of the contact points and of the members of the Network in accordance with the rules laid down in Title II;

3. it shall draw up and keep updated the information on judicial cooperation in civil and commercial matters and the legal systems of the Member States referred to in Title III, in accordance with the rules laid down in that Title.

Article 5

Contact points

1. The contact points shall be at the disposal of the authorities referred to in Article 2(1)(b) to (d) for the accomplishment of the tasks provided for by Article 3.

   The contact points shall also be at the disposal of the local judicial authorities in their own Member State for the same purposes, in accordance with rules to be determined by each Member State.
2. In particular, the contact points shall:
   (a) supply the other contact points, the authorities mentioned in Article 2(1)(b) to (d) and the local judicial authorities in their own Member State with all the information needed for sound judicial cooperation between the Member States in accordance with Article 3, in order to assist them in preparing operable requests for judicial cooperation and in establishing the most appropriate direct contacts;
   (b) seek solutions to difficulties arising on the occasion of a request for judicial cooperation, without prejudice to paragraph 4 of this Article and to Article 6;
   (c) facilitate coordination of the processing of requests for judicial cooperation in the relevant Member State, in particular where several requests from the judicial authorities in that Member State fall to be executed in another Member State;
   (d) collaborate in the organisation of, and participate in, the meetings referred to in Article 9;
   (e) assist with the preparation and updating of the information referred to in Title III, and in particular with the information system for the public, in accordance with the rules laid down in that Title.
3. Where a contact point receives a request for information from another member of the Network to which it is unable to respond, it shall forward it to the contact point or the member of the Network which is best able to respond to it. The contact point shall remain available for any such assistance as may be useful for subsequent contacts.
4. In areas where Community or international instruments governing judicial cooperation already provide for the designation of authorities responsible for

facilitating judicial cooperation, contact points shall address requesters to such authorities.

Article 6

Relevant authorities for the purposes of Community or international instruments relating to judicial cooperation in civil and commercial matters

1. The involvement of relevant authorities provided for by Community or international instruments relating to judicial cooperation in civil and commercial matters in the Network shall be without prejudice to the powers conferred on them by the instrument providing for their designation.

   Contacts within the Network shall be without prejudice to regular or occasional contacts between these authorities.
2. In each Member State the authorities provided for by Community or international instruments relating to judicial cooperation in civil and commercial matters and the contact points of the Network shall engage in regular exchanges of views and contacts to ensure that their respective experience is disseminated as widely as possible.
3. The contact points of the Network shall be at the disposal of the authorities provided for by Community or international instruments relating to judicial cooperation in civil and commercial matters and shall assist them in all practicable ways.

Article 7

Language knowledge of the contact points

To facilitate the practical operation of the Network, each Member State shall ensure that the contact points have adequate knowledge of an official language of the institutions of the European Community other than their own, given that they need to be able to communicate with the contact points in other Member States.

Member States shall facilitate and encourage specialised language training for contact point staff and promote exchanges of staff between contact points in the Member States.

Article 8

Communication facilities

The contact points shall use the most appropriate technological facilities in order to reply as efficiently and as swiftly as possible to requests made to them.

TITLE II

MEETINGS WITHIN THE NETWORK

Article 9

Meetings of the contact points

1. The contact points of the Network shall meet no less often than once each half year, in accordance with Article 12.
2. Each Member State shall be represented at these meetings by one or more contact points, who may be accompanied by other members of the Network, but there shall be no more than four representatives per Member State.
3. The first meeting of the contact points shall be held no later than 1 March 2003 without prejudice to the possibility of prior preparatory meetings.

Article 10

Purpose of periodic meetings of contact points

1. The purpose of the periodic meetings of contact points shall be to:
   (a) enable the contact points to get to know each other and exchange experience, in particular as regards the operation of the Network;
   (b) provide a platform for discussion of practical and legal problems encountered by the Member States in the course of judicial cooperation, with particular reference to the application of measures adopted by the European Community;
   (c) identify best practices in judicial cooperation in civil and commercial matters and ensure that relevant information is disseminated within the Network;
   (d) exchange data and views, in particular on the structure, organisation and content of and access to the available information mentioned in Title III;
   (e) draw up guidelines for progressively establishing the practical information sheets provided for by Article 15, in particular as regards the subject matter to be covered and the form of such information sheets;
   (f) identify specific initiatives other than those referred to in Title III which pursue comparable objectives.
2. The Member States shall ensure that experience in the operation of specific cooperation mechanisms provided for by Community or international instruments is shared at meetings of the contact points.

Article 11

Meetings of members of the Network

1. Meetings open to all members of the Network shall be held to enable them to get to know each other and exchange experience, to provide a platform for discussion of practical and legal problems met and to deal with specific questions. Meetings can also be held on specific issues.

2. Meetings shall be convened, where appropriate, in accordance with Article 12.
3. The Commission, in close cooperation with the Presidency of the Council and with the Member States, shall fix for each meeting the maximum number of participants.

Article 12
Organisation and proceedings of meetings of the Network

1. The Commission, in close cooperation with the Presidency of the Council and with the Member States, shall convene the meetings provided for by Articles 9 and 11. It shall chair them and provide secretarial services.
2. Before each meeting the Commission shall prepare the draft agenda in agreement with the Presidency of the Council and in consultation with the Member States via their respective contact points.
3. The contact points shall be notified of the agenda prior to the meeting. They may ask for changes to be made or for additional items to be entered.
4. After each meeting the Commission shall prepare a record, which shall be notified to the contact points.
5. Meetings of the contact points and of members of the Network may take place in any Member State.

TITLE III
INFORMATION AVAILABLE WITHIN THE NETWORK, AND INFORMATION SYSTEM FOR THE PUBLIC

Article 13
Information disseminated within the Network

1. The information disseminated within the network shall include:
   (a) the information referred to in Article 2(5);
   (b) any further information deemed useful by the contact points for the proper functioning of the Network.
2. For the purpose of paragraph 1, the Commission shall progressively establish a secure limited-access electronic information exchange system in consultation with the contact points.

Article 14
Information system for the public

1. An Internet-based information system for the public, including the dedicated website for the Network, shall be progressively established in accordance with Articles 17 and 18.

2. The information system shall comprise the following elements:
   (a) Community instruments in force or in preparation relating to judicial cooperation in civil and commercial matters;
   (b) national measures for the domestic implementation of the instruments in force referred to in point (a);
   (c) international instruments in force relating to judicial cooperation in civil and commercial matters to which the Member States are parties, and declarations and reservations made in connection with such instruments;
   (d) the relevant elements of Community case-law in the area of judicial cooperation in civil and commercial matters;
   (e) the information sheets provided for by Article 15.
3. For the purposes of access to the information mentioned in paragraph 2(a) to (d), the Network should, where appropriate, in its site, make use of links to other sites where the original information is to be found.
4. The site dedicated to the Network shall likewise facilitate access to comparable public information initiatives in related matters and to sites containing information relating to the legal systems of the Member States.

Article 15
Information sheets

1. The information sheets shall be devoted by way of priority to questions relating to access to justice in the Member States and shall include information on the procedures for bringing cases in the courts and for obtaining legal aid, without prejudice to other Community initiatives, to which the Network shall have the fullest regard.
2. Information sheets shall be of a practical and concise nature. They shall be written in easily comprehensible language and contain practical information for the public. They shall progressively be produced on at least the following subjects:
   (a) principles of the legal system and judicial organisation of the Member States;
   (b) procedures for bringing cases to court, with particular reference to small claims, and subsequent court procedures, including appeal possibilities and procedures;
   (c) conditions and procedures for obtaining legal aid, including descriptions of the tasks of non-governmental organisations active in this field, account being taken of work already done in the Dialogue with Citizens;
   (d) national rules governing the service of documents;
   (e) rules and procedures for the enforcement of judgments given in other Member States;
   (f) possibilities and procedures for obtaining interim relief measures, with particular reference to seizures of assets for the purposes of enforcement;

(g) alternative dispute-settlement possibilities, with an indication of the national information and advice centres of the Community-wide Network for the Extra-Judicial Settlement of Consumer Disputes;
(h) organisation and operation of the legal professions.

4. The information sheets shall, where appropriate, include elements of the relevant case-law of the Member States.
5. The information sheets may provide more detailed information for the specialists.

Article 16
Updating of information

All information distributed within the Network and to the public under Articles 13 to 15 shall be updated regularly.

Article 17
Role of the Commission in the public information system

The Commission shall:

1. be responsible for managing the information system for the public;
2. construct, in consultation with the contact points, a dedicated website for the Network on its Internet site;
3. provide information on relevant aspects of Community law and procedures, including Community case-law, in accordance with Article 14;
   (a) ensure that the format of the information sheets is consistent and that they include all information considered necessary by the Network;
   (b) thereafter arrange for them to be translated into the other official languages of the Institutions of the Community, and install them on the site dedicated to the Network.

Article 18
Role of contact points in the public information system

Contact points shall ensure that

1. the appropriate information needed to create and operate the information system is supplied to the Commission;
2. the information installed in the system is accurate;
3. the Commission is notified forthwith of any updates as soon as an item of information requires changing;
4. the information sheets relating to their respective Member States are progressively established, according to the guidelines referred to in Article 10(1)(e);
5. the broadest possible dissemination of the information sheets installed on the site dedicated to the Network is arranged in their Member State.

TITLE IV

FINAL PROVISIONS

Article 19

Review

1. No later than 1 December 2005, and at least every five years thereafter, the Commission shall present to the European Parliament, the Council and the Economic and Social Committee a report on the application of this Decision on the basis of information supplied by the contact points. The report shall be accompanied if need be by proposals for adaptations.
2. The report shall consider, among other relevant matters, the question of possible direct public access to the contact points of the Network, access to and involvement of the legal professions in its activities, and synergy with the Community-wide Network for the Extra-Judicial Settlement of Consumer Disputes. It shall also consider the relationship between the contact points of the Network and the competent authorities provided for in Community or international instruments relating to judicial cooperation in civil and commercial matters.

Article 20

Establishment of the basic components of the Network

No later than 1 June 2002, the Member States shall notify the Commission of the information required by Article 2(5).

Article 21

Date of application

This Decision shall apply from 1 December 2002, except for Articles 2 and 20 which shall apply from the date of notification of the Decision to the Member States to which it is addressed.

This Decision is addressed to the Member States in accordance with the Treaty establishing the European Community.

Done at Brussels, 28 May 2001.

For the Council
The President
T. BODSTROM

BIBLIOGRAPHY

Aalto P, 'Yksityisoikeuden alan yhteistyö EU:ssa, Tilanne Tampereen Eurooppa-neuvoston jälkeen' *Lakimies* 3/2000, 315–35.

Albors-Llorens A, 'Changes in the Jurisdiction of the European Court of Justice under the Treaty of Amsterdam' *Common Market Law Review* 6/1998, 1273–94.

Alpa G and Danovi R (eds), *Diritto contrattuale europeo e diritto dei consumatori, L'integrazione europea e il processo civile*, Guiffrè Editore, 2003.

Alter K, 'Explaining National Court Acceptance of European Court Jurisprudence: A Critical Evaluation of Theories of Legal Integration' in Slaughter A-M, Stone Sweet A, and Weiler J (eds), *The European Court and National Courts – Doctrine and Jurisprudence, Legal Change in Its Social Context*, Hart Publishing, Oxford, 1998, 227–52.

Alter K, *Establishing the Supremacy of European Law, The Making of an International Rule of Law in Europe*, Oxford University Press, Oxford, 2001.

Andenas M, 'National Paradigms of Civil Enforcement: Mutual Recognition or Harmonization in Europe?' in Andenas M, Hess B, and Oberhammer P (eds), *Enforcement Agency Practice in Europe*, British Institute of International and Comparative Law, London, 2005, 7–23.

Andenas M and Nazzini R, 'Market Integration, The Harmonization Process, and Enforcement Practices in the EU Member States' in Andenas M, Hess B, and Oberhammer P (eds), *Enforcement Agency Practice in Europe*, British Institute of International and Comparative Law, London, 2005, 53–101.

Andenas M, Hess B, and Oberhammer P (eds), *Enforcement Agency Practice in Europe*, British Institute of International and Comparative Law, London, 2005.

Andersson T, 'EG-Rätten och den svenska processrätten' *Juridisk Tidskrift* 4/1998–1999, 807–17.

Andersson T, 'Approximation of Procedural Law in Europe' in Storme M (ed), *Procedural Laws in Europe. Towards Harmonisation*, Maklu, Antwerp-Apeldoorn, 2003, 55–65.

Andersson T, 'The Symposium "Parallel and Conflicting Enforcement of Laws" in Thoresta, Sweden, 18–19 August 2004' *European Review of Private Law* 2/2005, 265–9 (2005a).

Andersson T, 'Harmonization and Mutual Recognition: How to Handle Mutual Distrust' in Andenas M, Hess B, and Oberhammer P (eds), *Enforcement Agency Practice in Europe*, British Institute of International and Comparative Law, London, 2005, 245–51 (2005b).

Andrews N, 'Towards a European Protective Order in Civil Matters' in Storme M (ed), *Procedural Laws in Europe. Towards Harmonisation*, Maklu, Antwerp-Apeldoorn, 2003, 267–85.

Armstrong K, 'Tackling Social Exclusion through OMC: Reshaping Boundaries of European Governance' in Boerzel T and Cichowski R (eds), *The State of the European Union, Vol 6: Law, Politics and Society*, Oxford University Press, Oxford, 2003.

Arnull A, 'Rights and Remedies, Restraint or Activism?' in Lonbay J and Biondi A (eds), *Remedies for Breach of EC Law*, John Wiley & Sons, Chichester, 1997, 15–22.

Arnull A, 'Taming the Beast? The Treaty of Amsterdam and the Court of Justice' in O'Keeffe D and Twomey P (eds), *Legal Issues of the Amsterdam Treaty*, Hart Publishing, Oxford, 1999, 109–21.

Arnull A, 'Protecting Fundamental Rights in Europe's New Constitutional Order' in Tridimas T and Nebbia P (eds), *European Union Law for the Twenty-First Century – Rethinking the New Legal Order*, Hart Publishing, Oxford, 2004, 95–141.

Azoulay L, 'The Judge and the Community's Administrative Governance' in Joerges C (ed), *Good Governance in Europe's Integrated Market*, Oxford University Press, Oxford, 2002, 109–37.

Baker C, 'Le titre exécutoire européen. Une avancée pour la libre circulation des décisions?' *La Semaine Juridique Édition Générale* 22/2003, 985–91.

Bambust I, 'La chambre nationale des huissiers de justice de Belgique et sa nouvelle vocation dans le cadre du Règlement (CE) N° 1348/2000 du Conseil: centre S.O.S entre le géocentrisme et l'héliocentrisme' in De Leval G and Storme M (eds), *Le droit processuel et judiciaire européen*, La Charte & Die Keure, Brussels and Bruges, 2003, 237–69.

Bandrac M et al, *Justice et droits fondamentaux. Etudes offertes à Jacques Normand*, Litec, Paris, 2003.

Barnard C and Scott J (eds), *The Law of the Single European Market – Unpacking the Premises*, Hart Publishing, Oxford, 2002.

Barrett G, 'Chapter 1: Cooperation in Justice and Home Affairs in the European Union – An Overview and a Critique' in Barrett G (ed), *Justice Cooperation in the EU, The Creation of a European Legal Space*, Institute of European Affairs, Dublin, 1997, 3–47.

Barrett G (ed), *Justice Cooperation in the EU, The Creation of a European Legal Space*, Institute of European Affairs, Dublin, 1997.

Barrett G, 'Introduction' in Barrett G (ed), *Creating a European Judicial Space, Prospects for Improving Judicial Cooperation in Civil Matters in the European Union*, Vol 30, Academy of European Law Trier, Budesanzeiger, Cologne, 2001, 7–14.

Barrett G (ed), *Creating A European Judicial Space, Prospects for Improving Judicial Cooperation in Civil Matters in the European Union*, Vol 30, Academy of European Law Trier, Budesanzeiger, Cologne 2001.

Barrocas M P, 'Europe Summary' in Platto C (ed), *Economic Consequences of Litigation Worldwide*, Kluwer Law International, The Hague, 1999, 137–42

Basedow J, 'The Communitarization of the Conflict of Laws under the Treaty of Amsterdam' *Common Market Law Review* 3/2000, 687–708.

Basedow J et al (eds), *Private Law in the International Arena – Liber Amicorum Kurt Siehr*, TMC Asser Press, The Hague, 2000.

Beaumont P, 'The Brussels Convention Becomes a Regulation: Implications for Legal Basis, External Competence, and Contract Jurisdiction' in Fawcett J (ed), *Reform and Development of Private International Law, Essays in Honour of Sir Peter North*, Oxford University Press, Oxford, 2002, 9–30.

Bell A S, *Forum Shopping and Venue in Transnational Litigation*, Oxford University Press, Oxford, 2003.

Berger K P, 'Harmonisation of European Contract Law. The Influence of Comparative Law' *International and Comparative Law Quarterly* 4/2001, 877–900.

Berger K P, 'European Private Law, "Lex Mercatoria" and Globalisation' in Hartkamp A, Hesselink M, Honduis E, Joustra C, Du Perron E, and Veldman M (eds), *Towards a European Civil Code*, Third Edition, Kluwer Law International, Nijmegen, 2004, 43–58.

Berliri M, 'Jurisdiction and Choice of Law in Cyberspace in Europe' *International Law Practicum* 2003, 48–51.

Bermann G, 'Proportionality and Subsidiarity' in Barnard C and Scott J (eds), *The Law of the Single European Market – Unpacking the Premises*, Hart Publishing, Oxford, 2002, 75–99.

Biavati P, 'Is Flexibility a Way to the Harmonization of Civil Procedural Law in Europe?' in Carpi F and Lupoi M (eds), *Essays on Transnational and Comparative Civil Procedure*, G. Giappichelli Editore, Turin, 2001, 85–104.

Biavati P, 'L'Art. 47 della Carta dei diritti e il processo comunitario: Spunti dal caso Mannesmannröhren' in Taruffo M and Varano V (eds), *Diritti Fondamentali e Guistizia Civile in Europa*, G. Giappichelli Editore, Turin, 2002, 207–17.

Blackburn R (ed), *Rights of Citizenship*, Mansell Publishing, London, 1993.

Boele-Woelki K, 'Unification and Harmonization of Private International Law in Europe' in Basedow J et al (eds), *Private Law in the International Arena – Liber Amicorum Kurt Siehr*, TMC Asser Press, The Hague, 2000, 61–77.

Boerzel T and Cichowski R (eds) *The State of the Union, Vol 6: Law. Politics and Society*, Oxford University Press, Oxford, 2003.

Borrás A, 'The Effect of the Adoption of Brussels I and Rome I on the External Competences of the EC and the Member States' in Meeusen J, Pertegás M, and Straetmans G (eds), *Enforcement of International Contracts in the European Union. Convergence and Divergence between Brussels I and Rome I*, Intersentia, Antwerp, 2004, 99–125.

Borrás A et al (eds), *Liber amicorum Georges A. L Droz: On the Progressive Unification of Private International Law*, Martinus Nijhoff, The Hague/Boston/London, 1996.

Boschiero N, 'The Forthcoming European Enforcement Order. Towards a European Law-Enforcement Area' *Rivista di diritto internazionale* 2/2003, 394–425.

Bottomore T, 'Citizenship and Social Class, Forty Years On' in Marshall and Bottomore, *Citizenship and Social Class*, Pluto Press, London, 1992, 55–93.

Boularbah H, 'Le cadre général des règles communautaires en matière de procédure civile: coopération judiciaire, droit judiciaire européen et droit processuel commun' in De Leval G and Storme M (eds), *Le droit processuel et judiciaire européen*, La Charte & Die Keure, Brussels and Bruges, 2003, 167–93.

Bourel P et al, *L'Influence des Communautés Européennes sur le Droit International Privé des Etats Membres*, Larcier, Brussels, 1981.

Boytha D, 'La libre circulation des jugements dans l'espace judiciaire européen en matière civil et commerciale' *Revue du droit de l'Union Européenne* 3/2006, 619–67.

Bridge J, 'Procedural Aspects of the Enforcement of European Community Law through the Legal Systems of the Member States' *European Law Review* 1/1984, 28–42.

Bruneau C, 'L'obtention des preuves en matière civile et commerciale au sein de l'Union européenne, Règlement CE n° 1206/2001 du Conseil du 28 mai 2001' *La Semaine Juridique Édition Générale* 39/2001, 1767–71.

Bussani M and Mattei U (eds), *The Common Core of European Private Law*, Kluwer Law International, The Hague, 2003.

Buxbaum H, 'Regulatory Policy in Transnational Litigation: The Influence of Judicial Globalization' in Mansel H-P et al (eds), *Festschrift für Erik Jayme, Band I*, Sellier, Munich, 2004, 73–86.

Cafaggi F (ed), *The Institutional Framework of European Private Law*, Oxford University Press, Oxford, 2006.

Candela Soriano M, 'Les exigences linguistiques: Une entrave légitime à la libre circulation?' *Cahiers de Droit Européen* 1/2002, 9–44.

Cappelletti M, 'Social and Political Aspects of Civil Procedure – Reforms and Trends in Western and Eastern Europe' *Michigan Law Review* 1970–1971, 847–86.

Cappelletti M, 'New Dimensions of Justice' in Storme M, *Rechtspraak in Opspraak*, Kluwer, Amsterdam, 1980, 131–42.

Cappelletti M (ed), *Access to Justice and the Welfare State*, Publications of the European University Institute, Sijthoff/Bruylant/Klett-Cotta/Le Monnier, 1981.

Cappelletti M, *The Judicial Process in Comparative Perspective*, Clarendon Press, Oxford, 1989.

Cappelletti M and Garth B, 'Access to Justice and the Welfare State an Introduction' in Cappelletti M (ed), *Access to Justice and the Welfare State*, Publications of the European University Institute, Sijthoff/Bruylant/Klett-Cotta/Le Monnier, 1981, 1–25.

Carlier J-Y and De Schutter O (eds), *La Charte des droits fondamentaux de l'Union européenne. Son apport à la protection des droits de l'homme en Europe*, Bruylant, Brussels, 2002.

Carpi F, 'Reflections on the Harmonization of Civil Procedural Law in Europe in Relation to the 1968 Brussels Convention' in *Scritti in onore di G. F. Mancini Vol II*, Dott. A. Giuffrè Editore, Milan, 1998, 111–23.

Carpi F, 'Prime considerazioni sulle garanzie processuali della Carta dell'Unione Europea' in Taruffo M and Varano V (eds), *Diritti Fondamentali e Guistizia Civile in Europa*, G. Giappichelli Editore, Turin, 2002, 219–26.

Carpi F and Lupoi M (eds), *Essays on Transnational and Comparative Civil Procedure*, G. Giappichelli Editore, Turin, 2001.

Caruso D, 'The Missing View of the Cathedral: The Private Law Paradigm of European Legal Integration' *European Law Journal* 1/1997, 3–32.

Castellain J, 'La transmission sécurisée et la signification des actes' in Isnard J and Normand J (eds), *Nouveaux droits dans un nouvel espace européen de justice: Le droit processuel et le droit de l'exécution*, Éditions Juridiques et Techniques, Paris, 2002, 77–84.

Caupin M-T and De Leval G (eds), *L'Efficacité de la Justice en Europe*, Larcier, Brussels, 2000.

Cherednychenko O, 'EU Fundamental Rights, EC Fundamental Freedoms and Private Law' *European Review of Private Law* 1/2006, 23–61.

Collins H, 'European Private Law and the Cultural Identity of States' *European Review of Private Law* 3/1995, 353–65.

Comoglio L P, 'L'effettività della tutela giurusdizonale nella Carta dei diritti fondamentali dell'Unione europea' in Taruffo M and Varano V (eds), *Diritti Fondamentali e Guistizia Civile in Europa*, G. Giappichelli Editore, Turin, 2002, 227–46.

Correa Delcasso J P, 'Le titre exécutoire européen et l'inversion du contentieux' *Revue International de Droit Comparé* 1/2001, 61–82.

Correa Delcasso J P, 'Propositions pour l'instauration d'une procédure harmonisée d'injonction de payer dans les pays de l'UE' in Storme M (ed), *Procedural Laws in Europe. Towards Harmonisation*, Maklu, Antwerp-Apeldoorn, 2003, 257–65.

Coulon J-M, 'La coopération judiciaire moteur de l'espace européen de justice' in Isnard J and Normand J (eds), *Nouveaux droits dans un nouvel espace européen de justice: Le droit processuel et le droit de l'exécution*, Éditions Juridiques et Techniques, Paris, 2002, 139–48.

Craig P, 'The Community Rights and the Charter' *European Review of Public Law* 1/2002, 195–224.

Craig P and De Búrca G, *EU Law – Text, Cases and Materials*, Second Edition, Oxford University Press, Oxford, 1998.

Craig P and De Búrca G, *The Evolution of EU Law*, Oxford University Press, Oxford, 1999.

Craig P and De Búrca G, *EU Law – Text, Cases and Materials*, Third Edition, Oxford University Press, Oxford, 2002.

Crauford Smith R, 'Remedies for Breaches of EU Law in National Courts: Legal Variation and Selection' in Craig P and De Búrca G, *The Evolution of EU Law*, Oxford University Press, Oxford, 1999, 287–320.

Crifò C, 'First Steps towards the Harmonisation of Civil Procedure: The Regulation Creating a European Enforcement Order for Uncontested Claims' *Civil Justice Quarterly* 2/2005, 200–18.

Crossick S et al, 'The Draft Constitutional Treaty: An Assessment' European Policy Centre, Issue Paper No. 5, 2003.

Cuniberti G, 'Forum non conveniens and the Brussels Convention' *International and Comparative Law Quarterly* 4/2005, 973–81.

Curtin D, 'Case Review: "Marshall II"' *Common Market Law Review* 3/1994, 631.

Curtin D, Kellerman A E, and Blockmans S (eds), *The EU Constitution: The Best Way Forward?*, TMC Asser Press, The Hague, 2005.

Dashwood A, Hacon R, and White R, *A Guide to the Civil Jurisdiction and Judgments Convention*, Kluwer Law and Taxation Publishers, Deventer, 1987.

De Boer T, 'Forum Preferences in Contemporary European Conflicts Law: The Myth of a "Neutral Choice"' in Mansel H-P et al (eds), *Festschrift für Erik Jayme*, Vol I, Sellier, Munich, 2004, 39–56.

De Búrca G, 'National Procedural Rules and Remedies: The Changing Approach of the Court of Justice' in Lonbay J and Biondi A (eds), *Remedies for Breach of EC Law*, John Wiley & Sons, Chichester, 1997, 37–46.

De Búrca G, 'Reappraising Subsidiarity's Significance after Amsterdam' Harvard Jean Monnet Working Paper 7/99, 1999.

De Búrca G, 'Fundamental Rights and Citizenship' in De Witte B (ed), *Ten Reflections on the Constitutional Treaty for Europe*, EUI Robert Schumann Centre, Florence, 2003, 11.

Dehousse R, 'Misfits: EU Law and the Transformation of European Governance' in Joerges C (ed), *Good Governance in Europe's Integrated Market*, Oxford University Press, Oxford, 2002, 207.

De Leval G, 'Le droit de l'éxecution' in Università di Catania (eds), *Trans-National Aspects of Procedural Law*, Vols I–III, Giuffrè Editore, Milan, 1998, 731–81.

De Leval G, 'La procédure uniforme du titre exécutoire européen' in Isnard J and Normand J (eds), *Nouveaux droits dans un nouvel espace européen de justice: Le droit processuel et le droit de l'exécution*, Éditions Juridiques et Techniques, Paris, 2002, 131–8.

De Leval G and Storme M (eds), *Le droit processuel et judiciaire européen*, La Charte & Die Keure, Brussels and Bruges, 2003.

Delicostopoulos I, *Le procès civil à l'épreuve du droit processuel européen*, LGDJ, Paris, 2003 (2003a).

Delicostopoulos J, 'Towards European Procedural Primacy in National Legal Systems' *European Law Journal* 5/2003, 599–613 (2003b).

Del Vecchio B, 'Notification et attestation de validité dans le processus de circulation des actes civils et judiciaires dans l'Union européenne' in Isnard J and Normand J (eds), *Nouveaux droits dans un nouvel espace européen de justice: Le droit processuel et le droit de l'exécution*, Éditions Juridiques et Techniques, Paris, 2002, 95–112.

Den Boer M, 'An Area of Freedom, Security and Justice: Bogged Down by Compromise' in O'Keeffe D and Twomey P (eds), *Legal Issues of the Amsterdam Treaty*, Hart Publishing, Oxford, 1999, 303–21.

Denning LJ, *Introduction to the European Court of Justice: Judges or Policy Makers?*, Bruges Group, London, 1990.

De Roo A, 'Alternative Dispute Resolution in Continental Civil Law: Something Old, Something New' in Barrett G (ed), *Creating A European Judicial Space, Prospects for Improving Judicial Cooperation in Civil Matters in the European Union*, Vol 30, Academy of European Law Trier, Budesanzeiger, Cologne, 2001, 97–104.

De Vareilles-Sommières P (ed), *Le Droit Privé Européen*, Economica, Paris, 1998.

De Vareilles-Sommières P, 'L'articulation du droit international privé et de la procédure' in Leroyer A-M and Jeuland E (eds), *Quelle cohérence pour l'espace judiciaire européen?*, Dalloz, Paris, 2004, 91–104.

De Vel G, 'La Contribution du Conseil de l'Europe à la création d'un espace juridique et judiciaire européen' in Barrett G (ed), *Creating A European Judicial Space, Prospects for Improving Judicial Cooperation in Civil Matters in the European Union*, Vol 30 Academy of European Law Trier, Budesanzeiger, Cologne, 2001, 27–34.

De Vos W and Rechberger W, 'Transnational Litigation and the Evolution of the Law of Evidence' in Università di Catania (eds), *Trans-National Aspects of Procedural Law*, Vols I–III, Giuffrè Editore, Milan, 1998, 687–727.

De Witte B, 'Sovereignty and European Integration: The Weight of Legal Tradition' in Slaughter A-M, Stone Sweet A, and Weiler J (eds), *The European Court and National Courts – Doctrine and Jurisprudence, Legal Change in Its Social Context*, Hart Publishing, Oxford 1998, 277–304.

De Witte B, 'The Process of Ratification and the Crisis Options: A Legal Perspective' in Curtin D, Kellerman A E, and Blockmans S (eds), *The EU Constitution: The Best Way Forward?*, TMC Asser Press, The Hague, 2005, 21.

De Witte B (ed), *Ten Reflections on the Constitutional Treaty for Europe*, EUI Robert Schuman Centre, Florence, 2003.

De Witte B and Forder C (eds), *The Common Law of Europe and the Future of Legal Education*, Kluwer Law, Deventer, 1992.

Diez-Picazo I, 'L'articolo 47 della Carta dei diritti fondamentali dell'Unione europea: La prospettiva spagnola' in Taruffo M and Varano V (eds), *Diritti Fondamentali e Guistizia Civile in Europa*, G. Giappichelli Editore, Turin, 2002, 43–51.

Dony M and Bribosia E (eds), *L'avenir du système juridictionnel de l'Union européenne*, Editions de l'Université de Bruxelles, Brussels, 2002.

Douchy M, 'Du conflit de conventions au conflit de sources' in Isnard J and Normand J (eds), *Nouveaux droits dans un nouvel espace européen de justice: Le droit processuel et le droit de l'exécution*, Éditions Juridiques et Techniques, Paris, 2002, 55–76.

Dougan M, 'Enforcing the Single Market: The Judicial Harmonisation of National Remedies and Procedural Rules' in Barnard C and Scott J (eds), *The Law of the Single European Market – Unpacking the Premises*, Hart Publishing, Oxford, 2002, 153–79.

Dougan M, 'The Convention's Draft Constitutional Treaty: Bringing Europe Closer to its Lawyers?' *European Law Review* 6/2003, 763–93.

Dougan M, *National Remedies Before the Court of Justice, Issues of Harmonisation and Differentiation*, Hart Publishing, Oxford and Portland, Oregon, 2004.

Drobnig U, 'Unification of National Law and the Uniformisation of the Rules of Private International Law' in Bourel P et al, *L'Influence des Communautés Européennes sur le Droit International Privé des Etats Membres*, Larcier, Brussels, 1981, 1–46.

Drobnig U, 'European Private International Law after the Treaty of Amsterdam: Perspectives for the Next Decade' *King's College Law Journal* 1/2000, 190–201.

Droz G and Gaudemet-Tallon H, 'La transformation de la Convention de Bruxelles du 27 septembre 1968 en Règlement du Conseil concernant la compétence judiciaire, la reconnaissance et l'exécution des décisions en matière civile et commerciale' *Revue Critique de Droit International Privé* 4/2001, 601–52.

Dubois O, *Les juridictions nationales, juge communautaire – Contribution à l'étude des transformations de la fonction juridictionnelle dans les États membres de l'Union européenne*, Dalloz, Paris, 2001.

Duintjer Tebbens H, 'Les règles de conflit contenues dans les instruments de droit dérivé' in Fuchs A, Muir Watt H, and Pataut E (eds), *Les conflits de lois et le système juridique communautaire*, Dalloz, Paris, 2004, 101–15.

Edward D, 'National Courts – the Powerhouse of Community Law' *Cambridge Yearbook of European Legal Studies* Vol 5, Hart Publishing, Oxford/Portland, Oregon, 2004, 1.

Ekelmans M, 'Le règlement 1348/2000 relatif à la signification et à la notification des actes judiciaires et extrajudiciaires' *Journal des Tribunaux* 6014/2001, 481–8.

Engström J, 'Effektivt Rättskydd i Förvirring – Nationell Process – och Sanktionsrätt i Ljuset av C-253/00 Munõz' *Europarättslig Tidskrift* 1/2003, 167–81.

Ervasti K, 'Lainkäytön funktiot' *Lakimies* 1/2002, 47–72.

Ervo L, 'Suomen prosessin kompastuskivet Euroopan ihmisoikeustuomioistuimen oikeuskäytännössä' in Männistö J (ed), *Prosessioikeudellisia Erityiskysymyksiä – Juhlajulkaisu Antti Jokela*, Turku University Press, Turku, 2004, 11–29.

Estella A, *The EU Principle of Subsidiarity and Its Critique*, Oxford University Press, Oxford, 2002.

European Consumer Law Group/Bureau Européen des Unions de Consommateurs (ECLG), *Jurisdiction and Applicable Law in Cross-Border Consumer Complaints – Socio-Legal Remarks on an Ongoing Dilemma Concerning Effective Legal Protection for Consumer-Citizens in the European Union*, ECLG/157/1998, available at http://www.europeanconsumerlawgroup.org/.

European Consumer Law Group/Bureau Européen des Unions de Consommateurs (ECLG), *Commission Proposal for a Directive on Mediation*, ECLG/122/2004, available at http://www.europeanconsumerlawgroup.org/.

Fallon M, 'Les droits fondamentaux liés à la citoyenneté de l'Union européenne sous les regards croisés du traité CE et de la Charte' in Carlier J-Y and De Schutter O (eds), *La Charte des droits fondamentaux de l'Union européenne. Son apport à la protection des droits de l´homme en Europe*, Bruylant, Brussels, 2002, 149–78.

Fallon M, 'La compétence internationale selon le droit judiciaire européen: émergence d'une compétence judiciaire européenne?' in De Leval G and Storme M (eds), *Le droit processuel et judiciaire européen*, La Charte & Die Keure, Brussels and Bruges, 2003, 25–62.

Fawcett J (ed), *Reform and Development of Private International Law, Essays in Honour of Sir Peter North*, Oxford University Press, Oxford, 2002.

Fentiman R, 'Civil Jurisdiction and Third States: *Owusu* and After' *Common Market Law Review* 2006, 705–34.

Fernández Arroyo D P, 'Exorbitant and Exclusive Grounds of Jurisdiction in European Private International Law: Will They Ever Survive?' in Mansel H-P et al (eds), *Festschrift für Erik Jayme*, Vol I, Sellier, Munich, 2004, 169–86.

Ferrera M, Matsaganis M, and Sacchi S, 'Open Co-ordination Against Poverty: The New EU Social Inclusion Process' *Journal of European Social Policy* 3/2002, 227.

Fouchard P (ed), *Vers un procès civil universel? Les règles transnationales de procédure civile de l'American Law Institute*, Editions Panthéon-Assas, Paris, 2001.

Frände D, 'Towards a Harmonized Criminal Justice System in the EU' in Frände D et al, *In the Footsteps of Tampere – Justice in the European Union*, University of Helsinki, Helsinki, 2006, 35–49.

Frände D et al, *In the Footsteps of Tampere – Justice in the European Union*, University of Helsinki, Helsinki, 2006.

Freudenthal M, 'The Simplification of Cross-Border Debt Collection' in Storme M (ed), *Procedural Laws in Europe. Towards Harmonisation*, Maklu, Antwerp-Apeldoorn, 2003, 363–8.

Freyhold, Vial & Partner Consultants, *The Cost of Legal Obstacles to the Disadvantage of Consumers in the Single Market*, Report for the EU Commission DG SANCO, 1998, available at http://europa.eu.int/comm/consumers/whatsnew/news:archives_1t99.htm.

Fricero N, 'L'acte introductif d'instance et la transmission des actes au regard de la convention européenne des droits de l'homme' in Isnard J and Normand J (eds), *Nouveaux droits dans un nouvel espace européen de justice: Le droit processuel et le droit de l'exécution*, Éditions Juridiques et Techniques, Paris, 2002, 45–53.

Fricero N, 'La consécration européenne du droit à l'exécution' in Isnard J and Normand J (eds), *L'aménagement du droit de l'exécution dans l'espace communautaire: bientôt les premiers instruments*, Éditions Juridiques et Techniques, Paris, 2003, 61–77 (2003a).

Fricero N, 'La libre exécution des jugements dans l'espace judiciaire européen: Un principe émergent?' in Bandrac M et al, *Justice et droits fondamentaux. Etudes offertes à Jacques Normand*, Litec, Paris, 2003, 173–83 (2003b).

Fuchs A, Muir Watt H, and Pataut E (eds), *Les conflits de lois et le système juridique communautaire*, Dalloz, Paris, 2004.

Galanter M, 'Justice in Many Rooms' in Cappelletti M (ed), *The Access to Justice and the Welfare State*, Publications of the European University Institute, Sijthoff/Bruylant/Klett-Cotta/Le Monnier, 1981, 147.

Gardner J P, *Hallmarks of Citizenship: A Green Paper*, British Institute of International and Comparative Law, London, 1994.

Gasparinetti M, 'Access to Justice: The State of Play' in Lonbay J (ed), *Enhancing the Legal Position of the European Consumer*, British Institute of International and Comparative Law, London, 1996, 227–30.

Gaudemet-Tallon H, 'Quel Juge?' in Fouchard P (ed), *Vers un procès civil universel? Les règles transnationales de procédure civile de l'American Law Institute*, Editions Panthéon-Assas, Paris, 2001, 67–71.

Gaudemet-Tallon H, *Compétence et exécution des jugements en Europe – Règlement n° 44/2001, Conventions de Bruxelles et Lugano*, Third Edition, Librairie Générale de Droit et de Jurisprudence, Paris, 2002.

Gaudemet-Tallon H, 'La cohérence des sources communautaires et internationales' in Leroyer A-M and Jeuland E (eds), *Quelle cohérence pour l'espace judiciaire européen?*, Dalloz, Paris, 2004, 67–85.

Geddes A, *Protection of Individual Rights under EC Law*, Butterworths, London, 1995.

Geimer R, 'The Brussels Convention – Successful Model and Old-Timer' *European Journal of Law Reform* 1/2002, 19–35.

Gillies L, 'Adapting international private law rules for electronic consumer contracts' in Rickett C and Telfer T (eds.) *International Perspectives on Consumers' Access to Justice*, Cambridge University Press, Cambridge, 2003, 359–83.

Girard-Thuilier P, 'La communication trans-frontière des juges' in Barrett G (ed), *Creating A European Judicial Space, Prospects for Improving Judicial Cooperation in Civil Matters in the European Union*, Vol 30 Academy of European Law Trier, Budesanzeiger, Cologne, 2001, 59–64.

Girerd P, 'L'article 68 CE: un renvoi préjudiciel d'interprétation et d'application incertaines' *Revue Trimestrielle de Droit Européen* 2/1999, 239–60.

Girerd P, 'Les principes d'équivalence et d'effectivité: encadrement ou désencadrement de l'autonomie procédurale des États membres' *Revue Trimestrielle de Droit Eur*opéen 1/2002, 75–102.

Girsberger D, 'The Internet and Jurisdiction Based on Contracts' *European Journal of Law Reform* 1/2002, 165–83.

Giussani A, 'The "Verbandsklage" and the Class Action: Two Models for Collective Litigation' in Storme M (ed), *Procedural Laws in Europe. Towards Harmonisation*, Maklu, Antwerp-Apeldoorn, 2003, 389–405.

Glenn H P, 'Globalization and Dispute Resolution' *Civil Justice Quarterly* 2000, 136–53.

Gonod P, 'L'espace administratif européen' in Leroyer A-M and Jeuland E (eds), *Quelle cohérence pour l'espace judiciaire européen?*, Dalloz, Paris, 2004, 135.

Gonzales Campos J D, 'La Cour de Justice des Communautés Européennes et le non-Droit international privé' in Mansel H-P et al (eds), *Festschrift für Erik Jayme*, Vol I, Sellier, Munich, 2004, 263–76.

Gottwald P, 'Recognition and Enforcement of Foreign Judgments under the Brussels Convention' in Miller C and Beaumont P (eds), *The Option of Litigating in Europe*, UK Comparative Law Series, Vol 14, 1993, 31–41.

Gottwald P, 'Principles and Current Problems of Uniform Procedural Law in Europe under the Brussels Convention' *St Louis–Warsaw Transatlantic Law Journal* 1/1997, 139–71.

Gout M, 'Welcoming Remarks: Global Forum on Access to Justice' *Fordham International Law Journal* 2000, 312–16.

Gröning L, 'EU:s straffrättsliga samarbete – En fråga om legitimitet' *Tidskrift utgiven av Juridiska Föreningen i Finland* 1/2005, 1–23.

Guinchard S et al, *Droit Processuel – Droit commun et droit comparé du procès*, Second Edition, Dalloz, Paris, 2003.

Haapaniemi P, *Kansallinen Toumioistuin EU-Oikeuden Soveltajana*, Kauppakaari Lakimiesliiton Kustannus, Jyväskylä, 1999.

Haibach G, 'The Mutual Recognition of Decisions in Civil and Commercial Matters in the European Union in the Light of the Full Faith and Credit Clause of the U.S. Constitution' *Maastricht Journal of European Comparative Law* 3/2003, 291–300.

Haibach G, 'The Commission Proposal for a Regulation Establishing a European Small Claims Procedure: An Analysis' *European Review of Private Law* 4/2005, 593–601.

Harding C, 'Member State Enforcement of European Community Measures: The Chimera of "Effective" Enforcement' *Maastricht Journal of European and Comparative Law* 4/1997, 5–24.

Harlow C, 'The Charter of Fundamental Rights: A Textual Critique' *European Review of Public Law* 1/2002, 255–71.

Harris J, 'Stays of Proceedings and the Brussels Convention' *International and Comparative Law Quarterly* 4/2005, 933–50.

Hartkamp A, Hesselink M, Honduis E, Du Perron E, and Joustra C (eds), *Towards a European Civil Code*, Second Edition, Kluwer Law, Nijmegen, 1998.

Hartkamp A, Hesselink M, Honduis E, Joustra C, Du Perron E, and Veldman M (eds), *Towards a European Civil Code*, Third Edition, Kluwer Law International, Nijmegen, 2004.

Hartley T C, 'Antisuit Injunctions and the Brussels Jurisdiction and Judgments Convention' *International and Comparative Law Quarterly* 1/2000, 166.

Hartley T C, 'The European Union and the Systematic Dismantling of the Common Law of Conflict of Laws' *International and Comparative Law Quarterly* 4/2005, 813–28.

Hartley T C, 'The Hague Choice-of-Court Convention' *European Law Review* 3/2006, 414–24.

Hartnell H, 'EUstitia: Institutionalizing Justice in the European Union' *Northwestern Journal of International Law and Business* 2002, 65–138.

Hazard G, 'Civil Litigation without Frontiers: Harmonisation and Unification of Procedural Law' General Report XI World Congress on Procedural Law, 1999, 3.

Heater D, *A Brief History of Citizenship*, Edinburgh University Press, Edinburgh, 2004.

Heffenan L, 'Community Courts post-Nice: A European Certiorari Revisited' *International and Comparative Law Quarterly* 4/2003, 907–33.

Heiskanen V and Kulovesi K (eds), *Function and Future of European Law*, Helsinki University Press, Helsinki, 1999.

Heiss H and Suprón-Heidel A, 'EU Enlargement: Aspects of (International) Procedural Law' *European Journal of Law Reform* 1/2002, 147–64.

Hess B, 'The Integrating Effect of European Civil Procedural Law' *European Journal of Law Reform* 1/2002, 3–17 (2002a).

Hess B, 'Le projet anglo-germano-suédois de titre exécutoire européen: Conditions nécessaires à la suppression de l'exequatur' in Isnard J and Normand J (eds), *Nouveaux droits dans un nouvel espace européen de justice: Le droit processuel et le droit de l'exécution*, Éditions Juridiques et Techniques, Paris, 2002, 121–30 (2002b).

Hess B, 'Nouvelles techniques de la coopération judiciaire transfrontière en Europe' *Revue Critique de Droit International Privé* 2/2003, 215–37.

Hess B, 'Le compétences externes de la Communauté européenne dans le cadre de l'article 65 CE' in Fuchs A, Muir Watt H, and Pataut E (eds), *Les conflits de lois et le système juridique communautaire*, Dalloz, Paris, 2004, 81–100 (2004a).

Hess B, *Study No JAI/A3/2002/02 on Making More Efficient the Enforcement of Judicial Decisions within the European Union: Transparency of Debtor's Assets, Attachment of Bank Accounts, Provisional Enforcement and Protective Measures*, 2004, published on the website of the Commission: http://www.

europa.eu.int/comm/justice_home/doc_centre/civil/studies/doc_civil_studies_en.htm (2004b).

Hess B, 'Comparative Analysis of the National Reports' in Andenas M, Hess B, and Oberhammer P (eds), *Enforcement Agency Practice in Europe*, British Institute of International and Comparative Law, London, 2005, 25–46 (2005a).

Hess B, 'Minimum Procedural Standards for Enforcement of Provisional and Protective Measures at European Level' in Andenas M, Hess B, and Oberhammer P (eds), *Enforcement Agency Practice in Europe*, British Institute of International and Comparative Law, London, 2005, 265–85 (2005b).

Himsworth C, 'Things Fall Apart: The Harmonisation of Community Judicial Procedural Protection Revisited' *European Law Review* 4/1997, 291–311.

Hodges C, 'Multiparty Actions: A European Approach' *Duke Journal of Comparative and International Law* 2001, 321–51.

Hodges C, 'Some Observations on Multi-Party Claims' in Storme M (ed), *Procedural Laws in Europe. Towards Harmonisation*, Maklu, Antwerp-Apeldoorn, 2003, 403–5.

Hoskins M, 'Tilting the Balance: Supremacy and National Procedural Rules' *European Law Review* 5/1996, 365.

Huber P, 'Playing the Same Old Song – German Courts, the "Napster" Case and the International Law of Service of Process' in Mansel H-P et al (eds), *Festschrift für Erik Jayme*, Vol 1, Sellier, Munich, 2004, 361–70.

Isnard J and Normand J (eds), *Nouveaux droits dans un nouvel espace européen de justice: Le droit processuel et le droit de l'exécution*, Éditions Juridiques et Techniques, Paris, 2002.

Isnard J and Normand J (eds), *L'aménagement du droit de l'exécution dans l'espace communautaire: bientôt les premiers instruments*, Éditions Juridiques et Techniques, Paris, 2003.

Israël J, 'Conflicts of Law and the EC after Amsterdam, A Change for the Worse?' *Maastricht Journal of European Comparative Law* 1/2000, 81–99.

Jacobs F G, 'Enforcing Community Rights and Obligations in National Courts: Striking the Balance' in Lonbay J and Biondi A (eds), *Remedies for Breach of EC Law*, John Wiley & Sons, Chichester, 1997, 25–46.

Jagtenberg R W, 'Cross-Border Mediation in Europe: Prospects and Pitfalls' in Barrett G (ed), *Creating a European Judicial Space, Prospects for Improving Judicial Cooperation in Civil Matters in the European Union*, Vol 30, Academy of European Law Trier, Budesanzeiger, Cologne, 2001, 91–6.

Jagtenberg R, Örücü E, and De Roo A (eds), *Transfrontier Mobility of Law*, Kluwer Law International, The Hague, 1995.

Jansen R, Koster D, and Van Zutphen R (eds), *European Ambitions of the National Judiciary*, Kluwer Law International, The Hague, 1997.

Jarvis M, *The Application of EC Law by National Courts – The Free Movement of Goods*, Clarendon Press, Oxford, 1998.

Jastrow S, 'Overview of Jurisdiction and Enforcement in Civil and Commercial Matters' EIPA Seminar Paper, 11–12 November 2004, Luxembourg.

Jayme E and Kohler C, 'L'interaction des règles de conflit contenues dans le droit dérivé de la Communauté européenne et des conventions de Bruxelles et de Rome' *Revue Critique de Droit Internationale Privé* 1/1995, 1–40.

Jessurun D'Oliveira H U, 'Towards a "European" Private International Law?' in De Witte B and Forder C (eds), *The Common Law of Europe and the Future of Legal Educat*ion, Kluwer Law, Deventer 1992, 265–83.

Jessurun D'Oliveira H U, 'Union Citizenship: Pie in the Sky?' in Rosas A and Antola E (eds), *A Citizen's Europe. In Search of a New Legal Order*, Sage Publications, London, 1995, 58–84.

Jessurun D'Oliveira H U, 'The EU and a Metamorphosis of Private International Law' in Fawcett J (ed), *Reform and Development of Private International Law, Essays in Honour of Sir Peter North*, Oxford University Press, Oxford, 2002, 111–36.

Jeuland E, 'Les lacunes du droit judiciaire européen' in Leroyer A-M and Jeuland E (eds), *Quelle cohérence pour l'espace judiciaire européen?*, Dalloz, Paris, 2004,105–16.

Joerges C, 'The Bright and the Dark Side of the Consumer's Access to Justice in the EU' *Global Jurist Topics* 2/2001, 1.

Joerges C, 'The Law's Problem with the Governance of the European Market' in Joerges C (ed), *Good Governance in Europe's Integrated Market*, Oxford University Press, Oxford, 2002, 3.

Joerges C (ed), *Good Governance in Europe's Integrated Market*, Oxford University Press, Oxford, 2002.

Johansson S (ed), *Kansainvälisen Siviiliprosessioikeuden Käsikirja*, Talentum, Helsinki, 2002.

Johnston A, 'Judicial Reform and the Treaty of Nice' *Common Market Law Review* 3/2001, 499–523.

Jolowicz J A, 'On the Nature and Purposes of Civil Procedural Law' in Scott I (ed), *International Perspectives on Civil Justice, Essays in Honour of Sir Jack I. H. Jacob Q.C.*, Sweet & Maxwell, London, 1990, 27–45.

Jolowicz J A, 'Fact-Finding: A Comparative Perspective' in Miller C and Beaumont P (eds), *The Option of Litigating in Europe*, UK Comparative Law Series Vol 14, 1993, 133–48.

Jolowicz J A, 'Introduction – Recourse Against Civil Judgments in the European Union: A Comparative Survey' in Jolowicz J A and Van Rhee C H (eds), *Recourse Against Judgments in the European Union*, Kluwer Law International, The Hague, 1999, 1–18.

Jolowicz J A, *On Civil Procedure*, Cambridge University Press, Cambridge, 2000.

Jolowicz J A and Van Rhee C H (eds), *Recourse Against Judgments in the European Union*, Kluwer Law International, The Hague, 1999.

Jongbloet A W, 'De dwangsom als een speciale sanctie in het Europees privaatrecht' (English Summary) in Storme M (ed), *Procedural Laws in Europe. Towards Harmonisation*, Maklu, Antwerp-Apeldoorn, 2003, 255.

Juenger F K, 'What's Wrong with Forum Shopping?' *Sydney Law Review* 1/1994, 4–13.

Juenger F K, 'Some Comments on European Procedural Harmonization' *American Journal of Comparative Law* 4/1997, 931–7.

Kakouris C N, 'Do the Member States Possess Judicial Procedural "Autonomy"?' *Common Market Law Review* 6/1997, 1389–412.

Kamàl Yuille L, 'No One's Perfect (Not Even Close): Reevaluating Access to Justice in the United States and Western Europe' *Columbia Journal of Transnational Law* 3/2004, 863–923.

Kaye P, *Methods of Execution of Orders and Judgments in Europe*, John Wiley & Sons, Chichester, 1995.

Kaye P, 'The European Convention on the Service of Judicial and Extra-judicial Documents' in Hoffman B von (ed), *European Private International Law*, Ars Aequi Libri, Nijmegen, 1998, 159–80.

Kennett W, 'Harmonization and the Judgments Convention: Historical Influences' *European Review of Private Law* 1/1993, 83–107.

Kennett W, 'Enforcement of Judgments – Chronique' *European Review of Private Law* 2/1997, 321–427.

Kennett W, 'Service of Documents in Europe' *Civil Justice Quarterly* 3/1998, 284–307.

Kennett W, *Enforcement of Judgments in Europe*, Oxford University Press, Oxford, 2000.

Kennett W, 'The Brussels I Regulation' *International and Comparative Law Quarterly* 3/2001, 725–37.

Kennett W, 'Aperçus comparatifs des différents modes d'exécution forcée des obligations pécuniaires dans l'Union européenne' in Isnard J and Normand J (eds), *Nouveaux droits dans un nouvel espace européen de justice: Le droit processuel et le droit de l'exécution*, Éditions Juridiques et Techniques, Paris, 2002, 255–65.

Kennett W, 'Enforcement: General Report' in Storme M (ed), *Procedural Laws in Europe. Towards Harmonisation*, Maklu, Antwerp-Apeldoorn, 2003, 81–111.

Kerameus K, 'Procedural Unification: The Need and the Limitations' in Scott I (ed), *International Perspectives on Civil Justice. Essays in Honour of Sir Jack I. H. Jacob Q.C.*, Sweet & Maxwell, London, 1990, 47–66.

Kerameus K, 'Procedural Harmonization in Europe' *American Journal of Comparative Law* 3/1995, 401–16.

Kerameus K, 'Political Integration and Procedural Convergence in the European Union' *American Journal of Comparative Law* 4/1997, 919–30.

Kerameus K, 'Procedural Implications of Civil Law Unification' in Hartkamp A, Hesselink M, Honduis E, Du Perron E, and Joustra C (eds), *Towards a European Civil Code*, Second Edition, Kluwer Law, Nijmegen, 1998, 121–32 (1998a).

Kerameus K, 'Provisional Remedies in Transnational Litigation. Second Part' in Università di Catania (eds), *Trans-National Aspects of Procedural Law*, Vols I–III, Giuffrè Editore, Milan, 1998, 1171–209 (1998b).

Kerameus K, 'La traduction des actes dans le règlement du 29 mai 2000' in Isnard J and Normand J (eds), *Nouveaux droits dans un nouvel espace européen de justice: Le droit processuel et le droit de l'exécution*, Éditions Juridiques et Techniques, Paris, 2002, 113–18.

Kerameus K, 'Procédure civile nationale et exigences communautaires' in Bandrac M et al, *Justice et droits fondamentaux. Etudes offertes à Jacques Normand*, Litec, Paris, 2003, 253–9.

Kerameus K, 'Procedural Implications of Civil Law Unification' in Hartkamp A, Hesselink M, Honduis E, Joustra C, Du Perron E, and Veldman M (eds), *Towards a European Civil Code*, Third Edition, Kluwer Law International, Nijmegen, 2004, 145–57.

Kightlinger M, 'A Solution to the Yahoo! Problem? The EC E-Commerce Directive as a Model for International Cooperation on Internet Choice of Law' *Michigan Journal of International Law* 3/2003, 719–47.

Knuts G, *Förfarandegarantier vid domstolsanknuten medling*, Suomalainen Lakimiesyhdistys A-sarja No. 270, Helsinki, 2005.

Koch H, 'Prozeβfürung bei komplexen Verfahren in Europa' (English Summary) in Storme M (ed), *Procedural Laws in Europe. Towards Harmonisation*, Maklu, Antwerp-Apeldoorn, 2003, 386.

Kodek G, 'Zwishen Subsidiaritätsprinzip und Europäischer rechtsidee: Gedanken zur Vereinheitlichung den Inkassoverfahrens' (English Summary) in Storme M (ed), *Procedural Laws in Europe. Towards Harmonisation*, Maklu, Antwerp-Apeldoorn, 2003, 361.

Kodek G, 'The Impact of the European Convention on Human Rights and Fundamental Liberties on Enforcement Practices' in Andenas M, Hess B, and Oberhammer P (eds), *Enforcement Agency Practice in Europe*, British Institute of International and Comparative Law, London, 2005, 303–33.

Kohler C, 'Practical Experience of the Brussels Jurisdiction and Judgments Convention in the Six Original Contracting States' *International and Comparative Law Quarterly* 3/1985, 563–83.

Kohler C, 'Interrogations sur les sources du droit international privé européen après le traité d'Amsterdam' *Revue Critique de Droit International Privé* 1/1999, 1–30.

Kohler C, 'Lo spazio giudiziario europeo in materia civile e il diritto internazionale privato comunitario' in Picone P (ed), *Diritto Internazionale Privato e Diritto Communitario*, CEDAM, Padua, 2004, 65–94.

Komninos A, 'New Prospects for Private Enforcement of EC Competition Law: *Courage v. Crehan* and the Community Right to Damages' *Common Market Law Review* 3/2002, 447.

Koopmans T, 'Towards a New "Ius Commune"' in De Witte B and Forder C (eds), *The Common Law of Europe and the Future of Legal Education*, Kluwer Law, Deventer 1992, 43–51.

Koppenol-Laforce M, 'International Procedural Law' in Snijders H J et al, *Access to Civil Procedure Abroad*, Kluwer Law International, The Hague/Boston, 1999, 25.

Kötz H, 'A Common Private Law for Europe: Perspectives for the Reform of Legal Education' in De Witte B and Forder C (eds), *The Common Law of Europe and the Future of Legal Education*, Kluwer Law, Deventer 1992, 31–43.

Koulu R, *Kansainvälisen prosessi – ja insolvenssioikeuden pääpiirteet*, Lakimiesliiton Kustannus Oy, Helsinki, 2001.

Koulu R, 'XII 1 Kansainvälinen Siviiliprosessioikeus' in Lappalainen J et al, *Prosessioikeus*, WSOY Lakitieto, Helsinki, 2003, 1083.

Koulu R, 'Kommer den alternativa tvistlösningen att europeiseras?' *Tidskrift utgiven av Juridiska Föreningen i Finland* 4–5/2005, 544–59.

Kruger T, 'The 20th Session of the Hague Conference: A New Choice of Court Convention and the Issue of EC Membership' *International and Comparative Law Quarterly* 2/2006, 447–56.

Labayle H, 'Un espace de liberté, de sécurité et de justice' *Revue Trimestrielle de Droit Européen* 4/1997, 813–63.

Labayle H, 'Les nouveaux domaines d'intervention de la Cour de justice: l'espace de liberté, de sécurité et de justice' in Dony M and Bribosia E (eds), *L'avenir du système juridictionnel de l'Union européenne*, Editions de l'Université de Bruxelles, Brussels, 2002, 73–103.

Labayle H, 'La cohérence institutionnelle de l'espace judiciaire européen. Propos introductifs' in Leroyer A-M and Jeuland E (eds), *Quelle cohérence pour l'espace judiciaire européen?*, Dalloz, Paris, 2004, 15–30.

Lakimiesliitto (ed), *Kansainvälinen Oikeusapu*, Suomen Lakimiesliiton Kustannus Oy, Mänttä, 1980.

Lappalainen J, *Siviiliprosessioikeus I*, Lakimiesliiton Kustannus, Helsinki, 1995.

Lappalainen J, *Siviiliprosessioikeus II*, Kauppakaari, Helsinki, 2001.

Lappalainen J et al, *Prosessioikeus*, WSOY Lakitieto, Helsinki, 2003.

La Torre M (ed), *European Citizenship: An Institutional Challenge*, Kluwer Law International, The Hague/London/Boston, 1998.

Laukkanen S, 'Coming Together of Minimum Standards for Summary Proceedings' in Storme M (ed), *Procedural Laws in Europe. Towards Harmonisation*, Maklu, Antwerp-Apeldoorn, 2003, 187–91.

Lavranos Nikolaos, 'Opinion 1/03, Lugano Convention, (Full Court) of 7 February 2006, not yet reported' *Common Market Law Review* 2006, 1087–110.

Lebeau D and Niboyet M-L, 'Regards croisés du processualiste et de l'internationaliste sur le règlement CE du 28 mai 2001 relatif à l'obtention des preuves civiles à l'étranger' *Gazette du Palais (Doctrine)* 2003, 221–33.

Lebessis N and Paterson J, *Evolution in Governance: What Lessons for the Commission? A First Assessment*, Working Paper of the Commission Forward Studies Unit, 1997.

Lebois M, 'Le Règlement (CE) no. 1206/2001 du Conseil du 28 mai 2001 relatif à la coopération entres les juridictions des Etats membres dans le domaine de l'obtention des preuves en matière civile ou commerciale' in De Leval G and Storme M (eds), *Le droit processuel et judiciaire européen*, La Charte & Die Keure, Brussels and Bruges, 2003, 271–93.

Legrand P, 'Legal Traditions in Western Europe: The Limits of Commonality' in Jagtenberg R, Örücü E, and De Roo A (eds), *Transfrontier Mobility of Law*, Kluwer Law International, The Hague, 1995, 63–84.

Legrand P, 'Against a European Civil Code' *Modern Law Review* 1/1997, 44–63.

Legrand P, 'On the Unbearable Localness of Law: Academic Fallacies and Unreasonable Observations' *European Review of Private Law* 1/2002, 61–76.

Legrand P, 'A Diabolical Idea' in Hartkamp A, Hesselink M, Honduis E, Joustra C, Du Perron E, and Veldman M (eds), *Towards a European Civil Code*, Third Edition, Kluwer Law International, Nijmegen, 2004, 245–72.

Leible S and Staudinger A, 'Article 65 of the EC Treaty in the EC System of Competencies' *European Legal Forum* 4/2000–2001, 225–335.

Leppänen T, 'Siviiliprosessin tehtävistä muuttavassa yhteiskunnassa' *Lakimies* 5/1998, 828–31.

Leroy E, 'L'aide juridique et judiciaire en droit européen' in De Leval G and Storme M (eds), *Le droit processuel et judiciaire européen*, La Charte & Die Keure, Brussels and Bruges, 2003, 295–327.

Leroyer A-M and Jeuland E (eds), Quelle *cohérence pour l'espace judiciaire européen?*, Dalloz, Paris, 2004.

Lesauvage C, 'Contribution de la Cour de justice des communautés européennes à la mise en œuvre d'un régime d'exécution des titres et décisions judiciaires' in Isnard J and Normand J (eds), *L'aménagement du droit de l'exécution dans l'espace communautaire: bientôt les premiers instruments*, Éditions Juridiques et Techniques, Paris, 2003, 45–59.

Leubsdorf J, 'The Myth of Civil Procedure Reform' in Zuckerman A A S (ed), *Civil Justice in Crisis, Comparative Perspectives of Civil Procedure*, Oxford University Press, Oxford, 1999, 53–67.

Lewis C, *Remedies and the Enforcement of European Community Law*, Sweet & Maxwell, London, 1996.

Likosky M (ed), *Transnational Legal Processes, Globalisation and Power Disparities*, Butterworths, Edinburgh, 2002.

Lindblom P H, 'The Privatization of Justice: Some Aspects of Recent Developments in American and Swedish Procedural Law' in Sumampouw M et al (eds), *Law and Reality, Essays on National and International Procedural Law in Honour of Cornelis Carel Albert Voskuil*, T.M.C. Asser Institute, Martinus Nijhoff, Dordrecht, 1992, 199–214.

Lindblom P H, 'Harmony of the Legal Spheres, A Swedish View on the Construction of a Unified European Procedural Law' *European Review of Private Law* 1/1997, 11–46 (1997a).

Lindblom P H, 'Integrera mera? Regeringsförhandlingar om (bl.a.) civilprocessrätten i EU!' *Svensk Juristtidning* 4/1997, 307–16 (1997b).

Lindblom P H, *Progressiv Process*, Iustus Förlag, Uppsala, 2000 (2000a).

Lindblom P H, 'Civilprocessens grundprinciper de lege ferenda. Synpunkter i anslutning till det aktuella civilprocessuella reformarbetet i England, Danmark, Finland, Norge och Sverige' *Svensk Juristtidning* 2/2000, 105–55 (2000b).

Lindblom P H, 'Grupptalan – världsläget år 2000' in Lindblom P H, *Progressiv Process*, Iustus Förlag, Uppsala, 2000, 427–42 (2000c).

Lindblom P H, 'Domstolarnas växande samhällsroll och processens förändrade funktioner – flosker eller fakta?' *Svensk Juristtidning* 3/2004, 229–62.

Lindblom P H, 'ADR – opium för rättsväsendet? Synpunkter på alternativ tvistlösning och valfri civil process' *Svensk Juristtidning* 2/2006, 101–30.

Lindell B, *Civilprocessen*, Andra Upplagan, Iustus Förlag, Uppsala, 2003.

Lindholm P, 'Oikeusavusta pohjoismaiden kesken' in Lakimiesliitto (ed), *Kansainvälinen Oikeusapu*, Suomen Lakimiesliiton kustannus Oy, Mänttä, 1980,11–27.

Liukkunen U, 'Perspectives on the Unification of Private International Law in Europe' in Frände D et al, *In the Footsteps of Tampere – Justice in the European Union*, University of Helsinki, Helsinki, 2006, 51–72.

Lodder A and Kaspersen H, *Directives: Guide to European Union Law on E-Commerce*, Kluwer Law International, The Hague, 2002.

Lonbay J (ed), *Enhancing the Legal Position of the European Consumer*, British Institute of International and Comparative Law, London, 1996.

Lonbay J and Biondi A (eds), *Remedies for Breach of EC Law*, John Wiley & Sons, Chichester, 1997.

Lööf R, 'Shooting from the Hip – Proposed Minimum Rights in Criminal Proceedings' *European Law Journal* 3/2006, 421.

Lopez-Tarruella A, 'The Public Policy Clause in the System of Recognition and Enforcement of the Brussels Convention' *European Legal Forum* 2/2000–2001, 122–35.

Louis J-V, 'La fonction juridictionnelle de Nice à Rome' *Journal des Tribunaux (Droit Européen)* 2003, 257–63.

McAuley S, 'Achieving the Harmonization of Transnational Civil Procedure: Will the ALI/UNIDROIT Project Succeed?' *The American Review of International Arbitration* 2/2004, 231–52.

McBarnet D, 'Transnational Transactions: Legal Work, Cross-Border Commerce and Global Regulation' in Likosky M (ed), *Transnational Legal Processes, Globalisation and Power Disparities*, Butterworths, Edinburgh, 2002, 98–113.

McClean D, *International Co-operation in Civil and Criminal Matters*, Oxford University Press, Oxford, 2002 (2002a).

McClean D, 'The Hague Conference's Judgments Project' in Fawcett J (ed), *Reform and Development of Private International Law, Essays in Honour of Sir Peter North*, Oxford University Press, Oxford, 2002, 255–71 (2002b).

McKendrick J, 'Modifying Procedural Autonomy: Better Protection for Community Rights' *European Review of Private Law* 4/2000, 565–87.

Mainstrat, *Study on the Application of Council Regulation (EC) No 1348/2000 on the Service of Judicial and Extra Judicial Documents in Civil and Commercial Matters*, published on the Commission website: http://www.europa.eu.int/comm./justice_home/doc_centre/civil/studies/doc/study_ec1348_2000_en.pdf.

Männistö J (ed), *Prosessioikeudellisia Erityiskysymyksiä – Juhlajulkaisu Antti Joke*la, Turku University Press, Turku, 2004.

Mansel H-P et al (eds), *Festschrift für Erik Jayme*, Vol I, Sellier, Munich, 2004.

Marias E (ed), *European Citizenship*, European Institute of Public Administration, Maastricht, 1994.

Markensinis B, 'Litigation-Mania in England, Germany and the USA: Are We so Very Different?' *Cambridge Law Journal* 2/1990, 233–76.

Markensinis B, 'Studying Judicial Decisions in the Common Law and the Civil Law: A Good Way of Discovering Some of the Most Interesting Similarities and Differences that Exist Between these Legal Families' in Van Hoecke M and Ost F (eds), *The Harmonisation of European Private Law*, Hart Publishing, Oxford, 2000, 117–34.

Marshall T H and Bottomore T, *Citizenship and Social Class*, Pluto Press, London, 1992.

Mattli W and Slaughter A-M, 'The Role of National Courts in the Process of European Integration: Accounting for Judicial Preferences and Constraints' in Slaughter A-M, Stone Sweet A, and Weiler J (eds), *The European Court and National Courts – Doctrine and Jurisprudence, Legal Change in Its Social Context*, Hart Publishing, Oxford 1998, 253–76.

Mayer P, 'L'utilité des règles transnationales de procédure civile: Une vue critique' in Fouchard P (ed), *Vers un procès civil universel? Les règles transnationales de procédure civile de l'American Law Institute*, Editions Panthéon-Assas, Paris, 2001, 23–7.

Mayntz R, 'The State and Civil Society in Modern Governance', Paper for VI Congresso Internacional del CLAD, at http://www.clad.org.ve/anales6/mayntz.html (2002).

Meeusen J, 'Fifteen Theses on Brussels I, Rome I and the European Union's Institutional Framework' in Meeusen J, Pertegás M, and Straetmans G (eds), *Enforcement of International Contracts in the European Union. Convergence and Divergence between Brussels I and Rome I*, Intersentia, Antwerp, 2004, 43–76.

Meeusen J, Pertegás M, and Straetmans G, 'General Report' in Meeusen J, Pertegás M, and Straetmans G (eds), *Enforcement of International Contracts in the European Union. Convergence and Divergence between Brussels I and Rome I*, Intersentia, Antwerp, 2004, 1–20.

Meeusen J, Pertegás M, and Straetmans G (eds), *Enforcement of International Contracts in the European Union. Convergence and Divergence between Brussels I and Rome I*, Intersentia, Antwerp, 2004.

Michalik P, 'Justice in Crisis: England and Wales' in Zuckerman A A S (ed), *Civil Justice in Crisis, Comparative Perspectives of Civil Procedure*, Oxford University Press, Oxford, 1999, 117–65.

Mignolet O, 'Le contenu des règles de procédure issues des règlements communautaires et leur sanction' in De Leval G and Storme M (eds), *Le droit processuel et judiciaire européen*, La Charte & Die Keure, Brussels and Bruges, 2003, 329–71.

Miller C and Beaumont P (eds), *The Option of Litigating in Europe*, UK Comparative Law Series Vol 14, 1993.

Milo J, 'Access to Justice Combating Late Payment in Business Transactions: How a New European Directive has Failed to Set a Substantial Minimum Standard Regarding National Provisions on Retention of Title' *European Review of Private Law* 3/2003, 379–93.

Moccia L, 'Du "marché" à la citoyenneté: A la recherche d'un droit privé européen durable et de sa base juridique' *Revue Internationale de Droit Comparé* 2/2004, 291–327.

Möller G, 'Kansainvälinen oikeusapu riita-asioissa' in *Kansainvälinen Oikeusapu*, Suomen Lakimiesliiton kustannus Oy, Mänttä, 1980, 76–104.

Möller G, 'The Date upon which a Finnish and a Swedish Court Become Seised for the Purpose of the European Judgment Conventions' in Borrás

A et al (eds), *Liber amicorum Georges A. L Droz: On the Progressive Unification of Private International Law*, Martinus Nijhoff, The Hague/Boston/London, 1996, 219.

Möllers T, 'The Role of Law in European Integration' *American Journal of Comparative Law* 4/2000, 679–711.

Monar J, 'Justice and Home Affairs in the Treaty of Amsterdam: Reform at the Price of Fragmentation' *European Law Review* 4/1998, 320–35 (1998a).

Monar J, 'A Dual Citizenship in the Making' in La Torre M (ed), *European Citizenship: An Institutional Challenge*, Kluwer Law International, The Hague/London/Boston, 1998, 167–265 (1998b).

Morijn J, 'Balancing Fundamental Rights and Common Market Freedoms in Union Law: Schmidberger and Omega in Light of the European Constitution' *European Law Journal* 1/2006, 15–40.

Mougenot D, 'Le règlement européen sur l'obtention des preuves' *Journal des Tribunaux* 2002, 17–21.

Mourre A, *Droit Judiciaire Privé Européen des Affaires, Droit Communautaire – Droit Comparé*, Bruylant, Brussels, 2003.

Mowbray A R, The *Development of Positive Obligations under the European Convention on Human Rights by the European Court of Human Rights*, Hart Publishing, Oxford/Portland, Oregon, 2004.

Muir Watt H, 'Evidence of an Emergent European Legal Culture: Public Policy Requirements of Procedural Fairness under the Brussels and Lugano Conventions' *Texas International Law Journal* 3/2001, 539–54 (2001a).

Muir Watt H, 'Quelle méthode?' in Fouchard P (ed), *Vers un procès civil universel? Les règles transnationales de procédure civile de l'American Law Institute*, Editions Panthéon-Assas, Paris, 2001, 39–50 (2001b).

Muir Watt H, 'Remarques liminaires sur l'espace européen en matière civile et commerciale' in Leroyer A-M and Jeuland E (eds), *Quelle cohérence pour l'espace judiciaire européen?*, Dalloz, Paris, 2004, 1–9.

Nascimbene B, 'Community Courts in the Area of Judicial Cooperation' *International and Comparative Law Quarterly* 2/2005, 489–97.

Neville Brown L, 'Reconciling Autonomy and Effectiveness' in Lonbay J and Biondi A (eds), *Remedies for Breach of EC Law*, John Wiley & Sons, Chichester, 1997, 67–72.

Niboyet M-L, 'La révision de la convention de Bruxelles du 27 septembre 1968 par le règlement du 22 décembre 2000' *Gazette Du Palais (Doctrine)* 2001, 943–9 (2001a).

Niboyet M-L, 'Quels litiges?' in Fouchard P (ed), *Vers un procès civil universel? Les règles transnationales de procédure civile de l'American Law Institute*, Editions Panthéon-Assas, Paris, 2001, 51–7 (2001b).

Niedwiedz M, 'European Community Competence and the Proposed Hague Jurisdiction Convention' in Snyder F (ed), *The European Union and Governance*, Bruylant, Brussels, 2003, 213–41.

Niemi-Kiesiläinen J, 'International Cooperation and Approximation of Laws in the Field of Civil Procedure' in Heiskanen V and Kulovesi K (eds), *Function and Future of European Law*, Helsinki University Press, Helsinki, 1999, 249–57.

Normand J, 'Le rapprochement des procédures civiles dans l'Union européenne' *European Review of Private Law* 4/1998, 383–99 (1998a).

Normand J, 'Un droit judiciaire privé européen?' in Vareilles-Sommières P (ed), *Le Droit Privé Européen*, Economica, Paris, 1998, 124–35 (1998b).

Normand J, 'La nécessité des procédures provisoires dans les litiges transnationaux – Première partie' in Università di Catania (eds), *Trans-National Aspects of Procedural Law*, Vols I–III, Giuffrè Editore, Milan, 1998, 1141–68 (1998c).

Normand J, 'Le titre exécutoire européen' in Alpa G and Danovi R (eds), *Diritto contrattuale europeo e diritto dei consumatori. L'integrazione europea e il processo civile*, Guiffrè Editore, Milan, 2003, 237–61.

Normand J, 'Conclusions' in Leroyer A-M and Jeuland E (eds), *Quelle cohérence pour l'espace judiciaire eoropéen?*, Dalloz, Paris, 2004, 167–81.

Nuyts A, 'Forum shopping et abus du forum shopping dans l'espace judiciaire européen' *Global Jurist Advances*, 1/2003, article 2, 1–33 (2003a).

Nuyts A, 'La théorie de l'éffet réflexe' in De Leval G and Storme M (eds), *Le droit processuel et judiciaire européen*, La Charte & Die Keure, Brussels and Bruges, 2003, 73–89 (2003b).

Oberhammer P, 'Die Rolle der Justiz' (English Summary) in Storme M (ed), *Procedural Laws in Europe. Towards Harmonisation*, Maklu, Antwerp-Apeldoorn, 2003, 441.

O'Brien W, 'The Hague Convention on Jurisdiction and Judgments: The Way Forward' *Modern Law Reveiw* 4/2003, 491–509.

O'Keeffe D and Twomey P (eds), *Legal Issues of the Amsterdam Treaty*, Hart Publishing, Oxford, 1999.

Oker-Blom M, 'Behovet av grupptalan – en argumentative övning' *Tidskrift utgiven av Juridiska Föreningen i Finland* 1–2/2006, 86–107.

O'Leary S, *European Union Citizenship. The Options for Reform*, Institute for Public Policy Research, London, 1996.

O'Leary S, 'The Options for Reform of European Union Citizenship' in O'Leary S and Tiilikainen T (eds), *Citizenship and Nationality Status in the New Europe*, Sweet & Maxwell, London, 1998, 81–116.

O'Leary S and Tiilikainen T (eds), *Citizenship and Nationality Status in the New Europe*, Sweet & Maxwell, London, 1998.

Opeskin B, 'The Price of Forum Shopping: A Reply to Professor Juenger' *Sydney Law Review* 1/1994, 14–27.

Øren J, 'International Jurisdiction over Consumer Contracts in e-Europe' *International and Comparative Law Quarterly* 3/2003, 665–95.

Osman F, 'Les actions collectives des consommateurs dans l'Union européenne: Un nouveau défi pour le droit international privé communautaire' in Université Jean Moulin, Faculté de Droit (eds), *Les effets des jugements nationaux dans les autres États membres de l'Union européenne*, Bruylant, Brussels, 2001, 89–117

Partsch P-E, *Le Droit International Privé Européen. De Rome à Nice*, Larcier, Brussels, 2003.

Pataut E, 'Qu'est-ce qu'un litige "intracommunautaire"? Réflexions autour de l'article 4 du Règlement Bruxelles I' in Bandrac M et al, *Justice et droits fondamentaux. Etudes offertes à Jacques Normand*, Litec, Paris, 2003, 365–85.

Pataut E, 'L'espace judiciaire européen: un espace cohérent?' in Leroyer A-M and Jeuland E (eds), *Quelle cohérence pour l'espace judiciaire européen?*, Dalloz, Paris, 2004, 31–49.

Paterson A, 'Financing Legal Services: A Comparative Perspective' in Miller C and Beaumont P (eds), *The Option of Litigating in Europe*, UK Comparative Law Series Vol 14, 1993, 149–73.

Paulino Pereira F R, 'Perspectives futures en matière de coopération judiciaire en Europe' in Barrett G (ed), *Creating A European Judicial Space, Prospects for Improving Judicial Cooperation in Civil Matters in the European Union*, Vol 30 Academy of European Law Trier, Budesanzeiger, Cologne, 2001, 43–8 (2001a).

Paulino Pereira F R, 'Signification et notification dans les États membres de l'Union européenne des actes judiciaires et extrajudiciaires en matière civile et commerciale' in Barrett G (ed), *Creating A European Judicial Space, Prospects for Improving Judicial Cooperation in Civil Matters in the European Union*, Vol 30 Academy of European Law Trier, Budesanzeiger, Cologne, 2001, 75–81 (2001b).

Perrot R, 'L'efficacité des procédures judiciaires au sein de l'Union européenne et les garanties des droits de la défense' in Caupin M-T and

De Leval G (eds), *L'Efficacité de la Justice en Europe*, Larcier, Brussels, 2000, 417–35.

Perrot R, 'L'inversion du contentieux (ou les processus de l'ordonnance sur requête)' in Bandrac M et al, *Justice et droits fondamentaux. Etudes offertes à Jacques Normand*, Litec, Paris, 2003, 387–99.

Picone P (ed), *Diritto Internazionale Privato e Diritto Communitario*, CEDAM, Padua, 2004.

Pipkorn J, 'Les méthodes de rapprochement des législations a l'intérieur de la CEE' in Bourel P et al, *L'Influence des Communautés Européennes sur le Droit International Privé des Etats Membres*, Larcier, Brussels, 1981, 13–46.

Platto C (ed), *Economic Consequences of Litigation Worldwide*, Kluwer Law International, The Hague, 1999.

Prechal S, 'EC Requirements for an Effective Remedy' in Lonbay J and Biondi A (eds), *Remedies for Breach of EC Law*, John Wiley & Sons, Chichester, 1997, 3–13.

Prechal S, 'Judge-made Harmonisation of National Procedural Rules: A Bridging Perspective' in Wouters J and Stuyck J (eds), *Principles of Proper Conduct for the Supranational, State and Private Actors in the European Union: Towards ad Ius Commune. Essays in Honour of Walter van Gerven*, Intersentia, Antwerp, 2001, 39–58.

Prechal S and Shelkoplyas N, 'National Procedures, Public Policy and EC Law. From Van Schijndel to Eco Swiss and Beyond' *European Review of Private Law* 5/2004, 589–611.

Raitio J, *The Principle of Legal Certainty in EC Law*, Kluwer Academic Publishers, Dordrecht, 2003.

Rancé P and De Baynast O, *L'Europe judiciaire. Enjeux et perspectives*, Dalloz, Paris, 2001.

Rechberger W and Kodek G (eds), *Orders for Payment in the European Union*, Kluwer Law International, The Hague/London/New York, 2001.

Remien O, 'European Private International Law, the European Community and Its Emerging Area of Freedom, Security and Justice' *Common Market Law Review* 1/2001, 53–86.

Rhodes R, *Understanding Governance: Policy Networks, Governance, Reflexivity and Accountability*, Open University Press, Buckingham, 1997.

Rickett C and Telfer T (eds), *International Perspectives on Consumers' Access to Justice*, Cambridge University Press, Cambridge, 2003.

Rissanen K, 'The Needs of Public Order. The Need to Enforce Judgments Across Borders within the Community. Herein "An Area of Justice and the European Union" ', in Sundström Z and Kauppi M (eds),

Access to Justice – The Architecture of the European Community Courts, Publications of the Finnish Association for European Law, Helsinki, 1999, 223–39.

Rissanen K, 'Perusoikeudet ja oikeusvaltioperiaate Euroopan unionissa' in *Juhlajulkaisu Pekka Hallberg*, Suomalainen Lakimiesyhdistys, Helsinki, 2004, 349.

Rosas A, 'Oikeus kansalliseen oikeudenkäyntiin EU-oikeuden mukaan' in *Juhlajulkaisu Pekka Hallberg*, Suomalainen Lakimiesyhdistys, Helsinki, 2004, 361–73.

Rosas A and Antola E (eds), *A Citizen's Europe. In Search of a New Legal Ord*er, Sage Publications, London, 1995.

Rossi L S, 'L'incidenza dei principi del diritto comunitario sul diritto internazionle privato: dalla "comunitarizzazione" alla "costituzionalizzione"', *Rivista di diritto internazionale privato e processuale*, 1/2004, 63–84.

Roth W-H, 'From Centros to Überseering: Free Movement of Companies, Private International Law, and Community Law' *International and Comparative Law Quarterly* 1/2003, 177–208.

Rouchaud A-M, 'Le renforcement de la coopération judiciaire' in Université Jean Moulin, Faculté de Droit (eds), *Les effets des jugements nationaux dans les autres États membres de l'Union européenne*, Bruylant, Brussels, 2001, 19–30.

Rouchaud A-M, 'Le renforcement de la coopération judiciaire' in Storme M (ed), *Procedural Laws in Europe. Towards Harmonisation*, Maklu, Antwerp-Apeldoorn, 2003, 449–59.

Rouchaud-Joët A-M, 'Le titre exécutoire européen' in De Leval G and Storme M (eds), *Le droit processuel et judiciaire européen*, La Charte & Die Keure, Brussels and Bruges, 2003, 451–5.

Salerno F, 'The Brussels Jurisdiction and Enforcement Convention' in Von Hoffman B (ed), *European Private International Law*, Ars Aequi Libri, Nijmegen, 1998, 115–58.

Salerno F, 'Il diritto processuale civile internazionale comunitario e le garanzie prosecutable fondamentali' in Picone P (ed), *Diritto Internazionale Privato e Diritto Communitario*, CEDAM, Padua, 2004, 95–123.

Sankari S, 'Placing the (Union) Citizen at the Heart of the Project – Futile Speech or Concrete Action?' in Frände et al, *In the Footsteps of Tampere – Justice in the European Union*, University of Helsinki, Helsinki, 2006, 73–116.

Scharpf F, 'European Governance: Common Concerns vs. The Challenge of Diversity,' *NYU Jean Monnet Working Paper* 6/2001.

Schermers H G, 'The International Extension of Procedural Law' in Sumampouw M et al (eds), *Law and Reality, Essays on National and International Procedural Law in Honour of Cornelis Carel Albert Voskuil*, T.M.C. Asser Institute, Martinus Nijhoff, Dordrecht, 1992, 279–90.

Schlosser P, 'Jurisdiction and International Judicial and Administrative Co-operation' *Recueil de Cours* 284 (2000), 13–418.

Schütte J, 'Judicial Co-operation in the Field of Criminal Law and Civil Law' in Jansen R, Koster D, and Van Zutphen R (eds), *European Ambitions of the National Judiciary*, Kluwer Law International, The Hague, 1997, 161–70.

Schütze R, '"Lis Pendens" and Related Actions' *European Journal of Law Reform* 1/2002, 57–68.

Schwartze A, 'Enforcement of Private Law: The Missing Link in the Process of European Harmonisation' *European Review of Private Law* 1/2000, 135–46.

Scott C, 'Regulation in the Age of Governance: The Rise of the Post-Regulatory State' Australian National University – National Europe Centre Paper No. 100, 2003.

Scott I (ed), *International Perspectives on Civil Justice, Essays in Honour of Sir Jack I. H. Jacob Q.C.*, Sweet & Maxwell, London, 1990.

Scott J and Trubek D, 'Mind the Gap: Law and New Approaches to Governance in the European Union' *European Law Journal* 1/2002, 1–18.

Serverin E, *Des procédures de traitement judiciaire des demandes de faible importance ou non contestées dans les droits des états-membres de l'Union européen*, Centre Nationale de la Recherche Scientifique IDHE, Paris, 2001.

Sevón L, 'Kansallinen tuomari yhteisön tuomarina: Prosessiautonomian periaate ja sen rajat' *Defensor Legis* 1/2003, 3–12.

Shelkoplyas N, *The Application of EC Law in Arbitration Proceedings*, Europa Law Publishing, Groningen, 2003.

Shúlleabháin M, 'Recent Developments in Cross-Border Enforcement' ERA Seminar Paper June 2007, Trier.

Slaughter A-M, 'Judicial Globalization' *Virginia Journal of International Law* 1999–2000, 1103–24.

Slaughter A-M, Stone Sweet A, and Weiler J (eds), *The European Court and National Courts – Doctrine and Jurisprudence, Legal Change in Its Social Context*, Hart Publishing, Oxford, 1998.

Snijders H J et al, *Access to Civil Procedure Abroad*, Kluwer Law International, The Hague/Boston, 1999.

Snyder F, *New Directions in European Community Law*, Weidenfeld & Nicolson, London 1990.

Snyder F, 'The Effectiveness of European Community Law: Institutions, Processes, Tools and Techniques' *Modern Law Review* 1/1993, 19–54.

Snyder F (ed), *The European Union and Governance*, Bruylant, Brussels, 2003.

Sommerlad H, 'Some Reflections on the Relationship between Citizenship, Access to Justice and the Reform of Legal Aid' *Journal of Law and Society* 3/2004, 345–66.

Spinelli J-P, 'Le passeport judiciaire européen' in Isnard J and Normand J (eds), *Nouveaux droits dans un nouvel espace européen de justice: Le droit processuel et le droit de l'exécution*, Éditions Juridiques et Techniques, Paris, 2002, 85–94.

Stadler A, 'From the Brussels Convention to Regulation 44/2001: Cornerstones of a European Civil Procedure' *Common Market Law Review* 2005, 1637–61.

Stoffel W, 'Place of Performance – Jurisdiction and Plaintiff's Interests in Contemporary Societies' *European Journal of Law Reform* 1/2002, 185–98.

Stone Sweet A, 'Constitutional Dialogues in the European Community' in Slaughter A-M, Stone Sweet A, and Weiler J (eds), *The European Court and National Courts – Doctrine and Jurisprudence, Legal Change in Its Social Context*, Hart Publishing, Oxford, 1998, 305–30.

Stoppenbrink K, 'Systemwechsel im internationalen Anerkennungsrecht: Von der EuGVVO zur geplanten Abschaffung des Exequaturs' (English abstract) *European Review of Private Law* 5/2002, 641.

Storme M, *Rechtspraak in Opspraak*, Kluwer, Amsterdam, 1980.

Storme M, 'Towards a Common European Procedural Law' in Heiskanen V and Kulovesi K (eds), *Function and Future of European Law*, Helsinki University Press, Helsinki, 1999, 233–46.

Storme M, 'Role and Status of the Judiciary as a State Power' in Carpi F and Lupoi M (eds), *Essays on Transnational and Comparative Civil Procedure*, G. Giappichelli Editore, Turin, 2001, 29–65.

Storme M (ed), *Approximation of Judiciary Law in the European Union*, Nijhoff, Dordrecht, 1994.

Storme M (ed), *Procedural Laws in Europe. Towards Harmonisation*, Maklu, Antwerp-Apeldoorn, 2003.

Storskrubb E, 'Alternative Dispute Resolution in Civil and Commercial Matters – Developments in the European Union' in Turunen S (ed),

Conflict Management – Riidanratkaisun uusi maailma, Edita, Helsinki, 2005, 285–314.

Storskrubb E, 'Steering the Tide – The Mid-Term Perspective for Civil Justice' in Frände D et al, *In the Footsteps of Tampere – Justice in the European Union*, University of Helsinki, Helsinki, 2006, 1–34.

Storskrubb E and Ziller J, 'Access to Justice in European Comparative Law' in Francoini F (ed) *Access to Justice as a Human Right*, Oxford University Press, Oxford, 2007, 177–203.

Straetmens G, 'The Consumer Concept in EC Law' in Meeusen J, Pertegás M, and Straetmans G (eds), *Enforcement of International Contracts in the European Union. Convergence and Divergence between Brussels I and Rome I*, Intersentia, Antwerp, 2004, 295–322.

Strömholm S, 'En gemenskapsrättslig internationell privaträtt? Konsekvenser för nordiskt samarbete, lagstiftning och juristutbildning' *Svensk Juristtidning* 5–6/2003, 521–36.

Stürner R, 'Einstweiliger Rechtsschutz: General Bericht' (English Summary) in Storme M (ed), *Procedural Laws in Europe. Towards Harmonisation*, Maklu, Antwerp-Apeldoorn, 2003, 185.

Stürner R, 'Procédure civile et culture juridique' *Revue Internationale de Droit Comparé* 4/2004, 797–824.

Sumampouw M et al (eds), *Law and Reality, Essays on National and International Procedural Law in Honour of Cornelis Carel Albert Voskuil*, T.M.C. Asser Institute, Martinus Nijhoff, Dordrecht, 1992.

Sundström Z and Kauppi M (eds), *Access to Justice – The Architecture of the European Community Courts*, Publications of the Finnish Association for European Law, Helsinki, 1999.

Suominen A, 'Ömesidigt erkännande av rättsliga beslut som hörnsten i det europeiska straffrättliga samarbetet' *Tidskrift utgiven av Juridiska Föreningen i Finland* 6/2006, 607–16.

Symeonides S, 'General Report' in Symeonides S (ed), *Private International Law at the End of the 20th Century: Progress or Regress?* Kluwer Law International, London, 2000, 3–79 (2000a).

Symeonides S (ed), *Private International Law at the End of the 20th Century: Progress or Regress?* Kluwer Law International, London, 2000 (2000b).

Szyszczak E, 'Making Europe More Relevant to Its Citizens: Effective Judicial Process' *European Law Review* 5/1996, 351–64.

Szyszczak E and Delicostopoulos J, 'Intrusions into National Procedural Autonomy: The French Paradigm' *European Law Review* 2/1997, 141–9.

Tagaras H, 'The European Enforcement Order (Regulation 805/2004)' EIPA Seminar Paper 11–12 November 2004, Luxembourg.

Takahashi K, 'External Competence Implications of the EC Regulation on Jurisdiction and Judgments' *International and Comparative Law Quarterly* 2/2003, 529–34.

Taruffo M and Varano V (eds), *Diritti Fondamentali e Guistizia Civile in Europa*, G. Giappichelli Editore, Turin, 2002.

Tarzia G, 'Une procédure civile sans frontières: Harmonisation et unification du droit procédural' *General Report XI World Congress on Procedural Law*, 1999, 25–36.

Tarzia G, 'Harmonisation ou unification transnational de la procédure civile' *Rivista di diritto internazionale privato e processuale* 4/2001, 869–84.

Tarzia G, 'Vers un concept européen du droit de l'exécution?' in Isnard J and Normand J (eds), *Nouveaux droits dans un nouvel espace européen de justice: Le droit processuel et le droit de l'exécution*, Éditions Juridiques et Techniques, Paris, 2002, 153–68.

Tarzia G, 'Rapidité, sécurité et efficacité de l'exécution transfrontalière en Europe' in Isnard J and Normand J (eds), *L'aménagement du droit de l'exécution dans l'espace communautaire: bientôt les premiers instruments*, Éditions Juridiques et Techniques, Paris, 2003, 79–92 (2003a).

Tarzia G, 'Exigences et garanties de l'exécution transfrontalière en Europe' in Bandrac M et al, *Justice et droits fondamentaux. Etudes offertes à Jacques Normand*, Litec, Paris, 2003, 449–59 (2003b).

Tenreiro M, 'L'accès du consommateur à la justice: une perspective européenne' in Barrett G (ed), *Creating A European Judicial Space, Prospects for Improving Judicial Cooperation in Civil Matters in the European Union*, Vol 30 Academy of European Law Trier, Budesanzeiger, Cologne, 2001, 111–17.

Tenreiro M. and Seoane J A, 'The Creation of a European Judicial Area in Civil and Commercial Matters: What Can the EU Do?' in Storme M (ed), *Procedural Laws in Europe. Towards Harmonisation*, Maklu, Antwerp-Apeldoorn, 2003, 461–71.

Thoma I, 'La définition et l'exercice des compétences externes de la Communauté européenne au domaine de la coopération dans les matières civiles ayant une incidence transfrontière' *European Review of Private Law* 3/2002, 397–416.

Tridimas T, 'The European Court of Justice and the Draft Constitution: A Supreme Court for the Union?' in Tridimas T and Nebbia P (eds),

European Union Law for the Twenty-First Century – Rethinking the New Legal Order, Hart Publishing, Oxford, 2004, 113.

Tridimas T and Nebbia P (eds), *European Union Law for the Twenty-First Century – Rethinking the New Legal Order*, Hart Publishing, Oxford, 2004.

Trocker N, 'Il diritto ad una tutela giurisdizionale effettiva nell'opera creatrice della Corte di giustizia della Comunità europea' in Taruffo M and Varano V (eds), *Diritti Fondamentali e Guistizia Civile in Europa*, G. Giappichelli Editore, Turin, 2002, 247–90.

Trocker N and Varano V (eds), *The Reforms of Civil Procedure in Comparative Perspective*, G. Giappichelli Editore, Turin, 2005.

Tubeuf C and Lebois M, 'Règlement 44/2001 du 22 décembre 2000. La reconnaissance et l'exécution des décisions judiciaires – Cadre général' in De Leval G and Storme M (eds), *Le droit processuel et judiciaire européen*, La Charte & Die Keure, Brussels and Bruges, 2003, 373–89.

Turunen S (ed), *Conflict Management. Riidanratkaisun uusi maailma*, Edita, Helsinki, 2005.

Twining W, 'Reviving General Jurisprudence' in Likosky M (ed), *Transnational Legal Processes, Globalisation and Power Disparities*, Butterworths, Edinburgh, 2002, 3–21.

Twomey P, 'European Citizenship and Human Rights: Actual Situation and Future Perspective' in Marias E (ed), *European Citizenship*, European Institute of Public Administration, Maastricht, 1994, 119–33.

Twomey P, 'Constructing a Secure Space: The Area of Freedom, Security and Justice' in O'Keeffe D and Twomey P (eds), *Legal Issues of the Amsterdam Treaty*, Hart Publishing, Oxford, 1999, 351–74.

Università di Catania (eds), *Trans-National Aspects of Procedural Law*, Vols I–III, Giuffrè Editore, Milan, 1998.

Université Jean Moulin, Faculté de Droit (eds), *Les effets des jugements nationaux dans les autres États membres de l'Union européenne*, Bruylant, Brussels, 2001.

Välimaa A, 'Todisteiden vastaanottamisesta riita-asioissa toisessa EU:n jäsenvaltiossa' *Defensor Legis* 5/2001, 850–70.

Van Compernolle J, 'Le droit à l'exécution: une nouvelle garantie du procès équitable' in De Leval G and Storme M (eds), *Le droit processuel et judiciaire européen*, La Charte & Die Keure, Brussels and Bruges, 2003, 475–83 (2003a).

Van Compernolle J, 'Le droit d'être jugé dans un délai raisonnable: Les effectivités d'un droit processuel autonome' in Bandrac M et al, *Justice et droits fondamentaux. Etudes offertes à Jacques Normand*, Litec, Paris, 2003, 471–82 (2003b).

Van den Bossche A-M, 'L'espace européen de justice et le (rapprochement du) droit judiciaire' in De Leval G and Storme M (eds), *Le droit processuel et judiciaire européen*, La Charte & Die Keure, Brussels and Bruges, 2003, 1–19.

Van Gerven W, 'Of Rights, Remedies and Procedures' *Common Market Law Review* 3/2000, 501–36.

Van Gerven W, 'The ECJ Case-Law as a Means of Unification of Private Law?' in Hartkamp A, Hesselink M, Honduis E, Joustra C, Du Perron E, and Veldman M (eds), *Towards a European Civil Code*, Third Edition, Kluwer Law International, Nijmegen, 2004, 101–23.

Van Gerven W, 'Bringing (Private) Laws Closer to Each Other at the European Level' in Cafaggi F (ed), *The Institutional Framework of European Private Law*, Oxford University Press, Oxford, 2006, 37–77.

Vanheukelen C, 'Le règlement 1348/2000 – Analyse et évaluation par un praticien du droit' in De Leval G and Storme M (eds), *Le droit processuel et judiciaire européen*, La Charte & Die Keure, Brussels and Bruges, 2003, 195–235.

Van Hoecke M and Ost F (eds), *The Harmonisation of European Private Law*, Hart Publishing, Oxford, 2000.

Van Rhee C, 'Civil Procedure: A European Ius Commune?' *European Review of Private Law* 4/2000, 589–611.

Van Rhee C H (ed), *European Traditions in Civil Procedure*, Intersentia, Antwerp, 2005.

Viitanen K, 'The Crisis of the Welfare State, Privatisation and Consumers' Access to Justice' in Wilhelmsson T and Hurri S (eds), *From Dissonance to Sense: Welfare State Expectations, Privatisation and Private Law*, Ashgate, Aldershot/Brookfield/Singapore/Sydney, 1999, 549–65.

Vincke F, 'Les entreprises européennes ont besoin de rapprochement' in Storme M (ed), *Procedural Laws in Europe. Towards Harmonisation*, Maklu, Antwerp-Apeldoorn, 2003, 15–24.

Virolainen J, 'Johdatus Prosessioikeuteen' in Lappalainen J et al, *Prosessioikeus*, WSOY Lakitieto, Helsinki, 2003, 35.

Vlas P, 'The Principle of Fair Trial in International Civil Litigation' in Sumampouw M et al (eds), *Law and Reality, Essays on National and International Procedural Law in Honour of Cornelis Carel Albert Voskuil*, T.M.C. Asser Institute, Martinus Nijhoff, Dordrecht, 1992, 391–406.

Von Hoffman B, 'The Europeanization of Private International Law' in Von Hoffman B (ed), *European Private International Law*, Ars Aequi Libri, Nijmegen, 1998, 13–17 (1998a).

Von Hoffman B, 'The Relevance of European Community Law' in Von Hoffman B (ed), *European Private International Law*, Ars Aequi Libri, Nijmegen, 1998, 19–37 (1998b).

Von Hoffman B (ed), *European Private International Law*, Ars Aequi Libri, Nijmegen, 1998.

Walker N, 'In Search of the Area of Freedom, Security and Justice: A Constitutional Odyssey' in Walker N (ed), *Europe's Area of Freedom, Security and Justice*, Oxford University Press, Oxford, 2004.

Walker N (ed), *Europe's Area of Freedom, Security and Justice*, Oxford University Press, Oxford, 2004.

Walter G, 'Helvetia docet' (English Summary) in Storme M (ed), *Procedural Laws in Europe. Towards Harmonisation*, Maklu, Antwerp-Apeldoorn, 2003, 77.

Walter G and Walther F, 'International Litigation: Past Experiences and Future Perspectives' in Carpi F and Lupoi M (eds), *Essays on Transnational and Comparative Civil Procedure*, G. Giappichelli Editore, Turin 2001, 155–98.

Ward A, *Judicial Review and the Rights of Private Parties in EC Law*, Oxford University Press, Oxford, 2000.

Weatherill S, *Cases and Material on EU Law*, Sixth Edition, Oxford University Press, Oxford, 2003.

Weatherill S, 'Why Harmonise?' in Tridimas T and Nebbia P (eds), *European Union Law for the Twenty-First Century – Rethinking the New Legal Order*, Hart Publishing, Oxford, 2004, 11 (2004a).

Weatherill S, 'Why Object to the Harmonization of Private Law by the EC?' *European Review of Private Law* 5/2004, 633–60 (2004b).

Weatherill S, 'Reflections on the EC's Competence to Develop a "European Contract Law"' *European Review of Private Law* 3/2005, 405.

Weinberg de Roca I, 'Private International Law in a Global World' in Mansel H-P et al (eds), *Festschrift für Erik Jayme*, Vol I, Sellier, Munich, 2004, 1001–10.

Westbrook J L, 'International Judicial Negotiation' *Texas International Law Journal* 2003, 567–86.

White R, 'Lawyers and the Courts' in Blackburn R (ed), *Rights of Citizenship*, Mansell Publishing, London, 1993, 236–53.

Wijffels A, 'European Private Law: A New Software-Package for an Outdated System?' in Van Hoecke M and Ost F (eds), *The Harmonisation of European Private Law*, Hart Publishing, Oxford, 2000, 101–16.

Wilderspin M, 'Cross-Border Access to Legal Aid' in Barrett G (ed), *Creating a European Judicial Space, Prospects for Improving Judicial Cooperation in Civil Matters in the European Union*, Vol 30 Academy of European Law Trier, Budesanzeiger, Cologne, 2001, 65–73.

Wilderspin M and Rouchard-Joët A-M, 'La compétence externe de la Communauté européenne en droit international privé' *Revue Critique de Droit International Privé* 1/2004, 1–48.

Wilhelmsson T, 'Europeiseringen av privaträtten: För ett fragmenterat utbyte av erfarenheter' *Tidskrift for Rettsvitenskap* 1–2/2001, 1–32.

Wilhelmsson T, 'The Abuse of the "Confident Consumer" as a Justification for EC Consumer Law', *Journal of Consumer Policy* 3/2004, 317.

Wilhelmsson T and Hurri S (eds), *From Dissonance to Sense: Welfare State Expectations, Privatisation and Private Law*, Ashgate, Dartmouth, 1999.

Willis A, 'The Problems of Cross-Border Litigation and Court-Assisted Alternative Dispute Resolution – A Solution in the Light of English Practice?' in Barrett G (ed), *Creating A European Judicial Space, Prospects for Improving Judicial Cooperation in Civil Matters in the European Union*, Vol 30 Academy of European Law Trier, Budesanzeiger, Cologne, 2001, 105–10.

Wouters J and Stuyck J (eds), *Principles of Proper Conduct for the Supranational, State and Private Actors in the European Union: Towards a Ius Commune. Essays in Honour of Walter van Gerven*, Intersentia, Antwerp, 2001.

Yessiou Faltsi P, 'Le droit de l'exécution selon la Cour européenne des droits de l'homme: analyse et prospective' in Isnard J and Normand J (eds), *Nouveaux droits dans un nouvel espace européen de justice: Le droit processuel et le droit de l'exécution*, Éditions Juridiques et Techniques, Paris, 2002, 195–237.

Zander M, 'Where Are We Heading with the Funding of Civil Litigation?' *Civil Justice Quarterly* 1/2003, 23–40.

Zilinsky M, 'Abolishing Exequatur in the European Union: The European Enforcement Order' *Netherlands International Law Review* 3/2006, 471–92.

Zuckerman A A S, 'Justice in Crisis: Comparative Dimensions of Civil Procedure' in Zuckerman A A S (ed), *Civil Justice in Crisis, Comparative Perspectives of Civil Procedure*, Oxford University Press, Oxford, 1999, 3–52.

Zuckerman A A. S, 'Conference on the "ALI-UNIDROIT Principles and Rules of Transnational Civil Procedure" hosted by the British Institute of International and Comparative Law, London May 24, 2002' *Civil Justice Quarterly* 2002, 322–5.

Zuckerman A A S (ed), *Civil Justice in Crisis, Comparative Perspectives of Civil Procedure*, Oxford University Press, Oxford, 1999.

INDEX